Chevrolet Cavalier & Pontiac Sunfire Automotive Repair Manual

by Rob Maddox, Mike Stubblefield and John H Haynes
Member of the Guild of Motoring Writers

Models covered:
All Chevrolet Cavalier and Pontiac Sunfire models
1995 through 2004

(1H9 - 38016)

ABCDE
FGHIJ
KLMN
2

Haynes Publishing Group
Sparkford Nr Yeovil
Somerset BA22 7JJ England

Haynes North America, Inc
861 Lawrence Drive
Newbury Park
California 91320 USA

Acknowledgements

Wiring diagrams originated exclusively for Haynes North America, Inc. by Valley Forge Technical Information Services.

A book in the Haynes Automotive Repair Manual Series

Printed in the U.S.A.

ISBN 1 56392 571 0

Library of Congress Control Number 2005920947

While every attempt is made to ensure that the information in this manual is correct, no liability can be accepted by the authors or publishers for loss, damage or injury caused by any errors in, or omissions from, the information given.

Contents

Haynes author, photographer and mechanic with 1997 Chevrolet Cavalier

About this manual

Its purpose

The purpose of this manual is to help you get the best value from your vehicle. It can do so in several ways. It can help you decide what work must be done, even if you choose to have it done by a dealer service department or a repair shop; it provides information and procedures for routine maintenance and servicing; and it offers diagnostic and repair procedures to follow when trouble occurs.

We hope you use the manual to tackle the work yourself. For many simpler jobs, doing it yourself may be quicker than arranging an appointment to get the vehicle into a shop and making the trips to leave it and pick it up. More importantly, a lot of money can be saved by avoiding the expense the shop must pass on to you to cover its labor and overhead costs. An added benefit is the sense of satisfaction and accomplishment that you feel after doing the job yourself.

Using the manual

The manual is divided into Chapters. Each Chapter is divided into numbered Sections, which are headed in bold type between horizontal lines. Each Section consists of consecutively numbered paragraphs.

At the beginning of each numbered Section you will be referred to any illustrations which apply to the procedures in that Section. The reference numbers used in illustration captions pinpoint the pertinent Section and the Step within that Section. That is, illustration 3.2 means the illustration refers to Section 3 and Step (or paragraph) 2 within that Section.

Procedures, once described in the text, are not normally repeated. When it's necessary to refer to another Chapter, the reference will be given as Chapter and Section number. Cross references given without use of the word "Chapter" apply to Sections and/or paragraphs in the same Chapter. For example, "see Section 8" means in the same Chapter.

References to the left or right side of the vehicle assume you are sitting in the driver's seat, facing forward.

Even though we have prepared this manual with extreme care, neither the publisher nor the author can accept responsibility for any errors in, or omissions from, the information given.

NOTE

A **Note** provides information necessary to properly complete a procedure or information which will make the procedure easier to understand.

CAUTION

A **Caution** provides a special procedure or special steps which must be taken while completing the procedure where the Caution is found. Not heeding a Caution can result in damage to the assembly being worked on.

WARNING

A **Warning** provides a special procedure or special steps which must be taken while completing the procedure where the Warning is found. Not heeding a Warning can result in personal injury.

Introduction to the Chevrolet Cavalier and Pontiac Sunfire

The Chevrolet Cavalier and Pontiac Sunfire is available in four-door sedan and two-door coupe body styles.

These models are available with two engine options. The transversely mounted 2.2-liter four-cylinder, pushrod engine, the 2.3L (1995) or 2.4L (1996 through 2002) engine with Dual Overhead-Camshafts (DOHC), or the 2.2L Dual Overhead Camshaft (DOHC) engine (2002 and later models). Both models are equipped with a sequential multi port electronic fuel injection system.

The engine transmits power to the front wheels through either a five-speed manual transaxle or a three or four-speed automatic transaxle via a pair of driveaxles.

The Cavalier and Sunfire features a steel uni-body and independent suspension with MacPherson strut/coil spring suspension at the front and shock absorbers and coil springs at the rear. The rack and pinion steering unit is mounted behind the engine with power-assist available as optional equipment.

Standard models are equipped with power assisted front disc and rear drum brakes. All models are equipped with an Anti-lock Brake System (ABS).

Vehicle identification numbers

Modifications are a continuing and unpublicized process in vehicle manufacturing. Since spare parts manuals and lists are compiled on a numerical basis, the individual vehicle numbers are essential to correctly identify the component required.

Vehicle Identification Number (VIN)

This very important identification number is located on a plate attached to the dashboard inside the windshield on the driver's side of the vehicle (see illustration). The VIN also appears on the Vehicle Certificate of Title and Registration. It contains information such as where and when the vehicle was manufactured, the model year and the body style.

VIN engine and model year codes

Two particularly important pieces of information found in the VIN are the engine code and the model year code. Counting from the left, the engine code letter designation is the 8th digit and the model year code designation is the 10th digit.

On the models covered by this manual the engine codes are:

4	2.2L OHV
D	2.3L OHC
T	2.4L OHC
F	2.2L OHC

On the models covered by this manual the model year codes are:

S	1995
T	1996
V	1997
W	1998
X	1999
Y	2000
1	2001
2	2002
3	2003
4	2004

Vehicle Safety Certification label

The Vehicle Safety Certification label is attached to the edge of the driver's side door (see illustration). The label contains the name of the manufacturer, the month and year of production, the Gross Vehicle Weight Rating (GVWR), the Gross Axle Weight Rating (GAWR) and the certification statement.

Tire placard

The tire placard (label) is attached to the driver's side door post (see illustration). The label contains the tire label code, the tire sizes (front, rear and spare) tire pressures, tire speed rating, maximum vehicle capacity weight, total seating occupancy and the VIN.

Engine identification numbers

The engine identification numbers can be found stamped on a pad on either the left rear of the cylinder block, behind the starter (2.2L OHV engine) or on the back of the timing cover

The Vehicle Identification Number (VIN) is stamped into a metal plate fastened to the dashboard on the driver's side - it's visible through the windshield

The Vehicle Safety Certification label is affixed to the drivers side door end or post

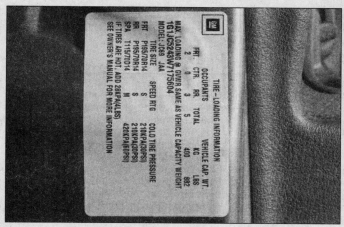

The tire placard (label) is affixed to the drivers side door end or post

Typical Engine Identification Number location

(2.3L and 2.4L OHC engines).

2.2L engine codes are stamped on the rear section of the engine block near the number 4 cylinder spark plug (see illustration).

2.3L and 1996 and 1997 2.4L engine codes are affixed on the label behind the timing cover (partial laser codes) and also stamped onto the engine block near the oil filter housing and below the starter assembly.

1998 and later 2.4L engine codes are located on the end surface of the cam cover while the VIN derivative is stamped on the bottom of the engine block in front of the transaxle extension.

On the 2002 and later 2.2L engine, the VIN derivative is located on a machined pad at the rear of the block, near the transaxle bellhousing.

Transaxle identification numbers

The transaxle identification information can be found on a bar code label located on the front of the transaxle (see illustration).

Vehicle Emissions Control Information (VECI) label

The emissions control information label is found under the hood, normally on the radiator support or the bottom side of the hood. This label contains information on the emissions control equipment installed on the vehicle, as well as tune-up specifications (see Chapter 6).

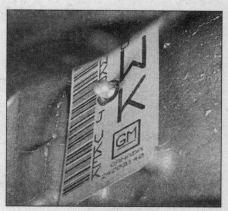

Location of the transaxle bar code label

Buying parts

Replacement parts are available from many sources, which generally fall into one of two categories - authorized dealer parts departments and independent retail auto parts stores. Our advice concerning these parts is as follows:

Retail auto parts stores: Good auto parts stores will stock frequently needed components which wear out relatively fast, such as clutch components, exhaust systems, brake parts, tune-up parts, etc. These stores often supply new or reconditioned parts on an exchange basis, which can save a considerable amount of money. Discount auto parts stores are often very good places to buy materials and parts needed for general vehicle maintenance such as oil, grease, filters, spark plugs, belts, touch-up paint, bulbs, etc. They also usually sell tools and general accessories, have convenient hours, charge lower prices and can often be found not far from home.

Authorized dealer parts department: This is the best source for parts which are unique to the vehicle and not generally available elsewhere (such as major engine parts, transmission parts, trim pieces, etc.).

Warranty information: If the vehicle is still covered under warranty, be sure that any replacement parts purchased - regardless of the source - do not invalidate the warranty!

To be sure of obtaining the correct parts, have engine and chassis numbers available and, if possible, take the old parts along for positive identification.

Maintenance techniques, tools and working facilities

Maintenance techniques

There are a number of techniques involved in maintenance and repair that will be referred to throughout this manual. Application of these techniques will enable the home mechanic to be more efficient, better organized and capable of performing the various tasks properly, which will ensure that the repair job is thorough and complete.

Fasteners

Fasteners are nuts, bolts, studs and screws used to hold two or more parts together. There are a few things to keep in mind when working with fasteners. Almost all of them use a locking device of some type, either a lockwasher, locknut, locking tab or thread adhesive. All threaded fasteners should be clean and straight, with undamaged threads and undamaged corners on the hex head where the wrench fits. Develop the habit of replacing all damaged nuts and bolts with new ones. Special locknuts with nylon or fiber inserts can only be used once. If they are removed, they lose their locking ability and must be replaced with new ones.

Rusted nuts and bolts should be treated with a penetrating fluid to ease removal and prevent breakage. Some mechanics use turpentine in a spout-type oil can, which works quite well. After applying the rust penetrant, let it work for a few minutes before trying to loosen the nut or bolt. Badly rusted fasteners may have to be chiseled or sawed off or removed with a special nut breaker, available at tool stores.

If a bolt or stud breaks off in an assembly, it can be drilled and removed with a special tool commonly available for this purpose. Most automotive machine shops can perform this task, as well as other repair procedures, such as the repair of threaded holes that have been stripped out.

Flat washers and lockwashers, when removed from an assembly, should always be replaced exactly as removed. Replace any damaged washers with new ones. Never use a lockwasher on any soft metal surface (such as aluminum), thin sheet metal or plastic.

Fastener sizes

For a number of reasons, automobile manufacturers are making wider and wider use of metric fasteners. Therefore, it is important to be able to tell the difference between standard (sometimes called U.S. or SAE) and metric hardware, since they cannot be interchanged.

All bolts, whether standard or metric, are sized according to diameter, thread pitch and length. For example, a standard 1/2 - 13 x 1 bolt is 1/2 inch in diameter, has 13 threads per inch and is 1 inch long. An M12 - 1.75 x 25

metric bolt is 12 mm in diameter, has a thread pitch of 1.75 mm (the distance between threads) and is 25 mm long. The two bolts are nearly identical, and easily confused, but they are not interchangeable.

In addition to the differences in diameter, thread pitch and length, metric and standard bolts can also be distinguished by examining the bolt heads. To begin with, the distance across the flats on a standard bolt head is measured in inches, while the same dimension on a metric bolt is sized in millimeters (the same is true for nuts). As a result, a standard wrench should not be used on a metric bolt and a metric wrench should not be used on a standard bolt. Also, most standard bolts have slashes radiating out from the center of the head to denote the grade or strength of the bolt, which is an indication of the amount of torque that can be applied to it. The greater the number of slashes, the greater the strength of the bolt. Grades 0 through 5 are commonly used on automobiles. Metric bolts have a property class (grade) number, rather than a slash, molded into their heads to indicate bolt strength. In

this case, the higher the number, the stronger the bolt. Property class numbers 8.8, 9.8 and 10.9 are commonly used on automobiles.

Strength markings can also be used to distinguish standard hex nuts from metric hex nuts. Many standard nuts have dots stamped into one side, while metric nuts are marked with a number. The greater the number of dots, or the higher the number, the greater the strength of the nut.

Metric studs are also marked on their ends according to property class (grade). Larger studs are numbered (the same as metric bolts), while smaller studs carry a geometric code to denote grade.

It should be noted that many fasteners, especially Grades 0 through 2, have no distinguishing marks on them. When such is the case, the only way to determine whether it is standard or metric is to measure the thread pitch or compare it to a known fastener of the same size.

Standard fasteners are often referred to as SAE, as opposed to metric. However, it should be noted that SAE technically refers to a non-metric fine thread fastener only.

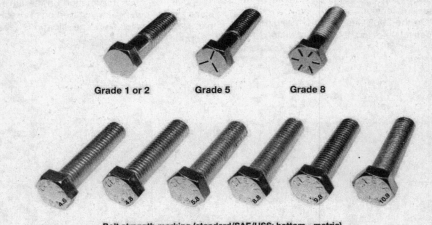

Grade 1 or 2   Grade 5   Grade 8

Bolt strength marking (standard/SAE/USS; bottom - metric)

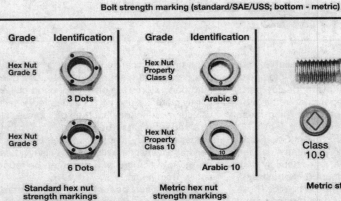

Grade	Identification	Grade	Identification
Hex Nut Grade 5	3 Dots	Hex Nut Property Class 9	Arabic 9
Hex Nut Grade 8	6 Dots	Hex Nut Property Class 10	Arabic 10
Standard hex nut strength markings		**Metric hex nut strength markings**	

Class 10.9   Class 9.8   Class 8.8

Metric stud strength markings

00-1 HAYNES

Coarse thread non-metric fasteners are referred to as USS sizes.

Since fasteners of the same size (both standard and metric) may have different strength ratings, be sure to reinstall any bolts, studs or nuts removed from your vehicle in their original locations. Also, when replacing a fastener with a new one, make sure that the new one has a strength rating equal to or greater than the original.

Tightening sequences and procedures

Most threaded fasteners should be tightened to a specific torque value (torque is the twisting force applied to a threaded component such as a nut or bolt). Overtightening the fastener can weaken it and cause it to break, while undertightening can cause it to eventually come loose. Bolts, screws and studs, depending on the material they are made of and their thread diameters, have specific torque values, many of which are noted in the Specifications at the beginning of each Chapter. Be sure to follow the torque recommendations closely. For fasteners not assigned a specific torque, a general torque value chart is presented here as a guide. These torque values are for dry (unlubricated) fasteners threaded into steel or cast iron (not aluminum). As was previously mentioned, the size and grade of a fastener determine the amount of torque that can safely be applied to it. The figures listed here are approximate for Grade 2 and Grade 3 fasteners. Higher grades can tolerate higher torque values.

Fasteners laid out in a pattern, such as cylinder head bolts, oil pan bolts, differential cover bolts, etc., must be loosened or tightened in sequence to avoid warping the component. This sequence will normally be shown in the appropriate Chapter. If a specific pattern is not given, the following procedures can be used to prevent warping.

Initially, the bolts or nuts should be assembled finger-tight only. Next, they should be tightened one full turn each, in a criss-cross or diagonal pattern. After each one has been tightened one full turn, return to the first one and tighten them all one-half turn, following the same pattern. Finally, tighten each of them one-quarter turn at a time until each fastener has been tightened to the proper torque. To loosen and remove the fasteners, the procedure would be reversed.

Component disassembly

Component disassembly should be done with care and purpose to help ensure that the parts go back together properly. Always keep track of the sequence in which parts are removed. Make note of special characteristics or marks on parts that can be installed more than one way, such as a grooved thrust washer on a shaft. It is a good idea to lay the disassembled parts out on a clean surface in the order that they were removed. It may also be helpful to make sketches or take instant photos of components before removal.

When removing fasteners from a component, keep track of their locations. Sometimes threading a bolt back in a part, or putting the washers and nut back on a stud, can prevent mix-ups later. If nuts and bolts cannot be returned to their original locations, they should be kept in a compartmented box or a series of small boxes. A cupcake or muffin tin is ideal for this purpose, since each cavity can hold the bolts and nuts from a particular area (i.e. oil pan bolts, valve cover bolts, engine mount bolts, etc.). A pan of this type is especially helpful when working on assemblies with very small parts, such as the carburetor, alternator, valve train or interior dash and trim pieces. The cavities can be marked with paint or tape to identify the contents.

Whenever wiring looms, harnesses or connectors are separated, it is a good idea to identify the two halves with numbered pieces of masking tape so they can be easily reconnected.

Gasket sealing surfaces

Throughout any vehicle, gaskets are used to seal the mating surfaces between two parts and keep lubricants, fluids, vacuum or pressure contained in an assembly.

Many times these gaskets are coated with a liquid or paste-type gasket sealing compound before assembly. Age, heat and pressure can sometimes cause the two parts to stick together so tightly that they are very difficult to separate. Often, the assembly can be loosened by striking it with a soft-face hammer near the mating surfaces. A regular hammer can be used if a block of wood is placed between the hammer and the part. Do not hammer on cast parts or parts that could be easily damaged. With any particularly

Metric thread sizes	Ft-lbs	Nm
M-6	6 to 9	9 to 12
M-8	14 to 21	19 to 28
M-10	28 to 40	38 to 54
M-12	50 to 71	68 to 96
M-14	80 to 140	109 to 154
Pipe thread sizes		
1/8	5 to 8	7 to 10
1/4	12 to 18	17 to 24
3/8	22 to 33	30 to 44
1/2	25 to 35	34 to 47
U.S. thread sizes		
1/4 - 20	6 to 9	9 to 12
5/16 - 18	12 to 18	17 to 24
5/16 - 24	14 to 20	19 to 27
3/8 - 16	22 to 32	30 to 43
3/8 - 24	27 to 38	37 to 51
7/16 - 14	40 to 55	55 to 74
7/16 - 20	40 to 60	55 to 81
1/2 - 13	55 to 80	75 to 108

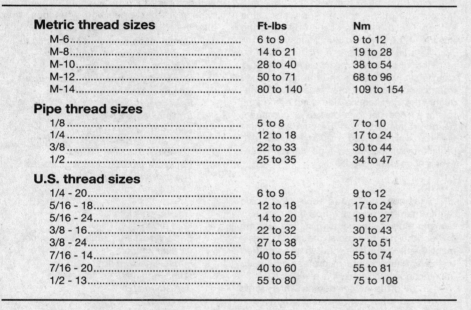

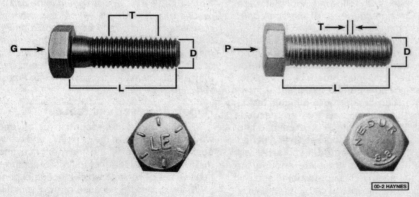

Standard (SAE and USS) bolt dimensions/grade marks

G   *Grade marks (bolt strength)*
L   *Length (in inches)*
T   *Thread pitch (number of threads per inch)*
D   *Nominal diameter (in inches)*

Metric bolt dimensions/grade marks

P   *Property class (bolt strength)*
L   *Length (in millimeters)*
T   *Thread pitch (distance between threads in millimeters)*
D   *Diameter*

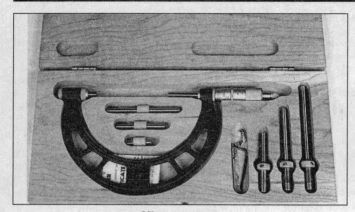

Micrometer set

Dial indicator set

stubborn part, always recheck to make sure that every fastener has been removed.

Avoid using a screwdriver or bar to pry apart an assembly, as they can easily mar the gasket sealing surfaces of the parts, which must remain smooth. If prying is absolutely necessary, use an old broom handle, but keep in mind that extra clean up will be necessary if the wood splinters.

After the parts are separated, the old gasket must be carefully removed and the gasket surfaces cleaned. If you're working on cast iron or aluminum parts, stubborn gasket material can be soaked with rust penetrant or treated with a special chemical to soften it so it can be easily scraped off. **Caution:** *Never use gasket removal solutions or caustic chemicals on plastic or other composite components.* A scraper can be fashioned from a piece of copper tubing by flattening and sharpening one end. Copper is recommended because it is usually softer than the surfaces to be scraped, which reduces the chance of gouging the part. Some gaskets can be removed with a wire brush, but regardless of the method used, the mating surfaces must be left clean and smooth. If for some reason the gasket surface is gouged, then a gasket sealer thick enough to fill scratches will have to be used during reassembly of the components. For most applications, a non-drying (or semi-drying) gasket sealer should be used.

Hose removal tips

Warning: *If the vehicle is equipped with air conditioning, do not disconnect any of the A/C hoses without first having the system depressurized by a dealer service department or a service station.*

Hose removal precautions closely parallel gasket removal precautions. Avoid scratching or gouging the surface that the hose mates against or the connection may leak. This is especially true for radiator hoses. Because of various chemical reactions, the rubber in hoses can bond itself to the metal spigot that the hose fits over. To remove a hose, first loosen the hose clamps that secure it to the spigot. Then, with slip-joint pliers, grab the hose at the clamp and rotate it around the spigot. Work it back and forth

until it is completely free, then pull it off. Silicone or other lubricants will ease removal if they can be applied between the hose and the outside of the spigot. Apply the same lubricant to the inside of the hose and the outside of the spigot to simplify installation.

As a last resort (and if the hose is to be replaced with a new one anyway), the rubber can be slit with a knife and the hose peeled from the spigot. If this must be done, be careful that the metal connection is not damaged.

If a hose clamp is broken or damaged, do not reuse it. Wire-type clamps usually weaken with age, so it is a good idea to replace them with screw-type clamps whenever a hose is removed.

Tools

A selection of good tools is a basic requirement for anyone who plans to maintain and repair his or her own vehicle. For the owner who has few tools, the initial investment might seem high, but when compared to the spiraling costs of professional auto maintenance and repair, it is a wise one.

To help the owner decide which tools are needed to perform the tasks detailed in this manual, the following tool lists are offered: *Maintenance and minor repair, Repair/overhaul* and *Special.*

The newcomer to practical mechanics should start off with the *maintenance and minor repair* tool kit, which is adequate for the simpler jobs performed on a vehicle. Then, as confidence and experience grow, the owner can tackle more difficult tasks, buying additional tools as they are needed. Eventually the basic kit will be expanded into the *repair and overhaul* tool set. Over a period of time, the experienced do-it-yourselfer will assemble a tool set complete enough for most repair and overhaul procedures and will add tools from the special category when it is felt that the expense is justified by the frequency of use.

Maintenance and minor repair tool kit

The tools in this list should be considered the minimum required for performance of routine maintenance, servicing and minor

repair work. We recommend the purchase of combination wrenches (box-end and open-end combined in one wrench). While more expensive than open end wrenches, they offer the advantages of both types of wrench.

> *Combination wrench set (1/4-inch to 1 inch or 6 mm to 19 mm)*
> *Adjustable wrench, 8 inch*
> *Spark plug wrench with rubber insert*
> *Spark plug gap adjusting tool*
> *Feeler gauge set*
> *Brake bleeder wrench*
> *Standard screwdriver (5/16-inch x 6 inch)*
> *Phillips screwdriver (No. 2 x 6 inch)*
> *Combination pliers - 6 inch*
> *Hacksaw and assortment of blades*
> *Tire pressure gauge*
> *Grease gun*
> *Oil can*
> *Fine emery cloth*
> *Wire brush*
> *Battery post and cable cleaning tool*
> *Oil filter wrench*
> *Funnel (medium size)*
> *Safety goggles*
> *Jackstands (2)*
> *Drain pan*

Note: *If basic tune-ups are going to be part of routine maintenance, it will be necessary to purchase a good quality stroboscopic timing light and combination tachometer/dwell meter. Although they are included in the list of special tools, it is mentioned here because they are absolutely necessary for tuning most vehicles properly.*

Repair and overhaul tool set

These tools are essential for anyone who plans to perform major repairs and are in addition to those in the maintenance and minor repair tool kit. Included is a comprehensive set of sockets which, though expensive, are invaluable because of their versatility, especially when various extensions and drives are available. We recommend the 1/2-inch drive over the 3/8-inch drive. Although the larger drive is bulky and more expensive, it has the capacity of accepting a very wide range of large sockets. Ideally, however, the mechanic should have a 3/8-inch drive set and a 1/2-inch drive set.

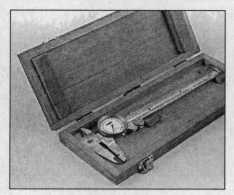

Dial caliper

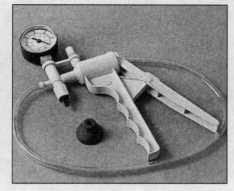

Hand-operated vacuum pump

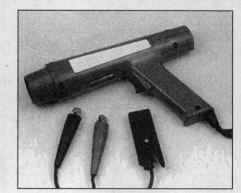

Timing light

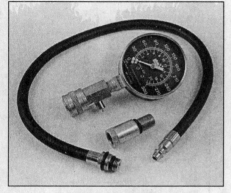

Compression gauge with spark plug hole adapter

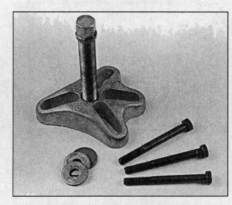

Damper/steering wheel puller

General purpose puller

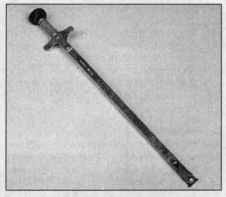

Hydraulic lifter removal tool

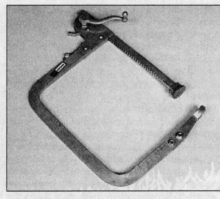

Valve spring compressor

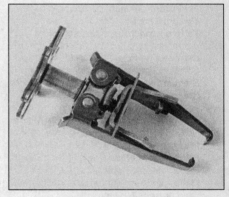

Valve spring compressor

Ridge reamer

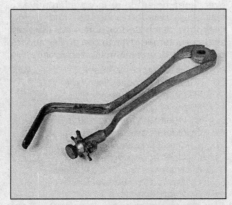

Piston ring groove cleaning tool

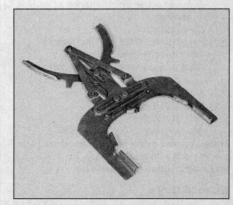

Ring removal/installation tool

Ring compressor

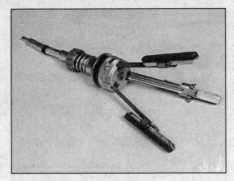

Cylinder hone

Brake hold-down spring tool

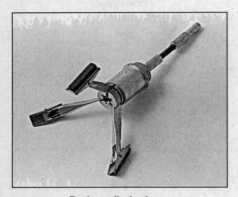

Brake cylinder hone

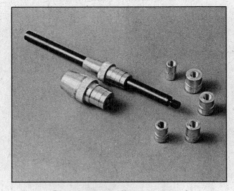

Clutch plate alignment tool

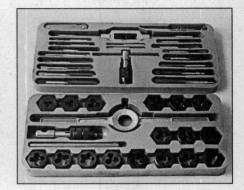

Tap and die set

Socket set(s)
Reversible ratchet
Extension - 10 inch
Universal joint
Torque wrench (same size drive as
    sockets)
Ball peen hammer - 8 ounce
Soft-face hammer (plastic/rubber)
Standard screwdriver (1/4-inch x 6 inch)
Standard screwdriver (stubby -
    5/16-inch)
Phillips screwdriver (No. 3 x 8 inch)
Phillips screwdriver (stubby - No. 2)
Pliers - vise grip
Pliers - lineman's
Pliers - needle nose
Pliers - snap-ring (internal and external)
Cold chisel - 1/2-inch
Scribe
Scraper (made from flattened copper
    tubing)
Centerpunch
Pin punches (1/16, 1/8, 3/16-inch)
Steel rule/straightedge - 12 inch
Allen wrench set (1/8 to 3/8-inch or
    4 mm to 10 mm)
A selection of files
Wire brush (large)
Jackstands (second set)
Jack (scissor or hydraulic type)

Note: Another tool which is often useful is an
electric drill with a chuck capacity of 3/8-inch
and a set of good quality drill bits.

Special tools

The tools in this list include those which
are not used regularly, are expensive to buy,
or which need to be used in accordance with
their manufacturer's instructions. Unless
these tools will be used frequently, it is not
very economical to purchase many of them.
A consideration would be to split the cost
and use between yourself and a friend or
friends. In addition, most of these tools can
be obtained from a tool rental shop on a temporary basis.

This list primarily contains only those
tools and instruments widely available to the
public, and not those special tools produced
by the vehicle manufacturer for distribution to
dealer service departments. Occasionally,
references to the manufacturer's special
tools are included in the text of this manual.
Generally, an alternative method of doing the
job without the special tool is offered. However, sometimes there is no alternative to
their use. Where this is the case, and the tool
cannot be purchased or borrowed, the work
should be turned over to the dealer service
department or an automotive repair shop.

Valve spring compressor
Piston ring groove cleaning tool
Piston ring compressor
Piston ring installation tool
Cylinder compression gauge
Cylinder ridge reamer
Cylinder surfacing hone
Cylinder bore gauge
Micrometers and/or dial calipers
Hydraulic lifter removal tool
Balljoint separator
Universal-type puller

Impact screwdriver
Dial indicator set
Stroboscopic timing light (inductive
    pick-up)
Hand operated vacuum/pressure pump
Tachometer/dwell meter
Universal electrical multimeter
Cable hoist
Brake spring removal and installation
    tools
Floor jack

Buying tools

For the do-it-yourselfer who is just starting to get involved in vehicle maintenance
and repair, there are a number of options
available when purchasing tools. If maintenance and minor repair is the extent of the
work to be done, the purchase of individual
tools is satisfactory. If, on the other hand,
extensive work is planned, it would be a good
idea to purchase a modest tool set from one
of the large retail chain stores. A set can usually be bought at a substantial savings over
the individual tool prices, and they often
come with a tool box. As additional tools are
needed, add-on sets, individual tools and a
larger tool box can be purchased to expand
the tool selection. Building a tool set gradually allows the cost of the tools to be spread
over a longer period of time and gives the
mechanic the freedom to choose only those
tools that will actually be used.

Tool stores will often be the only source
of some of the special tools that are needed,
but regardless of where tools are bought, try

to avoid cheap ones, especially when buying screwdrivers and sockets, because they won't last very long. The expense involved in replacing cheap tools will eventually be greater than the initial cost of quality tools.

Care and maintenance of tools

Good tools are expensive, so it makes sense to treat them with respect. Keep them clean and in usable condition and store them properly when not in use. Always wipe off any dirt, grease or metal chips before putting them away. Never leave tools lying around in the work area. Upon completion of a job, always check closely under the hood for tools that may have been left there so they won't get lost during a test drive.

Some tools, such as screwdrivers, pliers, wrenches and sockets, can be hung on a panel mounted on the garage or workshop wall, while others should be kept in a tool box or tray. Measuring instruments, gauges, meters, etc. must be carefully stored where they cannot be damaged by weather or impact from other tools.

When tools are used with care and stored properly, they will last a very long time. Even with the best of care, though, tools will wear out if used frequently. When a tool is damaged or worn out, replace it. Subsequent jobs will be safer and more enjoyable if you do.

How to repair damaged threads

Sometimes, the internal threads of a nut or bolt hole can become stripped, usually from overtightening. Stripping threads is an all-too-common occurrence, especially when working with aluminum parts, because aluminum is so soft that it easily strips out.

Usually, external or internal threads are only partially stripped. After they've been cleaned up with a tap or die, they'll still work. Sometimes, however, threads are badly damaged. When this happens, you've got three choices:

1) Drill and tap the hole to the next suitable oversize and install a larger diameter bolt, screw or stud.
2) Drill and tap the hole to accept a threaded plug, then drill and tap the plug to the original screw size. You can also buy a plug already threaded to the original size. Then you simply drill a hole to the specified size, then run the threaded plug into the hole with a bolt and jam nut. Once the plug is fully seated, remove the jam nut and bolt.
3) The third method uses a patented thread repair kit like Heli-Coil or Slimsert. These easy-to-use kits are designed to repair damaged threads in straight-through holes and blind holes. Both are available as kits which can handle a variety of sizes and thread patterns. Drill the hole, then tap it with the special included tap. Install the Heli-Coil and the hole is back to its original diameter and thread pitch.

Regardless of which method you use, be sure to proceed calmly and carefully. A little impatience or carelessness during one of these relatively simple procedures can ruin your whole day's work and cost you a bundle if you wreck an expensive part.

Working facilities

Not to be overlooked when discussing tools is the workshop. If anything more than routine maintenance is to be carried out, some sort of suitable work area is essential.

It is understood, and appreciated, that many home mechanics do not have a good workshop or garage available, and end up removing an engine or doing major repairs outside. It is recommended, however, that the overhaul or repair be completed under the cover of a roof.

A clean, flat workbench or table of comfortable working height is an absolute necessity. The workbench should be equipped with a vise that has a jaw opening of at least four inches.

As mentioned previously, some clean, dry storage space is also required for tools, as well as the lubricants, fluids, cleaning solvents, etc. which soon become necessary.

Sometimes waste oil and fluids, drained from the engine or cooling system during normal maintenance or repairs, present a disposal problem. To avoid pouring them on the ground or into a sewage system, pour the used fluids into large containers, seal them with caps and take them to an authorized disposal site or recycling center. Plastic jugs, such as old antifreeze containers, are ideal for this purpose.

Always keep a supply of old newspapers and clean rags available. Old towels are excellent for mopping up spills. Many mechanics use rolls of paper towels for most work because they are readily available and disposable. To help keep the area under the vehicle clean, a large cardboard box can be cut open and flattened to protect the garage or shop floor.

Whenever working over a painted surface, such as when leaning over a fender to service something under the hood, always cover it with an old blanket or bedspread to protect the finish. Vinyl covered pads, made especially for this purpose, are available at auto parts stores.

Booster battery (jump) starting

Observe these precautions when using a booster battery to start a vehicle:

a) Before connecting the booster battery, make sure the ignition switch is in the Off position.
b) Turn off the lights, heater and other electrical loads.
c) Your eyes should be shielded. Safety goggles are a good idea.
d) Make sure the booster battery is the same voltage as the dead one in the vehicle.
e) The two vehicles MUST NOT TOUCH each other!
f) Make sure the transaxle is in Neutral (manual) or Park (automatic).
g) If the booster battery is not a maintenance-free type, remove the vent caps and lay a cloth over the vent holes.

Connect the red jumper cable to the positive (+) terminals of each battery (see illustration).

Connect one end of the black jumper cable to the negative (-) terminal of the booster battery. The other end of this cable should be connected to a good ground on the vehicle to be started, such as a bolt or bracket on the body.

Start the engine using the booster battery, then, with the engine running at idle speed, disconnect the jumper cables in the reverse order of connection.

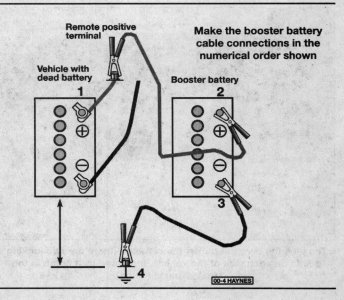

Make the booster battery cable connections in the numerical order shown

Jacking and towing

Jacking

Warning: *The jack supplied with the vehicle should only be used for changing a tire or placing jackstands under the frame. Never work under the vehicle or start the engine while this jack is being used as the only means of support.*

The vehicle should be on level ground. Place the shift lever in Park, if you have an automatic, or Reverse if you have a manual transaxle. Block the wheel diagonally opposite the wheel being changed. Set the parking brake.

Remove the spare tire and jack from stowage. Remove the wheel cover and trim ring (if so equipped) with the tapered end of the lug nut wrench by inserting and twisting the handle and then prying against the back of the wheel cover. Loosen the wheel lug nuts about 1/4-to-1/2 turn each.

Place the scissors-type jack under the side of the vehicle and adjust the jack height until it fits in the notch in the vertical rocker panel flange nearest the wheel to be changed. There is a front and rear jacking point on each side of the vehicle (**see illustrations**).

Turn the jack handle clockwise until the tire clears the ground. Remove the lug nuts and pull the wheel off. Replace it with the spare.

Install the lug nuts with the beveled edges facing in. Tighten them snugly. Don't attempt to tighten them completely until the vehicle is lowered or it could slip off the jack. Turn the jack handle counterclockwise to lower the vehicle. Remove the jack and tighten the lug nuts in a diagonal pattern.

Install the cover (and trim ring, if used) and be sure it's snapped into place all the way around.

Stow the tire, jack and wrench. Unblock the wheels.

Towing

As a general rule, the vehicle should be towed with the front (drive) wheels off the ground. If they can't be raised, place them on a dolly. The ignition key must be in the ACC position, since the steering lock mechanism isn't strong enough to hold the front wheels straight while towing.

Vehicles equipped with an automatic transaxle can be towed from the front only with all four wheels on the ground, provided that speeds don't exceed 30 mph and the distance is not over 40 miles. Before towing, check the transmission fluid level (see Chapter 1). If the level is below the HOT line on the dipstick, add fluid or use a towing dolly.

Caution: *Never tow a vehicle with an automatic transaxle from the rear with the front wheels on the ground.*

When towing a vehicle equipped with a manual transaxle with all four wheels on the ground, be sure to place the shift lever in neutral and release the parking brake.

Equipment specifically designed for towing should be used. It should be attached to the main structural members of the vehicle, not the bumpers or brackets.

Safety is a major consideration when towing and all applicable state and local laws must be obeyed. A safety chain system must be used at all times.

The jack fits over the rocker panel flange (there are two jacking points on each side of the vehicle, indicated by a notch in the rocker panel flange)

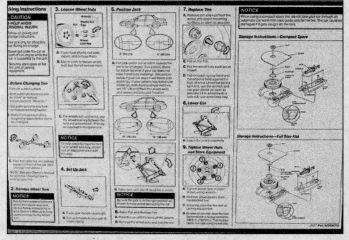

The vehicle is equipped with jacking instructions located in the trunk area

Automotive chemicals and lubricants

A number of automotive chemicals and lubricants are available for use during vehicle maintenance and repair. They include a wide variety of products ranging from cleaning solvents and degreasers to lubricants and protective sprays for rubber, plastic and vinyl.

Cleaners

Carburetor cleaner and choke cleaner is a strong solvent for gum, varnish and carbon. Most carburetor cleaners leave a dry-type lubricant film which will not harden or gum up. Because of this film it is not recommended for use on electrical components.

Brake system cleaner is used to remove brake dust, grease and brake fluid from the brake system, where clean surfaces are absolutely necessary. It leaves no residue and often eliminates brake squeal caused by contaminants.

Electrical cleaner removes oxidation, corrosion and carbon deposits from electrical contacts, restoring full current flow. It can also be used to clean spark plugs, carburetor jets, voltage regulators and other parts where an oil-free surface is desired.

Demoisturants remove water and moisture from electrical components such as alternators, voltage regulators, electrical connectors and fuse blocks. They are non-conductive and non-corrosive.

Degreasers are heavy-duty solvents used to remove grease from the outside of the engine and from chassis components. They can be sprayed or brushed on and, depending on the type, are rinsed off either with water or solvent.

Lubricants

Motor oil is the lubricant formulated for use in engines. It normally contains a wide variety of additives to prevent corrosion and reduce foaming and wear. Motor oil comes in various weights (viscosity ratings) from 0 to 50. The recommended weight of the oil depends on the season, temperature and the demands on the engine. Light oil is used in cold climates and under light load conditions. Heavy oil is used in hot climates and where high loads are encountered. Multi-viscosity oils are designed to have characteristics of both light and heavy oils and are available in a number of weights from 5W-20 to 20W-50.

Gear oil is designed to be used in differentials, manual transmissions and other areas where high-temperature lubrication is required.

Chassis and wheel bearing grease is a heavy grease used where increased loads and friction are encountered, such as for wheel bearings, balljoints, tie-rod ends and universal joints.

High-temperature wheel bearing grease is designed to withstand the extreme temperatures encountered by wheel bearings in disc brake equipped vehicles. It usually contains molybdenum disulfide (moly), which is a dry-type lubricant.

White grease is a heavy grease for metal-to-metal applications where water is a problem. White grease stays soft under both low and high temperatures (usually from -100 to +190-degrees F), and will not wash off or dilute in the presence of water.

Assembly lube is a special extreme pressure lubricant, usually containing moly, used to lubricate high-load parts (such as main and rod bearings and cam lobes) for initial start-up of a new engine. The assembly lube lubricates the parts without being squeezed out or washed away until the engine oiling system begins to function.

Silicone lubricants are used to protect rubber, plastic, vinyl and nylon parts.

Graphite lubricants are used where oils cannot be used due to contamination problems, such as in locks. The dry graphite will lubricate metal parts while remaining uncontaminated by dirt, water, oil or acids. It is electrically conductive and will not foul electrical contacts in locks such as the ignition switch.

Moly penetrants loosen and lubricate frozen, rusted and corroded fasteners and prevent future rusting or freezing.

Heat-sink grease is a special electrically non-conductive grease that is used for mounting electronic ignition modules where it is essential that heat is transferred away from the module.

Sealants

RTV sealant is one of the most widely used gasket compounds. Made from silicone, RTV is air curing, it seals, bonds, waterproofs, fills surface irregularities, remains flexible, doesn't shrink, is relatively easy to remove, and is used as a supplementary sealer with almost all low and medium temperature gaskets.

Anaerobic sealant is much like RTV in that it can be used either to seal gaskets or to form gaskets by itself. It remains flexible, is solvent resistant and fills surface imperfections. The difference between an anaerobic sealant and an RTV-type sealant is in the curing. RTV cures when exposed to air, while an anaerobic sealant cures only in the absence of air. This means that an anaerobic sealant cures only after the assembly of parts, sealing them together.

Thread and pipe sealant is used for sealing hydraulic and pneumatic fittings and vacuum lines. It is usually made from a Teflon compound, and comes in a spray, a paint-on liquid and as a wrap-around tape.

Chemicals

Anti-seize compound prevents seizing, galling, cold welding, rust and corrosion in fasteners. High-temperature ant-seize, usually made with copper and graphite lubricants, is used for exhaust system and exhaust manifold bolts.

Anaerobic locking compounds are used to keep fasteners from vibrating or working loose and cure only after installation, in the absence of air. Medium strength locking compound is used for small nuts, bolts and screws that may be removed later. High-strength locking compound is for large nuts, bolts and studs which aren't removed on a regular basis.

Oil additives range from viscosity index improvers to chemical treatments that claim to reduce internal engine friction. It should be noted that most oil manufacturers caution against using additives with their oils.

Gas additives perform several functions, depending on their chemical makeup. They usually contain solvents that help dissolve gum and varnish that build up on carburetor, fuel injection and intake parts. They also serve to break down carbon deposits that form on the inside surfaces of the combustion chambers. Some additives contain upper cylinder lubricants for valves and piston rings, and others contain chemicals to remove condensation from the gas tank.

Miscellaneous

Brake fluid is specially formulated hydraulic fluid that can withstand the heat and pressure encountered in brake systems. Care must be taken so this fluid does not come in contact with painted surfaces or plastics. An opened container should always be resealed to prevent contamination by water or dirt.

Weatherstrip adhesive is used to bond weatherstripping around doors, windows and trunk lids. It is sometimes used to attach trim pieces.

Undercoating is a petroleum-based, tar-like substance that is designed to protect metal surfaces on the underside of the vehicle from corrosion. It also acts as a sound-deadening agent by insulating the bottom of the vehicle.

Waxes and polishes are used to help protect painted and plated surfaces from the weather. Different types of paint may require the use of different types of wax and polish. Some polishes utilize a chemical or abrasive cleaner to help remove the top layer of oxidized (dull) paint on older vehicles. In recent years many non-wax polishes that contain a wide variety of chemicals such as polymers and silicones have been introduced. These non-wax polishes are usually easier to apply and last longer than conventional waxes and polishes.

Conversion factors

Length (distance)
Inches (in)	X	25.4	= Millimeters (mm)	X 0.0394	= Inches (in)
Feet (ft)	X	0.305	= Meters (m)	X 3.281	= Feet (ft)
Miles	X	1.609	= Kilometers (km)	X 0.621	= Miles

Volume (capacity)
Cubic inches (cu in; in³)	X 16.387 = Cubic centimeters (cc; cm³)	X 0.061	= Cubic inches (cu in; in³)
Imperial pints (Imp pt)	X 0.568 = Liters (l)	X 1.76	= Imperial pints (Imp pt)
Imperial quarts (Imp qt)	X 1.137 = Liters (l)	X 0.88	= Imperial quarts (Imp qt)
Imperial quarts (Imp qt)	X 1.201 = US quarts (US qt)	X 0.833	= Imperial quarts (Imp qt)
US quarts (US qt)	X 0.946 = Liters (l)	X 1.057	= US quarts (US qt)
Imperial gallons (Imp gal)	X 4.546 = Liters (l)	X 0.22	= Imperial gallons (Imp gal)
Imperial gallons (Imp gal)	X 1.201 = US gallons (US gal)	X 0.833	= Imperial gallons (Imp gal)
US gallons (US gal)	X 3.785 = Liters (l)	X 0.264	= US gallons (US gal)

Mass (weight)
Ounces (oz)	X 28.35 = Grams (g)	X 0.035	= Ounces (oz)
Pounds (lb)	X 0.454 = Kilograms (kg)	X 2.205	= Pounds (lb)

Force
Ounces-force (ozf; oz)	X 0.278 = Newtons (N)	X 3.6	= Ounces-force (ozf; oz)
Pounds-force (lbf; lb)	X 4.448 = Newtons (N)	X 0.225	= Pounds-force (lbf; lb)
Newtons (N)	X 0.1 = Kilograms-force (kgf; kg)	X 9.81	= Newtons (N)

Pressure
Pounds-force per square inch (psi; lbf/in²; lb/in²)	X 0.070 = Kilograms-force per square centimeter (kgf/cm²; kg/cm²)	X 14.223	= Pounds-force per square inch (psi; lbf/in²; lb/in²)
Pounds-force per square inch (psi; lbf/in²; lb/in²)	X 0.068 = Atmospheres (atm)	X 14.696	= Pounds-force per square inch (psi; lbf/in²; lb/in²)
Pounds-force per square inch (psi; lbf/in²; lb/in²)	X 0.069 = Bars	X 14.5	= Pounds-force per square inch (psi; lbf/in²; lb/in²)
Pounds-force per square inch (psi; lbf/in²; lb/in²)	X 6.895 = Kilopascals (kPa)	X 0.145	= Pounds-force per square inch (psi; lbf/in²; lb/in²)
Kilopascals (kPa)	X 0.01 = Kilograms-force per square centimeter (kgf/cm²; kg/cm²)	X 98.1	= Kilopascals (kPa)

Torque (moment of force)
Pounds-force inches (lbf in; lb in)	X 1.152 = Kilograms-force centimeter (kgf cm; kg cm)	X 0.868	= Pounds-force inches (lbf in; lb in)
Pounds-force inches (lbf in; lb in)	X 0.113 = Newton meters (Nm)	X 8.85	= Pounds-force inches (lbf in; lb in)
Pounds-force inches (lbf in; lb in)	X 0.083 = Pounds-force feet (lbf ft; lb ft)	X 12	= Pounds-force inches (lbf in; lb in)
Pounds-force feet (lbf ft; lb ft)	X 0.138 = Kilograms-force meters (kgf m; kg m)	X 7.233	= Pounds-force feet (lbf ft; lb ft)
Pounds-force feet (lbf ft; lb ft)	X 1.356 = Newton meters (Nm)	X 0.738	= Pounds-force feet (lbf ft; lb ft)
Newton meters (Nm)	X 0.102 = Kilograms-force meters (kgf m; kg m)	X 9.804	= Newton meters (Nm)

Vacuum
Inches mercury (in. Hg)	X 3.377 = Kilopascals (kPa)	X 0.2961	= Inches mercury
Inches mercury (in. Hg)	X 25.4 = Millimeters mercury (mm Hg)	X 0.0394	= Inches mercury

Power
Horsepower (hp)	X 745.7 = Watts (W)	X 0.0013	= Horsepower (hp)

Velocity (speed)
Miles per hour (miles/hr; mph)	X 1.609 = Kilometers per hour (km/hr; kph)	X 0.621	= Miles per hour (miles/hr; mph)

Fuel consumption*
Miles per gallon, Imperial (mpg)	X 0.354 = Kilometers per liter (km/l)	X 2.825	= Miles per gallon, Imperial (mpg)
Miles per gallon, US (mpg)	X 0.425 = Kilometers per liter (km/l)	X 2.352	= Miles per gallon, US (mpg)

Temperature
Degrees Fahrenheit = ($°C \times 1.8$) + 32   Degrees Celsius (Degrees Centigrade; °C) = ($°F - 32$) $\times$ 0.56

*It is common practice to convert from miles per gallon (mpg) to liters/100 kilometers (l/100km), where mpg (Imperial) x l/100 km = 282 and mpg (US) x l/100 km = 235

DECIMALS to MILLIMETERS

Decimal	mm	Decimal	mm
0.001	0.0254	0.500	12.7000
0.002	0.0508	0.510	12.9540
0.003	0.0762	0.520	13.2080
0.004	0.1016	0.530	13.4620
0.005	0.1270	0.540	13.7160
0.006	0.1524	0.550	13.9700
0.007	0.1778	0.560	14.2240
0.008	0.2032	0.570	14.4780
0.009	0.2286	0.580	14.7320
0.010	0.2540	0.590	14.9860
0.020	0.5080		
0.030	0.7620		
0.040	1.0160	0.600	15.2400
0.050	1.2700	0.610	15.4940
0.060	1.5240	0.620	15.7480
0.070	1.7780	0.630	16.0020
0.080	2.0320	0.640	16.2560
0.090	2.2860	0.650	16.5100
0.100	2.5400	0.660	16.7640
0.110	2.7940	0.670	17.0180
0.120	3.0480	0.680	17.2720
0.130	3.3020	0.690	17.5260
0.140	3.5560		
0.150	3.8100	0.700	17.7800
0.160	4.0640	0.710	18.0340
0.170	4.3180	0.720	18.2880
0.180	4.5720	0.730	18.5420
0.190	4.8260	0.740	18.7960
0.200	5.0800	0.750	19.0500
0.210	5.3340	0.760	19.3040
0.220	5.5880	0.770	19.5580
0.230	5.8420	0.780	19.8120
0.240	6.0960	0.790	20.0660
0.250	6.3500		
0.260	6.6040	0.800	20.3200
0.270	6.8580	0.810	20.5740
0.280	7.1120	0.820	21.8280
0.290	7.3660	0.830	21.0820
0.300	7.6200	0.840	21.3360
0.310	7.8740	0.850	21.5900
0.320	8.1280	0.860	21.8440
0.330	8.3820	0.870	22.0980
0.340	8.6360	0.880	22.3520
0.350	8.8900	0.890	22.6060
0.360	9.1440		
0.370	9.3980		
0.380	9.6520		
0.390	9.9060	0.900	22.8600
0.400	10.1600	0.910	23.1140
0.410	10.4140	0.920	23.3680
0.420	10.6680	0.930	23.6220
0.430	10.9220	0.940	23.8760
0.440	11.1760	0.950	24.1300
0.450	11.4300	0.960	24.3840
0.460	11.6840	0.970	24.6380
0.470	11.9380	0.980	24.8920
0.480	12.1920	0.990	25.1460
0.490	12.4460	1.000	25.4000

FRACTIONS to DECIMALS to MILLIMETERS

Fraction	Decimal	mm	Fraction	Decimal	mm
1/64	0.0156	0.3969	33/64	0.5156	13.0969
1/32	0.0312	0.7938	17/32	0.5312	13.4938
3/64	0.0469	1.1906	35/64	0.5469	13.8906
1/16	0.0625	1.5875	9/16	0.5625	14.2875
5/64	0.0781	1.9844	37/64	0.5781	14.6844
3/32	0.0938	2.3812	19/32	0.5938	15.0812
7/64	0.1094	2.7781	39/64	0.6094	15.4781
1/8	0.1250	3.1750	5/8	0.6250	15.8750
9/64	0.1406	3.5719	41/64	0.6406	16.2719
5/32	0.1562	3.9688	21/32	0.6562	16.6688
11/64	0.1719	4.3656	43/64	0.6719	17.0656
3/16	0.1875	4.7625	11/16	0.6875	17.4625
13/64	0.2031	5.1594	45/64	0.7031	17.8594
7/32	0.2188	5.5562	23/32	0.7188	18.2562
15/64	0.2344	5.9531	47/64	0.7344	18.6531
1/4	0.2500	6.3500	3/4	0.7500	19.0500
17/64	0.2656	6.7469	49/64	0.7656	19.4469
9/32	0.2812	7.1438	25/32	0.7812	19.8438
19/64	0.2969	7.5406	51/64	0.7969	20.2406
5/16	0.3125	7.9375	13/16	0.8125	20.6375
21/64	0.3281	8.3344	53/64	0.8281	21.0344
11/32	0.3438	8.7312	27/32	0.8438	21.4312
23/64	0.3594	9.1281	55/64	0.8594	21.8281
3/8	0.3750	9.5250	7/8	0.8750	22.2250
25/64	0.3906	9.9219	57/64	0.8906	22.6219
13/32	0.4062	10.3188	29/32	0.9062	23.0188
27/64	0.4219	10.7156	59/64	0.9219	23.4156
7/16	0.4375	11.1125	15/16	0.9375	23.8125
29/64	0.4531	11.5094	61/64	0.9531	24.2094
15/32	0.4688	11.9062	31/32	0.9688	24.6062
31/64	0.4844	12.3031	63/64	0.9844	25.0031
1/2	0.5000	12.7000	1	1.0000	25.4000

Safety first!

Regardless of how enthusiastic you may be about getting on with the job at hand, take the time to ensure that your safety is not jeopardized. A moment's lack of attention can result in an accident, as can failure to observe certain simple safety precautions. The possibility of an accident will always exist, and the following points should not be considered a comprehensive list of all dangers. Rather, they are intended to make you aware of the risks and to encourage a safety conscious approach to all work you carry out on your vehicle.

Essential DOs and DON'Ts

DON'T rely on a jack when working under the vehicle. Always use approved jackstands to support the weight of the vehicle and place them under the recommended lift or support points.

DON'T attempt to loosen extremely tight fasteners (i.e. wheel lug nuts) while the vehicle is on a jack - it may fall.

DON'T start the engine without first making sure that the transmission is in Neutral (or Park where applicable) and the parking brake is set.

DON'T remove the radiator cap from a hot cooling system - let it cool or cover it with a cloth and release the pressure gradually.

DON'T attempt to drain the engine oil until you are sure it has cooled to the point that it will not burn you.

DON'T touch any part of the engine or exhaust system until it has cooled sufficiently to avoid burns.

DON'T siphon toxic liquids such as gasoline, antifreeze and brake fluid by mouth, or allow them to remain on your skin.

DON'T inhale brake lining dust - it is potentially hazardous (see *Asbestos* below).

DON'T allow spilled oil or grease to remain on the floor - wipe it up before someone slips on it.

DON'T use loose fitting wrenches or other tools which may slip and cause injury.

DON'T push on wrenches when loosening or tightening nuts or bolts. Always try to pull the wrench toward you. If the situation calls for pushing the wrench away, push with an open hand to avoid scraped knuckles if the wrench should slip.

DON'T attempt to lift a heavy component alone - get someone to help you.

DON'T rush or take unsafe shortcuts to finish a job.

DON'T allow children or animals in or around the vehicle while you are working on it.

DO wear eye protection when using power tools such as a drill, sander, bench grinder, etc. and when working under a vehicle.

DO keep loose clothing and long hair well out of the way of moving parts.

DO make sure that any hoist used has a safe working load rating adequate for the job.

DO get someone to check on you periodically when working alone on a vehicle.

DO carry out work in a logical sequence and make sure that everything is correctly assembled and tightened.

DO keep chemicals and fluids tightly capped and out of the reach of children and pets.

DO remember that your vehicle's safety affects that of yourself and others. If in doubt on any point, get professional advice.

Asbestos

Certain friction, insulating, sealing, and other products - such as brake linings, brake bands, clutch linings, torque converters, gaskets, etc. - may contain asbestos. Extreme care must be taken to avoid inhalation of dust from such products, since it is hazardous to health. If in doubt, assume that they do contain asbestos.

Fire

Remember at all times that gasoline is highly flammable. Never smoke or have any kind of open flame around when working on a vehicle. But the risk does not end there. A spark caused by an electrical short circuit, by two metal surfaces contacting each other, or even by static electricity built up in your body under certain conditions, can ignite gasoline vapors, which in a confined space are highly explosive. Do not, under any circumstances, use gasoline for cleaning parts. Use an approved safety solvent.

Always disconnect the battery ground (-) cable at the battery before working on any part of the fuel system or electrical system. Never risk spilling fuel on a hot engine or exhaust component. It is strongly recommended that a fire extinguisher suitable for use on fuel and electrical fires be kept handy in the garage or workshop at all times. Never try to extinguish a fuel or electrical fire with water.

Fumes

Certain fumes are highly toxic and can quickly cause unconsciousness and even death if inhaled to any extent. Gasoline vapor falls into this category, as do the vapors from some cleaning solvents. Any draining or pouring of such volatile fluids should be done in a well ventilated area.

When using cleaning fluids and solvents, read the instructions on the container carefully. Never use materials from unmarked containers.

Never run the engine in an enclosed space, such as a garage. Exhaust fumes contain carbon monoxide, which is extremely poisonous. If you need to run the engine, always do so in the open air, or at least have the rear of the vehicle outside the work area.

If you are fortunate enough to have the use of an inspection pit, never drain or pour gasoline and never run the engine while the vehicle is over the pit. The fumes, being heavier than air, will concentrate in the pit with possibly lethal results.

The battery

Never create a spark or allow a bare light bulb near a battery. They normally give off a certain amount of hydrogen gas, which is highly explosive.

Always disconnect the battery ground (-) cable at the battery before working on the fuel or electrical systems.

If possible, loosen the filler caps or cover when charging the battery from an external source (this does not apply to sealed or maintenance-free batteries). Do not charge at an excessive rate or the battery may burst.

Take care when adding water to a non maintenance-free battery and when carrying a battery. The electrolyte, even when diluted, is very corrosive and should not be allowed to contact clothing or skin.

Always wear eye protection when cleaning the battery to prevent the caustic deposits from entering your eyes.

Household current

When using an electric power tool, inspection light, etc., which operates on household current, always make sure that the tool is correctly connected to its plug and that, where necessary, it is properly grounded. Do not use such items in damp conditions and, again, do not create a spark or apply excessive heat in the vicinity of fuel or fuel vapor.

Secondary ignition system voltage

A severe electric shock can result from touching certain parts of the ignition system (such as the spark plug wires) when the engine is running or being cranked, particularly if components are damp or the insulation is defective. In the case of an electronic ignition system, the secondary system voltage is much higher and could prove fatal.

Troubleshooting

Contents

This section provides an easy reference guide to the more common problems which may occur during the operation of your vehicle. These problems and their possible causes are grouped under headings denoting various components or systems, such as Engine, Cooling system, etc. They also refer you to the chapter and/or section which deals with the problem.

Remember that successful troubleshooting is not a mysterious black art practiced only by professional mechanics. It is simply the result of the right knowledge combined with an intelligent, systematic approach to the problem. Always work by a process of elimination, starting with the simplest solution and working through to the most complex - and never overlook the obvious. Anyone can run the gas tank dry or leave the lights on overnight, so don't assume that you are exempt from such oversights.

Finally, always establish a clear idea of why a problem has occurred and take steps to ensure that it doesn't happen again. If the electrical system fails because of a poor connection, check the other connections in the system to make sure that they don't fail as well. If a particular fuse continues to blow, find out why - don't just replace one fuse after another. Remember, failure of a small component can often be indicative of potential failure or incorrect functioning of a more important component or system.

Engine

1 Engine will not rotate when attempting to start

1   Battery terminal connections loose or corroded (Chapter 1).
2   Battery discharged or faulty (Chapter 1).
3   Automatic transaxle not completely engaged in Park (Chapter 7) or clutch pedal not completely depressed (Chapter 8).
4   Broken, loose or disconnected wiring in the starting circuit (Chapters 5 and 12).
5   Starter motor pinion jammed in flywheel ring gear (Chapter 5).
6   Starter solenoid faulty (Chapter 5).
7   Starter motor faulty (Chapter 5).
8   Ignition switch faulty (Chapter 12).
9   Starter pinion or flywheel teeth worn or broken (Chapter 5).
10   Defective fusible link (Chapter 12).

2 Engine rotates but will not start

1   Fuel tank empty.
2   Battery discharged (engine rotates slowly) (Chapter 5).
3   Battery terminal connections loose or corroded (Chapter 1).
4   Leaking fuel injector(s), faulty fuel pump, pressure regulator, etc. (Chapter 4).

5   Worn, faulty or incorrectly gapped spark plugs (Chapter 1).
6   Broken, loose or disconnected wiring in the starting circuit (Chapter 5).
7   Broken, loose or disconnected wires at the ignition coils or faulty coils or ignition module (Chapter 5).
8   Defective crankshaft sensor or PCM (Chapter 6).
9   Broken timing chain (Chapter 2).

3 Engine hard to start when cold

1   Battery discharged or low (Chapter 1).
2   Malfunctioning fuel system (Chapter 4).
3   Faulty coolant temperature sensor or intake air temperature sensor (Chapter 6).
4   Fuel injector(s) leaking (Chapter 4).
5   Faulty ignition system (Chapter 5).
6   Defective MAP sensor (see Chapter 6).

4 Engine hard to start when hot

1   Air filter clogged (Chapter 1).
2   Fuel not reaching the fuel injection system (Chapter 4).
3   Corroded battery connections, especially ground (Chapter 1).
4   Faulty coolant temperature sensor or intake air temperature sensor (Chapter 6).

5 Starter motor noisy or excessively rough in engagement

1   Pinion or flywheel gear teeth worn or broken (Chapter 5).
2   Starter motor mounting bolts loose or missing (Chapter 5).

6 Engine starts but stops immediately

1   Loose or faulty electrical connections at ignition coil (Chapter 5).
2   Insufficient fuel reaching the fuel injector(s) (Chapters 4).
3   Vacuum leak at the gasket between the intake manifold/plenum and throttle body (Chapter 4).
4   Fault in the engine control system (Chapter 6).
5   Intake air leaks, broken vacuum lines (see Chapter 4)

7 Oil puddle under engine

1   Oil pan gasket and/or oil pan drain bolt washer leaking (Chapter 2).
2   Oil pressure sending unit leaking (Chapter 2).
3   Valve covers leaking (Chapter 2).
4   Engine oil seals leaking (Chapter 2).

8 Engine lopes while idling or idles erratically

1   Vacuum leakage (Chapters 2 and 4).
2   Leaking EGR valve (Chapter 6).
3   Air filter clogged (Chapter 1).
4   Fuel pump not delivering sufficient fuel to the fuel injection system (Chapter 4).
5   Leaking head gasket (Chapter 2).
6   Camshaft lobes worn (Chapter 2).

9 Engine misses at idle speed

1   Spark plugs worn or not gapped properly (Chapter 1).
2   Faulty spark plug wires (Chapter 1).
3   Vacuum leaks (Chapters 2 and 4).
4   Faulty ignition coil(s) (Chapter 5).
5   Uneven or low compression (Chapter 2).
6   Faulty fuel injector(s) (Chapter 4).

10 Engine misses throughout driving speed range

1   Fuel filter clogged and/or impurities in the fuel system (Chapter 1).
2   Low fuel output at the fuel injector(s) (Chapter 4).
3   Faulty or incorrectly gapped spark plugs (Chapter 1).
4   Leaking spark plug wires (Chapters 1 or 5).
5   Faulty emission system components (Chapter 6).
6   Low or uneven cylinder compression pressures (Chapter 2).
7   Burned valves (Chapter 2).
8   Weak or faulty ignition system (Chapter 5).
9   Vacuum leak in fuel injection system, throttle body, intake manifold or vacuum hoses (Chapter 4).

11 Engine stumbles on acceleration

1   Spark plugs fouled (Chapter 1).
2   Problem with fuel injection system (Chapter 4).
3   Fuel filter clogged (Chapters 1 and 4).
4   Fault in the engine control system (Chapter 6).
5   Intake manifold air leak (Chapters 2 and 4).
6   EGR system malfunction (Chapter 6).

12 Engine surges while holding accelerator steady

1   Intake air leak (Chapter 4).
2   Fuel pump or fuel pressure regulator faulty (Chapter 4).
3   Problem with fuel injection system (Chapter 4).

4   Problem with the emissions control system (Chapter 6).

13   Engine stalls

1   Idle speed incorrect (Chapter 1).
2   Fuel filter clogged and/or water and impurities in the fuel system (Chapters 1 and 4).
3   Ignition components damp or damaged (Chapter 5).
4   Faulty emissions system components (Chapter 6).
5   Faulty or incorrectly gapped spark plugs (Chapter 1).
6   Faulty spark plug wires (Chapter 1).
7   Vacuum leak in the fuel injection system, intake manifold or vacuum hoses (Chapters 2 and 4).

14   Engine lacks power

1   Worn camshaft lobes (Chapter 2).
2   Burned valves or incorrect valve timing (Chapter 2).
3   Faulty spark plug wires or faulty coil (Chapters 1 and 5).
4   Faulty or incorrectly gapped spark plugs (Chapter 1).
5   Problem with the fuel injection system (Chapter 4).
6   Plugged air filter (Chapter 1).
7   Brakes binding (Chapter 9).
8   Automatic transaxle fluid level incorrect (Chapter 1).
9   Clutch slipping (Chapter 8).
10   Fuel filter clogged and/or impurities in the fuel system (Chapters 1 and 4).
11   Emission control system not functioning properly (Chapter 6).
12   Low or uneven cylinder compression pressures (Chapter 2).
13   Restricted exhaust system (Chapters 4).

15   Engine backfires

1   Emission control system not functioning properly (Chapter 6).
2   Faulty spark plug wires or coil(s) (Chapter 5).
3   Problem with the fuel injection system (Chapter 4).
4   Vacuum leak at fuel injector(s), intake manifold or vacuum hoses (Chapters 2 and 4).
5   Burned valves or incorrect valve timing (Chapter 2).

16   Pinging or knocking engine sounds during acceleration or uphill

1   Incorrect grade of fuel.
2   Problem with the engine control system

(Chapter 6).
3   Fuel injection system faulty (Chapter 4).
4   Improper or damaged spark plugs or wires (Chapter 1).
5   EGR valve not functioning (Chapter 6).
6   Vacuum leak (Chapters 2 and 4).

17   Engine runs with oil pressure light on

1   Low oil level (Chapter 1).
2   Idle rpm below specification (Chapter 1).
3   Short in wiring circuit (Chapter 12).
4   Faulty oil pressure sender (Chapter 2).
5   Worn engine bearings and/or oil pump (Chapter 2).

18   Engine diesels (continues to run) after switching off

1   Idle speed too high (Chapter 1).
2   Excessive engine operating temperature (Chapter 3).
3   Excessive carbon deposits on valves and pistons (Chapter 2).

Engine electrical system

19   Battery will not hold a charge

1   Alternator drivebelt defective or not adjusted properly (Chapter 1).
2   Battery electrolyte level low (Chapter 1).
3   Battery terminals loose or corroded (Chapter 1).
4   Alternator not charging properly (Chapter 5).
5   Loose, broken or faulty wiring in the charging circuit (Chapter 5).
6   Short in vehicle wiring (Chapter 12).
7   Internally defective battery (Chapters 1 and 5).

20   Alternator light fails to go out

1   Faulty alternator or charging circuit (Chapter 5).
2   Alternator drivebelt defective or out of adjustment (Chapter 1).
3   Alternator voltage regulator inoperative (Chapter 5).

21   Alternator light fails to come on when key is turned on

1   Warning light bulb defective (Chapter 12).
2   Fault in the printed circuit, dash wiring or bulb holder (Chapter 12).

Fuel system

22   Excessive fuel consumption

1   Dirty or clogged air filter element (Chapter 1).
2   Emissions system not functioning properly (Chapter 6).
3   Fuel injection system not functioning properly (Chapter 4).
4   Low tire pressure or incorrect tire size (Chapter 1).

23   Fuel leakage and/or fuel odor

1   Leaking fuel feed or return line (Chapters 1 and 4).
2   Tank overfilled.
3   Evaporative canister filter clogged (Chapters 1 and 6).
4   Problem with fuel injection system (Chapter 4).

Cooling system

24   Overheating

1   Insufficient coolant in system (Chapter 1).
2   Water pump defective (Chapter 3).
3   Radiator core blocked or grille restricted (Chapter 3).
4   Thermostat faulty (Chapter 3).
5   Electric coolant fan inoperative or blades broken (Chapter 3).
6   Radiator cap not maintaining proper pressure (Chapter 3).

25   Overcooling

1   Faulty thermostat (Chapter 3).
2   Inaccurate temperature gauge sending unit (Chapter 3)

26   External coolant leakage

1   Deteriorated/damaged hoses; loose clamps (Chapters 1 and 3).
2   Water pump defective (Chapter 3).
3   Leakage from radiator core or coolant reservoir bottle (Chapter 3).
4   Engine drain or water jacket core plugs leaking (Chapter 2).

27   Internal coolant leakage

1   Leaking cylinder head gasket (Chapter 2).
2   Cracked cylinder bore or cylinder head (Chapter 2).

28 Coolant loss

1   Too much coolant in system (Chapter 1).
2   Coolant boiling away because of over-heating (Chapter 3).
3   Internal or external leakage (Chapter 3).
4   Faulty pressure cap (Chapter 3).

29 Poor coolant circulation

1   Inoperative water pump (Chapter 3).
2   Restriction in cooling system (Chapters 1 and 3).
3   Thermostat sticking (Chapter 3).

Clutch

30 Pedal travels to floor - no pressure or very little resistance

1   Leaking clutch hydraulic release system or air in system (Chapter 8).
2   Broken release bearing or fork (Chapter 8).

31 Unable to select gears

1   Faulty transaxle (Chapter 7).
2   Faulty clutch disc or pressure plate (Chapter 8).
3   Faulty release cylinder or release bearing (Chapter 8).
4   Faulty shift lever assembly or rods (Chapter 8).

32 Clutch slips (engine speed increases with no increase in vehicle speed)

1   Clutch plate worn (Chapter 8).
2   Clutch plate is oil soaked by leaking rear main seal (Chapter 8).
3   Clutch plate not seated (Chapter 8).
4   Warped pressure plate or flywheel (Chapter 8).
5   Weak diaphragm springs (Chapter 8).
6   Clutch plate overheated. Allow to cool.
7   Faulty clutch self-adjusting mechanism (Chapter 8).

33 Grabbing (chattering) as clutch is engaged

1   Oil on clutch plate lining, burned or glazed facings (Chapter 8).
2   Worn or loose engine or transaxle mounts (Chapters 2 and 7).
3   Worn splines on clutch plate hub (Chapter 8).

4   Warped pressure plate or flywheel (Chapter 8).
5   Burned or smeared resin on flywheel or pressure plate (Chapter 8).

34 Transaxle rattling (clicking)

1   Release fork loose (Chapter 8).
2   Low engine idle speed (Chapter 1).

35 Noise in clutch area

Faulty bearing (Chapter 8).

36 Clutch pedal stays on floor

1   Broken release bearing or fork (Chapter 8).
2   Broken or disconnected clutch cable (Chapter 8).

37 High pedal effort

1   Binding clutch cable (Chapter 8).
2   Pressure plate faulty (Chapter 8).

Manual transaxle

38 Knocking noise at low speeds

1   Worn driveaxle constant velocity (CV) joints (Chapter 8).
2   Worn side gear shaft counterbore in differential case (Chapter 7A).*

39 Noise most pronounced when turning

Differential gear noise (Chapter 7A).*

40 Clunk on acceleration or deceleration

1   Loose engine or transaxle mounts (Chapters 2 and 7A).
2.   Worn differential pinion shaft in case.*
3   Worn side gear shaft counterbore in differential case (Chapter 7A).*
4   Worn or damaged inner CV joints (Chapter 8).

41 Clicking noise in turns

Worn or damaged outer CV joint (Chapter 8).

42 Vibration

1   Rough wheel bearing (Chapters 1 and 10).
2   Damaged driveaxle (Chapter 8).
3   Out of round tires (Chapter 1).
4   Tire out of balance (Chapters 1 and 10).
5   Worn CV joint (Chapter 8).

43 Noisy in neutral with engine running

1   Damaged input gear bearing (Chapter 7A).*
2   Damaged clutch release bearing (Chapter 8).

44 Noisy in one particular gear

1   Damaged or worn constant-mesh gears (Chapter 7A).*
2   Damaged or worn synchronizers (Chapter 7A).*
3   Bent reverse fork (Chapter 7A).*
4   Damaged fourth speed gear or output gear (Chapter 7A).*
5   Worn or damaged reverse idler gear or idler bushing (Chapter 7A).*

45 Noisy in all gears

1   Insufficient lubricant (Chapter 7A).
2   Damaged or worn bearings (Chapter 7A).*
3   Worn or damaged input gear shaft and/or output gear shaft (Chapter 7A).*

46 Slips out of gear

1   Worn or improperly adjusted linkage (Chapter 7A).
2   Transaxle loose on engine (Chapter 7A).
3   Shift linkage does not work freely, binds (Chapter 7A).
4   Input gear bearing retainer broken or loose (Chapter 7A).*
5   Dirt between clutch cover and engine housing (Chapter 7A).
6   Worn shift fork (Chapter 7A).*

47 Leaks lubricant

1   Driveshaft seals worn (Chapter 7A).
2   Excessive amount of lubricant in transaxle (Chapters 1 and 7A).
3   Loose or broken input gear shaft bearing retainer (Chapter 7A).*
4   Input gear bearing retainer O-ring and/or lip seal damaged (Chapter 7A).*
5   Vehicle speed sensor O-ring leaking (Chapter 7A).

48 Hard to shift

Shift linkage loose or worn (Chapter 7A).
* Although the corrective action necessary to remedy the symptoms described is beyond the scope of this manual, the above information should be helpful in isolating the cause of the condition so that the owner can communicate clearly with a professional mechanic.

Automatic transaxle

Note: *Due to the complexity of the automatic transaxle, it is difficult for the home mechanic to properly diagnose and service this component. For problems other than the following, the vehicle should be taken to a dealer or transaxle shop.*

49 Fluid leakage

1 Automatic transaxle fluid is a deep red color. Fluid leaks should not be confused with engine oil, which can easily be blown onto the transaxle by air flow.
2 To pinpoint a leak, first remove all built-up dirt and grime from the transaxle housing with degreasing agents and/or steam cleaning. Then drive the vehicle at low speeds so air flow will not blow the leak far from its source. Raise the vehicle and determine where the leak is coming from. Common areas of leakage are:
a) *Pan (Chapters 1 and 7)*
b) *Dipstick tube (Chapters 1 and 7)*
c) *Transaxle oil lines (Chapter 7)*
d) *Speed sensor (Chapter 7)*
e) *Driveaxle oil seals (Chapter 7)*

50 Transaxle fluid brown or has a burned smell

Transaxle fluid overheated (Chapter 1).

51 General shift mechanism problems

1 Chapter 7, Part B, deals with checking and adjusting the shift linkage on automatic transaxles. Common problems which may be attributed to poorly adjusted linkage are:
a) *Engine starting in gears other than Park or Neutral.*
b) *Indicator on shifter pointing to a gear other than the one actually being used.*
c) *Vehicle moves when in Park.*
2 Refer to Chapter 7B for the shift linkage adjustment procedure.

52 Transaxle will not downshift with accelerator pedal pressed to the floor

1 On non-electronically-controlled trans-

missions, check the throttle valve (TV) cable.
2 On electronically-controlled transaxles, this type of problem - which is caused by a malfunction in the control unit, a sensor or solenoid, or the circuit itself - is beyond the scope of this book. Take the vehicle to a dealer service department or a competent automatic transmission shop.

53 Engine will start in gears other than Park or Neutral

Neutral start switch out of adjustment or malfunctioning (Chapter 7B).

54 Transaxle slips, shifts roughly, is noisy or has no drive in forward or reverse gears

There are many probable causes for the above problems, but the home mechanic should be concerned with only one possibility - fluid level. Before taking the vehicle to a repair shop, check the level and condition of the fluid as described in Chapter 1. Correct the fluid level as necessary or change the fluid and filter if needed. If the problem persists, have a professional diagnose the cause.

Driveaxles

55 Clicking noise in turns

Worn or damaged outboard CV joint (Chapter 8).

56 Shudder or vibration during acceleration

1 Excessive toe-in (Chapter 10).
2 Incorrect spring heights (Chapter 10).
3 Worn or damaged inboard or outboard CV joints (Chapter 8).
4 Sticking inboard CV joint assembly (Chapter 8).

57 Vibration at highway speeds

1 Out of balance front wheels and/or tires (Chapters 1 and 10).
2 Out of round front tires (Chapters 1 and 10).
3 Worn CV joint(s) (Chapter 8).

Brakes
Note: *Before assuming that a brake problem exists, make sure that:*
a) *The tires are in good condition and properly inflated (Chapter 1).*
b) *The front end alignment is correct (Chapter 10).*

c) *The vehicle is not loaded with weight in an unequal manner.*

58 Vehicle pulls to one side during braking

1 Incorrect tire pressures (Chapter 1).
2 Front end out of alignment (have the front end aligned).
3 Front, or rear, tire sizes not matched to one another.
4 Restricted brake lines or hoses (Chapter 9).
5 Malfunctioning drum brake or caliper assembly (Chapter 9).
6 Loose suspension parts (Chapter 10).
7 Loose calipers (Chapter 9).
8 Excessive wear of brake shoe or pad material or disc/drum on one side.

59 Noise (high-pitched squeal when the brakes are applied)

Front and/or rear disc brake pads worn out. The noise comes from the wear sensor rubbing against the disc (does not apply to all vehicles). Replace pads with new ones immediately (Chapter 9).

60 Brake roughness or chatter (pedal pulsates)

1 Excessive lateral runout (Chapter 9).
2 Uneven pad wear (Chapter 9).
3 Defective disc (Chapter 9).

61 Excessive brake pedal effort required to stop vehicle

1 Malfunctioning power brake booster (Chapter 9).
2 Partial system failure (Chapter 9).
3 Excessively worn pads or shoes (Chapter 9).
4 Piston in caliper or wheel cylinder stuck or sluggish (Chapter 9).
5 Brake pads or shoes contaminated with oil or grease (Chapter 9).
6 Brake disc grooved and/or glazed (Chapter 1).
7 New pads or shoes installed and not yet seated. It will take a while for the new material to seat against the disc or drum.

62 Excessive brake pedal travel

1 Partial brake system failure (Chapter 9).
2 Insufficient fluid in master cylinder (Chapters 1 and 9).
3 Air trapped in system (Chapters 1 and 9).

63   Dragging brakes

1   Incorrect adjustment of brake light switch (Chapter 9).
2   Master cylinder pistons not returning correctly (Chapter 9).
3   Restricted brakes lines or hoses (Chapters 1 and 9).
4   Incorrect parking brake adjustment (Chapter 9).

64   Grabbing or uneven braking action

1   Malfunction of proportioning valve (Chapter 9).
2   Malfunction of power brake booster unit (Chapter 9).
3   Binding brake pedal mechanism (Chapter 9).

65   Brake pedal feels spongy when depressed

1   Air in hydraulic lines (Chapter 9).
2   Master cylinder mounting bolts loose (Chapter 9).
3   Master cylinder defective (Chapter 9).

66   Brake pedal travels to the floor with little resistance

1   Little or no fluid in the master cylinder reservoir caused by leaking caliper piston(s) (Chapter 9).
2   Loose, damaged or disconnected brake lines (Chapter 9).

67   Parking brake does not hold

Parking brake linkage improperly adjusted (Chapters 1 and 9).

Suspension and steering systems

Note: *Before attempting to diagnose the suspension and steering systems, perform the following preliminary checks:*

a) *Tires for wrong pressure and uneven wear.*
b) *Steering universal joints from the column to the rack and pinion for loose connectors or wear.*
c) *Front and rear suspension and the rack and pinion assembly for loose or damaged parts.*
d) *Out-of-round or out-of-balance tires, bent rims and loose and/or rough wheel bearings.*

68   Vehicle pulls to one side

1   Mismatched or uneven tires (Chapter 10).
2   Broken or sagging springs (Chapter 10).
3   Wheel alignment out-of-specifications (Chapter 10).
4   Front brake dragging (Chapter 9).

69   Abnormal or excessive tire wear

1   Wheel alignment out-of-specifications (Chapter 10).
2   Sagging or broken springs (Chapter 10).
3   Tire out-of-balance (Chapter 10).
4   Worn strut damper (Chapter 10).
5   Overloaded vehicle.
6   Tires not rotated regularly.

70   Wheel makes a thumping noise

1   Blister or bump on tire (Chapter 10).
2   Improper strut damper action (Chapter 10).

71   Shimmy, shake or vibration

1   Tire or wheel out-of-balance or out-of-round (Chapter 10).
2   Loose or worn wheel bearings (Chapters 1, 8 and 10).
3   Worn tie-rod ends (Chapter 10).
4   Worn lower balljoints (Chapters 1 and 10).
5   Excessive wheel runout (Chapter 10).
6   Blister or bump on tire (Chapter 10).

72   Hard steering

1   Lack of lubrication at balljoints, tie-rod ends and rack and pinion assembly (Chapter 10).
2   Front wheel alignment out-of-specifications (Chapter 10).
3   Low tire pressure(s) (Chapters 1 and 10).

73   Poor returnability of steering to center

1   Lack of lubrication at balljoints and tie-rod ends (Chapter 10).
2   Binding in balljoints (Chapter 10).
3   Binding in steering column (Chapter 10).
4   Lack of lubricant in steering gear assembly (Chapter 10).
5   Front wheel alignment out-of-specifications (Chapter 10).

74   Abnormal noise at the front end

1   Lack of lubrication at balljoints and tie-rod ends (Chapters 1 and 10).
2   Damaged strut mounting (Chapter 10).
3   Worn control arm bushings or tie-rod ends (Chapter 10).
4   Loose stabilizer bar (Chapter 10).
5   Loose wheel nuts (Chapters 1 and 10).
6   Loose suspension bolts (Chapter 10)

75   Wander or poor steering stability

1   Mismatched or uneven tires (Chapter 10).
2   Lack of lubrication at balljoints and tie-rod ends (Chapters 1 and 10).
3   Worn strut assemblies (Chapter 10).
4   Loose stabilizer bar (Chapter 10).
5   Broken or sagging springs (Chapter 10).
6   Wheels out of alignment (Chapter 10).

76   Erratic steering when braking

1   Wheel bearings worn (Chapter 10).
2   Broken or sagging springs (Chapter 10).
3   Leaking wheel cylinder or caliper (Chapter 10).
4   Warped rotors or drums (Chapter 10).

77   Excessive pitching and/or rolling around corners or during braking

1   Loose stabilizer bar (Chapter 10).
2   Worn strut dampers or mountings (Chapter 10).
3   Broken or sagging springs (Chapter 10).
4   Overloaded vehicle.

78   Suspension bottoms

1   Overloaded vehicle.
2   Worn strut dampers (Chapter 10).
3   Incorrect, broken or sagging springs (Chapter 10).

79   Cupped tires

1   Front wheel or rear wheel alignment out-of-specifications (Chapter 10).
2   Worn strut dampers (Chapter 10).
3   Wheel bearings worn (Chapter 10).
4   Excessive tire or wheel runout (Chapter 10).
5   Worn balljoints (Chapter 10).

80 Excessive tire wear on outside edge

1 Inflation pressures incorrect (Chapter 1).
2 Excessive speed in turns.
3 Front end alignment incorrect (excessive toe-in). Have professionally aligned.
4 Suspension arm bent or twisted (Chapter 10).

81 Excessive tire wear on inside edge

1 Inflation pressures incorrect (Chapter 1).
2 Front end alignment incorrect (toe-out). Have professionally aligned.

3 Loose or damaged steering components (Chapter 10).

82 Tire tread worn in one place

1 Tires out-of-balance.
2 Damaged or buckled wheel. Inspect and replace if necessary.
3 Defective tire (Chapter 1).

83 Excessive play or looseness in steering system

1 Wheel bearing(s) worn (Chapter 10).
2 Tie-rod end loose (Chapter 10).

3 Steering gear loose (Chapter 10).
4 Worn or loose steering intermediate shaft (Chapter 10).

84 Rattling or clicking noise in steering gear

1 Steering gear loose (Chapter 10).
2 Steering gear defective.

Notes

Chapter 1
Tune-up and routine maintenance

Contents

Specifications

Recommended lubricants and fluids

Note: *Listed here are manufacturer recommendations at the time this manual was written. Manufacturers occasionally upgrade their fluid and lubricant specifications, so check with your local auto parts store for current recommendations.*

Engine oil
  Type .... API "certified for gasoline engines"
  Viscosity .... See accompanying chart

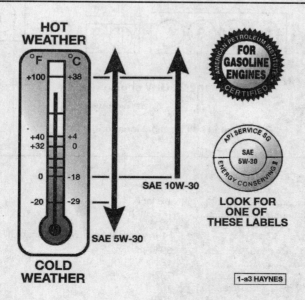

Engine oil viscosity chart - For best fuel economy and cold starting, select the lowest SAE viscosity grade for the expected temperature range

1-a3 HAYNES

Recommended lubricants and fluids (continued)

Automatic transaxle fluid	Dexron IIE or III Automatic Transaxle Fluid (ATF)
Manual transaxle lubricant	
1995 through 1999	Syncromesh Transmission fluid (GM part number 12345349)
2000 and later	Dexron IIE or III Automatic Transaxle Fluid (ATF)
Engine coolant	50/50 mixture of water and the specified ethylene glycol-based (green color) antifreeze or "DEX-COOL, silicate-free (orange-color) coolant - DO NOT mix the two types
Brake and clutch fluid	DOT 3 fluid
Power steering fluid	GM power steering fluid or equivalent
Chassis grease	SAE NLGI no. 2 chassis grease

Capacities*

Engine oil (with filter change)	
2.2L OHV engine and 2.3L and 2.4L OHC engines	4.0 quarts
2.2L OHC engine	5.0 quarts
Cooling system	Up to 10.5 quarts, depending on model
Automatic transaxle fluid (with filter replacement, torque converter not included)	
3-speed transaxles	7.0 quarts
4-speed transaxles	9.5 quarts
Manual transaxle gear lubricant	
2000 and earlier	2.0 quarts
2001 and later	1.8 quarts

All capacities approximate. Add as necessary to bring to appropriate level.

Ignition system

Spark plug type and gap	
2.2L OHV engine	
1998 and earlier	AC type 41-928 or equivalent @ 0.060 in.
1999 and 2000	AC type 41-928 or equivalent @ 0.050 in.
2001	AC type 41-928 or equivalent @ 0.040 in.
2.3L and 2.4L OHC engines	
1995 thru 1997	AC type 41-910 or equivalent @ 0.060 in.
1998 through 2000	AC type 41-942 or equivalent @ 0.050 in.
2001 and 2002	AC type 41-963 or equivalent @ 0.050 in.
2.2L OHC engine	AC type 41-981 or equivalent @ 0.042 in.
Firing order	1-3-4-2

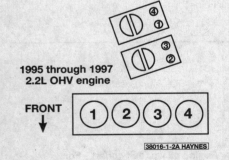

1995 through 1997 2.2L OHV engine

FRONT

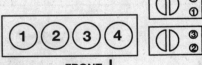

1998 and later 2.2L OHV engine

2.2L, 2.3L and 2.4L OHC engines

FRONT

Cylinder and coil terminal location

General

Coolant reservoir pressure cap rating	15 psi
Brake pad lining wear limit	1/8 inch
Brake shoe lining wear limit	1/16 inch

Torque specifications

Ft-lbs (unless otherwise indicated)

Automatic transaxle pan bolts	89 in-lbs
Engine oil drain plug	18
Spark plugs	132 in-lbs
Throttle body nuts/bolts	16
Wheel lug nuts	100

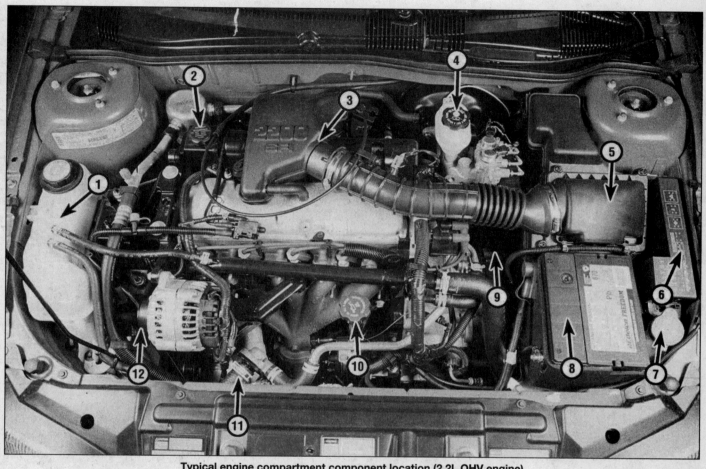

Typical engine compartment component location (2.2L OHV engine)

1 Pressurized engine coolant reservoir
2 Power steering fluid reservoir
3 Throttle body (underneath air intake plenum)
4 Brake master cylinder reservoir
5 Air filter housing
6 Engine compartment fuse and relay box
7 Windshield washer reservoir
8 Battery
9 Automatic transaxle fill and vent cap (located below master cylinder on transaxle)
10 Engine oil dipstick/fill tube
11 Upper radiator hose
12 Drivebelt

Typical engine compartment component location (2.2L OHC engine shown, 2.3L and 2.4L OHC engine compartments similar)

1   *Pressurized engine coolant reservoir*
2   *Power steering fluid reservoir*
3   *Resonator (the throttle body is located underneath the resonator)*
4   *Brake master cylinder reservoir*
5   *Air filter housing*
6   *Fuse and relay block*
7   *Windshield washer reservoir*

8   *Battery*
9   *Automatic transaxle fill and vent cap*
10   *Engine oil dipstick*
11   *Engine oil filler cap*
12   *Upper radiator hose*
13   *Clutch master cylinder reservoir, if equipped with a manual transaxle (not shown - this is an automatic)*

Typical front underside component location

1	Drivebelt	3	Front brake caliper	5	Automatic transaxle fluid pan
2	Strut assembly	4	Tie-rod end	6	Engine oil drain plug

Typical rear underside component location

1	Coil-over-shock assembly	3	Fuel filter	5	Exhaust pipe
2	Axle assembly	4	Fuel tank	6	Muffler

1 Chevrolet Cavalier and Pontiac Sunfire Maintenance schedule

The following maintenance intervals are based on the assumption that the vehicle owner will be doing the maintenance or service work, as opposed to having a dealer service department do the work. Although the time/mileage intervals are loosely based on factory recommendations, most have been shortened to ensure, for example, that such items as lubricants and fluids are checked/changed at intervals that promote maximum engine/driveline service life. Also, subject to the preference of the individual owner interested in keeping his or her vehicle in peak condition at all times, and with the vehicle's ultimate resale in mind, many of the maintenance procedures may be performed more often than recommended in the following schedule. We encourage such owner initiative.

When the vehicle is new it should be serviced initially by a factory authorized dealer service department to protect the factory warranty. In many cases the initial maintenance check is done at no cost to the owner (check with your dealer service department for more information).

Every 250 miles or weekly, whichever comes first

Check the engine oil level (Section 4)
Check the engine coolant level (Section 4)
Check the windshield washer fluid level (Section 4)
Check the brake fluid level (Section 4)
Check the tires and tire pressures (Section 5)

Every 3000 miles or 3 months, whichever comes first

All items listed above plus:
Check the power steering fluid level (Section 6)
Check the automatic transaxle fluid level (Section 7)
Change the engine oil and filter (Section 9)
Lubricate the chassis (Section 10)

Every 6000 miles or 6 months, whichever comes first

All items listed above plus:
Check and service the battery (Section 11)
Check the cooling system (Section 12)
Inspect and replace, if necessary, all underhood hoses (Section 13)
Check the engine drivebelt (Section 14)
Inspect the suspension and steering components (Section 15)
Check the brakes (Section 16)*
Rotate the tires (Section 17)
Inspect the exhaust system (Section 18)

Every 12,000 miles or 12 months, whichever comes first

Check the throttle body nut torque (Section 19)
Inspect and replace, if necessary, the windshield wiper blades (Section 20)
Inspect the seat belts (Section 21)
Replace the air filter and PCV inlet filter (Section 22)

Every 30,000 miles or 24 months, whichever comes first

All items listed above plus:
Inspect and replace, if necessary, the PCV valve (2.2L OHV engine) or oil/air separator (2.2L, 2.3L and 2.4L OHC engines) (Section 23)
Inspect and replace if necessary, the spark plug wires (2.2L) (Section 25)
Check the EGR valve (Section 24)
Replace the fuel filter (Section 26)
Inspect the fuel system (Section 27)
Change the automatic transaxle fluid and filter (Section 29)**
Service the cooling system (drain, flush and refill) (green-colored ethylene glycol anti-freeze only) (Section 28)

Every 50,000 miles or 3 years, whichever comes first

Change the fluid in the automatic transaxle (Section 29)
Change the fluid in the manual transaxle (Section 30)

Every 100,000 miles or 5 years, whichever comes first

Replace the spark plugs (platinum-tipped spark plugs) (Section 31)
Service the cooling system (drain, flush and refill) (orange-colored "DEX-COOL" silicate-free coolant only) (Section 28)

* If the vehicle frequently tows a trailer, is operated primarily in stop-and-go conditions or its brakes receive severe usage for any other reason, check the brakes every 3000 miles or three months.
** If operated under one or more of the following conditions, change the automatic transaxle fluid every 15,000 miles:
In heavy city traffic where the outside temperature regularly
Reaches 90-degrees F (32-degrees C) or higher
In hilly or mountainous terrain
Frequent trailer pulling

2 Introduction

This Chapter is designed to help the home mechanic maintain the Chevrolet Cavalier and the Pontiac Sunfire models with the goals of maximum performance, economy, safety and reliability in mind.

Included is a master maintenance schedule, followed by procedures dealing specifically with each item on the schedule. Visual checks, adjustments, component replacement and other helpful items are included. Refer to the **accompanying illustrations** of the engine compartment and the underside of the vehicle for the locations of various components.

Servicing your vehicle in accordance with the mileage/time maintenance schedule and the step-by-step procedures will result in a planned maintenance program that should produce a long and reliable service life. Keep in mind that it's a comprehensive plan, so maintaining some items but not others at the specified intervals won't produce the same results.

As you service your vehicle, you'll discover that many of the procedures can - and should - be grouped together because of the nature of the particular procedure you're performing or because of the close proximity of two otherwise unrelated components to one another.

For example, if the vehicle is raised, you should inspect the exhaust, suspension, steering and fuel systems while you're under the vehicle. When you're rotating the tires, it makes good sense to check the brakes since the wheels are already removed. Finally, let's suppose you have to borrow or rent a torque wrench. Even if you only need it to tighten the spark plugs, you might as well check the torque of as many critical fasteners as time allows.

The first step in this maintenance program is to prepare yourself before the actual work begins. Read through all the procedures you're planning to do, then gather up all the parts and tools needed. If it looks like you might run into problems during a particular job, seek advice from a mechanic or an experienced do-it-yourselfer.

Owner's Manual and VECI label information

Your vehicle owner's manual was written for your year and model and contains very specific information on component locations, specifications, fuse ratings, part numbers, etc. The Owner's Manual is an important resource for the do-it-yourselfer to have; if one was not supplied with your vehicle, it can generally be ordered from a dealer parts department.

Among other important information, the Vehicle Emissions Control Information (VECI) label contains specifications and procedures for applicable tune-up adjustments and, in some instances, spark plugs (see Chapter 6 for more information on the VECI label). The information on this label is the exact maintenance data recommended by the manufacturer. This data often varies by intended operating altitude, local emissions regulations, month of manufacture, etc.

This Chapter contains procedural details, safety information and more ambitious maintenance intervals than you might find in manufacturer's literature. However, you may also find procedures or specifications in your Owner's Manual or VECI label that differ with what's printed here. In these cases, the Owner's Manual or VECI label can be considered correct, since it is specific to your particular vehicle. **Caution:** *If the vehicle is equipped with a Delco Loc II or Theftlock audio system, make sure you have the correct activation code before disconnecting the battery.*

3 Tune-up general information

The term tune-up is used in this manual to represent a combination of individual operations rather than one specific procedure. If, from the time the vehicle is new, the routine maintenance schedule is followed closely and frequent checks are made of fluid levels and high wear items, as suggested throughout this manual, the engine will be kept in relatively good running condition and the need for additional work will be minimized due to lack of regular maintenance. This is even more likely if a used vehicle, which has not received regular and frequent maintenance checks, is purchased. In such cases, an engine tune-up will be needed outside of the regular routine maintenance intervals.

The first step in any tune-up or diagnostic procedure to help correct a poor running engine is a cylinder compression check. A compression check (see Chapter 2, Part D) will help determine the condition of internal engine components and should be used as a guide for tune-up and repair procedures. If, for instance, a compression check indicates serious internal engine wear, a conventional tune-up won't improve the performance of the engine and would be a waste of time and money. Because of its importance, the compression check should be done by someone with the right equipment and the knowledge to use it correctly.

The following procedures are those most often needed to bring a generally poor running engine back into a correct state of tune.

Minor tune-up

Check all engine-related fluids (Section 4)
Clean, inspect and test the battery (Section 11)
Check the cooling system (Section 12)
Check all underhood hoses (Section 13)
Check and adjust the drivebelts (Section 14)
Check the air filter (Section 22)
Check the PCV valve (Section 23)
Replace the spark plugs (Section 31)
Inspect the spark plug wires (Section 25)

Major tune-up

All items listed under Minor tune-up plus . . .
Replace the air filter (Section 22)
Replace the spark plug wires (Section 25)
Replace the fuel filter (Section 26)
Check the fuel system (Section 27)
Check the ignition timing (Chapter 5)
Check the charging system (Chapter 5)
Check the EGR system (Chapter 6)

4 Fluid level checks (every 250 miles or weekly)

Note 1: *The electronic instrument cluster on the dash utilizes several warning lamps to indicate low oil level (CHECK OIL), oil pressure problems (LOW OIL PRESSURE), low coolant level (LOW COOLANT LEVEL) and fuel/emissions systems failure (CHECK ENGINE). Refer to the appropriate Chapters and Sections to check the systems before serious engine trouble develops. Low fluid level checks can be remedied with correct maintenance. Refer to Chapter 2C for oil pressure checks and to Chapter 6 for fuel/emissions systems diagnostic procedures.*
Note 2: *The following are fluid level checks to be done on a 250 mile or weekly basis. Additional fluid level checks can be found in the specific maintenance procedures that follow. Regardless of intervals, be alert to fluid leaks under the vehicle, which would indicate a problem to be corrected immediately.*

1   Fluids are an essential part of the lubrication, cooling, brake and windshield washer systems. Because the fluids gradually become depleted and/or contaminated during normal operation of the vehicle, they must be periodically replenished. See *Recommended lubricants and fluids* at the beginning of this Chapter before adding fluid to any of the following components. **Note:** *The vehicle must be on level ground when fluid levels are checked.*

Engine oil

Refer to illustrations 4.2a, 4.2b, 4.2c, 4.4, 4.6a and 4.6b

2   Check the engine oil level with the dipstick **(see illustrations)**. The dipstick extends through a metal tube down into the oil pan. **Note:** *On 2.2L OHV models, the dipstick is an integral part of the oil filler cap.*

3   Check the oil level before driving the vehicle, or about 15 minutes after shutting off the engine. (If you check the oil immediately after driving the vehicle, some oil will still be in the upper part of the engine, so the indicated level on the dipstick will not be accurate.)

4   Pull the dipstick from the tube and wipe all the oil from the end with a clean rag or paper towel. Insert the clean dipstick all the

4.2a On 2.2L OHV models, the oil filler cap is located in front of the engine. Unscrew the cap and you'll find an integral dipstick

4.2b On 2.3L and 2.4L OHC engines, the engine oil dipstick is located on the backside of the engine compartment, between the valve cover and the firewall

4.2c On 2.2L OHC engines, the engine oil dipstick is located at the front right corner of the engine compartment

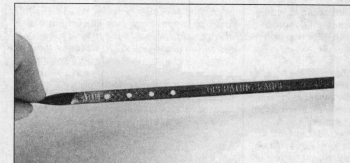

way back into the tube and pull it out again. Note the oil at the end of the dipstick. Add oil as necessary to keep the level above the ADD mark in the cross hatched area of the dipstick (see illustration).

5   Do not overfill the engine by adding too much oil. Overfilling can foul the spark plugs, cause oil leaks and even cause oil seals to fail.

6   Add oil to the engine after removing the twist-off cap located on the engine (2.2L OHV engine, see illustration 4.2a; other engines, see accompanying illustrations). Using a funnel will reduce spills.

7   Checking the oil level is an important preventive maintenance step. Slide your thumb and index finger up the dipstick before wiping off the oil. If you see (or feel) small dirt or metal particles clinging to the dipstick, change the oil (see Section 9). A consistently low oil level indicates oil leakage through damaged seals or gaskets or past worn rings or valve guides. If the oil looks milky in color or has water droplets in it, the cylinder head gasket might be blown or the cylinder head or block might be cracked. Check the engine immediately (see Chapter 2).

4.4 The oil level should be at or near the cross-hatched area on the dipstick. If it's below the ADD line, add enough oil to bring the level into the upper part of the cross-hatched area

Engine coolant

Refer to illustration 4.8

Warning: Do not allow antifreeze to contact your skin or the painted surfaces of the vehicle. Flush contaminated areas immediately with plenty of water. Do not store new coolant or leave old coolant lying around where it's accessible to children or pets - they're attracted by its sweet smell. Ingestion of even a small amount of coolant can be fatal! Wipe up garage floor and drip pan coolant spills immediately. Keep antifreeze containers covered and repair leaks in the cooling system immediately.

Caution: The manufacturer recommends using only DEX-COOL coolant for these systems. DEX-COOL is a long-lasting coolant designed for 100,000 miles or 5 years. Never mix green-colored ethylene glycol anti-freeze and orange-colored "DEX-COOL" silicate-free coolant because doing so will destroy the efficiency of the "DEX-COOL."

8   All models covered by this manual are equipped with a pressurized coolant recovery system. A plastic coolant reservoir, which is

4.6a On 2.3L and 2.4L OHC engines, the engine oil filler cap is located at the right rear corner of the valve cover

4.6b On 2.2L OHC engines, the oil filler cap is located on the left end of the valve cover

4.8 The coolant reservoir is located in the right (passenger's side) front corner of the engine compartment. Check the coolant level by observing the level through the translucent plastic; it should be at the FULL COLD mark. To add coolant, wait until the engine has completely cooled, then put a rag around the filler cap and slowly unscrew it

4.14 The windshield washer fluid reservoir is located at the left front corner of the engine compartment. Flip up the cap to add fluid

located at the right front corner of the engine compartment **(see illustration)**, is connected to the engine and radiator by three hoses. The level of the coolant in the reservoir rises and falls with engine temperature. The reservoir cap houses a spring-loaded "blow-off" or pressure valve and a vacuum valve. When the cooling system pressure exceeds the rated pressure (15 psi) of the cap, the spring-loaded valve in the cap opens, allowing hot coolant to vent. (The actual opening pressure of most "15 psi" caps will vary between 13 and 17 psi.) When the engine is turned off, the coolant cools down, creating a vacuum inside the coolant reservoir. When the vacuum inside the reservoir reaches a certain threshold, the vacuum valve in the cap opens, allowing the coolant to flow back to the radiator.

9 Check the coolant level in the reservoir regularly. **Warning:** *Do not remove the reservoir cap to check the coolant level when the engine is warm. The level in the reservoir varies with the temperature of the engine. When the engine is cold, the coolant level*

should be at or slightly above the FULL COLD mark on the reservoir **(see illustration 4.8)**. *If it isn't, add coolant to the reservoir (but only when the engine is cold!). Unscrew the cap from the reservoir and add a 50/50 mixture of ethylene glycol based green-colored antifreeze or orange-colored "DEX-COOL" silicate-free coolant and water* (see **Caution** above). *Once the engine has warmed up, the level should be at or near the FULL HOT mark.*

10 Drive the vehicle and recheck the coolant level. If only a small amount of coolant is needed to bring the system up to the correct level, it's okay to add just plain (distilled) water. However, adding water repeatedly will dilute the 50/50-antifreeze/water solution. In order to maintain the correct ratio of antifreeze and water, always top up the coolant level with the correct mixture. An empty gallon-size plastic water bottle makes a good container for mixing coolant with water. Do not use rust inhibitors or additives (they've already been added to the new coolant). General Motors specifies using "clean, drinkable" water; GM doesn't specify using distilled water (which is mineral free). However, if you live in an area where the tap water has a heavy mineral content, it's a good idea to use distilled water.

11 If the coolant level drops consistently,

there might be a leak in the system. Inspect the radiator, hoses, filler cap, drain plugs and water pump (see Section 12). If there are no obvious leaks, have a service station pressure-test the coolant reservoir cap.

12 If you have to remove the reservoir cap, wait until the engine has cooled completely, then wrap a thick cloth around the cap and turn it to the first stop. If coolant or steam escapes, let the engine cool down longer, then remove the cap.

13 Check the condition of the coolant. It should be relatively clear. If it's brown or rust-colored, drain, flush and refill the system. But even if coolant appears to be normal, the rust inhibitors wear out and other additives wear out, so it must still be replaced at the specified intervals.

Windshield washer fluid

Refer to illustration 4.14

14 The fluid for the windshield washer system is located in a plastic reservoir on the left side of the engine compartment **(see illustration)**. In milder climates, plain water can be used in the reservoir, but it should be kept no more than two-thirds full to allow for expansion if the water freezes. In colder climates, use windshield washer system antifreeze/cleaner (available at most auto parts stores) to lower the freezing point of the fluid. Mix the antifreeze/cleaner with water in accordance with the manufacturer's directions. **Caution:** *Do not use cooling system antifreeze. It will damage the paint.*

15 To help prevent icing in cold weather, warm the windshield with the defroster before using the windshield washer.

Battery electrolyte

Refer to illustration 4.16

16 All vehicles covered by this manual were equipped by the manufacturer with a permanently sealed battery, which has no filler caps. Water does not have to be added to one of these batteries at any time. However, if you or a previous owner have replaced the original maintenance-free battery with a conventional battery, check the battery electrolyte level regularly. Remove all the cell caps on top of the battery **(see illustration)**. Some maintenance-type batteries have individual caps; others have a pair of caps, each of which covers three cells. If the electrolyte level is low, add *distilled* water until the level is above the plates. On most conventional batteries, a "split-ring indicator" in each cell helps you judge when enough water has been added. Add water until the electrolyte level is just up to the bottom of the split ring indicator. Do not overfill the battery or it will spew out electrolyte when it is charging. **Caution:** *After adding distilled water to a maintenance-type battery, always wait several hours for the electrolyte in the plates to go into solution with the water before using or charging the battery. Trying to use or charge a battery that's just been topped up is not good for the battery, and could ruin it.*

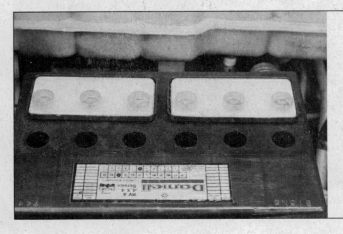

4.16 If your vehicle is equipped with an aftermarket maintenance-type battery, remove the cell caps to check the battery electrolyte level. Make sure that the plates in each cell are completely submerged.

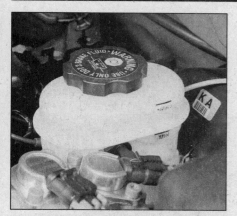

4.17 The fluid level inside the brake fluid reservoir can easily be checked by observing the level from the outside - fluid can be added to the reservoir after the cover is removed by prying up on the tabs

Brake fluid

Refer to illustration 4.17

17 Check the brake fluid level by looking through the plastic reservoir **(see illustration)** mounted on the master cylinder. The reservoir is on top of the master cylinder, which is mounted on the front of the power booster unit in the left (driver's side) rear corner of the engine compartment.

18 The fluid level should be between the MAX and MIN lines on the side of the reservoir **(see illustration 4.17)**. If the fluid level is low, wipe off the top of the reservoir and the lid with a clean rag to prevent dirt and grime

from contaminating the system, then open the reservoir filler cap.

19 When adding fluid, pour it carefully into the reservoir to avoid spilling it on surrounding painted surfaces. Be sure the specified fluid is used, since mixing different types of brake fluid can cause damage to the system. See *Recommended lubricants and fluids* at the front of this Chapter or your owner's manual. **Warning:** *Brake fluid can harm your eyes and damage painted surfaces, so use extreme caution when handling or pouring it. Do not use brake fluid that has been standing open or is more than one year old. Brake fluid absorbs moisture from the air. Excess moisture can cause a dangerous loss of braking effectiveness.*

20 At this time the fluid and master cylinder can be inspected for contamination. The system should be drained and refilled if deposits, dirt particles or water droplets are seen in the fluid.

21 After filling the reservoir to the correct level, make sure the lid completely snaps in place to prevent fluid leakage.

22 The brake fluid level in the master cylinder will drop slightly as the pads at each wheel wear down during normal operation. If the master cylinder requires repeated replenishing to keep it at the correct level, this is an indication of leakage in the brake system, which should be corrected immediately. Check all brake lines and connections (see Section 16 for more information).

23 If, when checking the master cylinder fluid level, you discover one or both reservoirs empty or nearly empty, the brake system should be bled (see Chapter 9).

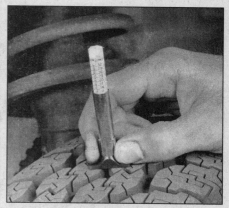

5.2 Use a tire tread depth gauge to monitor tire wear. Tread depth gauges are available at auto parts stores

5 Tire and tire pressure checks (every 250 miles or weekly)

Refer to illustrations 5.2, 5.3, 5.4a, 5.4b and 5.8

1 Periodic inspection of the tires may spare you the inconvenience of being stranded with a flat tire. It can also provide you with vital information regarding possible problems in the steering and suspension systems before major damage occurs.

2 The original tires on this vehicle are equipped with 1/2-inch wide bands that appear when tread depth reaches 1/16-inch, indicating the tires are worn out. Tread wear

UNDERINFLATION

CUPPING

Cupping may be caused by:
- Underinflation and/or mechanical irregularities such as out-of-balance condition of wheel and/or tire, and bent or damaged wheel.
- Loose or worn steering tie-rod or steering idler arm.
- Loose, damaged or worn front suspension parts.

OVERINFLATION

5.3 This chart will help you determine the condition of the tires, the probable cause(s) of abnormal wear and the corrective action necessary

INCORRECT TOE-IN OR EXTREME CAMBER

FEATHERING DUE TO MISALIGNMENT

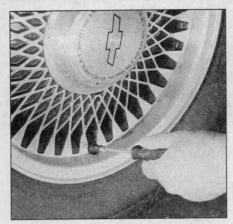

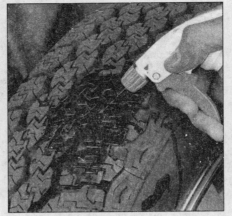

5.4a If a tire loses air on a steady basis, check the valve core first to make sure it's snug (special inexpensive wrenches are commonly available at auto parts stores)

5.4b If the valve core is tight, raise the corner of the vehicle with the low tire and spray a soapy water solution onto the tread as the tire is turned slowly. Leaks will cause small bubbles to appear

5.8 To extend the life of the tires, check the air pressure at least once a week with an accurate gauge. Don't forget the spare tire!

can be monitored with a simple, inexpensive device known as a tread depth indicator (see illustration).

3   Note any abnormal tread wear (see illustration). Tread pattern irregularities such as cupping, flat spots and more wear on one side than the other are indications of front end alignment and/or balance problems. If any of these conditions are noted, take the vehicle to a tire shop or service station to correct the problem.

4   Look closely for cuts, punctures and embedded nails or tacks. Sometimes a tire will hold air pressure for short time or leak down very slowly after a nail has embedded itself in the tread. If a slow leak persists, check the valve stem core to make sure it's tight (see illustration). Examine the tread for an object that may have embedded itself in the tire or for a "plug" that may have begun to leak (radial tire punctures are repaired with a plug that's installed in a puncture). If a puncture is suspected, it can be easily verified by spraying a solution of soapy water onto the suspected area (see illustration). The soapy

solution will bubble if there's a leak. Unless the puncture is unusually large, a tire shop or service station can usually repair the tire.

5   Carefully inspect the inner sidewall of each tire for evidence of brake fluid. If you see any, inspect the brakes immediately.

6   Correct air pressure adds miles to the lifespan of the tires, improves mileage and enhances overall ride quality. Tire pressure cannot be accurately estimated by looking at a tire, especially if it's a radial. A tire pressure gauge is essential. Keep an accurate gauge in the vehicle. The pressure gauges attached to the nozzles of air hoses at gas stations are often inaccurate.

7   Always check tire pressure when the tires are cold. Cold, in this case, means the vehicle has not been driven over a mile in the three hours preceding a tire pressure check. A pressure rise of four to eight pounds is not uncommon once the tires are warm.

8   Unscrew the valve cap protruding from the wheel or hubcap and push the gauge firmly onto the valve stem (see illustration).

Note the reading on the gauge and compare the figure to the recommended tire pressure shown on the label attached to the inside of the glove compartment door. Be sure to reinstall the valve cap to keep dirt and moisture out of the valve stem mechanism. Check all four tires and, if necessary, add enough air to bring them up to the recommended pressure.

9   Don't forget to keep the spare tire inflated to the specified pressure (refer to your owner's manual or the tire sidewall).

6   Power steering fluid level check (every 3000 miles or 3 months)

Refer to illustrations 6.2a, 6.2b and 6.6

1   Unlike manual steering, the power steering system relies on fluid which may, over a period of time, require replenishing.

2   The fluid reservoir for the power steering pump is located on the passenger side of the engine compartment (see illustrations).

3   For the check, the front wheels should

6.2a On vehicles with a 2.2L OHV engine, the power steering fluid reservoir is located at the right (passenger's side) rear corner of the engine compartment

6.2b On 2.2L, 2.3L and 2.4L OHC engines, the power steering fluid reservoir is located at the left (driver's side) front corner of the engine (2.2L OHC engine shown, 2.3L and 2.4L OHC engines similar)

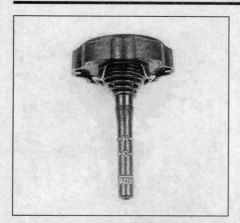

6.6 The marks on the dipstick indicate the safe fluid range

7.6 With the automatic transaxle at normal operating temperature, the fluid level must be maintained within the cross-hatched area on the dipstick

be pointed straight ahead and the engine should be off.

4   Use a clean rag to wipe off the reservoir cap and the area around the cap. This will help prevent any foreign matter from entering the reservoir during the check.

5   Twist off the cap and check the temperature of the fluid at the end of the dipstick with your finger.

6   Wipe off the fluid with a clean rag, reinsert it, then withdraw it and read the fluid level. The level should be at the HOT mark if the fluid was hot to the touch **(see illustration)**. It should be at the COLD mark if the fluid was cool to the touch.

7   If additional fluid is required, pour the specified type directly into the reservoir, using a funnel to prevent spills.

8   If the reservoir requires frequent fluid additions, all power steering hoses, hose connections, the power steering pump and the rack and pinion assembly should be carefully checked for leaks.

---

7   Automatic transaxle fluid level check (every 3000 miles or 3 months)

1   The automatic transaxle fluid level should be carefully maintained. Low fluid level can lead to slipping or loss of drive, while overfilling can cause foaming and loss of fluid.

2   With the parking brake set, start the engine, then move the shift lever through all the gear ranges, ending in Park. The fluid level must be checked with the transaxle at operating temperature and sitting level. **Note:** *Incorrect fluid level readings will result if the vehicle has just been driven at high speeds for an extended period, in hot weather in city traffic, or if it has been pulling a trailer. If any of these conditions apply, wait until the fluid has cooled (about 30 minutes).*

3-speed automatic transaxle

Refer to illustration 7.6

Note: On some 2000 and 2001 models, the 3-speed check is the same as the 4-

speed check below.

3   With the engine idling and the transaxle at normal operating temperature (driven 15 miles or idling five minutes), remove the dipstick from the filler tube. The dipstick is located at the rear section of the transaxle.

4   Wipe the fluid from the dipstick with a clean rag and push it back into the filler tube until the cap seats.

5   Pull the dipstick out again and note the fluid level.

6   The level should be within the crosshatched upper areas on the dipstick **(see illustration)**. If additional fluid is required, pour it directly into the tube using a funnel. It takes about one pint to raise the level from the lower mark to the upper edge of the cross-hatched area with the transaxle at normal operating temperature, so add the fluid a little at a time and keep checking the level until it's correct.

7   The condition of the fluid should also be checked along with the level. If the fluid at the end of the dipstick is a dark reddish-brown color, or if the fluid has a burned smell, the fluid should be changed. If you're in doubt about the condition of the fluid, purchase some new fluid and compare the two for color and smell.

4-speed automatic transaxle

8   On these models, it is not necessary to check the fluid level at regular intervals. If leaks or shifting problems lead you to suspect a low fluid level, refer to Section 29.

---

8   Manual transaxle lubricant level check (3,000 miles or 3 months)

1   The manual transaxle fluid level should be carefully maintained. Low fluid level can lead to gear and synchromesh scalding, chipping and gear damage.

2   With the engine OFF, the vehicle level and the engine temperature cold, remove the indicator from the fluid level vent plug and check the increments. If the oil level reads "ADD," it will be necessary to add the correct amount.

3   Use a narrow funnel designed to fit into the fill vent tube and slowly add the necessary transaxle fluid. Refer to the Specifications listed in this Chapter for the correct fluid type.

9   Engine oil and filter change (every 3000 miles or 3 months)

Refer to illustrations 9.2 and 9.7

1   Frequent oil changes are the best preventive maintenance the home mechanic can give the engine, because aging oil becomes diluted and contaminated, which leads to premature engine wear.

2   Make sure you have all the necessary

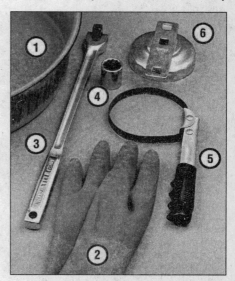

9.2 These tools are required when changing the engine oil and filter

1   Drain pan - *It should be fairly shallow in depth, but wide to prevent spills*

2   Rubber gloves - *When removing the drain plug and filter, you will get oil on your hands (the gloves will prevent burns)*

3   Breaker bar - *Sometimes the oil drain plug is tight, and a long breaker bar is needed to loosen it*

4   Socket - *To be used with the breaker bar or a ratchet (must be the correct size to fit the drain plug)*

5   Filter wrench - *This is a metal band-type wrench, which requires clearance around the filter to be effective*

6   Filter wrench - *This type fits on the bottom of the filter and can be turned with a ratchet or breaker bar (different-size wrenches are available for different types of filters)*

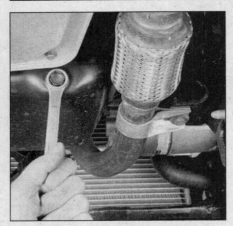

9.7 On vehicles with a 2.2L OHV engine, the engine oil drain plug is located at the right rear corner of the oil pan

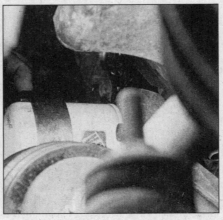

9.11 The oil filter is usually on very tight as well and will require a special wrench for removal (but do NOT use the wrench to tighten the new filter) (2.2L OHV engine and 2.3L and 2.4L OHC engines)

9.13 Lubricate the oil filter gasket with clean engine oil before installing the filter on the engine (2.2L OHV engine and 2.3L and 2.4L OHC engines)

tools before you begin this procedure (see illustration). You should also have plenty of rags or newspapers handy for mopping up any spills.

3   Access to the underside of the vehicle is greatly improved if the vehicle can be lifted on a hoist, driven onto ramps or supported by jackstands. **Warning:** *Do not work under a vehicle that is supported only by a hydraulic or scissors-type jack.*

4   If this is your first oil change, get under the vehicle and familiarize yourself with the locations of the oil drain plug and the oil filter. The engine and exhaust components will be warm during the actual work, so try to anticipate any potential problems before the engine and accessories are hot.

5   Park the vehicle on a level spot. Start the engine and allow it to reach its normal operating temperature. Warm oil and sludge will flow out more easily. Turn off the engine when it's warmed up. Remove the filler cap from the valve cover.

6   Raise the vehicle and support it securely on jackstands. **Warning:** *Never get beneath the vehicle when it is supported only by a jack. The jack provided with your vehicle is designed solely for raising the vehicle to remove and replace the wheels. Always use jackstands to support the vehicle when it becomes necessary to place your body underneath the vehicle.*

7   Being careful not to touch the hot exhaust components, place the drain pan under the drain plug in the bottom of the pan and remove the plug (see illustration). You may want to wear gloves while unscrewing the plug the final few turns if the engine is hot.

8   Allow the old oil to drain into the pan. It may be necessary to move the pan farther under the engine as the oil flow slows to a trickle. Inspect the old oil for the presence of metal shavings and chips.

9   After all the oil has drained, wipe off the drain plug with a clean rag. Even minute metal particles clinging to the plug would immediately contaminate the new oil.

10   Clean the area around the drain plug opening, reinstall the plug and tighten it to the torque listed in this Chapter's Specifications. Move the drain pan into position under the oil filter.

Vehicles with a 2.2L OHV engine or with a 2.3L or 2.4L OHC engine

Refer to illustrations 9.11 and 9.13

11   Loosen the oil filter (see illustration) by turning it counterclockwise with the filter wrench. Use a quality filter wrench of the correct size and be careful not to collapse the canister as you apply pressure. Once the filter is loose, use your hands to unscrew it from the block. Just as the filter is detached from the block, immediately tilt the open end up to prevent the oil inside the filter from spilling out. **Warning:** *The exhaust system may still be hot, so be careful.*

12   With a clean rag, wipe off the mounting surface on the block. If a residue of old oil is allowed to remain, it will smoke when the block is heated up. Also make sure that none of the old gasket remains stuck to the mounting surface. It can be removed with a scraper if necessary.

13   Compare the old filter with the new one to make sure they are the same type. Smear some clean engine oil on the rubber gasket of the new filter and screw it into place (see illustration). Because over-tightening the filter will damage the gasket, do not use a filter wrench to tighten the filter. Tighten it by hand until the gasket contacts the seating surface. Then seat the filter by giving it an additional 3/4-turn.

Vehicles with a 2.2L OHC engine

Refer to illustrations 9.14a, 9.14b and 9.14c

14   Vehicles with a 2.2L OHC engine use an oil filter element that's housed inside a receptacle located at the left front corner of the engine (see illustration). Unscrew the oil filter cap, then lift the cap and the oil filter from the filter receptacle in the engine (see illustration). Then separate the oil filter element from the cap (see illustration). Using a clean rag, remove all oil, dirt and sludge from the oil filter cap and from the rim around the oil filter receptacle. Install a new O-ring into the groove in the cap, then install the new filter element in the cap and insert both into the filter receptacle. Screw down the cap and tighten it securely.

9.14a On vehicles with a 2.2L OHC engine, the oil filter is housed inside a receptacle located at the front left corner of the engine. To replace the filter element, use a wrench to loosen the filter cap, unscrew the cap . . .

9.14c To detach the oil filter element from the filter cap, simply pull the two apart. Be sure to note which end of the filter element is installed in the cap. And be sure to replace the O-ring on the cap. There's also an O-ring on the lower end of the filter element; make sure that the new filter element has this O-ring. If not, install one

9.14b . . . and remove the cap and filter element as a single assembly

All vehicles

15   Remove all tools, rags, etc. from under the vehicle, being careful not to spill the oil in the drain pan, then lower the vehicle.

16   Add new oil to the engine through the oil filler cap in the valve cover. Use a funnel, if necessary, to prevent oil from spilling onto the top of the engine. Pour three quarts of fresh oil into the engine. Wait a few minutes to allow the oil to drain into the pan, then check the level on the oil dipstick (see Section 4 if necessary). If the oil level is at or near the upper hole on the dipstick, install the filler cap hand tight, start the engine and allow the new oil to circulate.

17   Allow the engine to run for about a minute. While the engine is running, look under the vehicle and check for leaks at the oil pan drain plug and around the oil filter. If either is leaking, stop the engine and tighten the plug or filter.

18   Wait a few minutes to allow the oil to trickle down into the pan, then recheck the level on the dipstick and, if necessary, add enough oil to bring the level to the upper hole.

19   During the first few trips after an oil change, make it a point to check frequently for leaks and correct oil level.

20   The old oil drained from the engine cannot be re-used in its present state and should be discarded. Check with your local refuse disposal company, disposal facility or environmental agency to see whether they will accept the oil for recycling. Don't pour used oil into drains or onto the ground. After the oil has cooled, it can be drained into a suitable container (capped plastic jugs, topped bottles, milk cartons, etc.) for transport to one of these disposal sites.

10   Chassis lubrication (every 3000 miles or 3 months)

Refer to illustration 10.1

1   Refer to *Recommended lubricants and fluids* at the front of this Chapter to obtain the

necessary grease, etc. You'll also need a grease gun **(see illustration)**. Occasionally plugs will be installed rather than grease fittings. If so, grease fittings will have to be purchased and installed.

2   Look under the vehicle and see if grease fittings or plugs are installed. If there are plugs, remove them and buy grease fittings, which will thread into the component. A dealer or auto parts store will be able to supply the correct fittings. Straight, as well as angled, fittings are available.

3   For easier access under the vehicle, raise it with a jack and place jackstands under the frame. Make sure it's safely sup-

10.1 Materials required for chassis and body lubrication

1   **Engine oil** - *Light engine oil in a can like this can be used for door and hood hinges*

2   **Graphite spray** - *Used to lubricate lock cylinders*

3   **Grease** - *Grease, in a variety of types and weights, is available for use in a grease gun. Check the Specification for your requirements*

4   **Grease gun** - *A common grease gun, shown here with a detachable hose and nozzle, is needed for chassis lubrication. After use, clean it thoroughly!*

ported by the stands. If the wheels are to be removed at this interval for tire rotation or brake inspection, loosen the lug nuts slightly while the vehicle is still on the ground.

4   Before beginning, force a little grease out of the nozzle to remove any dirt from the end of the gun. Wipe the nozzle clean with a rag.

5   With the grease gun and plenty of clean rags, crawl under the vehicle and begin lubricating the components.

6   Wipe one of the grease fittings clean and push the nozzle firmly over it. Pump the gun until the balljoint rubber seal is firm to the touch. Do not pump too much grease into the fitting as it could rupture the seal.

7   Wipe the excess grease from the components and the grease fitting. Repeat the procedure for the remaining fitting.

8   Clean and lubricate the parking brake cable, along with the cable guides and levers. This can be done by smearing some of the chassis grease onto the cable and its related parts with your fingers.

9   Open the hood and smear a little chassis grease on the hood latch mechanism. Have an assistant pull the hood release lever from inside the vehicle as you lubricate the cable at the latch.

10   Lubricate all the hinges (door, hood, etc.) with engine oil to keep them in correct working order.

11   The key lock cylinders can be lubricated with spray graphite or silicone lubricant, which is available at auto parts stores.

12   Lubricate the door weather-stripping with silicone spray. This will reduce chafing and retard wear.

11   Battery check, maintenance and charging (every 6000 miles or 6 months)

Refer to illustrations 11.1, 11.4, 11.5a, 11.5b and 11.5c

Warning: *Hydrogen gas is produced by the battery, so keep open flames and lighted tobacco away from it at all times. Always wear eye protection when working around the*

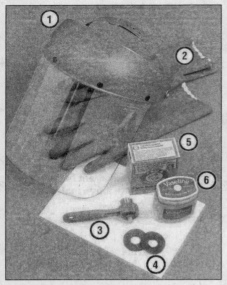

11.1 Tools and materials required for battery maintenance

1 *Face shield/safety goggles - When removing corrosion with a brush, the acidic particles can easily fly up into your eyes*
2 *Rubber gloves - Another safety item to consider when servicing the battery - remember that's acid inside the battery!*
3 *Battery terminal/cable cleaner - This wire brush cleaning tool will remove all traces of corrosion from the battery and cable*
4 *Treated felt washers - Placing one of these on each terminal, directly under the cable end, will help prevent corrosion (be sure to get the correct type for side-terminal batteries)*
5 *Baking soda - A solution of baking soda and water can be used to neutralize corrosion*
6 *Petroleum jelly - A layer of this on the battery terminal bolts will help prevent corrosion*

11.4 Check the tightness of the battery cable terminal bolts

11.5b Use the brush to finish the cleaning job

11.5a A tool like this one (available at auto parts stores) is used to clean the side terminal type battery contact area

11.5c The result should be a clean, shiny terminal area

battery. Rinse off spilled electrolyte immediately with large amounts of water. When removing the battery cables, always detach the negative cable first and hook it up last!
Caution: *If the vehicle is equipped with a Delco Loc II or Theftlock audio system, make sure you have the correct activation code before disconnecting the battery.*
1   Battery maintenance is an important procedure that will help ensure you aren't stranded because of a dead battery. Several tools are required for this procedure **(see illustration)**.
2   A sealed battery is standard equipment on all vehicles covered by this manual. Although this type of battery has many advantages over the older, capped cell type, and never requires the addition of water, it should still be routinely maintained according to the procedures that follow.

Check

3   The battery is located in the right front corner of the engine compartment. The exterior of the battery should be inspected periodically for damage such as a cracked case or cover.
4   Check the tightness of the battery cable terminals and connections to ensure good electrical connections and check the entire length of each cable for cracks and frayed conductors **(see illustration)**.
5   If corrosion (visible as white, fluffy deposits) is evident, remove the cables from the terminals, clean them with a battery brush and reinstall the cables **(see illustrations)**. Corrosion can be kept to a minimum by using special treated fiber washers available at auto parts stores or by applying a layer of petroleum jelly to the terminals and cables after they are assembled.
6   Make sure that the battery tray is in good condition and the hold-down clamp bolt is tight. If the battery is removed from the tray, make sure no parts remain in the bottom of the tray when the battery is reinstalled. When reinstalling the hold-down clamp bolt, do not overtighten it.
7   Information on removing and installing

the battery can be found in Chapter 5. Information on jump-starting can be found at the front of this manual. For more detailed battery checking procedures, refer to the *Haynes Automotive Electrical Manual*.

Cleaning

8   Corrosion on the hold-down components, battery case and surrounding areas can be removed with a solution of water and baking soda. Thoroughly rinse all cleaned areas with plain water.
9   Any metal parts of the vehicle damaged by corrosion should be covered with a zinc-based primer, then painted.

Charging

Warning: *When batteries are being charged, hydrogen gas, which is very explosive and flammable, is produced. Do not smoke or allow open flames near a charging or a recently charged battery. Wear eye protection when near the battery during charging. Also, make sure the charger is unplugged before connecting or disconnecting the battery from the charger.*
10   Slow-rate charging is the best way to restore a battery that's discharged to the

point where it will not start the engine. It's also a good way to maintain the battery charge in a vehicle that's only driven a few miles between starts. Maintaining the battery charge is particularly important in the winter when the battery must work harder to start the engine and electrical accessories that drain the battery are in greater use.

11   It's best to use a one or two-amp battery charger (sometimes called a "trickle" charger). They are the safest and put the least strain on the battery. They are also the least expensive. For a faster charge, you can use a higher amperage charger, but don't use one rated more than 1/10th the amp/hour rating of the battery. Rapid boost charges that claim to restore the power of the battery in one to two hours are hardest on the battery and can damage batteries that aren't in good condition. This type of charging should only be used in emergency situations.

12   The average time necessary to charge a battery should be listed in the instructions that come with the charger. As a general rule, a trickle charger will charge a battery in 12 to 16 hours.

13   Remove all of the cell caps (if equipped) and cover the holes with a clean cloth to prevent spattering electrolyte. Disconnect the negative battery cable and hook the battery charger leads to the battery posts (positive to positive, negative to negative), then plug in the charger. Make sure it is set at 12-volts if it has a selector switch.

14   If you're using a charger with a rate higher than two amps, check the battery regularly during charging to make sure it doesn't overheat. If you're using a trickle charger, you can safely let the battery charge overnight after you've checked it regularly for the first couple of hours.

15   If the battery has removable cell caps, measure the specific gravity with a hydrometer every hour during the last few hours of the charging cycle. Hydrometers are available inexpensively from auto parts stores - follow the instructions that come with the hydrometer. Consider the battery charged when there's no change in the specific gravity reading for two hours and the electrolyte in the cells is gassing (bubbling) freely. The specific gravity reading from each cell should be very close to the others. If not, the battery probably has a bad cell(s).

16   Some batteries with sealed tops have built-in hydrometers on the top that indicate the state of charge by the color displayed in the hydrometer window. Normally, a bright-colored hydrometer indicates a full charge and a dark hydrometer indicates the battery still needs charging. Check the battery manufacturer's instructions to be sure you know what the colors mean.

17   If the battery has a sealed top and no built-in hydrometer, you can hook up a digital voltmeter across the battery terminals to check the charge. A fully charged battery should read 12.5-volts or higher.

12   Cooling system check (every 6000 miles or 6 months)

Refer to illustration 12.4
Caution: *The manufacturer recommends using only DEX-COOL coolant for these systems. DEX-COOL is a long-lasting coolant designed for 100,000 miles or 5 years. Never mix green-colored ethylene glycol anti-freeze and orange-colored "DEX-COOL" silicate-free coolant because doing so will destroy the efficiency of the "DEX-COOL". If DEX-COOL is not available, check with your local auto parts store for the availability of coolant that is compatible for use in your vehicle's cooling system.*

1   Many major engine failures can be attributed to a faulty cooling system. If the vehicle is equipped with an automatic

Check for a chafed area that could fail prematurely.

Check for a soft area indicating the hose has deteriorated inside.

Overtightening the clamp on a hardened hose will damage the hose and cause a leak.

Check each hose for swelling and oil-soaked ends. Cracks and breaks can be located by squeezing the hose.

12.4 Hoses, like drivebelts, have a habit of failing at the worst possible time - to prevent the inconvenience of a blown radiator or heater hose, inspect them carefully as shown here

transaxle, the cooling system also cools the transaxle fluid and plays an important role in prolonging transaxle life.

2   The cooling system should be checked with the engine cold. Do this before the vehicle is driven for the day or after the engine has been shut off for at least three hours.

3   Remove the reservoir cap by turning it to the left until it reaches a stop. If you hear any hissing sounds (indicating there is still pressure in the system), wait until it stops. Now continue turning to the left until the cap can be removed. Thoroughly clean the cap, inside and out, with clean water. Also clean the filler neck on the radiator. All traces of corrosion should be removed. The coolant inside the radiator should be relatively transparent. If it is rust colored, the system should be drained and refilled (see Section 28). If the coolant level is not up to the top, add additional antifreeze/coolant mixture (see Section 4).

4   Carefully check the large upper and lower radiator hoses along with any smaller diameter heater hoses that run from the engine to the firewall. Inspect each hose along its entire length, replacing any hose that is cracked, swollen or shows signs of deterioration. Cracks may become more apparent if the hose is squeezed **(see illustration)**.

5   Make sure all hose connections are tight. A leak in the cooling system will usually show up as white or rust colored deposits on the areas adjoining the leak. If wire-type clamps are used at the ends of the hoses, it may be wise to replace them with more secure screw-type clamps.

6   Use compressed air or a soft brush to remove bugs, leaves, etc. from the front of the radiator or air conditioning condenser. Be careful not to damage the delicate cooling fins or cut yourself on them.

7   Every other inspection, or at the first indication of cooling system problems, have the cap and system pressure tested. If you don't have a pressure tester, most gas stations and repair shops will do this for a minimal charge.

13   Underhood hose check and replacement (every 6000 miles or 6 months)

General

1   **Warning:** *Replacement of air conditioning hoses must be left to a dealer service department or air conditioning shop that has the equipment to depressurize the system safely. Never remove air conditioning components or hoses until the system has been depressurized.*

2   High temperatures under the hood can cause the deterioration of the rubber and plastic hoses used for engine, accessory and emission systems operation. Periodic inspection should be made for cracks, loose

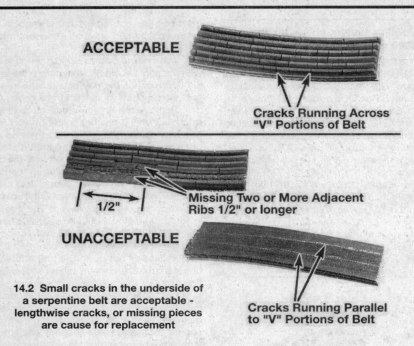

ACCEPTABLE

Cracks Running Across
"V" Portions of Belt

1/2"

Missing Two or More Adjacent
Ribs 1/2" or longer

UNACCEPTABLE

Cracks Running Parallel
to "V" Portions of Belt

14.2 Small cracks in the underside of a serpentine belt are acceptable - lengthwise cracks, or missing pieces are cause for replacement

clamps, material hardening and leaks. Information specific to the cooling system hoses can be found in Section 12.

3   Some, but not all, hoses are secured to the fittings with clamps. Where clamps are used, check to be sure they haven't lost their tension, allowing the hose to leak. If clamps aren't used, make sure the hose hasn't expanded and/or hardened where it slips over the fitting, allowing it to leak.

Vacuum hoses

4   It's quite common for vacuum hoses, especially those in the emissions system, to be color coded or identified by colored stripes molded into each hose. Various systems require hoses with different wall thickness, collapse resistance and temperature resistance. When replacing hoses, be sure the new ones are made of the same material.

5   Often the only effective way to check a hose is to remove it completely from the vehicle. If more than one hose is removed, be sure to label the hoses and fittings to ensure correct installation.

6   When checking vacuum hoses, be sure to include any plastic T-fittings in the check. Inspect the fittings for cracks and the hose where it fits over the fitting for distortion, which could cause leakage.

7   A small piece of vacuum hose (1/4-inch inside diameter) can be used as a stethoscope to detect vacuum leaks. Hold one end of the hose to your ear and probe around vacuum hoses and fittings, listening for the "hissing" sound characteristic of a vacuum leak. **Warning:** *When probing with the vacuum hose stethoscope, be careful not to allow your body or the hose to come into contact with moving engine components such as the drivebelt, cooling fan, etc.*

Fuel lines

Warning: *Gasoline is extremely flammable, so take extra precautions when you work on any part of the fuel system. Don't smoke or allow open flames or bare light bulbs near the work area, and don't work in a garage where a gas-type appliance (such as a water heater or clothes dryer) is present. If you spill any fuel on your skin, rinse it off immediately with soap and water. When you perform any kind of work on the fuel system, wear safety glasses and have a Class B type fire extinguisher on hand. The fuel system is under pressure, so if any lines must be disconnected, the pressure in the system must be relieved first (see Chapter 4 for more information).*

8   Check all fuel lines for deterioration and chafing. Check especially for cracks in areas where the tubing bends and just before fittings, such as where a line attaches to the fuel filter and fuel injection unit. Modular nylon fuel lines are used in conjunction with fuel system components. The nylon lines are flexible and are formed around bends, but will restrict fuel flow if kinked. Check the quick-connect fittings for damage or leakage.

9   High quality fuel line must be used for fuel line replacement. Never, under any circumstances, use vacuum line, clear plastic tubing or water hose for fuel lines. Replace defective nylon lines with components meeting original equipment specifications.

10   Spring-type clamps are commonly used on neoprene fuel lines. These clamps often lose their tension over a period of time, and can be "sprung" during the removal process. As a result spring-type clamps should be replaced with screw-type clamps whenever a hose is replaced.

Metal lines

11   Sections of steel tubing often used for fuel line between the fuel pump and fuel injection unit. Check carefully for cracks, kinks and flat spots in the line.

12   If a section of metal fuel line must be replaced, only seamless steel tubing should be used, since copper and aluminum tubing do not have the strength necessary to withstand normal engine vibration.

13   Check the metal brake lines where they enter the master cylinder and brake proportioning unit (if used) for cracks in the lines and loose fittings. Any sign of brake fluid leakage calls for an immediate thorough inspection of the brake system.

14   Drivebelt check and replacement (every 6000 miles or 6 months)

Refer to illustrations 14.2, 14.5 and 14.7

1   A single serpentine drivebelt is located at the front of the engine and plays an important role in the overall operation of the engine and its components. Due to its function and material make up, the belt is prone to wear and should be periodically inspected. The serpentine belt drives the alternator, power steering pump, water pump and air conditioning compressor.

2   With the engine off, open the hood and use your fingers (and a flashlight, if necessary), to move along the belt checking for cracks and separation of the belt plies. Also check for fraying and glazing, which gives the belt a shiny appearance **(see illustration)**. Both sides of the belt should be inspected, which means you will have to twist the belt to check the underside.

3   Check the ribs on the underside of the belt. They should all be the same depth, with none of the surface uneven.

4   The tension of the belt is maintained by the tensioner assembly and isn't adjustable. The belt should be checked at the mileage specified in the maintenance schedule at the front of this chapter, if the belt shows notice-

14.5 Using a wrench placed on the tensioner pulley bolt, rotate the tensioner clockwise to remove or install the belt

1-19

14.7 The serpentine drivebelt routing diagram is located on the radiator shroud (later model diagram shown)

15.3 Grab the top and bottom of the tire and pull in-and-out on it - Check for any noticeable movement that would indicate a loose wheel bearing assembly

Driveaxle boot check

Refer to illustration 15.7

6   The driveaxle boots are very important because they prevent dirt, water and foreign material from entering and damaging the constant velocity joints. Oil and grease can cause the boot material to deteriorate prematurely, so it's a good idea to wash the boots with soap and water.

7   Inspect the boots for tears and cracks as well as loose clamps (see illustration). If there is any evidence of cracks or leaking lubricant, they must be replaced as described in Chapter 8.

16 Brake check (every 6000 miles or 6 months)

Warning: *Brake system dust is hazardous to your health. DO NOT blow it out with compressed air, inhale it or use gasoline or solvents to remove it. Use brake system cleaner only.*

Note: *For detailed information of the brake system, refer to Chapter 9.*

1   In addition to the specified intervals, the brakes should be inspected every time the wheels are removed or whenever a defect is suspected. Raise the vehicle and place it securely on jackstands. Remove the wheels (see *Jacking and towing* at the front of the manual, if necessary).

Disc brakes

Refer to illustrations 16.3, 16.5 and 16.7

2   Disc brakes can be checked without removing any parts except the wheels. Extensive disc damage can occur if the pads are not replaced when needed.

3   The disc brake pads have built-in wear indicators (see illustration) which make a high-pitched squealing sound when the pads are worn. **Caution:** *Expensive damage to the disc can result if the pads are not replaced soon after the wear indicators start squealing.*

able damage or wear during these checks it should be replaced.

5   To replace the belt, rotate the tensioner pulley clockwise to release belt tension **(see illustration)**.

6   Remove the belt from the auxiliary components and slowly release the tensioner.

7   Route the new belt over the various pulleys, again rotating the tensioner to allow the belt to be installed, then release the belt tensioner. **Note:** *These models have a drivebelt routing decal on the radiator shroud to help during drivebelt installation* **(see illustration)**.

15 Steering, suspension and driveaxle boot check (every 6000 miles or 6 months)

Steering and suspension check

Refer to illustration 15.3

1   Indications of a fault in these systems are excessive play in the steering wheel before the front wheels react, excessive sway around corners, body movement over rough roads or binding at some point as the steering wheel is turned.

2   Raise the front of the vehicle periodically

and visually check the suspension and steering components for wear. Because of the work to be done, make sure the vehicle cannot fall from the stands.

3   Check the hub and bearing assembly. Do this by spinning the front wheels. Listen for any abnormal noises and watch to make sure the wheel spins true (doesn't wobble). Grab the top and bottom of the tire and pull in-and-out on it. Notice any movement that would indicate a loose bearing assembly **(see illustration)**. Often times, it will be necessary to drive the vehicle slowly and listen for grinding noises from the front end. The weight and load of the vehicle will make the symptoms pronounced. Refer to Chapter 10 for additional information.

4   From under the vehicle check for loose bolts, broken or disconnected parts and deteriorated rubber bushings on all suspension and steering components. Check the power steering hoses and connections for leaks. Check the shock absorbers or leaking fluid or damage.

5   Have an assistant turn the steering wheel from side-to-side and check the steering components for free movement, chafing and binding. If the steering doesn't react with the movement of the steering wheel, try to determine where the slack is located.

15.7 Check the driveaxle boots for wear or damage

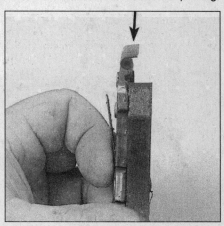

16.3 The disc brake pads are equipped with wear indicators that contact the disc and make a squealing sound when the pad has worn to its limit

16.5 With the wheels removed, the brake pad lining can be inspected through the caliper window and at each end of the caliper

16.7 Check for any sign of brake fluid leakage at the line fittings and the brake hoses

4   The disc brake calipers, which contain the brake pads, have an inner pad and outer pad in each caliper. All pads should be inspected.

5   Each caliper has a "window" to inspect the pads **(see illustration)**. If the pad material has worn to about 1/8-inch thick or less, the pads should be replaced.

6   If you're unsure about the exact thickness of the remaining lining material, remove the pads for further inspection or replacement (see Chapter 9).

7   Before installing the wheels, check for leakage and/or damage at the brake hoses and connections **(see illustration)**. Replace the hose or fittings as necessary, (see Chapter 9).

8   Check the condition of the brake disc. Look for score marks, deep scratches and overheated areas (they will appear blue or discolored). If damage or wear is noted, the disc can be removed and resurfaced by an automotive machine shop or replaced with a new one. See Chapter 9 for more detailed inspection and repair procedures.

Drum brakes

Refer to illustrations 16.14 and 16.16

9   Raise the vehicle and support it securely on jackstands. Block the front tires to prevent the vehicle from rolling; however, don't apply the parking brake or it will lock the drums in place.

10   Remove the wheels, referring to *Jacking and towing* at the front of this manual if necessary.

11   Mark the hub so it can be reinstalled in the same position. Use a scribe, chalk, etc. on the drum, hub and backing plate.

12   Remove the brake drum.

13   With the drum removed, carefully clean the brake assembly with brake system cleaner. **Warning:** *Don't blow the dust out with compressed air and don't inhale any of it (it is harmful to your health).*

14   Note the thickness of the lining material on both front and rear brake shoes. If the material has worn away to within 1/8-inch of the recessed rivets or metal backing, the shoes should be replaced **(see illustration)**. The shoes should also be replaced if they're cracked, glazed (shiny areas), or covered with brake fluid.

15   Make sure all the brake assembly springs are connected and in good condition.

16   Check the brake components for signs of fluid leakage. With your finger or a small screwdriver, carefully pry back the rubber cups on the wheel cylinder located at the top of the brake shoes **(see illustration)**. Any leakage here is an indication that the wheel cylinders should be replaced immediately (see Chapter 9). Also, check all hoses and connections for signs of leakage.

17   Wipe the inside of the drum with a clean rag and denatured alcohol or brake cleaner. Again, be careful not to breathe the dangerous asbestos dust.

18   Check the inside of the drum for cracks, score marks, deep scratches and "hard spots" which will appear as small discolored areas. If imperfections cannot be removed with fine emery cloth, the drum must be taken to an automotive machine shop for resurfacing.

19   Repeat the procedure for the remaining wheel. If the inspection reveals that all parts are in good condition, reinstall the brake drums, install the wheels and lower the vehicle to the ground.

Parking brake

20   The parking brake is operated by a hand lever and locks the rear brake system. The

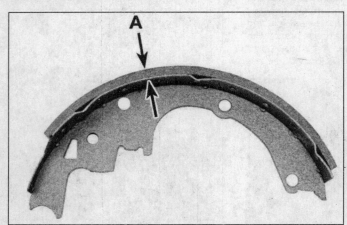

16.14 If the lining is bonded to the brake shoe, measure the lining thickness (A) from the outer surface to the metal shoe, as shown here; if the lining is riveted to the shoe, measure from the lining outer surface to the rivet head

16.16 Check for fluid leakage at both ends of the wheel cylinder dust covers

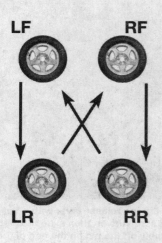

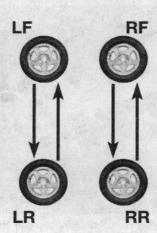

18.2a Check the flange connections for exhaust leaks - also check that the retaining nuts are securely tightened

17.2a Tire rotation diagram for non-directional radial tires

17.2b Tire rotation diagram for directional radial tires

easiest, and perhaps most obvious, method of periodically checking the operation of the parking brake assembly is to park the vehicle on a steep hill with the parking brake set and the transaxle in Neutral (be sure to stay in the vehicle during this check!). If the parking brake cannot prevent the vehicle from rolling, it needs service (see Chapter 9).

17 Tire rotation (every 6000 miles or 6 months)

Refer to illustrations 17.2a and 17.2b

1   The tires should be rotated at the specified intervals and whenever uneven wear is noticed.
2   Refer to the **accompanying illustrations** for the preferred tire rotation pattern.
3   Refer to the information in *Jacking and towing* at the front of this manual for the correct procedures to follow when raising the vehicle and changing a tire. If the brakes are to be checked, don't apply the parking brake as stated. Make sure the tires are blocked to

prevent the vehicle from rolling as it's raised.
4   Preferably, the entire vehicle should be raised at the same time. This can be done on a hoist or by jacking up each corner and then lowering the vehicle onto jackstands placed under the subframe rails. Always use four jackstands and make sure the vehicle is safely supported.
5   After rotation, check and adjust the tire pressures as necessary and be sure to tighten the lug nuts to the torque listed in this Chapter's Specifications.

18 Exhaust system check (every 6000 miles or 6 months)

Refer to illustrations 18.2a and 18.2b

1   With the engine cold (at least three hours after the vehicle has been driven), check the complete exhaust system from the engine to the end of the tailpipe. Ideally, the inspection should be done with the vehicle on a hoist to permit unrestricted access. If a hoist is not available, raise the vehicle and

support it securely on jackstands.
2   Check the exhaust pipes and connections for evidence of leaks, severe corrosion and damage. Make sure that all brackets and hangers are in good condition and tight **(see illustrations)**.
3   At the same time, inspect the underside of the body for holes, corrosion, open seams, etc. which may allow exhaust gases to enter the interior. Seal all body openings with silicone or body putty.
4   Rattles and other noises can often be traced to the exhaust system, especially the mounts and hangers. Try to move the pipes, muffler and catalytic converter. If the components can come in contact with the body or suspension parts, secure the exhaust system with new mounts.

19 Throttle body mounting nut torque check (every 12,000 miles or 12 months)

Refer to illustration 19.4

1   The throttle body unit is attached to the intake manifold by several bolts or nuts. These fasteners can sometimes work loose from vibration and temperature changes during normal engine operation and cause a vacuum leak.
2   If you suspect that a vacuum leak exists between the throttle body and intake manifold, obtain a length of hose about the diameter of fuel hose. Start the engine and place one end of the hose next to your ear as you probe around the base with the other end. You will hear a hissing sound if a leak exists (be careful of hot or moving engine components).
3   Remove the air cleaner assembly, tagging each hose to be disconnected with a piece of numbered tape to make reassembly easier.

18.2b Check the exhaust system hangers for damage and cracks

19.4 Tighten the throttle body mounting bolts to the torque listed in this Chapter's Specifications

20.3 Gently pry off the trim cap and check the tightness of the wiper arm retaining nut

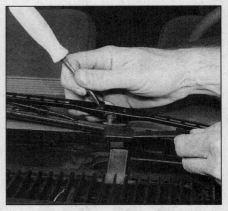

20.5 Lift the release lever with a flat-bladed screwdriver, then slide the blade assembly off the pin on the end of the wiper arm

4   Locate the mounting nuts or bolts at the base of the throttle body **(see illustration)**. Decide what special tools or adapters will be necessary, if any, to tighten the fasteners.

5   Tighten the nuts or bolts to the torque listed in this Chapter's Specifications. Do not overtighten them, as the threads could strip.

6   If, after the nuts or bolts are correctly tightened, a vacuum leak still exists, the throttle body must be removed and a new gasket installed. See Chapter 4 for more information.

7   After tightening the fasteners, reinstall the air cleaner and return all hoses to their original positions.

20 Windshield wiper blade inspection and replacement (every 12,000 miles or 12 months)

Refer to illustrations 20.3, 20.5 and 20.7

1   The windshield wiper and blade assemblies should be inspected periodically for damage, loose components and cracked or worn blade elements.

2   Road film can build up on the wiper

blades and affect their efficiency, so they should be washed regularly with a mild detergent solution.

3   The action of the wiping mechanism can loosen the bolts, nuts and fasteners, so they should be checked and tightened, as necessary, at the same time the wiper blades are checked **(see illustration)**.

4   If the wiper blade elements (sometimes called inserts) are cracked, worn or warped, they should be replaced with new ones.

5   Remove the wiper blade assembly from the wiper arm by inserting a screwdriver and lifting the release lever while pulling on the blade to release it **(see illustration)**.

6   With the blade removed from the vehicle, you can remove the rubber element from the blade.

7   Grasp the end of the wiper bridge securely with one hand and the element with the other. Detach the end of the element from the bridge claw and slide to free it, then slide the element out **(see illustration)**.

8   Compare the new element with the old for length, design, etc.

9   Slide the new element into the claw into place, notched end last and secure the claw into the notches.

10   Reinstall the blade assembly on the arm, wet the windshield and test for correct operation.

21 Seat belt check (every 12,000 miles or 12 months)

1   Check the seat belts, buckles, latch plates and guide loops for obvious damage and signs of wear.

2   See if the seat belt reminder light comes on when the key is turned to the Run or Start position. A chime should also sound.

3   The seat belts are designed to lock up during a sudden stop or impact, yet allow free movement during normal driving. Make sure the retractors return the belt against your chest while driving and rewind the belt fully when the buckle is unlatched.

4   If any of the above checks reveal problems with the seat belt system, replace parts as necessary.

22 Air filter replacement (every 12,000 miles or 12 months)

Refer to illustrations 22.2a and 22.2b

1   At the specified intervals, the air filter should be replaced with a new one. The filter should be inspected between changes.

2   The air filter is located inside the air filter housing which is mounted in the left front

20.7 Squeeze the end of the wiper element to free it from the bridge claw, then slide the element out

22.2a Remove the mounting screws from the air filter housing and . . .

22.2b . . . lift the air filter from the housing

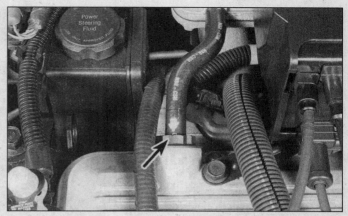

23.1 On 2.2L OHV models, the PCV valve is located at the right rear corner of the valve cover

corner of the engine compartment. Remove the mounting screws, separate the housing halves and lift the filter out **(see illustrations)**.

3   While the filter housing cover is off, be careful not to drop anything down into the air filter housing.

4   Wipe out the inside of the air filter housing with a clean rag.

5   Place the new filter in the air filter housing. Make sure it seats correctly.

6   The remainder of installation is the reverse of removal.

---

23   Positive Crankcase Ventilation (PCV) system check and replacement (every 30,000 miles or 24 months)

Note: *These models are equipped with three different crankcase ventilating systems. On 1997 and earlier 2.2L OHV models, the PCV valve is located on the right side of the valve cover. 1998 and later 2.2L engines are equipped with an oil/air separator located inside the valve cover that requires no maintenance. 2.3L and 2.4L OHC engines are equipped with an oil/air separator that is attached to the side of the engine block above the oil filter.*

2.2L OHV engine (1995 through 1997)

Refer to illustrations 23.1, 23.3a and 23.3b

1   The PCV valve is located on the right side of the valve cover **(see illustration)**.

2   To inspect the PCV valve, remove the hose from the nipple.

3   Unscrew the metal retainer and pull it out of the valve cover using a pair of needle-nose pliers **(see illustrations)**. Note its installed position and direction.

4   Make sure the PCV valve is not plugged with oil/dirt residue and that vacuum is allowed to pass through without obstruction.

5   Shake the PCV valve, listening for a rattle. If the valve doesn't rattle, replace it with a new one.

23.3a Unscrew the metal retainer from the valve cover (2.2L OHV engine)

23.3b Remove the PCV valve using a pair of needle-nose pliers (2.2L OHV engine)

6   When purchasing a replacement PCV valve, make sure it's for your particular vehicle, model year and engine size. Compare the old valve with the new one to make sure they are the same.

7   Push the valve into the end into the valve cover until it's seated.

8   Inspect the metal retainer for damage and replace it with a new one if necessary.

9   Push the PCV valve hose securely into position.

2.3L and 2.4L OHC engines

Refer to illustrations 23.10a and 23.10b

10   These models don't use a conventional PCV valve. Instead, they use an air/oil separator, which is located on the top of the intake manifold on (1995 only) 2.3L OHC engines **(see illustration)** and on the front side of the engine near the oil filter on 1996 through 2002 2.4L OHC engines **(see illustration)**. The air/oil separator separates the

23.10a On (1995 only) 2.3L OHC engines, the air/oil separator is located on top of the intake manifold

23.10b On 2.4L OHC engines, the air/oil separator is located on the front side of the engine block (oil filter removed for clarity)

25.3a Use a small screwdriver or awl to release the locking tab on the ignition wire hold-down bracket

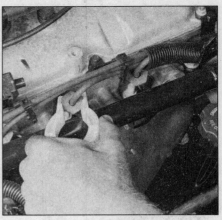

25.3b Using a special spark plug wire removal tool, grab the spark plug boot and pull carefully to separate the end from the spark plug

oil suspended in the crankcase vapors and allows it to drain back into the crankcase. Crankcase vapors are also allowed to pass through the separator and back into the air resonator to be burned in the normal combustion process. The air/oil separator might become clogged as a result of dirty oil that's been allowed to turn to sludge, but as long as you change the oil regularly the separator should function satisfactorily. However, if excess pressure builds up inside the engine, then the air/oil separator might very well be the cause. The usual symptoms are leaky engine seals, excess oil and sludge deposits on the oil dipstick and filler cap, dirty oil and excess crankcase pressure when the oil filler cap is removed. If you think the separator needs to be removed and cleaned, see "Positive Crankcase Ventilation (PCV) system - general information, inspection and component replacement" in Chapter 6.

2.2L OHC engine

11   This engine also uses an air/oil separator instead of a PCV valve, except that on this engine it's an integral part of the valve cover. The separator is not a routine maintenance item, but if the symptoms listed in Step 10 should occur, they might be caused by a clogged separator. To remove the valve cover, refer to Chapter 2C. For more information about the air/oil separator used on this engine, see "Positive Crankcase Ventilation (PCV) system - general information, inspection and component replacement" in Chapter 6.

24 Exhaust Gas Recirculation (EGR) system check (1995 2.2L OHV engine only) (every 30,000 miles or 24 months)

1   The EGR valve is located on the side of the cylinder head. Most of the time when a problem develops in this emissions system, it's due to a stuck or corroded EGR valve.
2   With the engine cold, to prevent burns,

push on the EGR valve diaphragm. Using moderate pressure, you should be able to press the diaphragm in and out within the housing.
3   If the diaphragm doesn't move or moves only with much effort, replace the EGR valve with a new one. If in doubt about the condition of the valve, compare the free movement of your EGR valve with a new valve.
4   Refer to Chapter 6 for more information on the EGR system.

25 Spark plug wire check and replacement (2.2L OHV engine) (every 30,000 miles or 24 months)

Refer to illustrations 25.3a and 25.3b
1   The spark plug wires should be checked at the recommended intervals and whenever new spark plugs are installed in the engine.
2   The wires should be inspected one at a time to prevent mixing up the order, which is essential for correct engine operation.
3   Disconnect the plug wire from the spark plug. To do this, grab the rubber boot, twist slightly and pull the wire off. Do not pull on the wire itself, only on the rubber boot **(see illustrations)**.
4   Check inside the boot for corrosion, which will look like a white crusty powder. Push the wire and boot back onto the end of the spark plug. It should be a tight fit on the plug. If it isn't, remove the wire and use pliers to carefully crimp the metal connector inside the boot until it fits securely on the end of the spark plug.
5   Using a clean rag, wipe the entire length of the wire to remove any built-up dirt and grease. Once the wire is clean, check for burns, cracks and other damage. Do not bend the wire excessively or pull the wire lengthwise - the conductor inside might break.
6   Check the remaining spark plug wires one at a time, making sure they are securely fastened at the coil packs and the spark plug when the check is complete.

7   If new spark plug wires are required, purchase a set for your specific engine model. Wire sets are available pre-cut, with the rubber boots already installed. Remove and replace the wires one at a time to avoid mix-ups in the firing order. **Note:** *If an accidental mix-up occurs, refer to the firing order diagrams at the beginning of this Chapter.*

26 Fuel filter replacement (every 30,000 miles or 24 months)

Refer to illustrations 26.3, 26.5, 26.6a and 25.6b
Warning: *Gasoline is extremely flammable, so take extra precautions when you work on any part of the fuel system. Don't smoke or allow open flames or bare light bulbs near the work area, and don't work in a garage where a gas-type appliance (such as a water heater or clothes dryer) is present. Since gasoline is carcinogenic, wear fuel-resistant gloves when there's a possibility of being exposed to fuel, and, if you spill any fuel on your skin, rinse it off immediately with soap and water. Mop up any spills immediately and do not store fuel-soaked rags where they could ignite. The fuel system is under constant pressure, so, if any fuel lines are to be disconnected, the fuel pressure in the system must be relieved first (see Chapter 4 for more information). When you perform any kind of work on the fuel system, wear safety glasses and have a Class B type fire extinguisher on hand.*
1   Relieve the fuel system pressure (see Chapter 4), then disconnect the cable from the negative terminal of the battery. **Caution:** *If the vehicle is equipped with a Delco Loc II or Theftlock audio system, make sure you have the correct activation code before disconnecting the battery.*
2   Raise the vehicle and support it securely on jackstands.
3   The fuel filter is located under the vehicle, between the fuel tank and the EVAP can-

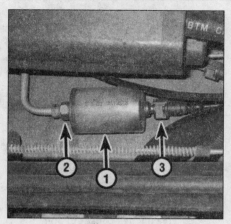

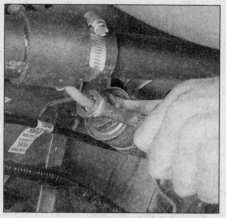

26.3 The fuel filter (1) is located under the vehicle, between the fuel tank and the EVAP canister. The inlet fitting (2) is a conventional tube nut on the end of the inlet line; the outlet fitting (3) is a quick-connect type fitting

26.5 To disconnect the fuel supply line from the fuel filter, loosen the fuel line fitting with a flare-nut wrench. Be sure to use a wrench on the stationary "nut" on the filter, to prevent the line from twisting

26.5a If the plastic quick-connect fitting has a plastic retainer wrapped around it, use a small screwdriver to pry the retainer open, then remove the retainer . . .

ister (see illustration).

4   Clean any dirt surrounding the fuel inlet and outlet line fittings, especially around the inside of the quick-connect fitting.

5   Using a flare-nut wrench, loosen the flare-nut fitting (see illustration) on the inlet side of the fuel filter. Be sure to use a back-up wrench on the "nut" that's located on the filter inlet. Note: Have spare rags or a small container to catch or wipe up extra gasoline that will spill from the filter assembly.

6   Remove the plastic retainer from the quick-connect fitting on the outlet side (see illustrations), if equipped (skip this step if there's no retainer). Then twist the quick-connect fitting 1/4-turn in each direction to loosen the seal. Push the fuel line into the filter, depress the plastic tabs (see illustration) and pull the fuel line from the fuel filter.

7   Remove the fuel filter from its mounting clamp.

8   Install the new fuel filter into the clamp. Note: Make SURE that the directional arrow on the fuel filter points in the direction of fuel flow.

9   Apply a few drops of clean engine oil

into the quick-connect fitting and press it onto the filter until it snaps into place. Pull in-an-out several times to ensure the fitting is securely installed. Slide the retainer into place, if equipped. Install the flare nut fitting and tighten it securely. Be sure to use a flare-nut wrench and a back-up wrench to prevent damage to the filter, fitting or fuel line.

10   Lower the vehicle, start the engine and check for fuel leaks at the filter.

27 Fuel system check (every 30,000 miles or 24 months)

Refer to illustration 27.4

Warning: Gasoline is extremely flammable, so take extra precautions when you work on any part of the fuel system. Don't smoke or allow open flames or bare light bulbs near the work area, and don't work in a garage where a gas-type appliance (such as a water heater or clothes dryer) is present. Since gasoline is carcinogenic, wear fuel-resistant gloves when there's a possibility of being exposed to fuel, and, if you spill any fuel on your skin, rinse it

off immediately with soap and water. Mop up any spills immediately and do not store fuel-soaked rags where they could ignite. The fuel system is under constant pressure, so, if any fuel lines are to be disconnected, the fuel pressure in the system must be relieved first (see Chapter 4 for more information). When you perform any kind of work on the fuel system, wear safety glasses and have a Class B type fire extinguisher on hand.

1   The fuel system is most easily checked with the vehicle raised on a hoist so the components underneath the vehicle are readily visible and accessible.

2   If the smell of gasoline is noticed while driving or after the vehicle has been in the sun, the system should be thoroughly inspected immediately.

3   Remove the gas tank cap and check for damage, corrosion and an unbroken sealing imprint on the gasket. Replace the cap with a new one if necessary.

4   With the vehicle raised, inspect the gas tank and the fuel filler neck hose for cracks and other damage (see illustration). The fuel filler hose, which connects the filler neck to the fuel tank, is especially critical. Warning: Do not, under any circumstances, try to repair

26.5b . . . squeeze the plastic tabs together and pull the quick-connect fitting off the fuel filter outlet pipe (if there's no retainer, ignore the first two parts of this step)

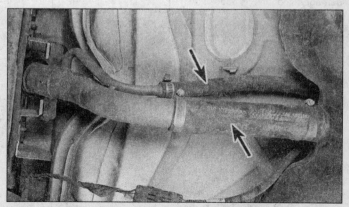

27.4 Check the fuel filler lines for cracks and deterioration and the hose clamps for tightness

28.6a The drain plug on earlier models, which is located at the lower right corner of the radiator, looks like this

28.6b On later models, the drain plug looks like this, but it's still in the same location (lower right corner of the radiator)

28.6c Use a small socket to open the bleeder screw (2.2L OHV model shown)

28.6d Location of the heater core bleeder plug (2.2L OHV model shown)

a fuel tank yourself (except rubber components). A welding torch or any open flame can easily cause the fuel vapors to explode if the correct precautions are not taken.

5   Carefully inspect all hoses and lines leading away from the fuel tank. Check for loose connections, deteriorated hoses, crimped lines and other damage. Follow the lines to the front of the vehicle, carefully inspecting them all the way. Repair or replace damaged sections as necessary.

28 Cooling system servicing (draining, flushing and refilling) (see maintenance schedule for service intervals)

Refer to illustrations 28.6a, 28.6b, 28.6c, 28.6d, 28.7a and 28.7b

Warning: *Make sure the engine is completely cool before performing this procedure.*

Caution: *The manufacturer recommends using only DEX-COOL coolant for these systems. DEX-COOL is a long-lasting coolant designed for 100,000 miles or 5 years. Never mix green-colored ethylene glycol anti-freeze and orange-colored "DEX-COOL" silicate-free coolant because doing so will destroy the efficiency of the "DEX-COOL." If DEX-COOL is not available, check with your local auto parts store for the availability of coolant that is compatible for use in your vehicle's cooling system.*

1   Periodically, the cooling system should be drained, flushed and refilled to replenish the antifreeze mixture and prevent formation of rust and corrosion, which can impair the performance of the cooling system and cause engine damage.

2   At the same time the cooling system is serviced, all hoses and the radiator cap should be inspected and replaced if defective (see Section 12).

3   Since antifreeze is a corrosive and poisonous solution, be careful not to spill any of the coolant mixture on the vehicle's paint or your skin. If this happens, rinse it off immediately with plenty of clean water. Consult local authorities about the dumping of antifreeze before draining the cooling system. In many areas, reclamation centers have been set up to collect automobile oil and drained antifreeze/water mixtures, rather than allowing them to be added to the sewage system.

4   With the engine cold, remove the reservoir pressure cap.

5   Move a large container under the radiator to catch the coolant as it's drained.

6   Drain the radiator by opening the drain plug **(see illustrations)**, which is located at the lower left front corner of the radiator. If the drain plug is corroded and can't be turned easily, or if the radiator isn't equipped with a plug, disconnect the lower radiator hose to allow the coolant to drain. Be careful not to get antifreeze on your skin or in your eyes. Some cooling systems are equipped with a bleeder screw; open the screw two or three turns **(see illustrations)**.

7   After the coolant stops flowing out of the radiator, move the container under the engine block drain plug and remove the plug

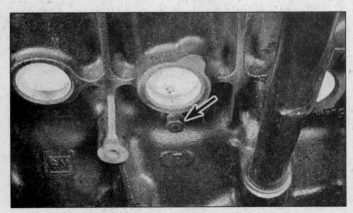

28.7a Location of the block drain plug (2.2L OHV models)

28.7b Location of the block drain plug (2.3L and 2.4L OHC models)

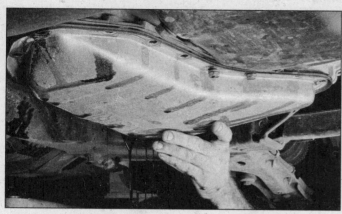

29.6 With the rear bolts in place but loose, pull the front of the pan down to drain the transaxle fluid

29.9a Remove the filter mounting bolts/nuts and . . .

(see illustrations). Note: *On some models, the knock sensor doubles as a block drain plug (see Chapter 6 for the location of the knock sensor on engines so equipped).*

8   Disconnect the hose from the coolant reservoir and remove the reservoir (see Chapter 3). Flush it out with clean water.

9   Remove the upper radiator hose from the radiator, then place a garden hose in the upper radiator opening and flush the system until the water runs clear at all drain points.

10   In severe cases of contamination or clogging of the radiator, remove it (see Chapter 3) and reverse flush it. This involves inserting the hose in the bottom radiator outlet to allow the water to run against the normal flow, draining through the top. A radiator repair shop should be consulted if further cleaning or repair is necessary.

11   When the coolant is regularly drained and the system refilled with the correct antifreeze/water mixture, there should be no need to use chemical cleaners.

12   To refill the system, install the block plugs or knock sensors, reconnect any radiator hoses and install the reservoir and the overflow hose.

13   On later models, make sure to use the correct coolant (see **Caution** above). The manufacturer recommends adding a cooling system sealer any time the coolant is changed. Slowly fill the radiator with the recommended mixture of antifreeze and water to the base of the filler neck. On models without

a radiator cap, add coolant to the coolant reservoir. Wait two minutes and recheck the coolant level, adding if necessary. Close the bleed screws (if equipped) when the coolant issuing from them is free of bubbles. **Note:** *The low coolant light may illuminate after the draining and flushing procedure has been completed. Start the engine and let it run until it reaches normal operating temperature, then let it completely cool down and add coolant as necessary. Repeat this procedure until the light goes out.*

14   Keep a close watch on the coolant level and the cooling system hoses during the first few miles of driving. Tighten the hose clamps and/or add more coolant as necessary. The coolant level should be a little above the HOT mark on the reservoir with the engine at normal operating temperature.

29   Automatic transaxle fluid and filter change (every 50,000 miles)

Refer to illustrations 29.6, 29.9a, 29.9b and 29.10

1   At the specified intervals, the transaxle fluid should be drained and replaced. Since the fluid will remain hot long after driving, perform this procedure only after the engine has cooled down completely.

2   Before beginning work, purchase the specified transaxle fluid (see *Recommended*

lubricants and fluids at the front of this Chapter) and a new filter.

3   Other tools necessary for this job include a floor jack, jackstands to support the vehicle in a raised position, a drain pan capable of holding at least eight quarts, newspapers and clean rags.

4   Raise the vehicle and support it securely on jackstands.

5   Place the drain pan underneath the transaxle pan. Remove the front and side pan mounting bolts, but only loosen the rear pan bolts approximately four turns.

6   Carefully pry the transaxle pan loose with a screwdriver, allowing the fluid to drain **(see illustration)**.

7   Remove the remaining bolts, pan and gasket. Carefully clean the gasket surface of the transaxle to remove all traces of the old gasket and sealant.

8   Drain the fluid from the transaxle pan, clean it with solvent and dry it with compressed air.

9   Remove the filter from the mount inside the transaxle **(see illustrations)**.

10   If the seal did not come out with the filter, remove it from the transaxle **(see illustration)**. Install a new filter and seal.

29.9b . . . lower it from the transaxle

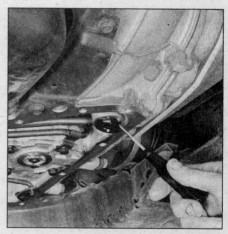

29.10 If necessary, use a screwdriver to remove the seal from the transaxle - be careful not to gouge the aluminum housing

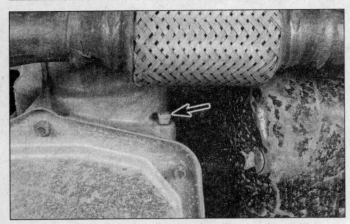

29.17 Location of the transaxle fluid level check plug (4-speed automatic transaxle)

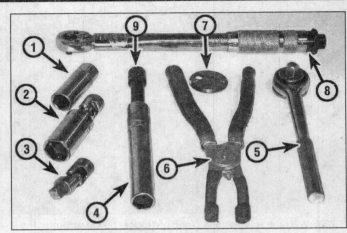

31.1 Tools for changing spark plugs

1   **(Basic) spark plug socket** - *This will have special padding inside to protect the spark plug's porcelain insulator*
2   **Spark plug socket with integral universal joint** - *Handy when you can't access the plugs from directly above*
3   **Universal joint** - *When used with a basic spark plug socket, gives you the same tool as No. 2*
4   **Elongated spark plug socket** - *On some (usually four-valve-per-cylinder) engines, the spark plugs are at the bottom of deep holes in the valve cover.*
5   **Ratchet** - *Standard hand tool to fit the spark plug socket*
6   **Spark plug wire boot removal tool** - *This handy tool will enable you to disconnect and reconnect spark plug wire boots easily and safely. It's especially handy for disconnecting plug wire boots when the engine is still hot!*
7   **Spark plug gap gauge** - *Plug gap gauges come in a variety of styles. This is one common type*
8   **Torque wrench** - *The only way to ensure that the plugs are tightened to the correct torque*
9   **Extension** - *Depending on the engine, you might need an extension to give you enough room to turn the ratchet handle*

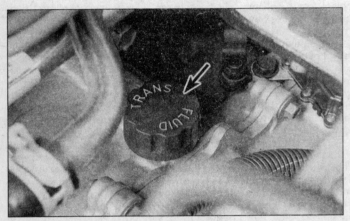

29.19 Location of the filler cap (4-speed automatic transaxle)

11   Make sure the gasket surface on the transaxle pan is clean, then install a new gasket on the pan. Put the pan in place against the transaxle and, working around the pan, tighten each bolt a little at a time until the final torque figure is reached.

12   Lower the vehicle and add approximately 3-1/2 quarts of the specified type of automatic transaxle fluid (see Section 7). **Note:** *This is only the initial amount of fluid that you'll add. More fluid will be required, but should be added in small amounts to prevent over-filling the transaxle.*

13   If you are working on a three-speed transaxle, refer to Section 7 for the fluid level checking procedure. If you're working on a four-speed automatic transaxle, proceed to Step 15.

14   Check under the vehicle for leaks during the first few trips.

Fluid level check (4-speed automatic transaxle)

Refer to illustration 29.17 and 29.19

15   The automatic transaxle fluid level should be carefully maintained. Low fluid level can lead to slipping or loss of drive, while overfilling can cause foaming and loss of fluid. **Warning:** *This procedure is poten-*

tially dangerous and is best left to a professional shop with a safe lifting apparatus. The vehicle must be kept level while being safely raised high enough for access to the check plug on the transaxle.

16   With the vehicle safely raised and supported, start the engine, then move the shift lever through all the gear ranges, ending in Park. **Note:** *Incorrect fluid level readings will result if the vehicle has just been driven at high speeds for an extended period, in hot weather in city traffic, or if it has been pulling a trailer. If any of these conditions apply, wait until the fluid has cooled (about 30 minutes).*

17   With the engine running and the transaxle at normal operating temperature (having idled for 3 to 5 minutes), locate the fluid level check plug on the transaxle. The check plug **(see illustration)** is located right above the right front corner of the transaxle oil pan, near the engine oil drain plug.

18   Place an oil container under the check plug and remove it. Observe the fluid as it drips into the pan, indicating correct fluid level.

19   The fluid level should be at the bottom of the check hole. If fluid pours out excessively, the transaxle may have been overfilled. Double-check to make sure the vehicle

is level. If no fluid drips from the check hole, add small amounts of fluid through the filler cap at the top of the transaxle until the level is at the bottom of the check hole **(see illustration)**. A long-necked funnel will be necessary to add fluid.

20   The condition of the fluid should also be checked along with the level. If the fluid in the drain pan is a dark reddish-brown color, or if the fluid has a burned smell, the fluid should be changed (see above). If you're in doubt about the condition of the fluid, purchase some new fluid and compare the two for color and smell.

21   Be sure to install the check plug and tighten it securely when you're done.

30   Manual transaxle lubricant change (every 50,000 miles)

1   Remove the drain plug and drain the fluid.

2   Reinstall the drain plugs securely.

3   Use a narrow funnel designed to fit into the fill vent tube and slowly add the necessary transaxle fluid. Refer to the Specifications listed in this Chapter for the correct fluid type.

31.5a Here's a wire type gauge being used to check the gap - if the wire does not slide between the electrodes with a slight drag, adjustment is required

31.5b To change the gap, bend the side electrode only, as indicated by the arrows, and be very careful not to crack or chip the porcelain insulator surrounding the center electrode

31 Spark plug check and replacement (see maintenance schedule for service intervals)

Refer to illustrations 31.1, 31.5a, 31.5b, 31.6, 31.8, 31.9 and 31.10
Note: *All of the engines covered by this manual are equipped with an Electronic Ignition (EI) system. On 2.2L OHV engines, a pair of coil packs and an ignition control module are mounted on the left end of the cylinder head, with spark plug wires connecting the spark plugs to the coil packs. The EI system on 2.2L, 2.3L and 2.4L OHC engines consists of an ignition control module and four ignition coils (one for each spark plug), all of which are integrated into a single assembly mounted directly on top of the valve cover. For more information about the ignition system, refer to Chapter 5.*

1   To replace the spark plugs, you'll need a few tools **(see illustration)**. They include a special spark plug socket (spark plug sockets are padded inside to prevent damage to the porcelain insulators on the plugs), an extension of the appropriate length and a ratchet.

You'll also need a spark plug gap gauge to check and adjust the gaps on the new spark plugs. Use a torque wrench to tighten the new spark plugs to the correct torque. A special spark plug boot removal tool is also handy - and. on some engines, indispensable - for disconnecting the plug wire boots from the plugs, and is a good idea on these models because the boots fit very tightly. It is a good idea to allow the engine to cool before removing or installing the spark plugs.

2   On 2.2L OHV models the spark plugs are located on the front side of the cylinder head. You'll need a spark plug socket, an extension and a ratchet to remove them. On 2.2L, 2.3L and 2.4L OHC engines the spark plugs are located in the middle of the cylinder head, between the intake and exhaust camshafts. To access the spark plugs on OHC engines, remove the ignition coil/ignition module assembly (see Chapter 5).

3   The best approach when replacing the spark plugs is to purchase the new ones in advance, adjust them to the correct gap and replace the spark plugs one at a time. When buying the new spark plugs, be sure to obtain

the correct spark plug type for your particular engine. The spark plug type can be found in the Specifications at the front of this Chapter and in your owner's manual. If these two sources list different spark plug types, consider the owner's manual correct.

4   Allow the engine to cool completely before attempting to remove any of the spark plugs. While you are waiting for the engine to cool, check the new spark plugs for defects and adjust the gaps.

5   Check the gap by inserting the gap gauge between the electrodes at the tip of the spark plug **(see illustration)**. The gap between the electrodes should be the same as the one specified on the Emissions Control Information label or at the beginning of this Chapter. The gauge should slide between the electrodes with a slight amount of drag. If the gap is incorrect, use the adjuster on the gauge body to bend the curved side electrode slightly until the correct gap is obtained **(see illustration)**. If the side electrode is not exactly over the center electrode, bend it with the adjuster until it is. Check for cracks in the porcelain insulator (if any are found, the spark plug must not be used).

6   With the engine cool, remove the spark plug wire from one spark plug. Pull only on the boot at the end of the wire - do not pull on the wire. A spark plug wire removal tool should be used if available **(see illustration)**. On 2.2L, 2.3L and 2.4L OHC engines it will be necessary to remove the ignition cover, the module, the coil pack assemblies and the spark plug boots as one complete assembly. Refer to Chapter 5 for additional information and illustrations.

7   If compressed air is available, use it to blow any dirt or foreign material away from the spark plug hole. The idea here is to eliminate the possibility of debris falling into the cylinder as the spark plug is removed.

8   The spark plugs on OHC engines are, for the most part, difficult to reach so a spark plug socket incorporating a universal joint will be necessary. Place the spark plug socket over the spark plug and remove it from the engine by turning it in a counterclockwise

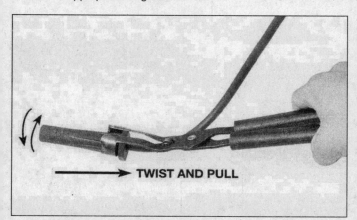

TWIST AND PULL

31.6 When removing the spark plug wires, pull only on the boot and use a twisting, pulling motion

31.8 Use an extension and socket to remove the spark plugs from the cylinder head

31.9 Apply a thin coat of anti-seize compound to the spark plug threads

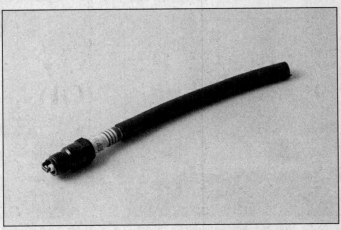

31.10 A length of snug-fitting rubber hose will save time and prevent damaged threads when installing the spark plugs

direction **(see illustration)**.

9   Compare the spark plug with the chart shown on the inside back cover of this manual to get an indication of the general running condition of the engine. Before installing the new spark plugs, it is a good idea to apply a thin coat of anti-seize compound to the threads **(see illustration)**.

10   Thread one of the new spark plugs into the hole until you can no longer turn it with your fingers, then tighten it with a torque wrench (if available) or the ratchet. It's a good idea to slip a short length of rubber hose over the end of the spark plug to use as a tool to thread it into place **(see illustration)**. The hose will grip the spark plug well enough to turn it, but will start to slip if the spark plug begins to cross-thread in the hole - this will prevent damaged threads and the accompanying repair costs.

11   Before pushing the spark plug wire onto the end of the spark plug, inspect it following the procedures outlined in Section 25.

12   Attach the spark plug wire to the new spark plug, again using a twisting motion on the boot until it's seated on the spark plug.

13   Repeat the procedure for the remaining spark plugs, replacing them one at a time to prevent mixing up the spark plug wires.

Chapter 2 Part A
Overhead valve (OHV) engine

Contents

Specifications

General

Displacement	134 cubic inches (2.2 liters)
Firing order	1-3-4-2
Compression pressure	See Chapter 2D
Oil pressure	See Chapter 2D

Torque specifications

	Ft-lbs (unless otherwise indicated)
Camshaft sprocket bolt	96
Crankshaft pulley-to-hub bolts	37
Crankshaft pulley center bolt	77
Cylinder head bolts (in sequence - see illustration 9.23)	
Step 1	
Short bolts	43
Long bolts	46
Step 2	Tighten an additional 90-degrees
Exhaust manifold fasteners	
1995 through 1997	115 in-lbs
1998 and later	118 in-lbs
Flywheel bolts	55
Driveplate bolts	52
Intake manifold fasteners	
1995 through 1997	
Upper intake manifold nuts	22
Lower intake manifold nuts	24
1998 and later	18
Timing chain cover bolts	97 in-lbs
Timing chain tensioner bolts	18
Oil pan bolts	89 in-lbs
Oil pump mounting bolt	32
Rocker arm nuts/bolts	
1995 through 1997	22
1998 and later	19
Valve cover bolts	89 in-lbs
Valve lifter anti-rotation bracket bolts	97 in-lbs

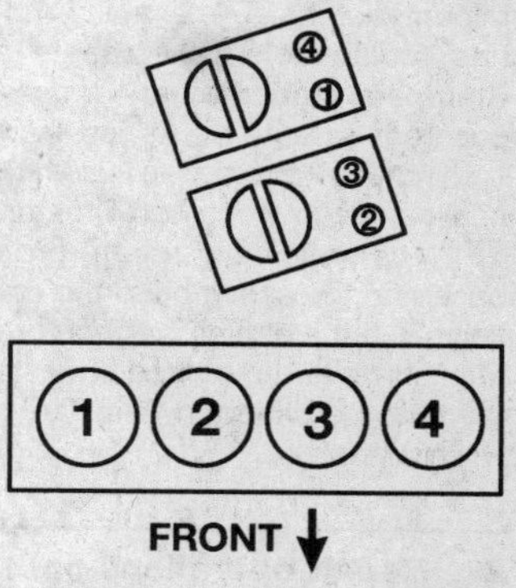

38016-1-2A HAYNES

1995-1997

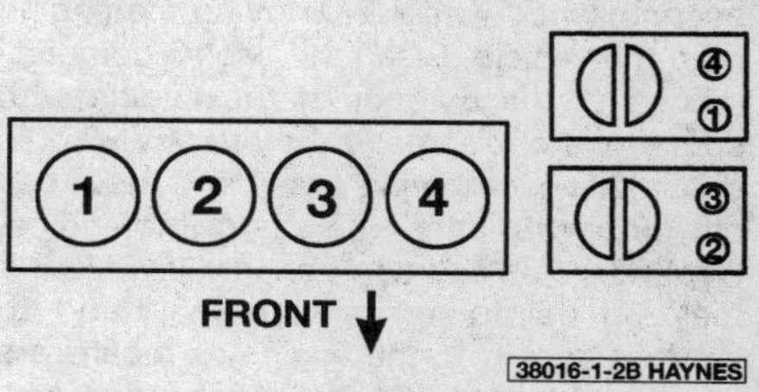

38016-1-2B HAYNES

1998 and later

4.6 Remove the valve cover bolts (arrows) and . . .

4.7 . . . lift the valve cover from the cylinder head

1   General information

Caution: *If the vehicle is equipped with a Delco Loc II or Theftlock audio system, make sure you have the correct activation code before disconnecting the battery. See the information at the front of this manual for the radio re-activation procedure.*

This Part of Chapter 2 is devoted to in-vehicle repair procedures for the 2.2 liter, four-cylinder overhead valve engine. This engine has a cast iron block and cast aluminum pistons. The aluminum cylinder head has replaceable valve seats and guides. Stamped steel rocker arms and tubular pushrods actuate the valves. Information concerning engine removal, installation and overhaul can be found in Part D of this Chapter.

The following repair procedures are based on the assumption the engine is in the vehicle. If the engine has been removed from the vehicle and mounted on a stand, many of the steps outlined in this Part of Chapter 2 will not apply.

2   Repair operations possible with the engine in the vehicle

Many major repair operations can be accomplished without removing the engine from the vehicle. Clean the engine compartment and the exterior of the engine with some type of degreaser before any work is done. It'll make the job easier and help keep dirt out of the internal areas of the engine. Depending on the components involved, it may be helpful to remove the hood to improve access to the engine as repairs are performed (refer to Chapter 11 if necessary). Cover the fenders to prevent damage to the paint. Special pads are available, but an old bedspread or blanket will also work.

If vacuum, exhaust, oil or coolant leaks develop, indicating a need for gasket or seal replacement, the repairs can generally be made with the engine in the vehicle. The intake and exhaust manifold gaskets, timing chain cover gasket, oil pan gasket, crankshaft oil seals and cylinder head gasket are all accessible with the engine in place.

Exterior engine components, such as the intake and exhaust manifolds, the oil pan (and the oil pump), the water pump, the starter motor, the alternator and the fuel system components can be removed for repair with the engine in place. Since the cylinder head can be removed without pulling the engine, valve component servicing can also be accomplished with the engine in the vehicle. Replacement of the timing chain and sprockets is also possible with the engine in the vehicle. In extreme cases caused by a lack of necessary equipment, repair or replacement of piston rings, pistons, connecting rods and rod bearings is possible with the engine in the vehicle. However, this practice is not recommended because of the cleaning and preparation work that must be done to the components involved.

3   Top Dead Center (TDC) for number one piston - locating

1   Top Dead Center (TDC) is the highest point in the cylinder each piston reaches as it travels up-and-down when the crankshaft turns. Each piston reaches TDC on the compression stroke and again on the exhaust stroke, but TDC generally refers to piston position on the compression stroke.
2   Positioning the piston(s) at TDC is an essential part of certain procedures such as camshaft removal and timing chain/sprocket removal.
3   Before beginning this procedure, be sure to place the transaxle in Neutral (or Park on automatic transaxle models), apply the parking brake and block the rear wheels. Disconnect the cable from the negative terminal of the battery. **Caution:** *If the vehicle is equipped with a Delco Loc II or Theftlock audio system, make sure you have the correct activation code before disconnecting the bat-tery. See the information at the front of this manual for the radio re-activation procedure.*
4   Remove the spark plugs (see Chapter 1).
5   When looking at the drivebelt end of the engine, normal crankshaft rotation is clockwise. In order to bring any piston to TDC, the crankshaft must be turned with a socket and ratchet attached to the bolt threaded into the center of the lower drivebelt pulley on the crankshaft.
6   Have an assistant turn the crankshaft with a socket and ratchet as described above while you hold a finger over the number one spark plug hole. **Note:** *See the Specifications for the number one cylinder location.*
7   When the piston approaches TDC, pressure will be felt at the spark plug hole. Have your assistant stop turning the crankshaft when the timing marks are aligned.
8   If the timing marks are bypassed, turn the crankshaft two complete revolutions clockwise until the timing marks are properly aligned.
9   After the number one piston has been positioned at TDC on the compression stroke, TDC for any of the remaining pistons can be located by turning the crankshaft one-half turn (180-degrees) to get to TDC for the next cylinder in the firing order.

4   Valve cover - removal and installation

Removal

Refer to illustrations 4.6 and 4.7

1   Disconnect the cable from the negative terminal of the battery. **Caution:** *If the vehicle is equipped with a Delco Loc II or Theftlock audio system, make sure you have the correct activation code before disconnecting the battery. See the information at the front of this manual for the radio re-activation procedure.*
2   Remove the air cleaner outlet duct from the throttle body to the air cleaner assembly.
3   On 1998 and later models, remove the

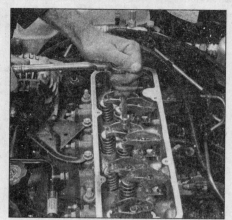

5.2 Remove the rocker arms one at a time and place them in a marked container to avoid assembly mistakes

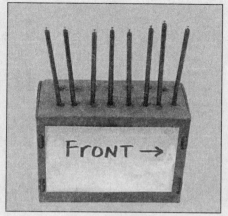

5.4 If more than one pushrod is being removed, store them in a perforated cardboard box to prevent mix-ups during installations (note the label indicating the front of the engine)

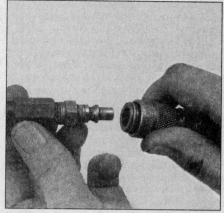

6.4 This is what the air hose adapter that threads into the spark plug looks like - they're commonly available from auto part stores

resonator from the throttle body and the resonator bracket that shields the fuel rail and harness connectors.

4   Remove the PCV hose from the valve cover.

5   Disconnect the accelerator cable, the throttle valve cable (automatic transaxle) and cruise control cable, if equipped.

6   Remove the valve cover bolts (see illustration).

7   Detach the valve cover from the cylinder head (see illustration). Note: *If the cover is stuck to the cylinder head, use a block of wood and hammer to dislodge it. If that doesn't work, try to slip a flexible putty knife between the cylinder head and cover to break the gasket seal. Don't pry at the cover-to-cylinder head joint or damage to the sealing surfaces may occur (leading to oil leaks in the future).*

Installation

8   The mating surfaces of the cylinder head and valve cover must be perfectly clean when the cover is installed. Use a gasket scraper to remove all traces of sealant or old gasket, then clean the mating surfaces with lacquer thinner or acetone (if there's sealant or oil on the mating surfaces when the cover is installed, oil leaks may develop). The cylinder head and cover are made of aluminum, so be extra careful not to nick or gouge the mating surfaces with the scraper.

9   Clean the mounting bolt threads with a die if necessary to remove any corrosion and restore damaged threads. Make sure the threaded holes in the cylinder head are clean - run a tap into them if necessary to remove corrosion and restore damaged threads.

10   Apply a thin coat of RTV-type sealant to the sealing flange on the cover and install a new gasket.

11   Place the valve cover on the cylinder head and install the mounting bolts. Tighten the bolts a little at a time to the torque listed in this Chapter's Specifications. Work from the center out in a spiral pattern.

12   Complete the installation by reversing the removal procedure.

5 Rocker arms and pushrods - removal, inspection and installation

Removal

Refer to illustrations 5.2 and 5.4

1   Refer to Section 5 and detach the valve cover from the cylinder head.

2   Beginning at the front of the cylinder head, loosen the rocker arm nuts (see illustration).

3   Remove the nuts, the rocker arms and the pivot balls and store them in marked containers (they must be reinstalled in their original locations).

4   Remove the pushrods and store them in order to make sure they don't get mixed up during installation (see illustration).

5   If the pushrod guides must be removed for any reason, make sure they're marked so they can be reinstalled in their original locations.

Inspection

6   Check each rocker arm for wear, cracks and other damage, especially where the pushrods and valve stems contact the rocker arm faces.

7   Make sure the hole at the pushrod end of each rocker arm is open.

8   Check each rocker arm pivot area for wear, cracks and galling. If the rocker arms are worn or damaged, replace them with new ones and use new pivot balls as well.

9   Inspect the pushrods for cracks and excessive wear at the ends. Roll each pushrod across a piece of plate glass to see if it's bent (if it wobbles, it's bent).

Installation

10   Lubricate the lower ends of the pushrods with clean engine oil or moly-base grease and install them in their original locations. Make sure each pushrod seats com-

pletely in the lifter socket.

11   Apply moly-base grease to the ends of the valve stems and the upper ends of the pushrods before positioning the rocker arms and installing the nuts.

12   Apply moly-base grease to the pivot balls to prevent damage to the mating surfaces before engine oil pressure builds up. Set the rocker arms in place, then install the pivot balls and nuts. Tighten the nuts to the torque listed in this Chapter's Specifications.

6 Valve springs, retainers and seals - replacement

Refer to illustrations 6.4, 6.9 and 6.17

Note: *Broken valve springs and defective valve stem seals can be replaced without removing the cylinder head. Two special tools and a compressed air source are normally required to perform this operation, so read through this Section carefully and rent or buy the tools before beginning the job. If compressed air isn't available, a length of nylon rope can be used to keep the valves from falling into the cylinder during this procedure.*

1   Refer to Section 4 and remove the valve cover.

2   Remove the spark plug from the cylinder which has the defective component. If all of the valve stem seals are being replaced, all of the spark plugs should be removed.

3   Turn the crankshaft until the piston in the affected cylinder is at top dead center on the compression stroke (see Section 3 for instructions). If you're replacing all of the valve stem seals, begin with cylinder number one and work on the valves for one cylinder at a time. Move from cylinder-to-cylinder following the firing order sequence (see this Chapter's Specifications).

4   Thread an adapter into the spark plug hole (see illustration) and connect an air hose from a compressed air source to it. Most auto parts stores can supply the air hose adapter. Note: *Many cylinder compres-*

sion gauges utilize a screw-in fitting that may work with your air hose quick-disconnect fitting.

5   Remove the nut, pivot ball and rocker arm for the valve with the defective part and pull out the pushrod. If all of the valve stem seals are being replaced, all of the rocker arms and pushrods should be removed (refer to Section 5).

6   Apply compressed air to the cylinder. **Warning:** *The piston may be forced down by compressed air, causing the crankshaft to turn suddenly. If the wrench used when positioning the number one piston at TDC is still attached to the bolt in the crankshaft nose, it could cause damage or injury when the crankshaft moves.*

7   The valves should be held in place by the air pressure.

8   If you don't have access to compressed air, an alternative method can be used. Position the piston at a point approximately 45-degrees before TDC on the compression stroke, then feed a long piece of nylon rope through the spark plug hole until it fills the combustion chamber. Be sure to leave the end of the rope hanging out of the engine so it can be removed easily. Use a large ratchet and socket to rotate the crankshaft in the normal direction of rotation (clockwise) until slight resistance is felt.

9   Stuff shop rags into the cylinder head holes above and below the valves to prevent parts and tools from falling into the engine, then use a valve spring compressor to compress the spring. Remove the keepers with small needle-nose pliers or a magnet **(see illustration)**. **Note:** *A couple of different types of tools are available for compressing the valve springs with the cylinder head in place. The type shown here utilizes the rocker arm stud and nut for leverage, while the other type grips the lower spring coils and presses on the retainer as the knob is turned. Both types work very well, although the lever type is usually less expensive.*

10   Remove the spring retainer and valve spring, then remove the valve guide seal. **Note:** *If air pressure fails to hold the valve in the closed position during this operation, the valve face or seat is probably damaged. If so, the cylinder head will have to be removed for additional repair operations.*

11   Wrap a rubber band or tape around the top of the valve stem so the valve won't fall into the combustion chamber, then release the air pressure. **Note:** *If a rope was used instead of air pressure, turn the crankshaft slightly in the direction opposite normal rotation.*

12   Inspect the valve stem for damage. Rotate the valve in the guide and check the end for eccentric movement, which would indicate the valve stem is bent.

13   Move the valve up-and-down in the guide and make sure it doesn't bind. If the valve stem binds, either the valve is bent or the guide is damaged. In either case, the cylinder head will have to be removed for repair.

6.9 Once the spring is depressed, the keepers can be removed with a small magnet or needle-nose pliers (a magnet is preferred to prevent dropping the keepers)

14   Reapply air pressure to the cylinder to retain the valve in the closed position, then remove the tape or rubber band from the valve stem. If a rope was used instead of air pressure, rotate the crankshaft in the normal direction of rotation until slight resistance is felt.

15   Lubricate the valve stem with engine oil and install a new valve guide seal. **Note:** *Intake and exhaust valve seals are different.*

16   Install the spring in position over the valve.

17   Install the valve spring retainer. Compress the valve spring and carefully install the keepers in the groove. Apply a small dab of grease to the inside of each keeper to hold it in place if necessary **(see illustration)**. Remove the pressure from the spring tool and make sure the keepers are seated.

18   Disconnect the air hose and remove the adapter from the spark plug hole. If a rope was used in place of air pressure, turn the crankshaft counterclockwise and pull it out of the cylinder.

19   Refer to Section 5 and install the rocker arm(s) and pushrod(s).

20   Install the spark plug(s) and hook up the wire(s).

21   Refer to Section 4 and install the valve cover.

22   Start and run the engine, then check for oil leaks and unusual sounds coming from the valve cover area.

---

7   Intake manifold - removal and installation

1995 through 1997 models
Upper intake manifold

1   Disconnect the cable from the negative terminal of the battery. **Caution:** *If the vehicle is equipped with a Delco Loc II or Theftlock audio system, make sure you have the correct activation code before disconnecting the battery.*

6.17 Apply a small dab of grease to the keepers before installation-it will hold them in place on the valve stem as the spring is released

2   Loosen the hose clamps and remove the air intake duct that connects the air filter housing to the throttle body.

3   Remove the throttle linkage cover, then disconnect the accelerator cable from the throttle linkage (see Chapter 4). If the vehicle is equipped with cruise control, also disconnect the cruise control cable from the throttle linkage. If the vehicle is equipped with an automatic transmission, disconnect the Throttle Valve (TV) cable (see Chapter 7B). **Note:** *It's not necessary to disengage the accelerator cable, cruise cable and TV cable from the cable bracket. Once you've disconnected the cables from the throttle linkage, unbolt the cable bracket and set the bracket and cables aside.*

4   Disconnect the electrical connectors from the Idle Air Control (IAC) valve, the Manifold Absolute Pressure (MAP) sensor and the Throttle Position (TP) sensor.

5   Disconnect the PCV hose and the power brake booster vacuum hose from the upper intake manifold.

6   Detach the vacuum distributor from the throttle body. (It's not necessary to disconnect the vacuum lines themselves; just set the vacuum distributor and the vacuum lines aside.)

7   Set the wiring harnesses for the fuel injectors and for the Exhaust Gas Recirculation (EGR) valve aside, then remove the upper intake manifold mounting bolts.

8   Remove the upper intake manifold and remove the old gasket from the lower intake manifold.

9   Carefully clean the gasket mating surfaces of the upper and lower intake manifolds. Be sure to remove all traces of old gasket material. Be extremely careful not to scratch or gouge the mating surface of either manifold.

10   Using a new gasket, place the upper intake manifold in position on the lower manifold. Then, starting with the bolt nearest the throttle linkage, work in a counterclockwise fashion and gradually and evenly tighten the

7.16 Unscrew this nut from the left end of the lower intake manifold and disconnect the Exhaust Gas Recirculation (EGR) pipe from the manifold. If the nut is difficult to loosen, spray some penetrant between the nut and the EGR pipe, wait awhile for it to soak in and try again (1995 through 1997 models)

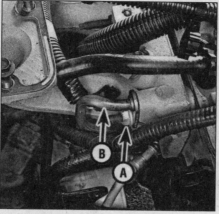

7.17 Remove this nut (A) and detach the fuel supply line (B) from the right end of the lower intake manifold (1995 through 1997 models)

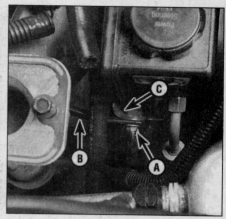

7.18 Remove this nut (A) to detach the lower intake manifold brace (B) from the power steering pump mounting bracket (C) (1995 through 1997 models)

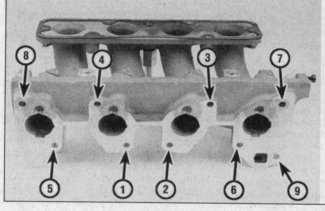

7.21 Lower intake manifold mounting nut tightening sequence (1995 through 1997 models)

upper intake manifold mounting bolts to the torque listed in this Chapter's Specifications. Installation is otherwise the reverse of removal.

Lower intake manifold

Refer to illustrations 7.16, 7.17, 7.18 and 7.21

11   Relieve the system fuel pressure (see Chapter 4).

12   Disconnect the cable from the negative terminal of the battery. **Caution:** *If the vehicle is equipped with a Delco Loc II or Theftlock audio system, make sure you have the correct activation code before disconnecting the battery.*

13   Remove the upper intake manifold (see Steps 2 through 8).

14   Disconnect the quick-connect fittings for the fuel supply and return lines (see Section 4 in Chapter 4). Plug the fuel supply and return line pipes to prevent dirt and moisture from entering the manifold.

15   Remove the power steering pump mounting bracket bolts, detach the pump mounting bracket and set the pump aside. (Don't disconnect the power steering fluid lines.)

16   Disconnect the EGR pipe from the lower intake manifold **(see illustration)**. If the vehicle is equipped with an automatic transmission, remove the transmission filler tube retaining nut and detach the dipstick tube bracket from the lower intake manifold. (The transmission dipstick tube bracket is bolted to the left rear corner of the lower intake manifold, right above the EGR pipe.)

17   Remove the nut that secures the flange for the fuel supply line pipe **(see illustration)** and detach the fuel supply line pipe from the lower intake manifold. Remove and discard the old O-ring seal.

18   Remove the nut **(see illustration)** that attaches the lower intake manifold brace to the power steering pump mounting bracket.

The other end of this brace is bolted to the underside of the lower intake manifold, so it's difficult to access at this time. Leave it attached to the manifold for now, then unbolt it after removing the manifold.

19   Remove the lower intake manifold mounting nuts and remove the lower intake manifold. Remove and discard the old gasket.

20   Carefully clean off all old gasket material from the mating surfaces of the lower intake manifold and the cylinder head. Be careful not to gouge or scratch the mating surfaces.

21   Using a new gasket, install the lower intake manifold and hand tighten the manifold mounting nuts, then tighten them in the indicated sequence **(see illustration)** to the torque listed in this Chapter's Specifications.

22   Installation is otherwise the reverse of removal.

23   When you're done, start the engine and check for air and fuel leaks.

1998 and later models

Refer to illustration 7.31

24   Relieve the system fuel pressure (see Chapter 4).

25   Disconnect the cable from the negative terminal of the battery. **Caution:** *If the vehicle is equipped with a Delco Loc II or Theftlock audio system, make sure you have the correct*

activation code before disconnecting the battery.

26   Loosen the hose clamps and remove the air intake duct. Also remove the "resonator" (the black plastic housing between the air intake duct and the throttle body) and remove the resonator mounting bracket.

27   If you're planning to *replace* the intake manifold, you'll have to swap the throttle body onto the new manifold. Remove the throttle body from the old manifold now, because it's easier to unbolt everything while the manifold is still attached to the cylinder head (see Chapter 4). If you're removing the intake manifold in order *to service something else* and plan to reuse the old intake manifold, then the throttle body can remain attached to the manifold. However, all of the following items must be disconnected from the throttle body:

a) *If the vehicle is equipped with cruise control, disconnect the cruise control cable from the cable bracket and from the throttle linkage.*

b) *Disconnect the accelerator cable from the cable bracket and from the throttle linkage (see Chapter 4).*

c) *Clearly label all vacuum lines or hoses that are connected to the throttle body, then disconnect them.*

7.31 Intake manifold mounting bolt and nut tightening sequence (1998 and later models)

8.8 Remove the oil filler tube mounting bracket bolt (arrow) and remove the tube

d) Disconnect the electrical connectors for the Manifold Absolute Pressure (MAP) sensor, the Throttle Position (TP) sensor and the Idle Air Control (IAC) valve (see Chapter 6 if you need help).

28   Remove the fuel rail and injector assembly (see Chapter 4).

29   Remove the intake manifold mounting nuts and bolts and remove the manifold.

30   Clean the gasket mating surfaces of the intake manifold and the cylinder head. Be careful not to gouge or scratch the mating surfaces.

31   Using a new gasket, place the intake manifold in position, install the manifold mounting nuts and bolts and tighten them in the indicated sequence **(see illustration)** to the torque listed in this Chapter's Specifications.

32   Installation is otherwise the reverse of removal.

33   When you're done, start the engine and check for air and fuel leaks.

8   Exhaust manifold - removal and installation

Removal

Refer to illustrations 8.8, 8.9 and 8.10

1   Disconnect the negative battery cable from the battery. **Caution:** *If the vehicle is equipped with a Delco Loc II or Theftlock audio system, make sure you have the correct activation code before disconnecting the battery. See the information at the front of this manual for the radio re-activation procedure.*

2   Remove the serpentine drivebelt from the engine (see Chapter 1).

3   Partially drain the coolant system (see Chapter 1).

4   Unplug the oxygen sensor lead.

5   Raise the front of the vehicle, support it securely on jackstands and apply the parking brake. Block the rear wheels to keep the vehicle from rolling off the jackstands. Unbolt the exhaust pipe from the manifold. Lower the vehicle.

6   Remove the alternator (see Chapter 5).

7   Remove the bolts from the exhaust manifold flange.

8   Remove the oil fill tube assembly **(see illustration)**.

9   Remove the heater outlet hose assembly **(see illustration)**.

10   Remove the exhaust manifold-to-cylinder head nuts/bolts **(see illustration)**, pull the manifold off the engine and lift it out of the exhaust pipe flange. Remove and discard the gasket.

11   Scrape all traces of gasket material off the exhaust manifold and cylinder head mating surfaces.

12   Clean all bolt and stud threads before installation. A wire brush can be used on the manifold mounting studs, while a tap works well when cleaning the bolt holes.

Installation

13   If a new manifold is being installed, transfer the oxygen sensor from the old manifold to the new one.

14   Install the exhaust manifold using a new

8.9 Remove the mounting clamps (arrows) and separate the heater outlet hoses from the pipes

8.10 Remove the exhaust manifold mounting nuts (arrows) from the cylinder head

9.6 Support the engine and remove the bolts (arrows) from the front engine mount

gasket. Tighten the nuts/bolts to the torque listed in this Chapter's Specifications. Work in a spiral pattern from the center out.

15   The remainder of installation is the reverse of removal. Refill the cooling system (see Chapter 1).

9   Cylinder head - removal and installation

Caution: *Allow the engine to cool completely before loosening the cylinder head bolts.*
Note: *On vehicles with high mileage or during an engine overhaul, camshaft lobe height should be checked prior to cylinder head removal (see Chapter 2, Part C, Section 13 for instructions).*

Removal

Refer to illustrations 9.6, 9.13a and 9.13b

1   Relieve the fuel pressure (see Chapter 4), then disconnect the negative battery cable from the battery. **Caution:** *If the vehicle is equipped with a Delco Loc II or Theftlock audio system, make sure you have the correct activation code before disconnecting the bat-*

9.13a To avoid mixing up the cylinder head bolts, use a new gasket to transfer the bolt hole pattern to a piece of cardboard, then punch holes to accept the bolts

tery. See the information at the front of this manual for the radio re-activation procedure.

2   Remove the alternator and brackets as described in Chapter 5. Remove the power steering pump and position the assembly to the side while keeping the power steering lines attached to the pump assembly.
3   Remove the intake manifold as described in Section 7.
4   Remove the exhaust manifold as described in Section 8.
5   Unbolt the drivebelt tensioner.
6   Support the engine from above using an engine support fixture (available at auto parts stores or equipment rental yards) or from below with a floor jack. Use a block of wood between the floor jack and the engine when raising it to prevent damage to the oil pan. Remove the front engine mount from the cylinder head **(see illustration)**.
7   Remove the front engine accessory bracket.
8   Disconnect any remaining wires, hoses, fuel and vacuum lines from the cylinder head. Be sure to label them to simplify reinstallation.

9   Disconnect the spark plug wires and remove the spark plugs. Be sure the plug wires are labeled to simplify reinstallation.
10   Remove the valve cover (see Section 4).
11   Remove the rocker arms and pushrods (see Section 5).
12   Remove the ignition coil assembly (coil packs, wires, ignition module) (see Chapter 5).
13   Using the new cylinder head gasket, outline the cylinders and bolt pattern on a piece of cardboard **(see illustration)**. Be sure to indicate the front of the engine for reference. Punch holes at the bolt locations. Loosen each of the cylinder head mounting bolts 1/4-turn at a time until they can be removed by hand **(see illustration)**. Store the bolts in the cardboard holder as they're removed - this will ensure they are reinstalled in their original locations, which is absolutely essential.
14   Lift the cylinder head off the engine. If it's stuck, don't attempt to pry it off - you could damage the sealing surfaces. Instead, use a hammer and block of wood to tap the cylinder head and break the gasket seal. Place the cylinder head on a block of wood to prevent damage to the gasket surface.
15   Remove the cylinder head gasket.
16   Refer to Chapter 2, Part C, for cylinder head disassembly and valve service procedures.

Installation

Refer to illustrations 9.19 and 9.23

17   If a new cylinder head is being installed, transfer all external parts from the old cylinder head to the new one.
18   If not already done, thoroughly clean the gasket surfaces on the cylinder head and the engine block. Do not gouge or otherwise damage the soft aluminum gasket surfaces.
19   To get the proper torque readings, the threads of the cylinder head bolts must be clean **(see illustration)**. This also applies to the threaded holes in the engine block. Run a tap through the holes to ensure they are clean.

9.13b Start with the outer bolts and work inward in a circular pattern to prevent warping the cylinder head

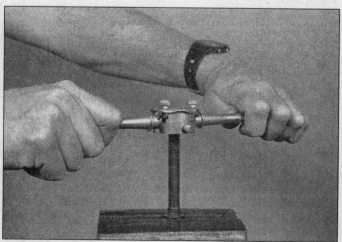

9.19 A die should be used to remove sealant and corrosion from the cylinder head bolt threads prior to installation

9.23 Cylinder head bolt tightening sequence

10.4a Remove the anti-rotation bracket bolts (arrows) and . . .

20   Place the gasket in position over the engine block dowel pins. Note any marks like "THIS SIDE UP" and install the gasket accordingly.

21   Carefully lower the cylinder head onto the engine, over the dowel pins and the gasket.

22   Install the bolts finger tight. Don't tighten any of the bolts at this time.

23   Tighten each of the bolts in 1/4-turn increments in the recommended sequence **(see illustration)**. Note that the different length bolts have different torque specifications. Continue tightening in the recommended sequence until the torque (and angle of rotation) specified in this Chapter's Specifications is reached.

24   The remaining installation steps are the reverse of removal.

25   Be sure to refill the cooling system and change the oil and filter (see Chapter 1).

10   Valve lifters - removal, inspection and installation

Removal

Refer to illustrations 10.4a, 10.4b, 10.5 and 10.6

1   A noisy valve lifter can be isolated when the engine is idling. Place a length of hose near the location of each valve while listening at the other end of the hose. Another method is to remove the valve cover and, with the engine idling, place a finger on each of the valve spring retainers, one at a time. If a valve lifter is defective it will be evident from the shock felt at the retainer as the valve seats. The most likely cause of a noisy valve lifter is a piece of dirt trapped inside the lifter.

2   Disconnect the cable from the negative battery terminal. **Caution:** *If the vehicle is equipped with a Delco Loc II or Theftlock audio system, make sure you have the correct activation code before disconnecting the battery. See the information at the front of this manual for the radio re-activation procedure.*

3   Remove the valve cover, the rocker

arms and pushrods and then remove the cylinder head (see Section 9).

4   Remove the anti-rotation brackets from the engine block **(see illustrations)**.

5   A magnetic pick-up tool or scribe can be positioned at the top of the lifter and used to raise it up and out of the bore **(see illustration)**. To remove a stuck lifter, a special hydraulic lifter removal tool may be used. Do not use pliers or other tools on the outside of the lifter body - they will damage the machined surface and render the lifter useless.

6   If you're removing more than one lifter at a time, store them in a marked container **(see illustration)**. They must be returned to the same locations. **Note:** *Refer to Chapter 2, Part C, for camshaft removal and inspection procedures.*

Inspection

Refer to illustrations 10.8a and 10.8b

7   Clean the lifters with solvent and dry them thoroughly without mixing them up.

8   Check each lifter wall and pushrod seat for scuffing, score marks and uneven wear **(see illustrations)**. Each roller (the surface that rides on the cam lobe) must be free of

10.4b . . . lift the anti-rotation brackets from the engine block

nicks, score marks or damage. If the lifter walls are damaged or worn (which isn't very likely), inspect the lifter bores in the engine block as well. If the pushrod seats are worn, check the pushrod ends.

9   On the roller lifters, check the rollers carefully for wear and damage and make sure they turn freely without excessive play.

10.5 Use a magnet to lift the hydraulic lifter from the engine block

10.6 If you're removing more than one lifter, keep them in order in a clearly labeled box

10.8a Check each lifter wall and pushrod seat for scuffing, score marks and uneven wear

10.8b The roller on roller lifters must turn freely - check for wear and excessive play as well

Installation

10 If new lifters are being installed, a new camshaft must also be installed. If the camshaft is replaced, then install new lifters as well (see Chapter 2, Part C). Never install used lifters unless the original camshaft is used and the lifters can be installed in their

original locations! When installing lifters, make sure they're coated with moly-base grease or engine assembly lube.
11 The remaining installation steps are the reverse of removal. There are several steps that must be performed carefully to avoid damaging the valvetrain components.
12 When installing the hydraulic lifters back into the bores, make sure that the flat sides of the lifters are aligned with the flat sides of the anti-rotation brackets. The roller will align parallel with the camshaft also.
13 Install the anti-rotation brackets onto the lifters, making sure they align correctly.
14 Tighten the anti-rotation bracket bolts to the torque listed in this Chapter's Specifications.

11 Crankshaft front oil seal - replacement

Refer to illustrations 11.5a and 11.5b
1 Disconnect the negative battery cable from the battery. **Caution:** *If the vehicle is equipped with a Delco Loc II or Theftlock audio system, make sure you have the correct activation code before disconnecting the battery. See the information at the front of this manual for the radio re-activation procedure.*
2 Remove the engine drivebelt (see Chapter 1).
3 Loosen the right front wheel lug nuts. Raise the vehicle and support it securely on jackstands.
4 Remove the right front wheel and the splash shield from the fenderwell. Remove the flywheel/driveplate inspection cover.
5 Have an assistant hold the ring gear on the flywheel (manual transaxle) or driveplate (automatic transaxle) to prevent the engine from rotating when loosening the pulley hub bolt **(see illustration)**. Remove the crankshaft pulley bolts and remove the pulley. Remove the pulley hub using a special crankshaft balancer/hub removal tool **(see illustration)**.
6 Pry the old oil seal out with a seal

removal tool or a screwdriver. Be very careful not to nick or otherwise damage the crankshaft in the process. Wrap the screwdriver tip with vinyl tape to protect the crankshaft.
7 Apply a thin coat of RTV-type sealant to the outer edge of the new seal. Lubricate the seal lip with multi-purpose grease or clean engine oil.
8 Place the seal squarely in position in the bore and drive it into place with a special seal driver tool.
9 If you don't have the special tool, carefully tap the seal into place with a large socket or piece of pipe and a hammer. The outer diameter of the socket or pipe should be the same size as the seal outer diameter. Make sure the seal is seated completely in the bore.
10 Install the crankshaft hub using a special crankshaft balancer/hub installation tool. If the special tool is not available, press the hub on using a large socket or section of pipe, washers and a long bolt of the correct size and thread pitch to thread into the crankshaft.
11 Install the pulley. Have an assistant hold the ring gear on the flywheel (manual transaxle) or driveplate (automatic transaxle) to prevent the engine from rotating when tightening the pulley hub bolt **(see illustration 11.5a)**.
12 Reinstall the remaining parts in the reverse order of removal.
13 Start the engine and check for oil leaks at the seal.

12 Timing chain cover, chain and sprockets - removal, inspection and installation

Cover removal
Refer to illustration 12.10
1 Disconnect the negative battery cable from the battery. **Caution:** *If the vehicle is equipped with a Delco Loc II or Theftlock audio*

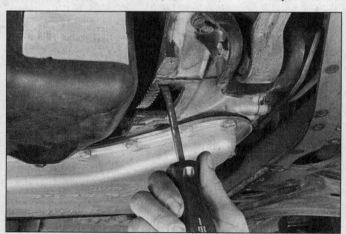

11.5a Have an assistant hold the ring gear with a large screwdriver as the pulley-to-crankshaft bolt is loosened or tightened

11.5b Use a puller to remove the crankshaft pulley and/or hub

12.10 Timing chain cover bolt locations

12.13 Align the camshaft and crankshaft sprocket timing marks
with the tabs on the timing chain tensioner (arrows)

system, make sure you have the correct activation code before disconnecting the battery. See the information at the front of this manual for the radio re-activation procedure.

2   Remove the engine drivebelt (see Chapter 1). Remove drivebelt tensioner.

3   Remove the power steering pump and position it to the side while keeping the power steering lines attached to the pump.

4   Remove the alternator (see Chapter 5) and the alternator brace from the engine.

5   Support the engine from above using an engine support fixture (available at auto parts stores or rental yards). Remove the front engine mount **(see illustration 9.6)**.

6   Remove the water pump pulley. Remove the engine accessory bracket.

7   Raise the vehicle and support it securely on jackstands.

8   Remove the oil pan (see Section 13).

9   Remove the crankshaft pulley and hub from the engine (see Section 11).

10   Remove the timing chain cover bolts and separate the cover from the engine **(see illustration)**.

11   Use a putty knife to break the cover loose from the engine, if necessary. Don't strike or pry on the cover, since it is made of plastic.

12   Use a gasket scraper to remove all traces of old gasket material and sealant from the cover and engine block. Clean the gasket sealing surfaces with lacquer thinner or acetone.

Timing chain removal

Refer to illustrations 12.13, 12.14 and 12.15

13   Temporarily install the crankshaft pulley hub and bolt. Rotate the crankshaft until the timing marks on the crankshaft and camshaft sprockets align with the tabs on the chain tensioner housing **(see illustration)**. **Note:** *Before removing the timing chain tensioner, check it carefully. Measure the distance from the hole in the bracket to the unworn surface of the timing chain tensioner shoe. It should not exceed 5/16 inch (8 mm). If out of limits, replace the tensioner, timing chain and both sprockets. This excessive play in the gears and chain can only be removed by installing new parts.*

14   Push the spring back on the timing chain tensioner and insert an appropriate size drill bit into the hole to retain it in the retracted position **(see illustration)**.

15   Use a prybar against two bolts in the crankshaft balancer hub (installed temporarily) to keep the engine from turning while removing the camshaft bolt **(see illustration)**. Do not turn the camshaft in the process (if you do, realign the timing marks before the sprocket is removed).

16   Use two large screwdrivers to carefully pry the camshaft sprocket off the camshaft dowel pin (it may come off easily with no tools required), and remove the sprocket and chain.

Inspection

17   Timing chains and sprockets should be replaced in sets. If you intend to install a new timing chain, remove the crankshaft sprocket with a puller and install a new one. Be sure to align the key in the crankshaft with the keyway in the sprocket during installation.

18   Clean the timing chain and sprockets with solvent and dry them with compressed air (if available). **Warning:** *Wear eye protection when using compressed air.*

19   Inspect the components for wear and damage. Look for teeth that are deformed, chipped, pitted and cracked.

20   The timing chain should be replaced with a new one if the engine has high mileage, the chain has visible damage, or total freeplay (without the tensioner) midway between the sprockets exceeds one inch. Failure to replace a worn timing chain may result in erratic engine performance, backfiring, loss of power and decreased fuel mileage. Loose chains can "jump" timing and in the worst case, will result in severe engine damage.

Installation

21   Mesh the timing chain with the camshaft sprocket, then engage it with the crankshaft sprocket. The timing marks should be aligned as shown in **illustration 12.13**. **Note:** *If the crankshaft has been disturbed, turn it until the*

12.14 Press the tensioner in and insert an appropriate size drill bit through the hole to retain the tensioner in the retracted position

12.15 Wedge a prybar against two bolts in the temporarily installed crankshaft hub to hold the crankshaft while loosening the camshaft sprocket bolt

13.10 Remove the oil pan mounting bolts (arrows; not all the bolts are visible in this photo)

15.3 Most flywheels and driveplates have locating dowels - if the one you're working on doesn't, make some marks to ensure correct installation

mark stamped on the crankshaft sprocket is pointing at the projection on the tensioner. If the camshaft was turned, install the sprocket temporarily and turn the camshaft until the timing marks align.

22 Install the camshaft sprocket bolt and tighten it to the torque listed in this Chapter's Specifications.

23 Press the timing chain against the tensioner, pull out the pin retaining the spring and release the tensioner.

24 Lubricate the chain and sprocket with clean engine oil. Rotate the engine through two complete revolutions and check the alignment of the timing marks again.

25 Install the timing chain cover, using a new gasket and tighten the cover bolts to the torque listed in this Chapter's Specifications.

26 Install the oil pan.

27 The remaining installation steps are the reverse of removal.

13 Oil pan - removal and installation

Removal

Refer to illustration 13.10

1 Warm up the engine, then drain the oil and remove the oil filter (see Chapter 1).

2 Disconnect the negative battery cable from the battery. **Caution:** *If the vehicle is equipped with a Delco Loc II or Theftlock audio system, make sure you have the correct activation code before disconnecting the battery. See the information at the front of this manual for the radio re-activation procedure.*

3 Raise the vehicle and support it securely on jackstands.

4 Remove the right engine splash shield and the exhaust pipe shield.

5 On air-conditioned models, remove the air conditioner brace at the starter and compressor bracket.

6 Remove the starter and bracket (see Chapter 5).

7 Remove the flywheel/driveplate inspection cover (see Chapter 7).

8 Remove the engine mount strut and remove the support bolts from the engine mount strut bracket. Lower the bracket slightly to gain clearance for oil pan removal.

9 Remove the oil filter extension (automatic transaxle equipped models only).

10 Remove the bolts and nuts securing the oil pan to the engine block **(see illustration)**.

11 Tap on the pan with a soft-face hammer to break the gasket seal, then detach the oil pan from the engine.

Installation

12 Using a gasket scraper, remove all traces of old gasket and/or sealant from the engine block and oil pan. Make sure the threaded bolt holes in the block are clean. Wash the oil pan with solvent and dry it thoroughly.

13 Check the gasket flanges for distortion, particularly around the bolt holes. If necessary, place the pan on a block of wood and use a hammer to flatten and restore the gasket surfaces. Clean the mating surfaces with lacquer thinner or acetone.

14 Place a 1/8-inch diameter bead of RTV sealant on the oil pan-to-block sealing flanges and the oil pan-to-front cover surface.

15 Apply a thin coat of RTV sealant to the ends of the rear oil pan seal down to the ears. Press the oil pan seal into position.

16 Carefully place the oil pan against the block.

17 Install the bolts/nuts and tighten them evenly to the torque listed in this Chapter's Specifications. Start with the bolts closest to the center of the pan and work out in a spiral pattern. Don't overtighten them or leakage may occur.

18 Reinstall components removed for access to the oil pan.

19 Add oil and install a new filter (see Chapter 1), run the engine and check for oil leaks.

14 Oil pump - removal and installation

1 Remove the oil pan (see Section 13).

2 Place a large drain pan under the engine.

3 Unbolt the pump from the rear main bearing cap.

4 Lower the pump and extension shaft from the engine.

5 Before installation, prime the pump with engine oil. Pour oil into the pick-up while the pump extension shaft is turned.

6 Attach the pump, extension shaft and retainer to the main bearing cap. While aligning the pump with the dowel pins at the bottom of the main bearing cap, align the top end of the extension shaft with the lower end of the oil pump drive. When aligned properly, it should slip into place easily.

7 Install the pump mounting bolt and tighten it to the torque listed in this Chapter's Specifications.

8 Install the oil pan (see Section 13) and add oil (see Chapter 1).

15 Flywheel/driveplate - removal and installation

Refer to illustrations 15.3 and 15.4

1 Raise the vehicle and support it securely on jackstands, then refer to Chapter 7 and remove the transaxle. If it's leaking, now would be a very good time to have the front pump seal/O-ring replaced (automatic transaxle only).

2 Remove the pressure plate and clutch disc (Chapter 8 - manual transaxle equipped vehicles). Now is a good time to check/replace the clutch components and pilot bearing.

3 If there is no dowel pin, make some marks on the flywheel/driveplate and crankshaft to ensure correct alignment during reinstallation **(see illustration)**.

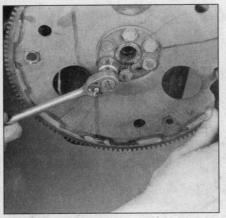

15.4 A large screwdriver wedged in the starter ring gear teeth or one of the holes in the driveplate can be used to keep the flywheel/driveplate from turning as the mounting bolts are removed

4   Remove the bolts that secure the flywheel/driveplate to the crankshaft **(see illustration)**. If the crankshaft turns, wedge a screwdriver through the openings in the driveplate (automatic transaxle) or against the flywheel ring gear teeth (manual transaxle). Since the flywheel is fairly heavy, be sure to support it while removing the last bolt.
5   Remove the flywheel/driveplate from the crankshaft.
6   Clean the flywheel to remove grease and oil. Inspect the friction surface for cracks, rivet grooves, burned areas and score marks. Light scoring can be removed with emery cloth. Check for cracked and broken ring gear teeth. Lay the flywheel on a flat surface and use a straightedge to check for warpage.
7   Clean and inspect the mating surfaces of the flywheel/driveplate and the crankshaft. If the crankshaft rear seal is leaking, replace it before reinstalling the flywheel/driveplate.
8   Position the flywheel/driveplate against the crankshaft. Be sure to align the dowel or marks made during removal. Before installing the bolts, apply thread locking compound to

16.2 Carefully pry the old oil seal out

the threads.
9   Keep the flywheel/driveplate from turning as described above while you tighten the bolts to the torque listed in this Chapter's Specifications.
10   The remainder of installation is the reverse of the removal procedure.

16   Rear main oil seal - replacement

Refer to illustration 16.2
1   Remove the flywheel/driveplate (see Section 15).
2   Using a flat-bladed screwdriver or seal removal tool, carefully remove the oil seal from the engine block **(see illustration)**. Be very careful not to damage the crankshaft surface while prying the seal out.
3   Clean the bore in the block and the seal contact surface on the crankshaft. Check the seal contact surface on the crankshaft for scratches and nicks that could damage the new seal lip and cause oil leaks - if the crankshaft is damaged, the only alternative is a new or different crankshaft. Inspect the seal bore for nicks and scratches. Carefully

smooth it with a fine file if necessary, but don't nick the crankshaft in the process.
4   A special tool is recommended to install the new oil seal. Lubricate the oil seal lips with clean engine oil or multi-purpose grease. Slide the seal onto the mandril until the dust lip bottoms squarely against the collar of the tool. **Note:** *If the special tool isn't available, carefully work the seal lip over the crankshaft and tap it into place with a hammer and punch.*
5   Align the dowel pin on the tool with the dowel pin hole in the crankshaft and attach the tool to the crankshaft by hand-tightening the bolts.
6   Turn the tool handle until the collar bottoms against the case, seating the seal.
7   Loosen the tool handle and remove the bolts. Remove the tool.
8   Check the seal and make sure it's seated squarely in the bore.
9   Install the flywheel/driveplate (see Section 15).
10   Install the transaxle.

17   Engine mounts - check and replacement

Refer to illustrations 17.7a, 17.7b, 17.7c and 17.7d
1   Engine mounts seldom require attention, but broken or deteriorated mounts should be replaced immediately or the added strain placed on the driveline components may cause damage or wear.

Check

2   During the check, the engine must be raised slightly to remove the weight from the mounts.
3   Raise the vehicle and support it securely on jackstands, then position a jack under the engine oil pan. Place a large block of wood between the jack head and the oil pan, then carefully raise the engine just enough to take the weight off the mounts. **Warning:** *DO NOT*

17.7a Strut mounting bolt locations (arrows)

17.7b Removing the engine mount/strut bracket from the bottom of the engine compartment

17.7c Remove the transaxle mounting bolts (arrows) to separate the mount

17.7d Remove the bracket from the front engine mount

place any part of your body under the engine when it's supported only by a jack!

4   Check the mounts to see if the rubber is cracked, hardened or separated from the metal plates. Sometimes the rubber will split right down the center.

5   Check for relative movement between the mount plates and the engine or frame (use a large screwdriver or pry bar to attempt to move the mounts). If movement is noted, lower the engine and tighten the mount fasteners.

Replacement

6   Disconnect the negative battery cable from the battery, then raise the vehicle and support it securely on jackstands (if not already done). **Caution:** *If the vehicle is equipped with a Delco Loc II or Theftlock audio system, make sure you have the correct activation code before disconnecting the battery. See the information at the front of this manual for the radio re-activation procedure.*

7   Raise the engine slightly with a jack or hoist. Remove the fasteners and detach the

mount from the frame bracket **(see illustrations)**.

8   Remove the mount-to-block bracket bolts/nuts and detach the mount.

9   Installation is the reverse of removal. Use thread locking compound on the threads and be sure to tighten everything securely.

10   Rubber preservative should be applied to the mounts to slow deterioration.

Notes

Chapter 2 Part B
2.3L and 2.4L overhead camshaft (OHC) engines

Contents

Specifications

General

Displacement	
2.3L engine............	138 cubic inches
2.4L engine............	146 cubic inches
Firing order	1-3-4-2
Compression pressure	See Chapter 2D
Oil pressure............	See Chapter 2D

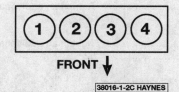

FRONT ↓

38016-1-2C HAYNES

Cylinder numbering on overhead
camshaft (OHC) engines

Camshafts and housings

Lobe lift (intake and exhaust)	
1995	0.3750 inch (9.525 mm)
1996 and later	
Intake	0.3540 inch (9.0 mm)
Exhaust	0.3460 inch (8.8 mm)
Lobe taper limit..	0.0018 to 0.0033 inch per 0.50 inch (0.046 to 0.083 mm per 14.0 mm)
Endplay	0.0009 to 0.0088 inch (0.025 to 0.225 mm)
Journal diameter	
No. 1	1.5720 to 1.5728 inch (39.93 to 39.95 mm)
All others	1.3751 to 1.3760 inch (34.93 to 34.95 mm)
Bearing oil clearance	0.0019 to 0.0043 inch (0.050 to 0.110 mm)
Lifters	
Bore diameter...	1.33381 to 1.3393 inch (33.989 to 34.019 mm)
Outside diameter	1.3369 to 1.3375 inch (33.959 to 33.975 mm)
Lifter-to-bore clearance	0.0006 to 0.0024 inch (0.014 to 0.060 mm)
Camshaft housing warpage limit	0.001 inch per 4.0 inch (0.025 mm per 100 mm)

Balance shafts and housing

Housing warpage maximum..	0.0030 inch (0.076 mm)
Chain slack (with 3 lb. applied to chain guide)	0.040 inch (1.0 mm)
Thrust plate thickness	0.1159 to 0.1199 inch (2.945 to 3.045 mm)

Torque specifications

Ft-lbs (unless otherwise indicated)

Balance shaft assembly-to-block bolts **(see illustration 14.19)**	
Step 1	
Bolts 9, 10 and 12...	18
Bolt 11...	30
Bolt 13...	39
Step 2	
Bolts 9, 10 and 12...	Tighten an additional 70-degrees
Bolt 11...	Tighten an additional 60-degrees
Balance shaft housing bolts **(see illustration 14.19)**	
Step 1	
Bolts 1, 2, 4, 5, 6 and 7......................................	89 in-lbs
Bolts 3 and 8...	132 in-lbs
Step 2	Tighten all bolts an additional 40-degrees
Balance shaft sprocket bolt (left hand thread)	
1995 through 1997	
Step 1..	22
Step 2..	Tighten an additional 45-degrees
1998 and later	
Step 1..	30
Step 2..	Tighten an additional 45-degrees
Balance shaft chain tensioner bolt	115 in-lbs
Balance shaft chain cover nut and bolt	115 in-lbs
Balance shaft thrust plate bolts.......................................	115 in-lbs
Balance shaft chain guide bolt	115 in-lbs
Camshaft housing-to-cylinder head bolts	
1995 and 1996	
Step 1..	132 in-lbs
Step 2..	Tighten an additional 90-degrees
1997 and later	
Step 1..	16
Step 2..	Tighten an additional 90-degrees
Camshaft cover-to-camshaft housing bolts (rear two on the intake camshaft housing)	
1995 and 1996	
Step 1..	132 in-lbs
Step 2..	Tighten an additional 30-degrees
1997 and later	
Step 1..	16
Step 2..	Tighten an additional 30-degrees
Camshaft sprocket-to-camshaft bolt	52
Crankshaft balancer-to-crankshaft bolt	
Step 1	129
Step 2	Tighten an additional 90-degrees
Crankshaft rear main oil seal housing bolts	106 in-lbs

Cylinder head bolts **(in sequence - see illustration 11.15)**
   1995
      Step 1
         Bolts 1 thru 8 30
         Bolts 9 and 10 26
      Step 2 .... Tighten all bolts an additional 90-degrees
   1996 and later models
      Step 1
         Bolts 1 thru 8 40
         Bolts 9 and 10 30
      Step 2 .... Tighten all bolts an additional 90-degrees
Engine mount-to-bracket bolts.. 96
Engine mount-to-body nuts... 55
Engine mount bracket-to-engine bolts *
   Step 1 44
   Step 2 .... Tighten an additional 90-degrees
Exhaust manifold nuts-to-cylinder head.. 31
Exhaust manifold brace
   Bolts 41
   Nuts 19
Flywheel-to-crankshaft bolts
   Step 1 22
   Step 2 .... Tighten an additional 45-degrees
Intake manifold-to-cylinder head nuts/bolts... 18
Oil pan bolts
   6 mm .... 106 in-lbs
   8 mm 18
Oil pump-to-balance shaft housing... 106 in-lbs
Timing chain cover-to-housing bolts... 106 in-lbs
Timing chain housing bolts.. 19
Timing chain housing-to-block stud.. 21
Timing chain tensioner... 89 in-lbs

* Replace with new bolts anytime they are removed.

1   General information

Caution: *If the vehicle is equipped with a Delco Loc II or Theftlock audio system, make sure you have the correct activation code before disconnecting the battery.*

   This Part of Chapter 2 is devoted to in-vehicle repair procedures for the 2.3L and 2.4L four-cylinder (Quad-4) engine. Information concerning engine removal, installation and engine block and cylinder head overhaul can be found in Part D of this Chapter. The following repair procedures are based on the assumption the engine is installed in the vehicle. If the engine has been removed from the vehicle and mounted on a stand, many of the steps outlined in this Part of Chapter 2 will not apply.

   These engines utilize a number of advanced design features to increase power output and improve durability. The aluminum cylinder head contains four valves per cylinder. A double-row timing chain drives two overhead camshafts - one for intake and one for exhaust. Lightweight bucket-type hydraulic lifters actuate the valves. Rotators are used on all valves for extended service life.

   A balance shaft assembly has been added to smooth power pulsations. This assembly is bolted to the bottom of the main bearing webs and is chain driven from the rear of the crank. The gerotor oil pump is driven by the balance shaft trailing shaft and is mounted to the rear of the balance shaft housing.

2   Repair operations possible with the engine in the vehicle

   Many major repair operations can be accomplished without removing the engine from the vehicle. Clean the engine compartment and the exterior of the engine with some type of degreaser before any work is done. It'll make the job easier and help keep dirt out of the internal areas of the engine.

   Depending on the components involved, it may be helpful to remove the hood to improve access to the engine as repairs are performed (refer to Chapter 11 if necessary). Cover the fenders to prevent damage to the paint. Special pads are available, but an old bedspread or blanket will also work.

   If vacuum, exhaust, oil or coolant leaks develop, indicating a need for gasket or seal replacement, the repairs can generally be made with the engine in the vehicle. The intake and exhaust manifold gaskets, timing chain housing gasket, oil pan gasket, crankshaft oil seals and cylinder head gasket are all accessible with the engine in place.

   Exterior engine components, such as the intake and exhaust manifolds, the oil pan (and the oil pump), the water pump, the starter motor, the alternator and the fuel system components can be removed for repair with the engine in place.

   Since the cylinder head can be removed without pulling the engine, camshaft and valve component servicing can also be accomplished with the engine in the vehicle. Replacement of the timing chain and sprockets is also possible with the engine in the vehicle.

   In extreme cases caused by a lack of necessary equipment, repair or replacement of piston rings, pistons, connecting rods and rod bearings is possible with the engine in the vehicle. However, this practice is not recommended because of the cleaning and preparation work that must be done to the components involved.

3   Top Dead Center (TDC) for number one piston - locating

Refer to illustration 3.1

1   Refer to Chapter 2A, Section 3 for the TDC locating procedure **(see illustration)**. The TDC locating procedure for these engines is the same as for the 2.2L OHV engine.

4   Intake manifold - removal and installation

Removal

1   Relieve the fuel system pressure as described in Chapter 4.
2   Detach the cable from the negative terminal of the battery. **Caution:** *If the vehicle is equipped with a Delco Loc II or Theftlock audio system, make sure you have the correct activation code before disconnecting the battery.*
3   Remove the accelerator cable (see Chapter 4), the cruise control cable (if, equipped) and the TV cable (automatic transaxle).
4   Label and disconnect the vacuum and breather hoses and electrical wires (MAP, IAT, EVAP, fuel injectors, etc.).
5   Remove the PCV oil/air separator (see Chapter 1).
6   Remove the oil fill cap and dipstick assembly. Unbolt the oil fill tube and detach it from the engine block, rotating it as necessary to gain clearance between the intake tubes.
7   Remove the alternator bracket bolt closest to the engine block with the stud end pointing UP.
8   Remove the EGR pipe from the EGR adapter (see Chapter 6).
9   Remove the intake manifold support brace.
10   Loosen the manifold mounting nuts/bolts in 1/4-turn increments until they can be removed by hand.
11   The manifold will probably be stuck to

the cylinder head and force may be required to break the gasket seal. If necessary, dislodge the manifold with a soft-face hammer. **Caution:** *Don't pry between the cylinder head and manifold or damage to the gasket sealing surfaces will result and vacuum leaks could develop.*

Installation

Refer to illustration 4.17
Note: *The mating surfaces of the cylinder head and manifold must be perfectly clean when the manifold is installed. Gasket removal solvents in aerosol cans are available at most auto parts stores and may be helpful when removing old gasket material stuck to the cylinder head and manifold (since the components are made of aluminum, aggressive scraping can cause damage). Be sure to follow the directions printed on the container.*
12   Use a gasket scraper to remove all traces of sealant and old gasket material, then clean the mating surfaces with lacquer thinner or acetone. If there's old sealant or oil on the mating surfaces when the manifold is reinstalled, vacuum leaks may develop.
13   Use a tap of the correct size to chase the threads in the bolt holes, then use compressed air (if available) to remove the debris from the holes. **Warning:** *Wear safety glasses or a face shield to protect your eyes when using compressed air. Use a die to clean and restore the stud threads.*
14   Position the gasket on the cylinder head. Make sure all intake port openings, coolant passage holes and bolt holes are aligned correctly.
15   Install the manifold, taking care to avoid damaging the gasket.
16   Thread the nuts/bolts into place by hand.
17   Tighten the nuts/bolts to the torque listed in this Chapter's Specifications following the recommended sequence **(see illustration)**. Work up to the final torque in three steps.
18   The remaining installation steps are the reverse of removal. Start the engine and check carefully for leaks at the intake manifold joints.

3.1 Timing marks (arrows) on the OHC engine

5   Exhaust manifold - removal and installation

Removal

Warning: *Allow the engine to cool completely before performing this procedure.*
1   Detach the cable from the negative terminal of the battery. **Caution:** *If the vehicle is equipped with a Delco Loc II or Theftlock audio system, make sure you have the correct activation code before disconnecting the battery.*
2   Unplug the oxygen sensor (see Chapter 6).
3   Remove the manifold heat shields.
4   Raise the vehicle and support it securely on jackstands, then remove the exhaust pipe-to-manifold nuts. The nuts are usually rusted in place, so penetrating oil should be applied to the stud threads before attempting to remove them. Loosen them a little at a time, working from side-to-side to prevent the flange from jamming.
5   Remove the exhaust manifold brace.
6   Separate the exhaust pipe flange from the manifold studs, then pull the pipe down slightly to break the seal at the manifold joint.
7   Loosen the exhaust manifold mounting

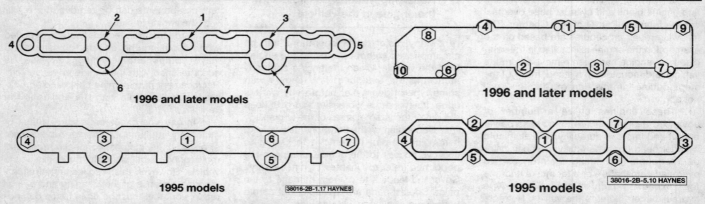

1996 and later models

1995 models

38016-2B-1.17 HAYNES

4.17 Intake manifold fastener tightening sequence

1996 and later models

1995 models

38016-2B-5.10 HAYNES

5.10 Exhaust manifold fastener tightening sequence

6.4 The crankshaft balancer can be held with a bar while the bolt is loosened or tightened

6.5 Use a puller that applies force to the crankshaft balancer hub - don't use a jaw-type puller that applies force to the outer edge or damage to the crankshaft balancer will occur

6.6 Pry the old seal out with a seal removal tool (shown here) or a screwdriver

nuts 1/4-turn at a time each, working from the inside out, until they can be removed by hand.

8   Separate the manifold from the cylinder head and remove it.

Installation

Refer to illustration 5.10

9   The manifold and cylinder head mating surfaces must be clean when the manifold is reinstalled. Use a gasket scraper to remove all traces of old gasket material and carbon deposits.

10   Using a new gasket, install the manifold and hand tighten the fasteners. Following the recommended sequence **(see illustration)**, tighten the bolts/nuts to the torque listed in this Chapter's Specifications.

11   The remaining installation steps are the reverse of removal.

6   Crankshaft front oil seal - replacement

Refer to illustrations 6.4, 6.5, 6.6, 6.9 and 6.11

1   Detach the cable from the negative terminal of the battery. **Caution:** *If the vehicle is equipped with a Delco Loc II or Theftlock audio system, make sure you have the correct activation code before disconnecting the battery.*

2   Remove the drivebelt (see Chapter 1).

3   With the parking brake applied and the shifter in Park (automatic) or in gear (manual), raise the front of the vehicle and support it securely on jackstands.

4   Remove the bolt from the front of the crankshaft. A breaker bar will probably be necessary, since the bolt is very tight. Insert a bar through a hole in the balancer to prevent the crankshaft from turning **(see illustration)**.

5   Using a puller that bolts to the crankshaft hub, remove the crankshaft balancer from the crankshaft **(see illustration)**.

6   Pry the old oil seal out with a seal removal tool **(see illustration)** or a screwdriver. Be very careful not to nick or otherwise damage the crankshaft in the process and don't distort the timing chain cover.

7   Apply a thin coat of RTV-type sealant to the outer edge of the new seal. Lubricate the seal lip with multi-purpose grease or clean engine oil.

8   Place the seal squarely in position in the bore with the spring side facing in.

9   Carefully tap the seal into place with a large socket or section of pipe and a hammer **(see illustration)**. The outer diameter of the socket or pipe should be the same size as the seal outer diameter.

10   Apply a thin layer of clean multi-purpose grease or clean engine oil to the seal contact surface of the crankshaft balancer hub.

11   Position the crankshaft balancer on the crankshaft and slide it through the seal until it bottoms against the crankshaft sprocket. Note that the slot (keyway) in the hub must be aligned with the Woodruff key in the end of the crankshaft **(see illustration)**. The crankshaft bolt can also be used to press the

crankshaft balancer into position.

12   Tighten the crankshaft bolt to the torque and angle of rotation listed in this Chapter's Specifications.

13   The remaining installation steps are the reverse of removal.

14   Start the engine and check for oil leaks at the seal.

7   Timing chain and sprockets - removal, inspection and installation

Note: *Special tools are required for this procedure. Read through the entire procedure and acquire the necessary tools and equipment before beginning work.*

Removal

Refer to illustrations 7.3, 7.5, 7.8, 7.10, 7.11, 7.12, 7.13, 7.15, 7.17 and 7.18

1   Detach the cable from the negative terminal of the battery. **Caution:** *If the vehicle is equipped with a Delco Loc II or Theftlock audio system, make sure you have the correct*

6.9 Install the new seal with a large socket or section of pipe

6.11 Align the keyway in the crankshaft balancer hub with the Woodruff key in the crankshaft (arrow)

7.3 Remove the three bolts and the engine mount bracket

7.5 Timing chain cover fastener locations (arrows)

7.8 Note how it's installed, then remove the oil slinger (arrow) from the crankshaft

7.10 Insert two 8 mm bolts (arrows) through the holes in the camshaft sprockets and into the holes in the timing chain housing - this locks the camshafts in the "timed" position

7.11 The mark on the crankshaft sprocket must align with the mark on the block (arrows)

activation code before disconnecting the battery.

2   Remove the coolant reservoir (see Chapter 3). Remove the drivebelt (see Chapter 1).

3   Support the engine from above, using an engine support fixture (available at rental yards), or from below using a floor jack. Use a wood block between the floor jack and the engine to prevent damage. Remove the front engine mount (see Section 17). Remove the engine mount bracket and discard the bolts **(see illustration). Caution:** *Replace the engine support bracket bolts with the manufacturers original type bolt anytime they are removed.*

4   Remove the crankshaft balancer (see Section 6).

5   Working from above, remove the upper timing chain cover fasteners **(see illustration)**.

6   Working from below, remove the lower timing chain cover fasteners.

7   Detach the timing chain cover vent hose and remove the cover and gaskets from the housing.

8   Slide the oil slinger off the crankshaft **(see illustration)**.

9   Temporarily reinstall the crankshaft balancer bolt to use when turning the crankshaft.

10   Turn the crankshaft clockwise until the camshaft sprocket's timing pin holes align with the holes in the timing chain housing. Insert 8 mm pins or bolts into the holes to maintain alignment **(see illustration)**.

11   The mark on the crankshaft sprocket should align with the mark on the engine block **(see illustration)**. The crankshaft sprocket keyway should point up and align with the centerline of the cylinder bores.

12   Remove the three timing chain guides **(see illustration)**.

13   Make sure all the slack in the timing

7.12 The three timing chain guides are wedged into the housing at four points (arrows) - just pull them out

7.13 The timing chain tensioner mounting bolt locations (1)

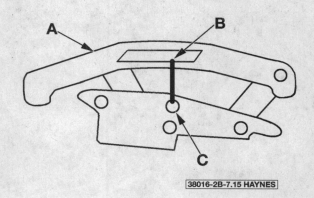

38016-2B-7.15 HAYNES

7.15 After retracting the tensioner shoe, insert a piece of wire (B) bent into a "U" shape between the tensioner shoe (A) and reset hole (C)

chain is above the tensioner assembly, then remove the chain tensioner assembly (see illustration).
14 The timing chain must be disengaged from the wear grooves in the tensioner shoe in order to remove the tensioner assembly. Slide a screwdriver blade under the timing chain while pulling the tensioner shoe out. Note: If difficulty is encountered when removing the chain tensioner, proceed as follows:

a) Hold the intake camshaft sprocket with an appropriate tool and remove the sprocket bolt and washer.
b) Remove the washer from the bolt and thread the bolt back into the camshaft by hand.
c) Remove the intake camshaft sprocket, using a three-jaw puller in the three relief holes in the sprocket, if necessary. Caution: Don't try to pry the sprocket off the camshaft or damage to the sprocket could occur.

15 Bend a piece of heavy wire into a "U", then apply light force to the tensioner shoe. While applying force, insert a small screwdriver into the reset hole (see illustration) and pry the ratchet pawl away from the ratchet teeth. When the shoe is fully retracted, insert the piece of bent wire into the hole and through the shoe to hold the shoe in place.
16 Remove the tensioner assembly retaining bolts and tensioner. Warning: The tensioner plunger is spring loaded and could come out with great force, causing personal injury. Remove the chain housing-to-block stud (timing chain tensioner shoe pivot).
17 Slip the timing chain off the sprockets (see illustration).
18 To remove the camshaft sprockets, loosen the bolts while holding the sprockets with a screwdriver or punch inserted through one of the holes. Mark the sprockets for identification (see illustration), remove the bolts, then pull on the sprockets by hand until they slip off the dowels. If necessary, use a small puller, with the legs inserted in the relief holes, to pull the sprockets off.
19 The crankshaft sprocket should slip off the crankshaft by hand. If not, use a pulley.

20 The idler sprocket and bearing are pressed into place. If replacement is necessary, remove the timing chain housing (see Section 8) and take it to a dealer service department or automotive machine shop. Special tools are required and the bearing must be replaced each time it's pressed out.

Inspection
21 Visually inspect all parts for wear and damage. Look for loose pins, cracks, worn rollers and side plates. Check the sprockets for hook-shaped, chipped and broken teeth. Note: Some scoring of the timing chain shoe and guides is normal. Replace the timing chain, sprockets, chain shoe and guides as a set if the engine has high mileage or fails the visual parts inspection.

Installation
Refer to illustration 7.22
22 Make sure the camshafts are positioned with the dowel pins at the top (see illustration). Install both camshaft sprockets (if removed). Apply thread locking compound to

7.17 Begin removing the chain at the exhaust camshaft sprocket

7.18 Mark the sprockets exhaust and intake (arrows), then remove the bolts and pull the sprockets off

7.22 The camshaft sprocket dowel pin(s) should be near the top prior to sprocket installation

8.11 Position a new gasket over the dowel pins (arrows)

the camshaft sprocket bolt threads and make sure the washers are in place. Hold the camshaft from turning as described in Step 18 and tighten the bolts to the torque listed in this Chapter's Specifications.

23 Recheck the positions of the camshaft and crankshaft sprockets for correct valve timing **(see illustrations 7.10 and 7.11)**. **Note:** *If the camshafts are out of position and must be rotated more than 1/8-turn in order to install the alignment pins:*

a) *The crankshaft must be rotated 90-degrees clockwise past Top Dead Center to give the valves adequate clearance to open.*

b) *Once the camshafts are in position and the alignment pins installed, rotate the crankshaft counterclockwise back to Top Dead Center.* **Caution:** *Do not rotate the crankshaft clockwise to TDC (valve or piston damage could occur).*

24 Slip the timing chain over the exhaust camshaft sprocket, then around the idler and crankshaft sprockets.

25 Remove the alignment pin from the intake camshaft. Using an appropriate tool, rotate the intake camshaft sprocket counterclockwise enough to mesh the timing chain with it. The chain run between the two camshaft sprockets will tighten. If the valve timing is correct, the intake camshaft alignment pin should slide in easily. If it doesn't index, the camshafts aren't timed correctly; repeat the procedure.

26 Leave the alignment pins installed for now and check the timing marks. With slack removed from the timing chain between the intake camshaft sprocket and the crankshaft sprocket, the timing marks on the crankshaft sprocket and the engine block should be aligned. If the marks aren't aligned, move the chain one tooth forward or backward, remove the slack and recheck the marks.

27 Reload the timing chain tensioner assembly to its "zero" position as follows:

a) *Use the bent wire from the chain tensioner locking procedure in illustration 7.15 or reform another if necessary.*

b) *Apply light force on the tensioner shoe to compress the plunger.*

c) *Insert a small screwdriver into the reset access hole and depress the shoe.*

d) *Install the locking wire or keeper into the access hole and the shoe.*

28 Install the tensioner assembly in the chain housing. Tighten the bolts to the torque specified in this Chapter. **Note:** *Recheck the plunger assembly installation - it's correctly installed when the long end is toward the crankshaft.*

29 Remove bent piece of wire, squeeze the plunger into the tensioner body then let go to unload the plunger assembly.

30 Remove the camshaft sprocket alignment pins.

31 Slowly rotate the crankshaft clockwise two full turns (720-degrees). Do not force it; if resistance is felt, recheck the installation procedure. Align the crankshaft timing mark with the mark on the engine block and temporarily reinstall the 8 mm alignment pins. The pins should slide in easily if the valve timing is correct. **Caution:** *If the valve timing is incorrect, severe engine damage could occur.*

32 Install the remaining components in the reverse order of removal, noting the following:

a) *Replace the engine mount bracket bolts with new bolts and tighten them to the torque listed in this Chapter's Specifications.*

b) *Check fluid levels, start the engine and check for proper operation and coolant/oil leaks.*

---

8   Timing chain housing - removal and installation

Refer to illustration 8.11

Warning: *Wait until the engine is completely cool before beginning this procedure.*

1 Detach the cable from the negative terminal of the battery. **Caution:** *If the vehicle is equipped with a Delco Loc II or Theftlock audio system, make sure you have the correct*

activation code before disconnecting the battery.

2 Drain the cooling system (see Chapter 1), then remove the heater hose from the thermostat housing to drain the coolant from the engine block.

3 Remove the timing chain and sprockets (see Section 7). If you're installing a replacement timing chain housing, remove the water pump (see Chapter 3).

4 Remove the timing chain housing-to-belt tensioner bracket brace.

5 Remove the four oil pan-to-timing chain housing bolts.

6 Remove the timing chain housing-to-block lower fasteners.

7 Remove the lowest cover retaining stud from the timing chain housing.

8 Remove the eight chain housing-to-camshaft housing bolts.

9 Using an engine support fixture or floor jack, raise the engine slightly for additional clearance.

10 Remove the timing chain housing and gaskets. Thoroughly clean the mating surfaces to remove any traces of old sealant or gasket material.

11 Install the timing chain housing with new gaskets **(see illustration)**. Tighten the bolts to the torque listed in this Chapter's Specifications.

12 The remaining steps are the reverse of removal.

---

9   Camshafts, lifters and housings - removal, inspection and installation

---

Note: *Special tools are required for this procedure. Read through the entire procedure and acquire the necessary tools and equipment before beginning work.*

Removal

Refer to illustrations 9.10, 9.11 and 9.14

1 Relieve the fuel system pressure (see Chapter 4).

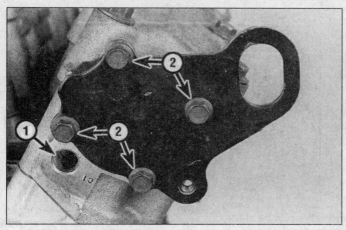

9.10 Oil pressure sending unit mounting hole (1) and engine lifting bracket bolts (2)

9.11 Gently lift the camshaft housing off the cylinder head and turn it over so the lifters don't fall out

2   Detach the cable from the negative terminal of the battery. **Caution:** *If the vehicle is equipped with a Delco Loc II or Theftlock audio system, make sure you have the correct activation code before disconnecting the battery.*

3   Position the engine at TDC on the compression stroke (see Section 3). Remove the timing chain and sprockets (see Section 7).

4   Remove the timing chain housing-to-camshaft housing bolts.

5   Remove the ignition coil and module assembly (see Chapter 5).

6   Remove the PCV oil/air separator from the side of the engine block (see Chapter 1). Remove the transaxle fluid level indicator and tube.

7   Without disconnecting the hoses, remove the power steering pump and secure it aside (see Chapter 10).

8   Disconnect the electrical connector from the camshaft position sensor.

9   Remove the fuel rail from the cylinder head and set it aside (see Chapter 4).

10   Disconnect the electrical connector from the oil pressure sending unit and unbolt the engine lifting bracket **(see illustration)**.

11   Loosen the camshaft housing-to-cylinder head bolts in 1/4-turn increments, in the reverse of the tightening sequence **(see illus-**

tration 9.28). Leave the two cover-to-housing bolts in place temporarily. Lift the housing off the cylinder head **(see illustration)**.

12   Remove the two camshaft cover-to-housing bolts. Push the cover off the housing by threading four of the housing-to-cylinder head bolts into the tapped holes in the cover. Carefully lift the camshaft out of the housing.

13   Remove all traces of old gasket material from the mating surfaces and clean them with lacquer thinner or acetone to remove any traces of oil.

14   Remove the oil seal from the intake camshaft **(see illustration)** and discard it.

15   Remove the lifters and store them in order so they can be reinstalled in their original locations. To minimize lifter bleed-down, store the lifters valve-side up, submerged in clean engine oil.

Inspection

Refer to illustrations 9.17a, 9.17b, 9.18 and 9.19

16   Refer to Chapter 2, Part C, for camshaft inspection procedures, but use this Chapter's Specifications. If the camshaft is damaged or worn beyond the specifications, replace the camshaft, do not attempt to salvage worn camshafts. Whenever a camshaft is replaced,

9.14 Remove the oil seal (arrow) from the intake camshaft

replace all the lifters actuated by the camshaft as well.

17   Visually inspect the lifters for wear, galling, score marks and discoloration from overheating **(see illustrations)**.

18   Measure each lifter bore inside diameter and record the results **(see illustration)**.

19   Measure each lifter outside diameter and record the results **(see illustration)**.

20   Subtract the lifter outside diameter from the corresponding bore inside diameter to

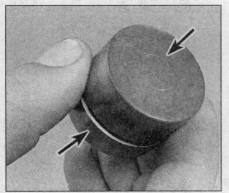

9.17a Check the camshaft lobe surfaces and the bore surfaces of the lifters for wear (arrows)

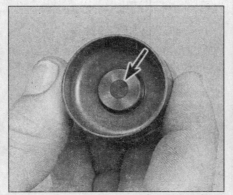

9.17b Check the valve-side of the lifters too, especially the valve stem contact area (arrow)

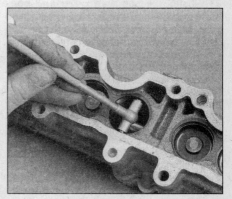

9.18 Use a telescoping gauge and micrometer to measure the lifter bores ...

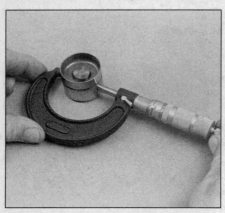

9.19 . . . then measure the lifters with a micrometer - subtract each lift diameter from the corresponding bore diameter to obtain the lifter-to-bore clearances

determine the clearance. Compare the results to this Chapter's specifications and replace parts as necessary.

Installation

Refer to illustrations 9.24 and 9.28

21   Using a new gasket, position the camshaft housing on the cylinder head and temporarily hold it in place with one bolt.

22   Coat the camshaft journals and lobes and the lifters with camshaft assembly lube and install them in their original locations.

23   On the intake camshaft only, lubricate the lip of the oil seal with clean engine oil, then position the seal on the camshaft journal with the spring side facing in.

24   Install the camshaft in the housing with the sprocket dowel pin UP (12 o'clock position) **(see illustration)**. Position the cover on the housing, holding it in place with the two bolts, as described previously.

25   Apply thread sealant to the threads of the camshaft housing and cover bolts.

26   Install new housing seals. **Note:** *Each housing seal is different shape and color. The intake seals are green with the inner seal configured differently than the outer seal. The exhaust seals are orange and they are also configured differently.*

27   Install the camshaft cover and bolts while positioning the oil seal (intake side only). Be sure the seal is installed to a precise 0.020 inch depth from the outer housing face.

28   Tighten the bolts in the sequence shown **(see illustration)** to the torque and angle of rotation listed in this Chapter's Specifications. Be sure to tighten the camshaft cover-to-housing bolts (rear two on the intake camshaft housing) at the prescribed lighter torque setting.

29   Install the power steering pump.

30   Install the remaining parts in the reverse order of removal.

31   Change the oil and filter (see Chapter 1). Add a can of engine oil supplement (GM part no. 1052367, or equivalent) if the camshafts and lifters have been replaced. **Note:** *If new lifters have been installed or the lifters bled*

9.24 The dowel pins (arrows) should be at the top (12 o'clock position)

down while the engine was disassembled, excessive lifter noise may be experienced after startup - this is normal. Use the following procedure to purge the lifters of air:

   a) *Start the engine and allow it to warm up at idle for five minutes.*

   b) *Increase engine speed to 2,000 rpm until the lifter noise is gone.*

   c) *Return the engine to idle for an additional five minutes.*

32   Road test the vehicle and check for oil and coolant leaks.

10   Valve springs, retainers and seals - replacement

Refer to illustrations 10.5 and 10.18

Note: *Broken valve springs and defective valve stem seals can be replaced without removing the cylinder head. Two special tools and a compressed air source are normally required to perform this operation, so read through this Section carefully and rent or buy the tools before beginning the job. If compressed air isn't available, a length of nylon rope can be used to keep the valves from falling into the cylinder during this procedure.*

1   Remove the spark plug from the cylinder

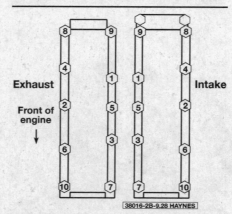

9.28 Camshaft housing-to-cylinder head bolt tightening sequence

which has the defective part. Due to the design of this engine, the intake and exhaust camshaft housings can be removed separately to service their respective components. If all of the valve stem seals are being replaced, all of the spark plugs and both camshaft housings should be removed.

2   Refer to Chapter 5 and remove the ignition coil assembly.

3   Remove the camshaft(s), lifters and housing(s) as described in Section 9.

4   Turn the crankshaft until the piston in the affected cylinder is at top dead center on the compression stroke (refer to Chapter 2, Part C, for instructions). If you're replacing all of the valve stem seals, begin with cylinder number one and work on the valves for one cylinder at a time. Move from cylinder-to-cylinder following the firing order sequence (see this Chapter's Specifications).

5   Thread an adapter into the spark plug hole **(see illustration)** and connect an air hose from a compressed air source to it. Most auto parts stores can supply the air hose adapter. **Note:** *Many cylinder compression gauges utilize a screw-in fitting that may work with your air hose quick-disconnect fitting.*

6   Apply compressed air to the cylinder. **Warning:** *The piston may be forced down by compressed air, causing the crankshaft to turn suddenly. If the wrench used when positioning the number one piston at TDC is still attached to the bolt in the crankshaft nose, it could cause damage or injury when the crankshaft moves.*

7   The valves should be held in place by the air pressure.

8   If you don't have access to compressed air, an alternative method can be used. Position the piston at a point approximately 45-degrees before TDC on the compression stroke, then feed a long piece of nylon rope through the spark plug hole until it fills the combustion chamber. Be sure to leave the end of the rope hanging out of the engine so it can be removed easily. Use a large ratchet and socket to rotate the crankshaft in the normal direction of rotation (clockwise) until slight resistance is felt.

9   Stuff shop rags into the cylinder head holes adjacent to the valves to prevent parts and tools from falling into the engine, then

10.5 This is what the air hose adapter that threads into the spark plug hole looks like - they're commonly available from auto parts stores

10.18 Apply a small dab of grease to each keeper before installation to hold it in place on the valve stem until the spring is released

use a valve spring compressor to compress the spring. Remove the keepers with small needle-nose pliers or a magnet.

10   Remove the retainer and valve spring, then remove the valve guide seal and rotator. **Note:** *If air pressure fails to hold the valve in the closed position during this operation, the valve face or seat is probably damaged. If so, the cylinder head will have to be removed for additional repair operations.*

11   Wrap a rubber band or tape around the top of the valve stem so the valve won't fall into the combustion chamber, then release the air pressure. **Note:** *If a rope was used instead of air pressure, turn the crankshaft slightly in a counterclockwise direction (opposite normal rotation).*

12   Inspect the valve stem for damage. Rotate the valve in the guide and check the end for eccentric movement, which would indicate the valve stem is bent.

13   Move the valve up-and-down in the guide and make sure it does not bind. If the valve stem binds, either the valve is bent or the guide is damaged. In either case, the cylinder head will have to be removed for repair.

14   Reapply air pressure to the cylinder to retain the valve in the closed position, then remove the tape or rubber band from the valve stem. If a rope was used instead of air pressure, rotate the crankshaft in the normal direction of rotation until slight resistance is felt.

15   Reinstall the valve rotator.

16   Lubricate the valve stem with engine oil and install a new guide seal.

17   Install the spring in position over the valve.

18   Install the valve spring retainer. Compress the valve spring and carefully install the keepers in the groove. Apply a small dab of grease to the inside of each keeper to hold it in place if necessary **(see illustration)**. Remove the pressure from the spring tool and make sure the keepers are seated.

19   Disconnect the air hose and remove the adapter from the spark plug hole. If a rope was used in place of air pressure, then turn the camshaft counterclockwise and pull it out of the cylinder.

20   Refer to Section 9 and install the camshaft(s), lifters and housing(s).

21   Install the spark plug(s) and the coil assembly.

22   Start and run the engine, then check for oil leaks and unusual sounds coming from the camshaft housings.

11   Cylinder head - removal and installation

Warning: *Wait until the engine is completely cool before beginning this procedure.*

Removal

1   Detach the cable from the negative terminal of the battery. **Caution:** *If the vehicle is equipped with a Delco Loc II or Theftlock audio system, make sure you have the correct activation code before disconnecting the battery.*

2   Drain the cooling system (see Chapter 1), then remove the heater hose from the thermostat housing to drain the coolant from the engine block.

3   Refer to Section 4 and remove the intake manifold. Refer to Section 5 and detach the exhaust manifold.

4   Remove the timing chain, camshafts and housings as described in Sections 7, 8 and 9.

5   Using the new cylinder head gasket, outline the cylinders and bolt pattern on a piece of cardboard to make a holder for the cylinder head bolts. Be sure to indicate the front of the engine for reference. Punch holes at the bolt locations **(see illustration 9.13a in Part A)**.

6   Loosen the cylinder head bolts in 1/4-turn increments until they can be removed by hand. Work from bolt-to-bolt in a pattern that's the reverse of the tightening sequence **(see illustration 11.15)**. Store the bolts in the cardboard holder as they're removed - this will ensure they are reinstalled in their original locations.

7   Lift the cylinder head off the engine. If resistance is felt, don't pry between the cylinder head and block as damage to the mating surfaces will result. To dislodge the cylinder head, place a wood block against the end of it and strike the wood block with a hammer. Store the cylinder head on wood blocks to prevent damage to the gasket sealing surfaces.

8   Cylinder head disassembly and inspection procedures are covered in detail in Chapter 2, Part C.

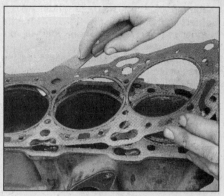

11.10 Remove the old gasket and clean the cylinder head thoroughly

Installation

Refer to illustrations 11.10 and 11.15

9   The mating surfaces of the cylinder head and block must be perfectly clean when the cylinder head is installed.

10   Use a gasket scraper to remove all traces of carbon and old gasket material **(see illustration)**, then clean the mating surfaces with lacquer thinner or acetone. If there's oil on the mating surfaces when the cylinder head is installed, the gasket may not seal correctly and leaks could develop. **Note:** *Since the cylinder head is made of aluminum, aggressive scraping can cause damage. Be extra careful not to nick or gouge the mating surface with the scraper. Use a vacuum cleaner to remove debris that falls into the cylinders.* **Caution:** *Do not use a wire brush or an abrasive pad to clean the cylinder head mating surface.*

11   Check the block and cylinder head mating surfaces for nicks, deep scratches and other damage. If damage is slight, it can be removed with a flat mill file; if it's excessive, machining may be the only alternative.

12   Use a nylon bristle brush to clean the threads in the cylinder head bolt holes. Mount each bolt in a vise and run a die down the threads to remove corrosion and restore the threads. Dirt, corrosion, sealant and damaged threads will affect torque readings.

13   Position the new gasket over the dowel pins in the block.

14   Carefully position the cylinder head on the block without disturbing the gasket.

15   Install the bolts in their original locations and tighten them finger tight. Following the

11.15 Cylinder head bolt TIGHTENING sequence

recommended sequence **(see illustration)**, tighten the bolts in several steps to the torque and angle of rotation listed in this Chapter's Specifications.

16   The remaining installation steps are the reverse of removal.

17   Refill the cooling system and change the oil and filter (see Chap-ter 1, if necessary).

18   Run the engine and check for leaks and proper operation.

12 Oil pan - removal and installation

Warning: *Wait until the engine is completely cool before beginning this procedure.*
Note: *The following procedure is based on the assumption the engine is installed in the vehicle. If it has been removed, simply unbolt the oil pan and detach it from the block.*

Removal

Refer to illustration 12.13

1   Detach the cable from the negative terminal of the battery. **Caution:** *If the vehicle is equipped with a Delco Loc II or Theftlock audio system, make sure you have the correct activation code before disconnecting the battery.*

2   Remove the right front wheel and the lower splash shield from the fenderwell.

3   Drain the engine oil and the coolant (see Chapter 1).

4   Remove the drivebelt (see Chapter 1).

5   Remove the air conditioning compressor from the bracket (see Chapter 3).

6   Remove the engine mount strut bracket (brace) from under the engine compartment (see Section 17).

7   Detach the radiator outlet pipes from the oil pan brackets.

8   Unbolt the exhaust manifold brace (see Section 5).

9   Remove the flywheel/driveplate inspection cover.

10   Remove the radiator outlet pipe from the lower radiator hose (see Chapter 3).

11   Disconnect and remove the oil level sensor from the oil pan.

12   Remove the oil pan-to-transaxle bolts.

13   Remove the oil pan mounting bolts **(see illustration)**..

14   Carefully separate the pan from the block. Don't pry between the block and pan or damage to the sealing surfaces may result and oil leaks may develop. **Note:** *The crankshaft may have to be rotated to gain clearance for oil pan removal.*

Installation

15   Clean the sealing surfaces with lacquer thinner or acetone. Make sure the bolt holes in the block are clean.

16   The gasket should be checked carefully and replaced with a new one if damage is noted. Minor imperfections can be repaired with RTV sealant. **Caution:** *Use only enough sealant to restore the gasket to its original size and shape. Excess sealant may cause*

part misalignment and oil leaks.

17   Carefully install the pan gasket and hold the pan against the block and install the bolts finger tight.

18   Tighten the bolts in three steps to the torque specified in this Chapter **(see illustration 12.13)**. Start at the center of the pan and work out toward the ends in a spiral pattern. Note that the bolts are not all tightened to the same torque figure.

19   The remaining steps are the reverse of removal. **Caution:** *Don't forget to refill the engine with oil and coolant before starting it* (see Chapter 1).

20   Start the engine and check carefully for oil leaks at the oil pan.

13 Oil pump - removal, inspection and installation

Removal

1   Remove the oil pan as described in Section 12.

2   Remove the balance shaft chain cover and tensioner (see Sec-tion 14).

3   Remove the oil pump mounting bolts and separate the oil pump from the balance shaft assembly.

4   Remove the oil pump cover and the gears from the oil pump housing.

Inspection

5   Clean all parts thoroughly.

6   Visually inspect all parts for wear, cracks and other damage. Replace the pump if it's defective, if the engine has high mileage or if the engine is being rebuilt.

Installation

6   Position the oil pump onto the balance shaft assembly. Tighten the mounting bolts to the torque listed in this Chapter's Specifications.

7   Install the balance shaft chain tensioner and cover (see Section 14).

8   Install the oil pan.

9   Add oil and run the engine. Check for oil pressure and leaks.

14 Balance shaft assembly - removal, inspection and installation

Note: *Special tools are normally required to perform this operation. Read through the entire Section carefully and acquire the necessary tools before beginning this procedure.*

Removal

1   Remove the oil pan (see Section 12). Remove the balance shaft chain cover.

2   Remove the oil pump (see Section 13).

3   Loosen, but don't remove, the balance shaft chain guide.

4   Remove the balance shaft driven sprocket. **Caution:** *The bolt is a left handed thread and must be loosened in a clockwise direction. Before removal of the driven sprocket, if it is to be reused, mark the face of the sprocket so it can be installed the same way it came off. The balance shaft may try to rotate as the bolt is loosened. Wedge a screwdriver in the flywheel/driveplate ring gear teeth to hold the crankshaft still (which will also prevent the balance shafts from turning).*

5   Just break loose the bolts holding the upper and lower housing halves together. DO NOT loosen or remove at this time. The bolts that retain only the balance shaft housing and do not extend into the engine block must be left alone at this time.

6   Remove the balance shaft assembly-to-block bolts. **Warning:** *Support the assembly securely before removal of the bolts.*

7   Remove the balance shaft assembly and place it on a workbench for disassembly and inspection.

Inspection

8   Remove the bolts and separate the upper and lower housing.

9   Pry out the oil pump pick-up screen. Clean or replace before reassembly.

10   Remove the thrust plate bolts and plate.

11   Inspect the thrust plate for gouges or burrs.

12   Remove each balance shaft and gear assembly.

13   Inspect all parts. Look for damage such

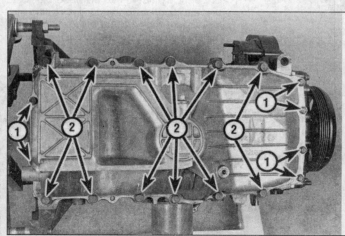

12.13 Oil pan bolt locations

1   16 mm bolts
2   8 mm bolts

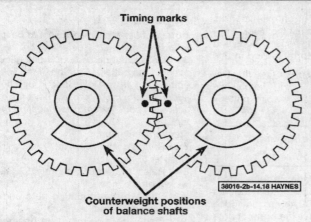

14.18 Be sure the timing marks are set correctly on the balance shaft gears

as nicks, cracks, scored bearing bores, damaged threaded holes, broken or worn guides, etc. and replace any necessary parts. **Caution:** *If the housing is damaged in any way, replace the entire assembly.*

14   Remove the bearings from the housings and inspect the bearings for scoring, over-heating, etc. in both the upper and lower housings. Replace if necessary. **Caution:** *Balance shafts must be replaced together. Any time balance shafts are replaced, the bearings must also be replaced.*

15   Inspect the chain for damaged links. **Caution:** *DO NOT replace individual links in the chain. The entire chain must be replaced if any damage is found. If the chain is to be replaced, the sprockets must also be replaced. Chain replacement requires removal of the crankshaft.*

Installation

Refer to illustrations 14.18 and 14.19

16   Assemble the thrust plate and tighten the bolts to the torque listed in this Chapter's Specifications.

17   Install the bearing halves in the upper and lower housings and lubricate the bearing faces with engine assembly lube.

18   Install the balance shafts in the hous-ings. Align the timing marks **(see illustration)**. **Caution:** *The engine will make noise or vibrate if the marks are not properly aligned.*

19   Assemble the upper and lower housings and tighten the bolts to 44 inch-lbs following the correct sequence **(see illustration)**. Final tightening will be done after the balance shaft assembly is installed on the block.

20   Place the number 1 piston at TDC (Top Dead Center), see Sec-tion 3.

21   Rotate the crankshaft, clockwise, 90-degrees.

22   Bolt the balance shaft assembly to the engine block. **Note:** *Use Locktite 242, or equivalent, thread locking compound on the housing-to-block bolts.*

23   Tighten the housing-to-block bolts, in sequence, to 44 inch-lbs **(see illustration 14.19)**. Make sure the balance shafts spin freely.

24   Tighten all bolts, in sequence **(see illustration 14.19)** to the torque listed in this Chapter's Specifications.

25   Install the oil pick-up screen. **Caution:** *The screen must not be installed until all bolts have be tightened to the final specification.*

26   Assemble the driveshaft sprocket and chain and bolt the sprocket to the balance shaft. **Caution:** *If reusing the old sprocket, be sure the mark, made on disassembly, shows.*

27   Immobilize the crankshaft as described in Step 4 and tighten the bolt to torque listed in this Chapter's Specifications. The balance shafts must not turn while the driven sprocket

is being tightened. Remember, the balance shaft sprocket bolt is reverse threaded, so turn it counter-clockwise to tighten.

28   Loosely install the chain tensioner and bolts.

29   Adjust the chain tension by inserting a 0.040-inch brass feeler gauge between the chain and chain guide. Apply light pressure (about 3 lbs) to the chain guide and tighten the chain guide bolt to the torque listed in this Chapter's Specifications. **Caution:** *A brass feeler gauge is necessary to measure chain clearance. A steel gauge will not bend and will give a incorrect chain-to-guide clearance.*

30   The remainder of the installation is the reverse of the removal procedure.

31   Add oil and a new filter, run the engine and check for leaks.

15   Flywheel/driveplate - removal and installation

This procedure is essentially the same for all engines. Refer to Chapter 2A and fol-low the procedure outlined there. Be sure to use the bolt torque listed in this Chapter's Specifications.

16   Rear main oil seal - replacement

Refer to illustrations 16.5, 16.6, 16.7 and 16.8

1   Remove the transaxle (see Chapter 7). Support the engine from above using an engine support fixture (available at rental yards). If the special support fixture is unavailable, position a jack under the engine oil pan. Place a large wood block between the jack head and the oil pan, then carefully raise the engine just enough to support the weight. **Warning:** *DO NOT place any part of your body under the engine when it's sup-ported only by a jack!*

2   If equipped with a manual transaxle, remove the pressure plate and clutch disc (see Chapter 8).

3   Remove the flywheel or driveplate (see Section 15).

4   Remove the seal housing-to-oil pan bolts.

5   Remove the seal housing-to-engine block bolts **(see illustration)**. Detach the seal housing and remove the old gasket material.

14.19 Balance shaft assembly tightening sequence

16.5 Remove the seal housing bolts (arrows)

16.6 After removing the housing from the engine, support it on wood blocks and drive out the old seal with a punch and hammer

6   Support the seal housing between two wood blocks on a workbench and drive the old seal out from the back side with a punch and hammer **(see illustration)**.
7   Drive the new seal into the housing with a wood block **(see illustration)**.
8   Lubricate the crankshaft seal journal and the lip of the new seal with multi-purpose grease or clean engine oil. Position a new gasket on the engine block **(see illustration)**.
9   Inspect the oil pan gasket. The gasket should be checked carefully and replaced with a new one if damage is noted. Minor imperfections can be repaired with RTV sealant. **Caution:** *Use only enough sealant to restore the gasket to its original size and shape. Excess sealant may cause part misalignment and oil leaks.*
10   Slowly and carefully push the new seal onto the crankshaft. The seal lip is stiff, so work it onto the crankshaft with a smooth

object such as the end of an extension as you push the housing against the block.
11   Install and tighten the housing bolts and the oil pan bolts to the torque listed in this Chapter's specifications.
12   Install the flywheel and clutch components.
13   Reinstall the transaxle.

17   Engine mounts - check and replacement

1   Engine mounts seldom require attention, but broken or deteriorated mounts should be replaced immediately or the added strain placed on the driveline components may cause damage or wear.

Check
2   During the check, the engine must be raised slightly to remove the weight from the mounts.
3   Raise the vehicle and support it securely on jackstands. Support the engine from above using an engine support fixture (available at rental yards). If the special support fixture is unavailable, position a jack under the engine oil pan. Place a large wood block between the jack head and the oil pan, then carefully raise the engine just enough to take the weight off the mounts. **Warning:** *DO NOT place any part of your body under the engine when it's supported only by a jack!*
4   Check the mounts to see if the rubber is cracked, hardened or separated from the metal plates. Sometimes the rubber will split right down the center.
5   Check for relative movement between the mount plates and the engine or frame (use a large screwdriver or pry bar to attempt to move the mounts). If movement is noted, lower the engine and tighten the mount fasteners.

Replacement
Note: *Rubber preservative should be applied to the mounts to slow deterioration.*
6   Detach the cable from the negative terminal of the battery. **Caution:** *If the vehicle is equipped with a Delco Loc II or Theftlock audio system, make sure you have the correct activation code before disconnecting the battery.*
Front engine mount
7   Remove the coolant reservoir (see Chapter 3).
8   Raise the engine slightly to take the weight off the mount.
9   Remove the mounting nuts and bolts and remove the engine mount.
10   Place the new mount in position and install the nuts. Gently lower the engine and tighten the nuts to the torque listed in this Chapter's Specifications.

Engine mount strut
11   Raise the vehicle and support it securely on jackstands. Remove the right lower splash shield.
12   Working under the mount, remove the nut from the through-bolt.
13   Raise the engine slightly to take the weight off the mount and separate the strut from the bracket.
14   Installation is the reverse of removal. Tighten the fasteners securely.

Engine mount strut bracket
15   Raise the vehicle and support it securely on jackstands. Remove the right lower splash shield.
16   Remove the engine mount strut.
17   Remove the engine mount strut bracket bolts and remove the bracket.
18   Installation is the reverse of removal. Tighten the bolts to the torque listed in this Chapter's Specifications.

16.7 Drive the new seal into the housing with a wood block - be careful not to cock the seal in the housing bore

16.8 Position a new gasket over the dowel pins (arrows)

Chapter 2 Part C
2.2L overhead camshaft (OHC) engine

Contents

Specifications

General

Firing order	1-3-4-2
Compression ratio	10:1
Compression pressure	See Chapter 2C
Bore	3.385 to 3.386 inches (85.9 to 86.0 mm)
Stroke	Not available
Displacement	134 cubic inches (2.2 liters)
Oil pressure	See Chapter 2C

FRONT OF VEHICLE → ❶ ② ③ ④   1-3-4-2

Cylinder locations and firing order

Timing chain tensioner

Timing chain tensioner compressed length	2.83 inches (72.0 mm)

Hydraulic lash adjuster

Lash adjuster bore diameter	0.4730 to 0.4739 inch (12.013 to 12.037 mm)
Lash adjuster diameter	0.4723 to 0.4728 inch (11.986 to 12.000 mm)
Lash adjuster-to-bore clearance	0.0005 to 0.0020 inch (0.013 to 0.051 mm)

Camshafts

Lobe lift (intake and exhaust)... Not available
Allowable lobe lift variation .... 0.005 inch (0.125 mm)
Endplay.. 0.0016 to 0.0057 inch (0.040 to 0.144 mm)
Journal diameter (all) .... 1.0604 to 1.0614 inches (26.935 to 26.960 mm)
Bearing inside diameter (all) .... 1.0630 to 1.0638 inches (27.00 to 27.021 mm)
Journal-to-bearing (oil) clearance .... 0.0015 to 0.0034 inch (0.040 to 0.086 mm)

Oil pump

Outer rotor-to-oil pump housing clearance limit .... 0.011 inch (0.277 mm)
Inner rotor-to-outer rotor tip clearance limit............................... 0.006 inch (0.150 mm)
Rotor-to-cover side clearance limit .... 0.005 inch (0.128 mm)

Torque specifications

Ft-lbs (unless otherwise indicated)

Camshaft sprocket bolts*
   Step 1... 63
   Step 2... Tighten an additional 30-degrees
Camshaft bearing cap bolts
   Intake camshaft rear cap bolts.. 19
   All other camshaft cap bolts .... 89 in-lbs
Crankshaft pulley bolt*
   Step 1... 74
   Step 2... Tighten an additional 75-degrees
Cylinder head bolts*
   Step 1 - Main bolts (1 through 10) 22
   Step 2 - Main bolts (1 through 10) .... Tighten an additional 155-degrees
   Step 3 - Front bolts (11 through 14) 25
Drivebelt tensioner bolt... 37
Flywheel/driveplate bolts
   Step 1... 39
   Step 2... Tighten an additional 25-degrees
Exhaust manifold-to-cylinder head nuts..................................... 13
Exhaust manifold heat shield bolts.. 18
Exhaust pipe-to-manifold nuts 22
Engine front cover perimeter bolts 18
Engine front cover water pump bolt 18
Intake manifold bolts/nuts .... 89 in-lbs
Oil pump cover-to-engine front cover screws............................. 53 in-lbs
Oil pump pressure relief valve plug 30
Oil pan-to-crankcase reinforcement bolts................................... 18
Oil pan-to-transaxle bolts 26
Balance shaft chain tensioner .... 89 in-lbs
Balance shaft chain guides
   Adjustable balance shaft chain guide bolts .... 89 in-lbs
   Small balance shaft chain guide bolts .... 89 in-lbs
   Upper balance shaft guide bolts .... 89 in-lbs
Balance shaft retainer bolts .... 89 in-lbs
Timing chain tensioner... 55
Timing chain guides
   Adjustable timing chain guide bolts .... 89 in-lbs
   Fixed timing chain guide bolts .... 89 in-lbs
   Upper timing chain guide bolts .... 89 in-lbs
Timing chain oiling nozzle bolt .... 89 in-lbs
Timing chain guide access hole plug 66
Valve cover bolts .... 89 in-lbs
Valve cover ground strap bolt .... 89 in-lbs
Water pump bolts 18
Water pump drain bolt.. 15

Bolt(s) must be replaced.

1   General information

This Part of Chapter 2 is devoted to in-vehicle repair procedures for the 2.2L DOHC (Double Overhead Camshaft), engine. All information concerning engine removal and installation and engine block overhaul can be found in Part D of this Chapter.

This engine is equipped with a single timing chain to drive the camshafts. The balance shaft chain drives the two balance shafts and the water pump sprocket. The balance shaft chain is mounted directly behind the camshaft timing chain.

The Specifications included in this Part of Chapter 2 apply only to the procedures contained in this Part. Information concerning engine removal and overhaul or replacement can be found in Chapter 2, Part D.

2   Repair operations possible with the engine in the vehicle

Many major repair operations can be accomplished without removing the engine from the vehicle.

Clean the engine compartment and the exterior of the engine with some type of degreaser before any work is done. It will make the job easier and help keep dirt out of the internal areas of the engine.

Depending on the components involved, it may be helpful to remove the hood to improve access to the engine as repairs are performed (refer to Chapter 11 if necessary). Cover the fenders to prevent damage to the paint. Special pads are available, but an old bedspread or blanket will also work.

If vacuum, exhaust, oil or coolant leaks develop, indicating a need for gasket or seal replacement, the repairs can generally be made with the engine in the vehicle. The intake and exhaust manifold gaskets, oil pan gasket, crankshaft oil seals and cylinder head gasket are all accessible with the engine in place.

Exterior engine components, such as the intake and exhaust manifolds, the oil pan, the oil pump, the water pump, the starter motor, the alternator and the fuel system components can be removed for repair with the engine in place.

Since the cylinder head can be removed without pulling the engine, camshaft and valve component servicing can also be accomplished with the engine in the vehicle. Replacement of the timing chain, balance shaft chain and sprockets is also possible with the engine in the vehicle. Balance shaft removal, however, will require removal of the engine.

In extreme cases caused by a lack of necessary equipment, repair or replacement of piston rings, pistons, connecting rods and rod bearings is possible with the engine in the vehicle. However, this practice is not recommended because of the cleaning and preparation work that must be done to the components involved.

3   Top Dead Center (TDC) for number one piston - locating

Refer to illustration 3.5

1   Top Dead Center (TDC) is the highest point in the cylinder that each piston reaches as it travels up-and-down during crankshaft rotation. Each piston reaches TDC on the compression stroke and again on the exhaust stroke, but TDC generally refers to piston position on the compression stroke.

2   Positioning the piston(s) at TDC is an essential part of certain other repair procedures discussed in this manual.

3   Before beginning this procedure, be sure to place the transmission in Neutral and apply the parking brake or block the rear wheels. Remove the spark plugs (see Chapter 1). Disable the ignition system by disconnecting the wiring harness connector from the ignition module or from each coil-on-plug assembly (see Chapter 5). Also disable the fuel system by unplugging the electrical connector in the wiring harness to the fuel injectors.

4   In order to bring any piston to TDC, the crankshaft must be turned using one of the methods outlined below. When looking at the front of the engine, normal crankshaft rotation is clockwise.

   a) *The preferred method is to turn the crankshaft with a socket and ratchet attached to the bolt threaded into the front of the crankshaft.*

   b) *A remote starter switch, which may save some time, can also be used. Follow the instructions included with the switch. Once the piston is close to TDC, use a socket and ratchet as described in the previous paragraph.*

   c) *If an assistant is available to turn the ignition switch to the Start position in short bursts, you can get the piston close to TDC without a remote starter switch. Make sure your assistant is out of the vehicle, away from the ignition switch, then use a socket and ratchet as described in Paragraph a) to complete the procedure.*

5   Insert a compression gauge into the number one cylinder spark plug hole. Turn

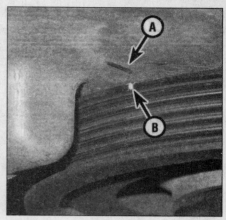

3.5 Timing marks - align the pointer on the engine front cover (A) with the notch in the crankshaft pulley (B)

the crankshaft (see Step 4 above) until compression registers on the gauge, then turn it slowly until the TDC mark on the timing chain cover is aligned with the notch on the crankshaft pulley **(see illustration)**.

6   After the number one piston has been positioned at TDC on the compression stroke, TDC for any of the remaining pistons can be located by turning the crankshaft and following the firing order. Divide the crankshaft pulley into two equal sections with chalk marks at each point, each indicating 180-degrees of crankshaft rotation. Rotating the engine past TDC no. 1 to the next mark will place the engine at TDC for cylinder no. 3.

4   Valve cover - removal and installation

Removal

Refer to illustrations 4.2, 4.3a, 4.3b, 4.4, 4.5 and 4.6

1   Disconnect the cable from the negative battery terminal (see Chapter 5, Section 1). Remove the ignition coil assembly from the valve cover (see Chapter 5).

2   Detach the PCV hose from the valve cover **(see illustration)**.

4.2 Squeeze the clamp and detach the PCV hose from the valve cover

4.3a Working on the timing chain end of the engine, disconnect the wiring harness from the bracket

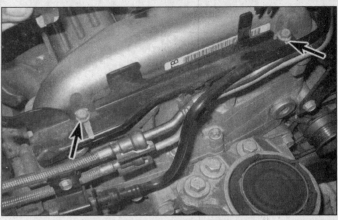

4.3b Remove the fuel line bracket bolts and position the assembly off to the side

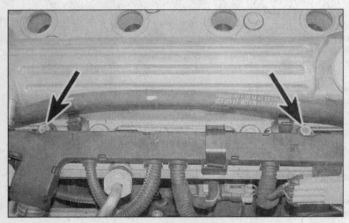

4.4 Remove these two nuts and detach the fuel injector wiring harness for access to the valve cover front mounting bolts

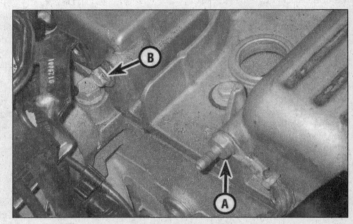

4.5 Remove the ground strap bolt (A) and the coolant tube bracket bolt (B)

3   Detach the wiring harness and the fuel line bracket from the timing chain end of the valve cover **(see illustrations)** and position the assembly away from the valve cover.

4   Remove the nuts and detach the fuel injector harness from the mounting studs **(see illustration)**.

5   Remove the bolts and detach the ground strap and coolant tube bracket from the valve cover **(see illustration)**.

6   Remove the valve cover bolts **(see illustration)** then lift the valve cover off. Tap gently with a soft-face hammer, if necessary, to break the gasket seal.

Installation

Refer to illustrations 4.8 and 4.9

7   Clean the gasket surfaces on the intake manifold, cylinder head and valve cover. Use a shop rag, lacquer thinner or acetone to wipe off all residue and gasket material from the sealing surfaces.

8   Insert a new valve cover gasket into the grooved recess in the valve cover. Make sure the gasket is positioned properly in the groove **(see illustration)**.

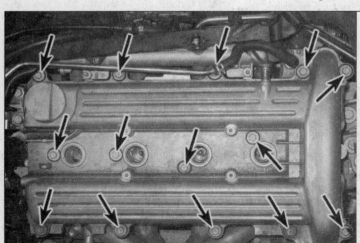

4.6 Location of the valve cover mounting bolts

4.8 Install the gasket into the grooved recess in the valve cover

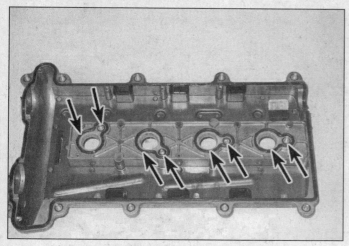

4.9 Be sure to change all the spark plug seals and
O-rings in the valve cover

5.6 Location of the intake manifold mounting bolts

9   Install new O-rings and spark plug seals in the valve cover **(see illustration)**.
10   The remainder of installation is the reverse of the removal Steps. Tighten the valve cover bolts evenly, starting with the center bolts and working out, to the torque listed in this Chapter's Specifications.
11   Reconnect the battery (see Chapter 5, Section 1).

5   Intake manifold - removal and installation

Removal

Refer to illustration 5.6
1   Disconnect the cable from the negative battery terminal (see Chapter 5, Section 1).
2   Remove the throttle body (see Chapter 4).
3   Disconnect any electrical connectors that would interfere with manifold removal. Open the wiring harness clips and detach all wiring harnesses from the manifold.
4   Disconnect any vacuum hoses con-

nected to the manifold (this will vary by year). Mark the hoses, if necessary, to ensure correct reassembly.
5   Remove the dipstick tube mounting bolt and position the dipstick to the side.
6   Remove the intake manifold mounting bolts and nuts **(see illustration)**.
7   Lift the intake manifold from the engine compartment.

Installation

8   Install a new gasket, if necessary. **Note:** *The intake manifold gasket does not need to be replaced unless it has become damaged during the removal process.* Make sure the mating surfaces of the manifold and cylinder head are clean.
9   Install the manifold over the studs on the cylinder head. Install the bolts and nuts and tighten them finger-tight.
10   Tighten the bolts to the torque listed in this Chapter's Specifications, starting with the center bolts and working towards the ends.
11   The remainder of installation is the reverse of the removal steps.

12   Reconnect the battery (see Chapter 5, Section 1).
13   Run the engine and check for vacuum leaks.

6   Exhaust manifold - removal and installation

Warning: *The engine must be completely cool before beginning this procedure.*

Removal

Refer to illustrations 6.2, 6.3, 6.5 and 6.7
1   Disconnect the cable from the negative battery terminal (see Chapter 5, Section 1).
2   If equipped, remove the AIR valve bracket nut, then remove the bolts and disconnect the AIR pipe from the exhaust manifold **(see illustration)**. **Note:** *It isn't necessary to detach the hose from the AIR valve.*
3   Remove the exhaust manifold heat shield **(see illustration)**.
4   Raise the vehicle and support it on jackstands.

6.2 Location of the AIR pipe and bracket fasteners

6.3 Location of the heat shield mounting bolts

6.5 Exhaust pipe-to-manifold nuts

6.7 Exhaust manifold mounting nuts

5   Detach the exhaust pipe from the manifold **(see illustration)**.
6   Follow the lead from the oxygen sensor up to its electrical connector, then unplug the connector. Also detach the lead from its retaining clip.
7   Remove the exhaust manifold mounting nuts and detach the manifold from the cylinder head **(see illustration)**.

Installation

8   Using a scraper, thoroughly clean the mating surfaces on the cylinder head, manifold and exhaust pipe. Remove the residue with a solvent such as acetone or lacquer thinner.
9   Check that the mating surfaces are perfectly flat and not damaged in any way. A warped or damaged manifold may require machining or, if severe enough, replacement. Install the new gasket to the cylinder head studs and place the manifold on the cylinder head. Tighten the nuts evenly, working from the center outwards, to the torque listed in this Chapter's Specifications.

10   Connect the exhaust pipe to the manifold and tighten the nuts evenly to the torque listed in this Chapter's Specifications.
11   The remainder of installation is the reverse of the removal steps.
12   Reconnect the battery (see Chapter 5, Section 1).
13   Run the engine and check for exhaust leaks.

---

7   Engine front cover - removal and installation

Removal

Refer to illustrations 7.7a and 7.7b
1   Disconnect the cable from the negative battery terminal (see Chapter 5, Section 1).
2   Drain the engine oil (see Chapter 1).
3   Remove the drivebelt (see Chapter 1).
4   Remove the drivebelt tensioner from the front cover.
5   Remove the crankshaft pulley (see Section 10).

6   Loosen the right front wheel lug nuts, then raise the front of the vehicle and support it securely on jackstands. Remove the right front wheel.
7   Loosen the engine cover fasteners gradually and evenly, then remove the fasteners **(see illustrations)**. **Note:** *Draw a sketch of the engine cover and cover fasteners. Identify the location of all bolts for installation in their original locations.*
8   Remove the water pump bolt from the engine front cover **(see illustration 7.7b)**.
9   Remove the front cover.
10   Remove the engine cover-to-block gasket.

Installation

11   Inspect and clean all sealing surfaces of the engine front cover and the block. **Caution:** *Be very careful when scraping on aluminum engine parts. Aluminum is soft and gouges easily. Severely gouged parts may require replacement.*
12   If necessary, replace the crankshaft front oil seal in the front cover (see Section 10).

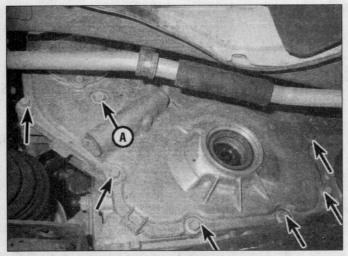

7.7a The engine cover mounting bolts can be accessed from below . . .

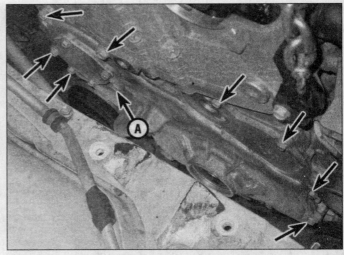

7.7b . . . and from above the engine compartment - don't forget the front cover/water pump bolt (A)

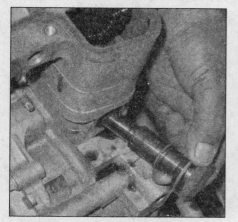

8.8 Remove the timing chain tensioner from the cylinder head

8.9 Remove the upper timing chain guide mounting bolts

8.10 Use a wrench on the hex drive on the camshaft to prevent the camshaft from turning while loosening the sprocket bolt

13   Install the front cover gasket on the engine block. **Note:** *The engine cover gasket is reusable. Make sure the gasket has not been damaged. Install a new gasket if necessary.*
14   Install the front cover and cover fasteners. Make sure the hub on the inner rotor is aligned with the flats on the crankshaft and the engine cover fasteners are in their original locations. Tighten the fasteners by hand until the cover is contacting the block around its entire periphery.
15   Install the long water pump bolt.
16   Tighten the bolts to the torque listed in this Chapter's Specifications.
17   Install the drivebelt and tensioner. Tighten the drivebelt tensioner to the torque listed in this Chapter's Specifications.
18   Install the crankshaft pulley (see Section 10).
19   Reinstall the remaining parts in the reverse order of removal.
20   Fill the crankcase with the recommended oil (see Chapter 1).
21   Reconnect the battery (see Chapter 5, Section 1).
22   Start the engine and check for leaks. Check all fluid levels.

8   Timing chain and sprockets - removal, inspection and installation

Removal

Refer to illustrations 8.8, 8.9, 8.10, 8.11a, 8.11b, 8.12, 8.14 and 8.15
1   Disconnect the cable from the negative battery terminal (see Chapter 5, Section 1).
2   Set the engine to TDC for cylinder number one (see Section 3).
3   Drain the engine oil (see Chapter 1).
4   Remove the drivebelt (see Chapter 1).
5   Remove the drivebelt tensioner from the front cover.
6   Remove the engine front cover (see Section 7).
7   Remove the valve cover (see Section 4).
8   Remove the timing chain tensioner **(see illustration)**.
9   Remove the upper timing chain guide **(see illustration)**.
10   Remove the exhaust camshaft sprocket bolt **(see illustration)**. Be sure to discard the bolt and install a new bolt on reassembly.
11   Remove the adjustable timing chain

8.11a Remove the adjustable timing chain guide mounting bolt . . .

guide **(see illustrations)**.
12   Unscrew the access bolt and remove the fixed timing chain guide upper mounting bolt **(see illustration)**.
13   Remove the fixed timing chain guide lower mounting bolt and lift the guide from the engine block.

8.11b . . . then lift the guide out through the top of the cylinder head

8.12 Access plug for the fixed timing chain guide upper mounting bolt

8.14 Use a wrench on the hex drive on the camshaft when loosening the camshaft sprocket bolt

14   Remove the intake camshaft sprocket bolt **(see illustration)**. Be sure to discard the bolt and install a new bolt on reassembly.
15   Remove the timing chain through the top of the cylinder head **(see illustration)**.
16   Remove the timing chain drive sprocket and slide the timing chain oiling nozzle off the engine block.

Inspection

17   Clean all parts with clean solvent and dry with compressed air, if available.
18   Inspect the chain tensioner for excessive wear or other damage. Be sure to drain all the oil out of the chain tensioner if it is to be reused.
19   Inspect the timing chain guides for deep grooves, excessive wear, or other damage.
20   Inspect the timing chain for excessive wear or damage.
21   Inspect the crankshaft and camshaft sprockets for chipped or broken teeth, excessive wear, or damage.
22   Replace any component that is in questionable condition.

Installation

Refer to illustrations 8.23, 8.25, 8.29, 8.33a, 8.33b, 8.33c, 8.33d and 8.33e
23   If the crankshaft has been rotated during this procedure, make sure the number one piston is at the top of it's stroke (TDC) (see Section 3). The timing mark (round dot) should point to 5 o'clock position on the crankshaft sprocket **(see illustration)**.
24   Install the intake camshaft sprocket onto the camshaft. Be sure to install a new bolt. Tighten the intake camshaft sprocket bolt lightly, finger tight at this time. **Caution:** *Do not turn the camshaft more than 1/2 turn to avoid any valve/piston contact. The camshafts should be positioned correctly before the timing chain is installed.*
25   Install the timing chain by lowering it from the top through the opening. Be sure the timing chain drops down around both sides of the cylinder block bosses. Be sure the bright colored link (copper) on the chain is aligned with the INT designation on the camshaft sprocket **(see illustration)**. **Note:** *The copper link will be installed at the intake camshaft sprocket (front) while the silver links will be installed at the crankshaft sprocket and the exhaust camshaft sprocket (rear).*
26   Drape the timing chain over the crankshaft sprocket and engage the plated link (silver) on the chain with the crankshaft sprocket timing mark located in the 5 o'clock position **(see illustration 8.23)**.
27   Install the adjustable timing chain guide. Install the bolts and tighten them to the torque listed in this Chapter's Specifications.
28   Install the exhaust camshaft sprocket onto the camshaft. Be sure to install a new bolt. Be sure the plated link (silver) on the chain is aligned with the EXH designation on the camshaft sprocket **(see illustration 8.25)**. Tighten the exhaust camshaft sprocket bolt lightly, finger tight at this time.

8.15   Carefully remove the timing chain and the intake camshaft sprocket through the top of the cylinder head

29   Install the fixed timing chain guide **(see illustration)**. Tighten the bolts to the torque listed in this Chapter's Specifications.
30   Install the upper timing chain guide **(see illustration 8.9)**. Tighten the bolts to the torque listed in this Chapter's Specifications.
31   Install a 24 mm wrench onto the intake camshaft hex as a back-up, and torque the intake camshaft bolt to the torque listed in

8.23   The round dot (alignment mark) on the sprocket should be in the 5 o'clock position. When installing the chain, one of the silver plated links must be aligned with this dot

this Chapter's Specifications.
32   Install a 24 mm wrench onto the exhaust camshaft hex as a back-up, and torque the exhaust camshaft bolt to the torque listed in this Chapter's Specifications.
33   Install the timing chain tensioner. The timing chain tensioner must be installed in its

8.25   The copper link must align with the INT on the intake camshaft and the silver link with the EXH on the exhaust camshaft

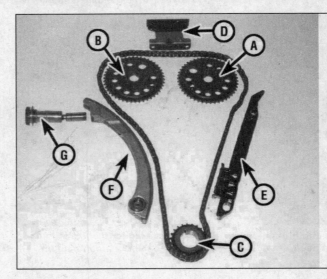

8.29   Timing chain component details

A   Intake camshaft sprocket
B   Exhaust camshaft sprocket
C   Crankshaft sprocket
D   Upper timing chain guide
E   Fixed timing chain guide
F   Adjustable timing chain guide
G   Timing chain tensioner

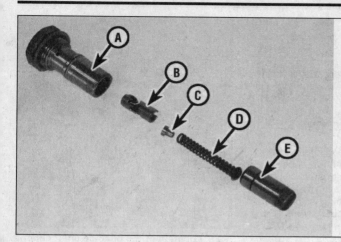

8.33a Timing tensioner details

A Timing chain tensioner body
B Ratchet cylinder
C Spring adjuster
D Spring
E Piston

8.33b When placing the piston in the vise, make sure the jaws of the vise only contact the flats of the piston

compressed state. Follow the steps to correctly compress the tensioner. **Caution:** *The timing chain tensioner must be installed in the compressed state. Do not install a tensioner in its released state. Damage to the tensioner and timing chain will occur.*

a) *Completely disassemble the tensioner and drain all the oil (see illustration). Inspect the tensioner body, the piston and all components for scoring or damage. If necessary, replace the tensioner with a new one.*
b) *Install the tensioner piston into the vise with the flats seated in the jaws of the vise (see illustration).*
c) *Install the ratchet cylinder into the piston, aligning the groove with the locating pin (see illustration).*
d) *Drive the ratchet cylinder into the piston with a flat-bladed screwdriver. Rotate the ratchet cylinder clockwise when it reaches the bottom (see illustration). The ratchet cylinder should be locked into position.*
e) *The tensioner must measure 2.83 inches (72 mm) from end-to-end (see illustration).*

34 Install the timing chain oiling nozzle.

Tighten the bolt to the torque listed in this Chapter's Specifications.
35 Apply a small amount of RTV sealant to the threads and install the timing chain guide access plug. Tighten the bolt to the torque listed in this Chapter's Specifications.
36 Install the valve cover (see Section 4).
37 Install the engine front cover (see Section 7).
38 The remainder of installation is the reverse of the removal Steps.
39 Reconnect the battery (see Chapter 5, Section 1).
40 Run the engine and check for oil or coolant leaks.

9 Balance shaft chain and balance shafts - removal, inspection and installation

Note: *This procedure covers removal of the balance shaft chain **and** balance shafts, but take note that the shafts themselves can only be removed from the engine block after the engine has been removed from the vehicle. If there is a problem with the balance shafts that does warrant their removal, the engine*

would have to be removed anyway, since replacement of the balance shaft bushings is a job that must be left to an automotive machine shop. If you're just removing or replacing the chain, ignore the steps that don't apply.

Removal
Refer to illustrations 9.5, 9.6 and 9.9
1 Disconnect the cable from the negative battery terminal (see Chapter 5, Section 1).
2 Drain the engine oil (see Chapter 1).
3 Remove the timing chain, timing chain guides and sprockets (see Section 8).
4 Check to make sure the engine is positioned at TDC for cylinder number 1 (see Section 3). **Caution:** *Do not rotate the engine to find TDC number 1 when the timing chain is removed unless the engine has been rotated accidentally. If the engine is not positioned at TDC number 1, the camshafts must be removed to prevent damage to the valves (see Section 11).*
5 Remove the balance shaft chain tensioner **(see illustration).**

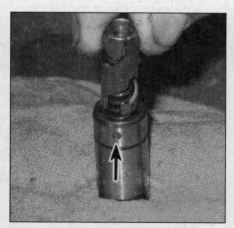

8.33c Align the groove in the ratchet cylinder with the pin in the piston

8.33d Using a flat-bladed screwdriver, drive the ratchet cylinder down to the bottom and rotate it clockwise to lock it into position

8.33e The tensioner should measure the correct length in its compressed state or it must be replaced with a new tensioner

6   Remove the adjustable balance shaft chain guide (see illustration).
7   Remove the small balance shaft chain guide (see illustration 9.6).
8   Remove the upper balance shaft chain guide (see illustration 9.6).
9   Remove the balance shaft drive chain (see illustration). Note: *To aid in removal, gather all the slack in the chain between the water pump sprocket and the crankshaft sprocket.*
10   If you're removing the balance shafts (engine removed from the vehicle), remove the balance shaft retainer bolts.
11   Remove the balance shafts from the engine block. Caution: *Mark each balance shaft to insure correct reassembly. The balance shafts are not interchangeable. Do not install the balance shaft into the wrong bore or extreme engine vibration will occur.*

Inspection

12   Clean all parts with clean solvent and dry with compressed air, if available.
13   Inspect the chain tensioners for excessive wear or other damage.
14   Inspect the balance shaft chain guides for deep grooves, excessive wear, or other damage.
15   Inspect the balance shaft chain for

excessive wear or damage.
16   Inspect the crankshaft and water pump sprockets for chipped or broken teeth, excessive wear, or damage.
17   Replace any component that is damaged.

Installation

Refer to illustration 9.18, 9.20, 9.21a, 9.21b, 9.26a, 9.26b and 9.28
18   If the crankshaft has been rotated during this procedure, make sure the number one piston is at the top of it's stroke (TDC) (see Section 3). The crankshaft timing mark (round dot) should point to 5 o'clock position on the crankshaft sprocket (see illustration). Caution: *Do not rotate the engine to find TDC number 1 after the timing chain has been removed unless the engine has been rotated accidentally. If the engine is not positioned at TDC number 1, the camshafts must be removed to prevent damage to the valves* (see Section 11).
19   Install the balance shafts into the bores and tighten the balance shaft retainer bolts to the torque listed in this Chapter's Specifications.
20   Align the balance shaft sprockets before installing the balance shaft chain. Starting with the intake side balance shaft, place the

9.5 Location of the balance shaft chain tensioner mounting bolts

alignment arrow pointing up, then temporarily install a drill bit into the alignment hole and the sprocket teeth to lock the balance shaft sprocket in place (see illustration).
21   Now position the exhaust side (rear) balance shaft sprocket with the arrow pointing down and aligned with the cutout in the retainer, then install a drill bit into the alignment hole to hold the sprocket (see illustrations).

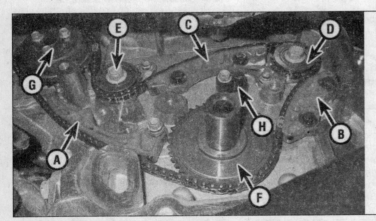

9.6 Balance shaft chain and guide details

A   Adjustable balance shaft chain guide
B   Small balance shaft chain guide
C   Upper balance shaft chain guide
D   Intake side (front) balance shaft sprocket
E   Exhaust side (rear) balance shaft sprocket
F   Crankshaft/balance shaft sprocket
G   Water pump sprocket
H   Timing chain oiling nozzle

9.9 Balance shaft sprocket/chain alignment marks (A) and retainer bolts (B)

9.18 The timing mark (round dot) should point to 5 o'clock (approximately) position on the crankshaft sprocket

9.20 With the arrow on the intake side balance shaft sprocket pointing up (and aligned with the cutout on the balance shaft retainer, not visible in this photo, but similar to the one shown in illustration 9.21a), install a drill bit into the hole to lock the sprocket in place

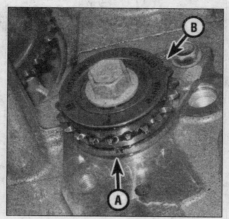

9.21a Location of the alignment notch for the sprocket arrow (A) and the alignment hole (B) on the exhaust side balance shaft sprocket

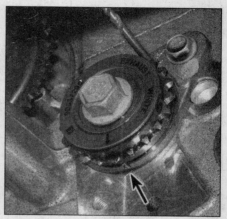

9.21b Install the drill bit into the exhaust balance shaft retainer to lock it into position

22   Install the balance shaft chain onto the balance shaft/crankshaft sprocket and the balance shafts. Align the colored links with the alignment marks on each sprocket. Posi-

9.26a Rotate the plunger 90-degrees, align the holes in the body and piston . . .

tion the copper-colored link onto the intake side balance shaft, aligning the mark with the colored link at approximately the 12 o'clock position (see illustration 9.9). Note: *The copper link will be installed at the intake balance shaft sprocket (front) while the silver links will be installed at the crankshaft sprocket and the exhaust balance shaft sprocket (rear).*
23   Working clockwise, position the second colored link (silver) on the crankshaft/balance shaft sprocket, aligning the mark on the sprocket with the colored link at the 6 o'clock position (see illustration 9.18).
24   Finally, pass the chain over the water pump sprocket, under the exhaust balance shaft sprocket and into position. Align the third colored link (silver) on the exhaust balance shaft sprocket, aligning the mark on the sprocket with the colored link at the 6 o'clock position.
25   Install the balance shaft chain guides (see illustration 9.6). Tighten the bolts to the torque listed in this Chapter's Specifications.
26   Reset the balance shaft chain tensioner. Turn the tensioner plunger 90-degrees in the bore and compress the tensioner plunger

(see illustration). Rotate the plunger back to the original position at 12 o'clock and install a paper clip through the hole in the body into the plunger (see illustration).
27   Install the balance shaft chain tensioner and torque the bolts to the Specifications listed in this Chapter.
28   Remove the drill bit to release the plunger (see illustration).
29   Recheck all the balance shaft chain timing marks.
30   Install the timing chain (see Section 8) and all components removed previously.
31   Reconnect the battery (see Chapter 5, Section 1).

---

10   Crankshaft pulley and front oil seal - removal and installation

---

Removal

Refer to illustrations 10.4, 10.5 and 10.7
1   Disconnect the cable from the negative battery terminal (see Chapter 5, Section 1).
2   Remove the drivebelt (see Chapter 1).
3   Raise the vehicle and support it securely on jackstands.

9.26b . . . then install a drill bit to retain the piston in the locked position

9.28 After the tensioner is installed and the bolts tightened, remove the drill bit

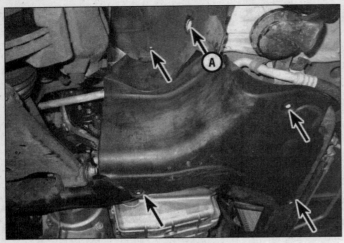

10.4 Remove the splash shield mounting bolts - one bolt can be removed through the access hole (A) in the inner fender splash shield

10.5 A large pin spanner can be used to prevent the pulley from rotating

4   Remove the splash shield from below the engine compartment **(see illustration)**.
5   Use a breaker bar and socket to remove the crankshaft pulley center bolt **(see illustration)**. Discard the bolt and obtain a new one for installation. **Note:** *It will be necessary to lock the pulley in position using a strap wrench or a large pin spanner. Be sure to wrap a length of old drivebelt around the pulley if you are using a strap wrench.*
6   Slide the puller off the nose of the crankshaft. If the pulley is stuck, use a puller that bolts to the three threaded holes in the pulley hub. Additionally, a spacer, such as a deep socket that just fit into the hole in the pulley and bears on the crankshaft, will be required to avoid damage to the crankshaft.
7   Use a seal puller to remove the crankshaft front oil seal **(see illustration)**. A screwdriver may be used instead, if the tip is wrapped with tape to avoid scratching the crankshaft.
8   Clean the seal bore and check it for nicks or gouges. Also examine the area of the hub that rides in the seal for signs of abnormal wear or scoring. For many popular engines, repair sleeves are available to restore a smooth finish to the sealing surface. Check with your auto parts store.

Installation

Refer to illustration 10.9
9   Coat the lip of the new seal with clean engine oil and drive it into the bore with a seal driver or a socket slightly smaller in diameter than the seal **(see illustration)**. The open side of the seal faces into the engine.
10   Using clean engine oil, lubricate the sealing surface of the hub. Install the crankshaft pulley/damper with a special installation tool, available at most auto parts stores. Do not use a hammer to install the pulley/damper. Install a new center bolt and tighten it to the torque listed in this Chapter's Specifications. **Note:** *You must use a new pulley bolt.*

11   The remainder of the installation is the reverse of the removal procedure.
12   Reconnect the battery (see Chapter 5, Section 1).

11 Camshafts and hydraulic lash adjusters - removal, inspection and installation

Note: *This is a difficult procedure, involving special tools. Read through the entire Section and obtain the necessary tools before beginning the procedure.*

Removal

Refer to illustrations 11.5a and 11.5b
1   Disconnect the cable from the negative battery terminal (see Chapter 5, Section 1).
2   Remove the valve cover (see Section 4).
3   Set the engine to TDC for cylinder number one (see Section 3), then turn the crankshaft counterclockwise until the engine

is set at 60-degrees *before* TDC. At this point, the diamond-shaped hole on the intake camshaft should be in the 12 o'clock position. **Caution:** *Do not remove the camshafts with the engine at TDC number 1 or the valves and pistons will be damaged.*
4   Remove the upper timing chain guide (see Section 8).
5   Install a special tool to secure the camshaft sprockets in position **(see illustrations)**. This camshaft locking tool (jig) can be purchased through a dealership parts department or at specialty automotive tool suppliers.
6   Remove the camshaft sprocket bolts and slide the camshaft sprockets forward, then tighten the wingnuts to hold the sprockets securely.

Intake camshaft

Refer to illustrations 11.7a, 11.7b, 11.8, 11.9 and 11.10
7   Each camshaft cap is marked with a number indicating its position **(see illustra-**

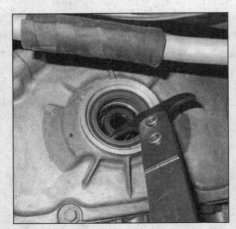

10.7 Use a seal puller to remove the old crankshaft seal, taking care not to damage the crankshaft or the seal bore in the cover

10.9 Driving the new front cover seal in with a seal driver

11.5a Install a camshaft locking tool to hold the sprockets and timing chain in place - make sure the camshaft sprockets are locked properly and the tool is bolted to the cylinder head

11.5b The diamond-shaped hole on the intake camshaft should be in the 12 o'clock position

tions). Loosen each bearing cap nut slowly and evenly, allowing the camshaft to lift from the cylinder head, parallel to the surface of the cylinder head. **Caution:** *The caps must be installed in their original locations. Keep all parts from each camshaft together; never mix parts from one camshaft with those for another.*

8   Remove the rocker arms **(see illustration)**.

9   Place the rocker arms in a suitable container, in order, so they can be reinstalled in their original positions **(see illustration)**.

10   Remove the hydraulic lash adjusters from their bores in the cylinder head **(see illustration)**. Store these with their corresponding rocker arms so they can be reinstalled in their original locations.

11.7a The camshaft bearing cap designations are stamped onto each cap

11.7b Make sure the arrow faces the timing chain end of the engine

11.8 Remove each rocker arm . . .

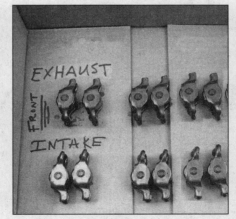

11.9 . . . and store them in an organized manner so they can be returned to their original locations

11.10 Pull the lash adjusters from their bores in the head and store them along with their corresponding rocker arms

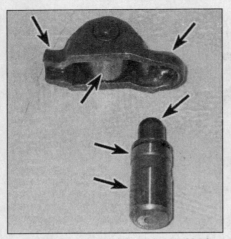

11.15 Check the rocker arms and lash adjusters for wear at the indicated points

11.18 Check the cam lobes for pitting, excessive wear, and scoring. If scoring is excessive, as shown here, replace the camshaft

11.19 Measure each camshaft lobe height with a micrometer

Exhaust camshaft

11   Mark the exhaust bearing caps in the original positions and remove them from the cylinder head. Each camshaft cap is designated with a number **(see illustrations 11.7a and 11.7b)**. Loosen each bearing cap nut slowly and evenly, allowing the camshaft to lift from the cylinder head, parallel to the surface of the cylinder head. **Caution:** *The camshaft bearing caps are numbered to identify the locations of the caps. The caps must be installed in their original locations. Keep all parts from each camshaft together; never mix parts from one camshaft with those for another.*

12   Mark the positions of the rocker arms so they can be reinstalled in their original locations, then remove the rocker arms.

13   Place the rocker arms in a suitable container so they can be separated and identified **(see illustration 11.9)**.

14   Lift the hydraulic lash adjusters from their bores in the cylinder head. Identify and separate the adjusters so they can be reinstalled in their original locations **(see illustration 11.10)**.

Inspection

Refer to illustrations 11.15, 11.18, 11.19, 11.20, 11.21 and 11.22

15   Check each hydraulic lash adjuster for excessive wear, scoring, pitting, or an out-of-round condition **(see illustration)**. Replace as necessary.

16   Measure the outside diameter of each adjuster at the top and bottom of the adjuster. Then take a second set of measurements at a right angle to the first. If any measurement is significantly different from the others, the adjuster is tapered or out of round and must be replaced. If the necessary equipment is available, measure the diameter of the lash adjuster and the inside diameter of the corresponding cylinder head bore. Subtract the diameter of the lash adjuster from the bore diameter to obtain the oil clearance. Compare the measurements obtained to

those given in this Chapter's Specifications. If the adjusters or the cylinder head bores are excessively worn, new adjusters or a new cylinder head, or both, may be required. If the valve train is noisy, particularly if the noise persists after a cold start, you can suspect a faulty lash adjuster.

17   Inspect the rocker arms for signs of wear or damage. The areas of wear are the tip that contacts the valve stem, the socket that contacts the lash adjuster and the roller that contacts the camshaft **(see illustration 11.15)**.

18   Examine the camshaft lobes for scoring, pitting, galling (wear due to rubbing), and evidence of overheating (blue, discolored areas). Look for flaking of the hardened surface layer of each lobe **(see illustration)**. If any such wear is evident, replace the camshaft.

19   Measure the lobe height of each cam lobe on the intake camshaft, and record your measurements **(see illustration)**. Compare the measurements for excessive variation; if the lobe heights vary more than 0.005 inch (0.125 mm), replace the camshaft. Compare the lobe height measurements on the

exhaust camshaft and follow the same procedure. Do not compare intake camshaft lobe heights with exhaust camshaft lobe heights, as they are different. Only compare intake lobes with intake lobes and exhaust lobes with exhaust lobes.

20   Inspect the camshaft bearing journals and the cylinder head bearing surfaces for pitting or excessive wear. If any such wear is evident, replace the component concerned. Using a micrometer, measure the diameter of each camshaft bearing journal at several points **(see illustration)**. If the diameter of any journal is less than specified, replace the camshaft.

21   To check the bearing journal oil clearance, remove the rocker arms and hydraulic lash adjusters (if not already done), use a suitable solvent and a clean lint-free rag to clean all bearing surfaces, then install the camshafts and bearing caps with a piece of Plastigage across each journal **(see illustration)**. Tighten the bearing cap bolts to the specified torque. Don't rotate the camshafts.

22   Remove the bearing caps and measure

11.20 Measure each journal diameter with a micrometer. If any journal is less than the specified minimum, replace the camshaft

11.21 Lay a strip of Plastigage on each camshaft journal, in line with the camshaft

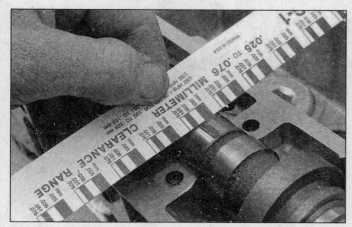

11.22 Compare the width of the crushed Plastigage to the scale on the package to determine the journal oil clearance

11.29 Camshaft and timing sprocket alignment details

the width of the flattened Plastigage with the Plastigage scale (see illustration). Scrape off the Plastigage with your fingernail or the edge of a credit card. Don't scratch or nick the journals or bearing caps.

23   If the oil clearance of any bearing is worn beyond the specified service limit, install a new camshaft and repeat the check. If the clearance is still excessive, replace the cylinder head.

24   To check camshaft endplay, remove the hydraulic lash adjusters, clean the bearing surfaces carefully, and install the camshafts and bearing caps. Tighten the bearing cap bolts to the specified torque, then measure the endplay using a dial indicator mounted on the cylinder head so that its tip bears on the camshaft end.

25   Lightly but firmly tap the camshaft fully toward the gauge, zero the gauge, then tap the camshaft fully away from the gauge and note the gauge reading. If the measured endplay is at or beyond the specified service limit, install a new camshaft thrust cap and repeat the check. If the clearance is still excessive, the camshaft or the cylinder head must be replaced.

Installation

Refer to illustration 11.29

26   Lubricate the rocker arms and hydraulic lash adjusters with engine assembly lubricant or fresh engine oil. Install the adjusters into their original bores, then install the rocker arms in their correct locations.

27   Lubricate the camshafts with camshaft installation lubricant and install them in their correct locations. Position the camshafts with the slots in the end of the camshafts positioned as shown in illustration 11.29, aligning them with the slots in the camshaft sprockets.

28   Install the camshaft bearing caps in their correct locations, except for the front end and rear end bearing caps on each camshaft. Install the cap bolts and tighten by hand until snug. Tighten the bolts in four to five steps, starting with the center cap and working to the outside caps, to the torque listed in this

Chapter's Specifications.

29   Slide the camshaft sprockets and timing chain along the guide pins toward the camshafts. Rotate the camshafts with an open-end wrench on the hex drive on each camshaft until the slots are aligned with the projections on the sprockets (see illustration). Install new bolts and tighten the camshaft sprockets to the torque listed in this Chapter's Specifications (see Section 8).

30   Remove the camshaft locking tool from the cylinder head. Then install the front and rear camshaft caps and tighten them to the torque listed in this Chapter's Specifications. Note that the rear cap on the intake camshaft is equipped with larger bolts and requires a different torque.

31   Install the upper timing chain guide (see Section 8). Rotate the engine by hand two revolutions - if you feel any resistance, stop and find out why.

32   The remainder of installation is the reverse of removal.

33   Reconnect the battery (see Chapter 5, Section 1).

12   Cylinder head - removal and installation

Caution: *The engine must be completely cool when the head is removed. Failure to allow the engine to cool off could result in head warpage.*

Removal

1   Disconnect the cable from the negative battery terminal (see Chapter 5, Section 1).

2   Wait until the engine is completely cool, then drain the cooling system (see Chapter 1).

3   Remove the drivebelt (see Chapter 1) and the drivebelt tensioner.

4   Remove the exhaust manifold (see Section 6).

5   Remove the intake manifold (see Section 5).

6   Remove the timing chain (see Section 8).

7   Label and disconnect the electrical connectors from the cylinder head that will interfere with removal. Use tape and mark each connector to insure correct reassembly.

8   Remove the cylinder head bolts and discard them, following the reverse of the tightening sequence (see illustration 12.16). Loosen the bolts in sequence 1/4-turn at a time. If the head is to be completely overhauled, refer to Section 11 for removal of the camshafts, rocker arms and hydraulic lash adjusters.

9   Use a prybar at the corners of the head-to-block mating surface to break the gasket seal. Do not pry between the cylinder head and engine block in the gasket sealing area.

10   Lift the cylinder head off the engine. If resistance is felt, place a wood block against the end and strike the wood block with a hammer. Store the cylinder head on wood blocks to prevent damage to the gasket sealing surfaces.

11   Remove the old cylinder head gasket. Before removing, note the correct orientation of the gasket for correct installation.

Installation

Refer to illustration 12.16

12   The mating surfaces of the cylinder head and block must be perfectly clean when the heads are installed. Use a gasket scraper to remove all traces of carbon and old gasket material, then clean the mating surfaces with lacquer thinner or acetone. If there's oil on the mating surfaces when the cylinder heads are installed, the gaskets may not seal correctly and leaks may develop. When working on the engine block, cover the open areas of the engine with shop rags to keep debris out during repair and reassembly. Use a vacuum cleaner to remove any debris that falls into the cylinders.

13   Check the engine block and cylinder head mating surfaces for nicks, deep scratches and other damage.

14   Use a tap of the correct size to chase the threads in the cylinder head bolt holes. Dirt, corrosion, sealant and damaged threads will affect torque readings.

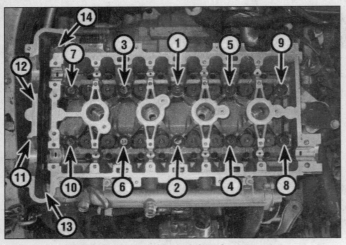

12.16 Cylinder head bolt tightening sequence

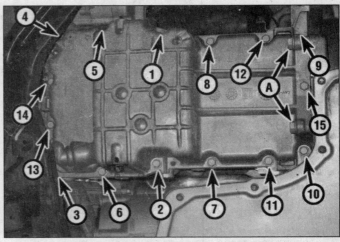

13.10 Oil pan bolt tightening sequence. Tighten the pan-to-transaxle bolts (A) until they're snug (but not too tight), then tighten the pan to block bolts in numerical order to the torque listed in this Chapter's Specifications, then tighten bolts (A) to the torque listed in this Chapter's Specifications

15   Make sure the new gasket is located on the dowels in the block.

16   Carefully position the cylinder head on the engine block without disturbing the gasket. Install new cylinder head bolts and, following the recommended sequence **(see illustration)**, tighten the bolts to the torque listed in this Chapter's Specifications. All the main cylinder head bolts (numbers 1 through 10) are tightened in the first Step and second Step. The four smaller bolts located on the front of the cylinder head are the only ones tightened in the third Step. Mark a stripe on each of the main cylinder head bolts to help keep track of the bolts that have been tightened the additional 155-degrees. **Note:** *The method used for the head bolt tightening procedure is referred to as a "torque-angle" method. A special torque angle gauge (available at most auto parts stores) is available to attach to a breaker bar and socket for better accuracy during the tightening procedure.*

17   Install the timing chain (see Section 8).

18   Install the exhaust manifold (see Section 6).

19   Install the intake manifold (see Section 5).

20   The remaining installation steps are the reverse of removal.

21   Reconnect the battery (see Chapter 5, Section 1).

22   Change the engine oil and filter (Chapter 1), then start the engine and check carefully for oil and coolant leaks.

13   Oil pan - removal and installation

Removal

1   Support the engine from above with an engine support fixture (available at some auto parts stores and most equipment rental yards).

2   Loosen the right-front wheel lug nuts, raise the front of the vehicle and support it securely on jackstands. Remove the right front wheel. Drain the engine oil (see Chapter 1).

3   Remove the splash shield from below the right side of the engine compartment **(see illustration 10.4)**.

4   Remove the lower air conditioning compressor mounting bolt (see Chapter 3). Loosen, but don't remove, the other compressor mounting bolts. Remove the engine mount strut and bracket.

5   Remove the dipstick and the dipstick tube (the tube is bolted to the intake manifold).

6   Remove the oil pan bolts. Follow the reverse of the tightening sequence **(see illustration 13.10)**.

7   Carefully remove the oil pan from the lower crankcase. **Caution:** *If the oil pan is difficult to separate from the lower crankcase, use a rubber mallet or a block of wood and a hammer to jar it loose. If it's stubborn and still won't come off, pry carefully on casting protrusions (not the mating surfaces!).*

Installation

Refer to illustration 13.10

8   Using a gasket scraper, thoroughly clean all old gasket material from the lower crankcase and oil pan. Remove residue and oil film with a solvent such as acetone or lacquer thinner.

9   Apply a 2 mm bead of RTV sealant to the perimeter of the oil pan, inboard of the bolt holes, and around the oil suction port. Allow the sealant to set-up before installing the oil pan to the engine (but be sure to install the pan in the time given by the sealant manufacturer).

10   Install the oil pan and bolts **(see illustration)**. Follow the correct torque sequence and tighten the bolts to the torque listed in this Chapter's Specifications.

11   The remaining installation is the reverse of removal. Be sure to tighten the wheel lug nuts to the torque listed in the Chapter 1 Specifications.

14   Oil pump - removal, inspection and installation

Removal

Refer to illustrations 14.5a and 14.5b

1   Drain the engine oil (see Chapter 1).

2   Remove the drivebelt (see Chapter 1).

3   Loosen the right-front wheel lug nuts, raise the front of the vehicle and support it securely on jackstands. Remove the right front wheel.

4   Remove the engine front cover (see Section 7).

5   Working on the backside of the engine cover, loosen the oil pump cover screws a little at a time until they're all loose **(see illustrations)**. When all of the screws are loose, remove the cover.

Inspection

Refer to illustrations 14.8a, 14.8b, 14.8c and 14.10

6   Note any identification marks on the rotors and withdraw the rotors from the pump body. If no marks can be seen, use a permanent marker and make your own to ensure that they will be installed correctly.

7   Thoroughly clean and dry the components.

8   Inspect the rotors for obvious wear or damage. If either rotor, the pump body or the cover is scored or damaged, the complete oil pump assembly must be replaced. Also check the inner-to-outer rotor tip clearance, the outer rotor-to-housing clearance, and the rotor-to-cover side clearance **(see illustrations)**.

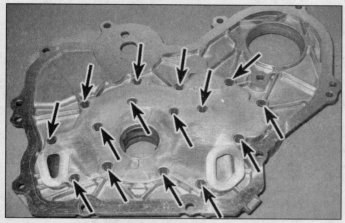

14.5a Location of the oil pump cover mounting screws

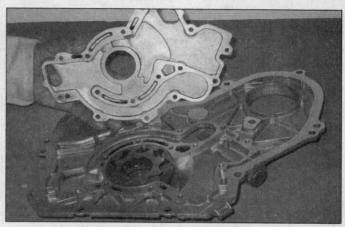

14.5b Lift the oil pump cover from the oil pump assembly

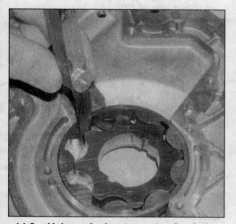

14.8a Using a feeler gauge to check the inner-to-outer rotor tip clearance . . .

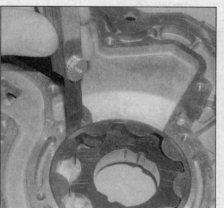

14.8b . . . and the outer rotor-to-housing clearance

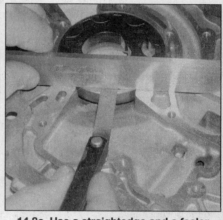

14.8c Use a straightedge and a feeler gauge to check the rotor-to-cover clearance

9   If the oil pump components are in acceptable condition, dip the rotors in clean engine oil and install them into the pump body with any identification marks positioned as noted during disassembly.

10   Remove the oil pressure relief valve components from the oil pump body. Thoroughly clean and dry the components. Inspect the components for obvious wear or damage. Install them in the correct order **(see illustration)**.

Installation

11   Install the rotors into the housing with the hub of the inner rotor facing the engine front cover. The inner rotor hub must be installed correctly or the engine front cover will not fasten properly.

12   Install the oil pump cover and screws and tighten by hand until snug. Then tighten the screws gradually and evenly to the torque listed in this Chapter's Specifications.

13   Install the engine front cover (see Section 7).

14   Refer to Chapter 1 and fill the engine with fresh engine oil. Install a new oil filter. Refill the cooling system.

15   Start the engine and check for leaks.

16   Run the engine and make sure oil pressure comes up to normal quickly. If it doesn't, stop the engine and find out the cause. Severe engine damage can result from running an engine with insufficient oil pressure!

15   Flywheel/driveplate - removal and installation

Removal

1   Raise the vehicle and support it securely on jackstands, then refer to Chapter 7 and remove the transaxle. If it's leaking, now would be a very good time to replace the front pump seal/O-ring (automatic transaxle only).

2   If you're working on a manual transaxle equipped vehicles, remove the pressure plate and clutch disc (see Chapter 8). Now is a good time to check/replace the clutch components.

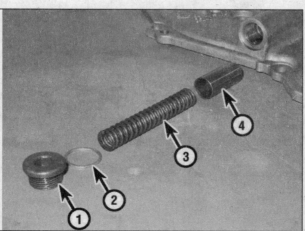

14.10 Oil pressure relief valve component details

1 *Oil pressure relief valve plug*
2 *Washer*
3 *Spring*
4 *Piston*

17.9a Location of the passenger side engine mount upper mounting bolts

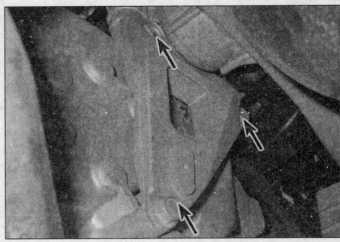

17.9b Location of the transaxle mount bracket, as seen from below - the transaxle mount can be accessed from above the transaxle

3   Use a center punch or paint to make alignment marks on the flywheel/driveplate and crankshaft to ensure correct alignment during reinstallation.

4   Remove the bolts that secure the flywheel/driveplate to the crankshaft. If the crankshaft turns, wedge a screwdriver in the ring gear teeth to jam the flywheel.

5   Remove the flywheel/driveplate from the crankshaft. Since the flywheel is fairly heavy, be sure to support it while removing the last bolt. Automatic transmission equipped vehicles have a spacer between the crankshaft and the driveplate.

Installation

6   Clean the flywheel to remove grease and oil. Inspect the surface for cracks, rivet grooves, burned areas and score marks. Light scoring can be removed with emery cloth. Check for cracked and broken ring gear teeth. Lay the flywheel on a flat surface and use a straightedge to check for warpage.

7   Clean and inspect the mating surfaces of the flywheel/driveplate and the crankshaft. If the crankshaft rear seal is leaking, replace it

before reinstalling the flywheel/driveplate (see Section 16).

8   Position the flywheel/driveplate against the crankshaft. Be sure to align the marks made during removal. Note that some engines have an alignment dowel or staggered bolt holes to ensure correct installation. Before installing the bolts, apply thread locking compound to the threads.

9   Wedge a screwdriver in the ring gear teeth to keep the flywheel/driveplate from turning and tighten the bolts to the torque listed in this Chapter's Specifications. Work up to the final torque in three or four steps.

10   The remainder of installation is the reverse of the removal procedure.

16   Rear main oil seal - replacement

1   The one-piece rear main oil seal is pressed into engine block and the crankcase reinforcement section. Remove the transaxle (see Chapter 7), the clutch components, if equipped (see Chapter 8) and the flywheel (see Section 15).

2   Pry out the old seal with a special seal removal tool or a flat-blade screwdriver. **Caution:** *To prevent an oil leak after the new seal is installed, be very careful not to scratch or otherwise damage the crankshaft sealing surface or the bore in the engine block.*

3   Clean the crankshaft and seal bore in the block thoroughly and de-grease these areas by wiping them with a rag soaked in lacquer thinner or acetone. Lubricate the lip of the new seal and the outer diameter of the crankshaft with engine oil.

4   Position the new seal onto the crankshaft. Make sure the edges of the new oil seal are not rolled over. **Note:** *When installing the new seal, if so marked, the words THIS SIDE OUT on the seal must face out, toward the rear of the engine.* Use a special rear main oil seal installation tool or a socket with the exact diameter of the seal to drive the seal in place. Make sure the seal is not off-set; it must be flush along the entire circumference of the engine block and the crankcase reinforcement section.

5   The remainder of installation is the reverse of removal.

17   Powertrain mounts - check and replacement

Check

1   Engine mounts seldom require attention, but broken or deteriorated mounts should be replaced immediately or the added strain placed on the driveline components may cause damage or wear.

2   During the check, the engine must be raised slightly to remove the weight from the mounts.

3   Raise the vehicle and support it securely on jackstands, then position a jack under the engine oil pan. Place a large block of wood between the jack head and the oil pan, then carefully raise the engine just enough to take

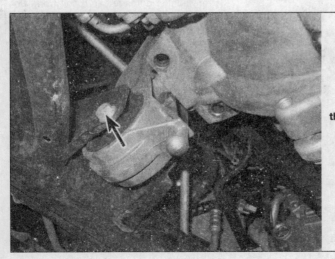

17.9c Location of the through-bolt on the front engine mount

17.9d Location of the rear engine mount through-bolt

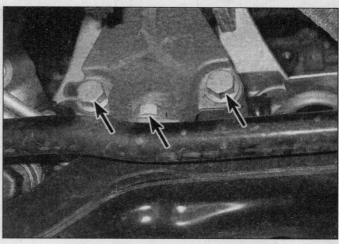

17.9e The rear engine mount bracket can be accessed from below

the weight off the mounts. **Warning:** *DO NOT place any part of your body under the engine when it's supported only by a jack!*

4   Check the mounts to see if the rubber is cracked, hardened or separated from the bushing in the center of the mount.

5   Check for relative movement between the mount and the engine or frame (use a large screwdriver or prybar to attempt to move the mounts). If movement is noted, lower the engine and tighten the mount fasteners.

Replacement

Refer to illustration 17.9a, 17.9b, 17.9c, 17.9d and 17.9e

6   Disconnect the negative battery cable from the battery (see Chapter 5, Section 1).

7   Raise the vehicle and support it securely on jackstands.

8   Place a large block of wood between the jack head and the oil pan, then carefully raise the engine just enough to take the weight off the mounts. **Caution:** *Do not disconnect more than one mount at a time*

unless the engine will be removed from the vehicle.

9   Remove the engine mount through-bolt/nuts and detach the mount from the chassis bracket **(see illustrations)**.

10   Remove the nuts holding the mount to the engine bracket.

11   Installation is the reverse of removal. Use thread-locking compound on the mount bolts and be sure to tighten them securely.

12   Reconnect the battery (see Chapter 5, Section 1).

Notes

Chapter 2 Part D
General engine overhaul procedures

Contents

Specifications

General

Displacement
2.2L OHV engine	134 cubic inches
2.3L OHC engine	138 cubic inches
2.4L OHC engine	146 cubic inches
2.2L OHC engine	134 cubic inches

Bore and Stroke
2.2L OHV engine	3.5 x 3.46 inches
2.3L OHC engine	3.62 x 3.35 inches
2.4L OHC engine	3.54 x 3.70 inches
2.2L OHC engine	3.44 x 3.73 inches
Cylinder compression	Lowest cylinder must be within 75 percent of highest cylinder

Oil pressure (engine at operating temperature)
2.2L OHV engine	56 psi at 3000 rpm
2.2L OHC engine	50 to 80 psi at 1,000 rpm
2.3L OHC engine	
At 900 rpm	15 psi
At 2000 rpm	30 psi
2.4L OHC engine	
At 900 rpm	10 psi
At 3000 rpm	30 psi

Torque specifications   **Ft-lbs** (unless otherwise indicated)

2.2L OHV engine
Connecting rod cap nuts	38
Main bearing cap bolts	70

2.2L OHC engine
Connecting rod cap bolts*	
Step 1	18
Step 2	Tighten an additional 100 degrees
Lower crankcase bolts* **(see illustration 10.19)**	
Step 1	15
Step 2	Tighten an additional 20 degrees
Lower crankcase perimeter bolts **(see illustration 10.30)**	18

Torque specifications (continued)

2.3L OHC and 2.4L OHC engines

Ft-lbs (unless otherwise indicated)

Connecting rod cap nuts
    Step 1 18
    Step 2 .... Tighten an additional 80 degrees
Main bearing cap bolts
    Step 1 15
    Step 2 .... Tighten an additional 90 degrees

* Bolt(s) must be replaced.

---

1   General information - engine overhaul

Refer to illustrations 1.1, 1.2, 1.3, 1.4, 1.5 and 1.6

Included in this portion of Chapter 2 are general information and diagnostic testing procedures for determining the overall mechanical condition of your engine.

The information ranges from advice concerning preparation for an overhaul and the purchase of replacement parts and/or components to detailed, step-by-step procedures covering removal and installation.

The following Sections have been written to help you determine whether your engine needs to be overhauled and how to remove and install it once you've determined it needs to be rebuilt. For information concerning in-vehicle engine repair, see Chapter 2A, 2B or 2C

The Specifications included in this Part are general in nature and include only those necessary for testing the oil pressure and checking the engine compression. Refer to Chapter 2A, 2B or 2C for additional engine Specifications.

It's not always easy to determine when, or if, an engine should be completely overhauled, because a number of factors must be considered.

High mileage is not necessarily an indication that an overhaul is needed, while low mileage doesn't preclude the need for an overhaul. Frequency of servicing is probably the most important consideration. An engine that's had regular and frequent oil and filter changes, as well as other required maintenance, will most likely give many thousands of miles of reliable service. Conversely, a neglected engine may require an overhaul very early in its service life.

Excessive oil consumption is an indication that piston rings, valve seals and/or valve guides are in need of attention. Make sure that oil leaks aren't responsible before deciding that the rings and/or guides are bad. Perform a cylinder compression check to determine the extent of the work required (see Section 3). Also check the vacuum readings under various conditions (see Section 4).

Check the oil pressure with a gauge installed in place of the oil pressure sending unit and compare it to this Chapter's Specifications (see Section 2). If it's extremely low, the bearings and/or oil pump are probably worn out.

Loss of power, rough running, knocking or metallic engine noises, excessive valve train noise and high fuel consumption rates may also point to the need for an overhaul, especially if they're all present at the same time. If a complete tune-up doesn't remedy the situation, major mechanical work is the only solution.

An engine overhaul involves restoring the internal parts to the specifications of a new engine. During an overhaul, the piston rings are replaced and the cylinder walls are reconditioned (rebored and/or honed) **(see illustrations 1.1 and 1.2)**. If a rebore is done by an automotive machine shop, new over-

1.1 An engine block being bored. An engine rebuilder will use special machinery to recondition the cylinder bores

1.2 If the cylinders are bored, the machine shop will normally hone the engine on a machine like this

1.3 A crankshaft having a main bearing journal ground

1.4 A machinist checks for a bent connecting rod, using specialized equipment

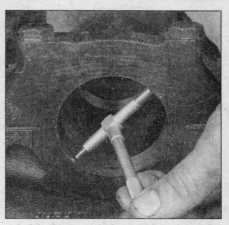

1.5 A bore gauge being used to check the main bearing bore

size pistons will also be installed. The main bearings, connecting rod bearings and camshaft bearings are generally replaced with new ones and, if necessary, the crankshaft may be reground to restore the journals **(see illustration 1.3)**. Generally, the valves are serviced as well, since they're usually in less-than-perfect condition at this point. While the engine is being overhauled, other components, such as the distributor, starter and alternator, can be rebuilt as well. The end result should be similar to a new engine that will give many trouble free miles. **Caution:** *Critical cooling system components such as the hoses, drivebelts, thermostat and water pump should be replaced with new parts when an engine is overhauled. The radiator should be checked carefully to ensure that it isn't clogged or leaking (see Chapter 3). If you purchase a rebuilt engine or short block, some rebuilders will not warranty their engines unless the radiator has been professionally flushed. Also, we don't recommend overhauling the oil pump - always install a new one when an engine is rebuilt.*

Overhauling the internal components on today's engines is a difficult and time-consuming task which requires a significant amount of specialty tools and is best left to a professional engine rebuilder **(see illustrations 1.4, 1.5 and 1.6)**. A competent engine rebuilder will handle the inspection of your old parts and offer advice concerning the reconditioning or replacement of the original engine; never purchase parts or have machine work done on other components until the block has been thoroughly inspected by a professional machine shop. As a general rule, time is the primary cost of an overhaul, especially since the vehicle may be tied up for a minimum of two weeks or more. Be aware that some engine builders only have the capability to rebuild the engine you bring them while other rebuilders have a large inventory of rebuilt exchange engines in stock. Also be aware that many machine shops could take as much as two weeks time to completely rebuild your engine depending on shop workload. Sometimes it makes more sense to simply exchange your engine for another engine that's already rebuilt to save time.

2 Oil pressure check

Refer to illustrations 2.2a, 2.2b, 2.2c, 2.2d and 2.3

1   Low engine oil pressure can be a sign of an engine in need of rebuilding. A "low oil pressure" indicator (often called an "idiot light") is not a test of the oiling system. Such indicators only come on when the oil pressure is dangerously low. Even a factory oil pressure gauge in the instrument panel is only a relative indication, although much better for driver information than a warning light. A better test is with a mechanical (not electrical) oil pressure gauge.

2   Locate the oil pressure sending unit on the engine block:

a) On the 2.2L OHV engine, the oil pressure sending unit is located on the rear (firewall) side of the engine block, near the oil filter **(see illustration)**.

b) On the 2.2L OHC engine, the oil pressure sending unit is located on the front left side of the engine block near the oil filter assembly **(see illustration)**.

1.6 Uneven piston wear like this indicates a bent connecting rod

2.2a On 2.2L OHV engines, the oil pressure sending unit is located on the front left side of the engine block near the oil filter

2.2b On 2.2L OHC engines, the oil pressure sending unit is located on the front side of the engine block, right below the oil filter housing

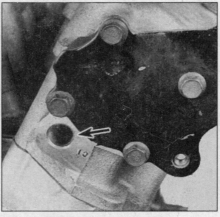

2.2c On 2.3L and 2.4L OHC engines, the oil pressure sending unit is located at the left end and on the backside of the intake cam box

2.2d On 2.3L and 2.4L OHC engines, there is also an oil galley plug in the left end of the exhaust cam box. If the oil pressure sending unit is too difficult to access, unscrew the plug and connect the hose for your oil pressure gauge here instead (the plug has already been unscrewed in this photo)

2.3 Remove the oil pressure sending unit and install an oil pressure gauge

3.6 Use a compression gauge with a threaded fitting for the spark plug hole, not the type that requires hand pressure to maintain the seal (2.2L OHC engine shown)

c) *On 2.3L and 2.4L OHC engines, the oil pressure sending unit is located at the left end and on the backside of the intake camshaft box* **(see illustration)**. *These engines also have an oil galley in the exhaust cam box that you can access by unscrewing a plug* **(see illustration)**.

3   Unscrew and remove the oil pressure sending unit and screw in the hose for your oil pressure gauge **(see illustration)**. If necessary, install an adapter fitting. Use Teflon tape or thread sealant on the threads of the adapter and/or the fitting on the end of your gauge's hose.

4   Connect an accurate tachometer to the engine, according to the tachometer manufacturer's instructions.

5   Check the oil pressure with the engine running (normal operating temperature) at the specified engine speed, and compare it to this Chapter's Specifications. If it's extremely low, the bearings and/or oil pump are probably worn out.

3   Cylinder compression check

Refer to illustration 3.6

1   A compression check will tell you what mechanical condition the upper end of your engine (pistons, rings, valves, head gaskets) is in. Specifically, it can tell you if the compression is down due to leakage caused by worn piston rings, defective valves and seats or a blown head gasket. **Note:** *The engine must be at normal operating temperature and the battery must be fully charged for this check.*

2   Begin by cleaning the area around the spark plugs before you remove them (compressed air should be used, if available). The idea is to prevent dirt from getting into the cylinders as the compression check is being done.

3   Remove all of the spark plugs from the engine (see Chapter 1).

4   Block the throttle wide open.

5   If you're working on a 2.2L OHV engine, disable the ignition system by unplugging the electrical connector(s) from the coil pack(s) (see Chapter 5) (on other engines the ignition system will already have been disabled because the coil assembly will already have been removed, to get the spark plugs out). Also disable the fuel system by unplugging the electrical connector in the harness to the fuel injectors (see Chapter 4) or by removing the fuel pump relay.

6   Install a compression gauge in the spark plug hole **(see illustration)**.

7   Crank the engine over at least seven compression strokes and watch the gauge. The compression should build up quickly in a healthy engine. Low compression on the first stroke, followed by gradually increasing pressure on successive strokes, indicates worn piston rings. A low compression reading on the first stroke, which doesn't build up during successive strokes, indicates leaking valves or a blown head gasket (a cracked head could also be the cause). Deposits on the undersides of the valve heads can also cause low compression. Record the highest gauge reading obtained.

8   Repeat the procedure for the remaining cylinders and compare the results to this Chapter's Specifications.

9   Add some engine oil (about three squirts from a plunger-type oil can) to each cylinder, through the spark plug hole, and repeat the test.

10   If the compression increases after the oil is added, the piston rings are definitely worn. If the compression doesn't increase significantly, the leakage is occurring at the valves or head gasket. Leakage past the valves may be caused by burned valve seats and/or faces or warped, cracked or bent valves.

11   If two adjacent cylinders have equally low compression, there's a strong possibility that the head gasket between them is blown.

The appearance of coolant in the combustion chambers or the crankcase would verify this condition.

12   If one cylinder is slightly lower than the others are, and the engine has a slightly rough idle, a worn lobe on the camshaft could be the cause.

13   If the compression is unusually high, the combustion chambers are probably coated with carbon deposits. If that's the case, the cylinder head(s) should be removed and decarbonized.

14   If compression is way down or varies greatly between cylinders, it would be a good idea to have a leak-down test performed by an automotive repair shop. This test will pinpoint exactly where the leakage is occurring and how severe it is.

4   Vacuum gauge diagnostic checks

Refer to illustrations 4.4 and 4.6

A vacuum gauge provides inexpensive but valuable information about what is going on in the engine. You can check for worn

4.4 A simple vacuum gauge can be handy in diagnosing engine condition and performance

Low, steady reading   Low, fluctuating needle   Regular drops

Irregular drops   Rapid vibration

Large fluctuation   Slow fluctuation

STD-O-OBR HAYNES

4.6 Typical vacuum gauge readings

rings or cylinder walls, leaking head or intake manifold gaskets, incorrect carburetor adjustments, restricted exhaust, stuck or burned valves, weak valve springs, improper ignition or valve timing and ignition problems.

Unfortunately, vacuum gauge readings are easy to misinterpret, so they should be used in conjunction with other tests to confirm the diagnosis.

Both the absolute readings and the rate of needle movement are important for accurate interpretation. Most gauges measure vacuum in inches of mercury (in-Hg). The following references to vacuum assume the diagnosis is being performed at sea level. As elevation increases (or atmospheric pressure decreases), the reading will decrease. For every 1,000 foot increase in elevation above approximately 2,000 feet, the gauge readings will decrease about one inch of mercury.

Connect the vacuum gauge directly to the intake manifold vacuum, not to ported (throttle body) vacuum **(see illustration)**. Be sure no hoses are left disconnected during the test or false readings will result.

Before you begin the test, allow the engine to warm up completely. Block the wheels and set the parking brake. With the transaxle in Park, start the engine and allow it to run at normal idle speed. **Warning:** *Keep your hands and the vacuum gauge clear of the fans.*

Read the vacuum gauge; an average, healthy engine should normally produce about 17 to 22 in-Hg with a fairly steady needle **(see illustration)**. Refer to the following vacuum gauge readings and what they indicate about the engine's condition:

1   A low steady reading usually indicates a leaking gasket between the intake manifold and cylinder head(s) or throttle body, a leaky vacuum hose, late ignition timing or incorrect camshaft timing. Check ignition timing with a timing light and eliminate all other possible causes, utilizing the tests provided in this Chapter before you remove the timing chain cover to check the timing marks.

2   If the reading is three to eight inches below normal and it fluctuates at that low reading, suspect an intake manifold gasket leak at an intake port or a faulty fuel injector.

3   If the needle has regular drops of about two-to-four inches at a steady rate, the valves are probably leaking. Perform a compression check or leak-down test to confirm this.

4   An irregular drop or down-flick of the needle can be caused by a sticking valve or an ignition misfire. Perform a compression check or leak-down test and read the spark plugs.

5   A rapid vibration of about four in-Hg vibration at idle combined with exhaust smoke indicates worn valve guides. Perform a leak-down test to confirm this. If the rapid vibration occurs with an increase in engine speed, check for a leaking intake manifold gasket or head gasket, weak valve springs, burned valves or ignition misfire.

6   A slight fluctuation, say one inch up and down, may mean ignition problems. Check all the usual tune-up items and, if necessary, run the engine on an ignition analyzer.

7   If there is a large fluctuation, perform a compression or leak-down test to look for a weak or dead cylinder or a blown head gasket.

8   If the needle moves slowly through a wide range, check for a clogged PCV system, incorrect idle fuel mixture, throttle body or

intake manifold gasket leaks.

9   Check for a slow return after revving the engine by quickly snapping the throttle open until the engine reaches about 2,500 rpm and let it shut. Normally the reading should drop to near zero, rise above normal idle reading (about 5 in-Hg over) and return to the previous idle reading. If the vacuum returns slowly and doesn't peak when the throttle is snapped shut, the rings may be worn. If there is a long delay, look for a restricted exhaust system (often the muffler or catalytic converter). An easy way to check this is to temporarily disconnect the exhaust ahead of the suspected part and redo the test.

5   Engine rebuilding alternatives

The do-it-yourselfer is faced with a number of options when purchasing a rebuilt engine. The major considerations are cost, warranty, parts availability and the time required for the rebuilder to complete the project. The decision to replace the engine block, piston/connecting rod assemblies and crankshaft depends on the final inspection results of your engine. Only then can you make a cost effective decision whether to have your engine overhauled or simply purchase an exchange engine for your vehicle.

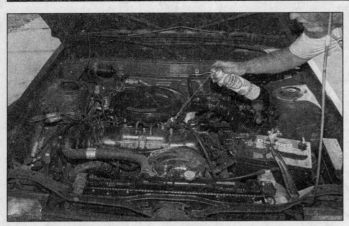

6.1 After tightly wrapping water-vulnerable components, use a spray cleaner on everything, with particular concentration on the greasiest areas, usually around the valve cover and lower edges of the block. If one section dries out, apply more cleaner

6.2 Depending on how dirty the engine is, let the cleaner soak in according to the directions and hose off the grime and cleaner. Get the rinse water down into every area you can get at; then dry important components with a hair dryer or paper towels

Some of the rebuilding alternatives include:

Individual parts - If the inspection procedures reveal that the engine block and most engine components are in reusable condition, purchasing individual parts and having a rebuilder rebuild your engine may be the most economical alternative. The block, crankshaft and piston/connecting rod assemblies should all be inspected carefully by a machine shop first.

Short block - A short block consists of an engine block with a crankshaft and piston/connecting rod assemblies already installed. All new bearings are incorporated and all clearances will be correct. The existing camshafts, valve train components, cylinder head and external parts can be bolted to the short block with little or no machine shop work necessary.

Long block - A long block consists of a short block plus an oil pump, oil pan, cylinder head, valve cover, camshaft and valve train

components, timing sprockets and chain or gears and timing cover. All components are installed with new bearings, seals and gaskets incorporated throughout. The installation of manifolds and external parts is all that's necessary.

Low mileage used engines - Some companies now offer low mileage used engines which is a very cost effective way to get your vehicle up and running again. These engines often come from vehicles that have been in totaled in accidents or come from other countries that have a higher vehicle turn over rate. A low mileage used engine also usually has a similar warranty like the newly remanufactured engines.

Give careful thought to which alternative is best for you and discuss the situation with local automotive machine shops, auto parts dealers and experienced rebuilders before ordering or purchasing replacement parts.

6   Engine removal - methods and precautions

Refer to illustrations 6.1, 6.2, 6.3 and 6.4

If you've decided that an engine must be removed for overhaul or major repair work, several preliminary steps should be taken. Read all removal and installation procedures carefully prior to committing to this job.

Locating a suitable place to work is extremely important. Adequate work space, along with storage space for the vehicle, will be needed. If a shop or garage isn't available, at the very least a flat, level, clean work surface made of concrete or asphalt is required.

Cleaning the engine compartment and engine before beginning the removal procedure will help keep tools clean and organized **(see illustrations 6.1 and 6.2)**.

An engine hoist will also be necessary. Make sure the hoist is rated in excess of the combined weight of the engine and transaxle. Safety is of primary importance, considering the potential hazards involved in removing the engine from the vehicle.

A vehicle hoist will be necessary for engine removal on four-cylinder engines with a manual transaxle, since on these models the engine/transaxle and subframe assembly must be lowered from the engine compartment, then the vehicle is raised and the powertrain unit is removed from under the vehicle. If the necessary equipment is not available, the engine will have to be removed by a qualified automotive repair facility.

If you're a novice at engine removal, get at least one helper. One person cannot easily do all the things you need to do to remove a big heavy engine and transaxle assembly from the engine compartment. Also helpful is to seek advice and assistance from someone who's experienced in engine removal.

6.3 Get an engine stand sturdy enough to firmly support the engine while you're working on it. Stay away from three-wheeled models: they have a tendency to tip over more easily, so get a four-wheeled unit

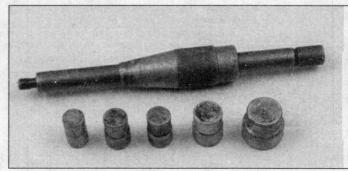

6.4 A clutch alignment tool will be necessary if you're working on a model with a manual transaxle

Plan the operation ahead of time. Arrange for or obtain all of the tools and equipment you'll need prior to beginning the job **(see illustrations 6.3 and 6.4)**. Some of the other equipment that you will need to safely and easily remove and install an engine:

Heavy-duty floor jack (ideally, with a transaxle jack-head adapter)
Complete set of wrenches and sockets
Wooden blocks (for placing between the floor jack and the vehicle, and between jackstands and the vehicle)
Plenty of rags
Cleaning solvent for mopping up spilled oil, coolant and gasoline.

Plan for the vehicle to be out of use for quite a while. A machine shop can do the work that is beyond the scope of the home mechanic. Machine shops often have a busy schedule, so before removing the engine, consult the shop for an estimate of how long it will take to rebuild or repair the components that may need work.

7 Engine - removal and installation

Refer to illustrations 7.6, 7.23a, 7.23b and 7.27

Warning 1: *Gasoline is extremely flammable, so take extra precautions when you work on any part of the fuel system. Don't smoke or allow open flames or bare light bulbs near the work area, and don't work in a garage where a gas-type appliance (such as a water heater or clothes dryer) is present. Since gasoline is carcinogenic, wear fuel-resistant gloves when there's a possibility of being exposed to fuel, and, if you spill any fuel on your skin, rinse it off immediately with soap and water. Mop up any spills immediately and do not store fuel-soaked rags where they could ignite. The fuel system is under constant pressure, so, if any fuel lines are to be disconnected, the fuel pressure in the system must be relieved first (see Chapter 4). When you perform any kind of work on the fuel system, wear safety glasses and have a Class B type fire extinguisher on hand.*
Warning 2: *The engine must be completely cool before beginning this procedure.*
Caution: *On some models there is a frontal impact sensor for the airbag system that is located near the hood latch on the radiator crossmember. The airbag(s) could deploy if the frontal impact sensor is disturbed, so be extremely careful when working in this area. Even though you probably won't be inside the vehicle while removing the engine (and therefore would not be injured by an accidental airbag deployment) an airbag is expensive and cannot be repacked. Once deployed it must be replaced. Refer to Chapter 12 for information about the frontal impact sensor and disarming the airbag system.*
Note: *Before getting started, read through the following steps carefully and thoroughly familiarize yourself with the engine removal*

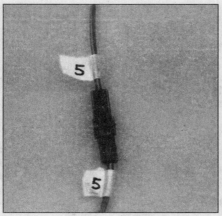

7.6 Label and number the wires on each side of each connection with masking tape before disconnecting it. Or use matching pieces of electrical tape, which is available in yellow, red, orange, green, blue, purple, etc.

procedure. Please be aware that this is a difficult procedure, which you should not attempt without the right tools and plenty of help. Because the following engine removal procedure is geared toward the home mechanic, it differs somewhat from the officially sanctioned General Motors procedure, which requires the availability of a vehicle hoist and a special engine fixture, both of which are expensive items for the weekend mechanic.
1 Relieve the fuel system pressure (see Chapter 4).
2 Disconnect the cable from the negative battery terminal. **Caution:** *If the vehicle is equipped with a Delco Loc II or Theftlock audio system, make sure you have the correct activation code before disconnecting the battery.*
3 Cover the fenders and cowl and remove the hood (see Chapter 11). Special pads are available to protect the fenders, but an old bedspread or blanket will also work.
4 Remove the air cleaner assembly and the intake ducts (see Chapter 4).
5 Label the vacuum lines, emissions system hoses, wiring connectors, ground straps and fuel lines to ensure correct reinstallation, then detach them. The relay panel and bracket can be detached as an assembly. Pieces of masking tape with numbers or letters written on them work well for marking wires and hoses **(see illustration)**.
6 If there's any possibility of confusion, make a sketch of the engine compartment and clearly label the lines, hoses and wires. If you have a camera, take reference photos of critical connections and the correct routing for cables, hoses, vacuum lines, wiring harnesses, etc. (A *digital* camera is really handy for this purpose.)
7 Raise the vehicle and support it securely on jackstands.
8 Drain the engine oil and remove the filter (see Chapter 1).
9 Drain the cooling system (see Chapter 1).

7.23a Attach the chain for the engine hoist to the engine lifting bracket on the front of the cylinder head . . .

10 Label and detach all coolant hoses from the engine (see Chapter 3).
11 Remove the coolant reservoir, the engine cooling fan and shroud and the radiator (see Chapter 3).
12 Remove the accessory drivebelt (see Chapter 1). Remove the crankshaft pulley/balancer (see Chapter 2).
13 Disconnect the fuel hoses that connect the under-vehicle metal fuel lines to the fuel injection system (see Chapter 4). Plug or cap all open fittings/lines.
14 Disconnect the accelerator cable (see Chapter 4) and, if equipped, the cruise control cable (which is removed the same way as the accelerator cable).
15 On 1995 through 2001 models with a 3T40 (three-speed) automatic transaxle, disconnect the throttle valve (TV) cable (see Chapter 7B).
16 Unbolt the power steering pump (see Chapter 10) and set it aside. Do NOT disconnect the pressure line and return hose. Make sure that the pump remains in an upright position in the engine compartment. (If you can't find a nearby place to set the pump upright, hang it with a coat hanger or with some other suitable wire to prevent it from falling over.)
17 Unbolt the air conditioning compressor (see Chapter 3) and set it aside. Do NOT disconnect the hoses.
18 Remove the starter and the alternator (see Chapter 5).
19 Detach the brake master cylinder from the power brake booster (see Chapter 9) to allow clearance for the transaxle. Position the master cylinder as far to the side as possible (or remove the unit completely, if necessary).
20 Disconnect the exhaust system from the engine (see Chapter 4).
21 Disconnect all electrical harnesses, cables, etc. from the transaxle (see Chapter 7).
22 Disconnect the driveaxles from the transaxle (see Chapter 8).
23 Connect an engine hoist to the lifting brackets on the engine **(see illustrations)**.

7.23b . . . and attach the other chain (or the other end of the chain) to the engine lifting bracket on the rear of the head

7.27 Carefully lift the engine/transaxle assembly from the engine compartment. Have an assistant man the hoist so that you can guide the engine/transaxle assembly past any obstacles until it clears the engine compartment

24   Raise the engine assembly slightly to take the weight off the mounts. **Warning:** *Do NOT place any part of your body under the engine while it's supported only by a hoist or other lifting device.*

25   Remove the engine and transaxle mounts. Remove everything - including all rubber insulators *and* mounting brackets - from the engine, the transaxle *and* the vehicle. You're going to remove the engine and the transaxle as a single assembly, so leaving any mounting bracket on the engine, the transaxle or in the engine compartment will make removal difficult, or impossible. As you disassemble and remove each engine or transaxle mount, store all the parts for that mount in a large sturdy plastic bag to ensure that the parts for various mounting brackets aren't mixed up while the engine is out. If any of the mounts look similar, it's a good idea to label each bag of mounting bracket parts.

26   Recheck to be sure nothing is still connecting the engine to the vehicle (or transaxle, where applicable). Disconnect anything still remaining.

27   Slowly raise the engine and transaxle as an assembly out of the vehicle. Check carefully to make sure nothing is hanging up as the hoist is raised **(see illustration)**.

28   Once the engine/transaxle assembly is out of the vehicle, remove the transaxle-to-engine block bolts (see Chapter 7). Carefully separate the engine from the transaxle. If you're working on a vehicle with an automatic transaxle, make sure that the torque converter stays in place. Clamp a pair of locking pliers to the bellhousing to keep the converter from sliding out. If you're working on a vehicle with a manual transaxle, make sure that the input shaft is completely disengaged from the clutch hub before trying to separate the transaxle from the engine.

29   On engines with a manual transaxle, remove the clutch (see Chapter 8), then remove the flywheel (see Chapter 2). On engines with an automatic transaxle, remove

the driveplate (see Chapter 2).

30   Mount the engine on an engine stand.

Installation

31   Remove the contents of each plastic bag and inspect the condition of the engine and transaxle mounts. If any of the rubber insulators are cracked, torn or deteriorated, replace them. If any of the mounting bracket bolts are bent or stripped, replace them.

32   If you're working on a vehicle with a manual transaxle, now is the time to decide whether to install a new clutch. Inspect the condition of the pressure plate and the clutch components (see Chapter 8). After installing the pressure plate and clutch assembly, apply a dab of high-temperature grease to the input shaft on the transaxle.

33   If you're working on an automatic transaxle equipped vehicle, take great care when installing the torque converter (see Chapter 7B).

34   After everything in Step 32 or 33 is inspected and installed, then reattach the transaxle to the engine. **Caution:** *Do NOT use the transaxle-to-engine bolts to force the transaxle and engine together. If something's not correctly aligned, using the bolts to force the engine and transaxle together will cause expensive damage!*

35   Carefully lower the engine/transaxle assembly into the engine compartment, then install the engine and transaxle mounts. Make sure that all mounts are correctly aligned. Tighten all mounting bracket bolts and nuts securely.

36   The remainder of installation is the reverse of removal. Double-check to make sure that everything is correctly connected.

37   Install a new oil filter and refill the engine with oil and refill the cooling system (see Chapter 1). If you drained the transaxle while it was removed, be sure to refill it too (see Chapter 1). Check the level of the power steering fluid and refill as necessary. Refill the

brake master cylinder and bleed the brake system (see Chapter 9).

38   Start the engine and check for leaks while it warms up. When the engine if warmed up and you have verified that there are no leaks anywhere, verify that all accessories are operating correctly.

39   Install the hood (see Chapter 11).

40   Test drive the vehicle.

---

8   Engine overhaul - disassembly sequence

1   It's much easier to remove the external components if the engine is mounted on a portable engine stand. A stand can often be rented quite cheaply from an equipment rental yard. Before the engine is mounted on a stand, the flywheel/driveplate should be removed from the engine.

2   If a stand isn't available, it's possible to remove the external engine components with it blocked up on the floor. Be extra careful not to tip or drop the engine when working without a stand.

3   If you're going to obtain a rebuilt engine, all external components must come off first, to be transferred to the replacement engine. These components include:

Clutch and flywheel (models with manual transaxle)
Driveplate (models with automatic transaxle)
Ignition system components
Emissions-related components
Engine mounts and mount brackets
Engine rear cover (spacer plate between flywheel/driveplate and engine block)
Intake/exhaust manifolds
Fuel injection components
Oil filter
Ignition coil pack(s) and spark plugs
Thermostat and housing assembly
Water pump

9.1 Before you try to remove the pistons, use a ridge reamer to remove the raised material (ridge) from the top of the cylinders

9.3 Checking the connecting rod endplay (side clearance)

9.4 If the connecting rods and caps are not marked, use permanent ink to mark the caps to the rods by cylinder number (for example, this would be the No. 4 connecting rod)

Note: *When removing the external components from the engine, pay close attention to details that might be helpful or important during installation. Note the installed position of gaskets, seals, spacers, pins, brackets, washers, bolts and other small items.*

4   If you're going to obtain a "short block" (assembled engine block, crankshaft, pistons and connecting rods), you'll need to exchange your old short block as a "core." Remove the timing chain or belt, cylinder head, oil pan, oil pump pick-up tube, oil pump and water pump from your engine. See *Engine rebuilding alternatives* for additional information regarding the different possibilities to be considered.

9   Pistons and connecting rods - removal and installation

Removal

Refer to illustrations 9.1, 9.3 and 9.4

Note: *Prior to removing the piston/connecting rod assemblies, remove the cylinder head and oil pan (see Chapter 2).*

1   Use your fingernail to feel if a ridge has formed at the upper limit of ring travel (about 1/4-inch down from the top of each cylinder). If carbon deposits or cylinder wear have produced ridges, they must be completely removed with a special tool **(see illustration)**. Follow the manufacturer's instructions provided with the tool. Failure to remove the ridges before attempting to remove the piston/connecting rod assemblies may result in piston breakage.

2   After the cylinder ridges have been removed, turn the engine so the crankshaft is facing up.

3   Before the main bearing cap assembly and connecting rods are removed, check the connecting rod endplay with feeler gauges. Slide them between the first connecting rod and the crankshaft throw until the play is

removed **(see illustration)**. Repeat this procedure for each connecting rod. The endplay is equal to the thickness of the feeler gauge(s). Check with an automotive machine shop for the endplay service limit (a typical endplay limit should measure between 0.005 to 0.015 inch). If the play exceeds the service limit, new connecting rods will be required. If new rods (or a new crankshaft) are installed, the endplay may fall under the minimum allowable. If it does, the rods will have to be machined to restore it. If necessary, consult an automotive machine shop for advice.

4   Check the connecting rods and caps for identification marks. If they aren't plainly marked, use paint or marker to clearly identify each rod and cap (1, 2, 3, etc., depending on the cylinder they're associated with) **(see illustration)**.

5   Remove the connecting rod cap bolts from the number one connecting rod. **Note:** *New connecting rod cap bolts must be used when reassembling the engine, but save the old bolts - they'll be required for the bearing*

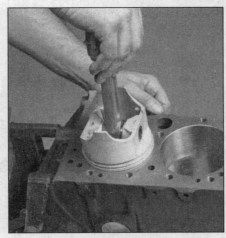

9.13 Install the piston ring into the cylinder then push it down into position using a piston so the ring will be square in the cylinder

oil clearance check during reassembly.

6   Remove the number one connecting rod cap and bearing insert. Don't drop the bearing insert out of the cap.

7   Remove the bearing insert and push the connecting rod/piston assembly out through the top of the engine. Use a wooden dowel to push on the connecting rod. If resistance is felt, double-check to make sure that all of the ridge was removed from the cylinder.

8   Repeat the procedure for the remaining cylinders.

9   After removal, reassemble the connecting rod caps and bearing inserts in their respective connecting rods and install the cap bolts finger tight. Leaving the old bearing inserts in place until reassembly will help prevent the connecting rod bearing surfaces from being accidentally nicked or gouged.

10   The pistons and connecting rods are now ready for inspection and overhaul at an automotive machine shop.

Piston ring installation

Refer to illustrations 9.13, 9.14, 9.15, 9.19a, 9.19b and 9.22

11   Before installing the new piston rings, the ring end gaps must be checked. It's assumed that the piston ring side clearance has been checked and verified correct.

12   Lay out the piston/connecting rod assemblies and the new ring sets so the ring sets will be matched with the same piston and cylinder during the end gap measurement and engine assembly.

13   Insert the top (number one) ring into the first cylinder and square it up with the cylinder walls by pushing it in with the top of the piston **(see illustration)**. The ring should be near the bottom of the cylinder, at the lower limit of ring travel.

14   To measure the end gap, slip feeler gauges between the ends of the ring until a gauge equal to the gap width is found **(see illustration)**. The feeler gauge should slide

ENGINE BEARING ANALYSIS

Debris

Babbitt bearing embedded with debris from machinings

Microscopic detail of debris

Microscopic detail of gouges

Overplated copper alloy bearing gouged by cast iron debris

Aluminum bearing embedded with glass beads

Microscopic detail of glass beads

Damaged lining caused by dirt left on the bearing back

Misassembly

Result of a lower half assembled as an upper - blocking the oil flow

Excessive oil clearance is indicated by a short contact arc

Polished and oil-stained backs are a result of a poor fit in the housing bore

Result of a wrong, reversed, or shifted cap

Overloading

Damage from excessive idling which resulted in an oil film unable to support the load imposed

Damaged upper connecting rod bearings caused by engine lugging; the lower main bearings (not shown) were similarly affected

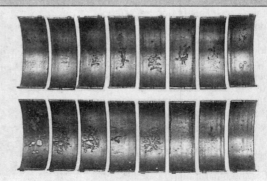

The damage shown in these upper and lower connecting rod bearings was caused by engine operation at a higher-than-rated speed under load

Misalignment

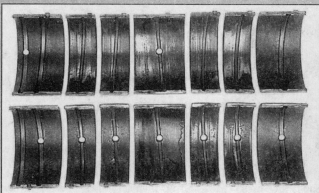

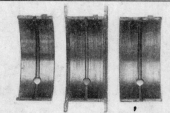

A poorly finished crankshaft caused the equally spaced scoring shown

A tapered housing bore caused the damage along one edge of this pair

A warped crankshaft caused this pattern of severe wear in the center, diminishing toward the ends

A bent connecting rod led to the damage in the "V" pattern

Lubrication

Result of dry start: The bearings on the left, farthest from the oil pump, show more damage

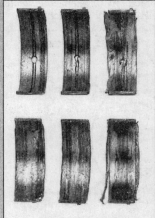

Result of a low oil supply or oil starvation

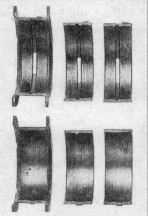

Severe wear as a result of inadequate oil clearance

Corrosion

Microscopic detail of corrosion

Corrosion is an acid attack on the bearing lining generally caused by inadequate maintenance, extremely hot or cold operation, or interior oils or fuels

Microscopic detail of cavitation

Example of cavitation - a surface erosion caused by pressure changes in the oil film

Damage from excessive thrust or insufficient axial clearance

Bearing affected by oil dilution caused by excessive blow-by or a rich mixture

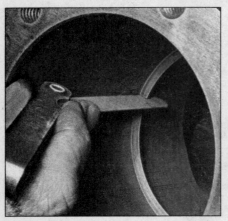

9.14 With the ring square in the cylinder, measure the ring end gap with a feeler gauge

9.15 If the ring end gap is too small, clamp a file in a vise as shown and file the piston ring ends - be sure to remove all raised material

9.19a Installing the spacer/expander in the oil ring groove

9.19b DO NOT use a piston ring installation tool when installing the oil control side rails

between the ring ends with a slight amount of drag. A typical ring gap should fall between 0.010 and 0.020 inch [0.25 to 0.50 mm] for compression rings and up to 0.030 inch [0.76 mm] for the oil ring steel rails. If the gap is larger or smaller than specified, double-check to make sure you have the correct rings before proceeding.

15   If the gap is too small, it must be enlarged or the ring ends may come in contact with each other during engine operation, which can cause serious damage to the engine. If necessary, increase the end gaps by filing the ring ends very carefully with a fine file. Mount the file in a vise equipped with soft jaws, slip the ring over the file with the ends contacting the file face and slowly move the ring to remove material from the ends. When performing this operation, file only by pushing the ring from the outside end of the file towards the vise **(see illustration)**.

16   Excess end gap isn't critical unless it's greater than 0.040 inch (1.01 mm). Again, double-check to make sure you have the correct ring type.

17   Repeat the procedure for each ring that will be installed in the first cylinder and for

each ring in the remaining cylinders. Remember to keep rings, pistons and cylinders matched up.

18   Once the ring end gaps have been checked/corrected, the rings can be installed on the pistons.

19   The oil control ring (lowest one on the piston) is usually installed first. It's composed of three separate components. Slip the spacer/expander into the groove **(see illustration)**. If an anti-rotation tang is used, make sure it's inserted into the drilled hole in the ring groove. Next, install the upper side rail in the same manner **(see illustration)**. Don't use a piston ring installation tool on the oil ring side rails, as they may be damaged. Instead, place one end of the side rail into the groove between the spacer/expander and the ring land, hold it firmly in place and slide a finger around the piston while pushing the rail into the groove. Finally, install the lower side rail.

20   After the three oil ring components have been installed, check to make sure that both the upper and lower side rails can be rotated smoothly inside the ring grooves.

21   The number two (middle) ring is installed

next. It's usually stamped with a mark, which must face up, toward the top of the piston. Do not mix up the top and middle rings, as they have different cross-sections. **Note:** *Always follow the instructions of the piston ring manufacturer. Different manufacturers might require different approaches.*

9.22 Use a piston ring installation tool to install the number 2 and the number 1 (top) rings - be sure the directional mark on the piston ring(s) is facing toward the top of the piston

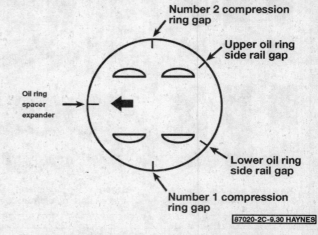

Number 2 compression ring gap

Upper oil ring side rail gap

Oil ring spacer expander

Lower oil ring side rail gap

Number 1 compression ring gap

87020-2C-9.30 HAYNES

9.30 Position the piston ring end gaps as shown

9.35 Use a plastic or wooden hammer handle to push the piston into the cylinder

9.37 Place Plastigage on each connecting rod bearing journal, parallel to the crankshaft centerline

9.41 Use the scale on the Plastigage package to determine the bearing oil clearance - be sure to measure the widest part of the Plastigage and use the correct scale; it comes with both standard and metric scales

22   Use a piston ring installation tool and make sure the identification mark is facing the top of the piston, then slip the ring into the middle groove on the piston **(see illustration)**. Don't expand the ring any more than necessary to slide it over the piston.
23   Install the number one (top) ring in the same manner. Make sure the mark is facing up. Be careful not to confuse the number one and number two rings.
24   Repeat the procedure for the remaining pistons and rings.

Installation

25   Before installing the piston/connecting rod assemblies, the cylinder walls must be perfectly clean, the top edge of each cylinder bore must be chamfered, and the crankshaft must be in place.
26   Remove the cap from the end of the number one connecting rod (refer to the marks made during removal). Remove the original bearing inserts and wipe the bearing surfaces of the connecting rod and cap with a clean, lint-free cloth. They must be kept spotlessly clean.

Connecting rod bearing oil clearance check

Refer to illustrations 9.30, 9.35, 9.37 and 9.41
27   Clean the back side of the new upper bearing insert, then lay it in place in the connecting rod.
28   Make sure the tab on the bearing fits into the recess in the rod. Don't hammer the bearing insert into place and be very careful not to nick or gouge the bearing face. Don't lubricate the bearing at this time.
29   Clean the back side of the other bearing insert and install it in the rod cap. Again, make sure the tab on the bearing fits into the recess in the cap, and don't apply any lubricant. It's critically important that the mating surfaces of the bearing and connecting rod are perfectly clean and oil free when they're assembled.
30   Position the piston ring gaps at the specified intervals around the piston as shown **(see illustration)**.

31   Lubricate the piston and rings with clean engine oil and attach a piston ring compressor to the piston. Leave the skirt protruding about 1/4-inch to guide the piston into the cylinder. The rings must be compressed until they're flush with the piston.
32   Rotate the crankshaft until the number one connecting rod journal is at BDC (bottom dead center) and apply a liberal coat of engine oil to the cylinder walls.
33   With the arrow on top of the piston facing the front (timing belt end or timing chain) of the engine, gently insert the piston/connecting rod assembly into the number one cylinder bore and rest the bottom edge of the ring compressor on the engine block. Install the pistons with the cavity mark(s) or arrow facing toward the timing belt or timing chain end of the engine.
34   Tap the top edge of the ring compressor to make sure it's contacting the block around its entire circumference.
35   Gently tap on the top of the piston with the end of a wooden or plastic hammer handle **(see illustration)** while guiding the end of the connecting rod into place on the crankshaft journal (a pair of wooden dowels would be helpful for this). The piston rings may try to pop out of the ring compressor just before entering the cylinder bore, so keep some downward pressure on the ring compressor. Work slowly, and if any resistance is felt as the piston enters the cylinder, stop immediately. Find out what's hanging up and fix it before proceeding. Do not, for any reason, force the piston into the cylinder - you might break a ring and/or the piston.
36   Once the piston/connecting rod assembly is installed, the connecting rod bearing oil clearance must be checked before the rod cap is permanently installed.
37   Cut a piece of the appropriate size Plastigage slightly shorter than the width of the connecting rod bearing and lay it in place on the number one connecting rod journal, parallel with the journal axis **(see illustration)**.
38   Clean the connecting rod cap bearing face and install the rod cap. Make sure the

mating mark on the cap is on the same side as the mark on the connecting rod **(see illustration 9.4)**.
39   Install the old rod bolts, at this time, and tighten them to the torque listed in this Chapter's Specifications. **Note:** *Use a thin-wall socket to avoid erroneous torque readings that can result if the socket is wedged between the rod cap and the bolt. If the socket tends to wedge itself between the fastener and the cap, lift up on it slightly until it no longer contacts the cap. DO NOT rotate the crankshaft at any time during this operation.*
40   Remove the fasteners and detach the rod cap, being very careful not to disturb the Plastigage. Discard the cap bolts at this time as they cannot be reused. **Note:** *You MUST use new connecting rod bolts.*
41   Compare the width of the crushed Plastigage, to the scale printed on the Plastigage envelope to obtain the oil clearance **(see illustration)**. The connecting rod oil clearance is usually about 0.001 to 0.002 inch. Consult an automotive machine shop for the clearance specified for the rod bearings on your engine.
42   If the clearance is not as specified, the bearing inserts may be the wrong size (which means different ones will be required). Before deciding that different inserts are needed, make sure that no dirt or oil was between the bearing inserts and the connecting rod or cap when the clearance was measured. Also, recheck the journal diameter. If the Plastigage was wider at one end than the other, the journal may be tapered. If the clearance still exceeds the limit specified, the bearing will have to be replaced with an undersize bearing. **Caution:** *When installing a new crankshaft always use a standard size bearing.*

Final installation

43   Carefully scrape all traces of the Plastigage material off the rod journal and/or bearing face. Be very careful not to scratch the

COMMON ENGINE OVERHAUL TERMS

B

Backlash - The amount of play between two parts. Usually refers to how much one gear can be moved back and forth without moving gear with which it's meshed.

Bearing Caps - The caps held in place by nuts or bolts which, in turn, hold the bearing surface. This space is for lubricating oil to enter.

Bearing clearance - The amount of space left between shaft and bearing surface. This space is for lubricating oil to enter.

Bearing crush - The additional height which is purposely manufactured into each bearing half to ensure complete contact of the bearing back with the housing bore when the engine is assembled.

Bearing knock - The noise created by movement of a part in a loose or worn bearing.

Blueprinting - Dismantling an engine and reassembling it to EXACT specifications.

Bore - An engine cylinder, or any cylindrical hole; also used to describe the process of enlarging or accurately refinishing a hole with a cutting tool, as to bore an engine cylinder. The bore size is the diameter of the hole.

Boring - Renewing the cylinders by cutting them out to a specified size. A boring bar is used to make the cut.

Bottom end - A term which refers collectively to the engine block, crankshaft, main bearings and the big ends of the connecting rods.

Break-in - The period of operation between installation of new or rebuilt parts and time in which parts are worn to the correct fit. Driving at reduced and varying speed for a specified mileage to permit parts to wear to the correct fit.

Bushing - A one-piece sleeve placed in a bore to serve as a bearing surface for shaft, piston pin, etc. Usually replaceable.

C

Camshaft - The shaft in the engine, on which a series of lobes are located for operating the valve mechanisms. The camshaft is driven by gears or sprockets and a timing chain. Usually referred to simply as the cam.

Carbon - Hard, or soft, black deposits found in combustion chamber, on plugs, under rings, on and under valve heads.

Cast iron - An alloy of iron and more than two percent carbon, used for engine blocks and heads because it's relatively inexpensive and easy to mold into complex shapes.

Chamfer - To bevel across (or a bevel on) the sharp edge of an object.

Chase - To repair damaged threads with a tap or die.

Combustion chamber - The space between the piston and the cylinder head, with the piston at top dead center, in which air-fuel mixture is burned.

Compression ratio - The relationship between cylinder volume (clearance volume) when the piston is at top dead center and cylinder volume when the piston is at bottom dead center.

Connecting rod - The rod that connects the crank on the crankshaft with the piston. Sometimes called a con rod.

Connecting rod cap - The part of the connecting rod assembly that attaches the rod to the crankpin.

Core plug - Soft metal plug used to plug the casting holes for the coolant passages in the block.

Crankcase - The lower part of the engine in which the crankshaft rotates; includes the lower section of the cylinder block and the oil pan.

Crank kit - A reground or reconditioned crankshaft and new main and connecting rod bearings.

Crankpin - The part of a crankshaft to which a connecting rod is attached.

Crankshaft - The main rotating member, or shaft, running the length of the crankcase, with offset throws to which the connecting rods are attached; changes the reciprocating motion of the pistons into rotating motion.

Cylinder sleeve - A replaceable sleeve, or liner, pressed into the cylinder block to form the cylinder bore.

D

Deburring - Removing the burrs (rough edges or areas) from a bearing.

Deglazer - A tool, rotated by an electric motor, used to remove glaze from cylinder walls so a new set of rings will seat.

E

Endplay - The amount of lengthwise movement between two parts. As applied to a crankshaft, the distance that the crankshaft can move forward and back in the cylinder block.

F

Face - A machinist's term that refers to removing metal from the end of a shaft or the face of a larger part, such as a flywheel.

Fatigue - A breakdown of material through a large number of loading and unloading cycles. The first signs are cracks followed shortly by breaks.

Feeler gauge - A thin strip of hardened steel, ground to an exact thickness, used to check clearances between parts.

Free height - The unloaded length or height of a spring.

Freeplay - The looseness in a linkage, or an assembly of parts, between the initial application of force and actual movement. Usually perceived as slop or slight delay.

Freeze plug - See Core plug.

G

Gallery - A large passage in the block that forms a reservoir for engine oil pressure.

Glaze - The very smooth, glassy finish that develops on cylinder walls while an engine is in service.

H

Heli-Coil - A rethreading device used when threads are worn or damaged. The device is installed in a retapped hole to reduce the thread size to the original size.

I

Installed height - The spring's measured length or height, as installed on the cylinder head. Installed height is measured from the spring seat to the underside of the spring retainer.

J

Journal - The surface of a rotating shaft which turns in a bearing.

K

Keeper - The split lock that holds the valve spring retainer in position on the valve stem.

Key - A small piece of metal inserted into matching grooves machined into two parts fitted together - such as a gear pressed onto a shaft - which prevents slippage between the two parts.

Knock - The heavy metallic engine sound, produced in the combustion chamber as a result of abnormal combustion - usually detonation. Knock is usually caused by a loose or worn bearing. Also referred to as detonation, pinging and spark knock. Connecting rod or main bearing knocks are created by too much oil clearance or insufficient lubrication.

L

Lands - The portions of metal between the piston ring grooves.

Lapping the valves - Grinding a valve face and its seat together with lapping compound.

Lash - The amount of free motion in a gear train, between gears, or in a mechanical assembly, that occurs before movement can begin. Usually refers to the lash in a valve train.

Lifter - The part that rides against the cam to transfer motion to the rest of the valve train.

M

Machining - The process of using a machine to remove metal from a metal part.

Main bearings - The plain, or babbit, bearings that support the crankshaft.

Main bearing caps - The cast iron caps, bolted to the bottom of the block, that support the main bearings.

O

O.D. - Outside diameter.

Oil gallery - A pipe or drilled passageway in the engine used to carry engine oil from one area to another.

Oil ring - The lower ring, or rings, of a piston; designed to prevent excessive amounts of oil from working up the cylinder walls and into the combustion chamber. Also called an oil-control ring.

Oil seal - A seal which keeps oil from leaking out of a compartment. Usually refers to a dynamic seal around a rotating shaft or other moving part.

O-ring - A type of sealing ring made of a special rubberlike material; in use, the O-ring is compressed into a groove to provide the sealing action.

Overhaul - To completely disassemble a unit, clean and inspect all parts, reassemble it with the original or new parts and make all adjustments necessary for proper operation.

P

Pilot bearing - A small bearing installed in the center of the flywheel (or the rear end of the crankshaft) to support the front end of the input shaft of the transmission.

Pip mark - A little dot or indentation which indicates the top side of a compression ring.

Piston - The cylindrical part, attached to the connecting rod, that moves up and down in the cylinder as the crankshaft rotates. When the fuel charge is fired, the piston transfers the force of the explosion to the connecting rod, then to the crankshaft.

Piston pin (or wrist pin) - The cylindrical and usually hollow steel pin that passes through the piston. The piston pin fastens the piston to the upper end of the connecting rod.

Piston ring - The split ring fitted to the groove in a piston. The ring contacts the sides of the ring groove and also rubs against the cylinder wall, thus sealing space between piston and wall. There are two types of rings: Compression rings seal the compression pressure in the combustion chamber; oil rings scrape excessive oil off the cylinder wall.

Piston ring groove - The slots or grooves cut in piston heads to hold piston rings in position.

Piston skirt - The portion of the piston below the rings and the piston pin hole.

Plastigage - A thin strip of plastic thread, available in different sizes, used for measuring clearances. For example, a strip of plastigage is laid across a bearing journal and mashed as parts are assembled. Then parts are disassembled and the width of the strip is measured to determine clearance between journal and bearing. Commonly used to measure crankshaft main-bearing and connecting rod bearing clearances.

Press-fit - A tight fit between two parts that requires pressure to force the parts together. Also referred to as drive, or force, fit.

Prussian blue - A blue pigment; in solution, useful in determining the area of contact between two surfaces. Prussian blue is commonly used to determine the width and location of the contact area between the valve face and the valve seat.

R

Race (bearing) - The inner or outer ring that provides a contact surface for balls or rollers in bearing.

Ream - To size, enlarge or smooth a hole by using a round cutting tool with fluted edges.

Ring job - The process of reconditioning the cylinders and installing new rings.

Runout - Wobble. The amount a shaft rotates out-of-true.

S

Saddle - The upper main bearing seat.

Scored - Scratched or grooved, as a cylinder wall may be scored by abrasive particles moved up and down by the piston rings.

Scuffing - A type of wear in which there's a transfer of material between parts moving against each other; shows up as pits or grooves in the mating surfaces.

Seat - The surface upon which another part rests or seats. For example, the valve seat is the matched surface upon which the valve face rests. Also used to refer to wearing into a good fit; for example, piston rings seat after a few miles of driving.

Short block - An engine block complete with crankshaft and piston and, usually, camshaft assemblies.

Static balance - The balance of an object while it's stationary.

Step - The wear on the lower portion of a ring land caused by excessive side and back-clearance. The height of the step indicates the ring's extra side clearance and the length of the step projecting from the back wall of the groove represents the ring's back clearance.

Stroke - The distance the piston moves when traveling from top dead center to bottom dead center, or from bottom dead center to top dead center.

Stud - A metal rod with threads on both ends.

T

Tang - A lip on the end of a plain bearing used to align the bearing during assembly.

Tap - To cut threads in a hole. Also refers to the fluted tool used to cut threads.

Taper - A gradual reduction in the width of a shaft or hole; in an engine cylinder, taper usually takes the form of uneven wear, more pronounced at the top than at the bottom.

Throws - The offset portions of the crankshaft to which the connecting rods are affixed.

Thrust bearing - The main bearing that has thrust faces to prevent excessive endplay, or forward and backward movement of the crankshaft.

Thrust washer - A bronze or hardened steel washer placed between two moving parts. The washer prevents longitudinal movement and provides a bearing surface for thrust surfaces of parts.

Tolerance - The amount of variation permitted from an exact size of measurement. Actual amount from smallest acceptable dimension to largest acceptable dimension.

U

Umbrella - An oil deflector placed near the valve tip to throw oil from the valve stem area.

Undercut - A machined groove below the normal surface.

Undersize bearings - Smaller diameter bearings used with re-ground crankshaft journals.

V

Valve grinding - Refacing a valve in a valve-refacing machine.

Valve train - The valve-operating mechanism of an engine; includes all components from the camshaft to the valve.

Vibration damper - A cylindrical weight attached to the front of the crankshaft to minimize torsional vibration (the twist-untwist actions of the crankshaft caused by the cylinder firing impulses). Also called a harmonic balancer.

W

Water jacket - The spaces around the cylinders, between the inner and outer shells of the cylinder block or head, through which coolant circulates.

Web - A supporting structure across a cavity.

Woodruff key - A key with a radiused backside (viewed from the side).

bearing - use your fingernail or the edge of a plastic card.

44   Make sure the bearing faces are perfectly clean, then apply a uniform layer of clean moly-base grease or engine assembly lube to both of them. You'll have to push the piston into the cylinder to expose the face of the bearing insert in the connecting rod.

45   Slide the connecting rod back into place on the journal, install the rod cap, install the new bolts and tighten them to the torque listed in this Chapter's Specifications. **Caution:** *Install new connecting rod cap bolts. Do NOT reuse old bolts - they have stretched and cannot be reused* (see Step 5).

46   Repeat the entire procedure for the remaining pistons/connecting rods.

47   The important points to remember are:

a) *Keep the back sides of the bearing inserts and the insides of the connecting rods and caps perfectly clean when assembling them.*

b) *Make sure you have the correct piston/rod assembly for each cylinder.*

c) *The arrow or mark on the piston must face toward the front (timing chain) end of the engine.*

d) *Lubricate the cylinder walls liberally with clean oil.*

e) *Lubricate the bearing faces when installing the rod caps after the oil clearance has been checked.*

48   After all the piston/connecting rod assemblies have been correctly installed, rotate the crankshaft a number of times by hand to check for any obvious binding.

49   As a final step, check the connecting rod endplay, as described in Step 3. If it was correct before disassembly and the original crankshaft and rods were reinstalled, it should still be correct. If new rods or a new crankshaft were installed, the endplay may be inadequate. If so, the rods will have to be removed and taken to an automotive machine shop for resizing.

10   Crankshaft - removal and installation

Removal

Refer to illustrations 10.1, 10.3, 10.4a and 10.4b

Note: *Before you can remove the crankshaft, you must remove the engine from the vehicle. Then remove the flywheel or driveplate, the crankshaft pulley, the timing belt or timing chain, the oil pan, the oil pump body, the oil filter and the piston/connecting rod assemblies. The rear main oil seal retainer must also be unbolted and separated from the block. Once all these components are removed, the crankshaft is ready for removal.*

1   Before the crankshaft is removed, measure the endplay. Mount a dial indicator with the indicator in line with the crankshaft and just touching the end of the crankshaft as shown **(see illustration)**.

10.1 Checking crankshaft endplay with a dial indicator

2   Pry the crankshaft all the way to the rear and zero the dial indicator. Next, pry the crankshaft to the front as far as possible and check the reading on the dial indicator. The distance traveled is the endplay. A typical crankshaft endplay will fall between 0.003 to 0.010 inch. If it is greater than that, check the crankshaft thrust surfaces for wear after it's removed. If no wear is evident, new main bearings should correct the endplay.

3   If a dial indicator isn't available, use feeler gauges instead. Gently pry the crankshaft all the way to the front of the engine. Slip feeler gauges between the crankshaft and the front face of the thrust bearing or washer to determine the clearance **(see illustration)**.

4   On 2.2L OHV engines, and on 2.3L and 2.4L OHC engines, check the main bearing caps to determine whether they're already marked to indicate their locations. They should be numbered consecutively from the front of the engine to the rear. If they aren't, mark their locations with number stamping dies or with a center punch **(see illustration)**. Number them consecutively, from the front of

10.4a To ensure that the main bearing caps are installed in the same position on the block, use a center punch (or number-stamping dies) to mark each main bearing cap (make the marks near the bolt heads)

10.3 Checking the crankshaft endplay with feeler gauges

the engine to the rear. Each main bearing cap should also have a directional arrow **(see illustration)**, which points toward the timing chain or timing belt end of the engine. Loosen each crankshaft main bearing cap bolt 1/4-turn at a time until all the bolts are unscrewed. Remove the bolts. Gently tap the caps with a soft-face mallet, then separate them from the engine block. Try not to drop the bearing inserts if they come off with the caps.

5   On 2.2L OHC engines, loosen the lower crankcase perimeter bolts and the lower crankcase bolts 1/4-turn at a time each, until they can be removed by hand. Follow the reverse of the tightening sequence **(see illustration 10.19)**. **Caution:** *The lower crankcase bolts must be replaced with new ones upon installation. Save the old bolts, however, as they will be used for the main bearing oil clearance check.* Remove the lower crankcase.

6   Carefully lift the crankshaft out of the engine. It may be a good idea to have an assistant available, since the crankshaft is quite heavy and awkward to handle. With the

10.4b The arrow on each main bearing cap points toward the front (timing chain or timing belt) end of the engine. Make sure that you install each cap with this arrow pointing the right way

10.17 Place the Plastigage onto the crankshaft bearing journal as shown

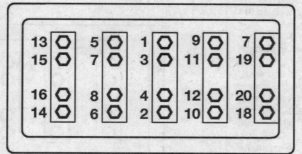

10.19 Lower crankcase bolt tightening sequence (2.2L OHC engine)

← Front

87020-2C-10.19a HAYNES

10.21 Use the scale on the Plastigage package to determine the bearing oil clearance - be sure to measure the widest part of the Plastigage and use the correct scale; it comes with both standard and metric scales

bearing inserts in place inside the engine block and main bearing caps and bridge or the lower crankcase, reinstall the caps and bridge or lower crankcase onto the engine block and tighten the bolts finger tight.

Installation

7   Crankshaft installation is the first step in engine reassembly. It's assumed at this point that the engine block and crankshaft have been cleaned, inspected and repaired or reconditioned.
8   Position the engine block with the bottom facing up.
9   Remove the mounting bolts and lift off the lower crankcase or bearing bridge and main bearing caps.
10   If they're still in place, remove the original bearing inserts from the block and from the main bearing caps or lower crankcase. Wipe the bearing surfaces of the block and bearing cap/lower crankcase saddle with a clean, lint-free cloth. They must be kept spotlessly clean. This is critical for determining the correct bearing oil clearance.

Main bearing oil clearance check

Refer to illustrations 10.17, 10.19 and 10.21
11   Without mixing them up, clean the back sides of the new upper main bearing inserts (with grooves and oil holes) and lay one in each main bearing saddle in the engine block. Each upper bearing (engine block) has an oil groove and oil hole in it. **Caution:** *The oil holes in the block must line up with the oil holes in the engine block inserts.* The thrust washer or thrust bearing insert must be installed in the correct location. **Note:** *The thrust bearing on the 2.2L OHC engine is located on the engine block number 2 journal.* Clean the back sides of the lower main bearing inserts and lay them in the corresponding location in the lower crankcase saddles (four-cylinder). Make sure the tab on the bearing insert fits into the recess in the block or main bearing caps. **Caution:** *Do not hammer the bearing insert into place and don't nick or*

gouge the bearing faces. *DO NOT apply any lubrication at this time.*
12   Clean the faces of the bearing inserts in the block and the crankshaft main bearing journals with a clean, lint-free cloth.
13   Check or clean the oil holes in the crankshaft, as any dirt here can go only one way - straight through the new bearings.
14   Once you're certain the crankshaft is clean, carefully lay it in position in the cylinder block.
15   Before the crankshaft can be permanently installed, the main bearing oil clearance must be checked.
16   Cut several strips of the appropriate size of Plastigage. They must be slightly shorter than the width of the main bearing journal.
17   Place one piece on each crankshaft main bearing journal, parallel with the journal axis as shown **(see illustration)**.
18   Clean the faces of the bearing inserts in the lower crankcase or main bearing caps. Hold the bearing inserts in place and install the lower crankcase or caps onto the crankshaft and cylinder block. DO NOT disturb the Plastigage.
19   Apply clean engine oil to all bolt threads prior to installation, install all the main bearing cap bolts finger-tight, then tighten them to the torque listed in this Chapter's Specifications. On 2.2L OHC engines, tighten the lower crankcase cap bolts in the sequence shown **(see illustration)** progressing in steps, to the torque listed in this Chapter's Specifications. DO NOT rotate the crankshaft at any time during this operation.
20   Remove the main bearing cap bolts. On 2.2L engines, remove them in the *reverse* order of the tightening sequence. Carefully lift the lower crankcase or main bearing caps straight up and off the block. Do not disturb the Plastigage or rotate the crankshaft. If the main bearing caps are difficult to remove, tap them gently from side-to-side with a soft-face hammer to loosen it.
21   Compare the width of the crushed Plastigage on each journal to the scale printed on the Plastigage envelope to determine the main bearing oil clearance **(see illustration)**. Check with an automotive machine shop for the oil clearance for your engine.
22   If the clearance is not as specified, the

bearing inserts might be the wrong size (which means different ones will be required). Before deciding if different inserts are needed, make sure that no dirt or oil was between the bearing inserts and the caps or block when the clearance was measured. If the Plastigage was wider at one end than the other, the crankshaft journal on which it was used might be tapered. If the clearance still exceeds the specified limit, the bearing insert(s) will have to be replaced with an undersize bearing insert(s). **Caution:** *When installing a new crankshaft always install a standard bearing insert set.*
23   Carefully scrape all traces of the Plastigage material off the main bearing journals and/or the bearing insert faces. Be sure to remove all residue from the oil holes. Use your fingernail or the edge of a plastic card - don't nick or scratch the bearing faces.

Final installation

Refer to illustration 10.30
24   Carefully lift the crankshaft out of the cylinder block.
25   Clean the bearing insert faces in the cylinder block, then apply a thin, uniform layer of moly-base grease or engine assem-

bly lube to each of the bearing surfaces. Be sure to coat the thrust faces as well as the journal face of the thrust bearing.

26   Make sure the crankshaft journals are clean, then lay the crankshaft back in place in the cylinder block.

27   Clean the bearing insert faces and apply the same lubricant to them. Clean the engine block and the mating surface of the lower crankcase or the bearing caps thoroughly. The surfaces must be free of oil residue. Install the lower crankcase.

28   Prior to installation, apply clean engine oil to all bolt threads, wiping off any excess, then install all bolts finger-tight. **Caution:** *Remember, new bolts must be used.*

29   Tighten the bolts to the torque listed in this Chapter's Specifications. On 2.2L OHC engines, be sure to follow the correct torque sequence **(see illustration 10.19).**

30   On 2.2L OHC engines, install the lower crankcase perimeter bolts and tighten them to the torque listed in this Chapter's Specifications **(see illustration).**

31   Recheck the crankshaft endplay with a feeler gauge or a dial indicator. The endplay should be correct if the crankshaft thrust faces aren't worn or damaged and if new bearings have been installed.

32   Rotate the crankshaft a number of times by hand to check for any obvious binding. It should rotate with a running torque of 50 in-lbs or less. If the running torque is too high, correct the problem at this time.

33   Install the new rear main oil seal (see Chapter 2).

11   Engine overhaul - reassembly sequence

1   Before beginning engine reassembly, make sure you have all the necessary new parts, gaskets and seals as well as the following items on hand:

Common hand tools
A 1/2-inch drive torque wrench
New engine oil
Gasket sealant
Thread locking compound

2   If you obtained a short block it will be necessary to install the cylinder head, the oil pump and pick-up tube, the oil pan, the water pump, the timing belt or chain and timing

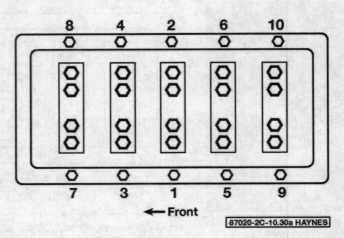

10.30 **Lower crankcase perimeter bolt tightening sequence (2.2L OHC engine)**

cover, and the valve cover (see Chapter 2). In order to save time and avoid problems, the external components must be installed in the following general order:

Thermostat and housing cover
Water pump
Intake and exhaust manifolds
Fuel injection components
Emission control components
Spark plug wires and spark plugs
Ignition coils or coil packs
Oil filter
Engine mounts and mount brackets
Clutch and flywheel (manual transaxle)
Driveplate (automatic transaxle)

12   Initial start-up and break-in after overhaul

Warning: *Have a fire extinguisher handy when starting the engine for the first time.*

1   Once the engine has been installed in the vehicle, double-check the engine oil and coolant levels.

2   With the spark plugs out of the engine and the ignition system and fuel pump disabled, crank the engine until oil pressure registers on the gauge or the light goes out.

3   Install the spark plugs, hook up the plug wires and restore the ignition system and fuel pump functions.

4   Start the engine. It may take a few moments for the fuel system to build up pressure, but the engine should start without a great deal of effort.

5   After the engine starts, it should be allowed to warm up to normal operating temperature. While the engine is warming up, make a thorough check for fuel, oil and coolant leaks.

6   Shut the engine off and recheck the engine oil and coolant levels.

7   Drive the vehicle to an area with minimum traffic, accelerate from 30 to 50 mph, then allow the vehicle to slow to 30 mph with the throttle closed. Repeat the procedure 10 or 12 times. This will load the piston rings and cause them to seat properly against the cylinder walls. Check again for oil and coolant leaks.

8   Drive the vehicle gently for the first 500 miles (no sustained high speeds) and keep a constant check on the oil level. It is not unusual for an engine to use oil during the break-in period.

9   At approximately 500 to 600 miles, change the oil and filter.

10   For the next few hundred miles, drive the vehicle normally. Do not pamper it or abuse it.

11   After 2,000 miles, change the oil and filter again and consider the engine broken in.

Chapter 3
Cooling, heating and air conditioning systems

Contents

Specifications

General

Coolant capacity	See Chapter 1
Coolant reservoir pressure cap rating	15 psi
Thermostat opening temperature	
2.2L OHV engine	195-degrees F
2.2L, 2.3L and 2.4L OHC engines	180-degrees F
Refrigerant type	R-134a
Refrigerant capacity	1.5 pounds
Refrigerant lubricant (PAG oil) capacity	
If only the accumulator is being replaced	1.5 ounces
If the compressor is also being replaced	2.5 ounces

Torque specifications

Ft-lbs (unless otherwise indicated)

Thermostat housing nuts/bolts
    2.2L OHV engine
        1995 .... 89 in-lbs
        1996 and later .... 124 in-lbs
    2.2L OHC engine .... 89 in-lbs
    2.3L and 2.4L OHC engines .... 124 in-lbs
Water pump bolts
    2.2L OHV engine
        Water pump mounting bolts 18
        Water pump pulley bolts 18
    2.2L OHC engine
        Water pump mounting bolts 18
        Water pump sprocket bolts .... 89 in-lbs
        Water pump access cover bolts .... 89 in-lbs
    2.3L and 2.4L OHC engines
        Water pump-to-timing chain housing nuts 19
        Water pump cover-to-water pump housing bolts .... 120 in-lbs
        Water pump cover-to-engine block bolts 19
        Radiator outlet pipe-to-water pump housing bolts .... 124 in-lbs

1   General information

All vehicles covered by this manual employ a pressurized engine cooling system with thermostatically-controlled coolant circulation. Coolant is drawn from the radiator by the water pump, which is mounted on the front of the engine block, then the coolant is circulated through the engine block, the intake manifold and the cylinder heads and finally back to the radiator.

On 2.2L OHV engines, the water pump is located at the front right corner of the engine block, right below the alternator. On 2.3L and 2.4L OHC engines, the water pump is located on the front of the engine block, below the exhaust manifold (which must be removed in order to access the pump). On 2.2L OHC engines, the water pump is located at the right rear corner of the engine block.

A wax-pellet type thermostat is located in the thermostat housing near the front of the engine. During warm up, the closed thermostat prevents coolant from circulating through the radiator. When the engine reaches its normal operating temperature, the thermostat opens and allows hot coolant to travel through the radiator, where it is cooled before returning to the engine.

On 1995 2.2L OHV models, the thermostat housing is located at the left end of the cylinder head, above the transaxle. On 1996 and later 2.2L OHV models, the thermostat is located in a housing up front, near the radiator. On 2.3L and 2.4L OHC models, the thermostat housing is an integral part of the metal coolant outlet line on the firewall side of the engine block. On 2.2L OHC engines, the thermostat housing is located at the left rear corner of the cylinder head. On 2.2L OHC engines the thermostat housing is difficult to see because it's hidden by cooling hoses and other components. If you have difficulty find-

ing it, just trace the lower radiator hose backwards from the left end of the radiator until you find the thermostat housing.

All models covered by this manual are equipped with a pressurized coolant recovery system. A plastic coolant reservoir, which is located at the right front corner of the engine compartment **(see illustration)**, is connected to the cooling system by three hoses. There are two inlet hoses (the two smaller hoses connected to the filler neck of the reservoir). One of the two inlet hoses routes hot coolant from the radiator to the reservoir; the other inlet hose routes hot coolant from the cylinder head. The outlet hose (the larger hose connected to the lower left front corner of the reservoir) routes coolant from the reservoir back to the cooling system. **Warning:** *Unlike a conventional coolant recovery tank, the pressure cap on the expansion tank must never be opened after the engine has warmed up, because of the danger of severe burns caused by steam or scalding coolant.*

The cap houses a spring-loaded "blow-off" or pressure valve and a vacuum valve. When the cooling system pressure exceeds the rated pressure (15 psi) of the cap, the spring-loaded valve in the cap opens, venting the system to the atmosphere. When the engine is turned off and the coolant cools down, the vacuum valve in the cap opens, equalizing the pressure.

The heating system works by directing air through the heater core mounted in the dash and then to the interior of the vehicle by a system of ducts. Temperature is controlled by mixing heated air with fresh air, using a system of doors in the ducts, and a blower motor.

The air conditioning system consists of an evaporator core (located under the dash), a condenser (in front of the radiator), an accumulator (in the engine compartment) and a belt-driven compressor (mounted at the front, or accessory belt, end of the engine).

2   Antifreeze - general information

Refer to illustration 2.4

Warning: *Do not allow antifreeze to come in contact with your skin or painted surfaces of the vehicle. Rinse off spills immediately with plenty of water. Antifreeze is highly toxic if ingested. Never leave antifreeze lying around in an open container or in puddles on the floor; children and pets are attracted by its sweet smell and may drink it. Check with local authorities about disposing of used antifreeze. Many communities have collection centers that will see that antifreeze is disposed of safely. Never dump used anti-freeze on the ground or pour it into drains.*

Caution: *The manufacturer recommends using only DEX-COOL coolant for these systems. DEX-COOL is a long-lasting coolant designed for 100,000 miles or 5 years. Never mix green-colored ethylene glycol anti-freeze and orange-colored "DEX-COOL" silicate-free coolant because doing so will destroy the efficiency of the "DEX-COOL." If DEX-COOL is not available, check with your local auto parts store for the availability of coolant that is compatible for use in your vehicle's cooling system.*

The cooling system should be filled with a water/ethylene glycol based antifreeze solution, which will prevent freezing down to at least -20-degrees F (even lower in cold climates). It also provides protection against corrosion and increases the coolant boiling point.

These models are filled with a new, long-life "DEX-COOL coolant," which the manufacturer claims is good for five years. If the coolant level is low, check all hose connections before adding antifreeze to the system. Antifreeze can leak through very minute openings.

The exact mixture of antifreeze to water

2.4 Use an inexpensive hydrometer (available at any auto parts store) to test the condition of your coolant

3.8 Thermostat cover bolt locations (2.2L OHV engine)

3.9 Note how it's installed, then remove the thermostat. When installing the thermostat, make sure that the spring end points toward the engine (2.2L OHV engine)

that you should use depends on the relative weather conditions. The mixture should contain at least 50-percent antifreeze, but should never contain more than 70-percent antifreeze. Consult the mixture ratio chart on the antifreeze container before adding coolant. Hydrometers are available at most auto parts stores to test the coolant **(see illustration)**. Use antifreeze that meets the vehicle manufacturer's specifications. Double-check with the hydrometer manufacturer concerning the specific gravity ratios between ethylene glycol and the modern DEX-COOL antifreeze solutions when measuring coolant strength.

3 Thermostat - check and replacement

Warning: *The engine must be completely cool when this procedure is performed.*
Caution: *Don't drive the vehicle without a thermostat! The computer may stay in open loop mode and emissions and fuel economy will suffer.*

Check

1 Before condemning the thermostat, check the coolant level, drivebelt tension and temperature gauge (or light) operation.
2 If the engine takes a long time to warm up, the thermostat is probably stuck open. Replace the thermostat.
3 If the engine runs hot, put your hand (carefully!) on the upper radiator hose. If the hose isn't hot, the thermostat is probably stuck shut. Replace the thermostat.
4 If the upper radiator hose is hot, then coolant is circulating and the thermostat is open. Refer to the *Troubleshooting* Section at the front of this manual for the cause of overheating.
5 If an engine has been running too hot for too long, it might have serious damage such as a leaking head gasket, a warped or cracked cylinder head and/or scuffed pistons (see Chapter 2).

Replacement

2.2L OHV engine

Refer to illustrations 3.8, 3.9 and 3.12
Warning: *The engine must be completely cool before beginning this procedure.*
6 Drain coolant (about 1 gallon) from the radiator, until the coolant level is below the thermostat housing (see Chapter 1).
7 Disconnect the radiator hose from the thermostat cover.
8 Remove the bolts and lift the cover off **(see illustration)**. It may be necessary to tap the cover with a soft-face hammer to break the gasket seal.
9 Note how it's installed, then remove the thermostat **(see illustration)**. Be sure to use a replacement thermostat with the correct opening temperature (see this Chapter's Specifications).
10 If a gasket was used, use a scraper or putty knife to remove all traces of old gasket material and sealant from the mating surfaces. **Caution:** *Be careful not to gouge or damage the gasket surfaces, because a leak could develop after assembly. Make sure no gasket material falls into the coolant passage; it's a good idea to stuff a rag in the passage. Wipe the mating surfaces with a rag saturated with lacquer thinner or acetone.*
11 Install the thermostat and make sure the correct end faces out - the spring is directed toward the engine.
12 Most models will not have a traditional gasket, but rather a rubber ring around the thermostat. If so, replace this ring and install the thermostat cover without gasket sealant **(see illustration)**. **Note:** *If a gasket was used, apply a thin coat of RTV sealant to both sides of the new gasket and position it on the engine side, over the thermostat, and make sure the gasket holes line up with the bolt holes in the housing.*
13 Carefully position the cover and install the bolts. Tighten them to the torque listed in this Chapter's Specifications - do not overtighten the bolts or the cover may crack or become distorted.

14 Reattach the radiator hose to the cover and tighten the clamp - now would be a good time to check and replace the hoses and clamps (see Chapter 1).
15 Refer to Chapter 1 and refill the system, then run the engine and check carefully for leaks.
16 Repeat steps 1 through 4 to verify that the thermostat corrected the problem.

2.3L and 2.4L OHC engines

Refer to illustrations 3.20, 3.22, 3.24, 3.25 and 3.28
Warning: *The engine must be completely cool before beginning this procedure.*
17 Drain the coolant from the radiator (see Chapter 1).
18 Remove the exhaust manifold heat shield (see Chapter 2B).
19 On 1995 through 1998 models, remove the heat shield that protects the outlet pipe on the thermostat housing. (You can access the cover bolts through the exhaust manifold runners.)
20 Remove the coolant inlet pipe from the thermostat housing **(see illustration)**.

3.12 Install a new rubber seal around the thermostat (2.2L OHV engine)

21   Raise the vehicle and secure it on jack-stands.

22   Remove the engine-to-transaxle support brace **(see illustration)**.

23   Disconnect the lower radiator hose from the coolant inlet pipe.

24   Detach the coolant inlet pipe from the oil pan and disconnect the coolant inlet pipe from the thermostat housing **(see illustration)**.

25   Note how it's installed, then remove the thermostat from the inlet pipe **(see illustration)**. Be sure to use a replacement thermostat with the correct opening temperature (see this Chapter's Specifications).

26   If the mating surfaces of the thermostat inlet pipe flange and the thermostat housing flange are sealed by a conventional gasket, use a scraper or putty knife to remove all traces of old gasket material and sealant from the mating surfaces. **Caution:** *Be careful not to gouge or damage the gasket surfaces, because a leak could develop after assembly. Make sure no gasket material falls into the coolant passage; it's a good idea to stuff a rag in the passage. Wipe the mating surfaces with a rag saturated with lacquer thinner or acetone.*

27   Install the thermostat in the thermostat inlet pipe. Make sure that the spring end of the thermostat faces out (away from the inlet pipe) as shown in the illustration **(see illustration 3.25)**.

28   Most models do not use a conventional gasket; they use a rubber O-ring type gasket around the thermostat. If the old thermostat had a rubber O-ring, install a new O-ring **(see illustration)**, then install the coolant inlet pipe without any gasket sealant on the mounting flanges. If a conventional gasket *was* used, apply a thin coat of RTV sealant to both sides of the new gasket. When installing the gasket, make sure that the gasket holes are aligned with the bolt holes in the thermostat housing.

29   Installation is otherwise the reverse of removal. Be sure to tighten the inlet pipe-to-thermostat housing bolts to the torque listed in this Chapter's Specifications. Tighten all other fasteners securely.

30   When you're done, refill the cooling system, then repeat steps 1 through 4 to verify that the new thermostat has corrected the problem.

2.2L OHC engine

Refer to illustrations 3.32, 3.35, 3.36 and 3.38
Warning: *The engine must be completely cool before beginning this procedure.*

31   Drain the cooling system (see Chapter 1). (If the coolant is still in good condition, you can save it and reuse it.)

32   Remove the water pump drain plug **(see illustration)** and drain the excess coolant into a container.

33   Trace the lower radiator hose to the engine to locate the thermostat housing.

34   It's not necessary to disconnect the lower radiator hose from the thermostat housing in order to remove the housing

3.20 Working from above, remove the coolant inlet pipe-to-thermostat housing bolts (exhaust manifold removed for clarity only; it's not necessary to actually remove the exhaust manifold) (2.3L and 2.4L OHC engines)

3.22 To detach the engine-to-transaxle support bracket, remove these bolts (2.3L and 2.4L OHC engines)

cover. However, if the hose is cracked, torn or otherwise deteriorated, now would be a good time to replace it. Loosen the hose clamp, then pull the hose off the thermostat

cover pipe. If the hose is stuck, grasp it near the end with a pair of adjustable pliers and twist it to break the seal, then pull it off. If this doesn't work, cut off the old hose with a utility knife. If the outer surface of the thermostat cover is already corroded, pitted, or other-

3.24 To disconnect the coolant inlet pipe from the lower radiator hose (the radiator outlet hose), loosen this hose clamp (A); to detach the coolant inlet pipe from the oil pan, remove this retaining stud (B) (2.3L and 2.4L OHC engines)

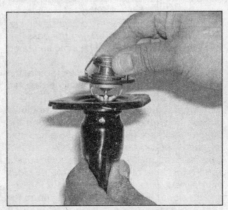

3.25 Before removing the thermostat from the coolant inlet pipe, note its installation orientation, with the spring facing out, away from the coolant inlet pipe flange; this is the same way that the thermostat must be installed (2.3L and 2.4L OHC engines)

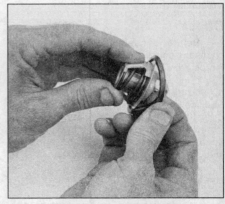

3.28 Install a new rubber O-ring on the thermostat as shown (2.3L and 2.4L OHC engines)

3.32 Location of the water pump drain plug (2.2L OHC engine)

wise deteriorated, it might become even more damaged when you disconnect the hose. If the cover is in bad shape, replace it now too.

35   Remove the thermostat cover **(see illustration)**. If the cover is stuck, tap it with a soft-face hammer to jar it loose. Be prepared for some coolant to spill as soon as you break the gasket seal.

36   Note how the thermostat is oriented in its installed position, with the spring end facing into the housing, then remove the thermostat **(see illustration)**.

37   Remove all traces of old gasket material and sealant from the gasket mating surfaces of the thermostat housing and the cover with a gasket scraper.

38   Install a new rubber gasket on the thermostat **(see illustration)**, then install the thermostat in the housing, spring-end first.

39   Installation is the reverse of removal. Be sure to tighten the thermostat cover bolts to the torque listed in this Chapter's Specifications.

40   When you're done, refill the cooling system (see Chapter 1), then repeat steps 1 through 4 to verify that the new thermostat has corrected the problem.

4   Engine cooling fan - replacement

Refer to illustrations 4.3, 4.4 and 4.5

Warning: *Keep your hands, tools and clothing away from the fan. To avoid injury or damage Do NOT operate the engine with a damaged fan. Do not try to repair fan blades. If the blades are damaged, replace the fan.*

1   Disconnect the cable from the negative terminal of the battery. **Caution:** *On models equipped with a Delco Loc II or Theftlock audio system, be sure the lockout feature is turned off before performing any procedure which requires disconnecting the battery.*

2   Disconnect the electrical connector from the fan motor.

3   Remove the bolts and detach the fan shroud from the radiator **(see illustration)**.

4   Lift up the fan assembly slightly to disengage its mounting tabs from the radiator, make sure that all wiring clips are disconnected, then guide the fan assembly out from the engine compartment **(see illustration)**, Be careful not to damage the radiator cooling fins.

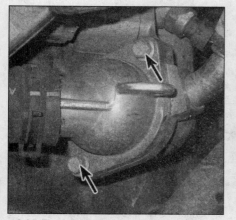

3.35 To detach the thermostat housing cover, remove these two bolts (2.2L OHC engine)

3.36 Note how the thermostat is oriented in its installed position, then remove it from the thermostat housing (2.2L OHC engine)

3.38 Install a new rubber gasket around the perimeter of the thermostat (2.2L OHC engine)

4.3 To detach the fan shroud from the radiator, remove the bolts that attach the shroud to the radiator support

4.4 To disengage the fan shroud mounting tabs from the radiator, lift it up slightly, then verify that nothing else is still attached or connected before removing the fan and shroud as a single assembly

4.5 To detach the fan from the fan motor, remove this nut

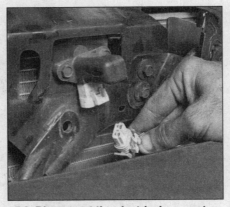

5.3 Disconnect the electrical connector from the airbag system's forward discriminating sensor. Cover the end of the sensor and connector to prevent dirt and moisture from contaminating it while it's unplugged

5.6 Disconnect the upper and lower transaxle cooler line fittings, preferable with a flare-nut wrench (only the lower line fitting is visible in this photo; the upper fitting is near the top of the side tank)

5   If you're removing the fan assembly in order to replace either the fan itself or the fan motor, then detach the fan retaining bolt from the fan assembly **(see illustration)**. If you removed the fan assembly simply to access some other component, such as the radiator, then skip this step. **Caution:** *If you're replacing the fan motor, it is extremely important to obtain a new motor with the correct part number, because different models have different amperage and/or wattage ratings, and installing a fan with insufficient power could result in overheating problems.*
6   Installation is the reverse of removal.

5   Radiator and coolant reservoir - removal and installation

Warning 1: *The models covered by this manual are equipped with airbags. Always disable the airbag system before working in the vicinity of the impact sensors, steering column or instrument panel to avoid the possibility of accidental deployment of the airbag(s), which could cause personal injury (see Chapter 12).*
Warning 2: *The engine must be completely cool when this procedure is performed.*

Radiator

Refer to illustrations 5.3, 5.6, 5.8a, 5.8b, 5.8c and 5.11

1   Disconnect the cable from the negative terminal of the battery. **Caution:** *On models equipped with a Delco Loc II or Theftlock audio system, be sure the lockout feature is turned off before performing any procedure which requires disconnecting the battery.*
2   Drain the cooling system as described in Chapter 1. Refer to the coolant **Warning** in Section 2.
3   Disable the airbag system (see Chapter 12). Disconnect the electrical connector from the airbag system's forward discriminating sensor **(see illustration)**, which is located on the hood latch support bracket, next to the latch. **Note:** *Some newer models use a slightly different airbag system so they might not be equipped with a forward discriminat-*

ing sensor. If a discriminating sensor is present, be very careful not to bump it against anything while handling the support bracket.
4   Remove the cooling fan and shroud assembly (see Section 4).
5   Loosen the hose clamps for the upper and lower radiator hoses, then disconnect both hoses from the radiator. Also disconnect the coolant reservoir inlet and outlet hoses from the radiator. Be prepared to catch any spilled coolant with a couple of drain pans and/or some shop rags.
6   On vehicles with an automatic transaxle, disconnect the automatic transaxle cooler lines (if equipped) from the left side tank of the radiator **(see illustration)**. Be careful not to kink the metal lines or round the corners of the fittings. If you have flare-nut wrenches use them to protect the fittings. If there are fixed nuts welded to the side tank, they were put there to protect the tank from being damaged when loosening and tightening the cooler line fittings. Put a back-up wrench on each welded nut while loosening the cooler line fitting. If there are no welded nuts on the tank, be extremely careful not to damage the tank. If the fittings are overtightened or corroded, they might be difficult to loosen. Spray a little penetrant on each fitting and wait awhile for

5.8a To detach the hood latch support bracket from the upper radiator crossmember, remove these two bolts

the threads to loosen up. Plug the ends of the disconnected lines to prevent leakage and to stop dirt from entering the system. Have a drip pan ready to catch any spills.
7   Remove the right and the left headlight

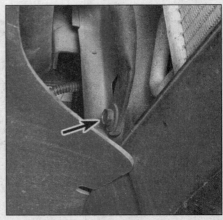

5.8b To detach the two support struts for the hood latch support bracket, trace each strut down its lower end and remove this bolt (lower end mounting bolt for right support strut shown, left support strut bolt identical)

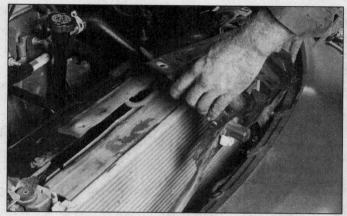

5.8c Carefully lift the hood latch support bracket off the upper radiator crossmember and set it aside. Be very careful with the support bracket if the forward discriminating sensor is still installed

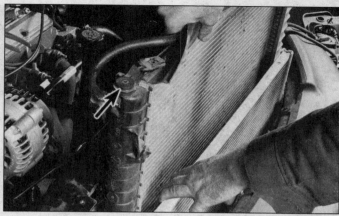

5.11 Carefully lift out the radiator from between the condenser and the upper radiator crossmember. Pull the condenser forward slightly as shown to give yourself a little more room. After removing the radiator, inspect the rubber insulators

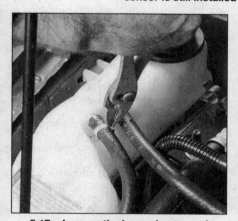

5.17a Loosen the hose clamps and disconnect the upper hoses from the coolant reservoir

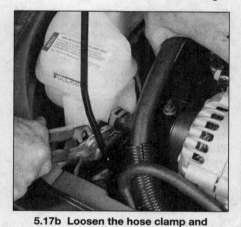

5.17b Loosen the hose clamp and disconnect the lower (outlet) hose from the coolant reservoir

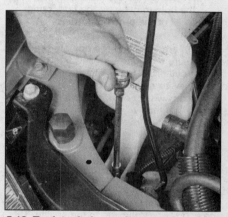

5.18 To detach the coolant reservoir from the engine compartment, remove this mounting bolt (the reservoir on your vehicle might have another bolt somewhere, so look for another bolt if the reservoir doesn't budge when you try to remove it)

5.19 Lift the coolant reservoir from the engine compartment and disconnect the electrical connector from the coolant level sensor

assemblies from the vehicle (see Chapter 12).

8   Remove the hood latch support bracket from the upper radiator crossmember **(see illustrations)**. It's not necessary to detach the hood latch or the airbag's forward discriminating sensor from the support bracket. Just set the support bracket aside so that it's clear of the radiator.

9   Remove the condenser mounting bolts from the radiator.

10   Remove the radiator upper mounting bolts, which are located at the upper left and right ends of the radiator, directly above the radiator's side tanks.

11   Carefully remove the radiator **(see illustration)**. Be careful not to damage the radiator or the condenser.

12   Before installing the radiator, replace any damaged radiator insulators **(see illustration 5.11)**. Also inspect the condition of all hose clamps and radiator hoses. If either radiator hose is cracked, torn or deteriorated, replace it. If there have been leaks or cooling problems, have the radiator cleaned and tested at a radiator shop.

13   Make sure that the lower insulators are in place, then carefully lower the radiator into

position. Make sure that the radiator lower locator pins are aligned with and fully seated in the lower insulators.

14   Installation is otherwise the reverse of removal.

15   When you're done, refill the cooling system with the correct mixture of antifreeze and bleed the air from the cooling system (see Chapter 1). Also check the automatic transaxle fluid level and add fluid if necessary (see Chapter 1).

Coolant reservoir

Refer to illustration 5.17a, 5.17b, 5.18 and 5.19

16   Drain the cooling system (see Chapter 1) until the coolant reservoir is empty. (Refer to the coolant **Warning** in Section 2.)

17   Disconnect the inlet and outlet hoses from the coolant reservoir **(see illustrations)**.

18   To detach the coolant reservoir from the engine compartment, remove the reservoir mounting bolts **(see illustration)**.

19   Lift up the coolant reservoir and disconnect the connector from the low coolant warning sensor **(see illustration)**.

6.2 If coolant is leaking from the weep hole, the water pump seal is defective. On some models the hole is on top of the water pump (like this 2.2L OHV engine); the hole may be on the underside of the pump on others

20   Before installing the coolant reservoir, make sure that it's clean and free of debris, which could be drawn into the radiator. The best way to clean a reservoir is to wash it with soapy water and a stiff bottle brush, then rinse it thoroughly.
21   Installation is the reverse of removal.

6   Water pump - check

Refer to illustrations 6.2 and 6.4
1   Water pump failure can cause overheating and serious damage to the engine. There are three ways to check the operation of the water pump while it is installed on the engine. If any one of the following quick-checks indicates water pump problems, it should be replaced immediately.
2   A seal protects the water pump impeller shaft bearing from contamination by engine coolant. If this seal fails, a weep hole in the water pump snout will leak coolant **(see illustration)** (an inspection mirror can be used to look at the underside of the pump if the hole isn't on top). If the weep hole is leaking, shaft bearing failure will follow. Replace the water pump immediately.
3   The water pump impeller shaft bearing can also prematurely wear out. When the bearing wears out, it emits a high-pitched squealing sound. If such a noise is coming from the water pump during engine operation, the shaft bearing has failed. Replace the water pump immediately. **Note:** *Do not confuse belt noise with bearing noise.*
4   To identify excessive bearing wear on a 2.2L OHV engine, grasp the water pump pulley and try to force it up-and-down or side-to-side **(see illustration)**. If you can move the pulley horizontally or vertically, the bearing is nearing the end of its service life. Replace the water pump. Don't mistake drivebelt slippage, which causes a squealing sound, for water pump bearing failure.

6.4 Check the pump for loose or rough bearings (2.2L OHV engines)

5   It's possible for a water pump to be bad, even if it doesn't howl or leak water. Sometimes the fins on the back of the impeller can corrode and wear down until the pump is no longer effective. The only way to check for this is to remove the pump for examination.

7   Water pump - removal and installation

Warning: *Wait until the engine is completely cool before starting this procedure.*
1   Disconnect the cable from the negative battery terminal. **Caution:** *On models equipped with a Delco Loc II or Theftlock audio system, make sure that the lockout feature is turned off before performing any procedure which requires disconnecting the battery.*
2   Drain the engine coolant (see Chapter 1).

2.2L OHV engine

Refer to illustrations 7.3 and 7.6
3   Loosen the water pump pulley bolts **(see illustration)**.
4   Remove the serpentine drivebelt (see Chapter 1).
5   Remove the water pump pulley from the water pump.
6   Remove the water pump mounting bolts **(see illustration)** and remove the pump. If the pump is stuck, strike it with a soft-face hammer or a wooden hammer handle to break the gasket seal. Do NOT pry between the pump and the block.
7   Remove all old gasket material from the gasket mating surface of the block. If you're planning to reinstall the old pump, clean the mating surfaces of the pump as well. Use a rag saturated with lacquer thinner or acetone to loosen the old gasket material.
8   Apply a thin layer of RTV sealant to both sides of the new gasket and install the gasket on the water pump.
9   Place the water pump in position and install the bolts finger tight. Make sure that the gasket doesn't slip out of position. Coat

7.3 Use a large flat-bladed screwdriver to lock the pulley in place and loosen the water pump pulley bolts (2.2L OHV engine)

the water pump bolts with thread sealant to prevent leaks. Don't forget to reinstall any mounting brackets, cable clips and/or grounds secured by the water pump mounting bolts/studs. Tighten the water pump mounting bolts/studs to the torque listed in this Chapter's Specifications.
10   The remainder of installation is the reverse of removal.
11   When you're done, refill the cooling system (see Chapter 1).
12   Reconnect the cable to the negative battery terminal.
13   Start the engine, then check the coolant level. Also check the water pump for leaks. Bleed any air from the cooling system (see Chapter 1).

2.3L and 2.4L OHC engines

Refer to illustration 7.20, 7.21, 7.22a, 7.22b and 7.25
Note: *In order to avoid an incorrect tightening sequence and leaky gasket mating surfaces, read this entire procedure before installing the water pump into the timing chain housing and the engine block.*

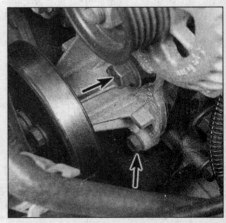

7.6 To detach the water pump from the engine, remove the four mounting bolts (two right bolts not visible in this photo) (2.2L OHV engine)

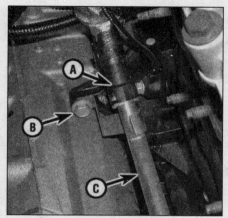

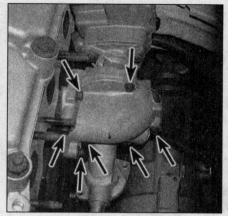

7.20 Remove the quick-connect fitting (A) and the retaining bolt (B) for the heater outlet pipe bracket, then remove the heater outlet pipe (C) from the water pump cover (2.3L and 2.4L OHC engines)

7.21 Water pump cover mounting bolts (2.3L and 2.4L OHC engines)

7.22a Remove all three water pump retaining nuts (lower nut not shown) (2.3L and 2.4L OHC engines)

14   Raise the vehicle and support it securely on jackstands.

15   Remove the exhaust manifold (see Chapter 2B). **Note:** *Do not rotate the flex coupling more than 4 degrees or damage to the flex coupling may occur.*

16   Disconnect the coolant inlet pipe from the water pump outlet hose, detach it from the engine, disconnect it from the thermostat housing and remove it (see Section 3).

17   Lower the vehicle.

18   Detach the brake booster vacuum hose from the camshaft housing.

19   Remove the front timing chain cover and the timing chain tensioner (see Chapter 2B). **Caution:** *The timing chain tensioner must be removed to unload chain tension before removing the water pump from the timing chain housing. If it isn't, the water pump will become jammed in the timing chain housing.*

20   Remove the heater outlet pipe from the water pump **(see illustration)**.

21   Remove the water pump cover bolts **(see illustration)** from the engine block and from the water pump, then remove the water pump cover from the timing chain housing.

22   Remove the water pump retaining nuts, then separate the water pump from the timing chain housing **(see illustrations)**.

23   Remove all old gasket material from the gasket sealing surfaces of the water pump cover, the water pump and the timing chain housing. Wipe the mating surfaces with a rag saturated with lacquer thinner or acetone.

24   Working on the bench, install the water pump cover and gasket on the water pump, but leave the bolts finger tight. Apply a thin layer of RTV sealant to both sides of the new gasket and install the gasket on the water pump. This entire procedure must be performed in a timely manner before the RTV sealant sets up and dries.

25   On 1995 (2.3L) models, lubricate the splines of the water pump drive **(see illustration)** with grease, then insert the pump into the timing chain housing. Make sure that the pump shaft is fully seated into the splines of the pump drive, then install the nuts finger tight.

26   On 1996 and later models (which use a sprocket instead), install the pump into the timing chain housing. Make sure that the driven sprocket is fully engaged with the timing chain. On all models, make sure that the

gasket doesn't slip out of position. Leave the water pump mounting nuts loose to allow repositioning of the pump when the block bolts are installed in the next step.

27   Install the water pump cover to engine block bolts and tighten them by hand.

28   Lubricate the O-ring on the metal outlet pipe with coolant and install it into the water pump housing. Hand tighten the bolts.

29   Now that the entire water pump housing assembly is installed and is fitted against the engine block, tighten the pump mounting fasteners in the following sequence to insure correct installation.

a) *Tighten the water pump-to-timing chain housing nuts to the torque listed in this Chapter's Specifications.*

b) *Tighten the water pump cover-to-water pump housing bolts to the torque listed in this Chapter's Specifications.*

c) *Tighten the water pump cover-to-engine block bolts to the torque listed in this Chapter's Specifications. Tighten the bottom bolts first then the top bolt.*

d) *Tighten the radiator outlet pipe-to-water pump housing to the torque listed in this Chapter's Specifications.*

30   Install the timing chain tensioner and the timing chain cover (see Chapter 2B).

31   Install the exhaust manifold (see Chapter 2B).

32   Install the exhaust pipe to the exhaust manifold.

33   The remainder of the installation procedure is the reverse of removal.

34   When you're done, refill the cooling system (see Chapter 1).

35   Start the engine and check the coolant level. Then inspect the water pump, metal lines and hoses for leaks. Bleed the cooling system (see Chapter 1).

2.2L OHC engine

Refer to illustration 7.45a, 7.45b, 7.46, 7.49a, 7.49b, 7.51a and 7.51b

36   Disconnect the cable from the negative battery terminal (see Chapter 5).

7.22b Pull the water pump from the timing chain housing (2.3L and 2.4L OHC engines)

7.25 Lubricate the splines of the water pump drive with grease (1995 2.3L OHC engine)

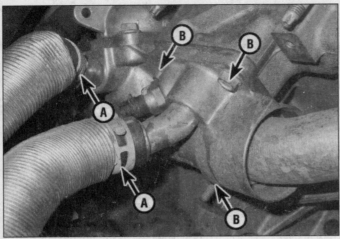

7.45a Remove the heater hoses (A) and thermostat housing mounting bolts (B) and separate the thermostat housing from the engine block and the water pump (2.2L OHC engine)

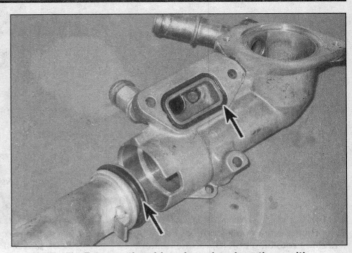

7.45b Remove the old seals and replace them with new ones (2.2L OHC engine)

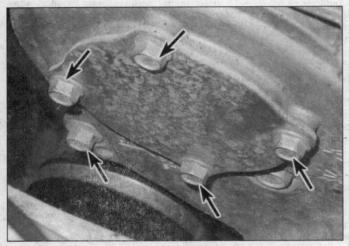

7.46 Remove the water pump access cover mounting bolts (2.2L OHC engine)

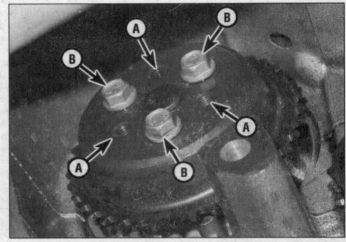

7.49a Before installing the special tool onto the water pump sprocket, note the location of the bolt holes for the sprocket tool (A) and the sprocket bolts (B) (2.2L OHC engine)

37   Drain the cooling system (see Chapter 1).

38   Remove the accessory drivebelt (see Chapter 1).

39   Remove the air intake duct and the air filter housing (see Chapter 4).

40   Remove the exhaust manifold heat shield (see Chapter 2C).

41   Remove the plug from the bottom of the water pump housing **(see illustration 3.32)** and drain the excess coolant into a container.

42   Remove the lower radiator hose.

43   On 2004 models, remove the thermostat housing pipe bolt from the front of the engine block.

44   Disconnect the ECT harness connector (see Chapter 6).

45   Disconnect the heater hoses and remove the thermostat housing mounting bolts **(see illustration),** then separate the thermostat housing from the engine block and the water pump. Discard the old seals

from the water pipe **(see illustration)** and replace them with new seals.

46   Remove the water pump access cover from the engine front cover **(see illustration).**

47   Loosen the right front wheel lug nuts. Raise the vehicle and support it securely on jackstands. Remove the right front wheel.

48   Remove the inner fender splash shield (see Chapter 11).

49   Install a special holding tool onto the water pump sprocket (tool J-43651, available from specialty tool manufacturers and some dealer service departments). A tool can be fabricated if necessary **(see illustrations).** Be sure to lock the tool carefully, not allowing any sprocket movement. The bolts of the special tool will thread into the holes in the water pump sprocket that aren't for the sprocket bolts. **Note:** *The water pump sprocket tool will lock the sprocket into position, allowing the balance shaft chain to remain in its timed state while the water*

7.49b Remove one sprocket bolt, install the special tool and lock the sprocket into position before removing the other two sprocket bolts (2.2L OHC engine)

7.51a Remove the two water pump bolts on the rear of the engine block . . .

pump is being replaced. If you're using a homemade tool like the one shown in the illustration, remove one of the water pump bolts first.

50 Remove the water pump pulley bolts.
51 Remove the two bolts attaching the water pump to the front and two bolts attaching to the rear of the engine block and remove the pump from the engine **(see illustrations)**. If the water pump is stuck, gently tap it with a soft-faced hammer to break the seal.
52 Clean the bolt threads and the threaded holes in the engine and remove any corrosion or sealant. Remove all traces of old gasket material from the sealing surfaces. Remove the sealing ring from the water pump (if the same pump is to be installed).
53 Install a new sealing ring into the groove in the pump. To install the new water pump, install a guide pin (threaded stud) into the water pump pulley to align the water pump sprocket with the water pump.
54 Install the water pump mounting bolts and tighten them loosely. Install two bolts into the water pump sprocket and tighten

them loosely. Remove the guide pin and install the third water pump sprocket bolt.
55 Tighten the water pump mounting bolts (two in the front and two in the rear of the engine block) to the torque listed in this Chapter's Specifications.
56 Tighten the water pump sprocket bolts to the torque listed in this Chapter's Specifications.
57 Install the water pump access cover and tighten the bolts to the torque listed in this Chapter's Specifications.
58 Install the thermostat housing and water pipe and tighten the bolts to the torque listed in this Chapter's Specifications. Lubricate the seal lightly with silicon gel before installing the water pipe into the water pump.
59 Installation is otherwise the reverse of removal.
60 Refill the cooling system when you're done.
61 Reconnect the cable to the negative battery terminal.
62 Start the engine and check for leaks.

8 Coolant temperature gauge sending unit - check and replacement

Check

1 The coolant temperature indicator system consists of a warning light or a temperature gauge on the dash and a coolant temperature sending unit mounted on the engine. On the models covered by this manual, the Engine Coolant Temperature (ECT) sensor, which is an information sensor for the Powertrain Control Module (PCM), also functions as the coolant temperature sending unit.
2 If an overheating indication occurs, check the coolant level in the system and then make sure all connectors in the wiring harness between the sending unit and the indicator light or gauge are tight.
3 When the ignition switch is turned to

START and the starter motor is turning, the indicator light (if equipped) should come on. This doesn't mean the engine is overheated; it just means that the bulb is good.
4 If the light doesn't come on when the ignition key is turned to START, the bulb might be burned out, the ignition switch might be faulty or the circuit might be open.
5 As soon as the engine starts, the indicator light should go out and remain off, unless the engine overheats. If the light doesn't go out, the wire between the sending unit and the light could be grounded; the sending unit might be defective (have it checked by a dealer service department); or the ignition switch might be faulty (see Chapter 12). Check the coolant to make sure it's correctly mixed; plain water, with no antifreeze, or coolant that's mainly water, might have too low a boiling point to activate the sending unit (see Chapter 1).

Replacement

6 See Chapter 6, *Information sensors - replacement*, for the replacement procedure.

9 Blower motor - replacement

Refer to illustrations 9.2, 9.3 and 9.4
Warning: *The models covered by this manual are equipped with airbags. Always disable the airbag system before working in the vicinity of the impact sensors, steering column or instrument panel to avoid the possibility of accidental deployment of the airbag(s), which could cause personal injury (see Chapter 12).*
1 Remove the lower right dash insulator panel (below the glove box) for access to the blower motor.
2 Disconnect the electrical connector from the blower motor and remove the three screws from the blower housing **(see illustration)**.
3 Pull the blower motor and fan straight down **(see illustration)**.

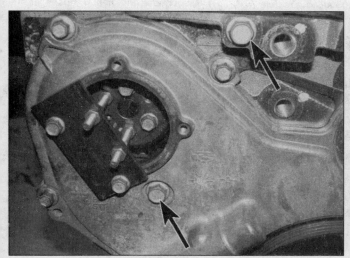

7.51b . . . and the front of the engine block (2.2L OHC engine)

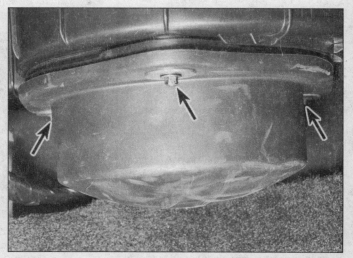

9.2 Remove the screws retaining the blower motor to the housing

9.3 Lower the blower motor and fan assembly straight down to remove it from the vehicle

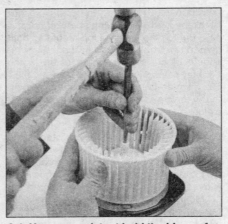

9.4 Have an assistant hold the blower fan while tapping the motor shaft with a narrow punch to carefully drive the shaft out of the fan

10.3 Disconnect the heater core hoses at the engine compartment firewall

10.5 Disconnect the ducts from the heater core cover

10.7a Remove the heater core cover bolts from the face of the assembly

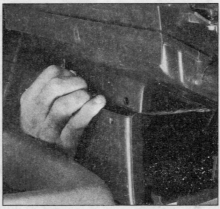

10.7b Remove the bolt from under the ledge area of the cover. Don't forget the recessed mounting bolt near the middle, rear section of the heater core cover

4   To remove the fan from the blower motor, use a narrow punch and tap the shaft out of the fan assembly **(see illustration)**.

5   Install the fan onto the motor and install the blower motor into the heater housing.

10   Heater core - removal and installation

Refer to illustrations 10.3, 10.5, 10.7a, 10.7b, 10.7c, 10.7d, 10.8a and 10.8b

Warning 1: *The models covered by this manual are equipped with airbags. Always disable the airbag system before working in the vicinity of the impact sensors, steering column or instrument panel to avoid the possibility of accidental deployment of the airbag(s), which could cause personal injury (see Chapter 12)*

Warning 2: *The air conditioning system is under high pressure. DO NOT loosen any fittings or remove any components until after the system has been discharged. Air conditioning refrigerant should be properly discharged into an EPA-approved container at a dealership service department or an automotive air conditioning facility. Always wear eye*

protection when disconnecting air conditioning system fittings.

1   Disconnect the cable from the negative battery terminal. **Caution:** *On models equipped with a Delco Loc II or Theftlock audio system, be sure the lockout feature is turned off before performing any procedure*

which requires disconnecting the battery.

2   Drain the cooling system (see Chapter 1).

3   Disconnect the heater hoses at the heater core inlet and outlet on the engine side

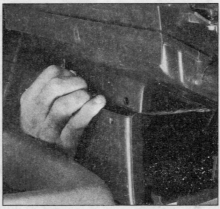

10.7c Separate the lower panel from the heater core housing

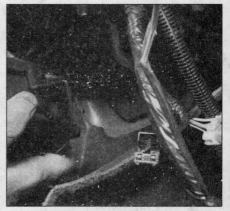

10.7d Pull the heater cover from the bottom to dislodge the condenser drain hoses

10.8a Remove the heater core straps from the assembly

10.8b Lower the forward section of the heater core and angle the assembly toward the rear of the vehicle to separate it from the heater core housing

11.3a Remove the screws retaining the heater/air conditioning control assembly to the instrument panel

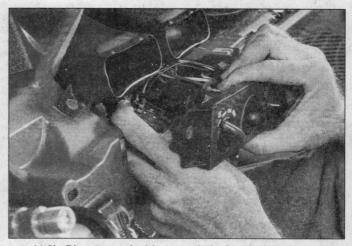

11.3b Disconnect the blower switch electrical connector

of the firewall (passenger side) **(see illustration)** and plug the open fittings. If the hoses are stuck to the pipes, cut them off.

4   From the inside of the car, remove the lower right dash insulator panel (below the glove box) and the glove box (see Chapter 11).

5   Disconnect the ducts from the heater cover **(see illustration)**.

6   Remove the instrument panel (see Chapter 11).

7   Remove the heater core cover **(see illustrations)**.

8   Remove the heater core clamp bolts and clamps **(see illustration)**, then slide the heater core out carefully **(see illustration)**.

9   Installation is the reverse of removal. **Note:** *When reinstalling the heater core, make sure any original insulating/sealing materials are in place around the heater core pipes and around the core.*

10   Refill the cooling system (see Chapter 1).

11   Start the engine and verify that the heater works correctly.

11   Heater and air conditioning control assembly - removal and installation

Refer to illustrations 11.3a, 11.3b, 11.3c, 11.3d, 11.3e and 11.3f

Warning: *The models covered by this manual are equipped with airbags. Always disable the airbag system before working in the vicinity of the impact sensors, steering column or instrument panel to avoid the possibility of accidental deployment of the airbag(s), which could cause personal injury (see Chapter 12).*

1   Disconnect the battery cable from the negative battery terminal. **Caution:** *On models equipped with a Delco Loc II or Theftlock audio system, be sure the lockout feature is turned off before performing any procedure which requires disconnecting the battery.*

2   Remove the main instrument panel bezel to allow access to the heater/air conditioning control mounting screws (see Chapter 11).

3   Remove the control assembly retaining

screws and pull the unit from the dash **(see illustrations)**. It can be pulled out just far enough to allow disconnecting the control cable end, electrical connections and vacuum harness (on air-conditioned models) from the control head. Use a small screw-

11.3c Disconnect the air conditioning and defogger switch electrical connector

11.3d Disconnect the vacuum harness

11.3e Disconnect the lighting harness assembly

11.3f Use a small screwdriver to pry apart the clips that retain the air conditioner control cable (If equipped)

driver to release the clips retaining the control cable.

4   To install the control assembly, reverse the removal procedure. **Caution:** *When reconnecting the vacuum harness to the control assembly, do not use any lubricant to make them slip on easier; it can affect vacuum operation. If necessary, use a drop of plain water to make reconnection easier.*

12   Air conditioning and heating system - check and maintenance

Warning: *The air conditioning system is under high pressure. DO NOT loosen any fittings or remove any components until after the system has been discharged. Air conditioning refrigerant must be properly discharged into an EPA-approved recovery container at a dealership service department or an automotive air conditioning repair facility. Always wear eye protection when disconnecting air conditioning system fittings.*

1   The following maintenance steps should be performed on a regular basis to ensure that the air conditioner continues to operate at peak efficiency:

a) *Check the drivebelt (see Chapter 1).*
b) *Check the condition of the hoses. Look for cracks, hardening and deterioration. Look at potential leak areas (hoses and fittings) for signs of refrigerant oil leaking out.* **Warning:** *Do not replace air conditioning hoses until the system has been discharged by a dealership or air conditioning repair facility.*
c) *Check the fins of the condenser for leaves, bugs and other foreign material. A soft brush and compressed air can be used to remove them.*
d) *Check the wire harness for correct routing, broken wires, damaged insulation, etc. Make sure the electrical connectors are clean and tight.*
e) *Maintain the correct refrigerant charge.*

2   The system should be run for about 10 minutes at least once a month. This is particularly important during the winter months

because long-term non-use can cause hardening of the internal seals.

3   Because of the complexity of the air conditioning system and the special equipment required to effectively work on it, accurate troubleshooting of the system should be left to a certified air conditioning technician.

4   If the air conditioning system doesn't operate at all, check the fuse panel. Check the HVAC fuse and the air conditioning compressor relay.

5   The most common cause of poor cooling is simply a low system refrigerant charge. If a noticeable drop in cool air output occurs, the following quick check will help you determine if the refrigerant level is low. For more complete information on the air conditioning system, refer to the *Haynes Automotive Heating and Air Conditioning Manual.*

Checking the refrigerant charge

Refer to illustration 12.9

6   Warm the engine up to normal operating temperature.

7   Place the air conditioning temperature

selector at the coldest setting and the blower at the highest setting. Open the doors (to make sure the air conditioning system doesn't cycle off as soon as it cools the passenger compartment).

8   With the compressor engaged - the clutch will make an audible click and the center of the clutch will rotate - feel the surface of the accumulator and the evaporator inlet pipe. If there's no perceptible difference between the inlet pipe and the accumulator, the system is properly charged. If there's a difference, there's something wrong with the system. It might be low charge, but it might be something else. To be sure, take the vehicle to a dealer service department or other qualified repair facility for further diagnosis.

9   Insert the business end of a thermometer into the dashboard vent nearest the evaporator **(see illustration)**. Then add refrigerant to the system until the indicated temperature is around 40 to 45-degrees F. If the ambient air temperature is very high, say 110-degrees F, the duct air temperature will probably not be as cool as it would be on a cooler day. But the air conditioned air inside the passenger compartment is generally about 30 to 40-

12.9 Install an automotive thermometer into the cooling duct closest to the evaporator core (right side duct)

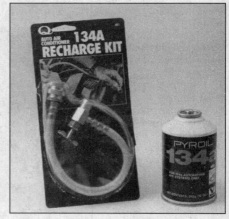
12.10 A basic charging kit for R-134a systems is available at most auto parts stores

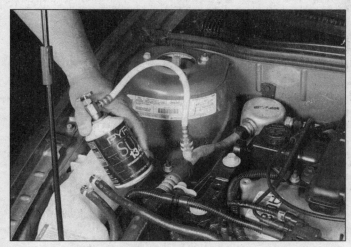

12.13 Add refrigerant to the low-side port only - the procedure is easier if you wrap the can with a warm, wet towel to prevent icing

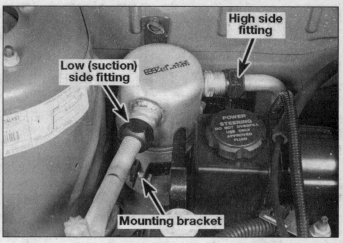

13.2 Disconnect the inlet and outlet lines, then remove the mounting bracket bolt

degrees F cooler than the ambient air. **Note:** *The humidity of the ambient air also affects the cooling capacity of the system. Higher ambient humidity lowers the effectiveness of the air conditioning system.*

Adding refrigerant

Refer to illustrations 12.10 and 12.13

10   Buy an automotive charging kit at an auto parts store. A charging kit includes a can of refrigerant, a tap valve and a short section of hose that can be attached between the tap valve and the system low side service valve **(see illustration).**

11   Hook up the charging kit by following the manufacturer's instructions. **Warning:** *DO NOT hook the charging kit hose to the system high side! The fittings on the charging kit are designed to fit* **only** *on the low side of the system.*

12   Back off the valve handle on the charging kit and screw the kit onto the refrigerant can, making sure first that the O-ring or rubber seal inside the threaded portion of the kit is in place. **Warning:** *Wear protective eyewear when dealing with pressurized refrigerant cans.*

13   Remove the dust cap from the low-side charging connection and attach the quick-connect fitting on the kit hose **(see illustration).**

14   Warm up the engine and turn on the air conditioner. Keep the charging kit hose away from the fan and other moving parts. **Note:** *The charging process requires the compressor to be running. Your compressor may cycle off if the pressure is low due to a low charge. If the clutch cycles off, you can disconnect the air conditioning compressor clutch connector near the compressor and apply battery voltage (+) using a jumper wire. This will keep the compressor ON.*

15   Turn the valve handle on the kit until the stem pierces the can, then back the handle out to release the refrigerant. You should be able to hear the rush of gas. Add refrigerant to the low side of the system until both the

accumulator surface and the evaporator inlet pipe feel about the same temperature . Allow stabilization time between each addition.

16   If you have an accurate thermometer, you can place it in the center air conditioning duct inside the vehicle and keep track of the "conditioned" air temperature. A charged system that is working correctly should put out air that is 40-degrees F, or about 30 to 40 degree cooler than the outside air temperature. However, if the ambient air temperature is very high, say 110-degrees F, then the air temperature at the duct probably won't be as cold as it would be if the outside air were a little cooler.

17   When the can is empty, turn the valve handle to the closed position and release the connection from the low-side port. Replace the dust cap. **Warning:** *Never add more than one can of refrigerant to the system (if more than one can is required, the system should be evacuated and leak tested).*

18   Remove the charging kit from the can and store the kit for future use with the piercing valve in the UP position, to prevent inadvertently piercing the can on the next use.

Heating systems

19   If the carpet under the heater core is damp, or if antifreeze vapor or steam is coming through the vents, the heater core is leaking. Remove it (see Section 10) and install a new unit (most radiator shops will not repair a leaking heater core).

20   If the air coming out of the heater vents isn't hot, the problem could stem from any of the following causes:

a) *The thermostat is stuck open, preventing the engine coolant from warming up enough to carry heat to the heater core. Replace the thermostat (see Section 3).*

b) *A heater hose is blocked, preventing the flow of coolant through the heater core. Feel both heater hoses at the firewall. They should be hot. If one of them is cold, there is an obstruction in one of the hoses or in the heater core, or the*

heater control valve is shut. Detach the hoses and back flush the heater core with a water hose. If the heater core is clear but circulation is impeded, remove the two hoses and flush them out with a water hose.

c) *If flushing fails to remove the blockage from the heater core, the core must be replaced (see Section 10).*

13   Air conditioning accumulator/drier - removal and installation

Removal

Refer to illustration 13.2

Warning: *The air conditioning system is under high pressure. DO NOT loosen any fittings or remove any components until after the system has been discharged. Air conditioning refrigerant must be properly discharged into an EPA-approved container at a dealership service department or an automotive air conditioning repair facility. Always wear eye protection when disconnecting air conditioning system fittings.*

1   Have the air conditioning system discharged (see **Warning** above). Disconnect the cable from the negative terminal of the battery. **Caution:** *On models equipped with a Delco Loc II or Theftlock audio system, be sure the lockout feature is turned off before performing any procedure which requires disconnecting the battery.*

2   Disconnect the refrigerant inlet and outlet lines **(see illustration).** Cap or plug the open lines immediately to prevent the entry of dirt or moisture.

3   Loosen the clamp bolt on the mounting bracket and slide the accumulator/drier assembly up and out of the compartment.

Installation

4   If you are replacing the accumulator/drier with a new one, add one ounce of fresh

14.5a Disconnect the electrical connector from the air conditioning compressor (2.2L OHV engine)

14.5b Disconnect the electrical connector (A) and the mounting bolt (B) that secures the refrigerant lines to the back of the compressor (2.3L and 2.4L OHC engines)

refrigerant oil to the new unit (oil must be R-134a compatible).

5   Place the new accumulator/drier into position in the bracket.

6   Install the inlet and outlet lines, using clean refrigerant oil on the new O-rings. Tighten the mounting bolt securely.

7   Connect the cable to the negative terminal of the battery.

8   Have the system evacuated, recharged and leak tested by the shop that discharged it.

14 Air conditioning compressor - removal and installation

Refer to illustrations 14.5a, 14.5b, 14.5c, 14.6a, 14.6b, 14.8a and 14.8b

Warning: *The air conditioning system is under high pressure. DO NOT loosen any fittings or remove any components until after the system has been discharged. Air conditioning refrigerant must be properly discharged into an EPA-approved container at a dealership service department or an automotive air conditioning repair facility. Always wear eye protection when disconnecting air conditioning system fittings.*

Note: *If you are replacing the compressor, you must also replace the accumulator/drier (see Section 13) and the expansion (orifice) tube (see Section 17).*

1   Have the air conditioning system discharged (see **Warning** above). Disconnect the cable from the negative terminal of the battery. **Caution:** *On models equipped with a Delco Loc II or Theftlock audio system, be sure the lockout feature is turned off before performing any procedure which requires disconnecting the battery.*

2   Clean the compressor thoroughly around the refrigerant line fittings.

3   Remove the serpentine drivebelt (see Chapter 1).

4   Raise the vehicle and support it securely

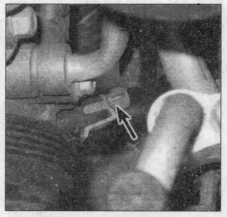

14.5c Disconnect the electrical connector from the air conditioning compressor (2.2L OHC engine)

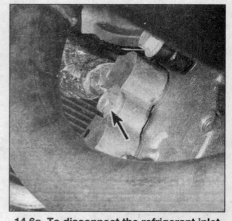

14.6a To disconnect the refrigerant inlet and outlet lines from the compressor on a 2.2L OHV engine, remove this bolt

on jackstands.

5   Disconnect the electrical connector from the air conditioning compressor **(see illustrations)**.

6   Disconnect the suction and discharge lines **(2.2L OHV engine, see illustration 14.6a; 2.3L and 2.4L OHC engines, see**

illustration 14.5b; 2.2L OHC engine, see illustration 14.6b) from the compressor. Both lines are mounted to the back of the compressor with a plate secured by one bolt. Plug the open fittings to prevent the entry of dirt and moisture, and discard the seals between the plate and compressor.

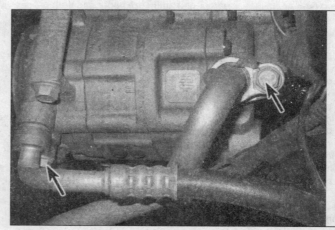

14.6b To disconnect the refrigerant inlet and outlet lines from the compressor on a 2.2L OHC engine, remove these two bolts

14.8a To detach the compressor from a 2.3L or 2.4L OHC engine, remove these four bolts

14.8b To detach the compressor from a 2.2L OHC engine, remove these three bolts

7   On 2.2L OHV engines, unbolt and remove the rear compressor mount. **Note:** *On some later models it is necessary to remove the right-side engine mount bolt and raise the engine to access the rear compressor mount bolts.*

8   Remove the compressor mounting bolts **(see illustrations)** and remove the compressor from the engine compartment.

9   If you're installing a new compressor, pour the oil from the old compressor into a graduated container and measure it. Then add the exact same amount of new PAG refrigerant oil to the new compressor. (This is a good rule-of-thumb when replacing the compressor. But always follow the manufacturer's directions, which will be included with the new replacement compressor.) **Note:** *Some replacement compressors come with refrigerant oil in them. Follow the directions with the compressor regarding the draining of excess oil prior to installation.* **Caution:** *The oil used must be labeled as compatible with R-134a refrigerant systems.*

10   Installation is the reverse of the disassembly. When installing the line fitting bolt to the compressor, be sure to use new O-ring seals, lubricated with a little clean refrigerant oil, then tighten the bolt securely.

11   Reconnect the cable to the negative battery terminal.

12   Have the system evacuated, recharged and leak tested by the shop that discharged it.

15   Air conditioning condenser - removal and installation

Warning 1: *The models covered by this manual are equipped with airbags. Always disable the airbag system before working in the vicinity of the impact sensors, steering column or instrument panel to avoid the possibility of accidental deployment of the airbag(s), which could cause personal injury (see Chapter 12).*

Warning 2: *The air conditioning system is under high pressure. DO NOT loosen any fittings or remove any components until after the system has been discharged. Air conditioning refrigerant must be properly discharged into an EPA-approved container at a dealership service department or an automotive air conditioning facility. Always wear eye protection when disconnecting air conditioning system fittings.*

1   Have the air conditioning system discharged (see **Warning** above). Disconnect the cable from the negative terminal of the battery. **Caution:** *On models equipped with a Delco Loc II or Theftlock audio system, be sure the lockout feature is turned off before performing any procedure which requires disconnecting the battery.*

2   Disconnect the refrigerant line fittings from the right side of the condenser and cap the open fittings to prevent the entry of dirt and moisture.

3   Remove the hood latch support (see Section 5).

4   Remove the right and left headlamp assemblies (see Chapter 12).

5   Raise the vehicle and support it securely on jackstands.

6   Disable the airbag system and remove the front airbag (crash) sensor from the mounting brackets (see Chapter 12).

7   Working in the engine compartment, remove the right side radiator mount. Make sure the hood latch mechanism and the airbag sensor harness are secured, out of the way.

8   Remove the condenser mounting bolts from the radiator.

9   Tilt the upper half of the radiator forward and dislodge the condenser insulator mounts from the radiator support.

10   Pull the condenser up between the radiator and the radiator support to remove it from the vehicle. **Caution:** *The condenser is made of aluminum - be careful not to damage it during removal.*

11   Installation is the reverse of removal. Be sure to use new, compatible O-rings on the refrigerant line fittings (lubricate the O-rings with clean refrigerant oil. If a new condenser is installed, add 1 ounce of new refrigerant oil to the system (oil must be R-134a compatible.

12   Have the system evacuated, recharged and leak tested by the shop that discharged it.

16   Air conditioning evaporator - removal and installation

Refer to illustrations 16.3, 16.5a, 16.5b, 16.6a, 16.6b, 16.6c, 16.7a and 16.7b

Warning 1: *The models covered by this manual are equipped with airbags. Always disable the airbag system before working in the vicinity of the impact sensors, steering column or instrument panel to avoid the possibility of accidental deployment of the airbag(s), which could cause personal injury (see Chapter 12).*

Warning 2: *The air conditioning system is under high pressure. DO NOT loosen any fittings or remove any components until after the system has been discharged. Air conditioning refrigerant must be properly discharged into an EPA-approved container at a dealership service department or an automotive air conditioning repair facility. Always wear eye protection when disconnecting air conditioning system fittings.*

1   Have the air conditioning system discharged (see **Warning** above). Disconnect the cable from the negative terminal of the battery. **Caution:** *On models equipped with a Delco Loc II or Theftlock audio system, be sure the lockout feature is turned off before performing any procedure which requires disconnecting the battery.*

2   Drain the cooling system (see Chapter 1).

3   Disconnect the air conditioning lines at the passenger side of the firewall **(see illustration)**.

16.3 Disconnect the refrigerant lines leading to the
evaporator core

16.5a Remove the heater core shroud mounting bolt and then
drop the assembly using the hinge and . . .

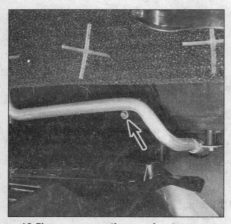

16.5b . . . access the rear heater core
shroud bolt by pulling down the assembly
to expose the rear section

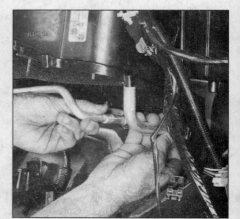

16.6a Remove the evaporator core inlet
line clamp and bolt

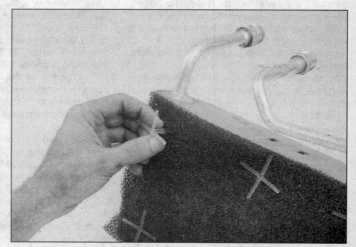

16.6b Pull the evaporator lines straight
back and out of the firewall

4   Follow the procedures in Section 11 for
removing the heater core. **Note:** *Remember,
this will require complete instrument panel
removal, heater housing disassembly and*

*heater core removal to gain access to the
evaporator core.*
5   Remove the evaporator protective
shroud **(see illustrations)**.
6   Remove the evaporator core clamp bolt

and clamp **(see illustration)**, then slide the
evaporator core out carefully **(see illustrations)**.
7   Check the core over carefully for signs
of leaks **(see illustrations)**.

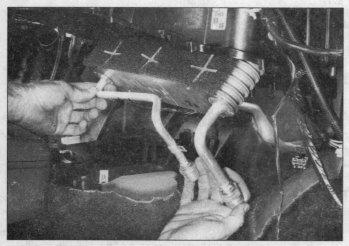

16.6c Angle the evaporator core inlet and outlet pipes down to
separate the core from the heater core box

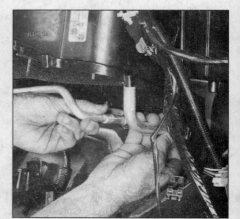

16.7a Pull the filter pad retainers straight out and lift the filter pad
from the evaporator core

16.7b Check the evaporator core for leaks, damage or cracks

17.3 Working from under the engine compartment, disconnect the high pressure line near the bottom of the engine compartment

8   If a new evaporator core is to be installed, save all of the sealing gaskets from the original unit and transfer them.

9   Installation is the reverse of the removal procedure. Lubricate all O-rings with clean refrigerant oil.

10   If a new evaporator has been installed, add 1 ounce of refrigerant oil (oil must be R-134a compatible). Have the system evacuated, recharged and leak tested by the shop that discharged it.

17   Air conditioning expansion (orifice) tube - removal and installation

Refer to illustrations 17.3, 17.4 and 17.5

Warning 2: *The air conditioning system is under high pressure. DO NOT loosen any fittings or remove any components until after the system has been discharged. Air condi-* *tioning refrigerant must be properly discharged into an EPA-approved container at a dealership service department or an automotive air conditioning repair facility. Always wear eye protection when disconnecting air conditioning system fittings.*

1   Have the air conditioning system discharged and the refrigerant recovered (see **Warning** above). Disconnect the cable from the negative terminal of the battery. **Caution:** *On models equipped with a Theftlock audio system, be sure the lockout feature is turned off before performing any procedure which requires disconnecting the battery.*

2   Remove the air cleaner and duct (see Chapter 4).

3   Disconnect the refrigerant high-pressure line at the fitting at the bottom of the engine compartment **(see illustration)**.

4   The expansion tube is a tube with a fixed-diameter orifice and a mesh filter at each end **(see illustration)**. When you separate the pipe at the fitting you will see one end of the orifice tube inside the pipe leading to the evaporator. Use needle-nose pliers to remove the orifice tube.

5   The orifice tube acts to meter the refrigerant, changing it from high-pressure liquid to low-pressure liquid. It is possible to reuse the orifice tube if **(see illustration)**:

 a) *The screens aren't plugged with grit or foreign material*
 b) *Neither screen is torn*
 c) *The plastic housing over the screens is intact*
 d) *The brass orifice inside the plastic housing is unrestricted*

6   Installation is the reverse of removal. Be sure to insert the expansion tube with the shorter end in first, toward the evaporator. **Caution:** *Always use a new O-ring when installing the expansion (orifice) tube.*

7   Retighten the fitting and refrigerant line, then have the system evacuated, recharged and leak-tested by the shop that discharged it.

17.4 Carefully remove the expansion tube using needle-nose pliers

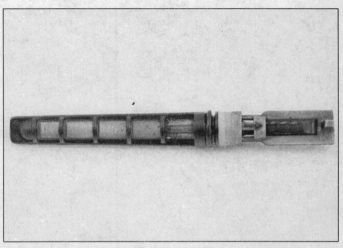

17.5 The expansion tube is equipped with a tapered mesh screen that must be cleaned and not have any holes or damage

Notes

Chapter 4
Fuel and exhaust systems

Contents

Specifications

General

Fuel pressure
  2.2L OHV engine (1995 through 2002)
    1995 through 2000
      Engine not running, with ignition key turned to ON
        Fuel pump running (pump primes system for
          1 to 2 seconds) .... 41 to 47 psi
        After fuel pump stops running .... 36 to 42 psi (for at least 10 minutes)
      Engine running at idle .... 31 to 44 psi
    2001 and 2002
      Engine not running, with ignition key turned to ON
        Fuel pump running (pump primes system for
          1 to 2 seconds) .... 53 to 59 psi
        After fuel pump stops running .... 38 to 54 psi (for at least 10 minutes)
      Engine running at idle .... 43 to 56 psi
  2.2L OHC engine (2002 on)
    Engine not running, with ignition key turned to ON
      Fuel pump running (pump primes system for 1 to 2 seconds) ... 50 to 60 psi
      After fuel pump stops running .... 45 to 55 psi (for at least one minute)
    Engine running at idle .... 40 to 57 psi
  2.3L (1995 only) and 2.4L OHC engines (1996 through 2002)
    1995 through 1998
      Engine not running, with ignition key turned to ON
        Fuel pump running (primes system for 1 to 2 seconds) ..... 41 to 47 psi
        After fuel pump stops running .... 36 to 42 psi (for at least 10 minutes)
      Engine running (at idle) .... 31 to 44 psi
    1999 through 2002
      Engine not running, with ignition key turned to ON
        Fuel pump running (primes system for 1 to 2 seconds) ..... 52 to 58 psi
        After fuel pump stops running .... 37 to 52 psi (for at least 10 minutes)
      Engine running (at idle) .... 42 to 55 psi

Injector resistance
  2.2L OHV engine
    1995 only .... 11.6 to 12.4 ohms
    1996 and 1997 .... 11.8 to 12.6 ohms
    1998 through 2000.. 1.95 to 2.3 ohms
    2001 and 2002 .... 11 to 14 ohms
  2.2L OHC engine (2002 on).. 11 to 14 ohms
  2.3L (1995 only) and 2.4L OHC engines
    1995 (2.3L engine) .... 1.95 to 2.15 ohms
    1996 through 1998 .... 1.95 to 2.3 ohms
    1999 and 2000 .... 11.4 to 12.6 ohms
    2001 and 2002 .... 11 to 14 ohms

Torque specifications

Ft-lbs (unless otherwise indicated)

Fuel pressure regulator mounting bolt(s)
  2.2L OHV engine
    1995 through 1997.. 31 in-lbs
    1998 and later .... 31 in-lbs
  2.2L OHC engine... 44 in-lbs
  2.3L and 2.4L OHC engines .... 102 in-lbs
Fuel rail mounting bolts
  2.2L OHV engine (1998 and later) 18
  2.2L OHC engine
  2.3L and 2.4L OHC engines 19
Throttle body bolts/nuts
  2.2L OHV engine (1998 and later) .... 89 in-lbs
  2.2L OHC engine... 89 in-lbs
  2.3L and 2.4L OHC engine .... 58 in-lbs

1   General information

Multiport Fuel Injection (MFI) system

All vehicles covered by this manual are equipped with a Multiport Fuel Injection (MFI) system. Although the details of each system vary in accordance with the engine type and model year, all systems include an electric in-tank fuel pump, a fuel filter, a fuel rail with four fuel injectors, a fuel pressure regulator, an air filter housing and a throttle body. The fuel pump delivers pressurized fuel to the fuel rail. The fuel pressure regulator maintains fuel pressure within the specified range. When the fuel pressure regulator opens, excess fuel is sent back to the fuel tank through return fuel line. The fuel injectors are small electric solenoid-operated valves that meter a precise amount of fuel into each intake port in accordance with a continuous stream of commands from "injector drivers" inside the Powertrain Command Module (PCM). The air filter housing prevents dirt and moisture from entering the engine. The throttle body meters the amount of air entering the engine.

Fuel pump and lines

Fuel is circulated from the fuel tank to the fuel injection system, and back to the fuel tank, through a series of metal and plastic fuel lines running along the underside of the vehicle.

The fuel pump circuit is controlled by a fuel pump relay mounted on the inner fender panel in the engine compartment. When the ignition is turned ON (not START), before the engine is started, the PCM energizes the fuel pump relay for two seconds, which activates the fuel pump long enough to prime the system and bring it up to operating pressure. After the system is pressurized, the pump relay is turned off by the PCM, which also turns off the pump. If the ignition key were then turned back to OFF, the pump would remain off, and the fuel system would slowly lose pressure. But if the ignition key is then turned to START, the PCM begins to supply power to the fuel pump relay again, and will do so as long as it receives reference pulses from the Crankshaft Position (CKP) sensor. A defective fuel pump relay effectively disables the fuel pump and prevents the engine from starting and running. **Note:** *Some early models are equipped with a combination fuel pump relay/oil pressure indicator switch. The switch is normally open until oil pressure reaches six psi, causing it to close. If oil pressure falls below two psi, the switch opens, shutting down the fuel pump. This switch is a fail-safe device used to stop the engine if oil pressure fails. If the fuel pump relay fails, the switch will provide battery voltage directly to the fuel pump. In the event of fuel pump relay and/or oil pressure switch problems, be sure to check both components. But before doing so, make sure that you disable the fuel pump by disconnecting the electrical connector from the pump.*

Exhaust system

The exhaust system includes the exhaust manifold (see Chapter 2), a series of exhaust pipes, the catalytic converter (see Chapter 6) and a muffler. The exhaust system is suspended from the underside of the vehicle by a series of rubber hangers. Anytime you're working underneath the vehicle, be sure to inspect these hangers. If they're broken, torn, cracked or otherwise deteriorated, replace them.

2   Fuel pressure relief procedure

Refer to illustration 2.3

Warning 1: *Gasoline is extremely flammable, so take extra precautions when you work on any part of the fuel system. Don't smoke or allow open flames or bare light bulbs near the work area, and don't work in a garage where a gas-type appliance (such as a water heater or a clothes dryer) is present. Since gasoline is carcinogenic, wear latex gloves when there's a possibility of being exposed to fuel, and, if you spill any fuel on your skin, rinse it off immediately with soap and water. Mop up any spills immediately and do not store fuel-soaked rags where they could ignite. The fuel system is under constant pressure, so, if any fuel lines are to be disconnected, the fuel pressure in the system must be relieved first. When you perform any kind of work on the fuel system, wear safety glasses and have a Class B type fire extinguisher on hand.*

Warning 2: *Always relieve the system fuel pressure before disconnecting fuel line connections. Failure to relieve fuel pressure could allow raw fuel to squirt out when a fuel line connection is disconnected, which might spray fuel in your eyes or onto your body and cause serious injury.*

Note: *After the fuel pressure has been relieved, it's a good idea to put a shop towel over a fuel line connection before disconnecting it in order to absorb any residual fuel that might leak out when the lines are opened.*

1   To minimize the risk of fire or personal injury, always relieve the fuel pressure before servicing any fuel system component.

2   Remove the fuel filler cap to relieve any pressure that has built up in the tank.

3   There are three ways that you can relieve the fuel system pressure on these vehicles:

a) *The easiest way is to simply raise the hood, open the engine compartment fuse and relay box, remove the fuel pump relay* **(see illustration)**, *start the engine and let it stall (it might not even start at all, which is fine). Whether the engine stalls or doesn't even start, the fuel pressure is now relieved, but it's still a good idea to put a shop towel around the first fuel fitting that you disconnect, to catch the residual fuel that will spill out.*

b) *If you're planning to replace the fuel pump/fuel level sending unit module or the fuel tank, raise the vehicle, place it securely on jackstands and disconnect the fuel pump electrical connector, which is located near the fuel tank. Then start the engine and allow it to run until the engine stalls (the engine might not even start at all if the residual fuel pressure is low enough). The fuel pressure is now relieved. It is a good idea to place shop towels around the fuel fitting to be disconnected to absorb any residual fuel that spills out.*

c) *The fuel rails on 2.2L OHC engines are equipped with a Schrader valve test port for connecting a fuel pressure gauge to measure fuel pressure. You can also use this Schrader valve to relieve system fuel pressure, if you have the right type of gauge, with a bleeder valve on it. You'll also need a suitable adapter to connect the pressure gauge hose to the Schrader valve* **(see illustrations 3.3b and 3.5)** *you can also use it to relieve system fuel pressure. Simply hook up your fuel pressure gauge to the Schrader valve, then open the bleeder valve and bleed off any residual fuel into a container suitable for gasoline. (Fuel pressure gauges with bleeder valves and hoses with the right adapters are available at most auto parts stores.)*

---

3   Fuel pump/fuel pressure - check

Warning: *Gasoline is extremely flammable, so take extra precautions when you work on any part of the fuel system. See the* **Warning** *in Section 2.*

Fuel pump operational check

1   The fuel pump is located inside the fuel tank, which muffles its sound when the engine is running. But you can actually hear the fuel pump. Sit inside the vehicle with the windows closed, turn the ignition key to ON (not START) and listen carefully for the whirring sound made by the fuel pump as it's briefly turned on by the PCM to pressurize the fuel system prior to starting the engine. You will only hear a soft whirring sound for a second or two, but that sound tells you that the pump is working. If you can't hear the pump, remove the fuel filler cap and have an assistant turn the ignition switch to ON while you listen for the sound of the pump. If the pump does not come on when the ignition key is turned to ON, check the fuel pump fuse and relay (both of which are located in the engine compartment fuse and relay box). If the fuse and relay are okay, check the wiring back to the fuel pump (see Section 5 if you need help locating the fuel pump electrical connector). If the fuse, relay and wiring are okay, the fuel pump is probably defective. If the pump runs continuously with the ignition key in its ON position, the Powertrain Control Module (PCM) is probably defective. Have the PCM checked by a dealer service department or other qualified repair shop.

Fuel pressure check

Refer to illustrations 3.3a, 3.3b, 3.4, 3.5, 3.8 and 3.9

Note: *The fuel filter must be in good condition for the following check. If it's dirty, the results of your measurements will be inaccurate. If you have any doubt about the condition of the fuel filter, install a new filter (see Chapter 1).*

2   Relieve the fuel system pressure (see Section 2).

3   For the following test, you will need a fuel pressure gauge and a hose and adapter setup suitable for connecting your gauge to the fuel system **(see illustrations)**. If you're going to measure the fuel pressure on a 2.2L

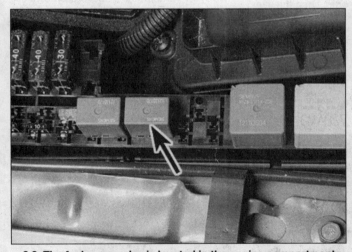

2.3 The fuel pump relay is located in the engine compartment fuse/relay box, near the air filter housing (the fuel pump relay might not be in the same location in the fuse box on your vehicle, so be sure to verify its location by referring to the fuse and relay guide, which is in your owner's manual and on the lid of the fuse box)

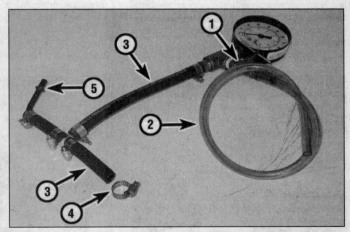

3.3a A typical fuel pressure gauge setup for measuring fuel pressure on a 2.2L OHV engine or on a 2.3L or 2.4L OHC engine (which do not have a Schrader valve test port on the fuel rail):

1) *Bleeder valve*
2) *Bleeder hose*
3) *Approved fuel hoses for tee-ing into the fuel system between the fuel supply hose or line and the fuel rail*
4) *Enough hose clamps to secure the hoses to the gauge, the fuel tee-fitting, the fuel supply line and the fuel rail*
5) *A flared section of metal fuel line*

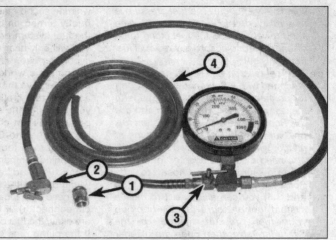

3.3b A typical fuel pressure gauge setup for measuring fuel pressure on 2.2L OHC engines (which have a Schrader valve test port on the fuel rail):

1) *Screw-on adapter for the quick-release fitting*
2) *Quick-release fitting for connecting the gauge hose to the Schrader valve*
3) *Bleeder valve*
4) *Bleeder hose*

OHV engine or on 2.3L or 2.4L OHC engines, you will be "tee-ing" into the fuel system between the fuel supply hose and the fuel rail, so you'll need a setup like the one shown in **illustration 3.3a**. If you're going to measure the fuel pressure on a 2.2L OHC engine, which has a Schrader valve test port on the fuel rail, use a setup similar to the one shown in **illustration 3.3b**.

4   On 2.2L OHV engines and on 2.3L and 2.4L OHC engines, connect a fuel pressure gauge between the fuel rail and the fuel supply line **(see illustration)**. You will need a fuel pressure gauge capable of measuring fuel pressure in the specified range (see Specifications). If the fuel line connection that you're going to tee into is equipped with quick-connect fittings (most models use them), then you will also need the correct adapters to hook up to the quick-connect fittings on the fuel lines. If it's necessary to use special fuel line adapters to connect to the fuel line quick-connect fittings, adapters can be fabricated from approved metal fuel line and the necessary quick-connect fittings.

5   On 2.2L OHC engines, locate the Schrader valve test port on the fuel supply line, unscrew the cap and connect your fuel pressure gauge **(see illustration)**.

6   Turn the ignition switch to ON (engine not running). The fuel pump should run for about two seconds, to prime the system, then it should stop. Note the reading on the gauge. After the pump stops running the pressure should hold steady and should be within the range listed in this Chapter's Specifications.

7   Start the engine and let it idle at normal operating temperature; the pressure should go down by 3 to 10 psi. Disconnect the vacuum hose from the fuel pressure regulator; the pressure should increase by 3 to 10 psi. If all the pressure readings are within the limits listed in this Chapter's Specifications, the system is operating correctly.

8   If the pressure doesn't drop by 3 to 10 psi after starting the engine or doesn't increase by a similar amount when the vacuum hose is disconnected from the fuel pressure regulator, apply 12 to 14 inches of vacuum to the pressure regulator **(see illustration)**. If the pressure still doesn't drop,

replace the fuel pressure regulator (see Section 15). If the pressure does drop, the regulator isn't getting a good vacuum signal from the intake manifold. The vacuum hose is probably cracked or loose. Inspect the vacuum hose carefully. If it's simply loose at one end, cut off a small part of the hose end, reconnect it and repeat this test. If the hose is cracked or torn somewhere between the two ends, replace the hose.

9   If the fuel pressure is not within specifications, check the following:

a) *If the pressure is higher than specified, check for vacuum to the fuel pressure regulator. Vacuum must fluctuate with the increase or decrease in engine rpm. If vacuum is present, check for a pinched or clogged fuel return hose or line. If the return line is OK, replace the regulator.*

b) *If the pressure is lower than specified, replace the fuel filter to rule out the possibility that a clogged filter is causing the lower-than-specified fuel pressure. If the pressure is still low, install a fuel line shut-off adapter between the pressure regulator and the return line (see illustration). You can fabricate your own fuel line shut-off adapter from approved fuel hose, a shut off valve (available at hardware stores) and the necessary hose clamps or quick-connect fittings to hook up your rig between the pressure regulator and the return line. Or, instead of a shut-off valve, use a section of fuel hose that you can pinch with a pair of pliers). With the valve open (or the hose not pinched), start the engine (if possible) and slowly close the valve or pinch the hose (only pinch the hose on the adapter you fabricated). If the pressure rises, replace the regulator (see Section 15).* **Warning:** *Don't allow the fuel pressure to exceed 60 psi. Also, don't attempt to restrict the return line by pinching it, as the nylon fuel line will be damaged.*

3.4 On 2.2L OHV engines (shown) and on 2.3L and 2.4L OHC engines, tee in a fuel pressure gauge between the fuel supply line and the fuel rail

3.5 On 2.2L OHC engines, unscrew the cap from the Schrader valve test port on the fuel line, then hook up your fuel pressure gauge to the test port (if your gauge has a bleeder valve, this setup can also be used for relieving fuel pressure)

3.8 Connect a vacuum pump to the fuel pressure regulator, apply vacuum to the fuel pressure regulator and check the fuel pressure - the fuel pressure should decrease as the vacuum increases

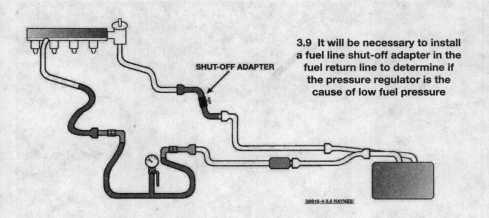

3.9 It will be necessary to install a fuel line shut-off adapter in the fuel return line to determine if the pressure regulator is the cause of low fuel pressure

SHUT-OFF ADAPTER

c) *If the pressure is still low with the fuel return line restricted, the fuel pump is probably defective (see Section 7).*

10   When the test is completed, relieve the fuel pressure (see Section 2) and disconnect the fuel pressure gauge. If you're working on a 2.2L OHV engine or a 2.3L or 2.4L OHC engine, reconnect the fuel supply line to the fuel rail. If you're working on a 2.2L OHC engine, don't forget to put the cap back on the Schrader valve test port.

---

4   Fuel lines and fittings - repair and replacement

Warning: *Gasoline is extremely flammable, so take extra precautions when you work on any part of the fuel system. See the* **Warning** *in Section 2.*

1   Always relieve the fuel pressure before servicing fuel lines or fittings on fuel-injected vehicles (see Section 2).
2   The fuel supply and return lines connect the fuel tank to the fuel rail on the engine. These lines are secured to the vehicle underbody by plastic clips. These clips also secure the vapor lines for the Evaporative Emission Control (EVAP) system. Be sure to inspect the fuel and EVAP lines for leaks, kinks and dents whenever you're servicing something underneath the vehicle.
3   Whenever you're working under the vehicle, be sure to inspect all fuel and EVAP lines for leaks, kinks, dents and other damage. Always replace a damaged fuel line or EVAP line immediately. Leaking fuel and EVAP lines will result in loss of fuel and excessive air pollution (leaking raw fuel emits unburned hydrocarbon vapors into the atmosphere).
4   If you find signs of dirt in the lines during disassembly, disconnect all lines and blow them out with compressed air. Be sure to inspect the fuel strainer on the fuel pump (see Section 7) for damage and deterioration. Also inspect the fuel filter (see Chapter 1).

Steel tubing

5   Because fuel lines used on fuel-injected vehicles are under high pressure, it is critical that they be replaced with lines of equivalent specification. If you have to replace a fuel or EVAP line, buy the replacement tubing from a Chevrolet or Pontiac dealer. If you're planning to buy your tubing somewhere else, make sure that you use steel tubing that meets the manufacturer's specifications. Don't use copper or aluminum tubing to replace steel tubing. These materials cannot withstand normal vehicle vibration.
6   Some steel fuel lines have threaded fittings. When loosening these fittings to service or replace components:

a) *Use a backup wrench while loosening and tightening the fittings.*
b) *If you're going to replace one of these fittings, use original equipment parts or parts that meet original equipment standards.*

Plastic tubing

7   Most of the fuel (and EVAP) lines on the vehicles covered in this manual are plastic. If you ever have to replace a plastic line, use only the original equipment plastic tubing. **Caution:** *When removing or installing plastic fuel line tubing, be careful not to bend or twist it too much, which can damage it. And damaged fuel lines MUST be replaced! Also, be aware that the plastic fuel tubing is NOT heat resistant, so keep it away from excessive heat. Nor is it acid-proof, so don't wipe it off with a shop rag that has been used to wipe off battery electrolyte. If you accidentally spill or wipe electrolyte on plastic fuel tubing, replace the tubing.*

Flexible hoses

Warning: *Use only original equipment replacement hoses or their equivalent. Unapproved hoses might fail when subjected to the high operating pressures of the fuel system.*

8   Don't route fuel hoses within four inches of exhaust system components or within ten inches of a catalytic converter. Make sure that no rubber hoses are installed directly against the vehicle, particularly in places where there is any vibration. If allowed to touch some vibrating part of the vehicle, a hose can easily become chafed and it might start leaking. A good rule of thumb is to maintain a minimum of 1/4-inch clearance around a hose (or metal line) to prevent contact with the vehicle underbody.

Fuel line and EVAP line fittings

9   The vehicles covered in this manual use two kinds of fuel line quick-connect fittings (metal or plastic) for most connections at the fuel pump, the fuel tank, under the vehicle and in the engine compartment. (A third type of plastic quick-connect fitting is used only at the EVAP canister and on the vent hose connection at the fuel tank for the EVAP canister vent solenoid.)
10   The procedure for releasing each type of fuel line fitting is different. But a few rules of thumb apply to all fittings:

a) *Inspect the fitting for dirt. If the fitting is dirty, clean it off before disassembling it. The seals in the fitting will stick to the fuel line as they age. Twist the fitting on the line, then push and pull the fitting until it moves freely.*
b) *Always disconnect all fuel line fittings from a fuel system component before removing the component.*
c) *When disconnecting a quick-connect fitting, inspect the condition of the retainer before reconnecting the fitting. The best strategy with respect to retainers is to simply replace the retainer every time that you disconnect the fitting.*
d) *When you disconnect a fitting with an O-ring inside, inspect the O-ring before reconnecting the fitting. Fuel line fittings are under the same pressure as the rest of the fuel system, so to avoid leaks (and fires!) make VERY SURE that the O-ring is good condition. Even better, simply replace it.*
e) *In most cases, the fitting itself is a non-removable part of the fuel line, so you might have to replace an entire fuel line if a fitting is damaged or defective.*

Metal collar quick-connect fittings

Disconnection

Refer to illustrations 4.12, 4.13a and 4.13b
Note 1: *You'll find these fittings at the connections between the fuel supply and return lines and the fuel rail.*
Note 2: *You'll need a special tool set (available at most auto parts stores) to disconnect these fittings.*
Note 3: *The photos accompanying the disconnection procedure depicted here shows the metal collar quick-connect fittings at the fuel rail of a 2.2L OHC engine, but the metal quick-connect fittings on other engines are similar.*

11   Relieve the fuel system pressure (see Section 2).
12   Pull down the end of the retainer (if equipped) that faces away from the fitting

4.12 Pull down the end of the retainer that's facing away from the connector, then remove the retainer by disengaging the other end from the female side of the fitting

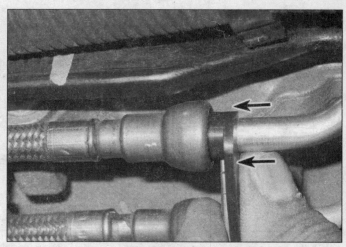

4.13a Here are a pair of metal collar quick-connect fittings; insert the special tool into the female side of the fitting . . .

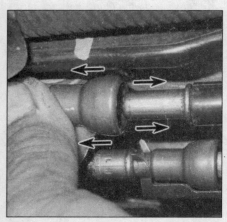

4.13b . . . then push it into the fitting and pull the two halves of the fitting apart

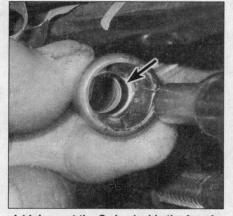

4.14 Inspect the O-ring inside the female side of the fitting; if it's cracked, torn or deteriorated, replace it

4.19a To release a plastic quick-connect fitting, depress the tabs on the connector housing with a small screwdriver, then continue pressing on them . . .

(see illustration), then remove it.

13   Using the correct disconnect tool (available at most auto parts stores) for the size of the fitting, insert the tool into the female side of the fitting, then push it into the fitting to release the locking tabs and pull the fitting apart **(see illustrations)**.

Reconnection

Refer to illustration 4.14

14   Inspect the O-ring **(see illustration)**. If it's dried out, cracked, torn or otherwise deteriorated, replace it.

15   Apply a few drops of clean engine oil to the male pipe end.

16   Push both sides of the fitting together until the retaining tabs snap into place. Pull on both sides of the fitting to verify that it's securely connected.

17   Install the retainer.

18   Start the engine and check for fuel leaks.

Plastic collar quick-connect fittings

Disconnection

Refer to illustrations 4.19a and 4.19b

19   To release this type of quick-connect fitting, depress the tabs of the retainer **(see illustration)**. Once the retainer is released, continue pressing on the tabs while pulling the two fuel lines apart **(see illustration)**.

20   Remove and discard the old retainer from the male side of the fitting.

21   Remove and discard the indicator ring from the male side of the fitting.

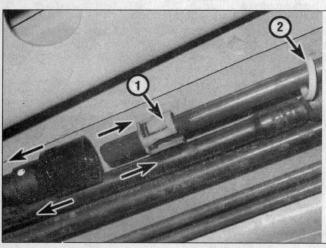

4.19b . . . until the two fuel lines are disconnected, then removed and discard the old retainer (1) and the indicator ring (2) (the indicator ring is used only during factory assembly; there is no need to replace it)

4.22 Inspect the old O-ring inside the female side of the fitting; if it's cracked, torn or deteriorated, replace it

4.23 Install a new retainer in the female side of the fitting; make sure that the release tabs are aligned with the windows in the connector

Reconnection

Refer to illustrations 4.22 and 4.23

22 Inspect the old O-ring inside the female side of the fitting **(see illustration)**. If it's dried out, cracked, torn or deteriorated, replace it.

23 Insert a new retainer in the female side of the fitting. Make sure that the release tabs are aligned with the "windows" of the connector **(see illustration)**.

24 Apply a few drops of engine oil to the tip of the male fuel line.

25 Push both sides of the fitting together until the retainer release tabs snap into place.

26 Pull on both sides of the fitting to verify that it's securely connected.

27 Start the engine and check for fuel leaks.

5 Fuel tank - removal and installation

Refer to illustrations 5.6, 5.7 and 5.10

Warning: *Gasoline is extremely flammable, so take extra precautions when you work on any part of the fuel system. See the* **Warning** *in Section 2.*

Note: *Don't begin this procedure until the fuel gauge indicates the tank is empty or nearly empty. If the tank must be removed when it isn't empty (for example, if the fuel pump malfunctions), siphon any remaining fuel from the tank prior to removal.*

1 Unless the vehicle has been driven far enough to completely empty the tank, it's a good idea to siphon the residual fuel out before removing the tank from the vehicle. **Warning:** *DO NOT start the siphoning action*

by mouth! Use a siphoning kit, available at most auto parts stores.

2 Relieve the fuel system pressure (see Section 2).

3 Disconnect the cable from the negative terminal of the battery. **Caution:** *If the vehicle is equipped with a Delco Loc II or Theftlock audio system, make sure you have the correct activation code before disconnecting the battery.*

4 Raise the vehicle and support it securely on jackstands placed underneath the jacking points.

5 Disconnect the exhaust rubber hangers and allow the rear portion of the exhaust system to rest on the rear axle. Remove the fuel tank heat shield, if equipped.

6 Disconnect the fuel filler neck hose and the filler neck EVAP line **(see illustration)**.

7 Disconnect the fuel feed and return lines **(see illustration)** and the EVAP line. You'll

5.6 To disconnect the fuel filler neck hose, loosen this hose clamp (1). To disconnect the filler neck EVAP hose, loosen the smaller hose clamp (2) next to it. To detach the fuel tank, remove the tank retaining strap bolts (3) (these are the rear strap bolts; to locate the front strap bolts, trace each strap to the front of the tank)

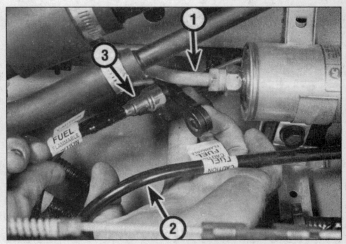

5.7 Fuel and EVAP lines at the fuel tank:

1   *Fuel supply line at the fuel filter*
2   *Fuel supply line from fuel filter*
3   *Fuel return line*

need a special tool to disconnect these fittings (see Section 4).

8   Support the fuel tank with a transmission jack or with a floor jack. If you're going to use a floor jack, be sure to place a piece of plywood between the tank and the jack head to protect the tank from damage.

9   Disconnect both fuel tank retaining strap bolts **(see illustration 5.6)** and remove the straps.

10   Lower the tank enough to disconnect the electrical connectors from the fuel pump/fuel level sending unit and, if equipped, the fuel tank pressure sensor **(see illustration)**.

11   Lower the tank to the floor.

12   Installation is the reverse of removal. Be sure to tighten the fuel tank retaining strap bolts securely.

6   Fuel tank cleaning and repair - general information

1   A professional with experience in this critical and potentially dangerous work should carry out all repairs to the fuel tank or filler neck. Even after cleaning and flushing of the fuel system, explosive fumes can remain and ignite during repair of the tank.

2   If the fuel tank is removed from the vehicle, it should not be placed in an area where sparks or open flames could ignite the fumes coming out of the tank. Be especially careful inside garages where a gas-type appliance is located, because it could cause an explosion.

7   Fuel pump/fuel level sending unit - removal and installation

Refer to illustrations 7.5a, 7.5b, 7.5c, 7.6, 7.8a and 7.8b

Warning: *Gasoline is extremely flammable, so take extra precautions when you work on*

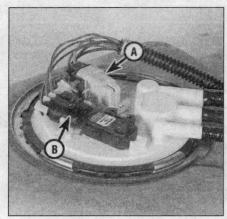

5.10 Lower the fuel tank enough to disconnect the electrical connectors from the fuel pump/fuel level sending unit (A) and, if equipped, the fuel tank pressure sensor (B)

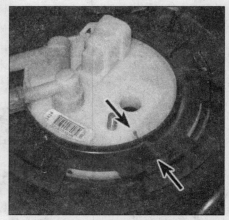

7.5a Make alignment marks on the fuel pump mounting flange and on the fuel tank to ensure correct realignment of the pump when installing it again

any part of the fuel system. See the **Warning** *in Section 2.*

1   Relieve the fuel system pressure (see Section 2).

2   Disconnect the cable from the negative battery terminal. **Caution:** *If the vehicle is equipped with a Delco Loc II or Theftlock audio system, make sure you have the correct activation code before disconnecting the battery.*

3   Remove the fuel tank (see Section 5).

4   Disconnect the electrical connectors from the fuel pump/fuel level sending unit and from the fuel tank pressure sensor **(see illustration 5.10)**.

5   The fuel pump/sending unit assembly is located inside the fuel tank. Before removing the pump on a 1999 or later model, mark the orientation of the fuel pump in relation to the fuel tank **(see illustration)**. On 1995 through 1998 models, push down on the fuel

pump/fuel level sending unit assembly and use a pair of snap-ring pliers to remove the big snap-ring that retains the fuel pump/fuel level sending unit **(see illustration)**. On 1999 and later models, use a pair of water pump pliers to unscrew the fuel pump/fuel level sending unit locknut by turning it counter-clockwise **(see illustration)**. If the locknut is too tight to loosen this way, use a hammer and a brass punch to loosen it (don't use a steel punch, which could produce sparks when struck by the hammer).

6   Lift the fuel pump/sending unit assembly from the fuel tank **(see illustration)**. **Caution:** *The fuel level float and sending unit are delicate. Do not bump them against the tank during removal or the accuracy of the sending unit may be affected.*

7   Inspect the condition of the O-ring around the opening of the tank. If it is dried, cracked or deteriorated, replace it.

8   Remove the fuel inlet strainer from the

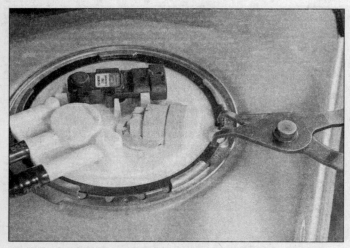

7.5b On 1995 through 1998 models, push down on the fuel pump/fuel level sending unit assembly and use a pair of snap-ring pliers to remove this big snap-ring

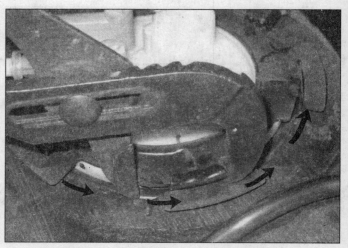

7.5c On 1999 and later models, use a large pair of water pump pliers to loosen and unscrew the fuel pump locknut; if the locknut is too tight to loosen this way, carefully tap it loose with a hammer and *brass* punch (using a steel punch could cause sparks)

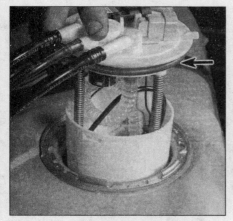

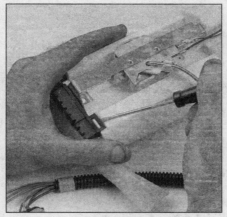

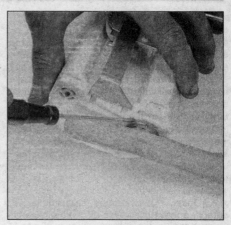

7.6 Carefully lift the fuel pump assembly out of the fuel tank. If necessary, angle the pump a little to protect the fuel level sending unit's float arm from damage. After removing the pump/sender assembly, inspect the O-ring that seals the tank opening; if it's cracked, torn or deteriorated, replace it

7.8a Pry on the plastic tab to remove the protective shield from the foot of the assembly

7.8b Carefully pry the fuel strainer from the inlet pipe

lower end of the fuel pump **(see illustrations)**. If it is dirty, clean it with a suitable solvent and blow it out with (low-pressure) compressed air. If it is too dirty to be cleaned, replace it.

9   If you are planning to replace the fuel pump, remove the fuel tank pressure sensor mounting screws and remove the pressure sensor from the top of the fuel pump assembly. Install the fuel tank pressure sensor on the new pump and tighten the screws securely.

10   The fuel pump and the fuel level sending unit are available separately. If you want to replace either component, then separate the two components (see Section 8).

11   Installation is the reverse of removal.

8   Fuel pump/fuel level sending unit - component replacement

Refer to illustrations 8.2 and 8.3
Warning: *Gasoline is extremely flammable, so take extra precautions when you work on any part of the fuel system. See the Warning in Section 2.*

1   Remove the fuel tank from the vehicle (see Section 5), then remove the fuel pump from the tank (see Section 7).

2   Disconnect the sending unit electrical connector **(see illustration)**.

3   On 1998 and earlier models, carefully separate the sending unit bracket from the base of the fuel pump assembly **(see illustration)**. To release the sending unit from the fuel pump module on 1999 and later models detach the sending unit retaining clips.

4   Installation is the reverse of removal.

9   Air filter housing - removal and installation

Air intake duct

Refer to illustration 9.2

1   It's usually easier to access the air filter housing after you've removed or disconnected the air intake duct. Removing the air intake duct is also necessary in order to remove the "resonator," which is the black plastic housing that sits atop the throttle body on most models. And even 1995 through 1997 2.2L OHV models, which do not use a resonator, still require removal of the air intake duct in order to remove the upper intake manifold/throttle body assembly.

2   To remove the air intake duct, simply loosen the hose clamp screws at both ends of the duct **(see illustration)**, then slide the clamps back.

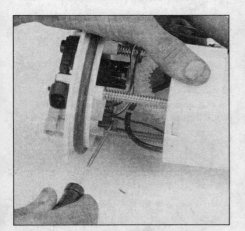

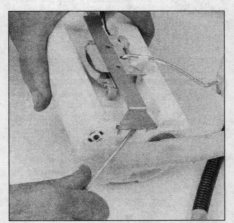

8.2 Disconnect the fuel level sending unit electrical connector from the fuel pump assembly

8.3 To remove the fuel level sending unit from the fuel pump on 1995 through 1998 models, pry this bracket loose from the base of the fuel pump assembly (on 1999 and later models, the sender is secured to the pump by plastic clips)

9.2 A typical air intake duct (2.2L OHC model shown, other models similar). To remove the duct, make sure that no cable or hose clips are attached to it and that all hoses and electrical connectors (such as the IAT sensor) are disconnected, then loosen the hose clamp screws and remove the duct

3   Before removing the air intake duct, always inspect it thoroughly for any cable or vacuum hose clips that might be attached to it. Disengage any cables or hoses from these clips and set them aside. Then look for any hoses, such as the fresh air inlet hose for the Positive Crankcase Ventilation (PCV) system, that might be connected to the air intake duct and disconnect them also. Finally, look for the electrical connector to the Intake Air Temperature (IAT) sensor, which is located on the air intake duct on some models. (It's not necessary to remove the IAT sensor to remove the air intake duct, but make sure that the electrical connector is disconnected.)

4   Once you've verified that nothing is attached to the air intake duct, carefully disengage it from the air filter housing and from the resonator (or, on 1995 through 1997 2.2L OHV models, the upper intake manifold) and remove it.

5   Installation is the reverse of removal.

Air filter housing

Refer to illustration 9.8

6   Disconnect the negative battery cable, then the positive cable from the battery and remove the battery (see Chapter 5). **Caution:** *If the vehicle is equipped with a Delco Loc II or Theftlock audio system, make sure you have the correct activation code before disconnecting the battery.*

7   Loosen the clamp that retains the air intake duct to the air cleaner and detach the duct from the housing **(see illustration 9.2)**.

8   If there are any wiring harness clips **(see illustration)** attached to the air filter housing cover, detach them.

9   Remove the battery (see Chapter 5). Then pull up on the fuse and relay box, which is retained by a couple of push retainers, and set it aside. (It's not necessary to remove the fuse and relay box, but you will need to give yourself a little room to work the air filter housing free.)

10   Lift up the air filter element housing to disengage the front locator pin from its

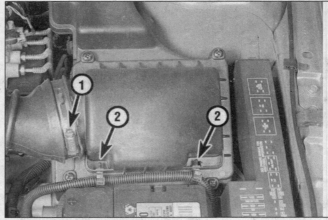

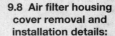

9.8 Air filter housing cover removal and installation details:

1)   *To detach the air intake duct from the air filter housing, loosen this hose clamp and pull off the duct*

2)   *To detach these wiring harness clips from the air filter housing, carefully pry them loose with a small screwdriver*

mounting grommet, then pull the air filter housing forward to disengage the rear locator pin from its grommet. Lift out the air filter housing.

11   Installation is the reverse of removal.

10   Accelerator cable - removal and installation

Removal

Refer to illustrations 10.1 and 10.2

1   Working inside the vehicle, under the dash, disconnect the accelerator cable from the accelerator pedal **(see illustration)**.

2   Where the accelerator cable goes through a hole in the firewall, it's secured to the hole by a plastic bushing and grommet **(see illustration)** that prevents water from entering the passenger compartment. To disengage the bushing from its hole in the firewall, squeeze its locking tabs together with a pair of needle-nose pliers, then push the cable through the hole into the engine compartment. (The locking tabs are located inside the vehicle, under the dash, so you'll need a flashlight and a pair of needle-nose pliers to do the job.)

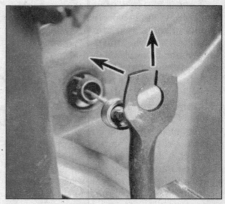

10.1 To disengage the lower end of the accelerator cable from the accelerator pedal, push the upper end of the pedal forward and thread the cable through the slot in the pedal arm

2.2L OHV engine

Refer to illustrations 10.3, 10.4a, 10.4b, 10.4c and 10.4d

3   Remove the throttle linkage cover **(see illustration)**.

4   Release the locking tab on the cruise

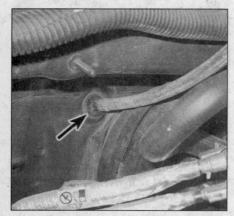

10.2 The accelerator cable is secured to its hole in the firewall by a plastic bushing and grommet that's locked into place from inside the vehicle

10.3 On 2.2L OHV engines, carefully pry the throttle linkage cover loose from its mounting bracket

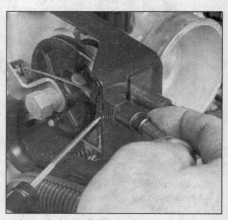

10.4a On 2.2L OHV engines, use a small screwdriver to release the locking tab that secures the cruise control cable to the accelerator cable bracket, slide the cruise cable out of the bracket . . .

10.4b ... then disconnect the cable from the pin on the throttle cam (1995 through 1997 2.2L OHV engine shown; later 2.2L engines similar)

10.4c On 2.2L OHV engines, use a small screwdriver to release the locking tab that secures the accelerator cable to the accelerator cable bracket, slide the cable out of the bracket . . .

10.4d ... then rotate the throttle cam in a clockwise direction to remove tension from the cable and disengage the cable end plug from the throttle cam by sliding the end plug out through its slot in the cam (1995 through 1997 2.2L OHV engine shown; later 2.2L engines similar)

control cable, detach the cruise control cable from the accelerator cable bracket, then disconnect the cruise control cable from the throttle cam (see illustrations). Release the locking tab on the accelerator cable, detach the accelerator cable from the accelerator cable bracket, then disconnect the accelerator cable from the throttle cam (see illustrations).

5   Note how the accelerator cable is routed in the engine compartment, then remove the cable. Pay particular attention to any cable clips, clamps or guides. Clearly label their location, what they're attached, to, etc. to ensure that the new cable will be correctly routed when installed.

2.3L and 2.4L OHC engines

Refer to illustration 10.6

6   Remove the throttle linkage cover (see illustration).

7   On models equipped with cruise control, detach the cruise control cable from the accelerator cable bracket.

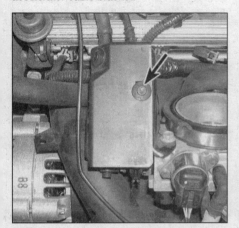

10.6 On 2.3L and 2.4L OHC engines, pry up the center part of this pop fastener, then remove the pop fastener and the throttle linkage cover

8   Rotate the throttle cam and disconnect the accelerator cable end plug from the throttle cam (see illustration 10.4d). Then squeeze the locking tabs on the cable housing and disengage the cable from the accelerator cable bracket.

9   Note how the accelerator cable is routed in the engine compartment, then remove the cable. Pay particular attention to any cable clips, clamps or guides. Clearly label their location, what they're attached, to, etc. to ensure that the new cable will be correctly routed when installed.

2.2L OHC engine

Refer to illustration 10.10

10   Disconnect the accelerator cable from the throttle cam (see illustration).

11   Disengage the accelerator cable from the cable bracket.

12   Note how the accelerator cable is routed in the engine compartment, then remove the cable. Pay particular attention to any cable clips, clamps or guides. Clearly label their location, what they're attached, to, etc. to ensure that the new cable will be correctly routed when installed.

Installation (all models)

13   Installation is the reverse of removal. Make sure that the cable is routed correctly and is not within two inches of any other moving parts.

14   When you're done, depress the accelerator pedal and verify that the cable operates smoothly and that it fully opens and closes the throttle plate inside the throttle body.

15   It's a good idea to apply silicone sealant to the accelerator cable housing where the cable goes through the hole in the firewall. Apply the sealant to the engine compartment side of the firewall.

11   Fuel injection system - general information

Refer to illustrations 11.1a and 11.1b

    The fuel injection system (see illustrations) consists of three sub-systems: the air induction system, the fuel delivery system, and electronic control system.

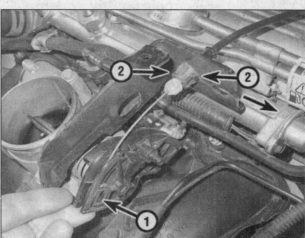

10.10 Accelerator cable details at the throttle cam (2.2L OHC engines)

1   Align the cable with the slot in the cam, then pull the cable through the slot

2   Squeeze the retainers on the cable housing to free it from the bracket, then pass the cable through the slot

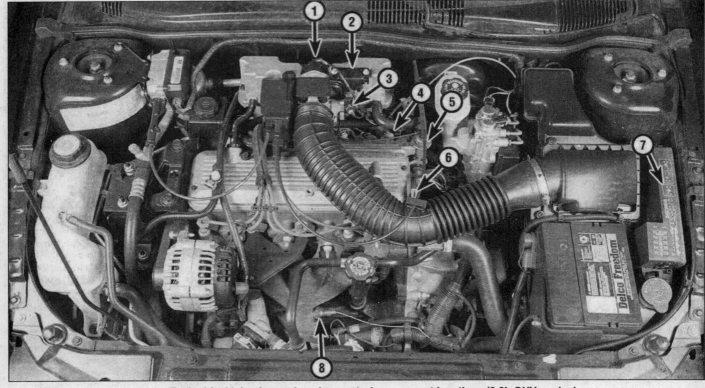

11.1a Typical fuel injection and engine control component locations (2.2L OHV engine)

1 Idle Air Control (IAC) valve	3 Throttle Position Sensor (TPS)
2 Manifold Absolute Pressure (MAP)	4 Fuel injectors
sensor	5 Fuel pressure regulator

6   Intake Air Temperature (IAT) sensor
7   Fuse/relay box (fuel pump relay inside)
8   Oxygen sensor

Air induction system

The air induction system consists of the air filter assembly, the air intake duct, the throttle body and the intake manifold. The throttle body contains a throttle plate that regulates the amount of air entering the intake manifold. The throttle plate is opened and closed by the accelerator cable. The lower part of the throttle body on some engines is heated by engine coolant to prevent icing in cold weather. The throttle body is also the location of the Throttle Position (TP) sensor and the Manifold Absolute Pressure (MAP) sensor. Another information sensor, the Intake Air Temperature (IAT) sensor, is located on the air intake duct or on the intake manifold. All of the air induction components (air filter housing, air intake duct and throttle body) are covered in this Chapter, except for the intake manifold, which is covered in Chapter 2, and the information sensors, which are covered in Chapter 6.

When the engine is idling, the Idle Air Control (IAC) system maintains the correct idle speed by regulating the amount of air that bypasses the (closed) throttle plate in response to a command from the Powertrain Control Module (PCM). The IAC system consists of the IAC valve (located on or near the throttle body), the PCM, and several information sensors, including the Engine Coolant Temperature (ECT) sensor, the Intake Air

Temperature (IAT) sensor and the Manifold Absolute Pressure (MAP) sensor. The IAC valve is activated and controlled by the PCM in response to the running conditions of the engine (cold or warm running, power steering pressure high or low, air conditioning system on or off, etc.). As the PCM receives data from the information sensors (vehicle speed, coolant temperature, air conditioning and/or power steering load, etc.) it adjusts the idle according to the demands of the engine and driver.

Electronic control system

For more information about the electronic control system, i.e. the PCM, its information sensors and output actuators, refer to Chapter 6.

Fuel delivery system

The fuel delivery system consists of the fuel pump, the fuel filter, the fuel pressure regulator, the fuel rail and fuel injectors, and the hoses, lines and pipes that carry fuel between all of these components.

The fuel pump is an in-tank design. Fuel is drawn through a "sock" (or strainer) at the pump inlet, then pumped out the other end of the pump and through a fuel filter, which is located right behind the tank. After the pressurized fuel has been filtered, it's pumped through the fuel supply line to the fuel injec-

tors. A fuel pressure regulator maintains the fuel pressure within the specified operating range. When the operating pressure exceeds the specified operating range, the pressure regulator opens and sends the excess fuel back to the fuel tank.

Each fuel injector is a solenoid-actuated, pintle-type design consisting of a solenoid, plunger, ball or needle valve, and housing. When the engine is running, there is always voltage on the "hot" side of each injector terminal. Injector "drivers" inside the PCM turn the injectors on and off by switching their ground paths on and off. The quantity of fuel injected each time an injector opens is determined by its "pulse width," which is the interval of time during which the valve is open.

12 Fuel injection system - general check

Refer to illustrations 12.7 and 12.9
Warning: *Gasoline is extremely flammable, so take extra precautions when you work on any part of the fuel system. See the* **Warning** *in Section 2.*
Note: *The following procedure is based on the assumption that the fuel pump is working and the fuel pressure is adequate (see Section 3).*

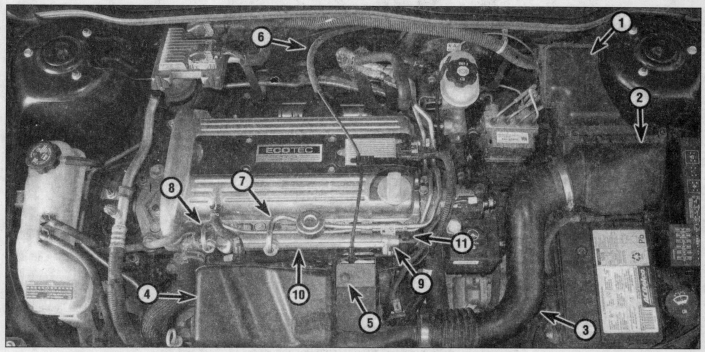

11.1b Typical fuel injection component locations (2.2L OHC engine)

1	Fuse/relay box (fuel pump relay inside)	
2	Air filter housing	
3	Air intake duct	
4	Resonator (throttle body is underneath)	
5	Throttle linkage cover	
6	Accelerator cable	
7	Fuel supply line	
8	Fuel return line	
9	Fuel pressure regulator	
10	Fuel rail (injectors underneath)	
11	Fuel pressure test port (Schrader valve)	

1   Check all electrical connectors that are related to the system. Check the ground wire connections for tightness. Loose connectors and poor grounds can cause many problems that resemble more serious malfunctions.

2   Verify that the battery is fully charged. The Powertrain Control Module (PCM), information sensors and output actuators (the fuel injectors are output actuators) depend on a stable voltage supply in order to meter fuel correctly.

3   Inspect the air filter element (see Chapter 1). A dirty or partially blocked filter will severely impede performance and economy.

4   Check all fuses related to the fuel system (see Chapter 12). If you find a blown fuse, replace it and see if it blows again. If it does, look for a wire shorted to ground in the circuit(s) protected by that fuse.

5   Check the air induction system between the throttle body and the intake manifold for air leaks, which will cause a lean air/fuel mixture ratio. (When the mixture ratio becomes excessively lean, the engine will misfire.) Also inspect the condition of all vacuum hoses connected to the intake manifold and to the throttle body. A loose or broken vacuum hose will allow false (unmetered) air into the intake manifold. The Manifold Absolute Pressure (MAP) sensor and the PCM can compensate for some false air, but if it's excessive, especially at idle and during other high-intake-manifold-vacuum conditions, the engine will misfire.

6   Remove the air intake duct from the

throttle body and look for dirt, carbon, varnish, or other residue in the throttle body, particularly around the throttle plate. If it's dirty, clean it with carb cleaner, a toothbrush and a clean shop towel.

7   With the engine running, place an automotive stethoscope against each injector, one at a time, and listen for a clicking sound that indicates operation **(see illustration)**. If you don't have a stethoscope, touch the tip of a long screwdriver against each injector and listen through the handle.

8   If you can hear the injectors operating,

but the engine is misfiring, then the electrical circuits are functioning correctly, but the injectors might be dirty or clogged. Try a commercial injector cleaning product (available at auto parts stores). If cleaning the injectors doesn't help, the injectors probably need to be replaced.

9   If an injector is not operating, i.e. it makes no clicking sound, disconnect the injector electrical connector and measure the resistance across the injector terminals with an ohmmeter **(see illustration)**. Compare your measurement with the resistance value

12.7 Use a stethoscope or screwdriver to determine if the injectors are working correctly

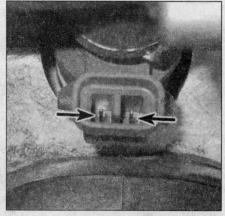

12.9 To measure the resistance of an injector solenoid coil winding, touch the tips of your ohmmeter probes to the two terminals of the fuel injector

listed in this Chapter's Specifications. Replace any injector whose resistance value does not fall within the specifications.

10   If the injector is not operating, but the resistance reading is within specifications, the PCM or the circuit between the PCM and the injector might be faulty.

13   Throttle body - inspection, removal and installation

Warning 1: *Gasoline is extremely flammable, so take extra precautions when you work on any part of the fuel system. See the* **Warning** *in Section 2.*

Warning 2: *DO NOT use any type of solvents or cleaners containing Methyl Ethyl Ketone (MEK) on the fuel system components as damage may occur to the throttle body and other fuel system components.*

Inspection

Refer to illustration 13.3

1   Loosen the hose clamp that secures the air intake duct to the throttle body and move the duct out of the way.

2   Have an assistant depress the accelerator pedal while you watch the throttle plate.

13.3 Spray carburetor cleaner into the throttle body to break away any carbon deposits or sludge that may have collected around the throttle plate

Verify that the throttle plate opens smoothly from idle position (almost fully closed) to wide-open throttle (fully open).

3   Spray carburetor cleaner into the throttle body, especially around the shaft area **(see illustration)** to free-up any binding caused by the accumulation of carbon deposits or sludge buildup.

4   Wiggle the throttle linkage cam while watching the throttle shaft inside the bore. If it's loose, it's excessively worn. Not only does a worn throttle plate shaft affect the smooth operation of the throttle plate, it also allows false (unmetered) air to enter the throttle body, which can cause driveability problems and lean misfires. Replace the throttle body unit.

Removal and installation

Warning: *Wait until the engine is completely cool before beginning this procedure.*

2.2L OHV engine

1995 through 1997 models

5   On these models, the throttle body is an integral part of the upper intake manifold. It cannot be replaced separately from the upper manifold. If the throttle body must be replaced, you must replace the upper intake manifold (see Section 7 in Chapter 2A).

1998 and later models

Refer to illustration 13.8

6   Disconnect the cable from the negative terminal of the battery. **Caution:** *If the vehicle is equipped with a Delco Loc II or Theftlock audio system, make sure you have the correct activation code before disconnecting the battery.*

7   Loosen the hose clamps that secure the air intake duct between the air filter housing and the resonator, then remove the intake duct. Remove the resonator (the black plastic housing between the air intake duct and the throttle body). To detach the resonator from the throttle body, remove the resonator mounting screw, loosen the hose clamp that secures the resonator to the throttle body and disconnect the fresh air inlet hose for the PCV system.

8   Disconnect the electrical connectors

from the Idle Air Control (IAC) valve, the Manifold Absolute Pressure (MAP) sensor and the Throttle Position (TP) sensor **(see illustration 13.8)**.

9   Clearly label all vacuum hoses connected to the throttle body **(see illustration 13.8)**, then disconnect them.

10   Disconnect the accelerator cable and, if equipped, the cruise control cable and/or the Throttle Valve (TV) cable **(see illustrations 10.4a and 10.4b)**. **Note:** *It's not necessary to disengage any of these cables from the cable bracket because the bracket will be unbolted in the next step. Just disconnect the cable(s) from the throttle linkage, then set the cable(s) and cable bracket aside after the bracket is unbolted.*

11   Remove the throttle body bolts **(see illustration 13.8)**. Note that the two left throttle body mounting bolts also secure the accelerator cable/cruise control cable/TV cable bracket. Remove the throttle body.

12   Remove the old throttle body gasket. Clean off all traces of old gasket material from the mating surfaces of the throttle body and from the intake manifold.

13   Using a new gasket, install the throttle body, install the throttle body mounting bolts (don't forget to reattach the bracket for the accelerator cable, cruise control cable and TV cable). Tighten the throttle body mounting bolts to the torque listed in this Chapter's Specifications.

14   Installation is otherwise the reverse of removal. When you're done, start the engine and verify that the throttle body operates correctly and that there are no air leaks.

2.3L and 2.4L OHC engines

Refer to illustrations 13.16 and 13.18

15   Disconnect the cable from the negative terminal of the battery. **Caution:** *If the vehicle is equipped with a Delco Loc II or Theftlock audio system, make sure you have the correct activation code before disconnecting the battery.*

16   Loosen the hose clamp that secures the air intake duct to the resonator and remove the intake duct. Remove the resonator (the black plastic housing between the air intake duct and the throttle body). To detach the

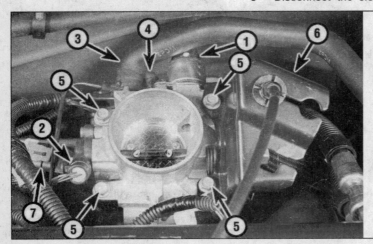

13.8   To remove the throttle body on 1998 and later 2.2L OHV models, disconnect or remove the following:

1   *Idle Air Control (IAC) valve electrical connector*
2   *Throttle Position (TP) sensor electrical connector*
3   *Power brake booster vacuum hose*
4   *Vacuum hose*
5   *Throttle body mounting bolts*
6   *Accelerator cable/cruise control cable/Throttle Valve (TV) cable bracket*
7   *Manifold Absolute Pressure (MAP) sensor electrical connector*

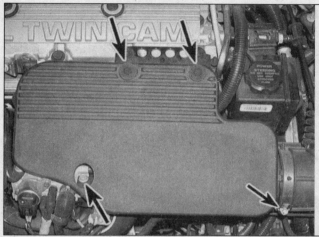

13.16 To detach the resonator on 2.4L OHC engines, loosen the hose clamp screw and disconnect the air intake duct from the resonator, remove the three resonator retaining bolts, then lift up the resonator and disconnect the PCV system fresh air inlet hose

13.18 To remove the throttle body on 2.4L OHC engines, disconnect or remove the following (everything but the throttle body mounting bolts has already been disconnected in this photo):

1   Idle Air Control (IAC) valve electrical connector
2   Manifold Absolute Pressure (MAP) sensor electrical connector
3   Throttle Position (TP) sensor electrical connector
4   Vacuum hose
5   Power brake booster vacuum hose
6   Throttle body mounting bolts

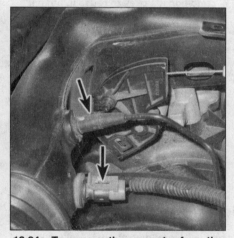

13.24a To remove the resonator from the throttle body on a 2.2L OHC engine, disconnect the electrical connector from the Intake Air Temperature (IAT) sensor and disconnect the vacuum line from the resonator . . .

resonator from the throttle body, remove the resonator mounting screws (see illustration), loosen the hose clamp that secures the resonator to the throttle body and disconnect the PCV system fresh air inlet hose.

17   Disconnect the accelerator cable and, if equipped, the cruise control cable and/or the Throttle Valve (TV) cable (see Section 10). Unbolt and remove the cable bracket.

18   Disconnect the electrical connectors for the Idle Air Control (IAC) valve, the Manifold Absolute Pressure (MAP) sensor and the Throttle Position (TP) sensor (see illustration).

19   Clearly label all vacuum hoses, then disconnect them from the throttle body.

20   Remove the throttle body mounting bolts and remove the throttle body. Remove the old throttle body gasket.

21   Using a new gasket, install the throttle body, install the throttle body mounting bolts and tighten them to the torque listed in this Chapter's Specifications.

22   Installation is otherwise the reverse of removal. When you're done, start the engine and verify that the throttle body operates correctly and that there are no air leaks.

2.2L OHC engine

Refer to illustrations 13.24a, 13.24b, 13.24c, 13.25 and 13.28

Warning: *Wait until the engine is completely cool before beginning this procedure.*

23   Disconnect the cable from the negative battery terminal (see Chapter 5).

24   Loosen the hose clamps that secure the air intake duct to the air filter housing and to the resonator and remove the air intake duct. Remove the resonator (see illustrations).

25   Disconnect the electrical connectors

13.24b . . . then loosen the hose clamp screw . . .

13.24c . . . carefully lift off the resonator and inspect it thoroughly to make sure that nothing else is attached or connected to it (like this crankcase ventilation hose, which is actually easier to disconnect from the valve cover) before removing it

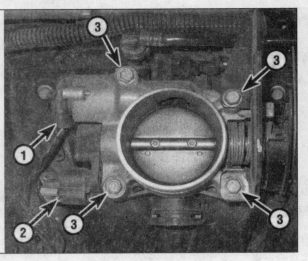

13.25 To remove the throttle body on 2.2L OHC engines, disconnect or remove the following:

1   Idle Air Control (IAC) valve electrical connector
2   Throttle Position (TP) sensor electrical connector
3   Throttle body mounting bolts (two left bolts also secure the bracket for the accelerator and cruise control cables to the throttle body)

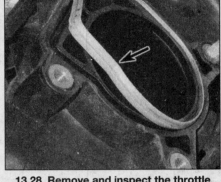

13.28 Remove and inspect the throttle body's O-ring type gasket; if it's in good condition it's okay to reuse it, but if it's cracked, torn or otherwise deteriorated, replace it (2.2L OHC engine)

from the Idle Air Control (IAC) valve and the Throttle Position (TP) sensor **(see illustration)**.

26   Disconnect the accelerator cable from the throttle cam (see Section 10). If the vehicle is equipped with cruise control, disconnect the cruise control cable from the throttle cam too. (Disconnect the cruise control cable from the throttle cam the same way you disconnected the accelerator cable.)

27   Remove the throttle body mounting bolts and nuts, remove the cable bracket for the accelerator cable and cruise control cable, then remove the throttle body.

28   Remove the throttle body gasket **(see illustration)** and inspect it. If the gasket isn't cracked, torn or otherwise deteriorated, it's okay to reuse it. But if it's damaged or worn, replace it. (If the vehicle is fairly old, it's a good idea to replace this gasket regardless of its apparent condition.)

29   Installation is the reverse of removal. Don't forget to reinstall the accelerator cable/cruise control cable bracket, then install the throttle body mounting bolts and nuts and tighten them to the torque listed in this Chapter's Specifications.

30   Start the engine and verify that the throttle body operates correctly and that there are no air leaks.

---

14   Fuel rail and injectors - removal and installation

2.2L OHV engine

1995 through 1997 models

Refer to illustrations 14.6a, 14.6b, 14.8 and 14.9

Warning: *Before disconnecting the fuel lines from the fuel rail, relieve the system fuel pressure (see Section 2).*

Note: *On these models, the lower intake manifold functions as the "fuel rail." There is no separate fuel rail. The fuel injectors are housed inside small receptacles in the lower intake manifold. These receptacles are supplied with fuel by a passage inside the lower manifold.*

1   Relieve the system fuel pressure (see Section 2).

2   Disconnect the cable from the negative terminal of the battery. **Caution:** *If the vehicle is equipped with a Delco Loc II or Theftlock audio system, make sure you have the correct activation code before disconnecting the battery.*

3   Remove the upper intake manifold (see Chapter 2A).

4   Remove the nut that secures the fuel return pipe bracket, then move the return pipe and bracket away from the fuel pressure regulator.

5   Remove the fuel pressure regulator (see Section 15).

6   Remove the fuel injector retainer screws, then carefully remove the injector retainer **(see illustrations)**. Make sure that you don't disturb the injectors or the fuel pressure regulator when you remove the retainer.

7   Disconnect the electrical connectors from the fuel injectors.

8   Before removing any of the fuel injectors, note their orientation. If you're planning to reuse the old injectors, it's a good idea to

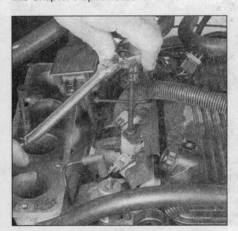

14.6a To detach the fuel injector retainer on a 1995 through 1997 2.2L OHV engine, remove the two retainer mounting screws (other screw not visible in this photo) . . .

14.6b . . . then carefully slide the retainer out of position. Make sure that you don't damage the injectors or the fuel pressure regulator when you remove the retainer

14.8 Use a screwdriver to carefully pry each injector out of its receptacle in the lower intake manifold

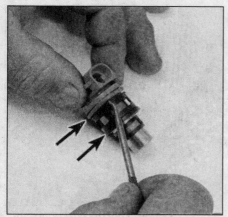

14.9 Remove the old O-rings from each injector and replace them with new ones. Coat the new O-rings with clean engine oil before installing the injectors

mark the orientation of each injector in relation to the lower intake manifold. Even if you're planning to install new injectors, the marks on the old injectors will help you orient the new units correctly. Remove the fuel injectors **(see illustration)**, then immediately cover each injector receptacle in the lower intake manifold to ensure that no dirt or moisture enters the fuel system.

9   Remove the old O-rings from each injector **(see illustration)** and discard them. **Warning:** *As soon as you remove each injector, verify that it still has a lower O-ring seal. The lower O-rings sometimes come off when the injector are removed from the lower intake manifold. If an O-ring remains inside the bottom of an injector receptacle, and you forget or neglect to remove it, then when the injector is installed with a new lower O-ring, it won't fully seat into its receptacle. This will cause a fuel leak, which can cause a fire.*

10   Before installing each injector - whether it's new or used - make sure that you install

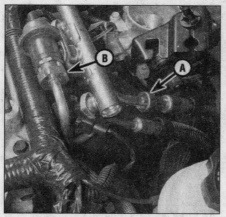

14.18 Disconnect the fuel supply line (A) and the return line (B). You'll need a special tool to disconnect the fuel supply line fitting (see Section 4), and be sure to use a back-up wrench on the regulator when loosening the fuel return line nut (1998 and later 2.2L OHV engine)

new upper and lower O-ring seals on each injector. Lubricate the new injector O-ring seals with clean engine oil, then carefully install the injectors. Make sure that each injector is fully seated into its receptacle. **Caution:** *Because bottom-feed fuel injectors are mounted in the intake manifold instead of a separate fuel rail assembly, it's critical that they're fully seated in their receptacles inside the intake manifold BEFORE the engine is started. If the injectors aren't seating correctly, the fuel pressure in the passage that supplies fuel to the injectors will force fuel past the seals and into the cylinders, which could damage the engine. To verify that the injectors are fully seated and the seals are sealing off the fuel supply passage, check the fuel pressure with the ignition key turned to ON, but don't start the engine (see Section 3). If the fuel pressure rises to its normal operat-*

ing range and remains steady, the fuel supply passage is correctly sealed.

11   Carefully install the injector retainer. Make sure that the injector retaining slots and the fuel pressure regulator are aligned with the slots in the retainer bracket.

12   Installation is otherwise the reverse of removal.

1998 and later models

Refer to illustrations 14.18, 14.19a, 14.19b, 14.20, 14.21a and 14.21b

13   Relieve the system fuel pressure (see Section 2).

14   Disconnect the cable from the negative terminal of the battery. **Caution:** *If the vehicle is equipped with a Delco Loc II or Theftlock audio system, make sure you have the correct activation code before disconnecting the battery.*

15   Loosen the hose clamps and remove the air intake duct. Remove the resonator.

16   Remove the bolt and two nuts from the top of the stamped steel bracket that covers the fuel rail, remove the three nuts on the backside of the bracket and remove the bracket.

17   Disconnect the electrical connectors from the fuel injectors and set the fuel injector harness aside.

18   Disconnect the fuel supply line quick-connect fitting and the threaded fuel return line fitting at the fuel pressure regulator **(see illustration)**. If you're not familiar with quick-connect fittings and how to disconnect them, see Section 4.

19   Remove the fuel rail retaining bolts, then carefully remove the fuel rail and the injectors as a single assembly **(see illustrations)**. **Caution:** *Use care when handling the fuel rail assembly to avoid damaging the injectors.*

20   Remove the fuel injectors from the fuel rail **(see illustration)**.

21   Remove the injector O-ring seals **(see illustrations)**.

22   Install the new O-rings on the injectors

14.19a The arrows in this photo indicate the fuel rail mounting brackets. Follow each bracket to its lower end and you'll find the mounting bolts. Remove the fuel rail mounting bolts . . .

14.19b . . . and separate the fuel rail and injectors from the intake manifold (1998 and later 2.2L OHV engine)

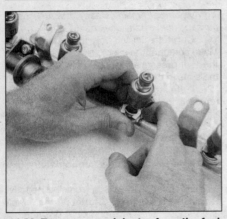

14.20 To remove an injector from the fuel rail, spread the retaining clip with a small screwdriver, then pull the injector from the fuel rail

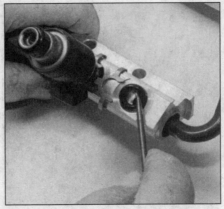

14.21a Carefully remove the injector seal from each injector bore in the fuel rail and install new O-rings. Don't mix up the O-rings - the O-rings that seal the fuel rail are *black*. Coat the new O-rings with clean engine oil before installing the injectors (1998 and later 2.2L OHV models)

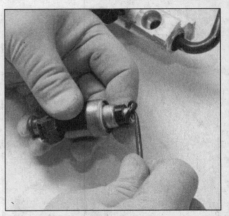

14.21b Carefully pry the old O-rings off the injectors and replace them with new ones. Coat the new O-rings with clean engine oil before installing the injectors

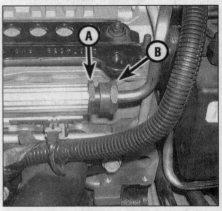

14.32 To disconnect the fuel supply line from the fuel rail, use a back-up wrench on nut A and loosen nut B with another wrench (2.3L and 2.4L OHC engines)

and lubricate them with a light film of engine oil. **Caution:** *Be sure to replace the injector O-rings with new O-rings of the correct color. Use brown O-rings on the engine side of each injector and black O-rings on the fuel rail side.*

23   Carefully insert the injectors into the fuel rail. Make sure that each injector is fully seated.

24   Secure the injectors with the retainer clips.

25   Installation is otherwise the reverse of removal.

2.3L and 2.4L OHC engines

Refer to illustrations 14.32, 14.33a, 14.33b, 14.34a, 14.34b and 14.35

26   Relieve the system fuel pressure (see Section 2).

27   Disconnect the cable from the negative battery terminal. **Caution:** *If the vehicle is equipped with a Delco Loc II or Theftlock audio system, make sure you have the correct activation code before disconnecting the battery.*

28   Remove the air intake duct and the resonator **(see illustration 13.15)**.

29   Disconnect the vacuum hose from the fuel pressure regulator.

30   Disconnect the electrical connector from the Camshaft Position (CMP) sensor (see Chapter 6).

31   Disconnect the fuel injector electrical connectors and set the injector harness aside. **Note:** *Apply a numbered tag to each connector with the corresponding cylinder number. Detach any wiring harness retainers from the fuel rail.*

32   Disconnect the fuel supply line from the fuel rail **(see illustration)**.

33   Detach the fuel line brackets **(see illustrations)** and remove the fuel line assembly.

34   Clean any debris from around the injectors. Remove the fuel rail mounting nuts/bolts **(see illustration)**. Gently rock the fuel rail and injectors to loosen the injectors. Lift up the fuel rail and disconnect the fuel return line from the fuel pressure regulator (see illustration). Remove the fuel rail and fuel injectors as a single assembly.

35   Remove the retaining clips and remove the injectors from the fuel rail assembly **(see illustration)**. Remove and discard the old injector O-rings **(see illustration 14.21b)**.

Note: *Whether you're replacing an injector or a leaking O-ring, it's always a good idea to remove all the injectors from the fuel rail and to replace all the O-rings.*

36   Coat the new O-rings with clean engine oil and slide them onto the injectors.

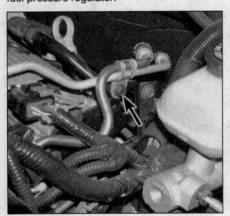

14.33a To detach the fuel line retaining brackets from the engine, remove this bolt . . .

14.33b . . . and this one (2.3L and 2.4L OHC engines)

14.34a To detach the fuel rail and injector assembly from the cylinder head, remove these two bolts . . .

14.34b ... then lift up the fuel rail assembly, remove the fuel return line flange bolt and disconnect the fuel return line from the fuel pressure regulator. Be sure to remove and discard the old O-ring (2.3L and 2.4L OHC engines)

14.35 To remove each injector from the fuel rail, slide the injector retainer to the side, then pull the injector straight up (2.3L and 2.4L OHC engines)

This activates the fuel pump for about two seconds, which builds up fuel pressure in the fuel lines and the fuel rail. Repeat this step two or three times, then inspect the fuel lines, the fuel rail, the fuel pressure regulator and the injectors for fuel leakage.

2.2L OHC engine

Refer to illustrations 14.45, 14.46, 14.47, 14.48a, 14.48b and 14.49

37   Insert each injector into its corresponding bore in the fuel rail, then secure it with the injector retaining clip.

38   Install the injector and fuel rail assembly on the intake manifold. Be sure to reconnect the fuel return line before seating the injectors.

When the fuel return line is reconnected to the fuel pressure regulator, seat the injectors, then tighten the fuel rail mounting nuts to the torque listed in this Chapter's Specifications.

39   The remainder of installation is the reverse of removal.

40   When you're done, turn the ignition switch to ON, but don't operate the starter.

41   Relieve the fuel system pressure (see Section 2) and equalize tank pressure by removing the fuel filler cap.

42   Disconnect the cable from the negative battery terminal (see Chapter 5).

43   Remove the air intake duct and the resonator (see Section 9).

44   Disconnect the vacuum line from the fuel pressure regulator (see Section 15).

45   Disconnect the fuel supply line and return lines from the fuel rail. Remove the old O-rings **(see illustration)** from the fuel line fittings and discard them.

46   Disconnect the electrical connectors from the fuel injectors **(see illustration)**.

47   Remove the fuel rail mounting bolts **(see illustration)**.

48   Remove the fuel rail and injectors as a single assembly **(see illustration)**. After

14.45 After unscrewing the fuel supply and return line fittings, remove and discard these O-rings. Be sure to install new O-rings before reconnecting the fuel lines to the fuel rail (2.2L OHC engine)

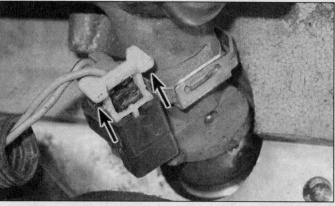

14.46 To disconnect the electrical connector from each fuel injector, pull up on the lock, then unplug the connector (2.2L OHC engine)

14.47 To detach the fuel rail from the cylinder head, remove these two mounting bolts (2.2L OHC engine)

14.48a Remove the fuel rail and the injectors as a single assembly. You might have to wiggle each injector a little to work it free from its mounting hole (2.2L OHC engine)

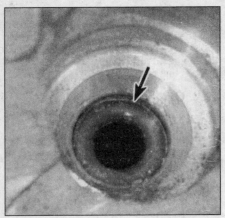

14.48b After removing the fuel rail and the injectors, check each hole and make sure that there's no O-ring in it. Sometimes the lower injector O-ring comes off and stays in the hole when the injector is removed (2.2L OHC engine)

14.49 To release an injector retainer, free it from the small lugs on each side of the injector and pull it off (2.2L OHC engine)

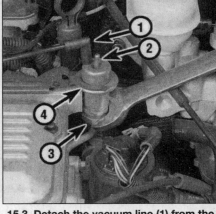

15.3 Detach the vacuum line (1) from the regulator (2), unscrew the return line (3) and unbolt the regulator from the manifold (the bolt is located behind the regulator). When installing, make sure the regulator is positioned below the retainer (4) (1995 through 1997 2.2L OHV engines)

removing the fuel rail and injectors, look inside each injector hole and make sure that no O-rings remain in the holes **(see illustration)**.

49   Remove the retainer that secures each fuel injector to the fuel rail and pull out the injector **(see illustration)**.

50   Remove the old O-rings from each injector **(see illustration 14.21b)** and discard them. Always install new O-rings on the injectors before reassembling the injectors and the fuel rail.

51   Lubricate the new O-rings with clean engine oil to ensure that they're not damaged when the injectors are installed into the fuel rail and into the intake manifold. And be sure to tighten the fuel rail mounting bolts to the torque listed in this Chapter's Specifications.

52   Installation is otherwise the reverse of removal. When you're done, start the engine and verify that there are no fuel leaks.

and discard the old fuel pressure regulator O-rings from the pressure regulator's inlet and outlet ports **(see illustration)**. Always replace both O-rings before reattaching the pressure regulator to the fuel rail.

6   If you're planning to reinstall the old fuel pressure regulator, remove the pressure regulator strainer from the inlet port. If the strainer is dirty, carefully clean it with an old toothbrush and fresh solvent. If you can't clean the strainer, replace it.

7   If you're planning to reuse the old fuel pressure regulator, install the strainer in the regulator's inlet port.

8   Install new O-rings in the fuel return line port and in the outlet port **(see illustration 15.5)**. When installing new O-rings, lubricate them with a light film of clean engine oil.

9   Installation is otherwise the reverse of removal. Be sure to tighten the fuel pressure regulator mounting bolt to the torque listed in this Chapter's Specifications.

10   When you're done, start the engine and check for leaks from the fuel supply line fit-

ting and the outlet fitting on the fuel pressure regulator

1998 and later models

Refer to illustrations 15.15 and 15.17

11   Relieve the fuel system pressure (see Section 2).

12   Disconnect the cable from the negative terminal of the battery. **Caution:** *If the vehicle is equipped with a Delco Loc II or Theftlock audio system, make sure you have the correct activation code before disconnecting the battery.*

13   Remove the resonator.

14   Remove the fuel rail bracket (which is retained by two bolts and a nut on the top and by three nuts on the back).

15   Disconnect the vacuum line from the fuel pressure regulator **(see illustration)**.

16   Disconnect the fuel return line from the

---

15   Fuel pressure regulator - replacement

2.2L OHV engine

1995 through 1997 models

Refer to illustrations 15.3 and 15.5

1   Relieve the fuel system pressure (see Section 2).

2   Disconnect the cable from the negative terminal of the battery. **Caution:** *If the vehicle is equipped with a Delco Loc II or Theftlock audio system, make sure you have the correct activation code before disconnecting the battery.*

3   Disconnect the vacuum line from the fuel pressure regulator **(see illustration)**.

4   Disconnect the fuel return line from the fuel pressure regulator.

5   Remove the pressure regulator mounting bolt and detach the fuel pressure regulator from the lower intake manifold. Remove

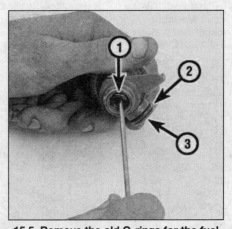

15.5 Remove the old O-rings for the fuel return line fitting (1) and the pressure regulator inlet fitting (2), then pull out the strainer (3) (not shown) from the inlet fitting, inspect it and clean it if necessary (1995 through 1997 2.2L OHV engine)

15.15 Detach the vacuum line (1), put a back-up wrench on the regulator (2), loosen the return line (3) with another wrench, then remove the regulator mounting bracket bolt (4) (1998 and later 2.2L OHV engines)

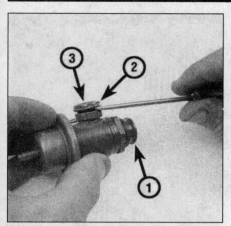

15.17 Remove the old O-rings from the fuel return line fitting (1) and the pressure regulator inlet fitting (2), then pull out the strainer (3) (not shown) from the inlet fitting, inspect it and clean it if necessary (1998 and later 2.2L OHV engine)

15.23 Remove this bolt to detach the regulator. Remove and discard the O-rings for the outlet port (shown) and the inlet port (not shown). If you're planning to reuse the old regulator, be sure to remove and clean the strainer in the inlet port (2.3L and 2.4L OHC engine)

15.31 To remove the fuel pressure regulator from the fuel rail on 2.2L OHC engines, disconnect the vacuum hose and remove the two mounting bolts

fuel pressure regulator.

17   Remove the pressure regulator mounting bolt and detach the fuel pressure regulator from the fuel rail. Remove and discard the old O-rings from the inlet and outlet ports (see illustration). Always replace both O-rings before reattaching the pressure regulator to the fuel rail.

18   If you're planning to reinstall the old fuel pressure regulator, remove the strainer from the pressure regulator's inlet port. If the strainer is dirty, carefully clean it with an old toothbrush and fresh solvent. If you can't clean the strainer, replace it. Install the strainer.

19   Install new O-rings in the inlet and outlet ports of the fuel pressure regulator (see illustration 15.5). When installing new O-rings, lubricate them with a light film of clean engine oil.

15.33a Remove and discard the old O-ring (1) and the plastic retainer (2) from the fuel pressure regulator and discard them; always use a new O-ring and retainer when installing the pressure regulator (2.2L OHC engine)

20   Installation is otherwise the reverse of removal. Be sure to tighten the fuel pressure regulator mounting bolt to the torque listed in this Chapter's Specifications.

21   When you're done, start the engine and check for leaks from the fuel supply line fitting and the outlet fitting on the fuel pressure regulator

2.3L and 2.4L OHC engines

Refer to illustration 15.23

22   Remove the fuel rail assembly (see Section 14).

23   Remove the fuel pressure regulator mounting bolt (see illustration).

24   Remove the fuel pressure regulator from the fuel rail. If the regulator feels "stuck" to the fuel rail, use a back-and-forth twisting motion while pulling it off.

25   If you're planning to reinstall the old fuel pressure regulator, remove the strainer from the pressure regulator's inlet port. If the strainer is dirty, carefully clean it with an old toothbrush and fresh solvent. If you can't clean the strainer, replace it. Install the strainer.

26   Install new O-rings in the inlet and outlet ports of the fuel pressure regulator. When installing new O-rings, lubricate them with a light film of clean engine oil.

27   Installation is otherwise the reverse of removal. Be sure to tighten the fuel pressure regulator mounting bolt to the torque listed in this Chapter's Specifications.

28   When you're done, start the engine and check for leaks from the fuel supply line fitting and the outlet fitting on the fuel pressure regulator

2.2L OHC engine

Refer to illustrations 15.31, 15.33a and 15.33b

29   Relieve the fuel system pressure (see Section 2).

30   Disconnect the cable from the negative battery terminal (see Chapter 5).

31   Disconnect the vacuum hose from the fuel pressure regulator (see illustration).

32   Remove the two bolts that attach the fuel pressure regulator to the fuel rail (see illustration 15.31) and remove the pressure regulator.

33   Remove the old O-ring and plastic retainer from the fuel pressure regulator (see illustration), remove the old O-ring from the pressure regulator bore (see illustration), discard all three and replace them with new ones.

34   Installation is the reverse of removal. Be sure to tighten the fuel pressure regulator mounting bolts to the torque listed in this Chapter's Specifications.

35   When you're done, start the engine and verify that there are no fuel leaks at the regulator.

15.33b Remove the old O-ring from the pressure regulator bore in the end of the fuel rail, discard it and replace it with a new one (2.2L OHC engine)

16.1a Inspect the rubber hangers for cracks, tears and deterioration. A damaged rubber hanger will allow the exhaust system to sag. It might even hit the ground on a rough road (2.2L OHV model shown, other models similar)

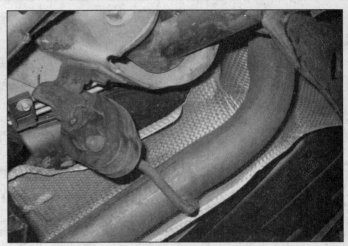

16.1b Another typical rubber exhaust hanger (2.2L OHC model shown, other models similar)

16 Exhaust system servicing - general information

Refer to illustrations 16.1a, 16.1b, 16.1c, 16.4a, 16.4b and 16.4c

Warning: *The vehicle's exhaust system generates very high temperatures and must be allowed to cool down completely before touching any of the components. Be especially careful around the catalytic converter, which stays hot longer than other exhaust components.*

1   The exhaust system consists of the exhaust manifolds, the catalytic converter, the muffler, the tailpipe and all connecting pipes, flanges and clamps. The exhaust system is isolated from the vehicle body and from chassis components by a series of rubber hangers **(see illustrations)**. Periodically inspect these hangers for cracks or other signs of deterioration, replacing them as nec-

essary. Some exhaust components are also supported by brackets **(see illustration)** bolted to the underside of the vehicle. Make sure that these brackets are tightly fastened to the exhaust system and to the vehicle and that they're neither cracked nor corroded.

2   Conduct regular inspections of the exhaust system to keep it safe and quiet. Look for any damaged or bent parts, open seams, holes, loose connections, excessive corrosion or other defects which could allow exhaust fumes to enter the vehicle. Do not repair deteriorated exhaust system components; replace them with new parts.

3   If the exhaust system components are extremely corroded, or rusted together, you'll need welding equipment and a cutting torch to remove them. The convenient strategy at this point is to have a muffler repair shop remove the corroded sections with a cutting torch. If you want to save money by doing it yourself, but you don't have a welding outfit

and cutting torch, simply cut off the old components with a hacksaw. If you have compressed air, there are special pneumatic cutting chisels (available from specialty tool manufacturers) that can also be used. If you decide to tackle the job at home, be sure to wear safety goggles to protect your eyes from metal chips and wear work gloves to protect your hands.

4   Replacement of exhaust system components is basically a matter of removing the heat shields, disconnecting the component and installing a new one. The heat shields and exhaust system hangers must be reinstalled in the original locations or damage could result. Due to the high temperatures and exposed locations of the exhaust system components, rust and corrosion can seize parts together. Penetrating oils are available to help loosen frozen fasteners. However, in some cases it may be necessary to cut the pieces apart with a hacksaw or cutting torch.

16.1c Make sure that the exhaust pipe brackets are neither cracked nor damaged. Always replace damaged brackets immediately

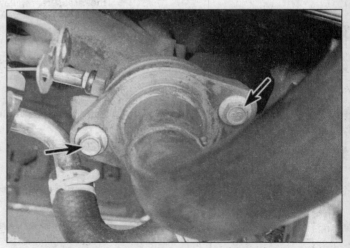

16.4a If exhaust system fasteners, like these exhaust manifold-to-exhaust pipe flange bolts, are difficult to loosen, spray penetrant onto them, wait awhile for it to loosen them up, then try again

16.4b Catalytic converter flange fasteners are also extremely difficult to loosen because catalysts operate at very high temperatures. Again, be sure to use penetrant to loosen up these fasteners before trying to remove them. And never use old, rusted and/or overheated fasteners to reattach exhaust system components

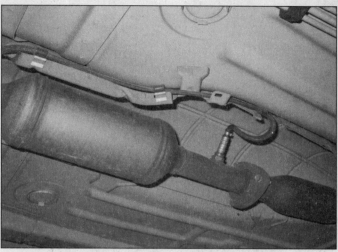

16.4c While you're waiting for the penetrant to loosen up the exhaust system fasteners, locate the downstream oxygen sensor, trace its lead to the connector, unplug the connector and remove the sensor (see Chapter 6 if you need help with removing the oxygen sensor)

(Only persons experienced in this work should employ this latter method.) Here are some simple guidelines to follow when repairing the exhaust system:

a) Work from the back to the front when removing exhaust system components.
b) Apply penetrating oil to the exhaust system component fasteners **(see illustrations)** to make them easier to remove.

c) While you're waiting for the penetrant to loosen up the exhaust system fasteners, always disconnect the electrical connector for the downstream oxygen sensor and remove the sensor before removing the exhaust pipe section that includes the catalytic converter **(see illustration)**.
d) Use new gaskets, hangers and clamps when installing exhaust systems components.

e) Apply anti-seize compound to the threads of all exhaust system fasteners during reassembly.
f) Be sure to allow sufficient clearance between newly installed parts and all points on the underbody to avoid overheating the floor pan and possibly damaging the interior carpet and insulation. Pay particularly close attention to the catalytic converter and heat shield.

Notes

Chapter 5
Engine electrical systems

Contents

Specifications

General

Firing order	1-3-4-2
Alternator regulated charging output	13 to 14.5 volts

1   General information

The engine electrical systems include all ignition, charging and starting components. Because of their engine-related functions, these components are discussed separately from chassis electrical devices such as the lights, the instruments, etc. (which are included in Chapter 12).

Precautions

Always observe the following precautions when working on the electrical system:

a) *Be extremely careful when servicing engine electrical components. They are easily damaged if checked, connected or handled improperly.*

b) *Never leave the ignition switched on for long periods of time when the engine is not running.*

c) *Never disconnect the battery cables while the engine is running.*

d) *Maintain correct polarity when connecting battery cables from another vehicle during jump starting - see the "Booster battery (jump) starting" Section at the front of this manual.*

e) *Always disconnect the negative cable from the battery before working on the electrical system, but read the following battery disconnection procedure first.*

It's also a good idea to review the safety-related information regarding the engine electrical systems located in the *"Safety first!"* Section at the front of this manual, before beginning any operation included in this Chapter.

Battery disconnection

The battery is located in the engine compartment on all vehicles covered by this manual. To disconnect the battery for service procedures that require battery disconnection, simply disconnect the cable from the *negative* battery terminal. Make sure that you isolate the cable to prevent it from coming into con-

tact with the battery negative terminal.

Some vehicle systems (radio, alarm system, power door locks, etc.) require battery power all the time, either to enable their operation or to maintain control unit memory (Powertrain Control Module, automatic transaxle control module, etc.), which would be lost if the battery were to be disconnected. So before you disconnect the battery, note the following points:

a) *Before connecting or disconnecting the cable from the negative battery terminal, make sure that you turn the ignition key and the lighting switch to their OFF positions. Failure to do so could damage semiconductor components.*

b) *On a vehicle with power door locks, it is a wise precaution to remove the key from the ignition and to keep it with you, so that it does not get locked inside if the power door locks should engage accidentally when the battery is reconnected!*

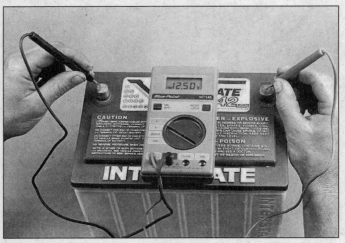

3.2 To test the open circuit voltage of the battery, touch the black probe of the voltmeter to the negative terminal and the red probe to the positive terminal of the battery; a fully charged battery should be about 12.5 volts

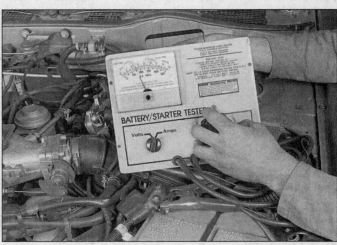

3.3 Some battery load testers (like this one) are equipped with an ammeter that allows you to vary the amount of the load on the battery (less expensive testers only have a load switch that puts the battery under a fixed load)

c) *After the battery has been disconnected, then reconnected (or a new battery has been installed) on vehicles with an automatic transaxle, the Transaxle Control Module (TCM) will need some time to relearn its adaptive strategy. As a result, shifting might feel firmer than usual. This is a normal condition and will not adversely affect the operation or service life of the transaxle. Eventually, the TCM will complete its adaptive learning process and the shift feel of the transaxle will return to normal.*

d) *The engine management system's PCM has some learning capabilities that allow it to adapt or make corrections in response to minor variations in the fuel system in order to optimize driveability and idle characteristics. However, the PCM might lose some or all of this information when the battery is disconnected. The PCM must go through a relearning process before it can regain its former driveability and performance characteristics. Until it relearns this lost data, you might notice a difference in driveability, idle and/or (if you have an automatic) shift "feel." To facilitate this relearning process, refer to "Enabling the PCM to relearn" below.*

Memory savers

Devices known as "memory savers" (typically, small 9-volt batteries) can be used to avoid some of the above problems. A memory saver is usually plugged into the cigarette lighter, and then you can disconnect the vehicle battery from the electrical system. The memory saver is designed to deliver sufficient current to maintain security alarm codes, PCM memory, the clock memory and radio presets.

Warning: *If you're going to work around any airbag system components, disconnect the battery and do not use a memory saver. If you*

do, the airbag could accidentally deploy and cause personal injury.

Caution: *Because memory savers deliver current to operate unswitched circuits when the battery is disconnected, make sure that the circuit that you're going to service is actually open before working on it!*

2   Battery - emergency jump starting

Refer to the *Booster battery (jump) starting* procedure at the front of this manual.

3   Battery - check and replacement

Check

Refer to illustrations 3.2 and 3.3

Warning: *Hydrogen gas is produced by the battery, so keep open flames and lighted cigarettes away from it at all times. Always wear eye protection when working around a battery. Rinse off spilled electrolyte immediately with large amounts of water.*

Caution 1: *Always disconnect the negative cable first and hook it up last or you might accidentally short out the battery with the tool you're using to loosen the cable clamps.*

Caution 2: *If the vehicle is equipped with a Delco Loc II or Theftlock audio system, make sure you have the correct activation code before disconnecting the battery.*

1   Disconnect the negative battery cable, then the positive cable from the battery.

2   Check the battery state of charge. Visually inspect the indicator eye on the top of the battery; if the indicator eye is black in color charge the battery as described in Chapter 1. Next perform an open voltage circuit test using a digital voltmeter **(see illustration)**.

Note: *The battery's surface charge must be*

removed before accurate voltage measurements can be made. Turn on the high beams for ten seconds, then turn them off and let the vehicle stand for two minutes. With the engine and all accessories Off, touch the negative probe of the voltmeter to the negative terminal of the battery and the positive probe to the positive terminal of the battery. The battery voltage should be 11.5 to 12.5 volts or slightly above. If the battery is less than the specified voltage, charge the battery before proceeding to the next test. Do not proceed with the battery load test unless the battery charge is correct.

3   Perform a battery load test. An accurate check of the battery condition can only be performed with a load tester (available at most auto parts stores). This test evaluates the ability of the battery to operate the starter and other accessories during periods of high current draw. Hook up a special load tester to the battery terminals **(see illustration)**. Load test the battery according to the manufacturer's instructions. This tool utilizes a carbon-pile-type variable resistor to increase the load demand (current draw) on the battery. Maintain the load on the battery for 15 seconds or less and observe that the battery voltage does not drop below 9.6 volts. If the battery condition is weak or defective, the tool will indicate this condition immediately.

Note: *Cold temperatures will cause the minimum voltage requirements to drop slightly. Follow the chart given in the manufacturer's instructions to compensate for cold climates. Minimum load voltage for freezing temperatures (32 degrees F) should be approximately 9.1 volts.*

Replacement

Refer to illustration 3.4

4   Disconnect the cable from the negative terminal of the battery FIRST **(see illustration)**, *then* disconnect the cable from the positive terminal. **Warning:** *Always discon-*

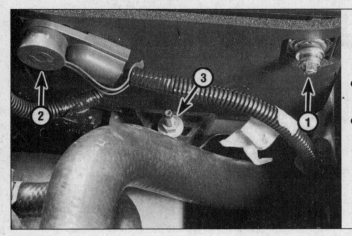

3.4 To remove the battery from the battery tray, disconnect the cable from the negative battery post (1), disconnect the cable from the positive terminal (2), then remove the battery hold-down clamp bolt (3)

nect the negative cable first and hook it up last or the battery may be shorted by the tool being used to loosen the cable clamps. **Caution:** *If the vehicle is equipped with a Delco Loc II or Theftlock audio system, make sure you have the correct activation code before disconnecting the battery.*

5   Remove the battery hold-down clamp bolt **(see illustration 3.4)** from the battery tray.

6   Carefully lift the battery out of the battery tray. **Warning:** *Always keep the battery in an upright position to reduce the possibility of electrolyte spills. If you spill electrolyte on yourself or the vehicle, rinse it off immediately with plenty of water.*

7   If you're installing a new battery, make sure you get one that's identical (same dimensions, amperage rating, cold cranking rating, etc.).

8   Inspect the condition of the battery tray. The battery tray and hold-down clamp should be clean and free from corrosion before installing the battery. If the tray or the hold-down clamp is corroded, try scrubbing it clean with baking soda and water. If the tray is still corroded, unbolt it and replace it.

9   If you're planning to install the old battery, make sure that the battery terminals and cable ends are clean and free of corrosion (see Chapter 1).

10   Set the battery in position in the tray. Don't tilt the battery or you might spill battery acid through the vent tube onto the tray or on components near the tray.

11   Install the hold-down clamp and bolt. The bolt should be snug, but overtightening it may damage the battery case.

12   Connect the battery cable for the positive terminal FIRST, then reconnect the cable for the negative terminal

4   Battery cables - check and replacement

1   Periodically inspect the entire length of each battery cable for damage, cracked or burned insulation and corrosion. Poor battery cable connections can cause starting prob-

lems and decreased engine performance.

2   Check the cable-to-terminal connections at the ends of the cables for cracks, loose wire strands and corrosion. The presence of white, fluffy deposits under the insulation at the cable terminal connection is a sign that the cable is corroded and should be replaced. Inspect the terminals for distortion, missing mounting bolts or nuts and corrosion.

3   When removing the cables, always *disconnect the negative cable FIRST* and *hook it up LAST* or you might accidentally short out the battery with the tool you're using to loosen the cable clamps. Even if you're only replacing the positive battery cable, be sure to disconnect the negative cable from the battery first.

4   Disconnect the old cables from the battery, then trace each of them to their opposite ends and detach them from the starter solenoid (positive cable) and ground bolts (negative cable). Note the routing of each cable to ensure correct installation. **Caution:** *If the vehicle is equipped with a Delco Loc II or Theftlock audio system, make sure you have the correct activation code before disconnecting the battery.*

5   If you're replacing either or both cables, take the old ones with you when buying the new ones. The replacements must be identical. Cables have characteristics that make them easy to identify: Positive cables are normally red, larger in diameter and have a larger diameter battery post and clamp; ground cables are normally black, smaller in diameter and have a slightly smaller battery post and clamp.

6   Clean the threads of the solenoid or ground connection with a wire brush to remove rust and corrosion. Apply a light coat of petroleum jelly to the threads to prevent future corrosion.

7   Attach the cable to the solenoid or ground connection and tighten the mounting nut/bolt securely.

8   Before connecting a new cable to the battery, make sure it reaches the battery post without having to be stretched.

9   Connect the positive cable first, followed by the negative cable.

5   Ignition system - general information

The Electronic Ignition (EI) systems used on all engines covered by this manual are the "distributorless" type. All of these engines have a firing order of 1-3-4-2. The EI system uses one ignition coil to fire *two* "companion" cylinders *simultaneously*. This term refers to the fact that anytime one cylinder is at Top Dead Center (TDC), so is its companion cylinder, except that one of them is at TDC on its compression stroke, while the other is at TDC on its exhaust stroke. One coil fires the plugs for cylinders 1 and 4; the other coil fires the plugs for cylinders 2 and 3. So, when the piston in cylinder No. 1 is at TDC on its compression stroke, the piston in cylinder No. 4 is at TDC on its exhaust stroke. When the first ignition coil fires No. 1 at TDC, most of the spark voltage goes to that cylinder because the pressure - and therefore the resistance - is high in that cylinder (the higher the resistance, the higher the voltage needed to jump the gap from the spark plug's center electrode to ground). Conversely, the piston in cylinder No. 4, which is at TDC on its exhaust stroke produces no pressure, and therefore no resistance, so little voltage is needed to jump the gap from the spark plug's center electrode to ground. The ignition coil for cylinders 2 and 3 works the same way. This design is known as a "waste spark" ignition.

On 2.2L OHV engines, the EI system consists of two ignition coils, the spark plug wires, the spark plugs, the Ignition Control Module (ICM), the Crankshaft Position (CKP) sensor and the Powertrain Control Module (PCM). The "drivers" that turn the ignition coils on and off are inside the ICM, which in turn is controlled by the PCM. All engines are also equipped with a knock sensor. (For more information about the CKP sensor, the knock sensor and the PCM, refer to Chapter 6.)

On 2.3L and 2.4L OHC engines, the EI system consists of two ignition coils, the spark plugs, the Ignition Control Module (ICM), the Crankshaft Position (CKP) sensor and the Powertrain Control Module (PCM). The "drivers" that turn the ignition coils on and off by opening and closing their ground paths are inside the ICM, which in turn is controlled by the PCM. All engines are also equipped with a knock sensor. (For more information about the CKP sensor, the knock sensor and the PCM, refer to Chapter 6.) The ignition module and the ignition coils are housed inside a single assembly that's mounted directly on top of the spark plugs (there are no spark plug wires). The two high-tension towers of each coil are connected to the spark plugs by long boots.

On 2.2L OHC engines, the EI system consists of the Ignition Control Module (ICM), the ignition coil pack, the spark plugs, the Crankshaft Position (CKP) sensor, the knock sensor and the Powertrain Control Module (PCM). (For more information about the CKP sensor, the knock sensor and the PCM, refer

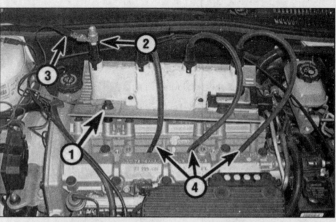

6.2b Spark tester details on an OHC engine:

1   *Ignition coil/control module cover removed and bolted to the valve cover*
2   *Spark tester installed in spark plug boot*
3   *Ground wire*
4   *Fabricated spark plug wires installed between spark plug boots and remaining spark plugs*

6.2a   To use a calibrated ignition tester on a 2.2L OHV engine, simply disconnect a spark plug wire, attach the tester to the spark plug wire, clip the tester to a convenient ground and crank over the engine. If there's enough power to fire the plug, sparks will be visible between the electrode tip and the tester body. Repeat this test for each plug

to Chapter 6.) These models are equipped with a single "coil-over-plug" coil pack/ignition control module that fits directly onto the four spark plugs. The ignition control module is mounted on the ignition coil pack, and it can be replaced separately. The coil pack assembly consists of two ignition coils. Each coil is connected to the spark plugs for two cylinders by a short boot, which contains a coil spring that carries voltage to the plugs. The ignition control module houses the "driver modules" that turn the ignition coils on and off by closing and opening their ground paths. The timing of these drivers is controlled by the PCM. The ignition control module is serviceable separately from the coil pack.

    The CKP, CMP and knock sensors are information sensors used by the PCM to control ignition timing and other engine operating parameters. The PCM also uses a number of other information sensors to make decisions regarding the correct ignition timing. These other sensors include the Throttle Position (TP) sensor, the Engine Coolant Temperature (ECT) sensor, the Mass Air Flow (MAF) sensor, the Intake Air Temperature (IAT) sensor, the Vehicle Speed Sensor (VSS) and the transmission gear position sensor or Transmission Range (TR) switch. For more information on the CKP, CMP, knock and these other sensors, refer to Chapter 6.

6   Ignition system - check

Refer to illustrations 6.2a and 6.2b
Warning: *Because of the high voltage generated by the ignition system, use extreme care when performing a procedure involving ignition components.*
1   If a malfunction occurs in the ignition system, check the following items:
   a)   *Make sure that the cable clamps at the battery terminals are clean and tight.*

   b)   *Test the condition of the battery (see Section 3). If it doesn't pass all the tests, replace it.*
   c)   *Check the ignition coil connections.*
   d)   *Check any relevant fuses in the engine compartment fuse and relay box (see Chapter 12). If they're burned, determine the cause and repair the circuit.*

2   Check the ignition spark at each plug, one at a time. Disconnect the spark plug wire from the number one spark plug and install a spark tester **(see illustrations)**. Then crank over the engine and note whether or not a spark is produced.
3   If sparks occur during cranking, sufficient voltage is reaching the plug to fire it (repeat the check for each cylinder to verify that the other coils are OK). However, be aware that even if spark is delivered to all four cylinders, the plugs themselves might be

7.2   On 1995 through 1999 2.2L OHV engines the ignition coil/ignition control module is located on the backside of the engine block (cylinder head removed for clarity)

A   *Mounting nut (1 of 3)*
B   *Electrical connectors*

fouled, so remove and inspect the plugs too (see Chapter 1).
4   If no sparks occur during cranking at one cylinder, inspect the primary wire connection at the coil. Make sure that it's clean and tight.
5   If no sparks or intermittent sparks occur during cranking at all cylinders, the PCM is probably defective. Have the PCM checked out by a dealer service department (testing the PCM is beyond the scope of the do-it-yourselfer because it requires expensive special tools).
6   If the spark plug is in good shape, the coil might be defective. Have it checked out by a dealer service department or other qualified repair shop.
7   Any additional testing of the ignition system must be done by a dealer service department or by an independent repair shop with the right tools.

7   Ignition coil and ignition control module - replacement

2.2L OHV engine
1995 through 1999 models
Refer to illustrations 7.2, 7.3 and 7.4
Warning: *Because of the location of the ignition coil/ignition control module assembly on these models, make sure that the engine is completely cooled down before trying to remove the coil/module assembly.*
1   Disconnect the cable from the negative terminal of the battery (see Section 1). **Caution:** *If the vehicle is equipped with a Delco Loc II or Theftlock audio system, make sure you have the correct activation code before disconnecting the battery.*
2   Raise the front end of the vehicle and place it securely on jackstands. Locate the

ignition coil/ignition control module assembly on the backside of the engine block **(see illustration)**.

3   Remove the mounting bracket bolts **(see illustration)**, lift up the coil/control module assembly and disconnect the electrical connectors from the ignition coil/ignition control module. If the spark plug wires are not already numbered, clearly label each wire, then disconnect the wires from the coil high-tension terminals and remove the coil/control module assembly.

4   To separate either of the ignition coils from the ignition control module, remove the coil mounting bolts and pull the two components apart **(see illustration)**.

5   Installation is the reverse of removal **(see illustration 7.4)**.

2000 and later models

Refer to illustration 7.7

6   Disconnect the cable from the negative terminal of the battery (see Section 1). **Caution:** *If the vehicle is equipped with a Delco Loc II or Theftlock audio system, make sure you have the correct activation code before disconnecting the battery.*

7   Locate the ignition coil/ignition control module assembly on the left end the cylinder head **(see illustration)**.

8   Remove the ignition coil/ignition control module mounting bracket bolts, lift up the coil/control module assembly and disconnect the electrical connectors from the ignition coil/ignition control module **(see illustration 7.3)**. If the spark plug wires are not already numbered, clearly label each plug wire, then disconnect the wires from the coil high-tension terminals and remove the coil/control module assembly.

9   To separate either of the ignition coils from the ignition control module, remove the coil mounting bolts and pull the two components apart.

10   Installation is the reverse of removal.

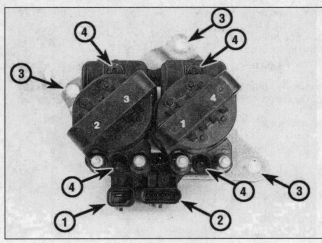

7.3 Ignition coil/ignition control module assembly (2.2L OHV engine)

1   Ignition coil primary terminal
2   Ignition control module terminal
3   Mounting bracket bolt holes
4   Ignition coil mounting bolts

2.3L and 2.4L OHC engines

Refer to illustrations 7.12, 7.13, 7.14a and 7.14b

11   Disconnect the cable from the negative terminal of the battery (see Section 1). **Caution:** *If the vehicle is equipped with a Delco Loc II or Theftlock audio system, make sure you have the correct activation code before disconnecting the battery.*

12   Disconnect the electrical connector from the ignition control module **(see illustration)**.

13   Remove the retaining bolts **(see illustration)** for the ignition coil/ignition control module cover and lift off the cover.

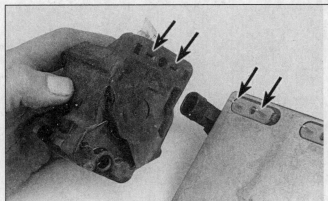

7.4 Remove the coil mounting bolts, then pull straight up. When installing a coil, carefully align the spade terminals on the ignition control module with their corresponding slots in the ignition coil

7.7 On 2000 and later 2.2L OHV models, the ignition coil/control module is located on the left end of the cylinder head, but the mounting arrangement is the same as the earlier unit (see illustrations 7.3 and 7.4)

7.12 On 2.3L and 2.4L OHC engines, you'll find the electrical connector for the ignition control module at the left end of the ignition coil/ignition control module cover. To disconnect the connector, depress the locking tab on top and pull out the connector

7.13 To detach the cover for the ignition coil and ignition control module, remove these retaining bolts (2.3L and 2.4L OHC engines)

14   Flip the cover upside down, remove the ignition coil housing mounting bolts **(see illustrations)** and remove the coil housing from the cover. Disconnect the ignition coil electrical connector and remove the ignition coils from the housing.

15   Remove the ignition module mounting bolts **(see illustration 7.14a)** and detach the module from the cover.

16   Installation is the reverse of removal.

2.2L OHC engine

Ignition control module

Refer to illustrations 7.18 and 7.20

17   Disconnect the cable from the negative battery terminal (see Section 1).

18   Disconnect the electrical connector from the ignition control module **(see illustration)**.

19   Remove the ignition control module mounting screws.

20   Remove the ignition control module and the "interconnect" **(see illustration)**.

21   If you're *replacing* the ignition control module, disconnect the interconnect from the

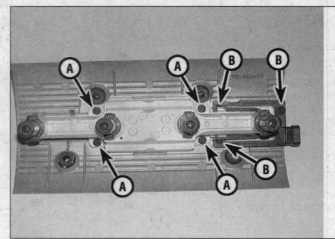

7.14a   Typical ignition/ignition control module assembly (2.3L and 2.4L OHC engines

- A   *Ignition coil housing mounting bolts*
- B   *Ignition control module mounting bolts*

module and plug it into the new module. The interconnect is an adapter plug that connects the terminals on the ignition control module to the terminals on the coil pack assembly. You'll have to swap it to the new module if you're replacing the old module. Either end of

the interconnect can be plugged into the ignition control module or the ignition coil pack. But pay attention to how the plug is oriented in relation to the terminals because it only goes in one way. One side of the interconnect - and one side of the terminals on the

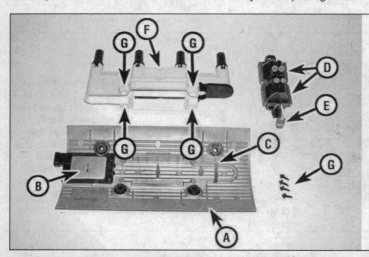

7.14b   Typical (disassembled) ignition coil/ignition control module assembly (2.3L and 2.4L OHC engines)

- A   *Ignition coil/ignition control module cover*
- B   *Ignition control module*
- C   *Ground strap*
- D   *Ignition coils (coils removed from housing for clarity)*
- E   *Ignition coil electrical connector*
- F   *Ignition coil housing (this is a later housing; earlier housings are black)*
- G   *Ignition coil housing mounting bolt holes and mounting bolts*

7.18   To remove the ignition control module from a 2.2L OHC engine, disconnect the electrical connector and remove the mounting screws

7.20   To remove the ignition control module from the valve cover on a 2.2L OHC engine, pull it straight up. To remove the "interconnect," simply disconnect it from the module and plug it into the new module

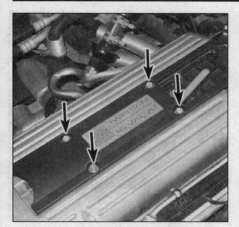

7.25 To detach the ignition coil pack assembly from the valve cover on a 2.2L OHC engine, remove these four bolts (the ignition control module is already removed in this photo, but it's not necessary to do so unless you're planning to replace the coil pack)

ignition control module and on the ignition coil pack - has rounded corners and the other side has square corners. The interconnect is equipped with a weather-resistant grommet. Make sure that this grommet is in good shape. If it's cracked, torn or deteriorated, replace it.

22 Installation is the reverse of removal. Tighten the ignition control module mounting screws to the torque listed in this Chapter's Specifications.

Ignition coil pack

Refer to illustrations 7.25, 7.26 and 7.27

23 Disconnect the cable from the negative battery terminal (see Section 1).

24 Disconnect the electrical connector from the ignition control module **(see illustration 7.18)**. It's not necessary to remove the ignition control module from the ignition

coil pack in order to *remove* the coil pack assembly, which is something you must do in order to remove the valve cover or to service the cylinder head components. However, if you're going to *replace* the ignition coil pack, you'll have to remove the ignition control module in order to remove the cover from the ignition coil pack **(see illustration 7.18)**.

25 Remove the four ignition coil pack mounting bolts **(see illustration)**.

26 Pull the ignition coil pack straight up, detaching the spark plug boots **(see illustration)**.

27 If you're replacing the ignition coil pack, remove the cover **(see illustration)** and install it on the new coil pack.

28 If you're replacing the ignition coil pack, remove the four boots from the coil pack and inspect them for cracks, tears and deterioration. If any of the boots are damaged, replace them.

29 Before installing the boots on the ignition coil pack, coat the interior of each boot with silicone dielectric compound.

30 Installation is otherwise the reverse of removal. Tighten the ignition coil pack mounting bolts to the torque listed in this Chapter's Specifications.

8 Charging system - general information and precautions

The charging system consists of a belt-driven alternator with an integral voltage regulator and the battery. These components work together to supply electrical power for the ignition system, the lights and all accessories.

All models are equipped with the CS type alternator. These alternators are non-serviceable and, if defective, must be exchanged as cores for new or rebuilt units.

The purpose of the voltage regulator is to limit the alternator's voltage to a preset

value. This prevents power surges, circuit overloads, etc., during peak voltage output. On all models with which this manual is concerned, the voltage regulator is mounted inside the alternator housing.

The charging system doesn't ordinarily require periodic maintenance. However, the drivebelt, battery and wires and connections should be inspected at the intervals outlined in Chapter 1.

The dashboard warning light should come on when the ignition key is turned to START, then go off immediately after the engine has started. If it stays on or comes on when the engine is running, a charging system problem has occurred (see Section 9).

Be very careful when making electrical circuit connections to a vehicle equipped with an alternator and note the following:

a) *When reconnecting wires to the alternator from the battery, be sure to note the polarity.*

b) *Before using arc welding equipment to repair any part of the vehicle, disconnect the wires from the alternator and the battery terminals.* **Caution:** *If the vehicle is equipped with a Delco Loc II or Theft-lock audio system, make sure you have the correct activation code before disconnecting the battery.*

c) *Never start the engine with a battery charger connected.*

d) *Always disconnect both battery leads before using a battery charger.*

e) *The alternator is turned by an engine drivebelt which could cause serious injury if your hands, hair or clothes become entangled in it with the engine running.*

f) *Because the alternator is connected directly to the battery, it could arc or cause a fire if overloaded or shorted out.*

g) *Wrap a plastic bag over the alternator and secure it with rubber bands before steam cleaning the engine.*

7.26 To remove the ignition coil pack assembly from the valve cover on a 2.2L OHC engine, grasp it firmly and pull straight up; the boots should come off with the coil pack. If any of them stay with the spark plugs, simply pull them off the plugs

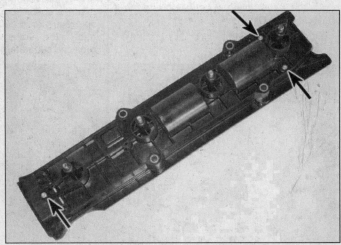

7.27 To separate the cover from the ignition coil pack on a 2.2L OHC engine, remove these three screws

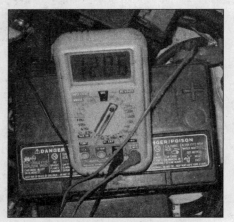

9.2 To measure standing voltage, put your multimeter in the "VOLTS" mode, connect the positive probe of the meter to the positive battery terminal and the negative probe to the negative terminal and note the reading, which should be around 12 volts. To measure charging voltage, start the engine and note the reading again, which should now be about 13.5 to 14.5 volts

9   Charging system - check

Refer to illustration 9.2

1   If the charging system malfunctions, don't immediately assume that the alternator is causing the problem. First check the following items:

a) *Ensure that the battery cable connections at the battery are clean and tight.*
b) *If the battery is not a maintenance-free type, check the electrolyte level and specific gravity. If the electrolyte level is low, add clean, mineral-free tap water. If the specific gravity is low, charge the battery.*
c) *Check the alternator wiring and connections.*
d) *Check the drivebelt condition and tension (see Chapter 1).*
e) *Check the alternator mounting bolts for looseness.*

10.3a Disconnect the wires from the rear of the alternator (2.2L OHV engine)

f) *Run the engine and check the alternator for abnormal noise.*

2   Use a voltmeter to check the battery voltage with the engine off. It should be at least 12 volts **(see illustration)**.
3   Start the engine and check the battery voltage again. It should now be approximately 13.5 to 14.5 volts.
4   If the charging voltage reading is zero, inspect the condition of the fusible link that's located in the wire between the alternator and the starter solenoid terminals. If a fusible link is badly blown, it will be obvious that a meltdown has occurred. If a visual inspection is inconclusive, use a continuity tester or ohmmeter to determine whether there is continuity through the fusible link. If the fusible link is blown, replace the fusible link and the wire in which it's located as a single assembly (available at dealer parts departments). The correct size of the fusible link should be printed on the outside of the link. Make sure that you obtain the correct fusible link and wire for the application. After replacing the fusible link, check the charging voltage again.
5   If the voltage reading is more or less than the specified charging voltage, the voltage regulator is defective. Replace the alternator (the voltage regulator cannot be replaced separately).

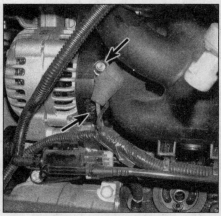

10.3b Disconnect the alternator electrical connections (2.3L and 2.4L OHC engines)

6   The charging system (battery) light on the instrument cluster lights up when the ignition key is turned to ON, but it should go out when the engine starts.
7   If the charging system light stays on after the engine has been started, there is a problem with the charging system. Before replacing the alternator, check the battery condition, alternator belt tension and electrical cable connections.
8   If replacing the alternator doesn't restore voltage to the specified range, have the charging system tested by a dealer service department or other qualified repair shop.

10   Alternator - removal and installation

Refer to illustrations 10.3a, 10.3b, 10.3c, 10.4a and 10.4b

1   Detach the cable from the negative terminal of the battery. **Caution:** *If the vehicle is equipped with a Delco Loc II or Theftlock audio system, make sure you have the correct activation code before disconnecting the battery.*
2   Remove the drivebelt (see Chapter 1).
3   Disconnect the electrical harnesses from the alternator **(see illustrations)**.
4   Remove the mounting bolts (2.2L OHV engine and 2.3L and 2.4L OHC engines, **see illustrations 10.4a and 10.4b;** 2.2L OHC engine, **see illustration 10.3c)** and separate the alternator from the engine.
5   If you're replacing the alternator, take the old one with you when purchasing the new one. Make sure that the new/rebuilt unit is identical to the old alternator. Look at the terminals - they should be the same in number, size and location as the terminals on the old alternator. Finally, look at the identification numbers - they'll be stamped into the housing or printed on a tag attached to the housing. Make sure that the numbers are the same on both alternators.
6   Many new/rebuilt alternators don't have a pulley installed, so you may have to switch

10.3c To remove the alternator from a 2.2L OHC engine, disconnect these two electrical connectors and remove the four mounting bolts

10.4a To detach the alternator from a 2.2L OHV engine, remove these two mounting bolts

10.4b To detach the alternator from a 2.3L or 2.4L OHC engine, remove these three mounting bolts (one bolt not visible)

12.3 Use an inductive-type ammeter to measure the current draw

the pulley from the old one to the new/rebuilt one. On some of the alternators used by the vehicles covered in this manual you might need a special puller to remove the pulley. If you don't have the right tool, ask the store where you're purchasing the alternator whether it can swap pulleys for you, or have the pulley swapped at a service station or automotive machine shop.

7   Installation is the reverse of removal. Be sure to tighten the alternator mounting bolts and nuts securely.

8   Check the charging voltage to verify that the alternator is operating correctly (see Section 9).

11 Starting system - general information and precautions

The starting system consists of the battery, the ignition switch, the clutch start switch (manual transaxles), the Transmission Range (TR) switch (automatic transaxles), the starter motor solenoid, the starter motor and the wires that connect these components. The solenoid is located on and is an integral part of the starter motor. The starter motor is located on the front left side of the engine block.

The starter motor on a vehicle with a manual transaxle can be operated only when the clutch pedal is depressed. The starter on a vehicle with an automatic transaxle can be operated only when the shift lever is in PARK or NEUTRAL. When the ignition key is turned to the START position, it closes the starter control circuit, which sends battery voltage to the clutch start switch or TR switch. When the clutch pedal is depressed (manual transaxle) or the shift lever is in PARK or NEUTRAL (automatic transaxle), battery voltage is sent to the starter solenoid, which sends current to the starter motor and moves a lever that engages the starter pinion gear with the flywheel ring gear to crank the engine.

Always observe the following precautions when working on the starting system:

a) *Excessive cranking of the starter motor can overheat it and cause serious damage. Never operate the starter motor for more than 15 seconds at a time without pausing for at least two minutes to allow it to cool.*

b) *The starter is connected directly to the battery and could arc or cause a fire if mishandled, overloaded or short-circuited.*

c) *Always detach the cable from the negative battery terminal before working on the starting system.* **Caution:** *If the vehicle is equipped with a Delco Loc II or Theftlock audio system, make sure you have the correct activation code before disconnecting the battery.*

12 Starter motor and circuit - check

Refer to illustrations 12.3 and 12.4

1   If a malfunction occurs in the starting circuit, do not immediately assume that the starter is causing the problem. First, check the following items:

a) *Make sure that the battery cable clamps are clean and tight where they connect to the battery.*

b) *Check the condition of the battery cables (see Section 4). Replace any defective battery cables with new parts.*

c) *Test the condition of the battery (see Section 3). If it does not pass all the tests, replace it with a new battery.*

d) *Check the starter solenoid wiring and connections. Refer to the wiring diagrams at the end of Chapter 12.*

e) *Check the starter mounting bolts for tightness.*

f) *Make sure that the shift lever is in PARK or NEUTRAL (automatic transaxle) or the clutch pedal is pressed (manual transaxle).*

g) *On vehicles with an automatic transaxle, check the adjustment of the Transmission Range (TR) switch (see Chapter 6). On vehicles with a manual transaxle, make sure that the clutch start switch is correctly installed (see Chapter 8).*

2   If the starter motor does not operate when the ignition switch is turned to the START position, check for battery voltage to the solenoid. Connect a test light or voltmeter to the starter solenoid switched terminal (the small wire) while an assistant turns the ignition switch to the START position. If voltage is not available, check the starting system circuit (see the wiring diagrams at the end of Chapter 12). If voltage is available but the starter motor does not operate, remove the starter (see Section 13) and bench test it (see Step 4).

3   If the starter turns over slowly, check the starter cranking voltage and the current draw from the battery. This test must be performed with the starter assembly on the engine. Crank the engine over (for 10 seconds or less) and observe the battery voltage. It should not drop below 8.0 volts on manual transaxle models or 8.5 volts on automatic transaxle models. Also, observe the current draw using an amp meter **(see illustration)**. It should not exceed 400 amps or drop below 250 amps. **Caution:** *The battery cables might overheat because of the large amount of current being drawn from the battery. Discontinue the testing until the starting system has cooled down.* If the starter motor cranking amp values are not within the correct range, replace it with a new unit. There are several conditions that may affect the starter cranking potential. The battery must be in good condition and the battery cold-cranking rating must not be under-rated for the particular application. Be sure to check the battery specifications carefully. The battery terminals and cables must be clean and not corroded. Also, in cases of extreme cold temperatures, make sure the battery and/or engine block is warmed before performing the tests.

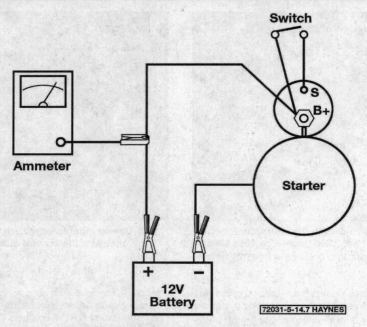

12.4 Starter motor bench testing details

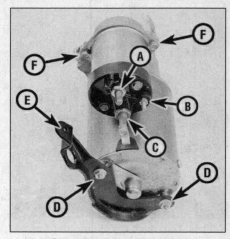

13.3 On earlier 2.2L OHV engines the starter motor/solenoid has a bracket that must be unbolted from the engine before the starter can be removed

A	Battery + terminal
B	Switch terminal (S)
C	Motor terminal (M)
D	Mounting bracket nuts
E	Mounting bracket-to-engine block bolt hole
F	Starter solenoid mounting bolts

4   If the starter is receiving voltage but does not activate, remove and check the starter/solenoid assembly on the bench **(see illustration)**. Most likely the solenoid is defective. In some rare cases, the engine may be seized so be sure to try and rotate the crankshaft pulley (see Chapter 2) before proceeding. With the starter/solenoid assembly mounted in a vise on the bench, install one jumper cable from the negative battery terminal to the body of the starter. Install the other jumper cable from the positive battery terminal to the B+ terminal on the starter. Install a starter switch and apply battery voltage to the solenoid S terminal (for 10 seconds or less) and see if the solenoid plunger, shift lever and overrunning clutch extends and rotates the pinion drive. If the pinion drive extends but does not rotate, the

solenoid is operating but the starter motor is defective. If there is no movement but the solenoid clicks, the solenoid and/or the starter motor is defective. If the solenoid plunger extends and rotates the pinion drive, the starter/solenoid assembly is working properly.

13   Starter motor - removal and installation

1   Disconnect the cable from the negative terminal of the battery. **Caution:** *If the vehicle is equipped with a Delco Loc II or Theftlock audio system, make sure you have the correct activation code before disconnecting the battery.*
2   Raise the front of the vehicle and sup-

port it securely on jackstands. Apply the parking brake and block the rear wheels to keep the vehicle from rolling off the jackstands.

2.2L OHV engine

Refer to illustrations 13.3, 13.4, 13.5 and 13.6
3   On 1995 through 1997 models with a manual transaxle, remove the "bending brace" that's bolted to the engine block and to the transaxle. The bending brace is attached to the engine by two bolts and to the transaxle by a third bolt. On these earlier models, you'll also need to remove the starter motor bracket **(see illustration)**, which is attached to the starter by two nuts, and to

13.4 On 2.2L OHV models, remove these two terminal nuts and disconnect the electrical wiring from the starter solenoid terminals

13.5 To detach the flywheel inspection plate on some 2.2L OHV models, remove these two bolts and two other bolts (not visible), which are located at the other end of the plate, between the oil pan and the transaxle pan

13.6 Starter motor mounting bolts - 2.2L OHV engine

13.9 After removing the air intake duct and resonator, remove the upper starter mounting bolt. The other (lower) bolt is easier to reach from below (2.3L and 2.4L OHC engines)

the engine block by a single bolt.

4   Working under the vehicle, clearly label, then disconnect the wires from the terminals on the starter motor and solenoid **(see illustration)**.

5   On models so equipped, remove the flywheel inspection plate **(see illustration)**.

6   Remove the starter motor mounting bolts **(see illustration)** and remove the starter. If the starter motor is shimmed, note the locations of the spacer shims. They must be reinstalled in the same positions.

7   Installation is the reverse of removal. Be sure to tighten the starter motor mounting bolt securely.

2.3L and 2.4L OHC engines

Refer to illustrations 13.9 and 13.10

8   Remove the air intake duct and resonator (see Chapter 4).

9   Remove the upper starter mounting bolt **(see illustration)**.

10   Clearly label, then disconnect the wires from the terminals on the starter motor

solenoid **(see illustration)**.

11   Raise the front of the vehicle and place it securely on jackstands.

12   Remove the lower starter mounting bolt **(see illustration 13.9)** and remove the starter.

13   Installation is the reverse of removal. Be sure to tighten the starter motor mounting bolts securely.

2.2L OHC engine

Refer to illustrations 13.15 and 13.16

14   Raise the front of the vehicle and place it securely on jackstands.

15   Disconnect the battery cable (the larger cable) and the starter control cable (the smaller cable) from the starter solenoid terminals **(see illustration)**.

16   Remove the starter motor mounting bolts **(see illustration)** and remove the starter motor.

17   Installation is the reverse of removal. Be sure to tighten the starter motor mounting bolts securely.

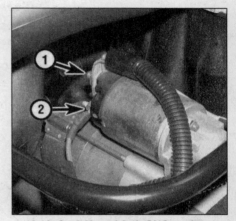

13.10 On 2.3L and 2.4L OHC engines, remove the terminal nuts and disconnect the battery cable (1) from the upper solenoid terminal and the strap that connects the lower solenoid terminal to the starter motor

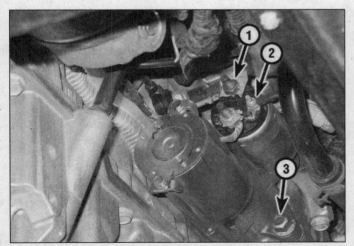

13.15 Disconnect the battery cable (1) and the starter solenoid wire (2) from the starter solenoid terminals. (3) is the lower mounting bolt (2.2L OHC engine)

13.16 To remove the upper starter motor upper mounting bolt, use a socket and extension (2.2L OHC engine)

14 Starter solenoid - removal and installation

Refer to illustration 14.5
Note: *Although it's possible to detach the solenoid from the starter on virtually all of the starter motors used by the vehicles covered in this manual, you should first verify that the solenoid or the starter used on your car is actually available separately. Some automotive parts stores only sell complete starter/solenoid assemblies. And even if your local parts supplier offers these components separately, you will find in most cases that a complete remanufactured starter motor/solenoid assembly is inexpensive enough to justify simply swapping your old starter/solenoid for a complete rebuilt unit. By the time the starter motor or the solenoid has worn out, the other component is probably in poor condition too, so even if it still works it will probably fail fairly*

soon, which means removing and disassembling the starter/solenoid again.

1   Disconnect the cable from the negative terminal of the battery. **Caution:** *If the vehicle is equipped with a Delco Loc II or Theftlock audio system, make sure you have the correct activation code before disconnecting the battery.*
2   Remove the starter motor (see Section 13).
3   Disconnect the strap from the solenoid to the starter motor terminal **(see illustration 13.3)**.
4   Remove the bolts that secure the solenoid to the starter motor.
5   Twist the solenoid in a clockwise direction to disengage the flange from the starter body **(see illustration)**.
6   Installation is the reverse of removal. Be sure to tighten the solenoid mounting bolts securely.

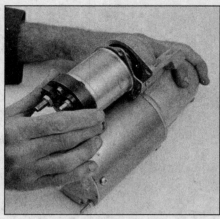

14.5 To remove the solenoid housing from the starter motor, remove the bolts (see illustration 13.3) and turn it clockwise

Chapter 6
Emissions and engine control systems

Contents

Specifications

Torque specifications

Ft-lbs (unless otherwise indicated)

Engine Coolant Temperature (ECT) sensor	
2.2L OHC engine	89 in-lbs
2.2L OHV engine	180 in-lbs
2.3L and 2.4L OHC engines	180 in-lbs
Knock Sensor (KS)	
2.2L OHC engine (retaining bolt)	18
2.2L OHV engine (screw-in type sensor, no retaining bolt)	168 in-lbs
2.3L and 2.4L OHC engines	
1995 through 1998 (screw-in type sensor, no retaining bolt)	170 in-lbs
1999 on (retaining bolt)	18

1 General information

Refer to illustration 1.7

The emission control systems and components are an integral part of the engine management system, which is referred to as the Multiport Fuel Injection (MFI) system on 1995 models and is called Sequential Fuel Injection (SFI) on 1996 and later models (see Chapter 4 for more information on the MFI and SFI systems). The SFI system also includes all the government-mandated diagnostic features of the second generation of on-board diagnostics, which is known as On-

Board Diagnostics II (OBD-II). The MFI system used on 1995 models is also equipped with (an early version of) OBD-II, but still uses the earlier two-digit Diagnostic Trouble Codes (DTCs).

At the center of the engine management systems is the on-board computer, which is known as the Powertrain Control Module (PCM). Using a variety of information sensors, the PCM monitors all of the important engine operating parameters (temperature, speed, load, etc.). It also uses an array of output actuators - such as the ignition coils, the fuel injectors, the Idle Air Control (IAC) valve, the Torque Converter Clutch (TCC) and vari-

ous solenoids and relays - to respond to and alter these parameters as necessary to maintain optimal performance, economy and emissions. The principal emission control systems used on the vehicles covered in this manual include the:

Catalytic converters
Evaporative Emission Control (EVAP) system
Exhaust Gas Recirculation (EGR) system
Positive Crankcase Ventilation (PCV) system
Torque Converter Clutch (TCC) system

The Sections in this Chapter include general descriptions and component replace-

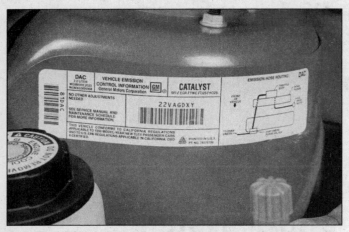

1.7 The VECI label specifies critical tune-up and/or adjustment procedures, if applicable, and provides a vacuum hose diagram that shows how vacuum-controlled emission components are connected

2.2 Scanners like these from Actron and the AutoXray are powerful diagnostic aids - programmed with comprehensive diagnostic information, they can tell you just about anything you want to know about your engine management system

ment procedures for most of the information sensors and output actuators, as well as the important components that are part of the systems listed above. Refer to Chapter 4 for more information on the air intake, fuel and exhaust systems, and to Chapter 5 for information on the ignition system. Refer to Chapter 1 for any scheduled maintenance for emission-related systems and components.

The procedures in this Chapter are intended to be practical, affordable and within the capabilities of the home mechanic. The diagnosis of most engine and emission control functions and driveability problems requires specialized tools, equipment and training. When servicing emission devices or systems becomes too difficult or requires special test equipment, consult a dealer service department or other qualified repair shop.

Although engine and emission control systems are very sophisticated on late-model vehicles, you can do most of the regular maintenance and some servicing at home with common tune-up and hand tools and relatively inexpensive meters. Because of the Federally mandated extended warranty that covers the emission control system, check with a dealer about warranty coverage before working on any emission-related systems. After the warranty has expired, you might want to perform some of the component replacement procedures in this Chapter to save money. Remember that the most frequent cause of emission and driveability problems is a loose electrical connector or a broken wire or vacuum hose, so before jumping to conclusions the first thing you should always do is to inspect all electrical connections, electrical wiring and vacuum hoses related to a system.

Pay close attention to any special precautions given in this Chapter. Remember that illustrations of various system components might not exactly match the component installed on the vehicle on which you're

working because of changes made by the manufacturer during production or from year to year.

A Vehicle Emission Control Information (VECI) label **(see illustration)** is located in the engine compartment. This label lists the emission control systems installed on the vehicle and, if applicable, contains emission-control and engine tune-up specifications and adjustment information. It also includes a vacuum hose routing diagram for emission-control components. When servicing the engine or emission systems, always check the VECI label in your vehicle. If any information in this manual contradicts what you read on the VECI label on your vehicle, always defer to the information on the VECI label.

---

2   On Board Diagnosis (OBD) system and Diagnostic Trouble Codes

Scan tool information

Refer to illustration 2.2

1   Hand-held scanners are handy for analyzing the engine management systems used on late-model vehicles. Because extracting the Diagnostic Trouble Codes (DTCs) from an engine management system is now the first step in troubleshooting many computer-controlled systems and components, even the most basic generic scan tools are capable of accessing a computer's DTCs. More powerful scan tools can also perform many of the diagnostics once associated with expensive factory scan tools. If you're planning to obtain a generic scan tool for your vehicle, make sure that it's compatible with the year, make and model of the vehicle(s) on which you plan to use it. Some of the more versatile scan tools accept removable cartridges, each of which contains the diagnostics for a particular manufacturer. An aftermarket generic scanner should work with any model covered

by this manual. But before purchasing a scan tool, contact the manufacturer of the scanner you're planning to buy and verify that it will work properly with the system you want to scan. If you don't plan to purchase a scan tool and don't have access to one, you can have the codes extracted by a dealer service department or other qualified repair shop.

2   With the advent of the Federally mandated emission control system known as On-Board Diagnostics-II (OBD-II), specially designed scanners were developed. Several tool manufacturers have released OBD-II scan tools for the home mechanic **(see illustration)**.

OBD-II system general description

Refer to illustration 2.4

3   All vehicles covered by this manual are equipped with the OBD-II system. This system consists of the on-board computer, known as the Powertrain Control Module (PCM), and information sensors that monitor various functions of the engine and send a constant stream of data to the PCM during engine operation. Unlike earlier on-board diagnostics systems, the OBD-II system doesn't just monitor everything, store Diagnostic Trouble Codes (DTCs) and illuminate a Malfunction Indicator Light (MIL) when there's a problem. *It even predicts the probable failure of systems and components when their data starts to become suspicious!*

4   The PCM is the "brain" of the electronically controlled OBD-II system. It receives data from a number of information sensors and switches. Based on the data that it receives from the sensors, the PCM constantly alters engine operating conditions to optimize driveability, performance, emissions and fuel economy. It does so by turning on and off and by controlling various output actuators such as relays, solenoids, valves and other devices. The PCM can only be accessed with an OBD-II scan tool plugged

2.4 The 16-pin Data Link Connector (DLC), also referred to as the diagnostic connector, is located under the left side of the dash

into the 16-pin Data Link Connector (DLC), which is located underneath the driver's end of the dashboard, near the steering column **(see illustration)**.

5   If your vehicle is still under warranty, virtually every fuel, ignition and emission control component in the OBD-II system is covered by a Federally mandated emissions warranty that is longer than the warranty covering the rest of the vehicle. Vehicles sold in California and in some other states have even longer emissions warranties than other states. Read your owner's manual for the terms of the warranty protecting the emission-control systems on your vehicle. It isn't a good idea to "do-it-yourself" at home while the vehicle emission systems are still under warranty because owner-induced damage to the PCM, the sensors and/or the control devices might VOID this warranty. So as long as the emission systems are still warranted, take the vehicle to a dealer service department if there's a problem.

Information sensors

6   **Camshaft Position (CMP) sensor** - The CMP sensor is a Hall effect switching device that produces a digital (ON-OFF) signal that the PCM uses to monitor the position of the camshaft. This data enables the CMP sensor to identify the position of the valvetrain so that it can time the firing sequence of the fuel injectors. On 1996 and later 2.2L OHV engines, the CMP sensor is on the backside of the engine block, right above the Knock Sensor (KS) and the Crankshaft Position (CKP) sensor (1995 2.2L OHV engines do not have a CMP sensor). 1995 2.3L OHC engines do not use a CMP sensor. On 2.4L OHC engines, the CMP sensor is located on the leading edge of the front camshaft housing. 2.2L OHC engines do not use a CMP sensor.

7   **Crankshaft Position (CKP) sensor** - The CKP sensor is a permanent magnet generator (also known as a variable reluctance sensor) that produces a variable AC voltage signal that the PCM uses to determine the

position of the crankshaft. The PCM uses data from the CKP sensor to synchronize ignition timing with fuel injector timing, to control spark knock and to detect misfires. On 2.2L OHV engines, the CKP sensor is located on the backside of the engine block, right next to the Knock Sensor (KS). On 2.3L and 2.4L OHC engines, the CKP sensor is located on the front side of the engine block, above and to the left of the oil filter. On 2.2L OHC engines, the CKP sensor is located on the front of the block, right above the starter motor.

8   **Engine Coolant Temperature (ECT) sensor** - The ECT sensor is a thermistor (temperature-sensitive variable resistor) that sends a voltage signal to the PCM, which uses this data to determine the temperature of the engine coolant. The ECT sensor tells the PCM when the engine is sufficiently warmed up to go into closed loop, helps the PCM control the air/fuel mixture ratio and ignition timing, and also helps the PCM determine when to turn the Exhaust Gas Recirculation (EGR) system on and off. On 2.2L OHV engines, the ECT sensor is either located on the thermostat housing (1995 through 1997 models), or on the coolant pipe, near the right front corner of the engine (1998 and later models). On 2.3L and 2.4L OHC engines, the ECT sensor is located at the left rear corner of the cylinder head. On 2.2L OHC engines, the ECT sensor is located on the thermostat housing, which is located on the left rear corner of the cylinder head.

9   **Fuel tank pressure sensor** - The fuel tank pressure sensor, which is located on top of the fuel tank (on the mounting flange of the fuel pump/fuel level sending unit module), measures the fuel tank pressure when the PCM tests the EVAP system. It's also used to control fuel tank pressure by signaling the EVAP system to purge the tank when the pressure becomes excessive.

10   **Inlet Air Temperature (IAT) sensor** - The IAT sensor monitors the temperature of the air entering the engine and sends a signal to the PCM. The PCM uses this information to help it determine spark timing and fuel injector "pulse width" (the interval of time during which an injector solenoid is energized by the PCM). The IAT sensor is located on the air intake duct on all engines.

11   **Knock Sensor (KS)** - The Knock Sensor (KS) is a "piezoelectric" crystal that oscillates in proportion to engine vibration. The oscillation of the piezoelectric crystal produces a voltage output that is monitored by the PCM, which retards the ignition timing when the oscillation exceeds a certain threshold. When the engine is operating normally, the Knock Sensor (KS) oscillates consistently and its voltage signal is steady. When detonation occurs, engine vibration increases, and the oscillation of the Knock Sensor (KS) exceeds a design threshold. Detonation is not only annoying (pinging or knocking sound), but, If allowed to continue, the engine can be damaged. On 2.2L OHV engines, the Knock Sen-

sor (KS) is located on the backside of the engine block, right next (and to the left) of the Crankshaft Position (CKP) sensor. On 2.3L and 2.4L OHC engines, the Knock Sensor (KS) is located on the backside of the block. On 2.2L OHV engines, the Knock Sensor (KS) is located on the front side of the block, near the starter motor.

12   **Manifold Absolute Pressure (MAP) sensor** - The MAP sensor monitors the pressure or vacuum downstream from the throttle plate, inside the intake manifold. The MAP sensor measures intake manifold pressure and vacuum on the absolute scale, i.e. from zero instead of from sea-level atmospheric pressure (14.7 psi). The MAP sensor converts the absolute pressure into a variable voltage signal that changes with the pressure. The PCM uses this data to determine engine load so that it can alter the ignition advance and fuel enrichment. On 1995 through 1997 2.2L OHV engines, the MAP sensor is located the upper intake manifold. On 1998 and later 2.2L OHV engines, the MAP sensor is located on the throttle body. On 2.2L OHC engines, the MAP sensor is located on the intake manifold, near the throttle body. On 2.3L and 2.4L OHC engines, the MAP sensor is located on the left side of the throttle body.

13   **Output Shaft Speed (OSS) sensor** - The OSS sensor is a magnetic pick-up coil located on the backside of the automatic transaxle, near the right inner CV joint. The OSS sensor provides the PCM with information about the rotational speed of the output shaft in the transaxle. The PCM uses this information to control shift timing and line pressure, and to determine when to apply or release the Torque Converter Clutch (TCC). There is also an Input Shaft Speed (ISS) sensor, which is similar in design and operation to the OSS, except that it provides the PCM with the rotational speed of the *input* shaft. The PCM uses the ISS to control line pressure and shift patterns, and to determine when to apply or release the Torque Converter Clutch (TCC). The OBD-II system also uses the ISS to calculate the appropriate gear ratio for the operating conditions and to calculate slippage in the TCC system. You can replace the OSS at home, but the ISS is inside the transaxle, so if it malfunctions have it serviced by an automatic transmission specialist.

14   **Oxygen sensors** - An oxygen sensor is a galvanic battery that generates a small variable voltage signal in proportion to the difference between the oxygen content in the exhaust stream and the oxygen content in the ambient air. The PCM uses the voltage signal from the upstream oxygen sensor to maintain a "stoichiometric" air/fuel ratio of 14.7:1 by constantly adjusting the "on-time" of the fuel injectors. There are *two* oxygen sensors: the *upstream* sensor is located on the exhaust manifold and a *downstream* oxygen sensor is located behind the catalyst.

15   **Throttle Position (TP) sensor** - The TP sensor is a potentiometer that receives con-

stant voltage input from the PCM and sends back a voltage signal that varies in relation to the opening angle of the throttle plate inside the throttle body. This voltage signal tells the PCM when the throttle is closed, half-open, wide open or anywhere in between. The PCM uses this data, along with information from other sensors, to calculate injector "pulse width" (the interval of time during which an injector solenoid is energized by the PCM). The TP sensor is located on the throttle body, on the end of the throttle plate shaft.

16   **Transmission Range (TR) switch** - The TR switch is located at the upper end of the manual shaft, on top of the automatic transaxle. The TR switch performs the same functions as a Park/Neutral Position (PNP) switch: it prevents the engine from starting in any gear other than Park or Neutral, and it closes the circuit for the back-up lights when the shift lever is moved to Reverse. But the TR switch is also connected to the PCM, which sends a voltage signal to the TR switch, which uses a series of step-down resistors that act as a voltage divider. The PCM monitors the voltage output signal from the switch, which corresponds to the position of the manual lever. Thus the PCM is able to determine the gear selected and is able to determine the correct pressure for the electronic pressure control system of the transaxle.

17   **Vehicle Speed Sensor (VSS)** - The VSS is a magnetic pick-up coil located on top of the manual transaxle, near the right inner CV joint. The VSS generates a pulsing voltage as long as vehicle speed exceeds three mph. This AC voltage output increases as the speed increases. The PCM uses this information to calculate vehicle speed, which it then sends to the instrument cluster for the speedometer and odometer and to the cruise control system.

Output actuators

18   **EVAP canister purge valve** - The EVAP canister purge valve is a PCM-controlled solenoid that controls the purging of evaporative emissions from the EVAP canister to the intake manifold. The EVAP purge solenoid is normally closed. But when ordered to do so by the PCM, it allows the fuel vapors that are stored in the EVAP canister to be drawn into the intake manifold, where they're mixed with intake air, then burned along with the normal air/fuel mixture, under certain operating conditions. On 2.2L OHV engines, the EVAP canister purge valve is located on the backside of the engine block, except for 1998 models, on which it's mounted on top of the valve cover. On 2.2L OHC engines, the EVAP canister purge valve is located to the left of the cylinder head, below and ahead of the brake master cylinder. On 2.3L OHC engines, the EVAP canister purge valve is located at the left end of the intake manifold, between the Idle Air Control (IAC) valve and the Intake Air Temperature (IAT) sensor. On 2.4L OHC engines, the EVAP

canister purge valve is located at the right front corner of the engine, below the alternator and above the air-conditioning compressor.

19   **EVAP canister vent solenoid** - The EVAP canister vent solenoid is located near the EVAP canister, which is located under the vehicle, near the fuel tank. The EVAP canister vent solenoid is part of the EVAP system's leak diagnostics. The vent solenoid is normally open, to allow outside air to flow through the vent, through the EVAP canister and into the fuel tank, which maintains atmospheric pressure inside the fuel tank. But when energized by the PCM, the vent solenoid closes and seals off the EVAP system for inspection and maintenance tests and for OBD-II leak and pressure tests.

20   **Exhaust Gas Recirculation (EGR) valve** - 1995 through 1998 2.2L OHV engines use an EGR system. When the engine is put under a load (hard acceleration, passing, going up a steep hill, pulling a trailer, etc.), combustion chamber temperature increases. When combustion chamber temperature exceeds 2500 degrees, excessive amounts of oxides of nitrogen (NOx) are produced. NOx is a precursor of photochemical smog. When combined with hydrocarbons (HC), other "reactive organic compounds" (ROCs) and sunlight, it forms ozone, nitrogen dioxide and nitrogen nitrate and other nasty stuff. The EGR valve allows exhaust gases to be recirculated back to the intake manifold where they dilute the incoming air/fuel mixture, which lowers the combustion chamber temperature and decreases the amount of NOx produced during high-load conditions. On 1995 2.2L OHV engines, the EGR valve is located at the left end of the cylinder head. The EGR valve on 1995 models is opened and closed by a separate control solenoid valve, which allows ported vacuum from the throttle body to open the EGR valve when directed to do so by the PCM. The EGR control solenoid valve on 1995 models is located on the front of the upper intake manifold, to the left of the Throttle Position (TP) sensor. 1996 and 1997 2.2L OHV engines use a "linear" EGR valve, which is also located at the same spot, on the left end of the cylinder head. Unlike the earlier (1995) EGR system, the linear system doesn't use a computer-controlled solenoid valve to direct ported vacuum to the EGR valve to open it. Instead, the linear type is all electronic. The PCM opens and closes it in response to input from the Throttle Position (TP) sensor and the Manifold Absolute Pressure (MAP) sensor. There is no separate EGR control solenoid valve on these models; the electronic control mechanism is an integral part of the EGR valve. On 1998 models (which also use a linear EGR valve system) the EGR valve is relocated to the left rear corner of the engine (to make room for the ignition coil pack, which was moved from the backside of the engine block to the left end of the head).

21   **Fuel injectors** - The fuel injectors,

which spray a fine mist of fuel into the intake ports, where it is mixed with incoming air, are inductive coils under PCM control. The injectors are installed in the intake ports that connect the intake manifold runners to the combustion chambers. For more information about the injectors, see Chapter 4.

22   **Idle Air Control (IAC) valve** - The IAC valve controls the amount of air allowed to bypass the throttle plate when the throttle plate is at its (nearly closed) idle position. The IAC valve is controlled by the PCM. When the engine is placed under an additional load at idle (high power steering pressure or running the air conditioning compressor during low-speed maneuvers, for example), the engine can run roughly, stumble and even stall. To prevent this from happening, the PCM opens the IAC valve to increase the idle speed enough to overcome the extra load imposed on the engine. The IAC valve is mounted on the throttle body. On 1995 through 1997 2.2L OHV engines, the IAC valve is mounted on top of the upper intake manifold. On 1998 and later 2.2L OHV engines and on all 2.2L, 2.3L and 2.4L OHC engines, the IAC valve is located on the throttle body.

23   **Ignition coils** - The ignition coils are under the control of the Powertrain Control Module (PCM). All engines use a coil pack assembly consisting of two ignition coils, each of which fires two cylinders. The coil packs used on 1995 through 1997 2.2L OHV engines are mounted on backside of the engine block. The coil packs on 1998 and later 2.2L OHV engines are mounted on the left end of the cylinder head. The coil packs used on OHC engines are mounted directly over the spark plugs (there are no spark plug wires) and are referred to as a "coil-over-plug" design. For more information about the ignition coils, see Chapter 5.

Obtaining and clearing Diagnostic Trouble Codes (DTCs)

24   All models covered by this manual are equipped with on-board diagnostics. When the PCM recognizes a malfunction in a monitored emission control system, component or circuit, it turns on the Malfunction Indicator Light (MIL) on the dash. The PCM will continue to display the MIL until the problem is fixed and the Diagnostic Trouble Code (DTC) is cleared from the PCM's memory. You'll need a scan tool to access any DTCs stored in the PCM.

25   Before outputting any DTCs stored in the PCM, thoroughly inspect ALL electrical connectors and hoses. Make sure that all electrical connections are tight, clean and free of corrosion. And make sure that all hoses are correctly connected, fit tightly and are in good condition (no cracks or tears). Also, make sure that the engine is tuned up. A poorly running engine is probably one of the biggest causes of emission-related malfunctions. Often, simply giving the engine a good tune-up will correct the problem.

Accessing the DTCs

26 On these models, all of which are equipped with On-Board Diagnostic II (OBD-II) systems, the Diagnostic Trouble Codes (DTCs) can only be accessed with a scan tool. Professional scan tools are expensive, but relatively inexpensive generic scan tools **(see illustration 2.2)** are available at most auto parts stores. Simply plug the connector of the scan tool into the Data Link Connector (DLC) or diagnostic connector **(see illustration 2.4)**, which is located under the lower edge of the dash, on the driver's side. Then follow the instructions included with the scan tool to extract the DTCs.

27 Once you have outputted all of the stored DTCs look them up on the accompanying DTC chart.

28 After troubleshooting the source of each DTC make any necessary repairs or replace the defective component(s).

Clearing the DTCs

29 Clear the DTCs with the scan tool in accordance with the instructions provided by the scan tool's manufacturer.

Diagnostic Trouble Codes

30 The accompanying tables are a list of the Diagnostic Trouble Codes (DTCs) that can be accessed by a do-it-yourselfer working at home (there are many, many more DTCs available to dealerships with proprietary scan tools and software, but those codes cannot be accessed by a generic scan tool). If, after you have checked and repaired the connectors, wire harness and vacuum hoses (if applicable) for an emission-related system, component or circuit, the problem persists, have the vehicle checked by a dealer service department or other qualified repair shop.

OBD Diagnostic Trouble Codes (DTCs) for 1995 models

Note: *Not all trouble codes apply to all models.*

Code	Probable cause
13	Open oxygen sensor circuit
14	Engine Coolant Temperature (ECT) sensor circuit, high temperature
15	Engine Coolant Temperature (ECT) sensor circuit, low temperature
19	Intermittent reference circuit for Crankshaft Position (CKP) sensor
21	Throttle Position (TP) sensor circuit, high signal voltage
22	Throttle Position (TP) sensor circuit, low signal voltage
23	Intake Air Temperature (IAT) sensor circuit, low temperature indicated
24	Vehicle Speed Sensor (VSS) circuit
25	Intake Air Temperature (IAT) sensor circuit, high temperature indicated
27	Quad-Driver Module (QDM 1) circuit
28	Quad-Driver Module (QDM 2) circuit
31	PRNDL error
32	Exhaust Gas Recirculation (EGR) flow check
33	Manifold Absolute Pressure (MAP) sensor circuit, high signal voltage
34	Manifold Absolute Pressure (MAP) sensor circuit, low signal voltage
35	Idle speed error
43	Knock Sensor (KS) (KS) circuit
44	Oxygen sensor circuit, lean exhaust indicated
45	Oxygen sensor circuit, rich exhaust indicated
51	EPROM error (faulty or incorrect EPROM)
53	Battery voltage error
55	Fuel lean monitor
66	Air conditioning refrigerant pressure sensor circuit
72	Loss of serial data

OBD-II Diagnostic Trouble Codes (DTCs) for 1996 and later models

Note: *Not all trouble codes apply to all models.*

Code	Probable cause
P0105	Manifold Absolute Pressure (MAP) sensor circuit or Throttle Position (TP) sensor circuit out of range
P0107	Manifold Absolute Pressure (MAP) sensor circuit, low voltage
P0108	Manifold Absolute Pressure (MAP) sensor circuit, high voltage
P0112	Intake Air Temperature (IAT) sensor circuit, excessively low voltage
P0113	Intake Air Temperature (IAT) sensor circuit, excessively high voltage
P0116	Engine Coolant Temperature (ECT) sensor performance
P0117	Engine Coolant Temperature (ECT) sensor circuit, low voltage
P0118	Engine Coolant Temperature (ECT) sensor circuit, high voltage
P0122	Throttle Position (TP) sensor circuit, very low signal voltage
P0123	Throttle Position (TP) sensor circuit, very high signal voltage
P0125	Engine Coolant Temperature (ECT) sensor circuit, engine takes too long to reach closed loop
P0128	Engine Coolant Temperature (ECT) sensor circuit, engine takes too long to warm up
P0130	Oxygen sensor circuit, engine not in closed loop
P0131	Oxygen sensor circuit, low voltage for excessive amount of time
P0132	Oxygen sensor circuit, high voltage for excessive amount of time
P0133	Oxygen sensor circuit, voltage response time too slow
P0134	Oxygen sensor circuit, voltage activity remains at or near bias voltage
P0135	Oxygen sensor heater circuit, heater current above or below threshold
P0137	Oxygen sensor circuit, low voltage for excessive amount of time
P0138	Oxygen sensor circuit, high voltage for excessive amount of time
P0140	Oxygen sensor circuit, voltage at or near bias voltage
P0141	Oxygen sensor heater circuit, heater current above or below threshold
P0171	PCM detects an excessively lean condition
P0172	PCM detects an excessively rich condition
P0201	Fuel injector control circuit No. 1, PCM detects incorrect voltage
P0202	Fuel injector control circuit No. 2, PCM detects incorrect voltage
P0203	Fuel injector control circuit No. 3, PCM detects incorrect voltage
P0204	Fuel injector control circuit No. 4, PCM detects incorrect voltage
P0300	Engine misfire detected by PCM
P0301	Misfire detected by PCM at cylinder No. 1

Code	Probable cause
P0302	Misfire detected by PCM at cylinder No. 2
P0303	Misfire detected by PCM at cylinder No. 3
P0304	Misfire detected by PCM at cylinder No. 4
P0325	Knock Sensor (KS) (KS) circuit not within normally expected range
P0326	Incorrect diagnosis of Knock Sensor (KS) (KS) circuit by PCM
P0336	Crankshaft Position (CKP) sensor circuit malfunction
P0340	PCM can't process signal from the Camshaft Position (CMP) sensor
P0341	PCM getting intermittent signal from Camshaft Position (CMP) sensor
P0420	Catalyst system efficiency has degraded below a certain threshold
P0440	Evaporative Emission (EVAP) system fails to hold sufficient vacuum
P0442	Evaporative Emission (EVAP) system, vacuum leak detected
P0446	Evaporative Emission (EVAP) system, vent system failure
P0452	Fuel Tank Pressure (FTP) sensor circuit, low voltage
P0453	Fuel Tank Pressure (FTP) sensor circuit, high voltage
P0506	Idle speed out of range (low) for a calibrated period of time
P0507	Idle speed out of range (high) for a calibrated period of time
P0601	PCM Read-Only Memory (ROM) problem
P0602	PCM not programmed

3.2 On 2.2L OHV engines, the CMP sensor (A) is located on the backside of the engine block, next to the Knock Sensor (KS) (B). To detach the CMP sensor from the block, remove the mounting bolt (C). To remove the KS from the block, unscrew it (exhaust manifold and cylinder head removed for clarity)

3 Camshaft Position (CMP) sensor - replacement

Note: *2.3L OHC engines do not use a CMP sensor.*

2.2L OHV engine

Refer to illustration 3.2

1 Raise the front end of the vehicle and place it securely on jackstands.
2 Locate the CMP sensor **(see illustra-**tion) on the backside of the engine block, to the left of the knock sensor.
3 Disconnect the electrical connector from the CMP sensor.
4 Remove the CMP sensor retaining bolt.
5 Remove the CMP sensor.
6 Installation is the reverse of removal.

2.4L OHC engine

Refer to illustration 3.7

7 Disconnect the electrical connector from the CMP sensor **(see illustration)**.

3.7 To detach the CMP sensor (A) from the front camshaft housing on a 2.4L OHC engine, disconnect the electrical connector (B) and remove the sensor retaining bolt (C). After removing the CMP sensor, remove and discard the old sensor O-ring and replace it with a new one

4.2 To detach the CKP sensor (A) from a 2.2L OHV engine, disconnect the electrical connector (B) and remove the sensor retaining bolt (C) (1995 through 1999 model shown, with ignition coil assembly removed for clarity; on 2000 through 2002 models, the ignition coil has been relocated, but the CKP sensor is still in this same location)

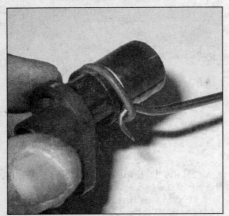

4.17 Be sure to remove and discard the old CKP sensor O-ring (CKP sensor for 2.2L OHC engine shown; other sensor O-rings similar)

8   Remove the CMP sensor retaining bolt.
9   Remove the CMP sensor.
10   Remove and discard the old CMP sensor O-ring.
11   Install a new CMP sensor O-ring.
12   Installation is otherwise the reverse of removal.

---

4   Crankshaft Position (CKP) sensor - replacement

2.2L OHV engine

Refer to illustration 4.2
1   Raise the front of the vehicle and place it securely on jackstands.
2   Locate the CKP sensor on the backside of the engine block (see illustration). On 1995 through 1999 engines, look for the CKP

4.8 To detach the CKP sensor (A) from a 2.3L or 2.4L OHC engine, disconnect the electrical connector (B) and remove the sensor retaining bolt (C) (oil filter removed for clarity)

sensor directly below the ignition coil assembly, which is also mounted on the backside of the block. The CKP sensor is in the same location on 2000 through 2002 models, except that the coil assembly has been moved to the left end of the cylinder head.
3   Disconnect the electrical connector from the CKP sensor.
4   Remove the CKP sensor retaining bolt and remove the sensor.
5   Remove and discard the old CKP sensor O-ring (see illustration 4.17). Even if you're planning to reuse the old CKP sensor, install a new O-ring when installing the CKP sensor.
6   Installation is the reverse of removal.

2.3L and 2.4L OHC engines

Refer to illustration 4.8
7   Raise the front of the vehicle and place it securely on jackstands.
8   Locate the CKP sensor right above the oil filter (see illustration).
9   Disconnect the electrical connector from the CKP sensor.
10   Remove the CKP sensor retaining bolt and remove the CKP sensor.
11   Remove and discard the old CKP sensor O-ring (see illustration 4.17). Even if you're planning to reuse the old CKP sensor, install a new O-ring when installing the CKP sensor.
12   Installation is the reverse of removal.

2.2L OHC engine

Refer to illustrations 4.15 and 4.17
13   Raise the vehicle and place it securely on jackstands.
14   Remove the starter motor (see Chapter 5).
15   Disconnect the electrical connector from the CKP sensor (see illustration).
16   Unscrew the CKP sensor mounting bolt and remove the CKP sensor.
17   Even if you're planning to reuse the old

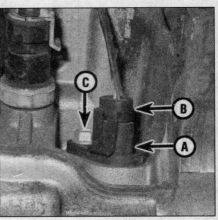

4.15 To detach the CKP sensor (A) from a 2.2L OHC engine, disconnect the electrical connector (B) and remove the sensor retaining bolt (C)

CKP sensor, be sure to remove the old O-ring (see illustration) and discard it. Always install a new O-ring when installing the CKP sensor.
18   Installation is the reverse of removal.

---

5   Engine Coolant Temperature (ECT) sensor - replacement

2.2L OHV engine

Refer to illustration 5.2a, 5.2b and 5.5
Warning: *Wait until the engine is completely cool before beginning this procedure.*
1   Drain the cooling system (see Chapter 1). (It's not necessary to fully drain the coolant, but it must be drained to a level that's below the lever of the ECT sensor.)
2   Locate the ECT sensor. On 1995 through 1997 models, the ECT sensor is

5.2a On 1995 through 1997 2.2L OHV engines, the ECT sensor (A) is located on the thermostat housing at the left end of the cylinder head. To remove the ECT sensor, disconnect the electrical connector (B) and unscrew the sensor

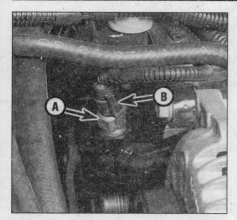

5.2b On 1998 and later 2.2L OHV engines, the ECT sensor (A) is located on the coolant pipe, at the right front corner of the cylinder head, right behind the alternator. To remove the ECT sensor, disconnect the electrical connector (B) and unscrew the sensor

located on the thermostat housing at the left end of the cylinder head **(see illustration)**. On 1998 and later models, the ECT sensor is located in the coolant pipe, at the right front corner of the cylinder head, near the alternator **(see illustration)**.
3   Disconnect the electrical connector from the ECT sensor.
4   Unscrew the ECT sensor and remove it.
5   Wrap the threads of the new ECT sensor with Teflon tape **(see illustration)**.
6   Installation is the reverse of removal. Be sure to tighten the ECT sensor to the torque listed in this Chapter's Specifications.
7   Refill the cooling system when you're done (see Chapter 1).

2.3L and 2.4L OHC engines

Refer to illustration 5.9
Warning: *Wait until the engine is completely cool before beginning this procedure.*

5.16 On 2.2L OHC engines, disconnect the electrical connector from the ECT sensor, which is located at the lower left corner of the cylinder head, on the thermostat housing

5.5 To prevent coolant from leaking past the threads, be sure to wrap the threads of the ECT sensor with Teflon tape before installing the sensor

8   Drain the cooling system (see Chapter 1). (It's not necessary to fully drain the coolant, but it must be drained to a level that's below the lever of the ECT sensor.)
9   Locate the ECT sensor on the thermostat housing at the left end of the cylinder head **(see illustration)**.
10   Disconnect the electrical connector from the ECT sensor.
11   Unscrew the ECT sensor and remove it.
12   Wrap the threads of the new ECT sensor with Teflon tape **(see illustration 5.5)**.
13   Installation is the reverse of removal. Be sure to tighten the ECT sensor to the torque listed in this Chapter's Specifications.
14   Refill the cooling system when you're done (see Chapter 1).

2.2L OHC engine

Refer to illustrations 5.16 and 5.17
Warning: *Wait until the engine is completely cool before beginning this procedure.*
15   Drain the cooling system (see Chapter 1). (It's not necessary to fully drain the coolant, but it must be drained to a level

5.17 Use a deep socket, a six-inch extension and a ratchet to unscrew the ECT sensor from 2.2L OHC engines

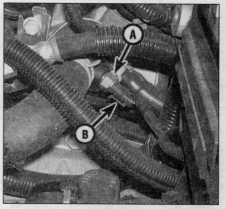

5.9 On 2.3L and 2.4L OHC engines, the ECT sensor (A) is located on the thermostat housing at the left end of the cylinder head. To remove the ECT sensor, disconnect the electrical connector (B) and unscrew the sensor

that's below the lever of the ECT sensor.)
16   Disconnect the electrical connector from the ECT sensor **(see illustration)**.
17   Unscrew the ECT sensor **(see illustration)** and remove it.
18   Wrap the threads of the ECT sensor with Teflon tape **(see illustration 5.5)**.
19   Installation is the reverse of removal. Be sure to tighten the ECT sensor to the torque listed in this Chapter's Specifications.
20   Refill the cooling system when you're done (see Chapter 1).

---

6   Inlet Air Temperature (IAT) sensor - replacement

2.2L OHV engine

Refer to illustration 6.1
1   Locate the IAT sensor on the air intake duct and disconnect the electrical connector **(see illustration)**.

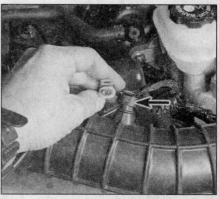

6.1 On 2.2L OHV engines, the IAT sensor is located on the air intake duct. To remove the IAT sensor, disconnect the electrical connector, then pull the sensor straight out from its mounting hole in the air intake duct

6.9 On 2.4L OHC engines, the IAT sensor is located on the air intake duct. To remove the IAT sensor, disconnect the electrical connector, then pull the sensor straight out from its mounting hole in the air intake duct

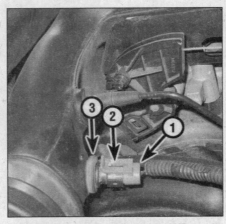

6.13 On 2.2L OHC engines, the IAT sensor (1) is located on the air intake resonator. Disconnect the electrical connector (2), then pull the sensor straight out of its grommet (3)

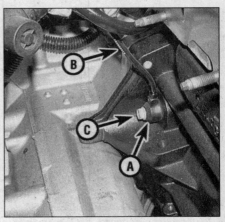

7.15 To remove the Knock Sensor (A) from a 1999 through 2002 2.4L OHC engine, trace the electrical lead (B) up to the electrical connector and disconnect it, then remove the retaining bolt (C)

2   To remove the IAT sensor from the air intake duct, simply pull it straight out. If the IAT sensor is difficult to remove, try wiggling it from side-to-side and pulling on it at the same time.

3   Installation is the reverse of removal. To prevent an air leak, make sure that the IAT sensor fits tightly into its mounting hole in the air intake duct. If it's loose, unfiltered air will enter the air intake duct. Sometimes a small leak can be stopped with the application of a small amount of silicone sealant around the mating surfaces of the air intake duct and the IAT sensor. If that doesn't work, you might have to replace the air intake duct.

2.3L and 2.4L OHC engines

2.3L OHC engine

4   Locate the IAT sensor on top of the intake manifold between intake runners three and four.

5   Disconnect the electrical connector from the IAT sensor.

6   Unscrew the sensor from the intake manifold.

7   Wrap the threads of the new IAT sensor with Teflon tape to prevent air leaks, screw in the sensor until it stops, then tighten it *slightly*. (There is no torque specification for the IAT sensor on these models.)

8   Installation is otherwise the reverse of removal.

2.4L OHC engine

Refer to illustration 6.9

9   Locate the IAT sensor on the air intake duct **(see illustration)**.

10   Disconnect the electrical connector from the IAT sensor.

11   To remove the IAT sensor from the air intake duct, simply pull it straight out. If the IAT sensor is difficult to remove, try wiggling it from side-to-side and pulling on it at the same time.

12   Installation is the reverse of removal. To prevent an air leak, make sure that the IAT sensor fits tightly into its mounting hole in the air intake duct. If it's loose, unfiltered air will enter the air intake duct. Sometimes a small leak can be stopped with the application of a small amount of silicone sealant around the mating surfaces of the air intake duct and the IAT sensor. If that doesn't work, you might have to replace the air intake duct.

2.2L OHC engine

Refer to illustration 6.13

13   Locate the IAT sensor in the resonator **(see illustration)**.

14   Disconnect the electrical connector from the IAT sensor.

15   To remove the IAT sensor from the resonator, pull it straight out.

16   While the IAT sensor is removed, inspect the condition of the grommet. If it's cracked, torn or otherwise deteriorated, replace it (or you will soon an air leak).

17   Installation is the reverse of removal.

---

7   Knock Sensor (KS) - replacement

2.2L OHV engine

1   Raise the vehicle and place it securely on jackstands.

2   Locate the KS on the backside of the engine block **(see illustration 3.2)**.

3   Disconnect the electrical connector from the KS.

4   Unscrew and remove the KS.

5   The threads of the new KS should already be coated with thread sealant. If they aren't, wrap the threads with Teflon tape to prevent leaks.

6   Screw in the sensor and tighten it to the torque listed in this Chapter's Specifications.

7   Installation is otherwise the reverse of removal.

2.3L and 2.4L OHC engines

8   Raise the front of the vehicle and place it securely on jackstands.

1995 through 1998 models

9   Locate the Knock Sensor (KS) at the left end of the backside of the engine block.

10   Disconnect the electrical connector from the KS.

11   Unscrew and remove the KS.

12   The threads of the new KS should already be coated with thread sealant. If they aren't, wrap the threads with Teflon tape to prevent leaks.

13   Screw in the sensor and tighten it to the torque listed in this Chapter's Specifications.

14   Installation is otherwise the reverse of removal.

1999 through 2002 models

Refer to illustration 7.15

15   Locate the knock sensor on the backside of the engine block **(see illustration)**.

16   Trace the electrical lead from the KS up to the electrical connector and disconnect the connector.

17   Remove the KS retaining bolt and remove the KS.

18   Installation is the reverse of removal. Be sure to tighten the KS retaining bolt to the torque listed in this Chapter's Specifications.

2.2L OHC engine

Refer to illustration 7.22

19   Disconnect the cable from the negative battery terminal (see Chapter 5). **Caution:** *On models equipped with a Delco-Loc II or Theftlock audio system, make sure that the lockout feature is turned off before disconnecting the battery cable.*

20   Raise the front of the vehicle and place it securely on jackstands.

21   Remove the starter motor (see Chapter 5).

22   Disconnect the Knock Sensor (KS) elec-

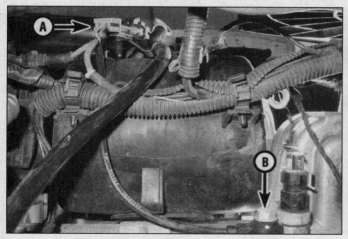

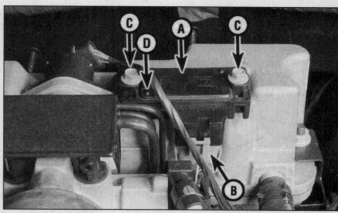

7.22 To remove the Knock Sensor from a 2.2L OHC engine, disconnect the electrical connector (A) and remove the sensor retaining bolt (B)

8.1 To remove the MAP sensor (A) from a 1995 through 1997 2.2L OHV engine, disconnect the electrical connector (B) and remove the sensor retaining bolts (C). Be sure to replace the old sensor seal, which is located underneath the MAP sensor, directly below the atmospheric vent hole (D)

trical connector **(see illustration)**.
23 Remove the KS retaining bolt.
24 Remove the KS.
25 Installation is the reverse of removal. Be sure to tighten the Knock Sensor (KS) retaining bolt to the torque listed in this Chapter's Specifications.

8 Manifold Absolute Pressure (MAP) sensor - replacement

2.2L OHV engine
1995 through 1997 models
Refer to illustration 8.1
1 Disconnect the MAP sensor electrical connector **(see illustration)**.
2 Remove the MAP sensor retaining bolts and remove the MAP sensor.
3 Remove the old sealing grommet from the MAP sensor and discard it. Always use a

new grommet when installing the MAP sensor, regardless of whether you're installing the old sensor or a new one.
4 Installation is the reverse of removal.

1998 and later models
Refer to illustration 8.5
5 On these models, the MAP sensor **(see illustration)** is located between the throttle body and the intake manifold, so you'll have to remove the throttle body to remove the MAP sensor (see Chapter 4).
6 Disconnect the electrical connector from the MAP sensor if you haven't already done so.
7 Remove the MAP sensor from the intake manifold.
8 Installation is the reverse of removal.

2.3L and 2.4L OHC engines
Refer to illustration 8.10
9 Remove the resonator from the throttle

body (see Chapter 4).
10 Disconnect the electrical connector and the vacuum line from the MAP sensor **(see illustration)**.
11 Remove the MAP sensor mounting bracket bolt (this is also one of the four throttle body mounting bolts).
12 Installation is the reverse of removal. Be sure to tighten the MAP sensor/throttle body mounting bolt to the torque listed in the Chapter 4 Specifications.

2.2L OHC engine
Refer to illustrations 8.14 and 8.16
13 Remove the resonator (see Chapter 4).
14 Disconnect the MAP sensor electrical connector **(see illustration)**.
15 To remove the MAP sensor from the intake manifold, turn it clockwise slightly to disengage it from the rear retainer, then lift it straight up. If it's stuck, carefully pry it loose with a screwdriver.

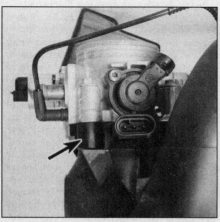

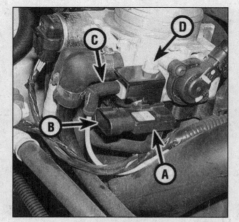

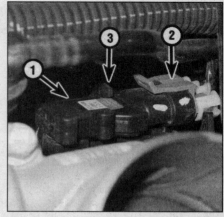

8.5 To remove the MAP sensor from a 1998 and later 2.2L OHV engine, remove the throttle body (see Chapter 4), then disconnect the MAP sensor electrical connector and remove the sensor from the manifold

8.10 To remove the MAP sensor (A) from a 2.4L OHC engine, unplug the electrical connector (B) (already disconnected here), detach the vacuum line (C) and remove the MAP sensor mounting bolt (D)

8.14 To remove the MAP sensor (1) on a 2.2L OHC engine, unplug the electrical connector (2), rotate the sensor just enough to disengage it from the rear retainer (3), then pull the sensor straight up

8.16 Remove and discard the old MAP sensor sealing grommet and install a new grommet before installing the MAP sensor

9.2 Disconnect the electrical connector from the Output Shaft Speed sensor

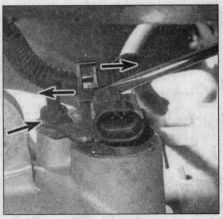

9.3 Open up the clip that secures the electrical harness to the OSS sensor (by prying it in opposite directions), then remove the retaining bolt

16   Remove the old sealing grommet from the MAP sensor (see illustration) and discard it. Always use a new grommet when installing the MAP sensor, regardless of whether you're installing the old sensor or a new one.
17   Installation is the reverse of removal.

9   Output Shaft Speed (OSS) sensor - replacement

Refer to illustrations 9.2 and 9.3
Note: *This sensor is used only on models with an automatic transaxle.*
1   Raise the front of the vehicle and place it securely on jackstands.
2   Disconnect the electrical connector from the OSS sensor (see illustration).
3   Disengage the electrical harness from the bracket that's attached to the OSS sensor (see illustration).
4   Remove the OSS sensor retaining bolt and remove the OSS sensor.
5   Remove the old O-ring from the OSS sensor and discard it. Be sure to use a new O-ring when installing the OSS sensor (even if you're planning to reuse the old OSS sensor).
6   Installation is the reverse of removal.

10   Oxygen sensors - general information and replacement

General information

1   An oxygen sensor is a galvanic battery that produces a very small voltage output in response to the amount of oxygen in the exhaust gases. This voltage signal is the "input" side of the feedback loop between the oxygen sensor and the Powertrain Control Module (PCM). Without it, the PCM would be unable to correct the injector on-time (which determines the air/fuel ratio) to maintain the "perfect" (known as *stoichiometric*)

air/fuel ratio of 14.7:1 that the catalyst needs for optimal operation.
2   All vehicles covered by this manual have On-Board Diagnostics II (OBD-II) engine management systems, which means they have the ability to verify the accuracy of the basic feedback loop between the oxygen sensor and the PCM. They accomplish this by using an oxygen sensor *ahead of* the catalytic converter and another oxygen sensor *behind* the catalytic converter.
3   By comparing the amount of oxygen in the post-catalyst exhaust gas to the oxygen content of the exhaust gas before it enters the catalyst, the PCM can determine the efficiency of the converter.
4   All vehicles covered by this manual have *two* heated oxygen sensors: one *upstream* sensor (ahead of the catalytic converter) and a *downstream* oxygen sensor (after the catalyst).
5   The upstream and downstream oxygen sensors on all models are heated to speed up the warm-up time during which the sensors are unable to produce an accurate voltage signal.
6   The circuit for each oxygen sensor heater is controlled by the PCM, which opens the ground side of the circuit to shut off the heater as soon as the sensor reaches its normal operating temperature.
7   Special care must be taken whenever a sensor is serviced.

   a) *Oxygen sensors have a permanently attached pigtail and an electrical connector that cannot be removed. Damaging or removing the pigtail or electrical connector will render the sensor useless.*
   b) *Keep grease, dirt and other contaminants away from the electrical connector and the louvered end of the sensor.*
   c) *Do not use cleaning solvents of any kind on an oxygen sensor.*
   d) *Oxygen sensors are extremely delicate. Do not drop a sensor or throw it around or handle it roughly.*

   e) *Make sure that the silicone boot on the sensor is installed in the correct position. Otherwise, the boot might melt and it might prevent the sensor from operating correctly.*

Replacement

Note: *Because it is installed in the exhaust manifold or pipe, both of which contract when cool, an oxygen sensor can be very difficult to loosen when the engine is cold. Rather than risk damage to the sensor or its mounting threads, start and run the engine for a minute or two, then shut it off. Be careful not to burn yourself during the following procedure.*

Upstream oxygen sensor

Refer to illustrations 10.9a, 10.9b and 10.9c
8   Disconnect the upstream oxygen sensor electrical connector. **Note:** *On some vehicles the oxygen sensor connector for the upstream sensor is easy to find because the electrical lead for the sensor is fairly short, so the connector is near the sensor. On others, the connector will be more difficult to locate because the lead is longer and the connector is farther from the sensor. The easiest way to locate the oxygen sensor connector is to trace the electrical lead from the sensor to the connector.*
9   Locate the upstream oxygen sensor (see illustrations) on the exhaust manifold. Unscrew the upstream oxygen sensor with an oxygen sensor socket (see illustration). (On most vehicles, it's virtually impossible to put a wrench on the upstream oxygen sensor because there simply isn't enough space to move the wrench. An oxygen sensor socket, which is available at most automotive parts stores, is much easier to use in a tight space than a wrench.) If the sensor is difficult to loosen, spray some penetrant onto the sensor threads and allow it to soak in for awhile.
10   If you're going to install the old sensor, apply anti-seize compound to the threads of the sensor to facilitate future removal.

10.9a On 2.2L OHV engines, the upstream oxygen sensor is located on the left (driver's) side of the exhaust manifold, right above the manifold-to-exhaust pipe flange

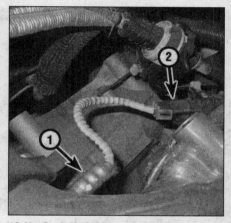

10.9b On 2.2L OHC engines, the upstream oxygen sensor (1) is located on the left (driver's) side of the exhaust manifold, right above the manifold-to-exhaust pipe flange. Before unscrewing the sensor from the manifold, disconnect the electrical connector (2)

10.9c Because of the tight space, it's difficult to put a wrench on an upstream oxygen sensor on most models. Instead, use an oxygen sensor socket to unscrew the sensor from the exhaust manifold

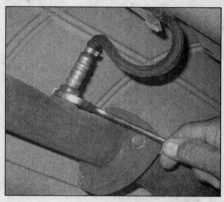

10.15a The downstream oxygen sensor is located behind the catalytic converter on all models

10.15b To remove the downstream oxygen sensor, simply unscrew it with a wrench. Because there's (usually) plenty of room to work down here, you can use a big wrench instead of an oxygen sensor socket to remove the sensor

11 If you're going to install a new oxygen sensor, it's not necessary to apply anti-seize compound to the threads. The threads on new sensors already have anti-seize compound on them.

12 Installation is otherwise the reverse of removal.

Downstream oxygen sensor

Refer to illustrations 10.15a and 10.15b

13 Raise the vehicle and place it securely on jackstands.

14 Disconnect the oxygen sensor electrical connector. **Note:** *On some vehicles the oxygen sensor connector for the downstream sensor is easy to find because the electrical lead for the sensor is fairly short, so the connector is near the sensor. On others, the connector will be more difficult to locate because the lead is longer and the connector is farther from the sensor. The easiest way to locate the oxygen sensor connector is to trace the electrical lead from the sensor to the connector.*

15 Find the downstream oxygen sensor **(see illustration)**, which is always located right behind the catalytic converter. Unlike upstream oxygen sensors, downstream sensors can be removed with a wrench **(see illustration)** because there's plenty of room to work. If the sensor is difficult to loosen, spray some penetrant onto the sensor threads and allow it to soak in for awhile. **Note:** *On most models it's not necessary to use an oxygen sensor socket on the downstream sensor because there is usually enough room to put a wrench on the sensor.*

16 If you're going to install the old sensor, apply anti-seize compound to the threads of the sensor to facilitate future removal. If you're going to install a new oxygen sensor, it's not necessary to apply anti-seize compound to the threads. The threads on new sensors already have anti-seize compound on them.

17 Installation is otherwise the reverse of removal.

11 Throttle Position (TP) sensor - replacement

2.2L OHV engine

1995 through 1997 models

Refer to illustration 11.2

1 Remove the air intake duct or resonator if it's in the way (see Chapter 4).

2 Disconnect the electrical connector from the TP sensor **(see illustration)**.

3 Remove the TP sensor mounting screws and remove the TP sensor.

4 To install the TP sensor, make sure that the throttle plate is at its idle position (nearly closed), align the slot in the backside of the TP sensor with the blade on the end of the throttle plate shaft, push the TP sensor onto the throttle body, then align the mounting holes on the TP sensor with the mounting holes in the throttle body by rotating the TP sensor counterclockwise.

11.2 To detach the TP sensor from the throttle body on 1995 through 1997 2.2L OHV engines, disconnect the electrical connector and remove the two mounting screws

11.9 To detach the TP sensor from the throttle body on 1998 through 2002 2.2L OHV engines, disconnect the electrical connector, then remove the two mounting screws

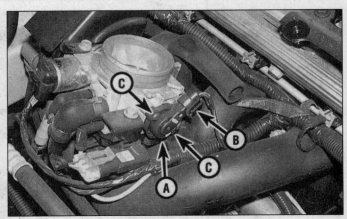

11.14 On 2.3L and 2.4L OHC engines, the TP sensor (A) is located on the left side of the throttle body. To detach the sensor, disconnect the electrical connector (B) and remove the mounting screws (C)

11.21 To remove the TP sensor from the throttle body on a 2.2L OHC engine, disconnect the electrical connector and remove the sensor mounting screws

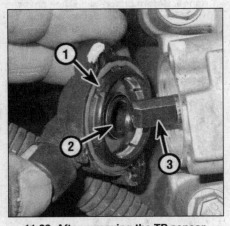

11.22 After removing the TP sensor, remove and discard the old sensor O-ring (1); when installing the TP sensor, make sure that the flat sides of the hub (2) are aligned with the flat sides of the throttle shaft (3)

TP sensor with the blade on the end of the throttle plate shaft, push the TP sensor onto the throttle body, then align the mounting holes on the TP sensor with the mounting holes in the throttle body by rotating the TP sensor counterclockwise.

18   Before installing the TP sensor mounting screws coat the threads of the screws with a non-hardening thread-locking compound. Installation is otherwise the reverse of removal.

2.2L OHC engine

Refer to illustrations 11.21 and 11.22

19   Remove the air intake duct or resonator if it's in the way (see Chapter 4).

20   Remove the resonator (see Chapter 4).

21   Disconnect the TP sensor electrical connector **(see illustration)**.

22   Remove the TP sensor mounting screws **(see illustration 11.21)** and remove the TP sensor **(see illustration)**.

23   Remove the old TP sensor O-ring **(see illustration 11.22)** and discard it. Install a new O-ring before you install the TP sensor, whether you're installing the old sensor or a new unit.

24   When installing the TP sensor make sure that the flats on the throttle plate shaft are aligned with the flats inside the TP sensor **(see illustration 11.22)**.

25   Before installing the TP sensor mounting screws coat the threads of the screws with a non-hardening thread-locking compound.

26   Installation is otherwise the reverse of removal.

12   Transmission Range (TR) switch - replacement

Removal

Refer to illustrations 12.3, 12.4, 12.5 and 12.6

Note 1: *You'll need a special alignment tool (J41545, or a suitable equivalent) to adjust the TR switch.*

Note 2: *1995 and 1996 models are equipped*

5   Before installing the TP sensor mounting screws coat the threads of the screws with a non-hardening thread-locking compound. Installation is otherwise the reverse of removal.

1998 through 2002 models

Refer to illustration 11.9

6   Remove the air intake duct or resonator if it's in the way (see Chapter 4).

7   Remove the resonator (see Chapter 4).

8   Disconnect the electrical connector from the TP sensor.

9   Remove the TP sensor mounting screws **(see illustration)** and remove the TP sensor. Also remove and discard the old TP sensor O-ring.

10   To install the TP sensor, make sure that the throttle plate is at its idle position (nearly closed), align the slot in the backside of the TP sensor with the blade on the end of the throttle plate shaft, push the TP sensor onto the throttle body, then align the mounting holes on the TP sensor with the mounting holes in the throttle body by rotating the TP sensor counterclockwise.

11   Before installing the TP sensor mounting screws coat the threads of the screws with a non-hardening thread-locking compound. Installation is otherwise the reverse of removal.

2.3L and 2.4L OHC engines

Refer to illustration 11.14

12   Remove the air intake duct or resonator if it's in the way (see Chapter 4).

13   Remove the resonator (see Chapter 4).

14   Disconnect the electrical connector from the TP sensor **(see illustration)**.

15   Remove the TP sensor mounting screws and remove the TP sensor.

16   If you're removing or replacing the TP sensor on any 2.4L OHC engine, be sure to remove and discard the old TP sensor O-ring (the TP sensor on 1995 2.3L OHC models doesn't use an O-ring).

17   To install the TP sensor, make sure that the throttle plate is at its idle position (nearly closed), align the slot in the backside of the

12.3 Use a screwdriver or a trim panel removal tool (shown) to pop the end of the shift control cable loose from the TR switch lever

12.4 Disconnect the electrical connectors from the TR switch

12.5 Using large water pump pliers to immobilize the lever, loosen this nut and detach the lever from the TR switch

with a PNP switch that can be adjusted with a gauge pin or drill bit (see Chapter 7B). On 1997 and later models, the switch is adjusted with a special tool (J-41545, or a suitable equivalent) like the one shown here.

1   Disconnect the cable from the negative battery terminal. **Caution:** *On models equipped with a Delco-Loc II or Theftlock audio system, make sure that the lockout feature is turned off before disconnecting the battery cable.*

2   Set the parking brake then place the shift lever in the NEUTRAL position.

3   Locate the TR switch on top of the transaxle. Disconnect the shift control cable from the TR switch lever **(see illustration)**.

4   Disconnect the electrical connectors from the TR switch **(see illustration)**.

5   Remove the TR switch lever nut **(see illustration)** and remove the lever.

6   Remove the TR switch mounting bolts **(see illustration)** and remove the switch.

Installation

Refer to illustrations 12.8a and 12.8b

Note: *The following procedure applies to a new or old TR switch that's being installed on the transaxle, as well as a TR switch that's already installed, but out of adjustment.*

7   Make sure that the shift lever is still in NEUTRAL.

8   To install the TR switch, align the flats on the transaxle shift shaft with the flats on the TR switch **(see illustration)**, then loosely install the TR switch mounting bolts. Install the special TR switch alignment tool **(see illustration)** and rotate the TR switch until the tool falls into place. When the TR switch is correctly aligned, tighten the switch mounting bolts securely.

9   Installation is otherwise the reverse of removal. Be sure to tighten the TR switch lever nut securely (and hold it with a pair of water pump pliers while doing so).

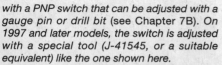

12.6 To detach the TR switch from the transaxle, remove these two mounting bolts

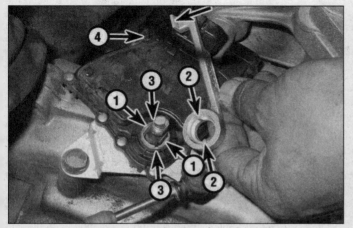

12.8a To install the TR switch, align the flats (1) on the transaxle shift shaft with the flats on the switch, slide the switch onto the shaft and loosely install the switch mounting bolts; to install the alignment tool, align the lugs (2) on the tool with the notches (3) in the switch and align the lug on the other end of the tool with the raised ridge (4) on the switch . . .

12.8b . . . then install the tool and rotate the switch slightly until the alignment tool drops into place (and looks like this), then tighten the TR switch mounting bolts to the torque listed in this Chapter's Specifications

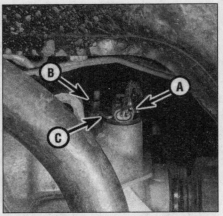

13.2 To remove the VSS, disconnect the electrical connector (A), remove the retainer mounting bolt (B) and remove the retainer (C), then pull the VSS straight out

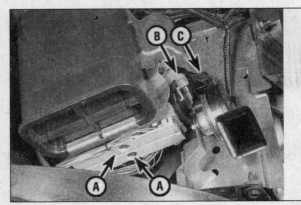

14.3 On 1995 through 2001 models, the PCM is located inside the right front fender (fender removed for clarity). Disconnect the horn electrical connector (B) and remove the horn mounting bracket bolt (C). Then remove the two electrical connector retaining screws (A) and carefully unplug both connectors

14.7a To release the PCM from its mounting bracket, remove this upper mounting bolt (viewed from above, headlight removed for clarity) . . .

14.7b . . . and this lower mounting bolt (1995 through 2001 models)

14.8 Carefully remove the PCM from underneath the vehicle (1995 through 2001 models)

13   Vehicle Speed Sensor (VSS) - replacement

Refer to illustration 13.2

1   Raise the vehicle and place it securely on jackstands.
2   Locate the VSS on top of the transaxle, near the right inner CV joint **(see illustration)**.
3   Disconnect the electrical connector from the VSS.
4   Remove the VSS retainer mounting bolt or stud.
5   Remove the VSS retainer.
6   Pull out the VSS.
7   Remove and discard the old VSS O-ring.
8   Coat the new O-ring with a little clean engine oil, apply a light coat of grease to the VSS driven gear, then insert the VSS into its mounting hole in the transaxle. Push the VSS down until it's fully seated.
9   Installation is otherwise the reverse of removal.

14   Powertrain Control Module (PCM) - removal and installation

Caution: *To avoid electrostatic discharge damage to the PCM, handle the PCM only by its case. Do not touch the electrical terminals during removal and installation. If available, ground yourself to the vehicle with an anti-static ground strap, available at computer supply stores.*
Note 1: *The procedures in this section apply only to removing and installing the PCM that is already installed in your vehicle. If you need a new PCM, it must be programmed with new software and calibrations. This procedure requires the use of GM's TECH-2 scan tool and GM's latest PCM-programming software, so you WILL NOT BE ABLE TO REPLACE THE PCM AT HOME.*
Note 2: *The PCM is a highly reliable component and rarely requires replacement. Because the PCM is the most expensive part of the engine management system, you should be absolutely certain that it has failed before replacing it. If in doubt, have the system tested by an experienced driveability technician at a dealer service department or other qualified repair shop.*

1995 through 2001 models

Refer to illustrations 14.3, 14.7a, 14.7b and 14.8

1   Disconnect the cable from the negative terminal of the battery (see Chapter 5). **Caution:** *On models equipped with a Delco-Loc II or Theftlock audio system, make sure that the lockout feature is turned off before disconnecting the battery cable.*
2   Loosen the lug nuts for the right front wheel, raise the front of the vehicle and place it securely on jackstands, then remove the right front wheel.
3   The PCM **(see illustration)** is located below the right front corner of the engine compartment, inside the right front fender.
4   Remove the right front inner fender splash shield (see Chapter 11).
5   Disconnect the electrical connector from the horn and remove the horn assembly (see Chapter 12).
6   Disconnect the electrical connectors from the PCM. **Note:** *Each connector should be color-coded so there should be no need to label the connectors. However, if the connectors on the PCM you're removing are not color-coded, be sure to label them to avoid damage to the connectors and/or the PCM terminals when reconnecting everything.*
7   Remove the PCM mounting bracket bolts **(see illustrations)**.
8   Carefully remove the PCM **(see illustration)**.
9   If the PCM is encased in a protective cover, remove the cover from the PCM.
10   Installation is the reverse of removal.

14.12 To release the PCM electrical connectors on 2002 and later models, depress the locking tab on top of each connector with a screwdriver and flip the lever off the connector, then pull the connector straight up

14.13 To remove the PCM from its mounting bracket, release the two retaining clips on the front edge of the PCM mounting bracket, then lift the front edge of the PCM and lift it out

15.2a To remove the IAC valve (A) on 1995 through 1997 2.2L OHV engines, disconnect the electrical connector (B) and remove the two mounting bolts (C)

15.2b To remove the IAC valve On 1998 through 2002 2.2L OHV engines, disconnect the electrical connector and remove the two mounting bolts (throttle body removed for clarity)

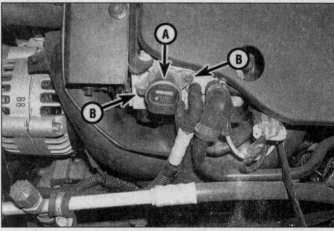

15.2c To remove the IAC valve (A) on 2.3L and 2.4L OHC engines, disconnect the electrical connector (already unplugged in this photo) and remove the two mounting screws (B)

2002 and later models

Refer to illustrations 14.12 and 14.13

11   Disconnect the cable from the negative battery terminal (see Chapter 5). **Caution:** *On models equipped with a Delco-Loc II or Theftlock audio system, make sure that the lockout feature is turned off before disconnecting the battery cable.*

12   Locate the PCM in the right rear corner of the engine compartment. Disconnect the electrical connectors from the PCM **(see illustration)**.

13   Release the two retaining clips on the front edge of the PCM mounting bracket **(see illustration)**.

14   To remove the PCM from its mounting bracket, lift the front edge of the PCM and slide it toward the front of the vehicle.

15   Installation is the reverse of removal.

15   Idle Air Control (IAC) valve - replacement

Refer to illustrations 15.2a, 15.2b, 15.2c, 15.2d, 15.4, 15.5, 15.9a and 15.9b

1   On 1995 through 1997 models 2.2L OHV engines locate the IAC valve on the backside of the upper intake manifold. On 1998 through 2002 models 2.2L OHV engines, remove the resonator (see Chapter 4), then locate the IAC valve on the backside of the throttle body. On 2.3L and 2.4L OHC engines, locate the IAC valve on top of the throttle body. On 2.2L OHC engines the IAC valve is located on the backside of the throttle body.

2   Disconnect the electrical connector from the Idle Air Control (IAC) valve **(see illustrations)**.

15.2d On 2.2L OHC engines, the IAC valve is located on the backside of the throttle body. To detach the IAC valve from the throttle body, disconnect the electrical connector, then remove the two IAC valve mounting screws

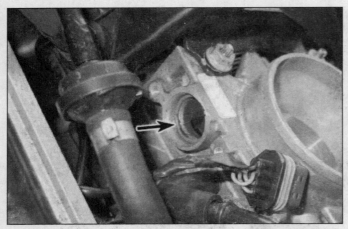

15.4 Be sure to remove and discard the old IAC valve O-ring from the IAC valve mounting hole in the throttle body. Always install a new O-ring before installing the IAC valve (2.2L OHC engine shown, others similar)

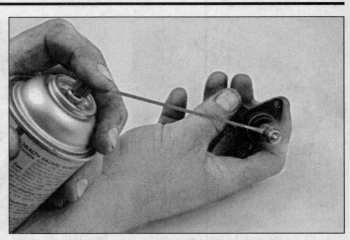

15.5 To remove any deposits that might prevent a good seal between the IAC valve's pintle valve and its seat, clean the pintle valve, pintle valve seat and the O-ring sealing surface with carburetor cleaner

15.9a Measure the distance (A) between the mounting flange and the tip of the pintle valve. If it exceeds 1-1/8 inches (28 mm) . . .

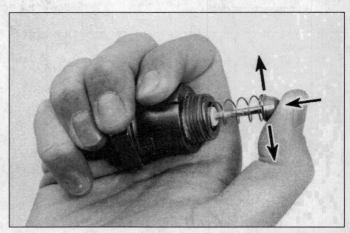

15.9b . . . grasp it as shown and, using a side-to-side motion with your thumb, firmly press it into the valve until the distance is no more than 0.79 inch (20 mm)

3   Unscrew the two IAC valve mounting screws and remove the valve from the upper intake manifold.

4   Remove the old IAC valve O-ring **(see illustration)** and discard it.

5   Using carburetor cleaner (NOT methyl ethyl ketone) and a parts cleaning brush, remove all carbon deposits from the O-ring sealing surface, the pintle valve **(see illustration)**, the pintle valve seat and the air passage.

6   Inspect the pintle valve and the seat. Shiny spots are okay, and indicate normal wear (they don't necessarily indicate misalignment or a bent pintle shaft). Inspect the air passage. If it still has heavy deposits on it even after it's been cleaned, remove the upper intake manifold (see Chapter 2A) and clean it more thoroughly.

7   Inspect the condition of the IAC valve electrical terminals. Make sure that the pins are straight and make good contact with the connector.

8   Before installing the IAC valve, the position of the pintle must be checked. If the pintle is extended too far, damage to the assembly may occur.

9   If you're installing the old IAC valve, measure the distance from the surface of the mounting flange to the tip of the pintle **(see illustration)**. If the distance is greater than 1-1/8 inch, reduce the distance by applying firm pressure onto the pintle to retract it. Try some side-to-side motion in the event the pintle binds **(see illustration)**. (It's a good idea to measure this distance on a new IAC valve as well, although most valves are already correctly adjusted at the factory.)

10   Position the new O-ring on the IAC valve. Lubricate the O-ring with a light film of engine oil. Install the IAC valve and tighten the valve or the mounting screws securely.

11   Reconnect the electrical connector to the IAC valve. **Note:** *No adjustment is made to the IAC assembly after reinstallation. The IAC resetting is controlled by the PCM when the engine is started.*

16   Catalytic converter - general information, check and replacement

Note: *Because of a Federally-mandated extended warranty which covers emission-related components such as the catalytic converter, check with a dealer service department before replacing the converter at your own expense.*

General description

1   A catalytic converter (or catalyst) is an emission control device in the exhaust system that reduces certain pollutants in the exhaust gas stream. There are two types of converters. An oxidation catalyst reduces hydrocarbons (HC) and carbon monoxide (CO). A reduction catalyst reduces oxides of nitrogen (NOx). A catalyst that can reduce *all three pollutants* is known as a "Three-Way Catalyst" (TWC). All models covered by this manual are equipped with TWCs.

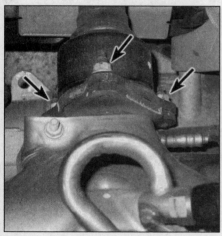

16.5 To disconnect the upper end of the catalytic converter/exhaust pipe assembly from the exhaust manifold flange, remove these three nuts (2.2L OHC engine shown, other engines similar)

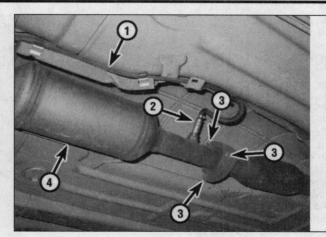

16.7 To disconnect the rear end of the catalytic converter/exhaust pipe assembly from the resonator pipe flange, trace the downstream oxygen sensor electrical lead (1) to its connector and unplug it, remove the oxygen sensor (2) and remove the three flange bolts (3) (2.2L OHC model shown, other models similar)

Check

2   The test equipment for a catalytic converter (a "loaded-mode" dynamometer and a 5-gas analyzer) is expensive. If you suspect that the converter on your vehicle is malfunctioning, take it to a dealer or authorized emission inspection facility for diagnosis and repair.

3   Whenever you raise the vehicle to service underbody components, inspect the converter for leaks, corrosion, dents and other damage. Carefully inspect the welds and/or flange bolts and nuts that attach the front and rear ends of the converter to the exhaust system. If you note any damage, replace the converter.

4   Although catalytic converters don't break too often, they can become clogged or even plugged up. The easiest way to check for a restricted converter is to use a vacuum gauge to diagnose the effect of a blocked exhaust on intake vacuum.

a)   *Connect a vacuum gauge to an intake manifold vacuum source (see Chapter 2).*

b)   *Warm the engine to operating temperature, place the transaxle in Park (automatic models) or Neutral (manual models) and apply the parking brake.*

c)   *Note the vacuum reading at idle and jot it down.*

d)   *Quickly open the throttle to near its wide-open position and then quickly get off the throttle and allow it to close. Note the vacuum reading and jot it down.*

e)   *Do this test three more times, recording your measurement after each test.*

f)   *If your fourth reading is more than one in-Hg lower than the reading that you noted at idle, the exhaust system might be restricted (the catalytic converter could be plugged, OR an exhaust pipe or muffler could be restricted).*

Replacement

Refer to illustrations 16.5 and 16.7
Warning: *Make sure that the exhaust system is completely cooled down before proceeding. If the vehicle has just been driven, the catalytic converter can be hot enough to cause serious burns.*

5   Open the hood and remove the three upper exhaust pipe-to-exhaust manifold flange nuts **(see illustration)**.

6   Raise the vehicle and place it securely on jackstands.

7   Remove the three bolts that attach the exhaust pipe behind the catalytic converter to the resonator pipe flange **(see illustration)**. If they're difficult to loosen, spray the threads with some penetrant, wait awhile and try again. **Note:** *The photos accompanying this procedure are of a 2.2L OHC model with a catalyst, two short pipes welded to either end and a three-hole mounting flange at the end of each pipe. Most models use this same setup. If your vehicle doesn't use a flange behind the catalyst, but is welded to the rear exhaust pipe instead, you will have to either cut it off yourself with hacksaw or have it cut off at an automotive repair shop.*

8   Remove the catalytic converter.

9   Remove and discard the old flange gaskets.

10   Installation is the reverse of removal. Be sure to use new gaskets at both mounting flanges. Use new nuts at the front flange and new bolts at the rear flange. Coat the threads of the nuts and bolts with anti-seize compound to facilitate future removal. Tighten the fasteners securely.

---

17   Evaporative emissions control (EVAP) system - general information and component replacement

---

General description

1   The **Evaporative Emissions Control (EVAP) system** prevents fuel system vapors (which contain unburned hydrocarbons) from escaping into the atmosphere. On warm days, vapors trapped inside the fuel tank expand until the pressure reaches a certain threshold, at which point the fuel vapors are routed from the fuel tank through the fuel vapor vent valve and the fuel vapor control valve to the EVAP canister, where they're stored temporarily, until they can be consumed by the engine during normal operation. When the conditions are right (engine warmed up, vehicle up to speed, moderate or heavy load on the engine, etc.) the Powertrain Control Module (PCM) opens the canister purge solenoid, which allows the fuel vapors to be drawn from the canister into the intake manifold, where they mix with the air/fuel mixture before being consumed in the combustion chambers. This system is complex and virtually impossible to troubleshoot without the right tools and training. However, the following description should give you a good idea of how the system works and where the components are located:

2   The **EVAP canister**, which contains activated charcoal, is the repository for storing the fuel vapors. You'll have to raise the vehicle to inspect or replace the canister (or the EVAP canister vent solenoid valve) but the canister is designed to be maintenance-free and should last the life of the vehicle. On 1995 through 1998 models, the EVAP canister is located at the right front corner of the vehicle, inside the void ahead of the right front wheel housing and behind the front bumper cover. On 1999 and later models, the EVAP canister is located underneath the vehicle, right behind the fuel tank.

3   The **fuel tank pressure sensor**, which is located on top of the mounting flange for the in-tank fuel pump/fuel level sending unit module, monitors the pressure inside the tank, and transmits its measurement to the PCM during an OBD-II leak test. You'll have to raise the vehicle and remove the fuel tank in order to access the fuel tank pressure sensor.

4   The **EVAP canister vent solenoid valve** is normally open. But it seals off the EVAP system for inspection and maintenance (I/M 240) testing and for OBD-II leak and pressure tests. On 1995 2.2LOHV engines,

there is no vent solenoid; these models are equipped with a fresh air vent that allows fresh air into the EVAP canister all the time. In 1996 the fresh air vent was replaced by a canister vent solenoid that admits outside air into the canister during purge mode, but shuts off the outside air to create a vacuum inside the fuel tank so that the PCM can run a diagnostic check on the EVAP system's integrity. On 1996 through 1998 models, the vent solenoid is located right above and behind the EVAP canister, which is located at the right front corner of the vehicle, inside the void ahead of the right front wheel housing and behind the front bumper cover. On 1999 and later models, the vent solenoid is located to the right of the EVAP canister, which is located underneath the vehicle, right behind the fuel tank.

5   The **EVAP canister purge solenoid valve**, which is under the control of the Powertrain Control Module (PCM), regulates the flow of vapors being purged from the EVAP canister into the intake manifold. The canister purge solenoid is normally closed. It opens only when directed to do so by the PCM, which uses the availability of intake manifold vacuum and data from various information sensor inputs to determine when and how long to open the valve. The interval of time during which the purge valve is opened by the PCM is known as its "duty cycle." On 1995 2.2L OHV engines, the canister purge solenoid valve is located on the front side of the upper intake manifold, right below the Manifold Absolute Pressure (MAP) sensor. On 1996, 1997 and 1999 through 2002 2.2L OHV engines, the canister purge solenoid is located on the backside of the engine block. The purge solenoid valve is near the ignition coil pack on 1996 and 1997 engines, and is above the oil filter on 1999 through 2002 models. On 1998 2.2L OHV engines, the purge solenoid is located on the upper rear edge of the valve cover. On 2.3L OHC engines the purge solenoid is located at the throttle body, between the Intake Air Temperature (IAT) sensor and the Idle Air Control (IAC) valve. On all 2.4L OHC engines, the purge solenoid valve is located at the right front corner of the engine, above the air conditioning compressor and below the alternator. On all 2.2L OHC engines, the purge valve is located at the left end of the engine, right behind the power steering reservoir.

General system checks

6   The most common symptom of a faulty EVAP system is a strong fuel odor (particularly during hot weather). If you smell fuel while driving or (more likely) right after you park the vehicle and turn off the engine, check the fuel filler cap first. Make sure that it's screwed onto the fuel filler neck all the way. If the odor persists, inspect all EVAP hose connections, both in the engine compartment and under the vehicle. You'll have to raise the vehicle and place it securely on jackstands to inspect most of the EVAP system, since it's located under the vehicle. Be

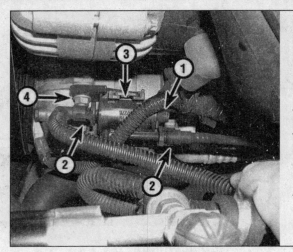

17.17 Typical EVAP canister purge solenoid valve assembly (1996 through 2002 2.4L OHC engines)

1 Disconnect the electrical connector
2 Disconnect the inlet and outlet purge lines
3 Release the locking tabs with a small screwdriver to disengage the canister purge valve from its mounting bracket
4 The mounting bracket is attached to the alternator by a single nut

sure to inspect each hose attached to the canister for damage and leakage along its entire length. Repair or replace as necessary. Inspect the canister for damage and look for fuel leaking from the bottom. If fuel is leaking or the canister is otherwise damaged, replace it.

7   Poor idle, stalling, and poor driveability can be caused by a defective fuel vapor vent valve or canister purge solenoid, a damaged canister, cracked hoses, or hoses connected to the wrong tubes. Fuel loss or fuel odor can be caused by fuel leaking from fuel lines or hoses, a cracked or damaged canister, or a defective vapor valve.

8   To check for excessive fuel vapor pressure in the fuel tank, remove the gas cap and listen for the sound of pressure release. If the fuel tank emits a "whooshing" sound when you open the filler cap, fuel tank vapor pressure is excessive. Inspect the canister vapor hoses and the canister inlet port for blockage or collapsed hoses. Also inspect the vapor vent valve. A complete test can only be done with a proprietary OBD-II scan tool (see Section 2), which will run a series of checks to detect excessive pressure. You'll have to take the vehicle to a dealer service department to have the EVAP system professionally diagnosed.

Component replacement

EVAP canister purge solenoid valve

2.2L OHV engine

9   Disconnect the cable from the negative battery cable (see Chapter 5). **Caution:** *On models equipped with a Delco-Loc II or Theftlock audio system, make sure that the lockout feature is turned off before disconnecting the battery cable.*
10   On 1996, 1997 and 1999 through 2002 models, raise the vehicle and place it securely on jackstands.
11   Locate the EVAP canister purge solenoid valve (see Step 5).
12   Disconnect the canister purge solenoid valve's electrical connector.
13   Disconnect the inlet and outlet purge line fittings from the canister purge solenoid

valve. Cap the lines to prevent dirt, dust and moisture from entering the EVAP system while the lines are open.
14   Remove the canister purge solenoid valve. On some of these models, the purge solenoid valve is attached to a small bracket, which is bolted to the engine. On others, the purge solenoid valve is clipped to a bracket and can be detached from the bracket separately. On models that require you to remove the canister purge solenoid valve and its mounting bracket as a single assembly, separate the canister purge solenoid from the mounting bracket.
15   Installation is the reverse of removal.

2.3L and 2.4L OHC engines
Refer to illustration 17.17
16   Disconnect the cable from the negative battery terminal. **Caution:** *On models equipped with a Delco-Loc II or Theftlock audio system, make sure that the lockout feature is turned off before disconnecting the battery cable.*
17   Locate the EVAP canister purge solenoid valve. On 1995 2.3L OHC engines, it's located at the throttle body, between the Intake Air Temperature (IAT) sensor and the Idle Air Control (IAC) valve. On all 2.4L OHC engines, the purge solenoid valve is located at the right front corner of the engine, above the air conditioning compressor and below the alternator **(see illustration)**.
18   Disconnect the electrical connector from the EVAP canister purge solenoid valve.
19   Clearly label the inlet and outlet purge lines, then disconnect the inlet and outlet purge line fittings from the canister purge solenoid valve. If they're quick-connect fittings and you're unfamiliar with these types of fittings, refer to Section 4 in Chapter 4 for help with disconnecting them. Cap the lines to prevent dirt, dust and moisture from entering the EVAP system while the lines are open.
20   Disengage the EVAP canister purge solenoid valve from its mounting bracket.
21   It's not necessary to remove the mounting bracket for the canister purge solenoid valve unless it's damaged or you need to remove it to access some other component

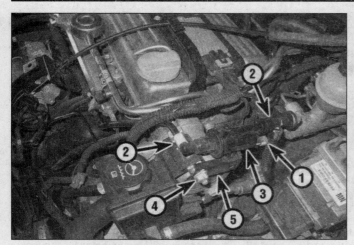

17.24 EVAP canister purge solenoid valve assembly (2.2L OHC engines)

1 *Electrical connector*
2 *Inlet and outlet purge lines (see Section 4, Chapter 4)*
3 *EVAP canister purge solenoid valve*
4 *Mounting nut*
5 *Mounting bracket*

17.38 A typical EVAP canister vent solenoid valve assembly on 1999 and later models

1 *EVAP canister vent solenoid valve*
2 *Loosen this hose clamp and disconnect the vent hose from the vent solenoid valve*
3 *Pry here until the solenoid valve pops loose from its mounting bracket on the crossmember*
4 *Trace this electrical harness up to the vent solenoid valve electrical connector, then unplug the connector*

that you want to remove or replace. If you need to remove the mounting bracket, it's secured by a single nut.

22 Installation is the reverse of removal

2.2L OHC engine

Refer to illustration 17.24

23 Disconnect the cable from the negative battery terminal. **Caution:** *On models equipped with a Delco-Loc II or Theftlock audio system, make sure that the lockout feature is turned off before disconnecting the battery cable.*

24 Locate the EVAP canister purge solenoid valve at the left end of the engine, right behind the power steering fluid reservoir **(see illustration)**.

25 Disconnect the electrical connector from the EVAP canister purge solenoid valve.

26 Clearly label the inlet and outlet purge lines, then disconnect the inlet and outlet purge line fittings from the canister purge solenoid valve. If they're quick-connect fittings and you're unfamiliar with these types of fittings, refer to Section 4 in Chapter 4 for help with disconnecting them. Cap the lines to prevent dirt, dust and moisture from entering the EVAP system while the lines are open.

27 Remove the EVAP canister purge solenoid valve mounting bracket nut and remove the bracket and the purge solenoid valve as a single assembly.

28 Separate the EVAP canister purge solenoid valve from the mounting bracket.

29 Installation is the reverse of removal.

EVAP canister vent solenoid valve

1996 through 1998 models

30 Loosen the right front wheel lug nuts, raise the front of the vehicle, place it securely on jackstands and remove the right front wheel.

31 Remove the liner from the right front wheelhousing (see Chapter 11).

32 Locate the EVAP canister vent solenoid valve, which is located right above and behind the EVAP canister.

33 Disconnect the electrical connector from the EVAP canister vent solenoid valve.

34 Loosen the hose clamp and disconnect the vent hose from the vent solenoid valve.

35 Remove the EVAP canister vent solenoid from its mounting bracket.

36 Installation is the reverse of removal.

1999 and later models

Refer to illustration 17.38

37 Raise the rear of the vehicle and place it securely on jackstands.

38 Locate the canister vent solenoid valve, which is located to the right of the EVAP canister **(see illustration)**.

39 Disconnect the electrical connector from the EVAP canister vent solenoid valve.

40 Loosen the hose clamp and disconnect the vent hose from the vent solenoid valve.

41 Insert a prybar or a large screwdriver between the EVAP canister vent solenoid valve and the crossmember and pry the vent solenoid valve forward until it disengages from its mounting bracket on the crossmember.

42 Pull down the EVAP canister vent solenoid down, remove the locking clip from the electrical connector and disconnect the electrical connector.

43 Installation is the reverse of removal.

EVAP canister

44 Disconnect the cable from the negative battery terminal. **Caution:** *On models equipped with a Delco-Loc II or Theftlock audio system, make sure that the lockout feature is turned off before disconnecting the battery cable.*

1995 through 1998 models

Refer to illustration 17.46

45 Loosen the right front wheel lug nuts. Raise the front end of the vehicle and place it securely on jackstands. Remove the right front wheel. Remove the splash shield (see Chapter 11).

46 Locate the canister **(see illustration)**.

47 Disconnect the hoses from the EVAP canister.

48 Remove the canister mounting bolt and remove the canister and its mounting bracket.

17.46 A typical EVAP canister assembly on 1995 through 1998 models

1 *EVAP canister*
2 *Line to EVAP canister purge solenoid valve*
3 *Line to EVAP canister vent solenoid valve*
4 *Hose to fuel tank*
5 *EVAP canister mounting bracket bolt*

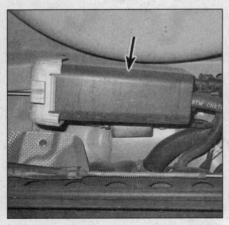

17.52 On 1999 and later models the EVAP canister is located behind the fuel tank

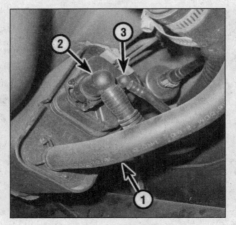

17.53 Disconnect these three hoses from the EVAP canister on 1999 and later models

1   *Vent hose to EVAP canister vent solenoid valve*
2   *EVAP vapor line*
3   *EVAP purge line*

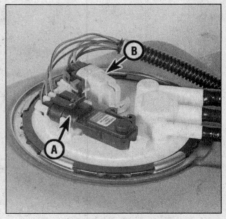

17.58 After lowering the fuel tank, disconnect the connector for the fuel tank pressure sensor (A), then carefully disengage the sensor from its retaining clips. (B) is the connector for the fuel pump

49   Separate the canister from its mounting bracket.
50   Installation is the reverse of removal.

1999 and later models

Refer to illustrations 17.52 and 17.53
51   Raise the rear of the vehicle and place it securely on jackstands.
52   Locate the EVAP canister behind the fuel tank **(see illustration)**.
53   Disconnect the hoses from the EVAP canister **(see illustration)**.
54   Remove the EVAP canister mounting bracket retaining bolt and remove the EVAP canister and mounting bracket as a single assembly. Then separate the EVAP canister from the mounting bracket.
55   Installation is the reverse of removal.

Fuel tank pressure sensor

Refer to illustration 17.58
56   Disconnect the cable from the negative battery terminal. **Caution:** *On models equipped with a Delco-Loc II or Theftlock audio system, make sure that the lockout feature is turned off before disconnecting the battery cable.*
57   Raise the vehicle and place it securely on jackstands. Lower the fuel tank far enough to access the fuel pump (see Chapter 4).
58   Disconnect the electrical connector from the fuel tank pressure sensor **(see illustration)**.
59   Remove the fuel tank pressure sensor from the fuel pump mounting flange.
60   Installation is the reverse of removal.

---

18   Exhaust Gas Recirculation (EGR) system - general information and component replacement

General description

1   Oxides of nitrogen, nitrogen oxide, or simply NOx, is a compound that is formed in the combustion chambers when the oxygen and nitrogen in the incoming air mix together.

NOx is a natural byproduct of high combustion chamber temperatures (2500 degrees Fahrenheit and higher). When NOx is emitted from the tailpipe, it mixes with reactive organic compounds (ROCs), hydrocarbons (HC) and sunlight to form ozone and photochemical smog.
2   The EGR system reduces NOx by recirculating exhaust gases from the exhaust manifold, through the EGR valve and intake manifold, then back to the combustion chambers, where it mixes with the incoming air/fuel mixture before being consumed. These recirculated exhaust gases "dilute" the incoming air/fuel mixture, which cools the combustion chambers, thereby reducing NOx emissions.
3   The EGR system consists of the Powertrain Control Module (PCM), the EGR valve and various information sensors (ECT, TP, MAP, IAT, RPM and VSS sensors) that the PCM uses to determine when to open the EGR valve. When the PCM closes the power/control circuit for the EGR valve, a solenoid inside the EGR valve is energized. This creates an electromagnetic field, which causes an armature to pull up, lifting the pintle off its seat. The exhaust gas then flows from the exhaust manifold port to the intake manifold.
4   Once activated by the PCM, the EGR valve uses a position feedback circuit to control the position of the pintle valve. The feedback circuit, which functions like a potentiometer, puts out a variable output voltage signal with an operating range between 0.5 and 5.4 volts. This variable output enables the PCM to control the position of the pintle with a high degree of precision. A pintle position sensor monitors the position of the pintle, and the PCM adjusts the current to match the actual pintle position to the optimal pintle position.
5   If there is too much EGR flow at idle,

cruise or during cold running conditions, the engine will stop after a cold start, stop at idle after deceleration, surge during cruising speeds or idle roughly. If there is too little EGR flow, combustion chamber temperature can become too high during acceleration or under a heavy load, which can cause spark knock (detonation) and/or engine overheating.

Component replacement

2.2L OHV engine

1995 models

6   On these models, the EGR valve is located at the left end of the cylinder head and is opened and closed by a separate control solenoid valve, which allows ported vacuum from the throttle body to open the EGR valve when directed to do so by the PCM. The EGR control solenoid valve on 1995 models is located on the front of the upper intake manifold, to the left of the Throttle Position (TP) sensor (in the exact same location that the MAP sensor is located on 1996 and 1997 models).
7   To remove the EGR control solenoid valve, disconnect the electrical connector, clearly label the vacuum hoses, disconnect the vacuum hoses from the solenoid valve and remove the solenoid valve mounting bolt. Installation is the reverse of removal.
8   To remove the EGR valve, disconnect the vacuum signal line from the EGR valve, remove the EGR valve mounting bolt and remove the valve.
9   Remove and discard the old EGR valve gasket.
10   Installation is the reverse of removal.

1996 and 1997 models

Refer to illustration 18.11
11   1996 and 1997 2.2L OHV engines use a "linear" EGR valve **(see illustration)**, which is also located at the same spot, on the left end of the cylinder head. Unlike the 1995 EGR

18.11 On 1996 and 1997 2.2L OHV engines, the EGR valve is located at the left end of the cylinder head. Unplug the electrical connector and unscrew the mounting bolts to remove it (head removed for clarity)

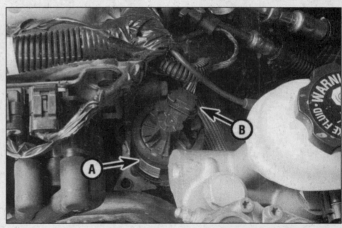

18.18 On 1998 2.2L OHV engines, the EGR valve (A) was relocated slightly, to the left rear corner of the cylinder head. Unplug the electrical connector (B) and remove the mounting bolts at the base of the valve

system, the linear system doesn't use a computer-controlled solenoid valve to direct ported vacuum to the EGR valve to open it. Instead, the linear type is electronically controlled by the PCM. The PCM opens and closes the EGR valve in response to input from the Throttle Position (TP) sensor and the Manifold Absolute Pressure (MAP) sensor. There is no separate EGR control solenoid valve on these models; the electronic control mechanism is an integral part of the EGR valve.

12 To remove the EGR valve disconnect the electrical connector from the valve.

13 Remove the EGR mounting bolts **(see illustration 18.11)** and remove the EGR valve.

14 Remove the old EGR valve gasket and discard it.

15 Clean the gasket mounting surfaces of the EGR valve and the housing on which it's installed. Be sure to remove all traces of gasket material from the intake manifold and, if you're planning to reinstall the old EGR valve, from the valve as well. Clean both mating surfaces with a cloth dipped in acetone or lacquer thinner.

16 Using a new gasket, install the EGR valve and tighten the mounting bolts securely.

17 Reconnect the electrical connector to the EGR valve.

1998 models
Refer to illustration 18.18

18 On 1998 models the EGR valve is relocated to the left rear corner of the engine **(see illustration),** to make room for the ignition coil pack, which was moved from the backside of the engine block to the left end of the head. The procedure for removing and installing the EGR valve on 1998 models is essentially the same as for 1996 and 1997 models, so refer to Steps 12 through 17.

2.4L OHC engine
Refer to illustration 18.19

19 1996 through 1998 2.4L OHC engines also use a linear EGR valve system. The EGR valve **(see illustration)** is located at the left front corner of the engine and is removed and installed exactly the same way as the EGR valve on 2.2L OHV engines, so refer to Steps 12 through 17.

19 Positive Crankcase Ventilation (PCV) system - general information, inspection and component replacement

General information
Refer to illustrations 19.3a, 19.3b, 19.4, 19.5 and 19.6

1 The Positive Crankcase Ventilation (PCV) system reduces hydrocarbon emissions by scavenging crankcase vapors, which are rich in unburned hydrocarbons. The PCV system used by the vehicles covered in this manual is somewhat different from conventional PCV systems because it doesn't rely on intake manifold vacuum to scavenge blow-by gases from the engine crankcase. In a conventional PCV system, a pressure differential in the crankcase is produced by intake manifold vacuum, which is accomplished by connecting the crankcase to a manifold vacuum source with a hose between the valve cover and the throttle body or intake manifold. Intake manifold vacuum draws crankcase vapors into the intake manifold, where they mix with the air/fuel mixture before being consumed in the combustion chambers. A fresh air inlet hose, which connects the air intake duct to the valve cover, allows fresh air to be drawn into the crankcase by the same intake vacuum source, thus equalizing the pressure in the bottom end. The result is a continuous loop of fresh air drawn into the crankcase, where it mixes with crankcase vapors before being drawn into the manifold by intake vacuum. A PCV valve regulates the flow of gases into the intake manifold in proportion to the amount of intake vacuum available. At idle, when intake vacuum is very high, the PCV valve restricts the flow of vapors so that the engine doesn't run poorly. As the throttle plate opens and intake vacuum begins to diminish, the PCV valve opens more to allow vapors to

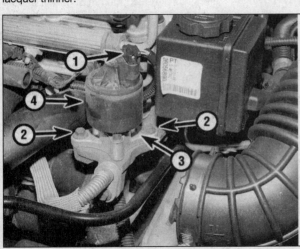

18.19 Typical linear EGR valve used on 1996 through 1998 2.4L OHC engines:

1 *Electrical connector*
2 *Mounting bolts*
3 *EGR valve mounting base (comes off with EGR valve)*
4 *Linear EGR valve*

19.3a On 1995 through 1997 2.2L OHV engines, the fresh air inlet to the crankcase is a sleeve that is located between the air intake duct and the valve cover

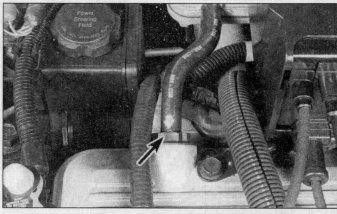

19.3b On 1995 through 1997 2.2L OHV engines, the crankcase ventilation hose and the PCV valve are located between the valve cover and the upper intake manifold. To remove the PCV valve, see Chapter 1

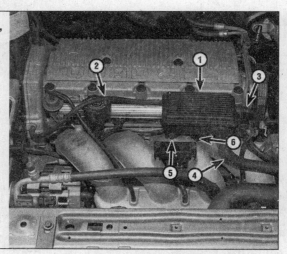

19.4 On 1995 2.3L OHC engines, the air/oil separator (1) is located on top of the intake manifold. To detach the air/oil separator from the manifold, disconnect or remove the following:

1   Air/oil separator
2   Crankcase ventilation hose
3   Hose to intake manifold
4   Hose to air/oil separator
5   Mounting bolts/screws (only one is visible in this photo)
6   Hose to dipstick/oil filler tube (underneath the separator)

19.5 To detach the air/oil separator (A) from the block on 2.4L OHC engines, remove these bolts

flow more freely.

2   The vehicles covered in this manual have a crankcase ventilation system that uses only one hose, between the valve cover and the air intake duct. There is no second hose and no PCV valve.

3   On 1995 through 1997 2.2L OHV engines, the PCV system consists of a fresh air inlet connection between the air intake duct and a pipe on the valve cover (see illustration), and the crankcase ventilation hose and PCV valve between the valve cover and the upper intake manifold (see illustration). On 1998 and later 2.2L OHV engines, there's a fresh air inlet hose between the air intake duct and the valve cover, but there's no PCV valve or crankcase ventilation hose. Instead, blow-by vapors are drawn up from the crankcase to an air/oil separator on the underside of the valve cover, and from there they are drawn into the resonator, which sits directly atop the valve cover.

4   On 2.3L OHC engines (1995 only), the PCV system consists of a crankcase vent air/oil separator, which is mounted on top of the intake manifold (see illustration) and the hoses connecting it to the air intake duct, the intake manifold, the dipstick/engine oil filler

tube and the timing chain cover. The hose to the intake manifold contains a 0.60-inch (1.52-mm) orifice. Also inside this hose is an anti-icing heater assembly that is turned on when the ignition key is turned to ON.

5   On 2.4L OHC engines, the PCV system consists of a crankcase vent air/oil separator, which is mounted on the front side of the engine block (see illustration). By moving the air/oil separator from the intake manifold to the crankcase, the system used on 1995 2.3L OHC models was simplified because several hoses were eliminated. In this system there are only two hoses: One hose, which connects the timing chain cover to the air/oil separator, directs crankcase vapors from the crankcase to the separator. The other hose directs crankcase vapors from the separator to the intake manifold. Because the separator is bolted to the block, there is no hose to drain the separated oil back to the crankcase through the dipstick filler tube; they're simply drained directly back to the block from the separator.

6   On 2.2L OHC engines, the PCV system consists of the single hose between the valve cover and the air intake duct (see illustration), and the crankcase ventilation housing

(or simply, the vent housing) permanently affixed to the underside of the valve cover. Crankcase blow-by vapors are directed through internal passages in the engine block and cylinder head up to a vent housing, from which they're drawn through the hose into the air intake duct, then through the throttle body and manifold and into the combustion chambers where they're consumed along with the air/fuel mixture.

Check

7   An engine that is operated without a properly functioning crankcase ventilation system can be damaged. So whenever you're servicing the engine, be sure to inspect the PCV system hose(s) for cracks, tears and other damage. Disconnect the hose(s) and inspect it/them for damage and obstructions. If a hose is clogged, clean it out. If you're unable to clean it satisfactorily, replace it.

8   A plugged PCV hose might cause any or all of the following conditions: A rough idle, stalling or a slow idle speed, oil leaks or

19.6 On 2.2L OHC engines, the PCV fresh air inlet hose to the crankcase is located between the resonator and the valve cover. To detach the hose, simply loosen both hose clamp screws and pull off the hose

sludge in the engine. So if the engine is running roughly, stalling and *idling at a lower than normal speed*, or is losing oil, or has oil in the throttle body or air intake manifold plenum, or has a build-up of sludge, a PCV system hose might be clogged. Repair or replace the hose(s) as necessary. On 2.3L and 2.4L OHC engines, remove and clean or replace the housing for the air/oil separator. On 2.2L OHC engines, remove the valve cover (see Chapter 2C) and inspect the air/oil separator. Make sure that it's clean by blowing it out with compressed air.

9   A leaking PCV hose might cause any or all of the following conditions: a rough idle, stalling or a high idle speed. So if the engine is running roughly, stalling and *idling at a higher than normal speed*, a PCV system hose might be leaking. Repair or replace the hose(s) as necessary.

10   Here's an easy functional check of the PCV system on a vehicle with a fresh air inlet hose and a crankcase ventilation hose with a PCV valve in it:

1   *Disconnect the PCV hose.*
2   *Start the engine and let it warm up to its normal idle.*
3   *Verify that there is vacuum at the PCV hose. If there is no vacuum, look for a plugged hose or manifold port. Also look for a hose that collapses when it's blocked (i.e. when vacuum is applied). Replace clogged or deteriorated hoses.*
4   *Remove the engine oil dipstick and install a vacuum gauge on the upper end of the dipstick tube.*
5   *Block off the PCV system fresh air passage.*
6   *Run the engine at 1500 rpm for 30 seconds, then read the vacuum gauge while the engine is running at 1500 rpm.*

7   *If there's vacuum present, the crankcase ventilation system is operating correctly.*
8   *If there's NO vacuum present, the engine might be drawing in outside air. The PCV system won't function correctly unless the engine is a sealed system. Inspect the valve cover(s), oil pan gasket or other sealing areas for leaks.*
9   *If the vacuum gauge indicates positive pressure, look for a plugged hose or engine blow-by.*

11   If the PCV system is functioning correctly, but there's evidence of engine oil in the throttle body or air filter housing, it could be caused by excessive crankcase pressure. Have the crankcase pressure tested by a dealer service department.

12   In the PCV system, excessive blow-by (caused by worn rings, pistons and/or cylinders, or by constant heavy loads) is discharged into the intake manifold and consumed. If you discover heavy sludge deposits or a dilution of the engine oil, even though the PCV system is functioning correctly, look for other causes (see Troubleshooting and Chapter 2D) and correct them as soon as possible.

Component replacement
2.2L OHV engine

Fresh air inlet "hose"

13   The fresh air inlet "hose" is actually just a short nylon sleeve between the air intake duct and the valve cover **(see illustration 19.3a)**. To replace the sleeve, remove the air intake duct (see Chapter 4 if necessary) and pull the sleeve out of the valve cover with a pair of needle-nose pliers.

14   Installation is the reverse of removal.

PCV valve and crankcase ventilation hose

15   Refer to Chapter 1. Removing and inspecting the PCV valve and crankcase ventilation hose is a regularly scheduled maintenance item.

1995 2.3L OHC engine

16   Clearly label all the hoses connected to the air/oil separator **(see illustration 19.4)**, then remove the three mounting screws and remove the separator.

17   Inspect the orifice at the pipe for the hose that connects the separator to the intake manifold. If this orifice becomes clogged up, it will lead to a buildup of sludge inside the PCV system hoses and oil leaks at the front and rear crankshaft seals. To verify that the orifice is open, try to blow through it with compressed air. If the orifice is clogged, replace the separator.

18   Installation is the reverse of removal.

1996 through 2002 2.4L OHC engine

19   Remove the intake manifold (see Chapter 2B).

20   Raise the front of the vehicle and place it securely on jackstands.

21   Clearly label the two hoses connected to the air/oil separator (one hose connects the timing chain cover to the separator and the other hose connects the separator to the intake manifold).

22   Remove the six separator mounting bolts **(see illustration 19.5)** and remove the separator.

23   Remove and discard the old air/oil separator gasket.

24   If there is any residual gasket material on the mating surfaces of the separator or the engine block, clean it off with a gasket scraper.

25   Installation is the reverse of removal. Tighten the separator mounting bolts to the torque listed in this Chapter's Specifications.

2.2L OHC engine

Crankcase ventilation hose (PCV hose)

26   Disconnect the hose from the resonator and from the valve cover **(see illustration 19.6)**.

27   Installation is the reverse of removal.

Crankcase vent housing

28   Remove the valve cover (see Chapter 2C). The vent housing is an integral component of the valve cover (it's riveted to the underside of the valve cover). It cannot be replaced separately.

29   Installation is the reverse of removal.

Notes

Chapter 7 Part A
Manual transaxle

Contents

Specifications

General
Lubricant type .... See Chapter 1

Torque specifications   Ft-lbs
Back-up light switch 24
Transaxle-to-engine bolts 55

1 General information

The vehicles covered by this manual are equipped with either a 5-speed manual or an automatic transaxle. Information on the manual transaxle is included in this Part of Chapter 7. Information on the automatic transaxle is in Part B.

The 1995 through 1999 models are equipped with a 5-speed Isuzu transaxle, while the 2000 and later models are equipped with a 5-speed Getrag transaxle. On all models, the transaxle consists of a transmission and differential housed in a single all-aluminum assembly. Because of its complexity, the special tools needed to overhaul it, and the difficulty of obtaining replacement parts, overhauling this unit is beyond the scope of the average home mechanic. The information in this chapter is limited to general diagnosis, external adjustments and removal and installation.

Depending on the cost, it may be a good idea to consider replacing the old unit with either a rebuilt or used transaxle instead of a new one. Your local dealer or transmission shop should be able to supply information concerning cost, availability and exchange policy. Regardless of how you decide to remedy a transaxle problem, however, you will save money by removing and installing it yourself.

2 Shift cables - removal and installation

1 Disconnect the shift and select cables from the levers on the transaxle. The cables can be pried from the pins on the levers with a screwdriver.
2 Remove the center console (see Chapter 11).
3 Disconnect the shift and select cables from the shift control assembly. The cables can be pried from the pins on the shift control assembly with a screwdriver. To detach the cables from their bracket on the shift control assembly base, pry off the large retaining plate.
4 Remove the screws from the right sill plate, remove the plate, then pull the carpet back for access to the cables.
5 Remove the cable grommet retainer screws (1995 and 1996 models) or pry loose the grommet (1997 and later models).
6 Pull the cables through into the passenger compartment and remove them from the vehicle.
7 Installation is the reverse of removal.

3   Shift control assembly - removal and installation

1   Remove the shift lever knob, console and shift boot (Chapter 11).
2   Disconnect the shift and select cables from the shift control assembly (see Section 2).
3   Remove the large shift cable retainer plate and detach the cables from their bracket on the shift control assembly base.
4   Remove the shift control assembly retaining nuts and remove the shift control assembly.
5   Installation is the reverse of removal.

4   Back-up light switch - check and replacement

Check

1   Turn the ignition key to the On position and move the shift lever to the Reverse position. The switch should close the back-up light circuit and turn on the back-up lights.
2   If it doesn't, check the back-up light fuse (see Chapter 12).
3   If the fuse is okay, verify that there's voltage available on the battery side of the switch (with the ignition turned to On).
4   If there's no voltage on the battery side of the switch, check the wire between the fuse and the switch; if there is voltage, put the shift lever in reverse and see if there's voltage on the ground side of the switch.
5   If there's no voltage on the ground side of the switch, replace the switch (see below); if there is voltage, note whether one or both back-up lights are out.
6   If only one bulb is out, replace it; if they're both out, the bulbs could be the problem, but it's more likely that the wire between the switch and the bulbs has an open somewhere.

Replacement

7   The back-up light switch is located on top of the left end (driver's side) of the transaxle.
8   Unplug the electrical connector from the switch.
9   Unscrew the switch with a *socket*. Do NOT use an open-end wrench.
10   Installation is the reverse of removal. Be sure to tighten the new switch to the torque listed in this Chapter's Specifications.

5   Manual transaxle - removal and installation

Removal

Refer to illustration 5.2
1   Disconnect the negative cable from the battery. **Caution**: *If the vehicle is equipped with a Delco Loc II or Theftlock audio system,*

5.2 During transmission removal, support the engine with a support fixture designed for this purpose. They are often available from rental yards

make sure you have the correct activation code before disconnecting the battery.
2   The engine must be supported during transaxle removal with an engine support tool **(see illustration)**. If this tool isn't available, support the engine with a hoist that can hold it high enough to allow the transaxle to be lowered from the engine compartment with the vehicle raised.
3   Working in the passenger compartment, remove the left sound insulator (see Chapter 11).
4   Disconnect the clutch master cylinder pushrod from the clutch pedal (see Chapter 8).
5   Remove the air cleaner and duct assembly from the throttle body (see Chapter 4).
6   Detach the wiring harness from its mounting bracket.
7   Remove the upper transaxle mount-to-transaxle bolts.
8   Disconnect the clutch actuator cylinder line and remove the clutch master cylinder from the clutch actuator cylinder (see Chapter 8).
9   Detach the wire harness from the mount bracket.
10   Disconnect the ground cables from their transaxle mounting studs.
11   Unplug the electrical connector from the back-up light switch.
12   Detach the vent tube from the transaxle.
13   Remove the rear transaxle-to-engine bolts.
14   Lower the engine to facilitate removal and installation of the transaxle.
15   Loosen the front wheel lug nuts, raise the vehicle and place it securely on jackstands. Remove the front wheels.
16   Drain the transaxle fluid (Chapter 1).
17   Remove the left front inner splash shield.
18   Unplug both front ABS wheel speed sensor connectors (see Chapter 9) and set the harnesses aside. It's not necessary to remove the sensor. Make sure the harnesses and connectors are safely out of harm's way where they won't be damaged.
19   Remove the flywheel housing cover bolts.

20   Remove the vehicle speed sensor from the transaxle (see Chapter 6).
21   Remove the left and right balljoint nuts and separate the balljoints from the steering knuckles.
22   Remove the left stabilizer link pin and remove the left U-bolt from the stabilizer bar (see Chapter 10).
23   Remove the left suspension support attaching bolts.
24   Detach the driveaxles from the transaxle (see Chapter 8).
25   Remove the front lower transaxle mount.
26   Support the transaxle with a jack, preferably a transmission jack made for this purpose. Chain the transaxle to the jack to make sure it doesn't fall off during removal.
27   Remove the rest of the transaxle-to-engine bolts.
28   Make a final check that all wiring, cables, etc. are disconnected from the transaxle.
29   Separate the transaxle from the engine by carefully prying the bellhousing away from the engine.
30   Lower the transaxle and remove it from the left side of the engine compartment.
31   The clutch components can now be inspected (Chapter 8). In most cases, new clutch components should be installed as a matter of course when the transaxle is removed.

Installation

32   With the clutch components installed and properly aligned (see Chapter 8), carefully raise the transaxle into place, guide the right side driveaxle into the transaxle and slide the input shaft into place in the clutch hub splines.
33   Install the transaxle-to-engine bolts. Tighten the bolts to the torque listed in this Chapter's Specifications.
34   Install the front transaxle mount and tighten the nuts and bolts securely.
35   Install the flywheel housing cover and tighten the bolts securely.
36   Install the driveaxles (see Chapter 8).
37   Install the left suspension support and

tighten the bolts securely.

38   Install the left stabilizer bar U-bolt (see Chapter 10).

39   Attach the left and right balljoints to the steering knuckles (see Chapter 10).

40   Install the left stabilizer bar link (see Chapter 10).

41   Reroute the ABS harnesses and connectors and plug the connectors into the front wheel speed sensors.

42   Install the front inner splash shield.

43   Install the wheels.

44   Install the vehicle speed sensor (see Chapter 6).

45   Lower the vehicle.

46   Connect the ground cables to their transaxle mounting studs.

47   Attach the vent tube to the transaxle.

48   Plug in the connector for the back-up light switch.

49   Install the upper transaxle-to-engine bolts and tighten them to the torque listed in this Chapter's Specifications.

50   Connect the clutch master cylinder to the clutch release cylinder (see Chapter 8).

51   Install the rear transaxle mount and tighten the nuts and bolts securely.

52   Attach the wiring harness to the mount bracket.

53   Remove the engine support.

54   Connect the shift and select cables to the shift levers and to the shift cable bracket.

55   Install the air cleaner and ducting (see Chapter 4).

56   Connect the clutch master cylinder pushrod to the clutch pedal (see Chapter 8).

57   Install the left sound insulator (see Chapter 11).

58   Fill the transaxle with the specified lubricant (see Chapter 1).

59   Connect the negative battery cable.

6   Manual transaxle overhaul - general information

Overhauling a manual transaxle is a difficult job for the do-it-yourselfer. It involves the disassembly and reassembly of many small parts. Numerous clearances must be precisely measured and, if necessary, changed with select fit spacers and snap-rings. As a result, if transaxle problems arise, it can be removed and installed by a competent do-it-yourselfer, but overhaul should be left to a transmission repair shop. Rebuilt transaxles may be available - check with your dealer parts department and auto parts stores. At any rate, the time and money involved in an overhaul is almost sure to exceed the cost of a rebuilt unit.

Nevertheless, it's not impossible for an inexperienced mechanic to rebuild a transaxle if the special tools are available and the job is done in a deliberate, step-by-step manner so nothing is overlooked.

The tools necessary for an overhaul include internal and external snap-ring pliers, a bearing puller, a slide hammer, a set of pin punches, a dial indicator and possibly a hydraulic press. In addition, a large, sturdy workbench and a vise or transaxle stand will be required.

During disassembly of the transaxle, make careful notes of how each piece comes off, where it fits in relation to other pieces and what holds it in place. Note how the parts are installed when you remove them; this will make it much easier to get the transaxle back together.

Before taking the transaxle apart for repair, it will help if you have some idea what area of the transaxle is malfunctioning. Certain problems can be closely tied to specific areas in the transaxle, which can make component examination and replacement easier. Refer to the Troubleshooting section at the front of this manual for information regarding possible sources of trouble.

Notes

Chapter 7 Part B
Automatic transaxle

Contents

Specifications

Torque specifications

	Ft-lbs
Park/Neutral Position switch retaining bolts	18
Transaxle-to-engine bolts	
All bolts except lower bolt	71
Lower bolt	41

1 General information

Due to the complexity of the clutches and the hydraulic control system, and because of the special tools and expertise required to perform an automatic transmission overhaul, it should not be undertaken by the home mechanic. Therefore, the procedures in this Chapter are limited to general diagnosis, routine maintenance and adjustment and transmission removal and installation.

If the transmission requires major repair work it should be left to a dealer service department or an automotive or transmission repair shop. You can, however, remove and install the transmission yourself and save the expense, even if the repair work is done by a transmission specialist.

Adjustments that the home mechanic may perform include those involving the throttle valve cable, the shift linkage and the neutral safety switch. **Caution:** *Never tow a disabled vehicle equipped with an automatic transaxle at speeds greater than 30 mph or distances over 50 miles unless the front wheels are off the ground. Failure to observe this precaution may result in severe transmission damage caused by lack of lubrication.*

2 Diagnosis - general

Note: *Automatic transaxle malfunctions may be caused by five general conditions: poor engine performance, improper adjustments, hydraulic malfunctions, mechanical malfunctions or malfunctions in the computer or its* signal network. *Diagnosis of these problems should always begin with a check of the easily repaired items: fluid level and condition (see Chapter 1), shift linkage adjustment (see Section 3) and throttle linkage adjustment (see Section 5). Next, perform a road test to determine if the problem has been corrected or if more diagnosis is necessary. If the problem persists after the preliminary tests and corrections are completed, additional diagnosis should be done by a dealer service department or transmission repair shop. Refer to the* Troubleshooting *section at the front of this manual for transaxle problem diagnosis.*

Preliminary checks

1   Drive the vehicle to warm the transaxle to normal operating temperature.
2   Check the fluid level as described in Chapter 1:

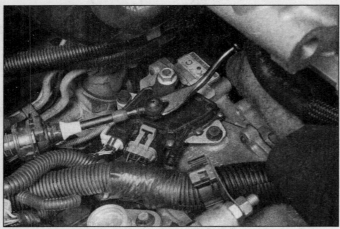

3.2 To disconnect the shift cable from the transaxle manual lever, pry it off the pin on the lever with a prying tool or screwdriver

3.3 To disengage the shift cable from the cable bracket on the transaxle, remove this locking clip, then squeeze the two locking tangs (arrow indicates one tang, other tang on other side of cable housing) and pull the cable housing from the bracket

   a) *If the fluid level is unusually low, add enough fluid to bring the level within the designated area of the dipstick, then check for external leaks.*

   b) *If the fluid level is abnormally high, drain off the excess, then check the drained fluid for contamination by coolant. The presence of engine coolant in the automatic transmission fluid indicates that a failure has occurred in the internal radiator walls that separate the coolant from the transmission fluid (see Chapter 3).*

   c) *If the fluid is foaming, drain it and refill the transaxle, then check for coolant in the fluid or a high fluid level.*

3   Check the engine idle speed. **Note:** *If the engine is malfunctioning, do not proceed with the preliminary checks until it has been repaired and runs normally.*

4   Check the Throttle Valve (TV) cable for freedom of movement. Adjust it if necessary (see Section 5). **Note:** *The TV cable may function properly when the engine is shut off and cold, but it may malfunction once the engine is hot. Check it cold and at normal engine operating temperature.*

5   Inspect the shift control cable (see Section 3). Make sure that it's properly adjusted and that the linkage operates smoothly.

Fluid leak diagnosis

6   Most fluid leaks are easy to locate visually. Repair usually consists of replacing a seal or gasket. If a leak is difficult to find, the following procedure may help.

7   Identify the fluid. Make sure it's transmission fluid and not engine oil or brake fluid (automatic transmission fluid is a deep red color).

8   Try to pinpoint the source of the leak. Drive the vehicle several miles, then park it over a large sheet of cardboard. After a minute or two, you should be able to locate the leak by determining the source of the fluid dripping onto the cardboard.

9   Make a careful visual inspection of the suspected component and the area immediately around it. Pay particular attention to gasket mating surfaces. A mirror is often helpful for finding leaks in areas that are hard to see.

10   If the leak still cannot be found, clean the suspected area thoroughly with a degreaser or solvent, then dry it.

11   Drive the vehicle for several miles at normal operating temperature and varying speeds. After driving the vehicle, visually inspect the suspected component again.

12   Once the leak has been located, the cause must be determined before it can be properly repaired. If a gasket is replaced but the sealing flange is bent, the new gasket will not stop the leak. The bent flange must be straightened.

13   Before attempting to repair a leak, check to make sure that the following conditions are corrected or they may cause another leak. **Note:** *Some of the following conditions cannot be fixed without highly specialized tools and expertise. Such problems must be referred to a transmission shop or a dealer service department.*

Gasket leaks

14   Check the pan periodically. Make sure the bolts are tight, no bolts are missing, the gasket is in good condition and the pan is flat (dents in the pan may indicate damage to the valve body inside).

15   If the pan gasket is leaking, the fluid level or the fluid pressure may be too high, the vent may be plugged, the pan bolts may be too tight, the pan sealing flange may be warped, the sealing surface of the transaxle housing may be damaged, the gasket may be damaged or the transaxle casting may be cracked or porous. If sealant instead of gasket material has been used to form a seal between the pan and the transaxle housing, it may be the wrong sealant.

Seal leaks

16   If a transaxle seal is leaking, the fluid level or pressure may be too high, the vent may be plugged, the seal bore may be damaged, the seal itself may be damaged or improperly installed, the surface of the shaft protruding through the seal may be damaged or a loose bearing may be causing excessive shaft movement.

17   Make sure the dipstick tube seal is in good condition and the tube is properly seated. Periodically check the area around the speedometer gear or sensor for leakage. If transmission fluid is evident, check the O-ring for damage. Also inspect the side gear shaft oil seals for leakage.

Case leaks

18   If the case itself appears to be leaking, the casting is porous and will have to be repaired or replaced.

19   Make sure the oil cooler hose fittings are tight and in good condition.

Fluid comes out vent pipe or fill tube

20   If this condition occurs, the transaxle is overfilled, there is coolant in the fluid, the case is porous, the dipstick is incorrect, the vent is plugged or the drain back holes are plugged.

3   Shift cable - replacement and adjustment

Replacement

Refer to illustration 3.2, 3.3, 3.5a, 3.5b and 3.6

1   Disconnect the negative battery cable. **Note:** *If the vehicle is equipped with a Delco Loc II or Theftlock system, make sure you have the correct activation code before disconnecting the battery (see Chapter 12).*

2   Disconnect the shift cable from the transaxle manual lever **(see illustration)**.

3   Disengage the shift cable from the cable bracket on the transaxle **(see illustration)**.

4   Remove the shift lever knob (see Section 4) and the console (see Chapter 11).

5   Pry out the locking clip and disengage the cable from the bracket at the front of the

3.5a To disengage the shift cable from the bracket on the shift lever base, remove this locking clip . . .

3.5b . . . squeeze the locking tangs together, then disengage the cable from the bracket

3.6 To disconnect the shift cable from the pin on the shift lever, simply pry it loose

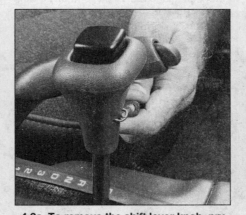

4.2a To remove the shift lever knob, pry out this locking clip . . .

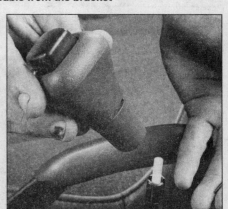

4.2b . . . then pull the knob straight up

shift lever base **(see illustrations)**.

6   Disconnect the shift cable from the pin on the shift lever **(see illustration)**.

7   Remove the sill plate, pull up the carpet and trace the cable to the cable grommet (the point at which it goes through the firewall). Pry out the grommet and pull the cable through the hole and remove it.

8   Installation is the reverse of removal. When you're done installing the new cable, be sure to adjust it.

Adjustment

9   Place the manual lever on the transaxle in the Neutral position. This is accomplished by rotating the lever clockwise from the Park position, through Reverse and into Neutral.

10   Place the shift lever inside the car in Neutral.

11   Push the tab on the cable adjuster at the cable bracket on the transaxle. The cable will automatically adjust itself.

12   Make sure the engine will start in the Park and Neutral positions only.

13   If the engine can be started in any position other than Park or Neutral, check the adjustment of the Park-Neutral Position Switch (see Section 7), then adjust and check the shift cable again.

14   If the cable still can't be adjusted properly, have the vehicle examined by a dealer service department.

4   Shift lever assembly - removal and installation

Removal

Refer to illustrations 4.2a, 4.2b and 4.6

1   Disconnect the negative battery cable. **Note:** *If the vehicle is equipped with a Delco Loc II or Theftlock system, make sure you have the correct activation code before disconnecting the battery* (see Chapter 12).

2   Remove the shift lever knob **(see illustrations)**.

3   Remove the console (see Chapter 11).

4   Disconnect the shift cable from the shift lever (see Section 3).

5   Unplug the electrical connector.

6   Remove the shift lever assembly retaining nuts **(see illustration)** and remove the shift lever assembly.

Installation

7   Place the shift lever in position on the mounting studs and install the nuts. Tighten the nuts securely.

8   Installation is the reverse of removal. Adjust the shift cable (see Section 3) when you're done.

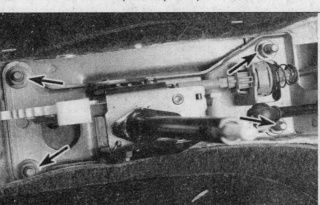

4.6 To detach the shift lever assembly from the floorpan, remove these four nuts (arrows)

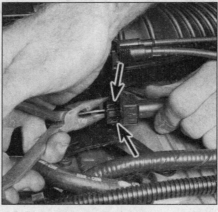

5.2 Disconnect the TV cable from the throttle lever at the throttle body

5.3 Disengage the TV cable housing from the cable bracket by compressing the tangs (arrows) and pushing the housing through the bracket

5.5 To detach the TV cable from the transaxle, remove this bolt (arrow)

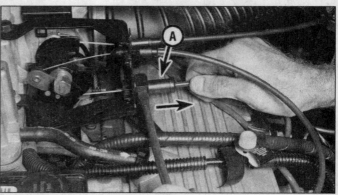

5.6 Pull up on the TV cable until the end of the cable is visible, then disengage it from the transaxle link

5.9 To adjust the TV cable, depress the adjustment button with a screwdriver or other suitable tool, move the slider (A) back (in direction of arrow) against the fitting until it stops, then release the adjustment button

5   Throttle Valve (TV) cable (3T40 transaxle) - replacement and adjustment

1   The Throttle Valve cable controls transaxle line pressure, which determines the shift "feel" and the timing of part-throttle and detent downshifts. The TV cable is attached to the throttle lever on the throttle body and to a link inside the transaxle.

Replacement

Refer to illustrations 5.2, 5.3, 5.5 and 5.6

2   Disconnect the TV cable from the throttle lever at the throttle body **(see illustration)**.
3   To disengage the TV cable housing from the cable bracket, compress the tangs and push the housing out of the bracket **(see illustration)**.
4   Disconnect any clips or straps retaining the cable to the transaxle.
5   Remove the bolt that secures the TV cable to the transaxle **(see illustration)**.
6   Pull up on the TV cable until the end of the cable is visible, then disengage it from the transaxle link **(see illustration)**.

7   Installation is the reverse of removal. Adjust the cable when you're done.

Adjustment

Refer to illustration 5.9

8   To check TV cable freeplay, pull on the upper end of the cable. It should travel a short distance with light resistance due to the small coiled return spring. To verify that the TV cable, lever and plunger are moving freely, pull the cable farther out to move the lever into contact with the plunger (this compresses the heavier TV spring). When released, the cable should return to its closed position. If the cable doesn't operate as described, turn off the engine (the engine must be turned off during adjustment), and adjust the TV cable as follows.
9   Depress the adjustment button **(see illustration)** and hold it down.
10   Pull the cable housing out until the slider mechanism hits the stop.
11   Release the adjustment button.
12   Remove the floormat.
13   Firmly depress the accelerator pedal all the way to the floor (wide-open throttle).
14   Verify that the cable moves freely.

15   Road test the vehicle. Sometimes, the cable will operate okay when the engine is cold, but will fail to operate properly when the engine is warmed up. If delayed or only full-throttle shifts still occur, try adjusting the cable one more time. If the problem persists, have the vehicle checked by a dealer service department or transmission shop.

6   Park/Lock system - description, adjustment and cable replacement

Warning: *The models covered by this manual are equipped with airbags. Always disable the airbag system before working in the vicinity of the impact sensors, steering column or instrument panel to avoid the possibility of accidental deployment of the airbag(s), which could cause personal injury (see Chapter 12).*

Description

1   The Park/Lock cable prevents the shift lever from being moved out of Park unless the brake pedal is depressed simultaneously.

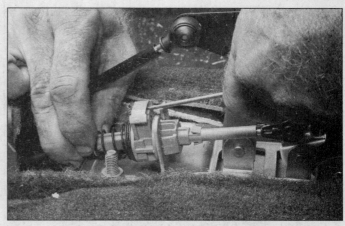

6.4 There must be no gap between the metal terminal stop (A) and the protruding end of the plastic collar (B). If there is a gap between the terminal stop and the collar, as there is in this photo, adjust the cable

6.9 To release the Park/Lock cable, raise the locking tab on the cable housing at the cable bracket on the shift lever base; to lock the cable into place, press the locking tab on the cable housing back into the housing

When the car is started, a solenoid is energized, locking the shift lever in Park; when the brake pedal is depressed, the solenoid is deenergized, unlocking the shift lever so that it can be moved into some other gear.

Check and adjustment

Refer to illustrations 6.4 and 6.9

2   Remove the left sound insulator trim panel from underneath the left end of the dash (see Chapter 11).

3   Locate the forward end of the Park/Lock cable.

4   The terminal stop on the steering column end of the Park-Lock cable must be touching the blue or white plastic collar that protrudes from the ignition switch. To check it:

a) *Turn the ignition key to the Lock position.*
b) *Put the shift lever in the Park position.*
c) *Note the position of the terminal stop (the metal plug on the end of the cable). There must be no gap between the metal terminal stop and the protruding end of the plastic collar (see illustration). If there's a gap between the terminal stop and the collar, adjust the cable. The plastic collar must be either flush or recessed about 0.04 inch (1 mm) into the ignition park-lock housing. If the plastic collar isn't in the correct position, adjust the cable.*

5   The plastic collar must have no more than 0.06 inch (1.5 mm) of travel. To check it:

a) *Put the key lock cylinder in the Lock position.*
b) *Put the shift lever in the Park position.*
c) *Gently, squeeze the park lock button on the shift lever until you feel resistance.*
d) *Verify that the plastic collar travels no more than 0.06 inch (1.5 mm) and that the shift lever doesn't come out of the Park position.*

6   With the ignition key turned to the On position, verify that the shift lever moves through all gear positions.

7   While moving the shift lever through all gear positions, verify that the ignition key can't be turned to the Lock position.

8   Verify that the ignition key can be removed when it's in the Lock position and the shift lever is in the Park position.

9   If the Park/Lock cable fails any of the above five tests, adjust it as follows.

a) *Put the shift lever in Park.*
b) *Turn the ignition key to Lock.*
c) *Remove the shift lever knob (see Section 3).*
d) *Remove the console (see Chapter 11).*
e) *Raise the locking tab on the cable housing at the cable bracket on the shift lever base (see illustration). This releases the Park/Lock cable.*
f) *Adjust the outer cable "conduit" (the cable sheathing) to correctly position the white plastic housing in the ignition switch (see illustration 6.4). There must be no gap between the metal terminal stop and the protruding end of the white plastic collar. The white plastic collar must either be flush or recessed about 0.04 inch (1 mm) into the ignition park lock housing.*

g) *Press the locking tab on the cable housing back into the housing.*

10   Following Steps 4 through 8 above, check the cable as described. Make sure it passes all five checks.

Cable replacement

Refer to illustrations 6.18 and 6.19

11   Remove the shift lever knob (see Section 3).

12   Remove the console, left sound insulator and steering column knee bolster panel (see Chapter 11).

13   Unbolt and lower the steering column.

14   Put the shift lever in the Park position.

15   Turn the ignition key to the Run position.

16   Insert a screwdriver blade into the slot in the ignition switch inhibitor, depress the cable latch and detach the cable from the inhibitor.

17   Raise the locking tab on the cable housing at the shift lever base to the up position **(see illustration 6.9)**.

18   Snap the rear end of the cable loose from the pin on the Park/Lock lever **(see illustration)**.

6.18 Pry the cable loose from the pin on the Park/Lock lever

6.19 To disengage the housing from the cable bracket, depress the two cable housing latches on the sides of the cable housing

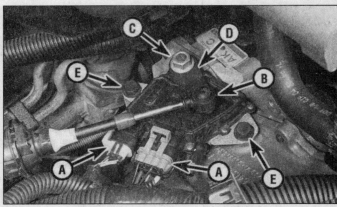

7.4 The Park/Neutral Position switch is located on top of the transaxle; to remove the switch, unplug the electrical connectors (A), disconnect the shift cable (B) from the manual lever, remove the manual lever retaining nut (C) and manual lever (D), and remove the switch retaining bolts (E)

19   Depress the two cable housing latches on the sides of the cable housing **(see illustration)** and disengage the housing from the cable bracket.

20   Remove any cable clips and remove the Park/Lock cable.

21   Make sure the cable locking tab is in the up position and the shift lever is in Park.

22   With the ignition key in the Run position (this is very important), snap the cable into the inhibitor housing.

23   Turn the ignition key to the Lock position.

24   Snap the rear end of the cable onto the pin on the park/lock lever.

25   Push the nose of the cable connector forward to remove the slack.

26   With no load on the connector nose, snap down the cable housing locking tab.

27   Check the operation of the park/lock cable as follows.

  a) *With the shift lever in Park and the key in Lock, make sure the shift lever cannot be moved to another position and the key can be removed.*

  b) *With the key in Run and the shift lever in Neutral, make sure the key cannot be turned to Lock.*

28   If it operates as described above, the park/lock cable system is properly adjusted. Proceed to Step 30.

29   If the park/lock system does not operate as described, return the cable connector lock to the up position and repeat the adjustment procedure. Push the cable connector down and recheck the operation.

30   If the key cannot be removed in the Park position, snap the locking tab to the up position and move the nose of the cable connector rearward until the key can be removed from the ignition switch.

31   Install the cable into the retaining clips.

32   Raise the steering column into position, install the bolts and tighten them securely.

33   Install the steering column knee bolster, the left sound insulator and the console (see Chapter 11).

34   Install the shift lever knob (see Section 3).

7   Park/Neutral Position (PNP) switch (1995 and 1996 models) - replacement

Refer to illustrations 7.4 and 7.13

1   If the vehicle you are working on is a 1997 or later model, refer to "Transmission Range (TR) switch" in Chapter 6.

2   Disconnect the negative cable from the battery. **Note:** *If the vehicle is equipped with a Delco Loc II or Theftlock system, be sure you have the correct code before disconnecting the battery. See the information at the front of this manual for the radio re-activation procedure.*

3   Apply the parking brake and put the shift lever in Neutral.

4   Locate the Park/Neutral Position (PNP) switch **(see illustration)**, which is mounted on the transaxle at the manual lever.

5   Disconnect the shift cable from the manual lever (see Section 3).

6   Unplug the electrical connector(s) from the PNP switch **(see illustration 7.4)**.

7   Remove the switch retaining screws or

bolts **(see illustration 7.4)** and detach the switch.

8   Remove the manual lever retaining nut and remove the manual lever **(see illustration 7.4)**.

9   Remove the Park/Neutral Position switch.

10   Put the shift shaft in the Neutral position.

11   Align the flats of the shift shaft with the flats of the Park/Neutral Position switch and install the switch.

12   Install the switch mounting bolts. If you're installing the old switch, don't tighten them yet. If you're installing a new switch, tighten the bolts to the torque listed in this Chapter's Specifications.

13   If you're installing the old switch, insert a 3/32-inch gauge pin or drill bit into the service adjustment hole **(see illustration)** and rotate the switch until the pin drops into the second hole; the pin or drill bit should drop into the holes to a depth of 9/64-inch. Tighten the switch mounting bolts to the torque listed in this Chapter's Specifications. Remove the gauge pin or drill bit. Verify that the engine will start only in Park or Neutral. If it starts in any other gear, readjust the switch.

14   If you're installing a new switch, align the service adjustment holes with the mount-

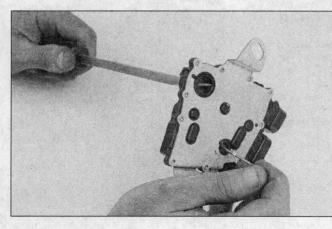

7.13 To adjust the old Park/Neutral Position switch, insert a 3/32-inch gauge pin or drill bit into the service adjustment hole and rotate the switch until the pin drops into the second hole; the pin or drill bit should drop into the holes to a depth of 9/64-inch

8.4 Rubber-type driveaxle oil seals (arrow) can be pried out of the transaxle housing with a screwdriver; be careful not to damage the splines of the axleshaft (transaxle removed for clarity)

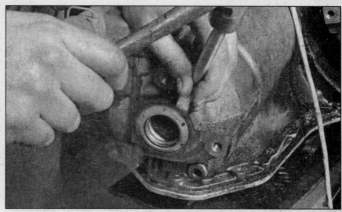

8.5 Dislodge metal-type driveaxle oil seals by working around the outer circumference with a chisel and hammer (transaxle removed for clarity)

ing boss on the transaxle. Put the manual lever in the Neutral position, but do NOT rotate the switch; the switch is pinned in the Neutral position. If it has been rotated and the pin is broken, adjust the switch as described in the previous step. Verify that the engine will start only in Park or Neutral. If it starts in any other gear, readjust the switch.

15 The remainder of installation is the reverse of removal.

8 Oil seal replacement

1 Oil leaks frequently occur due to wear of the driveaxle oil seals. Replacement of these seals is relatively easy, since the repairs can usually be performed without removing the transaxle from the vehicle.

Driveaxle oil seals

Refer to illustrations 8.4 and 8.5

2 The driveaxle oil seals are located in the sides of the transaxle, where the driveaxles are attached. If leakage at the seal is suspected, raise the vehicle and support it securely on jackstands. If the seal is leaking, fluid will be found on the sides of the transaxle.

3 Remove the driveaxles (see Chapter 8).

4 On rubber-type seals, use a screwdriver or prybar to carefully pry the oil seal out of the transaxle bore. Be careful not to damage the splines on the output shaft **(see illustration)**. If the oil seal cannot be removed with a screwdriver or prybar, a special oil seal removal tool (available at auto parts stores) will be required.

5 On metal-type seals, use a hammer and chisel to pry up the outer lip of the seal to dislodge it so it can be pried out of the housing **(see illustration)**.

6 Compare the old seal to the new one to be sure it's the correct one.

7 Coat the outside and inside diameters of the new seal with a small amount of transmission fluid.

8 Using a large section of pipe or a large

deep socket as a drift, install the new oil seal. Drive it into the bore squarely and make sure it's completely seated.

9 Install the driveaxle(s). Be careful not to damage the lip of the new seal.

Speedometer gear seal

10 Disconnect the speedometer cable, if equipped, from the transaxle (see Chapter 10). **Note:** *Some later models may use a vehicle speed sensor and an electric speedometer instead of a conventional mechanical speedometer, so there is no cable. However, the drive gear assembly - and the seals themselves - are similar to a conventional mechanical speedometer drive gear assembly and its seals.*

11 On models with a mechanical speedometer, remove the retainer clip that secures the speedometer cable, remove the speedometer driven gear and sleeve assembly and discard the O-ring.

12 On models with an electric speedometer, unplug the VSS connector, remove the governor cover or (on some models) the speed sensor housing, and discard the O-ring.

13 Installation is the reverse of removal. Be sure to dip the new O-ring into clean automatic transmission fluid before installing it.

9 Transaxle mount - check and replacement

1 Insert a large screwdriver or prybar between the mount bracket and the rubber portion of the mount and pry up.

2 The transaxle should not move excessively away from the mount. If it does, or if the rubber is torn or badly cracked, replace the mount.

3 To replace a mount, support the transaxle with a jack, remove the nuts and bolts and remove the mount. It may be necessary to raise the transaxle slightly to provide enough clearance to remove the mount.

4 Installation is the reverse of removal.

10 Transaxle - removal and Installation

Removal

Refer to illustrations 10.5, 10.9, 10.18a and 10.18b

1 Disconnect the negative battery cable. **Caution:** *If the vehicle is equipped with a Delco Loc II or Theftlock system, make sure you have the correct activation code before disconnecting the battery (see Chapter 12).*

2 Remove the intake air duct (see Chapter 4).

3 Disconnect the shift cable from transaxle (see Section 3).

4 Disconnect the TV cable from the transaxle on models equipped with a 3T40 transaxle (see Section 5).

5 Disconnect the vent hose **(see illustration)**.

6 Clearly label, then unplug, all electrical connectors.

7 Detach the power steering pump assembly (see Chapter 10) and set it aside.

8 Attach a suitable lifting device to the engine and raise the engine sufficiently to

10.5 Detach the vent hose (arrow) from the top of the transaxle

10.9 To detach the upper part of the transaxle from the engine, remove these nuts (arrows); be sure to label all ground wires, such as the two shown here, to ensure that they are reattached correctly

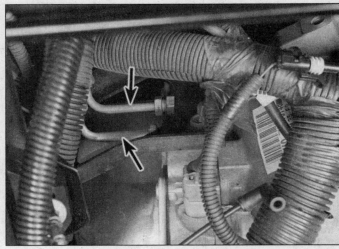

10.18a To detach the oil cooler lines (arrows) from a 3T40 transaxle, unscrew the tube nuts at the transaxle

support the weight of the engine. **Note:** *The engine must remain supported while the transaxle is out of the vehicle.*

9   Remove the upper transmission-to-engine bolts **(see illustra-tion)**.

10   Loosen the front wheel lug nuts, raise the vehicle and support it securely on jackstands. Remove the front wheels.

11   Remove the left splash shield.

12   Remove the front ABS wheel speed sensors and harnesses (see Chapter 9) and set them aside.

13   Remove the driveaxles (see Chapter 8).

14   Remove the engine-to-transaxle brace.

15   Remove the three torque converter cover bolts and remove the cover.

16   Remove the starter motor (see Chapter 5).

17   Mark the relationship of the torque converter to the driveplate and remove the flywheel-to-torque converter bolts.

18   Disconnect and plug the transaxle cooler lines **(see illustrations)**.

19   Disconnect all ground wires.

20   Remove the cooler line bracket.

21   Remove the exhaust brace.

22   Support the transaxle with a jack.

23   Remove the transaxle mount-to-body bolts.

24   Remove the transaxle mount bracket-to-transaxle bolts and remove the mount and bracket assembly.

25   Remove the nut and bolt from the heater core hose pipe-to-transaxle bracket.

26   Remove the remaining transaxle-to-engine bolts.

27   Remove the transaxle from the engine by sliding it toward the left side of the vehicle.

Installation

28   Installation is the reverse of removal, with attention paid to the following points:

a) *Tighten all transaxle-to-engine bolts to the torque listed in this Chapter's Specifications.*

b) *The front end alignment should be checked by a dealer or alignment shop.*

c) *Adjust the TV cable (see Section 5).*

d) *Check the transaxle fluid level (see Chapter 1).*

10.18b To detach the oil cooler lines (arrows) from a 4T40E transaxle, remove this nut (arrow)

Chapter 8
Clutch and driveaxles

Contents

Specifications

Clutch

Fluid type	See Chapter 1
CV joint boot length **(see illustrations 11.3u and 11.3v)**	
1995 models	
Ball-and-cage type joint	5-1/4 inches
Tripot type joint	
29/32 inch diameter axleshaft	7-1/2 inches
1-1/32 inch diameter axleshaft	6-11/16 inches
1996 and 1997 models (all)	4-29/32 inches
1998 and later models	
2.2L engine	4.0 inches
2.4L engine	4-29/32 inches

Torque specifications

	Ft-lbs (unless otherwise indicated)
Clutch master cylinder mounting nuts	180 in-lbs
Clutch pressure plate-to-flywheel bolts	
2.2L	180 in-lbs, then rotate 30-degrees
2.3L, 2.4L	180 in-lbs, then rotate 45-degrees
Driveaxle/hub nut	185
Intermediate shaft support bolts	48
Wheel lug nuts	See Chapter 1

1 General information

The information in this Chapter deals with the components from the rear of the engine to the front wheels, except for the transaxle, which is dealt with in Chapters 7A and 7B. For the purposes of this Chapter, these components are grouped into two categories: clutch and driveaxles. Separate Sections within this Chapter offer general descriptions and checking procedures for both groups.

Since nearly all the procedures covered in this Chapter involve working under the vehicle, make sure it's securely supported on sturdy jackstands or a hoist where the vehicle can be easily raised and lowered.

2 Clutch - description and check

1   All vehicles with a manual transaxle use a single dry plate, diaphragm spring type clutch. The clutch disc has a splined hub which allows it to slide along the splines of the transaxle input shaft. The clutch and pressure plate are held in contact by spring pressure exerted by the diaphragm in the pressure plate.

2   The clutch release system is operated by hydraulic pressure. The hydraulic release system consists of the clutch pedal, a master cylinder and fluid reservoir, the clutch fluid hydraulic line, and an integral clutch release cylinder and release bearing assembly.

3   When pressure is applied to the clutch pedal to release the clutch, hydraulic pres-

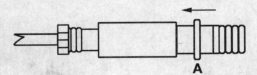

38016-8-3.2 HAYNES

3.2 To disconnect the clutch hydraulic line, push in the release slide (A), hold it there and pull the line and fitting apart

3.6 If you're going to re-use the same pressure plate, mark the relationship of the pressure plate to the flywheel

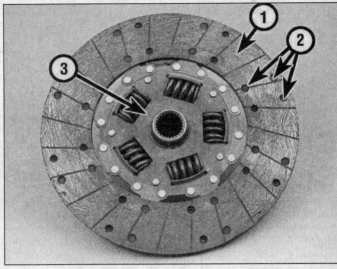

3.10 Examine the clutch disc for evidence of excessive wear, such as smeared friction material, chewed-up rivets, worn hub splines and distorted damper cushions or springs

1 *Lining* - wears down in use
2 *Rivets* - secure the lining and can damage the flywheel or pressure plate if allowed to contact the surfaces
3 *Markings* - usually says something like "Flywheel side"

sure is exerted against the release bearing, which pushes against the fingers of the diaphragm spring of the pressure plate assembly, which in turn releases the clutch disc.

4   Terminology can be a problem regarding the clutch components because common names have in some cases changed from that used by the manufacturer. For example, the driven plate is also called the clutch plate or disc, the pressure plate assembly is also referred to as the clutch cover, the clutch release bearing is also called a throw-out bearing, and the actuator cylinder is also known as a release or slave cylinder.

5   Unless you're replacing components that are obviously damaged, make the following preliminary checks to determine the nature of the clutch system failure.

a) *Check the fluid level in the clutch master cylinder (see Chapter 1). If the fluid level is low, add fluid as necessary and inspect the hydraulic clutch system for leaks. If the master cylinder reservoir has run dry, bleed the system (see Section 6) and retest the clutch operation.*

b) *Check "clutch spin down time": run the engine at normal idle speed with the transaxle in Neutral (not with the clutch pedal depressed), depress the clutch pedal, wait several seconds and shift the transaxle into Reverse. You should not hear a grinding noise, the most likely cause of which is a defective pressure plate or clutch disc.*

c) *Check for complete clutch release: run the engine (with the parking brake applied) and hold the clutch pedal about*

1/2-inch from the floor. Shift the transaxle between 1st gear and Reverse several times. If the shift is not smooth, component failure is indicated. Check the release cylinder pushrod travel. With the clutch pedal depressed completely the release cylinder pushrod should extend substantially. If it doesn't, check the fluid level in the clutch master cylinder.

d) *Visually inspect the clutch pedal bushing at the top of the clutch pedal to make sure there is no sticking or excessive wear.*

3   Clutch components - removal, inspection and installation

Warning: *Dust produced by clutch wear and deposited on clutch components may contain asbestos, which is hazardous to your health. DO NOT blow it out with compressed air and DO NOT inhale it. DO NOT use gasoline or petroleum based solvents to remove the dust. Brake system cleaner should be used to flush the dust into a drain pan. After the clutch components are wiped clean with a rag, dispose of the contaminated rags and cleaner in a labeled, covered container.*

Removal

Refer to illustrations 3.2 and 3.6

1   Access to the clutch components is normally accomplished by removing the transaxle, leaving the engine in the vehicle. If, of course, the engine is being removed for major overhaul, then the opportunity should

always be taken to check the clutch for wear and replace worn components as necessary. However, the relatively low cost of the clutch components compared to the time and labor involved in gaining access to them warrants their replacement any time the engine or transaxle is removed, unless they are new or in near-perfect condition. The following procedures assume that the engine will stay in place.

2   Disconnect the clutch hydraulic line from the clutch release cylinder **(see illustration)**. Have rags handy as some fluid will be lost as the line is disconnected. **Caution:** *Don't allow brake fluid to come into contact with paint, as it will damage the finish.*

3   Remove the clutch master cylinder assembly (see Section 4).

4   Remove the transaxle from the vehicle (see Chapter 7A).

5   To support the clutch disc during removal, install a clutch alignment tool through the clutch disc hub **(see illustration 3.14)**.

6   Carefully inspect the flywheel and pressure plate for indexing marks. The marks are usually an X, an O or a white letter. If they cannot be found, scribe marks yourself so the pressure plate and the flywheel will be in the same alignment during installation **(see illustration)**.

7   Slowly loosen the pressure plate-to-flywheel bolts. Work in a diagonal pattern and loosen each bolt a little at a time until all spring pressure is relieved. Then hold the pressure plate securely and completely remove the bolts, followed by the pressure plate and clutch disc.

NORMAL FINGER WEAR

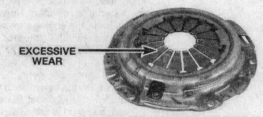

EXCESSIVE
WEAR

EXCESSIVE FINGER WEAR

BROKEN OR BENT FINGERS

3.12a Replace the pressure plate if excessive wear is noted

3.12b Examine the pressure plate friction surface for score
marks, cracks and evidence of overheating (blue spots)

3.14 Center the clutch disc in the pressure plate with a
clutch alignment tool

Inspection

Refer to illustrations 3.10, 3.12a and 3.12b

8   Ordinarily, when a problem occurs in the clutch, it can be attributed to wear of the clutch driven plate assembly (clutch disc). However, all components should be inspected at this time.

9   Inspect the flywheel for cracks, heat checking, score marks and other damage. If the imperfections are slight, a machine shop can resurface it to make it flat and smooth. Refer to Chapter 2 for the flywheel removal procedure.

10   Inspect the lining on the clutch disc. There should be at least 1/16-inch of lining above the rivet heads. Check for loose rivets, distortion, cracks, broken springs and other obvious damage **(see illustration)**. As mentioned above, ordinarily the clutch disc is replaced as a matter of course, so if in doubt about the condition, replace it with a new one.

11   Inspect the clutch release cylinder and bearing (see Section 5).

12   Check the machined surface and the diaphragm spring fingers of the pressure plate **(see illustrations)**. If the surface is grooved or otherwise damaged, replace the pressure plate assembly. Also check for obvious damage, distortion, cracking, etc. Light glazing can be removed with emery cloth or sandpa-

per. If a new pressure plate is indicated, new or factory rebuilt units are available.

Installation

Refer to illustrations 3.14 and 3.21

13   Before installation, carefully wipe the flywheel and pressure plate machined surfaces clean. It's important that no oil or grease is on these surfaces or the lining of the clutch disc. Handle these parts only with clean hands.

14   Position the clutch disc and pressure plate with the clutch held in place with an alignment tool **(see illustration)**. Make sure it's installed properly (most replacement clutch plates will be marked "flywheel side" or something similar - if not marked, install the clutch disc with the damper springs or cushion toward the transaxle).

15   Tighten the pressure plate-to-flywheel bolts only finger tight, working around the pressure plate.

16   Center the clutch disc by ensuring the

alignment tool is through the splined hub and into the recess in the crankshaft. Wiggle the tool up, down or side-to-side as needed to bottom the tool. Tighten the pressure plate-to-flywheel bolts a little at a time, working in a crisscross pattern to prevent distortion of the cover. After all of the bolts are snug, tighten them to the torque listed in this Chapter's Specifications. Remove the alignment tool.

17   Using high-temperature grease, lubricate the inner groove of the release bearing (see Section 4). Also place grease on the transaxle input shaft bearing retainer.

18   Install the clutch release cylinder and bearing (see Section 5).

19   Install the transaxle (see Chapter 7A).

20   Install the clutch master cylinder (see Section 4).

21   Connect the clutch hydraulic line to the clutch release cylinder **(see illustration)**.

22   Bleed the clutch hydraulic system (see Section 6).

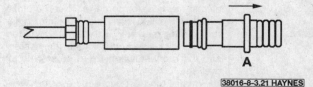

3.21 To connect the clutch
hydraulic line, pull back on
the release slide (A), hold it
there, and push the line
into the fitting until you
hear a click

38016-8-3.21 HAYNES

4 Clutch master cylinder - removal and installation

1   Remove the sound insulator from under the left side of the dashboard (see Chapter 11).
2   Using a flashlight, locate the clutch master cylinder pushrod. Disconnect the pushrod from the clutch pedal.
3   Remove the two nuts which attach the clutch master cylinder to the firewall. Detach the clutch master cylinder from the firewall.
4   Detach the clutch master cylinder remote reservoir from the firewall.
5   Disconnect the clutch hydraulic line from the clutch release cylinder **(see illustration 3.2)**. Have rags handy as some fluid will be lost as the line is removed. **Caution:** *Don't allow brake fluid to come into contact with paint, as it will damage the finish.*
6   Remove the clutch master cylinder, remote reservoir and clutch hydraulic line as a single assembly.
7   Installation is the reverse of removal. Be sure to tighten the clutch master cylinder nuts to the torque listed in this Chapter's Specifications. To reconnect the clutch hydraulic line at the clutch release cylinder, refer to illustration 3.21.
8   When you're done, bleed the clutch hydraulic system (see Sec-tion 6).

5 Clutch release cylinder and bearing - removal, inspection and installation

Warning: *Dust produced by clutch wear and deposited on clutch components may contain asbestos, which is hazardous to your health. DO NOT blow it out with compressed air and DO NOT inhale it. DO NOT use gasoline or petroleum-based solvents to remove the dust. Brake system cleaner should be used to flush it into a drain pan. After the clutch components are wiped clean with a rag, dispose of the contaminated rags and cleaner in a labeled, covered container.*

Removal

1   Remove the clutch master cylinder (see Section 4).
2   Remove the transaxle (see Chapter 7A).
3   Slide the clutch release cylinder and bearing assembly off the transaxle input shaft.

Inspection

4   Hold the bearing by the outer race and rotate the inner race while applying pressure. If the bearing doesn't turn smoothly or if it's noisy, replace the bearing/hub assembly with a new one. Wipe the bearing with a clean rag and inspect it for damage, wear and cracks. Don't immerse the bearing in solvent - it's sealed for life and to do so would ruin it. Also check the release cylinder for leaks. A thin coating of hydraulic fluid near the seal is

acceptable, but a liberal amount of fluid indicates a damaged seal. If the release cylinder and bearing assembly is noisy or leaking, replace it.

Installation

5   Fill the inner groove of the release bearing with high-temperature grease. Also apply a light coat of the same grease to the transaxle input shaft splines.
6   Slide the release cylinder and bearing onto the input shaft.
7   Apply a light coat of high-temperature grease to the face of the release bearing where it contacts the pressure plate diaphragm fingers.
8   Install the transaxle (see Chapter 7A).
9   Install the clutch master cylinder (see Section 4).
10   Bleed the clutch hydraulic system (see Section 6).

6 Clutch hydraulic system - bleeding

1   The hydraulic system should be bled of all air whenever any part of the system has been removed or if the fluid level has been allowed to fall so low that air has been drawn into the master cylinder. The procedure is similar to bleeding a brake system.
2   Fill the master cylinder with new brake fluid conforming to DOT 3 specifications. **Caution:** *Do not reuse any of the fluid coming from the system during the bleeding operation or use fluid which has been inside an open container for an extended period of time.*
3   Raise the vehicle and place it securely on jackstands to gain access to the release cylinder, which is located on the left side of the clutch housing.
4   Locate the bleeder valve on the clutch release cylinder (right above the fitting for the hydraulic fluid line). Remove the dust cap which fits over the bleeder valve and push a length of plastic hose over the valve. Place the other end of the hose into a clear container with about two inches of brake fluid in it. The hose end must be submerged in the fluid.
5   Have an assistant depress the clutch pedal and hold it. Open the bleeder valve on the release cylinder, allowing fluid to flow through the hose. Close the bleeder valve when fluid stops flowing from the hose. Once closed, have your assistant release the pedal.
6   Continue this process until all air is evacuated from the system, indicated by a full, solid stream of fluid being ejected from the bleeder valve each time and no air bubbles in the hose or container. Keep a close watch on the fluid level inside the clutch master cylinder reservoir; if the level drops too low, air will be sucked back into the system and the process will have to be started all over again.
7   Install the dust cap and lower the vehi-

cle. Check carefully for proper operation before placing the vehicle in normal service.

7 Clutch start switch - check and replacement

1   Remove the left side under-dash panel.

Check

2   Verify that the engine will not start when the clutch pedal is released. Now, depress the clutch pedal - the engine should start.
3   Locate the switch at the upper end of the clutch pedal and unplug the electrical connector.
4   Using an ohmmeter, verify that there is continuity between the terminals of the clutch start switch when the pedal is depressed. There should be no continuity when the pedal is released.
5   If the switch does not work as described, replace it.

Replacement

6   Unplug the electrical connector from the switch.
7   Detach the clutch pedal position switch from the clutch pedal bracket.
8   Installation is the reverse of removal. The switch is self-adjusting, so there's no need for adjustment.
9   Verify that the engine doesn't start when the clutch pedal is released, and does start when the pedal is depressed.

8 Driveaxles - general information and inspection

1   Power is transmitted from the transaxle to the wheels through a pair of driveaxles. The inner end of each driveaxle is splined into the differential side gears, or onto a splined intermediate axleshaft. The outer ends of the driveaxles are splined to the axle hubs and locked in place by a large nut.
2   The inner ends of the driveaxles are equipped with sliding constant velocity joints, which are capable of both angular and axial motion. Most inner joint assemblies consist of a tripot bearing and a joint housing (outer race) in which the joint is free to slide in and out as the driveaxle moves up and down with the wheel; some inner joints on 1995 models are the "cross-groove," or "ball-and-cage" type, which consists of six ball bearings riding between an inner race and outer race and held in position by a cage. The inner joints can be disassembled, cleaned, inspected and repacked, but they cannot be overhauled. If any parts are damaged, an inner joint must be replaced as a unit.
3   The outer CV joints are the cross-groove," or "ball-and-cage," type. The outer joints are capable of angular but not axial movement. The outer joints can be disassembled, cleaned, inspected and repacked,

9.5 To hold the hub/disc while breaking loose the driveaxle hub nut, jam a punch into the cooling vanes of the disc

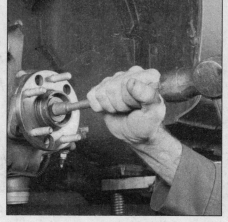

9.6 Using a brass punch, strike the end of the driveaxle sharply with a hammer; when it breaks free, it will move noticeably

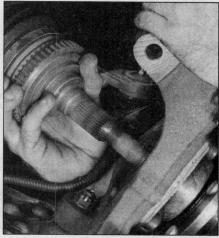

9.9 Pull the steering knuckle out and slide the end of the driveaxle out of the hub

but they cannot be overhauled. If any parts are damaged, an outer joint must be replaced as a unit.

4   The boots should be inspected periodically for damage and leaking lubricant. Torn CV joint boots must be replaced immediately or the joints can be damaged. Boot replacement involves removal of the driveaxle (see Section 9). **Note:** *Some auto parts stores carry "split" type replacement boots, which can be installed without removing the driveaxle from the vehicle. This is a convenient alternative; however, the driveaxle should be removed and the CV joint disassembled and cleaned to ensure the joint is free from contaminants such as moisture and dirt which will accelerate CV joint wear.* The most common symptom of worn or damaged CV joints, besides lubricant leaks, is a clicking noise in turns, a clunk when accelerating after coasting and vibration at highway speeds. To check for wear in the CV joints and driveaxle shafts, grasp each axle (one at a time) and rotate it in both directions while holding the CV joint housings, feeling for play indicating worn splines or sloppy CV joints. Also check the driveaxle shafts for cracks, dents and distortion.

9 Driveaxle - removal and installation

Removal

Refer to illustrations 9.5, 9.6, 9.9 and 9.10

1   Disconnect the cable from the negative terminal of the battery. **Caution:** *If the stereo in your vehicle is equipped with an anti-theft system, make sure you have the correct activation code before disconnecting the battery.*
2   Set the parking brake.
3   Loosen the front wheel lug nuts, raise the vehicle and support it securely on jackstands.

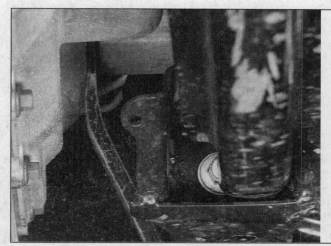

9.10 To separate the inner end of the driveaxle from the transaxle, pry on the CV joint housing like this with a large screwdriver or prybar - you may need to give the prybar a sharp rap with a brass hammer

4   Remove the wheel.
5   Remove the driveaxle/hub nut and washer. To prevent the disc/hub from turning, wedge a long punch into the brake disc cooling vanes and allow it to rest against the caliper anchor **(see illustration)**.
6   To loosen the driveaxle from the hub splines, tap the end of the driveaxle with a soft-faced hammer or a hammer and a brass punch **(see illustration)**. **Note:** *Don't attempt to push the end of the driveaxle through the hub yet. Applying force to the end of the driveaxle, beyond just breaking it loose from the hub, can damage the driveaxle or transaxle.* If the driveaxle is stuck in the hub splines and won't move, it may be necessary to remove the brake disc (see Chapter 9) and push it from the hub with a two-jaw puller after Step 8 is performed.
7   Place a drain pan underneath the transaxle to catch the lubricant that will spill out when the driveaxles are removed.
8   Separate the strut from the steering knuckle (see Chapter 10).
9   Pull out on the steering knuckle and

detach the driveaxle from the hub **(see illustration)**. Don't let the driveaxle hang by the inner CV joint after the outer end has been detached from the steering knuckle, as the inner joint could become damaged. Support the outer end of the driveaxle with a piece of wire, if necessary.
10   Carefully pry the inner CV joint out of the transaxle **(see illustration)** or off the splined end of the intermediate shaft (right driveaxle only, on vehicles so equipped).
11   Refer to Chapter 7 for the driveaxle oil seal replacement procedure.

Installation

12   Installation is the reverse of the removal procedure, but with the following additional points:

a) *Seat the inner CV joint in the differential side gear by positioning the end of a large screwdriver in the groove in the CV joint housing and tapping it into position with a hammer. Once this has been done pull out on the joint housing to make sure the retaining ring has seated.*

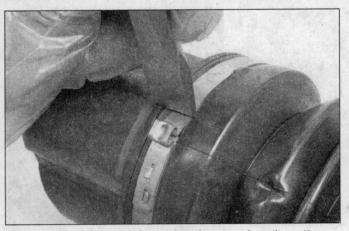

11.3a Cut off the boot seal retaining clamps, using wire cutters or a chisel and hammer

11.3b Slide the housing off the spider assembly

b) *Tighten the strut-to-knuckle bolts/nuts to the torque listed in the Chapter 10 Specifications.*
c) *Install a new driveaxle/hub nut and tighten it to the torque listed in this Chapter's Specifications.*
d) *Install the wheel and lug nuts, lower the vehicle and tighten the lug nuts to the torque listed in the Chapter 1 Specifications.*
e) *Check the transaxle lubricant and add, if necessary, to bring it to the proper level (see Chapter 1).*

10   Intermediate shaft - removal and installation

1   Loosen the right front wheel lug nuts. Raise the vehicle and support it securely on jackstands. Remove the right wheel.
2   Remove the right driveaxle assembly (see Section 9).
3   Unbolt the intermediate shaft support bracket from the engine block.

4   Carefully pull the intermediate shaft assembly from the transaxle. Make sure the splines on the inner end of the shaft don't damage the side-gear seal lip. Remove the intermediate shaft assembly.
5   Turn the shaft and verify that the bearing is in good condition. If the bearing makes grinding noises when the shaft is turned, have the bearing pressed off and a new one installed by an automotive machine shop.
6   Installation is the reverse of removal. Be sure to tighten the intermediate shaft support bolts to the torque listed in this Chapter's Specifications.

11   Driveaxle boot - replacement

Note: *If the CV joint boots must be replaced, explore all options before beginning the job. Complete rebuilt driveaxles are available on an exchange basis, which eliminates much time and work. Whichever route you choose to take, check on the cost and availability of parts before disassembling the vehicle.*

1   Remove the driveaxle (see Section 10).
2   Place the driveaxle in a vise lined with rags to avoid damage to the axleshaft. Check the CV joint for excessive play in the radial direction, which indicates worn parts. Check for smooth operation throughout the full range of motion for each CV joint. If a boot is torn, disassemble the joint, clean the components and inspect for damage due to loss of lubrication and possible contamination by foreign matter.

Inner CV joint

Refer to illustrations 11.3a through 11.3w
Note: *Some 1995 models use a "ball-and-cage" type inner CV joint instead of the usual tripot design. Aside from a wire retainer ring which must be removed before the ball-and-cage assembly can be removed from the CV joint housing, this unit is similar in construction to the outer CV joint, which is covered in the sequence beginning with illustration 11.4a.*
3   To replace the inner boot, refer to the accompanying illustrations **(see illustrations 11.3a through 11.3w).**

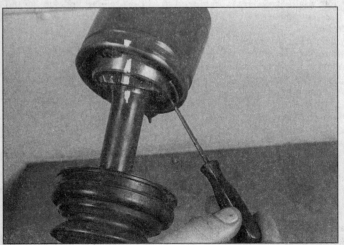

11.3c On models with a ball-and-cage inner joint, pry out the wire ring bearing retainer with a screwdriver

11.3d Slide the boot towards the center of the driveaxle

11.3e If the spider is positioned by a stop ring, spread the ends of the stop ring apart and slide it towards the center of the shaft

11.3f If the spider is not positioned by a stop ring, make a mark on the axleshaft (such as the white paint mark shown here), measure the distance from your mark to the tripot, and jot down this measurement for reassembly; when it's reinstalled, the spider must be placed in exactly the same position on the axleshaft splines

11.3g Slide the spider assembly back to expose the retaining ring and pry off the ring

11.3h Carefully tap the spider off the axleshaft with a brass punch (but don't hit it so hard that it flies off, or you'll be picking up needle bearings!)

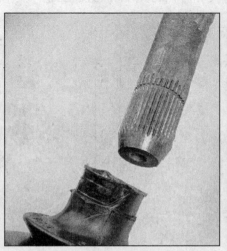

11.3i When you slide the spider off the driveaxle, hold the bearings in place with your hand; even better, use tape or a cloth wrapped around the spider bearing assembly to retain them

11.3j Slide the boot off the axleshaft (and the stop ring, if equipped)

11.3k Clean all of the old grease out of the housing and spider assembly, then remove each bearing, one at time

11.3l Carefully disassemble each section of the spider assembly, clean the needle bearings with solvent and inspect the rollers, spider cross, bearings and housing for scoring, pitting and other signs of abnormal wear

11.3m Apply a coat of CV joint grease to the inner bearing surfaces to hold the needle bearings in place and slide the bearing over them

11.3n Wrap the axleshaft splines with tape to avoid damaging the boot, then slide the small clamp and boot onto the axleshaft

11.3o Slide the spider stop ring, if equipped, onto the axleshaft, past the groove in which it seats

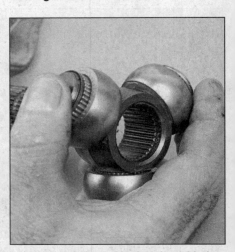

11.3p Install the spider bearing with the recess in the counterbore facing the end of the driveaxle

11.3q Use a screwdriver to install the spider retaining ring, then slide the spider assembly against it and install the stop ring, if equipped, in its groove; on units with no stop ring, position the spider the same distance from your mark that it was at prior to disassembly

11.3r Pack the housing with half of the grease furnished with the new boot and place the remainder in the boot

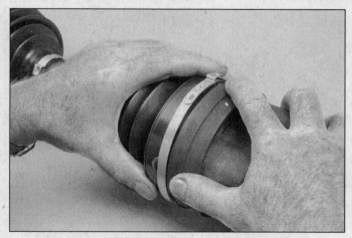

11.3s With the retaining clamps in place (but not tightened), install the tripot housing

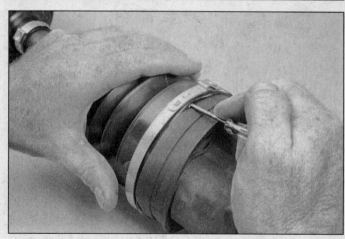

11.3t Seat the boot in the housing and axle seal grooves - a small screwdriver can make the job easier (make sure the boot isn't dimpled, stretched or out of shape)

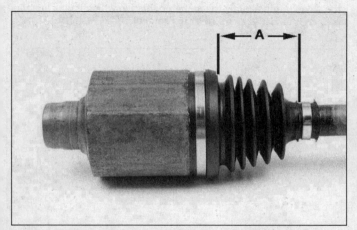

11.3u BEFORE tightening the clamps, adjust the length of the joint so that the indicated distance (measured from the inner ridge for the small clamp to the edge of the end of the boot folds on 1998 and later 2.2L models . . .

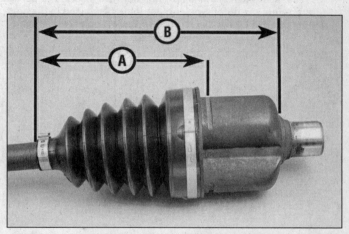

11.3v . . . or from the small end of the boot to the groove in the CV joint housing [A] on all others except 1995 models with tripot inner joints - on those models, measure dimension B) is the same as the dimension listed in this Chapter's Specifications

11.3w With the joint at the proper length, equalize the pressure in the boot by inserting a small screwdriver between the boot and the housing, then secure the boot clamps with special pliers (available at auto parts stores)

Outer CV joint

Refer to illustrations 11.4a through 11.4u

4 Refer to the accompanying illustrations and perform the outer CV joint boot replacement procedure (**see illustrations 11.4a through 11.4v**).

11.4a Cut off the band retaining the boot to the shaft, then slide the boot toward the center of the shaft

11.4b Some outer CV joints can be removed by spreading apart the ends of an internal snap-ring, then sliding off (or tapping off, if necessary) the CV joint assembly (you can identify this type by the large recess into which the snap-ring pliers are inserted to spread the snap-ring; the other type of outer joint, discussed in the next caption, doesn't have this recess, so there's no way to spread the snap-ring)

11.4c On joints that aren't retained by a snap-ring, clean all grease off the axleshaft and paint a mark on the shaft, then measure the distance from your mark to the face of the inner race and record this measurement; the inner race must be installed on the axleshaft in exactly the same position in which it was installed prior to removal

11.4d Outer CV joints without a recess for spreading apart the internal snap-ring must be removed with a slide hammer; you'll need an adapter) and a slide hammer setup such as the one shown here

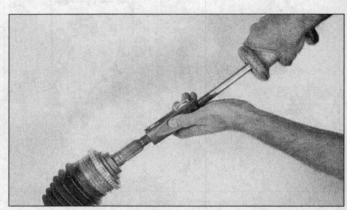

11.4e With the axleshaft firmly clamped down in a bench vise and the adapter gripping the driveaxle/hub nut, carefully extract the outer CV joint from the axleshaft

11.4f Press down on the inner race far enough to allow a ball bearing to be removed - if it's difficult to tilt, gently tap the cage and inner race with a brass punch and hammer

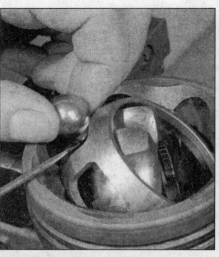

11.4g Pry the balls out of the cage, one at a time

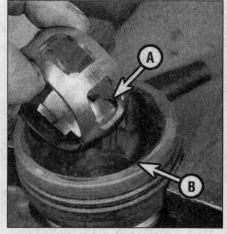

11.4h Tilt the inner race and cage 90-degrees, then align the windows in the cage (A) with the lands of the housing (B) and rotate the inner race up and out of the outer race

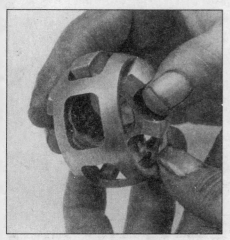

11.4i Align the inner race lands with the cage window and rotate the inner race out of the cage

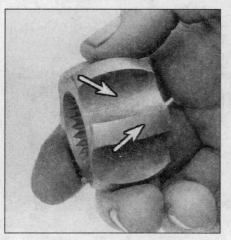

11.4j After cleaning the components with solvent, check the inner race lands and grooves for pitting and score marks

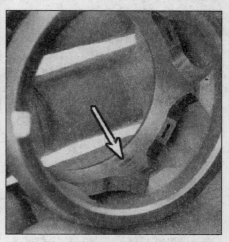

11.4k Check the cage for cracks, pitting and score marks - shiny spots are normal and don't affect operation

11.4l With the race and cage tilted at 90-degrees, lower the assembly into the housing

11.4m Rotate the assembly by gently tapping with a hammer and brass punch, then . . .

11.4n . . . press the balls into the cage windows, repeating until all of the balls are installed

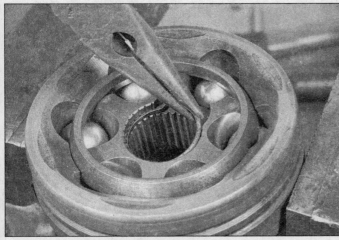

11.4o On models so equipped, use needle-nose pliers to lower a new snap-ring into the groove . . .

11.4p . . . then seat it into the groove with snap-ring pliers

11.4q Apply grease through the splined hole, then insert a wooden dowel (with a diameter slightly less than that of the axle) through the splined hole and push down - the dowel will force the grease into the joint - repeat until the bearing is completely packed

11.4r Install the small clamp and the boot on the driveaxle and apply grease to the inside of the axle boot until . . .

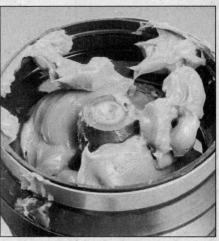

11.4s . . . the level is up to the end of axle

11.4t Position the CV joint assembly on the driveaxle, aligning the splines, then use a soft-face hammer to drive the joint onto the driveaxle until the snap-ring is seated in the groove (models with a snap-ring) or until the inner race of the joint is the same distance from the paint mark (applied as in Step 11.4) as it was on removal

11.4u Seat the inner end of the boot in the groove and install the retaining clamp, then do the same on the other end of the boot - tighten boot clamps with the special tool (see illustration 11.3w)

Chapter 9   Brakes

Contents

Specifications

General

Brake fluid type	See Chapter 1

Disc brakes

Pad minimum thickness	See Chapter 1
Disc minimum thickness	Refer to the dimension cast into the disc
Disc runout (maximum)	0.003 inch
Disc thickness variation (maximum)	0.0005 inch

Rear drum brakes

Shoe lining minimum thickness	See Chapter 1
Drum maximum diameter	Refer to the dimension cast into the drum
Drum taper (maximum)	0.003 inch
Out-of-round (maximum)	0.002 inch

Torque specifications

	Ft-lbs (unless otherwise indicated)
Brake hose-to-caliper banjo bolt	33
Caliper mounting bolts	38
Wheel cylinder-to-backing plate bolts	180 in-lbs
Master cylinder-to-power brake booster nuts	20
Power brake booster retaining nuts	20

1   General information

All vehicles covered by this manual are equipped with hydraulically operated front and rear brake systems. The front brakes are disc type, and the rear brakes are drum type. All brakes are self-adjusting.

The hydraulic system consists of two separate circuits. The master cylinder has separate reservoirs for the two circuits; in the event of a leak or failure in one hydraulic circuit, the other circuit will remain operative. A visual warning of circuit failure, air in the system, or other pressure differential conditions in the brake system is given by a warning light activated by a failure warning switch in the master cylinder.

The parking brake mechanically operates the rear brakes only. It's activated by a pull-handle in the center console between the front seats.

The power brake booster, located in the engine compartment on the firewall, uses engine manifold vacuum and atmospheric pressure to provide assistance to the hydraulically operated brakes.

After completing any operation involving the disassembly of any part of the brake system, always test drive the vehicle to check for proper braking performance before resuming normal driving. Test the brakes while driving on a clean, dry, flat surface. Conditions other than these can lead to inaccurate test results. Test the brakes at various speeds with both light and heavy pedal pressure. The vehicle should stop evenly without pulling to one side or the other. Avoid locking the brakes because this slides the tires and diminishes braking efficiency and control.

Tires, vehicle load and front end alignment are factors which also affect braking performance.

2   Anti-lock Brake System (ABS) and Enhanced Traction System (ETS) - general information

Anti-lock Brake System (ABS)

Refer to illustrations 2.2, 2.4a and 2.4b

A four-wheel Anti-lock Brake System (ABS) maintains vehicle maneuverability, directional stability, and optimum deceleration under severe braking conditions on most road surfaces. It does so by monitoring the rotational speed of the wheels and controlling the brake line pressure to the wheels during braking. This prevents the wheels from locking up on slippery roads or during hard braking.

On 1995 through 1999 models, the hydraulic control unit/motor pack assembly (see illustration), which is located in the left front corner of the engine compartment, is bolted to the left side of the master cylinder. The control unit/motor pack controls hydraulic pressure to the front calipers and rear wheel cylinders by modulating hydraulic pressure to prevent wheel lock-up.

On 1995 through 1999 models, the Electronic Brake Control Module (EBCM) is located above the left (driver's side) kick panel. The EBCM monitors the ABS system and controls the anti-lock valve solenoids. It accepts and processes information received from the brake switch and wheel speed sensors to control the hydraulic line pressure and avoid wheel lock-up. It also monitors the system and stores fault codes which indicates specific problems.

On 2000 and later models, the Electronic Brake Control Module/Brake Pressure Modulator Valve (EBCM/BPMV) is a separate unit that is located to the left side of the master cylinder. This system operates the ABS system in the same manner as the previous two different assemblies.

Each wheel speed sensor assembly consists of a variable reluctance sensor and a "toothed ring," with an air gap between them. The front wheel speed sensors (see illustration) are mounted on the inner side of each steering knuckle; the toothed rings are installed on the outer CV joints. The rear sensors (see illustration) are installed in the rear brake backing plates; the toothed rings are installed on the back side of each hub and bearing unit. The air gap between the sensors and the toothed rings is not adjustable, and the sensors themselves are not rebuildable. If a rear sensor or ring malfunctions, the entire hub and bearing assembly must be replaced. The front sensor can be replaced separately.

A wheel speed sensor measures wheel speed by monitoring the rotation of the

2.2 The hydraulic control unit/motor pack assembly is an integral part of the master cylinder assembly (1995 through 1999)

2.4a The front wheel speed sensors are mounted on the inner side of the steering knuckles, in close proximity to the toothed rings on the outer CV joints

2.4b The rear wheel speed sensors are mounted in the rear drum brake backing plates; the toothed rings (not visible in this photo) are installed on the inner side of the flange for each hub and bearing unit

toothed ring. As the teeth of the ring move through the magnetic field of the sensor, an AC voltage is generated. This signal frequency increases or decreases in proportion to the speed of the wheel. The EBCM monitors these three signals for changes in wheel speed; if it detects the sudden deceleration of a wheel, i.e. wheel lockup, the EBCM activates the ABS system.

The ABS system has self-diagnostic capabilities. Each time the vehicle is started, the EBCM runs a self-test. The red BRAKE warning light should come on briefly then go out. The EBCM also monitors the ABS system continuously during vehicle operation. If the ABS INOP light on the dash comes on while you're driving, there is a fault somewhere in the ABS system and the ABS system may be inoperative, but the brakes should still function in their non-ABS mode. Take the vehicle to a dealer service department or other qualified repair shop immediately and have the ABS serviced.

If the ABS INOP light *flashes*, however, there is a more serious fault in the ABS system which may have affected the regular braking system. Pull over immediately and have the vehicle towed to a dealer or other qualified repair shop for service.

Although a special electronic tester is necessary to properly diagnose the system, the home mechanic can perform a few preliminary checks before taking the vehicle to a dealer service department or repair shop which is equipped with this tester.

a) Make sure the brake calipers are in good condition.
b) Check the electrical connector at the controller.
c) Check the fuses.
d) Follow the wiring harness to the speed sensors and brake light switch and make sure all connections are secure and the wiring isn't damaged.

If the above preliminary checks don't rectify the problem, the vehicle should be diagnosed by a dealer service department or other qualified repair shop.

Enhanced Traction System (ETS)

The Enhanced Traction System (ETS) limits wheel slip during acceleration by cutting fuel to certain cylinders, by retarding the ignition, by upshifting the transaxle, or by some combination of the three. The EBCM monitors wheel speed through the ABS wheel speed sensors. When one or more wheels begins to spin faster than the others, the EBCM calculates the reduction in torque needed to stop wheelspin and restore traction. Depending on the torque reduction necessary, the calculated torque reduction is some combination of fuel cutoff, spark retard, and/or upshifting the transaxle. This recommendation is relayed from the EBCM to the Power Train Control Module (PCM), which manipulates fuel cutoff and spark retard to produce the requisite torque. If the wheels still spin, the PCM requests an upshift to the next higher gear.

3   Disc brake pads - replacement

Refer to illustrations 3.3 and 3.4a through 3.4j
Warning: *Disc brake pads must be replaced on both front wheels at the same time - never replace the pads on only one wheel. Also, the dust created by the brake system is harmful to your health. Never blow it out with compressed air and don't inhale any of it. An approved filtering mask should be worn when working on the brakes. Do not, under any circumstances, use petroleum-based solvents to clean brake parts. Use brake system cleaner only!*
1   Loosen the front wheel lug nuts, raise the front of the vehicle and support it securely on jackstands. Apply the parking brake. Remove the front wheels.
2   Remove about two-thirds of the fluid from the master cylinder reservoir and discard it. **Caution:** *Do not spill brake fluid on painted surfaces.* Position a drain pan under the brake assembly and clean the caliper and surrounding area with brake system cleaner.
3   Position a large C-clamp over the caliper and squeeze the piston back into its bore **(see illustration)** to provide room for the new brake pads. As the piston is depressed to the bottom of its caliper bore, the fluid in the master cylinder will rise. Make sure it doesn't overflow. If necessary, siphon off some of the fluid.
4   Work on one brake assembly at a time. Follow the accompanying photos, beginning with **illustration 3.4a**. Be sure to stay in order and read the caption under each illustration.
5   While the pads are removed, inspect the caliper for seal leaks (evidenced by moisture around the piston boot) and for any damage to the piston dust boots. If excessive moisture is evident, rebuild the caliper (see Section 4). When you're done, make sure you tighten the caliper bolts to the torque listed in this Chapter's Specifications.

3.3 Depress the piston into the caliper with a large C-clamp

3.4c While you're replacing the pads, hang the caliper with a piece of wire

3.4a Before getting started, wash the front brake assembly with brake cleaner to protect yourself from brake dust, which might contain asbestos, a known carcinogen

3.4b To detach the front caliper from the steering knuckle, remove these two bolts (upper and lower arrows); don't remove the banjo bolt (center arrow) for the brake hose unless you intend to overhaul the caliper

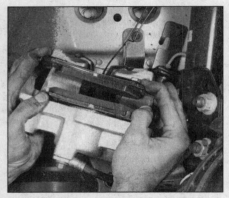

3.4d Remove the outer brake pad

3.4e Remove the inner brake pad

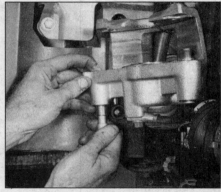

3.4f Pull the two caliper guide pins out of their sleeves, clean them, inspect them for wear, replacing as necessary . . .

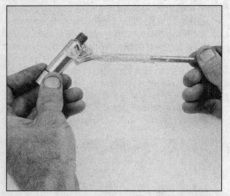

3.4g . . . then lubricate them with silicone grease and install them in the caliper

3.4h Apply anti-squeal compound to the backing plates of the new pads

3.4i Install the new inner pad

6   Install the brake pads on the opposite wheel, then install the wheels and lower the vehicle. Tighten the lug nuts to the torque listed in the Chapter 1 Specifications.

7   Pump the brakes several times to seat the pads against the disc, then check the fluid level and add some, if necessary (see Chapter 1).

8   Check the operation of the brakes before driving the vehicle in traffic. Try to avoid heavy brake applications until the brakes have been applied lightly several times to seat the pads.

4   Disc brake caliper - removal, overhaul and installation

Warning: *The dust created by the brake system is harmful to your health. Never blow it out with compressed air and don't inhale any of it. An approved filtering mask should be worn when working on the brakes. Do not, under any circumstances, use petroleum-based solvents to clean brake parts. Use brake system cleaner only!*

Note: *If an overhaul is indicated (usually because of fluid leaks, a stuck piston or broken bleeder screw) explore all options before beginning this procedure. New and factory rebuilt calipers are available on an exchange*

basis, which makes this job quite easy. If you decide to rebuild the calipers, make sure rebuild kits are available before proceeding. Always rebuild or replace the calipers in pairs - never rebuild just one of them.

Removal

1   Remove the cover from the brake fluid reservoir and siphon off two-thirds of the fluid into a container and discard it.

2   Loosen the wheel lug nuts, raise the front or rear of the vehicle and place it securely on jackstands. Remove the front or rear wheel.

3   Reinstall one wheel lug nut (flat side toward the disc) to hold the disc in place. Don't remove both calipers at the same time. Instead, remove only one caliper at a time so you can use the other assembled unit for reference.

4   Push the caliper piston back into its bore with a C-clamp **(see illustration 3.3)**. As the piston is depressed to the bottom of the caliper bore, the fluid in the master cylinder will rise. Make sure that it does not overflow.

5   Remove the banjo fitting bolt holding the brake hose, then remove and discard the sealing washers found on either side of the

3.4j Install the new outer pad, then install the caliper and tighten the caliper guide pins to the torque listed in this Chapter's Specifications

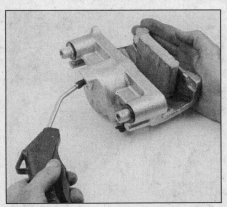

4.10 Using a block of wood as a cushion, ease the piston out of the caliper bore with compressed air

4.11 Pry the dust boot out of the caliper bore with a screwdriver - make sure you don't nick or gouge anything

4.12 To remove the seal from the caliper bore, use a plastic or wooden tool, such as a pencil

4.16 Lubricate the piston bore and seal with clean brake fluid before installing the new seal in the caliper bore groove

4.17 Install a new dust boot in the piston groove

4.18 Lubricate the piston with clean brake fluid, insert it squarely in the bore and carefully push it into the caliper

banjo fitting. Always use new sealing washers when reinstalling the brake hose.

6   To prevent brake fluid leakage and contamination, plug the openings in the caliper and brake hose. **Note:** *If you're just removing the caliper for access to other components, don't disconnect the hose.*

7   Remove the caliper (see Section 3) and separate the caliper from the disc.

8   Remove the brake pads from the caliper (see Section 3).

Overhaul

Refer to illustrations 4.10, 4.11, 4.12, 4.16, 4.17, 4.18 and 4.19

Note: *Purchase a brake caliper overhaul kit for your particular vehicle before beginning this procedure.*

9   Clean the exterior of the brake caliper with brake system cleaner (never use gasoline, kerosene or any petroleum-based solvents), then place the caliper on a clean workbench.

10   Place a wooden block or shop rag in the caliper as a cushion, then use compressed air to remove the piston from the caliper **(see illustration)**. Use only enough air pressure to ease the piston out of the bore. If the piston is blown out, even with the cushion in place, it may be damaged. **Warning:** *Never place*

your fingers in front of the piston in an attempt to catch or protect it when applying compressed air - serious injury could occur.

11   Carefully pry the dust boot out of the caliper bore **(see illustration)**.

12   Using a wooden or plastic tool, remove the piston seal from the groove in the caliper bore **(see illustration)**. Metal tools may cause bore damage.

13   Remove the caliper bleeder valve, then remove and discard the sleeves and bushings from the caliper ears. Also discard all rubber parts.

14   Clean the remaining parts with brake fluid or brake system cleaner. Allow them to drain and then shake them vigorously to remove as much fluid as possible.

15   Carefully examine the piston for nicks and burrs and loss of plating. If surface defects are present, parts must be replaced. Check the caliper bore in a similar way, but light polishing with crocus cloth is permissible to remove light corrosion and stains. Discard the mounting bolts if they are corroded or damaged.

16   When assembling, lubricate the piston bore and seal with clean brake fluid; position the seal in the caliper bore groove. Make sure the seal seats properly and isn't twisted **(see illustration)**.

17   Lubricate the piston with clean brake fluid, then install a new boot in the piston groove **(see illustration)**.

18   Insert the piston squarely into the caliper bore, then apply force to bottom the piston in the bore **(see illustration)**.

19   Position the dust boot in the caliper counterbore, then use a seal driver to drive it into position **(see illustration)**. If you don't have a seal driver, carefully tap the boot into place with a blunt punch, contacting only the

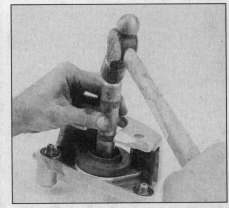

4.19 Use a hammer and seal driver to seat the boot in the caliper

5.5 Check the runout of the brake disc with a dial indicator

5.6a The minimum allowable thickness of the disc is cast into the hub area

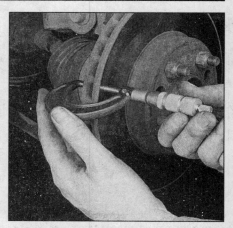

5.6b Use a micrometer to check the thickness of the disc and compare this measurement to the minimum allowable thickness cast into the disc

outer circumference (casing) of the boot. Make sure that the boot is evenly installed below the caliper face.

20   Install the bleeder valve.

21   Installation is the reverse of removal. Always use new sealing washers when connecting the brake hose. Tighten the caliper guide pins or mounting bolts to the torque listed in this Chapter's Specifications. Be sure to fill the master cylinder and bleed the brakes (see Section 10).

5   Brake disc - inspection, removal and installation

Refer to illustrations 5.5, 5.6a and 5.6b

1   Loosen the wheel lug nuts, raise the vehicle and place it securely on jackstands. Remove the wheel.

2   Remove the caliper assembly (see Section 4). It is not necessary to disconnect the brake hose. After removing the caliper mounting bolts, hang the caliper out of the way on a piece of wire. Never hang the caliper by the brake hose because damage to the hose will occur.

3   Inspect the disc surfaces. Light scoring or grooving is normal, but deep grooves or

severe erosion is not. If pulsating has been noticed during application of the brakes, suspect disc runout.

4   Reinstall the wheel lug nuts - flat side toward the disc - to hold the disc in a flat, vertical plane during the following inspection. You may have to place washers under the lug nuts in order for them to tighten onto the disc.

5   Attach a dial indicator to the caliper mounting bracket, turn the disc and note the amount of runout **(see illustration)**. Check both inner and outer surfaces. If the runout is more than the specified allowable maximum, the disc must be removed from the vehicle and taken to an automotive machine shop for resurfacing.

6   The minimum thickness of the disc is cast into the inside surface of the hub part of the disc **(see illustration)**. Using a micrometer, measure the thickness of the disc **(see illustration)**. If it is less than the specified minimum, replace the disc. Also measure the disc thickness at several points to determine variations in the surface. Any variation over 0.0005-inch may cause pedal pulsations during brake application. If this condition exists and the disc thickness is not below the minimum, the disc can be removed and taken to an automotive machine shop for resurfacing.

7   If the disc needs to be removed for repair or replacement, it can be pulled off after the lug nuts are removed.

6   Drum brake shoes - replacement

Refer to illustrations 6.4a through 6.4x, 6.5a through 6.5q and 6.6

Warning: *Drum brake shoes must be replaced on both rear wheels at the same time - never replace the shoes on only one wheel. Also, the dust created by the brake system is harmful to your health. Never blow it out with compressed air and don't inhale any of it. An approved filtering mask should be worn when working on the brakes. Do not, under any circumstances, use petroleum-based solvents to clean brake parts. Use brake cleaner only!*

Caution: *Whenever the brake shoes are replaced, the return and hold-down springs should also be replaced. Due to the continuous heating/cooling cycle the springs are subjected to, they lose tension over a period of time and may allow the shoes to drag on the drum and wear at a much faster rate than normal.*

Note: *All four rear shoes must be replaced at the same time, but to avoid mixing up parts, work on only one brake assembly at a time.*

1   Put the shift lever in Park (automatic transaxle) or Reverse (manual transaxle). Release the parking brake.

2   Loosen the wheel lug nuts, raise the rear of the vehicle and support it securely on jackstands. Block the front wheels to keep the vehicle from rolling off the jackstands. Remove the rear wheels.

3   Remove the brake drum. **Note:** *If the brake drum is stuck, make sure the parking brake is completely released, then apply some penetrating oil to the hub-to-brake drum joint. Allow the oil to soak in, then try to pull the drum off. If the drum still won't come off, the brake shoes will have to be retracted.*

6.4a Before removing anything, clean the brake assembly with brake system cleaner - DO NOT use compressed air to blow the dust out of the brake assembly!

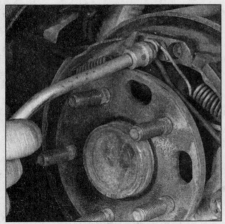

6.4b Remove the return springs with a brake spring tool

6.4c Remove the hold-down springs and pins by pushing the retainer in with and turning it 90-degrees - the tool shown here is available at most auto parts stores

6.4d Lift up on the actuator lever and remove the actuating link from the anchor pin pivot along with the actuator lever and return spring (arrows)

6.4e Spread the shoes apart at the top and remove the parking brake strut

6.4f With the shoe assembly spread to clear the hub flange, lift it away from the backing plate

6.4g Disconnect the parking brake lever from the cable and remove the shoe assembly

This is done by slackening the parking brake cables (see Section 12), then tapping off the brake drum with a rubber mallet.

4   To replace the brake shoes on 1995 through 2002 models, refer to the accompanying photographs, beginning with **illustra-**

tion 6.4a. Be sure to follow the sequence step-by-step and read each caption.
5   To replace the brake shoes on 2003 and

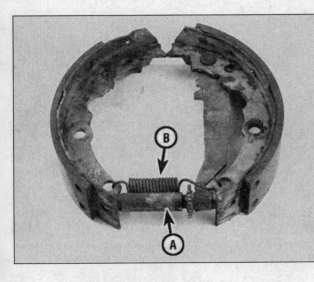

6.4h Remove the adjusting screw (A) and spring (B) from the shoe assembly - be sure to note the how they're positioned

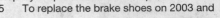

6.4i Remove the parking brake lever by prying off the C-clip

6.4j Install the parking brake lever on the new brake shoe and press the C-clip into place with needle-nose pliers

6.4k Lubricate the contact surfaces of the backing plate with high-temperature brake grease

6.4l Lubricate the adjuster screw threads and socket end prior to installation

6.4m Connect the parking brake lever to the cable

6.4n Spread the brake assembly apart sufficiently to clear the hub flange and raise it into position

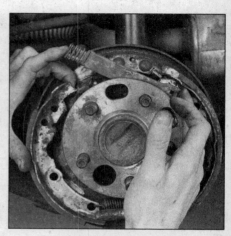

6.4o Install the parking brake strut and spring

later models, refer to the accompanying photographs, beginning with **illustration 6.5a**.
6   Before reinstalling the drum, check it for cracks, score marks, deep scratches and

hard spots, which will appear as blue discolored areas. If the hard spots can't be removed with fine emery cloth or if any of the other conditions listed above exist, the drum

6.4p Make sure the parking brake strut is positioned in the shoes properly (arrows)

6.4q Install the primary brake shoe hold-down pin and spring

6.4r Attach the actuator link and lever to the secondary brake shoe

6.4s Install the actuator lever
return spring

6.4t Install the secondary brake shoe
hold-down pin and spring

6.4u Install the return springs

6.4v Center the brake shoe assembly so the drum will
slide over it

6.4w Turn the adjusting screw so the drum fits snugly over the
shoes, then back-off the adjustment until the drum can be turned
without the shoes dragging

6.4x Remove the glaze from the drum
with sandpaper or emery cloth, using a
swirling motion

6.5a Brake drum
components (2003 and
later models)

1   Leading shoe
2   Parking brake lever
3   Actuator spring
4   Wheel cylinder
5   Adjuster actuator
6   Adjuster screw
    assembly
7   Trailing shoe
8   Retractor spring

6.5b Disconnect the actuator spring from the adjuster actuator

6.5c Pull the retractor spring out of its hole in the trailing shoe . . .

6.5d . . . and also from the leading shoe

6.5e Unscrew the bolt that retains the guide for the parking brake cable

6.5f Remove the trailing shoe and adjuster actuator, then the adjuster screw assembly (arrow)

6.5g Pull the retractor spring out of the way, then remove the leading shoe and parking brake lever

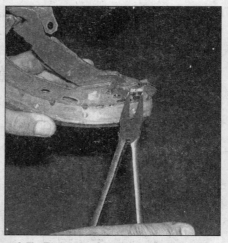

6.5h Force the C-clip off the post and detach the leading shoe from the parking brake lever. Note: *It isn't necessary to detach the parking brake cable from the lever*

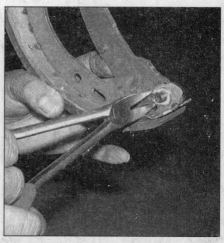

6.5i Attach the new leading shoe to the parking brake lever and secure it with a new C-clip

6.5j Clean the backing plate, then lubricate the shoe contact areas with a thin film of high-temperature grease

6.5k Position the leading shoe on the backing plate and install the end of the retractor spring in its hole

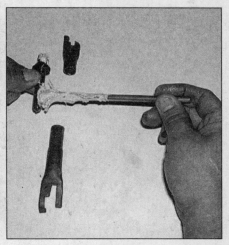

6.5l Clean the adjuster screw assembly, then lubricate the threads and socket end with high-temperature grease

6.5m Install the adjuster screw assembly, making sure that it engages correctly with the leading shoe and the parking brake lever

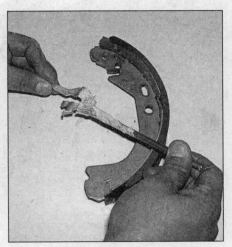

6.5n Lubricate the adjuster actuator . . .

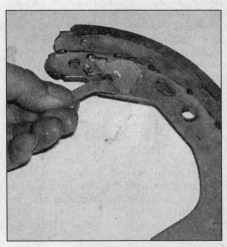

6.5o . . . and install it on the trailing shoe

6.5p Position the trailing shoe on the backing plate, making that that it (and the adjuster actuator) engage correctly with the adjuster screw assembly, then insert the retractor spring into its hole in the shoe

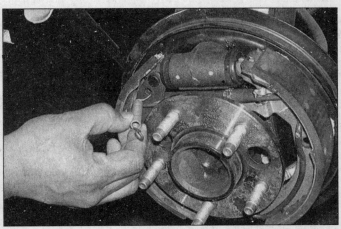

6.5q Insert the actuator spring into its hole in the leading shoe, then stretch it across and connect it to the adjuster actuator. Install the parking brake cable guide to the anchor at the bottom of the shoes and tighten the bolt securely

6.6 The maximum allowable diameter is cast into the brake drum

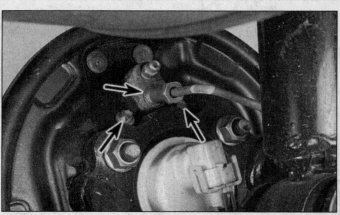

7.2 Unscrew the brake line fitting (upper arrow) from the rear of the wheel cylinder with a flare-nut wrench to prevent rounding off the corners of the nut, then remove the wheel cylinder retaining bolts (lower arrows)

must be taken to an automotive machine shop to have it resurfaced. **Note:** *The drums should be resurfaced, regardless of the surface appearance, to impart a smooth finish and ensure a perfectly round drum (which will eliminate brake pedal pulsations related to out-of-round drums). At the very least, if you don't have the drums resurfaced, remove the glaze from the surface with sandpaper or emery cloth using a swirling motion. If the drum won't "clean up" before the maximum (discard) diameter is reached in the machining operation, install a new one. The maximum diameter is cast into each brake drum* **(see illustration).**

7   Install the brake drum. If the shoes are still interfering with the drum, retract them (see Step 4 in Section 12). When the drum is turned, make sure the shoes don't drag on the drum.

8   Mount the wheel, install the lug nuts, then lower the vehicle.

9   Make a number of forward and reverse stops to adjust the brakes until satisfactory pedal feel is obtained. After adjustment, make sure that both wheels turn freely.

7   Wheel cylinder - removal, overhaul and installation

Refer to illustrations 7.2 and 7.5
Note: *Obtain a wheel cylinder rebuild kit before beginning this procedure.*

1   Remove the brake shoes (see Section 6).

2   Remove the brake line fitting from the rear of the wheel cylinder **(see illustration).** Use a flare-nut wrench, if available, to prevent rounding off the corners of the fitting. Cap the brake line to prevent contamination and excessive fluid loss.

3   Remove the wheel cylinder retaining bolts from the rear of the backing plate.

4   Remove the cylinder and place it on a clean workbench.

5   Remove the bleeder valve, seals, pistons, boots and spring assembly from the

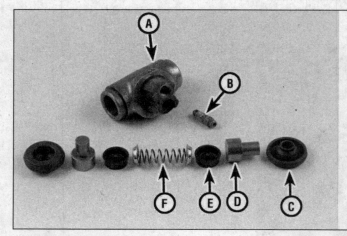

7.5 A typical wheel cylinder assembly

A   Wheel cylinder body
B   Bleeder screw
C   Boot
D   Piston
E   Seal
F   Spring

cylinder body **(see illustration).**

6   Clean the wheel cylinder with brake fluid or brake system cleaner. Do not, under any circumstances, use petroleum-based solvents to clean brake parts.

7   Use filtered, unlubricated compressed air to remove excess fluid from the wheel cylinder and to blow out the passages.

8   Check the cylinder bore for corrosion and scoring. Crocus cloth may be used to remove light corrosion and stains, but the cylinder must be replaced with a new one if the defects cannot be removed easily, or if the bore is scored.

9   Lubricate the new seals with clean brake fluid.

10   Assemble the brake cylinder, making sure the lips of the seals face inward, and the boots are properly seated.

11   Place the wheel cylinder in position on the backing plate. Thread the brake line fitting into the cylinder, being careful not to cross-thread it. Don't tighten the fitting yet.

12   Install the wheel cylinder retaining bolts and tighten them to the torque listed in this Chapter's Specifications. Now tighten the brake line fitting securely.

13   Bleed the brake system (see Section 10).

8   Master cylinder - removal and installation

Caution: On 1995 through 1999 models, *the master cylinder and ABS hydraulic unit/motor pack can be detached from the power brake booster as a single assembly, but the master cylinder itself must not be detached from the hydraulic unit/motor pack. If the master cylinder must be unbolted from the hydraulic unit/motor pack, it must be done at a dealer service department, after the dealer has used a Tech-1 scan tool to relieve tension on the gears inside the ABS unit. This procedure can only be performed with the master cylinder/hydraulic unit/motor pack assembly operational. If the master cylinder must be replaced (unbolted from the hydraulic unit/motor pack), have it done by a dealer service department or other qualified repair shop.*

Removal

Refer to illustrations 8.3 and 8.4

1   Completely cover the front fender and cowling area of the vehicle; brake fluid can ruin painted surfaces if it is spilled.

2   Remove the brake fluid from the master

8.3 Unplug the electrical connectors for the fluid level warning switch (center arrow) and the ABS solenoids (two right arrows); to detach the master cylinder from the power brake booster, remove the two mounting nuts (upper arrows) (1995 through 1999)

8.4 Unscrew the four brake line fittings with a flare-nut wrench (1995 through 1999)

cylinder reservoir and discard it. **Caution:** *Do not spill brake fluid on painted surfaces.* Place a drain pan or bundle of rags or newspapers under the master cylinder assembly and clean the area around the brake line fittings with brake system cleaner.

3   On 1995 through 1999 models, unplug the electrical connectors for the fluid warning switch and the ABS solenoids **(see illustration)**. On 2000 and later models, unplug the electrical connector for the fluid warning switch.

4   Disconnect the brake line fittings **(see illustration)**. Use a flare-nut wrench, if available, to prevent rounding off the corners of the fittings. Rags or newspapers should be placed under the master cylinder to soak up the fluid that will drain out.

5   Remove the two master cylinder mounting nuts **(see illustration 8.3)**, and remove the master cylinder from the vehicle. Do not bend the hydraulic lines running to the combination valve. Plug the ends of both of the lines immediately to prevent air from entering the ABS modulator and to protect the system from moisture and dirt.

Installation

6   Anytime the master cylinder is removed, the brake hydraulic system must be bled. It's much easier to bleed the rest of the system quickly and effectively if you "bench bleed" the master cylinder before installing it on the vehicle. Bench bleed the master cylinder as follows.

7   Insert threaded plugs of the correct size into the four brake line outlet holes (1995 through 1999 models), or two brake line outlet holes (2000 and later models). Fill the reservoir with brake fluid (the master cylinder should be supported in such a manner that brake fluid will not spill out during the bench bleeding procedure).

8   Loosen one plug at a time and push the piston assembly into the bore to force air from the master cylinder. To prevent air from being drawn back into the cylinder, the

appropriate plug must be tightened before allowing the piston to return to its original position.

9   Stroke the piston three or four times for each outlet to assure that all air has been expelled.

10   Refill the master cylinder reservoirs and install the diaphragm and cap assembly. **Note:** *The reservoir should only be filled to the top of the reservoir divider to prevent overflowing when the cap and diaphragm are installed.*

11   The remainder of installation is the reverse of removal. Make sure you bleed the rest of the system when you're done (see Section 10).

9   Brake hoses and lines - inspection and replacement

Inspection

1   About every six months, loosen the wheel lug nuts, raise the vehicle, place it securely on jackstands, remove the wheels, and inspect the flexible hoses which connect the steel brake lines with the front and rear brake assemblies. Look for cracks, chafing, leaks, blisters and any other damage. These are important and vulnerable parts of the brake system, so your inspection should be thorough. You'll need a flashlight and mirror to do the job right. If a hose exhibits any of the above conditions, replace it as follows.

Brake hose

Refer to illustrations 9.2 and 9.3

2   Using an open-end wrench on the hose fitting to keep the hose from turning, disconnect the brake line from the hose fitting, being careful not to bend the frame bracket or brake line **(see illustration)**.

3   Use pliers to remove the U-clip from the female fitting at the bracket **(see illustration)**, then remove the hose from the bracket.

4   At the caliper end of the hose, remove

9.2 Using an open-end wrench on the brake hose, loosen the brake line from the hose fitting with a flare-nut wrench, being careful not to bend the frame bracket or brake line

9.3 Use pliers to remove the U-clip from the female fitting at the bracket, then remove the hose from the bracket

the banjo bolt from the fitting block, then remove the hose and the sealing washers on either side of the fitting block.

5   When installing the hose, always use new sealing washers on either side of the fitting block and lubricate all bolt threads with clean brake fluid before installing them.

6   With the fitting flange engaged with the caliper locating ledge, attach the hose to the caliper and tighten it to the torque listed in this Chapter's Specifications.

7   Without twisting the hose, install the female fitting in the hose bracket (it will fit the bracket in only one position).

8   Install the U-clip retaining the female fitting to the frame bracket.

9   Attach the brake line to the hose fitting and tighten it securely.

10   When the brake hose installation is complete, there should be no kinks in the hose. Also make sure that the hose does not contact any part of the suspension. If you're replacing a front brake hose, verify this by turning the wheels to the extreme left and right positions. If the hose contacts anything, disconnect it and correct the installation as necessary.

11   Fill the master cylinder reservoir and bleed the system (see Section 10).

Steel brake lines

12   When replacing brake lines, be sure to buy the correct replacement parts. Don't use copper or any other tubing for brake lines.

13   Prefabricated brake lines, with the ends already flared and fittings installed, are available at auto parts stores and dealer service departments. If necessary, carefully bend the line to the proper shape. A tube bender is recommended for this. **Caution:** *Don't crimp or damage the line.*

14   When installing the new line, make sure it's securely supported in the brackets with plenty of clearance between moving or hot components.

15   After installation, check the master cylinder fluid level and add fluid as necessary. Bleed the brake system as outlined in the next Section and test the brakes carefully before driving the vehicle in traffic.

---

10   Brake hydraulic system - bleeding

Refer to illustration 10.28

1   Bleeding the hydraulic system is necessary to remove air whenever it is introduced into the brake system.

2   The manufacturer specifies that it will be necessary to bleed the *entire* system whenever air is allowed into *any* part of the system.

3   Before beginning the bleeding procedure, the ABS pistons in the hydraulic unit must be returned to the top of their travel. To do this, start the engine and let it run for 10 seconds. Watch the ABS light - it should turn off after three seconds or so. **Warning:** *If the light doesn't go off, a GM Tech 1 scan tool must be connected to diagnose the problem.*

Have the vehicle towed to a dealer service department or other repair shop equipped with the necessary tool.

4   If the light turned off like it is supposed to, turn the ignition off and repeat the procedure. If the light goes off again after three seconds, the brakes can now be bled.

5   Have an assistant on hand, as well as a supply of new brake fluid, an empty clear container, a length of clear plastic tubing to fit over the bleeder valve and a wrench to open and close the bleeder valve.

6   Remove the cap from the brake fluid reservoir and add fluid, if necessary (see Chapter 1). Don't allow the fluid level to drop too low during this procedure - check it frequently. Reinstall the cap.

7   Bleed the master cylinder as follows:

1995 through 1999 models
Models without bleeder valves on the hydraulic modulator

8   Disconnect the two forward brake lines from the master cylinder with a flare-nut wrench **(see illustration 8.4)**.

9   Fill the reservoir with brake fluid until fluid begins to flow from the two forward outlets.

10   Reconnect the forward lines to the master cylinder and tighten the tube nut fittings.

11   Slowly depress and hold down the brake pedal.

12   Loosen the fittings again and allow any air in the fluid to be purged, then retighten the fittings.

13   Slowly release the pedal and wait 15 seconds.

14   Repeat this procedure until all air is removed from the two front outlets.

15   Disconnect the two rear tube nut fittings and repeat this procedure until all air is expelled from those ports as well. Proceed to Step 17.

Models with bleeder valves on the hydraulic modulator

16   Attach the bleeder hose to the rearmost bleeder valve on the modulator assembly. With the other end of the hose in a jar partially filled with clean brake fluid, open the valve slowly and have an assistant depress the brake pedal. Keep the pedal down until fluid flows. Close the valve and release the brake pedal. Repeat this until no air is evident as the fluid enters the jar, then repeat the procedure for the forward bleeder valve. After bleeding the hydraulic modulator assembly, bleed the rest of the braking systems as described below.

2000 and later models

17   Make sure that the brake master cylinder is filled to the MAX line with the specified brake fluid.

18   Make sure that the rear brake line fitting at the master cylinder is tight. Loosen and disconnect the front brake line fitting from the front port of the master cylinder, wait until some brake fluid bleeds out of the port, then

reconnect and tighten the fitting.

19   Have a helper slowly press the brake pedal down as far as it will go and then hold it there.

20   Loosen the front brake line fitting again, this time just enough to allow brake fluid and bubbles escape. Then tighten the fitting again and have the helper slowly release the brake pedal.

21   Wait 15 seconds, then repeat this procedure several more times until all air bubbles have been bled from the front port of the master cylinder.

22   Once all the air has been purged from the front port, top up the master cylinder and repeat this entire procedure at the rear brake port. Repeat as many times as necessary until all air has been bled from the rear port.

23   After both ports have been bled of all air, make sure that both brake line connections are tight.

All models

24   When all air has been removed from the master cylinder, slowly depress the brake pedal and verify that the pedal feels firm. If it does, you're done. If it doesn't, proceed to the next step and bleed the rest of the system.

25   Check the fluid level again, adding fluid as necessary. Do not use old brake fluid. It contains moisture which will allow the fluid to boil, rendering the brakes useless. When bleeding, make sure the fluid coming out of the bleeder is not only free of bubbles, but clean also.

26   Raise the vehicle and support it securely on jackstands.

27   Beginning at the right rear brake, loosen the bleeder screw slightly, then tighten it to a point where it's snug but can still be loosened quickly and easily.

28   Place one end of the tubing over the bleeder screw and submerge the other end in brake fluid in the container **(see illustration)**.

10.28 When bleeding the brakes, a hose is connected to the bleeder screw and then submerged in brake fluid - air will be seen as bubbles in the tube and container (all air must be expelled before moving to the next brake or component)

11.7 To detach the power brake booster from the firewall, remove these two lower nuts (arrows) and the two upper nuts (not visible in this photo)

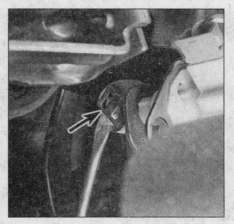

11.8 The booster pushrod is attached to a pin at the top of the brake pedal; the pushrod is retained by a small spring clip which can be pried off with a screwdriver

12.4 To adjust either rear brake assembly, push the actuator off the star wheel with a screwdriver (the actuator must be held off the star wheel to turn the wheel counterclockwise), then rotate the star wheel adjuster counterclockwise to retract the brake shoes, or clockwise to expand the shoes (1995 through 2002 models)

29   Open the bleeder screw and have your assistant slowly depress the brake pedal and hold the pedal firmly depressed. Watch for air bubbles to exit the submerged end of the tube. When the fluid flow slows, tighten the screw, then have your assistant slowly release the pedal. Wait five seconds before proceeding.
30   Repeat Step 29 until no more air is seen leaving the tube, then tighten the bleeder screw and proceed to the left rear brake, right front brake and left front brake, in that order. Be sure to check the fluid in the master cylinder reservoir frequently.
31   After bleeding the right rear wheel brake, repeat Steps 27 through 30 on the left rear brake, right front brake and the left front brake, in that order.
32   Lower the vehicle and check the fluid level in the brake fluid reservoir, adding fluid as necessary.
33   Check the operation of the brakes. The pedal should feel solid when depressed, with no sponginess. If necessary, repeat the entire process. **Warning:** *Do not operate the vehicle if you are in doubt about the effectiveness of the brake system.*

11   Power brake booster - check, removal and installation

Operating check

1   Depress the pedal and start the engine. If the pedal goes down slightly, operation is normal.
2   Depress the brake pedal several times with the engine running and make sure that there is no change in the pedal reserve distance.

Airtightness check

3   Start the engine and turn it off after one or two minutes. Depress the brake pedal several times slowly. If the pedal goes down far-

ther the first time but gradually rises after the second or third depression, the booster is airtight.
4   Depress the brake pedal while the engine is running, then stop the engine with the pedal depressed. If there is no change in the pedal reserve travel after holding the pedal for 30 seconds, the booster is airtight.

Removal and installation

Refer to illustrations 11.7 and 11.8
Note: *Dismantling of the power brake unit requires special tools. If a problem develops, it is recommended that a new or factory-exchange unit be installed rather than trying to overhaul the original booster.*
5   Remove the mounting nuts which hold the master cylinder to the power brake unit (see Section 8). Move the master cylinder forward, but be careful not to bend or kink the lines leading to the master cylinder. If there is any strain on the lines, disconnect them at the master cylinder and plug the ends.
6   Disconnect the vacuum hose leading to the front of the power brake booster. Cover the end of the hose.
7   Inside the vehicle, loosen the four nuts that secure the booster to the firewall **(see illustrations)**. Do not remove these nuts at this time.
8   Disconnect the power brake pushrod from the brake pedal **(see illustration)**. Do not force the pushrod to the side when disconnecting it.
9   Now remove the four booster mounting nuts and carefully lift the unit out of the engine compartment.
10   When installing, loosely install the four mounting nuts, then connect the pushrod to the brake pedal. If the old retaining clip doesn't snap into place, replace it with a new clip. Tighten the booster retaining nuts to the torque listed in this Chapter's Specifications. Reconnect the vacuum hose. Install the master cylinder (see Section 8). If the brake lines were disconnected from the master cylinder, bleed the brake system to eliminate any air

which has entered the system (see Section 10).

12   Parking brake - adjustment (1995 through 2002 models)

Refer to illustration 12.4
Note: *On 2003 and later models, the parking brake is self-adjusting. If parking brake lever travel is excessive, or won't hold the vehicle on an incline, adjust or replace the rear brake shoes (see Section 6).*
1   These models are equipped with a self-adjusting parking brake lever assembly that automatically takes up slack in the cables as they stretch. There is no need to adjust the parking brake cables manually during their service life. However, whenever new rear brake shoes are installed on the rear drum brakes, make sure the new shoes are properly adjusted; the automatic cable adjuster mechanism can't do its job if the rear shoes are out of adjustment. It's also a good idea to check cable adjustment whenever the brake shoes are replaced, or the brake drum is removed for some other reason.
2   Loosen the rear wheel lug nuts, raise the rear of the vehicle and support it securely on jackstands. Block the front wheels. Remove the rear wheels.
3   Remove the rear drums.
4   Using a screwdriver, lift the actuator off the adjuster wheel **(see illustration)**. Using a brake adjusting tool, or another screwdriver, turn the adjuster wheel until the shoes drag on the drum as the drum is turned. Since there are no adjustment holes in the brake backing plates on these vehicles, you'll have to expand the shoes a bit, then install the drum, expand the shoes a bit, install the drum, etc. until you feel the drum drag against the shoes. Then back off the adjuster

13.8 Squeeze the tangs on the cable retainer and disengage the front parking brake cable from the bracket on the parking brake lever base

13.9 Pull on the front cable to rotate the reel until the pawl drops into the notch

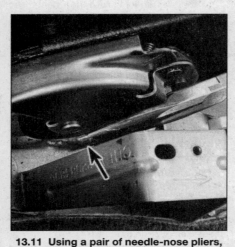

13.11 Using a pair of needle-nose pliers, disengage the plug (arrow) on the end of the front cable from the reel mechanism

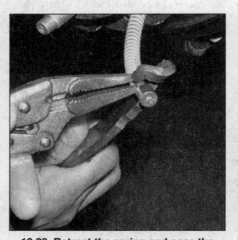

13.20 Retract the spring and pass the cable through the slot in the parking brake lever (2003 and 2004 models)

13.21 Squeeze the retainer and pull the parking brake cable through the brake backing plate

wheel a little until the drum rotates freely.

5　Adjust the other rear brake the same way.

6　Apply the parking brake and verify that the shoes hold the drums. Release the parking brake and make sure that both rear wheels turn freely and that there is no brake drag in either direction.

7　Remove the jackstands and lower the vehicle.

13　Parking brake cables - replacement

Front cable

Refer to illustrations 13.8, 13.9 and 13.11

1　Raise the vehicle and place it securely on jackstands.

2　The rear part of the front cable is attached to the floorpan by a clip which is an integral part of the cable. Remove the clip retaining screw and detach the clip from the floorpan.

3　Pull the front cable toward the rear of the vehicle to put some slack in the cable and hold it there.

4　Disengage the front cable from the rear cable at the cable junction.

5　Lower the vehicle.

6　Remove the center console (see Chapter 11) and, on Pontiacs, the shift lever boot.

7　Fully release the parking brake lever.

8　Squeeze the tangs of the cable retainer together **(see illustration)** and disengage the cable from the parking brake lever bracket.

9　Pull on the cable to rotate the ratcheting reel until the pawl drops into the notch, locking the reel into place **(see illustration)**.

10　Slowly release the cable and allow the

13.22 Disengage the rear parking brake cable from the front cable junction

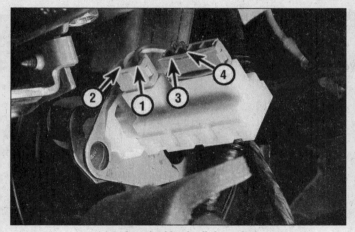

14.1 A typical brake light switch

1   Voltage in (brake light circuit)
2   Voltage out (brake light circuit)
3   Voltage in (cruise control circuit)
4   Voltage out (cruise control circuit)

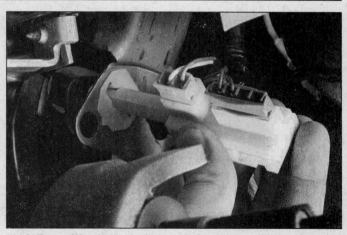

14.9 To remove the brake light switch, simply pull it straight out, then unplug the electrical connectors; to install the switch, depress the brake pedal, insert the switch into its bracket and push it in until it's fully seated, then slowly pull the brake pedal to the rear until you no longer hear any "clicking" sounds

notch to catch the leg of the pawl spring.

11   Disengage the plug on the end of the cable from the reel assembly **(see illustration)**.

12   Remove the left rocker panel/door sill plate.

13   Remove the grommet and retainer from the floorpan.

14   The forward part of the front cable is attached to the floorpan by a retaining clip. Bend this clip open and disengage the cable.

15   Remove the front parking brake cable.

16   Installation is the reverse of removal.

Rear cable

Refer to illustrations 13.20, 13.21 and 13.22

17   Fully release the parking brake lever.

18   Loosen the rear wheel lug nuts, raise the rear of the vehicle and place it securely on jackstands. Remove the rear wheel(s).

19   Remove the rear drum and disassemble the brake assembly (see Section 6).

20   Detach the cable from the rear shoe parking brake lever **(see the accompanying illustration or illustration 6.4g)**.

21   Squeeze the cable retainer with a pair of pliers **(see illustration)** and pull the cable through the backing plate.

22   Disengage the rear cable from the front cable at the cable junction **(see illustration)**.

23   Disconnect the cable from all clips and brackets.

24   Installation is the reverse of removal.

14   Brake light switch - check, adjustment and replacement

Check

Refer to illustration 14.1

1   The brake light switch **(see illustration)** is located on the brake pedal bracket. You'll need to remove the knee bolster (the trim panel beneath the steering column) to get to the switch and connector.

2   With the brake pedal in the fully released position, the switch plunger is pressed into the switch housing, and the brake light circuit is open. When the brake pedal is depressed, the plunger protrudes from the switch, which closes the circuit and sends current to the brake lights. On models with cruise control, the brake light switch is also a switch for the cruise control system when the system is operating. With the brake pedal in the released position, the circuit is closed; when the brake pedal is depressed, the brake light switch opens the circuit and cuts off current to the cruise control module, which turns off the cruise control system.

3   If the brake lights are inoperative, check the fuse (see Chapter 12).

4   If the fuse is okay, verify that voltage is available at the switch by backprobing the connector **(see illustration 14.1)**.

5   If there's no voltage to the switch, use a

test light to find the open circuit condition between the fuse panel and the switch. If there is voltage to the switch, close the switch (depress the brake pedal) and verify that there's voltage on the other side of the switch.

6   If there's no voltage on the other side of the switch with the brake pedal depressed, replace the switch (see Step 7). If voltage is available, check for voltage at the brake lights. If no power is present at the brake light sockets, look for an open circuit condition between the switch and the brake lights.

Replacement

Refer to illustration 14.9

7   Remove the knee bolster.

8   Unplug the electrical connector(s) from the switch.

9   Remove the switch from the bracket **(see illustration)**.

10   The switch must be adjusted as it's installed (see below).

Adjustment

11   Depress the brake pedal, insert the switch into its bracket and push it in until it's fully seated.

12   Slowly pull the brake pedal to the rear until you no longer hear any "clicking" sounds. The switch should now be adjusted.

13   The remainder of installation is the reverse of removal.

Notes

Chapter 10
Suspension and steering systems

Contents

Specifications

Torque specifications

Ft-lbs (unless otherwise indicated)

Front suspension

Balljoint-to-steering knuckle nut	
2002 and earlier	41 (up to 50, to install cotter pin)
2003 and later	41, plus an additional 180-degrees rotation
Control arm	
Front bushing bolt	
1998 and earlier	89, plus an additional 180-degrees rotation
1999 and later	79
Rear vertical bushing bolt	125
Hub and bearing assembly-to-steering knuckle bolts	70
Stabilizer bar	
Link nuts	156 in-lbs
Bushing clamp bolts	49
Strut assembly	
Strut-to-steering knuckle nuts	133
Strut-to-body nuts	18
Strut-to-body bolt	18
Strut damper shaft nut	52
Crossmember bolts	
1995 and 1996 models	96
1997 models	71, plus an additional 180-degrees rotation
1998 models	
Left rear outboard bolts	71, plus an additional 90-degrees rotation
Right rear outboard bolts	71, plus an additional 90-degrees rotation
Rear inboard bolts	71, plus an additional 90-degrees rotation
Front bolts	66, plus an additional 90-degrees rotation
1999 through 2003	71
2004	71, plus an additional 90-degrees rotation

Rear suspension

Hub and bearing assembly retaining bolts	44
Rear axle beam trailing arm pivot bolts	
1995 through 1999	44
2000 and later	88
Shock absorber and coil spring assembly	
Lower shock bolt/nut	52
Upper shock nut and bolts	
1995 through 1999	21
2000 and later	18

Torque specifications

Steering   **Ft-lbs** (unless otherwise indicated)

Steering gear mounting bolts 89
U-joint coupling pinch bolt 30
Power steering pump mounting bolts 22
Steering wheel nut 30
Tie-rod end-to-steering knuckle nuts .... 84 in-lbs, plus an additional 210-degrees
Wheel lug nuts .... See Chapter 1

1.1 Front suspension and steering components

1	Strut and spring assembly	4	Stabilizer link	7	Steering gear boot
2	Steering knuckle	5	Control arm	8	Tie-rod
3	Balljoint	6	Stabilizer bar	9	Tie-rod end

1   General information

Refer to illustrations 1.1 and 1.2

The front suspension **(see illustration)** is a MacPherson strut design. The upper ends of the struts are attached to the body; the lower ends of the struts are bolted to the steering knuckles. The lower ends of the steering knuckles are attached to the control arms by balljoints. The inner ends of the control arms are attached to the crossmember. A stabilizer bar reduces body lean during cornering. The stabilizer is attached to the crossmember by a pair of bushing clamps and to the control arms by link bolts.

The rear suspension **(see illustration)** is a semi-independent design which uses an axle beam with integral trailing arms and a

pair of shock absorber/coil spring assemblies. The axle trailing arms are attached to the body. The upper ends of the shocks are attached to the vehicle body; the lower ends are bolted to the axle beam.

The rack-and-pinion steering gear, which is located behind the engine/transaxle assembly, is bolted to the suspension crossmember. The steering gear turns the steering knuckles via a pair of tie-rod assemblies, each of which consists of an inner tie-rod and a tie-rod end. The inner tie-rods are attached to the steering gear; the outer tie-rods, or tie-rod ends, are attached to the steering knuckles. All models are equipped with power steering.

Warning: *Whenever any of the suspension or steering fasteners are loosened or removed, they must be inspected and, if necessary,*

replaced with new ones of the same part number or of original equipment quality and design. Torque specifications must be followed for proper reassembly and component retention. Never attempt to heat or straighten any suspension or steering components. Instead, replace any bent or damaged part with a new one.

Note 1: *These vehicles have a combination of standard and metric fasteners on the various suspension and steering components, so it would be a good idea to have both types of tools available when beginning work.*

Note 2: *On models equipped with a Delco Loc II or Theftlock audio system, be sure the lockout feature is turned off and make sure you have the correct activation code before performing any procedure which requires disconnecting the battery.*

1.2 Rear suspension components

1   *Shock absorber and coil spring assembly*   2   *Rear axle beam assembly*   3   *Rear axle pivot bolts*

2   Stabilizer bar and bushings - removal and installation

Removal

Refer to illustrations 2.2, 2.3 and 2.4

1   Loosen the lug nuts on both front wheels, raise the front of the vehicle and sup-port it securely on jackstands. Apply the parking brake and block the rear wheels to keep the vehicle from rolling off the jack-stands. Remove the front wheels.

2   Remove the nuts from the upper ends of the link bolts that connect the stabilizer bar to the control arms **(see illustration)**. Note the order in which the bushings, spacers and washers are installed on the links; they must be installed in exactly the same order in which they're removed.

3   Support the rear of the crossmember with a jack, then remove the rear center and outer crossmember retaining bolts **(see illus-tration)**. Lower the crossmember about three inches.

4   Remove the stabilizer bar bushing clamp bolts and bushing clamps from the

2.2 To disconnect the stabilizer bar from the link bolts that connect it to the control arms, remove the link bolt nut (arrow) from each end; make sure that you note the order in which the bushings, spacers and washers on the link are installed

2.3 To lower the rear part of the crossmember, remove these four bolts (arrows); be sure to put a sturdy floor jack under the crossmember before unbolting it

2.4 To detach the stabilizer bar from the crossmember, remove the bushing clamp bolt (arrow) and clamp from each bushing

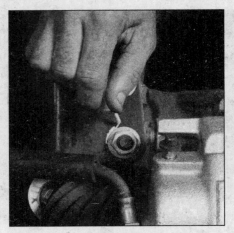

3.2 To mark the relationship of the strut to the steering knuckle, paint or scribe lines around the nuts

3.3 To remove the strut-to-knuckle bolts, drive them out with a hammer and brass punch

upper side of the crossmember **(see illustration)**.

5   Remove the stabilizer bar and bushings through the wheel well.

6   Inspect the stabilizer bushings for wear and damage and replace them if necessary. To ease installation of the new bushings, spray the inside and outside of the bushings with a silicone-based lubricant. Do not use petroleum-based lubricants on rubber parts. Inspect the link bushings, spacers and washers for wear and replace as necessary.

Installation

7   Install the stabilizer bar bushings and clamps, guide the stabilizer through the wheel well, over the crossmember and into position.

8   Center the stabilizer bar, install the bushing clamp bolts and hand tighten them.

9   Install the spacers, bushings and washers on the links in the same order in which they were removed. Tighten the link nuts to the torque listed in this Chapter's Specifications.

10   Tighten the bushing clamp bolts to the torque listed in this Chapter's Specifications.

11   Raise the crossmember, install the crossmember retaining bolts and tighten them to t he torque listed in this Chapter's Specifications.

12   Install the wheels and lower the vehicle. Tighten the lug nuts to the torque listed in the Chapter 1 Specifications.

3   Strut and coil spring assembly (front) - removal, inspection and installation

Removal

Refer to illustrations 3.2, 3.3 and 3.5

1   Loosen the wheel lug nuts, raise the front of the vehicle and support it securely on jackstands. Apply the parking brake and block the rear wheels to keep the vehicle

from rolling off the jackstands. Remove the wheel.

2   Mark the strut-to-steering knuckle relationship by making a line around the strut-to-steering knuckle nuts **(see illustration)**.

3   Remove the nuts from the strut-to-knuckle bolts and knock the bolts out with a brass punch and a hammer **(see illustration)**.

4   Separate the strut from the steering knuckle. Be careful not to overextend the inner CV joint or stretch the brake hose. If necessary, support the control arm with a jack.

5   Support the strut and spring assembly with one hand and remove the upper strut mounting nuts and bolt **(see illustration)**. Remove the strut and spring assembly.

Inspection

6   Check the strut body for leaking fluid, dents, cracks and other obvious damage which would warrant repair or replacement.

7   Check the coil spring for chips and cracks in the spring coating (this will cause premature spring failure due to corrosion). Inspect the spring seat for hardening, cracks and general deterioration.

8   If wear or damage is evident, replace the strut and/or coil spring as necessary (see Section 4).

Installation

9   Guide the strut assembly up into the fenderwell and insert the upper mounting studs through the holes in the shock tower. Once the studs protrude from the shock tower, install the nuts and bolt so the strut won't fall back through. This may require an assistant, since the strut is quite heavy and awkward.

10   Slide the steering knuckle into the strut flange and insert the two bolts. Install the nuts, align the marks you made prior to disassembly and tighten the nuts to the torque listed in this Chapter's Specifications.

3.5 Remove the strut upper mounting nuts and bolt (arrows) while supporting the strut assembly

11   Install the wheel, lower the vehicle and tighten the wheel lug nuts to the torque listed in the Chapter 1 Specifications.

12   Tighten the upper mounting nuts and bolt to the torque listed in this Chapter's Specifications.

13   Drive the vehicle to a dealer service department or an alignment shop to have the front wheel alignment checked and, if necessary, adjusted (this is only necessary if the strut has been modified for camber adjustment).

4   Strut/shock absorber or coil spring - replacement

1   If the struts/shock absorbers or coil springs exhibit the telltale signs of wear (leaking fluid, loss of damping capability, chipped, sagging or cracked coil springs) explore all options before beginning any work. The strut/shock absorber assemblies are not serviceable and must be replaced if a problem develops. However, strut assem-

4.3a Mark the relationship of the coil spring to the upper spring seat and insulator and to the strut mount . . .

4.3b . . . and to the lower seat of the strut

4.4 Following the tool manufacturer's instructions, install the spring compressor on the spring and compress it sufficiently to relieve all pressure from the upper spring seat

4.5 Using a wrench on the damper shaft to prevent it from turning, loosen the damper shaft nut

4.6a Remove the washer . . .

4.6b . . . and the strut mount; inspect the bearing in the mount for smooth operation and the rubber portion of the mount for cracking and general deterioration, if the bearing doesn't turn smoothly, or if there's any separation of the rubber, replace the mount

4.7 Remove the upper spring seat and insulator from the damper shaft; inspect the insulator for cracking and hardness and, if necessary, replace it

blies complete with springs may be available on an exchange basis, which eliminates much time and work. Whichever route you choose to take, check on the cost and availability of parts before disassembling your vehicle. **Warning:** *Disassembling a strut is potentially dangerous and utmost attention must be directed to the job, or serious injury may result. Use only a high-quality spring compressor and carefully follow the manufacturer's instructions furnished with the tool. After removing the coil spring from the strut assembly, set it aside in a safe, isolated area.*

Disassembly

Refer to illustrations 4.3a, 4.3b, 4.4, 4.5, 4.6a, 4.6b, 4.7, 4.8 and 4.9

2   Remove the strut and spring assembly (see Section 3) or shock absorber/coil spring assembly (see Section 9). Mount the strut assembly in a vise. Line the vise jaws with wood or rags to prevent damage to the unit and don't tighten the vise excessively.

3   Mark the relationship of the coil spring to the upper insulator and mount and to the lower seat **(see illustrations)**.
4   Following the tool manufacturer's instructions, install the spring compressor (which can be obtained at most auto parts stores or at equipment rental yards) on the spring and compress it sufficiently to relieve all pressure from the upper spring seat **(see illustration)**. This can be verified by wiggling the spring.
5   Loosen the damper shaft nut **(see illustration)**.
6   Remove the washer and strut mount **(see illustrations)**. Inspect the bearing in the strut mount for smooth operation. If it doesn't turn smoothly, replace the strut mount. Check the rubber portion of the strut mount for cracking and general deterioration. If there is any separation of the rubber, replace it.
7   Remove the upper spring seat and insulator from the damper shaft **(see illustration)**. Check the insulator for cracking and hardness; replace it if necessary.

4.8 Remove the rubber jounce bumper and dust shield from the damper shaft

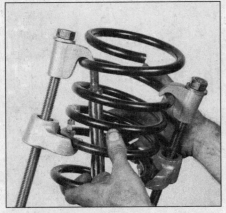

4.9 Carefully lift the compressed spring from the assembly and set it in a safe place; Do NOT *place your head near the end of the spring!*

4.12 Place the coil spring onto the lower insulator, with the end of the spring butted against the spring stop on the insulator

8   Remove the rubber jounce bumper and dust shield from the damper shaft **(see illustration)**.

9   Carefully lift the compressed spring from the assembly **(see illustration)** and set it in a safe place. **Warning:** *Never place your head near the end of the spring!*

10 Check the lower insulator for wear, cracking and hardness and replace it if necessary.

Reassembly

Refer to illustrations 4.12, 4.15a, 4.15b and 4.16

11 If the lower insulator is being replaced, set it into position with the dropped portion seated in the lowest part of the seat. Extend the damper rod to its full length and install the rubber bumper.

12 Place the coil spring onto the lower insulator, with the end of the spring butted against the spring stop on the insulator **(see illustration)**.

13 Install the dust shield and rubber jounce bumper.

14 Install the upper insulator and spring seat.

15 Install the strut mount and washer **(see illustrations)**.

4.15a Install the strut mount . . .

4.15b . . . and washer

16 Install the nut and tighten it securely **(see illustration)**.

17 Install the strut/spring assembly (see Section 3) or shock absorber/coil spring assembly (see Section 9).

18 Repeat this entire procedure for the other strut or shock absorber/coil spring assembly.

19 After the vehicle has been lowered to the ground, tighten the damper shaft nuts to the torque listed in this Chapter's Specifications.

5   Control arm - removal and installation

Removal

Refer to illustrations 5.3, 5.4, 5.5, 5.6a and 5.6b

1   Loosen the wheel lug nuts, raise the front of the vehicle and support it securely on jackstands. Apply the parking brake and block the rear wheels to keep the vehicle from rolling off the jackstands. Remove the wheel(s).

2   Disconnect the stabilizer bar from the control arm being removed (see Section 2). (If only one control arm is being removed, disconnect only that end of the stabilizer bar; if both control arms are being removed, disconnect both ends.)

4.16 Hold the damper shaft from turning, then tighten the nut securely (unless you have a special socket with a "window" in it for the back-up wrench, you won't be able to torque the nut until the strut assembly is installed in the vehicle and the vehicle is on the ground)

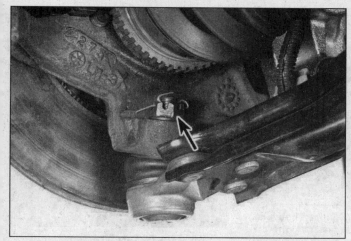

5.3 Remove the cotter pin and loosen - but don't remove - the nut (arrow) from the balljoint stud

5.4 Pop the balljoint out of the steering knuckle by striking the knuckle ballstud boss sharply with a hammer as shown

5.5 Once the ballstud is loose, separate the control arm from the steering knuckle by prying the ballstud out of the hole with a large prybar as shown

5.6a The front control arm pivot bolt (arrow) is accessed from the front of the suspension crossmember

5.6b To separate the rear part of the control arm from the suspension crossmember, remove the vertical bushing bolt (arrow)

3   Remove the cotter pin and loosen the balljoint stud-to-steering knuckle nut **(see illustration)**.

4   Using a hammer, strike the ballstud boss on the steering knuckle **(see illustration)**. until the ballstud pops loose from the knuckle. If the ballstud is frozen in the knuckle, you may have to use a special balljoint separator or a picklefork tool. Keep in mind that a picklefork will damage or destroy the boot, so it should be used only as a last resort.

5   Remove the nut from the ballstud. Using a large prybar positioned between the control arm and steering knuckle, separate the ballstud from the knuckle **(see illustration)**. **Caution:** *When removing the balljoint from the knuckle, be careful not to overextend the inner CV joint or it may be damaged.*

6   Remove the front control arm pivot bolt and the rear vertical bushing bolt **(see illustrations)** and detach the control arm.

7   The control arm bushings are replace-able, but special tools and expertise are necessary to do the job. Carefully inspect the bushings for hardening, excessive wear and cracks. If they appear to be worn or deteriorated, take the control arm to a dealer service department or other repair shop.

Installation

8   Position the control arm in the suspension crossmember and install the front pivot bolt and the rear vertical bushing bolt. Do not tighten them completely at this time.

9   Insert the balljoint stud into the steering knuckle boss, install the castellated nut and tighten it to the torque listed in this Chapter's Specifications. If necessary, tighten the nut a little more (up to, but not beyond, the specified maximum listed in the Specifications) if the cotter pin hole doesn't line up with an opening on the nut. Install a new cotter pin.

10   Install the stabilizer bar-to-control arm link bolt, bushings, spacers and washers (see Section 2) and tighten the link nut to the

torque listed in this Chapter's Specifications.

11   Install the wheel and lower the vehicle. Tighten the lug nuts to the torque listed in the Chapter 1 Specifications.

12   With the weight of the vehicle on the suspension, tighten the control arm pivot bolt and the rear vertical bushing bolt to the torque listed in this Chapter's Specifications. **Note:** *You can raise the suspension with a floor jack positioned under the balljoint to simulate normal ride height.* **Caution:** *If the bolts aren't tightened with the weight of the vehicle on the suspension, control arm bushing damage may occur.*

6   Balljoints - check and replacement

Check

Refer to illustration 6.3

1   Raise the front of the vehicle and sup-

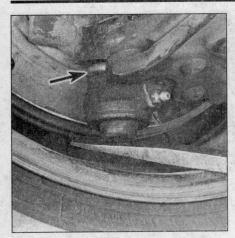

6.3a Check for movement between the balljoint and steering knuckle when prying up

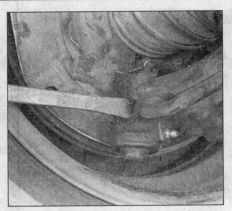

6.3b With the prybar positioned between the steering knuckle boss and the balljoint, pry down and check for play in the balljoint - if there's any play, replace the balljoint

7.6 A No. 55 Torx bit is required to remove the hub bolts - DO NOT use an Allen wrench or the bolts will be damaged

port it securely on jackstands. Apply the parking brake and block the rear wheels to keep the vehicle from rolling off the jackstands.

2   Visually inspect the rubber dust boot for damage, deterioration and leaking grease. If the boot is damaged, deteriorated or leaking, replace the balljoint.

3   Place a large prybar under the balljoint and resting on the wheel, then try to pry the balljoint up while feeling for movement between the balljoint and steering knuckle **(see illustration)**. Now, pry between the control arm and the steering knuckle and try to lever the control arm down while feeling for movement between the balljoint and steering knuckle **(see illustration)**. If any movement is evident in either check, the balljoint is worn out.

4   Have an assistant grasp the tire at the top and bottom and move the top of the tire in-and-out. Touch the balljoint stud castellated nut. If any looseness is felt, suspect a worn out balljoint stud or a widened hole in the steering knuckle boss. If the latter problem exists, the steering knuckle should be replaced as well as the balljoint.

5   Separate the control arm from the steering knuckle (Section 5). Using your fingers (don't use pliers), try to twist the stud in the socket. If the stud turns, replace the balljoint.

Replacement

6   Loosen the wheel lug nuts, raise the front of the vehicle and support it securely on jackstands. Apply the parking brake and block the rear wheels to keep the vehicle from rolling off the jackstands. Remove the wheel.

7   Separate the control arm from the steering knuckle (see Section 5). Temporarily insert the balljoint stud back into the steering knuckle (loosely). This will ease balljoint removal after Step 9 has been performed, as well as hold the assembly stationary while drilling out the rivets.

8   Using a 1/8-inch drill bit, drill a pilot hole

into the center of each balljoint-to-control arm rivet. Be careful not to damage the CV joint boot in the process.

9   Using a 1/2-inch drill bit, drill the head off each rivet. Work slowly and carefully to avoid deforming the holes in the control arm.

10   Loosen (but don't remove) the stabilizer bar-to-control arm link nut. Pull the control arm and balljoint down to remove the balljoint stud from the steering knuckle, then dislodge the balljoint from the control arm.

11   Position the new balljoint on the control arm and install the bolts (supplied in the balljoint kit) from the top of the control arm. Tighten the bolts to the torque specified in the new balljoint instruction sheet.

12   Insert the balljoint into the steering knuckle, install the castellated nut, tighten it to the torque listed in this Chapter's Specifications and install a new cotter pin. It may be necessary to tighten the nut some to align the cotter pin hole with an opening in the nut, which is acceptable (up to, but not beyond, the maximum torque, listed in this Chapter's Specifications). Never loosen the castellated nut to allow cotter pin insertion.

13   Tighten the stabilizer bar-to-control arm link nut to the torque listed in this Chapter's Specifications.

14   Install the wheel, lower the vehicle and tighten the lug nuts to the torque listed in the Chapter 1 Specifications.

---

7   Hub and bearing assembly (front) - removal and installation

---

Refer to illustrations 7.6 and 7.7
Warning: *Dust created by the brake system may contain asbestos, which is harmful to your health. Never blow it out with compressed air and don't inhale any of it. Do not, under any circumstances, use petroleum-based solvents to clean brake parts. Use brake cleaner or denatured alcohol only.*
Note: *The hub and bearing assembly is a*

sealed unit. If worn or damaged, it must be replaced.

1   Loosen the wheel lug nuts, raise the front of the vehicle and support it securely on jackstands. Apply the parking brake and block the rear wheels to keep the vehicle from rolling off the jackstands. Remove the wheel.

2   Disconnect the stabilizer bar from the control arm (see Section 2).

3   Remove the balljoint-to-steering knuckle nut and separate the control arm from the knuckle (see Section 5).

4   Remove the caliper from the steering knuckle and hang it out of the way with a piece of wire (see Chapter 9).

5   Pull the disc off the hub and remove the driveaxle (see Chapter 8 if necessary).

6   Remove the hub retaining bolts from the steering knuckle **(see illustration)**. Remove the disc shield.

7   Wiggle the hub and bearing assembly back-and-forth and pull it out of the steering knuckle **(see illustration)**.

7.7 Pull the hub and bearing assembly and the disc shield out of the steering knuckle

9.2 Remove this single nut (arrow) from the trunk space (the other two bolts, the threads of which are visible in this photo, are removed from underneath after the vehicle is raised)

9.4 To disconnect the lower end of the shock absorber from the rear axle beam, remove this nut and bolt (arrows)

8   Clean the mating surfaces on the steering knuckle, bearing flange and knuckle bore.
9   Install a new O-ring around the rear of the hub assembly and push it up against the bearing flange. Lubricate the outside diameter of the bearing and the seal lips with high-temperature grease and insert the hub and bearing into the steering knuckle. Position the disc shield and install the three bolts. Tighten them to the torque listed in this Chapter's Specifications.
10   Install the driveaxle (see Chapter 8).
11   Attach the control arm to the steering knuckle (see Section 5).
12   Reconnect the stabilizer bar to the control arm (see Section 2).
13   Install the brake disc and caliper (see Chapter 9).
14   Install the hub nut and tighten it securely to seat the driveaxle in the hub. Prevent the axle from turning by inserting a screwdriver through the caliper and into a disc cooling vane.
15   Install the wheel, lower the vehicle and tighten the lug nuts to the torque listed in this Chapter's Specifications.
16   Tighten the hub nut to the torque listed in the Chapter 8 Specifications.

8   Steering knuckle and hub - removal and installation

Warning: *Dust created by the brake system may contain asbestos, which is harmful to your health. Never blow it out with compressed air and don't inhale any of it. Do not, under any circumstances, use petroleum-based solvents to clean brake parts. Use brake cleaner or denatured alcohol only.*

Removal

1   Loosen the wheel lug nuts, raise the front of the vehicle and support it securely on jackstands. Apply the parking brake and block the rear wheels to keep the vehicle from rolling off the jackstands. Remove the wheel.

2   Remove the hub nut. Insert a screwdriver through the caliper and into a disc cooling vane to prevent the driveaxle from turning.
3   Remove the caliper and suspend it out of the way with a piece of wire. Lift the disc off the hub.
4   Mark the position of the two strut-to-knuckle nuts and remove them **(see illustration 3.2)**. Don't drive out the bolts at this time.
5   Separate the control arm balljoint from the steering knuckle (see Section 5).
6   Attach a puller to the hub flange and push the driveaxle out of the hub (see Chapter 8). Hang the driveaxle with a piece of wire to prevent damage to the inner CV joint.
7   Support the knuckle and drive out the two strut-to-knuckle bolts with a hammer and brass punch. Separate the steering knuckle from the strut.

Installation

8   Position the knuckle in the strut and insert the two splined bolts. Tap the bolts into place and install the nuts, but don't tighten them at this time.

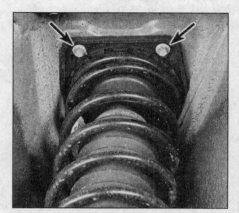

9.5 To detach the upper end of the shock absorber and coil spring assembly from the vehicle body, remove these two bolts (arrows)

9   Install the driveaxle in the hub.
10   Connect the control arm to the steering knuckle and tighten the castellated nut to the torque listed in this Chapter's Specifications. Install a new cotter pin.
11   Align the strut-to-knuckle nuts with the previously applied marks and tighten them to the torque listed in this Chapter's Specifications.
12   Install the brake disc and caliper.
13   Tighten the hub nut securely to seat the driveaxle in the hub.
14   Install the wheel, lower the vehicle and tighten the lug nuts to the torque listed in the Chapter 1 Specifications.
15   Tighten the hub nut to the torque listed in the Chapter 8 Specifications.

9   Shock absorber and coil spring assembly (rear) - removal and installation

Refer to illustrations 9.2, 9.4 and 9.5
Caution: *Don't remove both shock absorbers at the same time. They limit the downward travel of the rear suspension and damage to the brake hoses and lines may occur if the suspension is allowed to hang.*
1   Open the trunk and peel back the side trim panel to expose the upper shock mount.
2   Remove the mount *nut* **(see illustration)**. (The two *bolts* you see must be removed from the wheel well side, after the vehicle is raised and the wheel is removed.)
3   Loosen the wheel lug nuts, raise the rear of the vehicle and support it securely on jackstands. Block the front wheels to keep the vehicle from rolling off the jackstands. Remove the rear wheels.
4   Support the trailing arm with a jack and remove the lower shock absorber mounting nut and bolt **(see illustration)**.
5   Remove the two upper mount bolts **(see illustration)** and detach the shock absorber and coil spring from the vehicle. Check the shock absorber for dents and leaking fluid. Check the coil spring for chips and cracks.

10.3a Remove the four hub and bearing assembly bolts with a no. 55 Torx bit

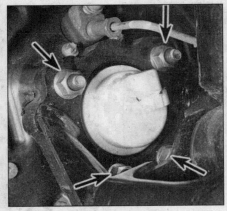

10.3b Put a wrench on these nuts (arrows) as you unscrew each Torx bolt

10.4a Angle the hub and bearing assembly out through the brake assembly

10.4b Temporarily reinstall two bolts (arrows) to retain the brake assembly to the trailing arm, rather than let it hang by the brake line

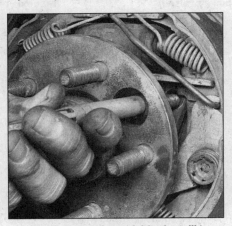

10.5 A magnet is useful for installing the bolts

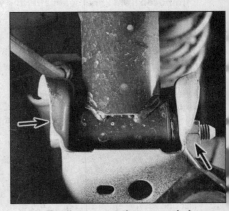

11.7 To disconnect the rear axle beam from the vehicle, remove the pivot bolt and nut (arrows) from the forward end of each trailing arm

6   Inspect the upper mount for cracks, hardening, separation and other damage.
7   If any of these conditions are found, replace the shock absorber or coil spring as necessary (see Section 4 for the disassembly and reassembly procedure - it's similar to a front strut).
8   Installation is the reverse of the removal procedure.

10 Hub and bearing assembly (rear) - removal and installation

Warning: *Dust created by the brake system may contain asbestos, which is harmful to your health. Never blow it out with compressed air and don't inhale any of it. Do not, under any circumstances, use petroleum-based solvents to clean brake parts. Use brake cleaner or denatured alcohol only.*

Removal

Refer to illustrations 10.3a, 10.3b, 10.4a, 10.4b and 10.5
Note: *The rear hub and bearing assembly is a sealed unit; if it's worn or damaged, it must be replaced.*

1   Loosen the wheel lug nuts, raise the rear of the vehicle and support it securely on jackstands. Block the front wheels to keep the vehicle from rolling off the jackstands. Remove the wheel.
2   Pull the brake drum off the hub. If difficulty is encountered, refer to Chapter 9 for the removal procedure.
3   Using a no. 55 Torx bit on the bolts and a wrench on the nuts (on the backside of the backing plate), remove the four hub-to-trailing arm bolts, accessible by turning the hub flange so the circular cutout exposes each bolt **(see illustrations)**. Save the upper rear bolt for last, because there isn't much clearance between the bolt and the parking brake strut.
4   Remove the hub and bearing assembly, maneuvering it out through the brake assembly. Reinstall two bolts through the brake backing plate into the trailing arm to avoid hanging the brake assembly by the hydraulic line **(see illustrations)**.

Installation

5   Position the hub and bearing assembly on the trailing arm and align the holes in the backing plate. Install the bolts, beginning with the upper rear bolt. A magnet is useful

for guiding the bolts through the hub flange and into position **(see illustration)**. After all four bolts have been installed, tighten them to the torque listed in this Chapter's Specifications.
6   Install the brake drum and wheel. Lower the vehicle and tighten the wheel lug nuts to the torque listed in the Chapter 1 Specifications.

11 Rear axle beam - removal, inspection and installation

Warning: *Dust created by the brake system may contain asbestos, which is harmful to your health. Never blow it out with compressed air and don't inhale any of it. Do not, under any circumstances, use petroleum-based solvents to clean brake parts. Use brake cleaner or denatured alcohol only.*

Removal

Refer to illustration 11.7
1   Loosen the wheel lug nuts, raise the rear of the vehicle and place it securely on jackstands. Block the front wheels and remove the rear wheels.

12.3a Remove the airbag module retaining screws (the other screw is in the same location on the other side of the steering column)

2   Remove the rear brake drums (see Chapter 9).
3   Disconnect the brake lines from the wheel cylinders and disconnect the brake hoses from the brake lines (see Chapter 9). Plug the brake lines to prevent moisture and contamination from entering the brake system.
4   Detach the brake backing plates from the axle beam and suspend them from the coil springs with pieces of wire. It isn't necessary to remove the brake shoes or the parking brake cable from the backing plate.
5   Support the axle beam with a floor jack. Place a block of wood between the axle and the jack head to protect the axle.
6   Disconnect the lower ends of the shock absorbers from the axle beam (see Section 9).
7   Remove the pivot bolts from the forward ends of the axle beam trailing arms **(see illustration)**.
8   Remove the axle beam assembly.

Inspection

9   Inspect the trailing arm bushings for cracks, deformation and wear. If they're damaged or worn out, take the axle beam assembly to a dealer service department or an automotive machine shop to have the old ones pressed out and new ones pressed in.

Installation

10   Installation is the reverse of removal. Be sure to tighten all fasteners to the torque listed in this Chapter's Specifications, but make sure to tighten the pivot bolts after the suspension is at normal ride height.
11   Lower the vehicle and tighten the wheel lug nuts to the torque listed in the Chapter 1 Specifications.
12   Bleed the brakes (see Chapter 9).

12 Steering wheel - removal and installation

Refer to illustrations 12.3a, 12.3b, 12.4, 12.6 and 12.7

Warning: *These models have airbags. Always*

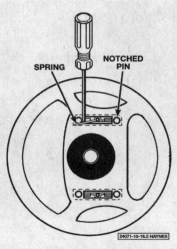

12.3b On 2003 and later models, the airbag module is retained by spring clips. Insert a screwdriver into the holes in the backside of the steering wheel and pry the clips away from the airbag module retaining pins

turn the steering wheel to the straight ahead position, place the ignition switch in the Lock position, remove the Air Bag fuse and unplug the yellow Connector Position Assurance (CPA) connectors at the base of the steering column and under the right side of the instrument panel before working in the vicinity of the impact sensors, steering column or instrument panel to avoid the possibility of accidental deployment of the airbag, which could cause personal injury (see Chapter 12).
Caution: *On models equipped with a Delco Loc II or Theftlock audio system, be sure the lockout feature is turned off before performing any procedure which requires disconnecting the battery.*
1   Disconnect the cable from the negative battery terminal.
2   Disable the airbag system (see Chapter 12 and **Warning** above).
3   On 1995 through 2002 models, remove the airbag module retaining screws **(see illustration)**. On 2003 and later models, the airbag module is retained by four spring clips. Insert a screwdriver into the holes in the backside of the steering wheel and disengage the clips from the retaining posts **(see illustration)**.
4   Remove the airbag module and unplug the electrical connectors **(see illustration)**.
Warning: *Carry the airbag module with the trim side facing away from you. Set the airbag module in an isolated area with the trim side facing up.*
5   Remove the steering wheel retaining nut.
6   The steering wheel and the steering shaft should already be marked **(see illustration)**. If they're not, mark their relationship to one another before removing the steering wheel.
7   Remove the steering wheel with a puller

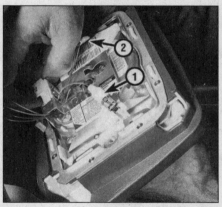

12.4 Unplug the electrical connectors for the airbag module (the big yellow connector), the horn lead (1) and the horn ground (2)

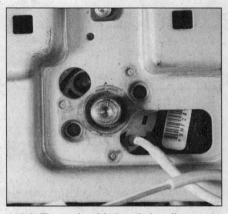

12.6 There should already be alignment marks on the steering wheel and steering shaft; if not, make alignment marks on the steering wheel hub and shaft at 12 o'clock

(see illustration). Warning: *Don't allow the steering shaft to turn with the steering wheel removed. If for some reason the steering shaft does turn, refer to Section 8 in Chapter 12 for the airbag coil centering procedure.*

12.7 Use a steering wheel puller to separate the steering wheel from the shaft - DO NOT attempt to remove the wheel with a hammer!

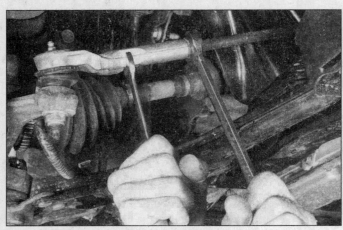

13.2a Before removing the tie-rod end, loosen the jam nut . . .

13.2b . . . and mark the position of the tie-rod end on the inner tie-rod

8   Installation is the reverse of removal. Be sure to tighten the steering wheel nut to the torque listed in this Chapter's Specifications.
9   To enable the airbag system, refer to Chapter 12.

13 Tie-rod ends - removal and installation

Refer to illustrations 13.2a, 13.2b and 13.3

1   Loosen the wheel lug nuts, raise the vehicle and place it securely on jackstands. Remove the wheel.
2   Loosen the tie-rod end jam nut **(see illustration)** and mark the position of the tie-rod end on the threaded portion of the tie-rod **(see illustration)**.
3   Remove the cotter pin and loosen (but do not remove) the castle nut from the tie-rod end balljoint stud, then install a small puller **(see illustration)** and break loose the tie-rod

13.3 To separate the tie-rod end from the steering knuckle, loosen - but don't remove - the ballstud nut, then install a balljoint removal tool (shown) or a small puller to pop the ballstud out of the knuckle (DO NOT pound on the stud!)

end from the steering knuckle. Remove the nut and detach the tie-rod end.
4   Unscrew the old tie-rod end and install the new one. Make sure the new tie-rod end is aligned with the mark you made on the threads of the tie-rod.
5   Installation is the reverse of removal. Be sure to tighten the tie-rod end balljoint nut to the torque listed in this Chapter's Specifications. Tighten the jam nut securely.

14 Steering gear boots - replacement

Refer to illustrations 14.4a and 14.4b

1   If a steering gear boot is torn, dirt and moisture can damage the steering gear. Replace it.
2   Loosen the wheel lug nuts, raise the vehicle and place it securely on jackstands. Remove the front wheels.
3   Disconnect the tie-rod ends from the steering knuckles and remove them from the tie-rods (see Section 13). Also remove the jam nuts.
4   Remove the boot clamps **(see illustration)** and slide the boots off the tie-rods.

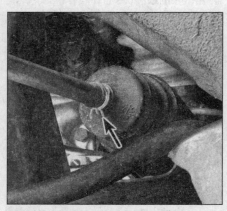

14.4a Squeeze the outer boot clamp with a pair of pliers and slide it down the tie-rod

5   Installation is the reverse of removal. Be sure to use new clamps on the boots.

15 Steering gear - removal and installation

Refer to illustrations 15.7, 15.8 and 5.11
Warning 1: *These models have airbags. Always turn the steering wheel to the straight ahead position, place the ignition switch in the Lock position, remove the Air Bag fuse and unplug the yellow Connector Position Assurance (CPA) connectors at the base of the steering column and under the right side of the instrument panel before working in the vicinity of the impact sensors, steering column or instrument panel to avoid the possibility of accidental deployment of the airbag, which could cause personal injury (see Chapter 12).*
Warning 2: *Make sure the steering shaft is not turned while the steering gear is removed or you could damage the airbag system. To prevent the shaft from turning, turn the ignition key to the lock position before beginning work or run the seat belt through the steering wheel and clip the seat belt into place.*

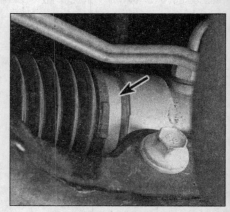

14.4b Cut off the inner boot clamps (arrow) with diagonal cutters and slide off the old boots

15.7 Remove the steering gear mounting bolts (arrows)

15.8 Unscrew these tube nuts (arrows) and disconnect the power steering pressure and return lines from the steering gear

1   Park the vehicle with the wheels pointing straight ahead.
2   Remove the left side under-dash panel.
3   Follow the steering column down towards the firewall and locate the intermediate shaft upper pinch bolt. Mark the relationship of the intermediate shaft to the steering shaft, then remove the bolt.
4   Loosen the wheel lug nuts, raise the vehicle and support it securely on jackstands.
5   Remove the front wheels.
6   Disconnect the tie-rod ends from the steering knuckles (see Section 13).
7   Remove the steering gear mounting bolts **(see illustration)**.
8   Place a drain pan under the left (driver's side) of the steering gear, then disconnect the pressure and return hoses attached to the power steering gear assembly **(see illustration)**. **Note:** *If available, use a flare-nut wrench to prevent rounding-off the fittings.* Plug the ends of the disconnected hoses and the holes in the power steering housing to prevent contamination.
9   Remove the plastic shroud protecting the lower intermediate shaft U-joint coupling.
10   Mark the relationship of the lower intermediate shaft U-joint coupling to the steering gear.

11   Remove the pinch bolt from the intermediate shaft-to-steering gear U-joint **(see illustration)**.
12   Remove the intermediate shaft assembly.
13   Support the suspension crossmember with a floor jack.
14   Remove the two rear suspension crossmember retaining bolts and the four other crossmember bolts, then lower the crossmember slightly to provide sufficient clearance for removal of the steering gear.
15   Remove the steering gear through the left wheel well.
16   Installation is the reverse of removal. Be sure to tighten all fasteners to the torque listed in this Chapter's Specifications.
17   Top up the power steering pump reservoir when you're done and bleed the power steering system (see Section 17).

16   Power steering pump - removal and installation

Removal

Refer to illustrations 16.4, 16.5, 16.6 and 16.7
1   Disconnect the cable from the negative battery terminal. **Caution:** *If the stereo in your vehicle is equipped with an anti-theft system, make sure you have the correct activation code before disconnecting the battery.*

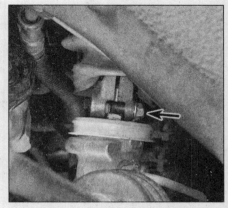

15.11 Mark the relationship of the lower U-joint coupling to the steering gear input shaft, then remove the pinch bolt (arrow)

2   Remove the drivebelt on 2.2L engines (see Chapter 1). Remove the air intake duct from the engine on 2.3L and 2.4L engines (see Chapter 4).
3   Disconnect the inlet and outlet hoses from the power steering pump.
4   Unbolt the power steering pump from the bracket on 2.2L engines **(see illustration)** or from the rear of the camshaft housing on 2.3L and 2.4L engines.
5   Remove the pump **(see illustration)**.

16.4 To remove the power steering pump, on 2.2L engines remove this bolt (arrow) and the other two bolts, which are accessed through the holes in the pulley

16.5 Remove the power steering pump (2.2L OHV engine shown)

16.6 A typical power steering pump pulley removal tool

16.7 A typical power steering pump pulley installation tool

6   On 2.2L engines, remove the pulley from the power steering pump with a suitable pulley removal tool **(see illustration)**. Pulley removal and installation tools are available at most auto parts stores.

7   Install the pulley on the new pump using a special installation tool **(see illustration)**. **Caution:** *Do not use a press to install the pulley.* The pulley should be installed so the face of the pulley is flush with the end of the pump shaft.

8   Installation is the reverse of removal. Tighten the pump bolts and the fittings securely.

9   Prime the pump by turning the pulley in the reverse direction to that of normal rotation (counterclockwise as viewed from the front) until air bubbles cease to emerge from the fluid when observed through the reservoir filler cap.

10   Install the drivebelt (see Chapter 1).

11   Bleed the power steering system (see Section 17).

17   Power steering system - bleeding

1   This is not a routine operation and normally will only be required when the system has been dismantled and reassembled.

2   Fill the reservoir to the correct level with fluid of the recommended type and allow it to remain undisturbed for at least two minutes.

3   Start the engine and run it for two or three seconds only. Check the reservoir and add more fluid as necessary.

4   Repeat the operations described in the preceding paragraph until the fluid level remains constant.

5   Raise the front of the vehicle until the wheels are clear of the ground.

6   Start the engine and increase the speed to about 1500 rpm. Now turn the steering wheel gently from stop-to-stop. Check the reservoir fluid level.

7   Lower the vehicle to the ground and, with the engine still running, move the vehicle forward sufficiently to obtain full right lock followed by full left lock. Recheck the fluid level. If the fluid in the reservoir is extremely foamy, allow the vehicle to stand for a few minutes with the engine switched off and then repeat the previous operations. At the same time, check the belt tightness and check for a bent or loose pulley. Check also to make sure the power steering hoses are not touching any other part of the vehicle, especially sheet metal or the exhaust manifold.

8   The procedures above will normally remedy an extreme foam condition and/or an objectionably noisy pump (low fluid level and/or air in the power steering fluid are the leading causes of this condition). If, however, either or both conditions persist after a few trials, the power steering system will have to be thoroughly checked. Do not drive the vehicle until the condition(s) have been remedied.

18   Wheels and tires - general information

Refer to illustration 18.1

All vehicles covered by this manual are equipped with metric-sized fiberglass or steel-belted radial tires **(see illustration)**. Use of other size or type of tires may affect the ride and handling of the vehicle. Don't mix different types of tires, such as radials and bias belted, on the same vehicle as handling may be seriously affected. It's recommended that tires be replaced in pairs on the same axle, but if only one tire is being replaced, be sure it's the same size, structure and tread design as the other. Because tire pressure has a substantial effect on handling and wear, the pressure on all tires should be checked at least once a month or before any extended trips (see Chapter 1).

Wheels must be replaced if they are bent, dented, leak air, have elongated bolt

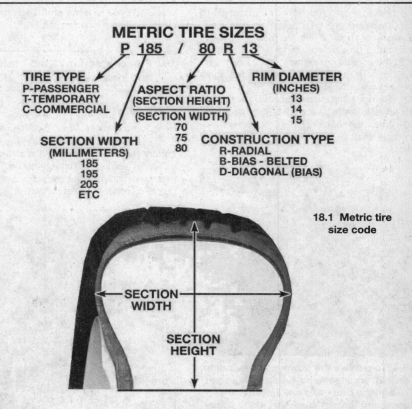

18.1 Metric tire size code

holes, are heavily rusted, out of vertical symmetry or if the lug nuts won't stay tight. Wheel repairs that use welding or peening are not recommended.

Tire and wheel balance is important to the overall handling, braking and performance of the vehicle. Unbalanced wheels can adversely affect handling and ride characteristics as well as tire life. Whenever a tire is installed on a wheel, the tire and wheel should be balanced by a shop with the proper equipment.

19 Front end alignment - general information

Refer to illustration 19.1

A front end alignment refers to the adjustments made to the front wheels so they are in proper angular relationship to the suspension and the ground **(see illustration)**. Front wheels that are out of proper alignment not only affect steering control, but also increase tire wear. Camber and toe-in are the only angles that can be adjusted on the vehicles covered by this manual, but caster should also be measured to determine if any suspension parts are bent.

Getting the proper front wheel alignment is a very exacting process, one in which complicated and expensive machines are necessary to perform the job properly. Because of this, you should have a technician with the proper equipment perform these tasks. We will, however, use this space to give you a basic idea of what is involved with front end alignment so you can better understand the process and deal intelligently with the shop that does the work.

Camber is the tilting of the front wheels from vertical when viewed from the front of the vehicle. On the vehicles covered in this

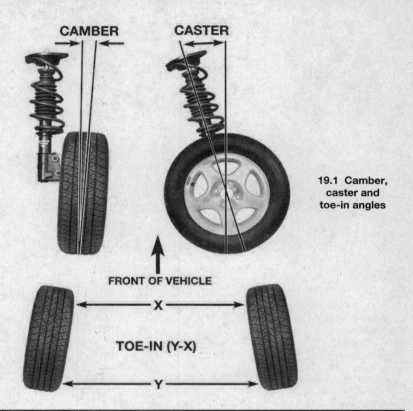

19.1 Camber, caster and toe-in angles

manual, camber can only be adjusted by elongating the lower strut-to-knuckle hole.

Caster is the tilting of the top of the front steering axis from the vertical: a tilt toward the rear is positive caster and a tilt toward the front is negative caster. Caster is not adjustable on these vehicles.

Toe-in is the turning in of the front wheels. The purpose of a toe specification is to ensure parallel rolling of the front wheels.

In a vehicle with zero toe-in, the distance between the front edges of the wheels will be the same as the distance between the rear edges of the wheels. The actual amount of toe-in is normally only a fraction of an inch. Toe-in adjustment is controlled by the position of the tie-rod end on the tie-rod. Incorrect toe-in will cause the tires to wear improperly by making them scrub against the road surface.

Notes

Chapter 11 Body

Contents

1   General information

Warning: *The models covered by this manual are equipped with airbags. Always disable the airbag system (see Chapter 12) before working in the vicinity of the impact sensors, steering column or instrument panel. Failure to follow these procedures may cause accidental deployment of the airbag, which could cause personal injury.*
Caution: *If the vehicle is equipped with a Delco Loc II or Theftlock audio system, make sure you have the correct activation code before disconnecting the battery.*

The models covered by this manual are designed with a "unibody" type construction. The major body components, floor pan and front and rear frame side rails are welded together to create a rigid structure which supports the remaining body components, drivetrain, front and rear suspension components and other mechanical components.

Certain body components are particularly vulnerable to accident damage and can be unbolted and repaired or replaced. Among these parts are the body moldings, front fenders, doors, bumpers, the hood, trunk lid and all glass.

Only general body maintenance practices and body panel repair procedures within the scope of the do-it-yourselfer are included in this Chapter.

2   Body - maintenance

1   The condition of your vehicle's body is very important, because the resale value depends a great deal on it. It's much more difficult to repair a neglected or damaged body than it is to repair mechanical components. The hidden areas of the body, such as the wheel wells, the frame and the engine compartment, are equally important, although they don't require as frequent attention as the rest of the body.
2   Once a year, or every 12,000 miles, it's a good idea to have the underside of the body steam cleaned. All traces of dirt and oil will be removed and the area can then be inspected carefully for rust, damaged brake lines, frayed electrical wires, damaged cables and other problems. The front suspension components should be greased after completion of this job.
3   At the same time, clean the engine and the engine compartment with a steam cleaner or water-soluble degreaser.
4   The wheel wells should be given close attention, since undercoating can peel away and stones and dirt thrown up by the tires can cause the paint to chip and flake, allowing rust to set in. If rust is found, clean down to the bare metal and apply an anti-rust paint.
5   The body should be washed about once a week. Wet the vehicle thoroughly to soften the dirt, then wash it down with a soft sponge and plenty of clean soapy water. If the surplus dirt is not washed off very carefully, it can wear down the paint.
6   Spots of tar or asphalt thrown up from the road should be removed with a cloth soaked in solvent.
7   Once every six months, wax the body and chrome trim. If a chrome cleaner is used to remove rust from any of the vehicle's plated parts, remember that the cleaner also removes part of the chrome, so use it sparingly.

3   Vinyl trim - maintenance

Don't clean vinyl trim with detergents, caustic soap or petroleum-based cleaners. Plain soap and water works just fine, with a soft brush to clean dirt that may be ingrained. Wash the vinyl as frequently as the rest of the vehicle. After cleaning, application of a high-quality rubber and vinyl protectant will help prevent oxidation and cracks. The protectant can also be applied to weatherstripping, vacuum lines and rubber hoses, which often fail as a result of chemical degradation, and to the tires.

4   Upholstery and carpets - maintenance

1   Every three months remove the floor mats and clean the interior of the vehicle (more frequently if necessary). Use a stiff whisk broom to brush the carpeting and loosen dirt and dust, then vacuum the upholstery and carpets thoroughly, especially along seams and crevices.
2   Dirt and stains can be removed from carpeting with basic household or automotive carpet shampoos available in spray cans. Follow the directions and vacuum again, then use a stiff brush to bring back the "nap" of the carpet.
3   Most interiors have cloth or vinyl upholstery, either of which can be cleaned and maintained with a number of material-specific cleaners or shampoos available in auto supply stores. Follow the directions on the product for usage, and always spot-test any upholstery cleaner on an inconspicuous area (bottom edge of a back seat cushion) to ensure that it doesn't cause a color shift in the material.
4   After cleaning, vinyl upholstery should be treated with a protectant. **Note:** *Make sure the protectant container indicates the product can be used on seats - some products may make a seat too slippery.* **Caution:** *Do not use protectant on vinyl-covered steering wheels.*
5   Leather upholstery requires special care. It should be cleaned regularly with saddlesoap or leather cleaner. Never use alcohol, gasoline, nail polish remover or thinner to clean leather upholstery.
6   After cleaning, regularly treat leather upholstery with a leather conditioner, rubbed in with a soft cotton cloth. Never use car wax on leather upholstery.
7   In areas where the interior of the vehicle is subject to bright sunlight, cover leather seating areas of the seats with a sheet if the vehicle is to be left out for any length of time.

5   Body repair - minor damage

Flexible plastic body panels (front and rear bumper fascia)

The following repair procedures are for minor scratches and gouges. Repair of more serious damage should be left to a dealer service department or qualified auto body shop. Below is a list of the equipment and materials necessary to perform the following repair procedures on plastic body panels. Although a specific brand of material may be mentioned, it should be noted that equivalent products from other manufacturers may be used instead.

> *Wax, grease and silicone removing solvent*
> *Cloth-backed body tape*
> *Sanding discs*
> *Drill motor with three-inch disc holder*
> *Hand sanding block*
> *Rubber squeegees*
> *Sandpaper*
> *Non-porous mixing palette*
> *Wood paddle or putty knife*
> *Curved tooth body file*
> *Flexible parts repair material*

1   Remove the damaged panel, if necessary or desirable. In most cases, repairs can be carried out with the panel installed.
2   Clean the area(s) to be repaired with a wax, grease and silicone removing solvent applied with a water-dampened cloth.
3   If the damage is structural, that is, if it extends through the panel, clean the backside of the panel area to be repaired as well. Wipe dry.
4   Sand the rear surface about 1-1/2 inches beyond the break.
5   Cut two pieces of fiberglass cloth large enough to overlap the break by about 1-1/2 inches. Cut only to the required length.
6   Mix the adhesive from the repair kit according to the instructions included with the kit, and apply a layer of the mixture approximately 1/8-inch thick on the backside of the panel. Overlap the break by at least 1-1/2 inches.
7   Apply one piece of fiberglass cloth to the adhesive and cover the cloth with additional adhesive. Apply a second piece of fiberglass cloth to the adhesive and immediately cover the cloth with additional adhesive insufficient quantity to fill the weave.
8   Allow the repair to cure for 20 to 30 minutes at 60-degrees to 80-degrees F.
9   If necessary, trim the excess repair material at the edge.
10   Remove all of the paint film over and around the area(s) to be repaired. The repair material should not overlap the painted surface.
11   With a drill motor and a sanding disc (or a rotary file), cut a "V" along the break line approximately 1/2-inch wide. Remove all dust and loose particles from the repair area.
12   Mix and apply the repair material. Apply a light coat first over the damaged area; then continue applying material until it reaches a level slightly higher than the surrounding finish.
13   Cure the mixture for 20 to 30 minutes at 60-degrees to 80-degrees F.
14   Roughly establish the contour of the area being repaired with a body file. If low

areas or pits remain, mix and apply additional adhesive.
15   Block sand the damaged area with sandpaper to establish the actual contour of the surrounding surface.
16   If desired, the repaired area can be temporarily protected with several light coats of primer. Because of the special paints and techniques required for flexible body panels, it is recommended that the vehicle be taken to a paint shop for completion of the body repair.

Steel body panels

See photo sequence

Repair of minor scratches

17   If the scratch is superficial and does not penetrate to the metal of the body, repair is very simple. Lightly rub the scratched area with a fine rubbing compound to remove loose paint and built-up wax. Rinse the area with clean water.
18   Apply touch-up paint to the scratch, using a small brush. Continue to apply thin layers of paint until the surface of the paint in the scratch is level with the surrounding paint. Allow the new paint at least two weeks to harden, then blend it into the surrounding paint by rubbing with a very fine rubbing compound. Finally, apply a coat of wax to the scratch area.
19   If the scratch has penetrated the paint and exposed the metal of the body, causing the metal to rust, a different repair technique is required. Remove all loose rust from the bottom of the scratch with a pocket knife, then apply rust inhibiting paint to prevent the formation of rust in the future. Using a rubber or nylon applicator, coat the scratched area with glaze-type filler. If required, the filler can be mixed with thinner to provide a very thin paste, which is ideal for filling narrow scratches. Before the glaze filler in the scratch hardens, wrap a piece of smooth cotton cloth around the tip of a finger. Dip the cloth in thinner and then quickly wipe it along the surface of the scratch. This will ensure that the surface of the filler is slightly hollow. The scratch can now be painted over as described earlier in this section.

Repair of dents

20   When repairing dents, the first job is to pull the dent out until the affected area is as close as possible to its original shape. There is no point in trying to restore the original shape completely as the metal in the damaged area will have stretched on impact and cannot be restored to its original contours. It is better to bring the level of the dent up to a point which is about 1/8-inch below the level of the surrounding metal. In cases where the dent is very shallow, it is not worth trying to pull it out at all.
21   If the back side of the dent is accessible, it can be hammered out gently from behind using a soft-face hammer. While doing this, hold a block of wood firmly against the opposite side of the metal to absorb the hammer

blows and prevent the metal from being stretched.

22 If the dent is in a section of the body which has double layers, or some other factor makes it inaccessible from behind, a different technique is required. Drill several small holes through the metal inside the damaged area, particularly in the deeper sections. Screw long, self-tapping screws into the holes just enough for them to get a good grip in the metal. Now the dent can be pulled out by pulling on the protruding heads of the screws with locking pliers.

23 The next stage of repair is the removal of paint from the damaged area and from an inch or so of the surrounding metal. This is done with a wire brush or sanding disk in a drill motor, although it can be done just as effectively by hand with sandpaper. To complete the preparation for filling, score the surface of the bare metal with a screwdriver or the tang of a file, or drill small holes in the affected area. This will provide a good grip for the filler material. To complete the repair, see the subsection on filling and painting later in this Section.

Repair of rust holes or gashes

24 Remove all paint from the affected area and from an inch or so of the surrounding metal using a sanding disk or wire brush mounted in a drill motor. If these are not available, a few sheets of sandpaper will do the job just as effectively.

25 With the paint removed, you will be able to determine the severity of the corrosion and decide whether to replace the whole panel, if possible, or repair the affected area. New body panels are not as expensive as most people think and it is often quicker to install a new panel than to repair large areas of rust.

26 Remove all trim pieces from the affected area except those which will act as a guide to the original shape of the damaged body, such as headlight shells, etc. Using metal snips or a hacksaw blade, remove all loose metal and any other metal that is badly affected by rust. Hammer the edges of the hole to create a slight depression for the filler material.

27 Wire brush the affected area to remove the powdery rust from the surface of the metal. If the back of the rusted area is accessible, treat it with rust inhibiting paint.

28 Before filling is done, block the hole in some way. This can be done with sheet metal riveted or screwed into place, or by stuffing the hole with wire mesh.

29 Once the hole is blocked off, the affected area can be filled and painted. See the following subsection on filling and painting.

Filling and painting

30 Many types of body fillers are available, but generally speaking, body repair kits which contain filler paste and a tube of resin hardener are best for this type of repair work. A wide, flexible plastic or nylon applicator will

be necessary for imparting a smooth and contoured finish to the surface of the filler material. Mix up a small amount of filler on a clean piece of wood or cardboard (use the hardener sparingly). Follow the manufacturer's instructions on the package, otherwise the filler will set incorrectly.

31 Using the applicator, apply the filler paste to the prepared area. Draw the applicator across the surface of the filler to achieve the desired contour and to level the filler surface. As soon as a contour that approximates the original one is achieved, stop working the paste. If you continue, the paste will begin to stick to the applicator. Continue to add thin layers of paste at 20-minute intervals until the level of the filler is just above the surrounding metal.

32 Once the filler has hardened, the excess can be removed with a body file. From then on, progressively finer grades of sandpaper should be used, starting with a 180-grit paper and finishing with 600-grit wet-or-dry paper. Always wrap the sandpaper around a flat rubber or wooden block, otherwise the surface of the filler will not be completely flat. During the sanding of the filler surface, the wet-or-dry paper should be periodically rinsed in water. This will ensure that a very smooth finish is produced in the final stage.

33 At this point, the repair area should be surrounded by a ring of bare metal, which in turn should be encircled by the finely feathered edge of good paint. Rinse the repair area with clean water until all of the dust produced by the sanding operation is gone.

34 Spray the entire area with a light coat of primer. This will reveal any imperfections in the surface of the filler. Repair the imperfections with fresh filler paste or glaze filler and once more smooth the surface with sandpaper. Repeat this spray-and-repair procedure until you are satisfied that the surface of the filler and the feathered edge of the paint are perfect. Rinse the area with clean water and allow it to dry completely.

35 The repair area is now ready for painting. Spray painting must be carried out in a warm, dry, windless and dust free atmosphere. These conditions can be created if you have access to a large indoor work area, but if you are forced to work in the open, you will have to pick the day very carefully. If you are working indoors, dousing the floor in the work area with water will help settle the dust which would otherwise be in the air. If the repair area is confined to one body panel, mask off the surrounding panels. This will help minimize the effects of a slight mismatch in paint color. Trim pieces such as chrome strips, door handles, etc., will also need to be masked off or removed. Use masking tape and several thickness of newspaper for the masking operations.

36 Before spraying, shake the paint can thoroughly, then spray a test area until the spray painting technique is mastered. Cover the repair area with a thick coat of primer. The thickness should be built up using several thin layers of primer rather than one thick

one. Using 600-grit wet-or-dry sandpaper, rub down the surface of the primer until it is very smooth. While doing this, the work area should be thoroughly rinsed with water and the wet-or-dry sandpaper periodically rinsed as well. Allow the primer to dry before spraying additional coats.

37 Spray on the top coat, again building up the thickness by using several thin layers of paint. Begin spraying in the center of the repair area and then, using a circular motion, work out until the whole repair area and about two inches of the surrounding original paint is covered. Remove all masking material 10 to 15 minutes after spraying on the final coat of paint. Allow the new paint at least two weeks to harden, then use a very fine rubbing compound to blend the edges of the new paint into the existing paint. Finally, apply a coat of wax.

6 Body repair - major damage

1 Major damage must be repaired by an auto body/frame repair shop with the necessary welding and hydraulic straightening equipment.

2 If the damage has been serious, it is vital that the structure be checked for proper alignment or the vehicle's handling characteristics may be adversely affected. Other problems, such as excessive tire wear and wear in the driveline and steering may occur.

3 Due to the fact that all of the major body components (hood, fenders, etc.) are separate and replaceable units, any seriously damaged components should be replaced rather than repaired. Sometimes these components can be found in a wrecking yard that specializes in used vehicle components, often at considerable savings over the cost of new parts.

7 Hinges and locks - maintenance

Once every 3000 miles, or every three months, the hinges and latch assemblies on the doors, hood and trunk should be given a few drops of light oil or lock lubricant. The door latch strikers should also be lubricated with a thin coat of grease to reduce wear and ensure free movement. Lubricate the door and trunk locks with spray-on graphite lubricant.

8 Windshield and fixed glass - replacement

Replacement of the windshield and fixed glass requires the use of special fast setting adhesive/caulk materials. These operations should be left to a dealer or a shop specializing in glass work.

These photos illustrate a method of repairing simple dents. They are intended to supplement *Body repair - minor damage* in this Chapter and should not be used as the sole instructions for body repair on these vehicles.

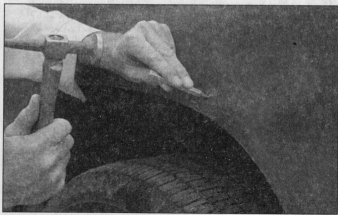

1 If you can't access the backside of the body panel to hammer out the dent, pull it out with a slide-hammer-type dent puller. In the deepest portion of the dent or along the crease line, drill or punch hole(s) at least one inch apart . . .

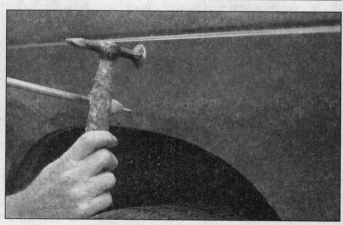

2 . . . then screw the slide-hammer into the hole and operate it. Tap with a hammer near the edge of the dent to help 'pop' the metal back to its original shape. When you're finished, the dent area should be close to its original contour and about 1/8-inch below the surface of the surrounding metal

3 Using coarse-grit sandpaper, remove the paint down to the bare metal. Hand sanding works fine, but the disc sander shown here makes the job faster. Use finer (about 320-grit) sandpaper to feather-edge the paint at least one inch around the dent area

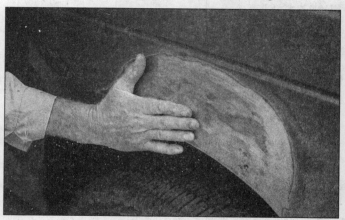

4 When the paint is removed, touch will probably be more helpful than sight for telling if the metal is straight. Hammer down the high spots or raise the low spots as necessary. Clean the repair area with wax/silicone remover

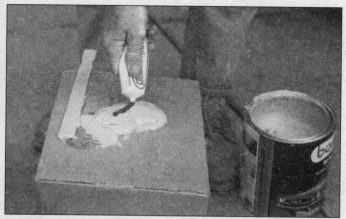

5 Following label instructions, mix up a batch of plastic filler and hardener. The ratio of filler to hardener is critical, and, if you mix it incorrectly, it will either not cure properly or cure too quickly (you won't have time to file and sand it into shape)

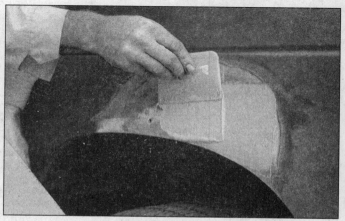

6 Working quickly so the filler doesn't harden, use a plastic applicator to press the body filler firmly into the metal, assuring it bonds completely. Work the filler until it matches the original contour and is slightly above the surrounding metal

7 Let the filler harden until you can just dent it with your fingernail. Use a body file or Surform tool (shown here) to rough-shape the filler

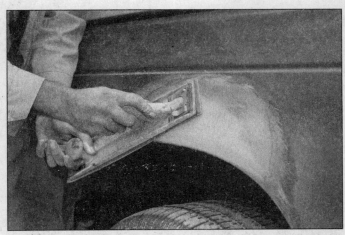

8 Use coarse-grit sandpaper and a sanding board or block to work the filler down until it's smooth and even. Work down to finer grits of sandpaper - always using a board or block - ending up with 360 or 400 grit

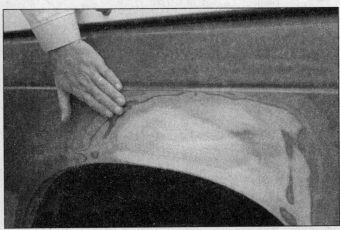

9 You shouldn't be able to feel any ridge at the transition from the filler to the bare metal or from the bare metal to the old paint. As soon as the repair is flat and uniform, remove the dust and mask off the adjacent panels or trim pieces

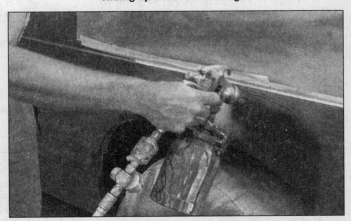

10 Apply several layers of primer to the area. Don't spray the primer on too heavy, so it sags or runs, and make sure each coat is dry before you spray on the next one. A professional-type spray gun is being used here, but aerosol spray primer is available inexpensively from auto parts stores

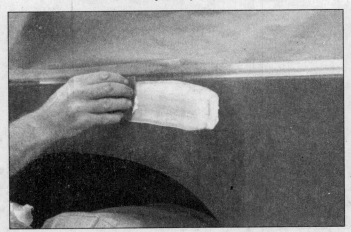

11 The primer will help reveal imperfections or scratches. Fill these with glazing compound. Follow the label instructions and sand it with 360 or 400-grit sandpaper until it's smooth. Repeat the glazing, sanding and respraying until the primer reveals a perfectly smooth surface

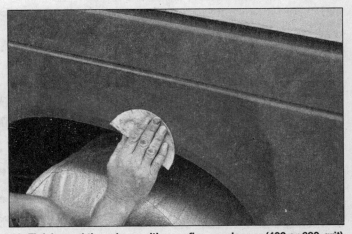

12 Finish sand the primer with very fine sandpaper (400 or 600-grit) to remove the primer overspray. Clean the area with water and allow it to dry. Use a tack rag to remove any dust, then apply the finish coat. Don't attempt to rub out or wax the repair area until the paint has dried completely (at least two weeks)

9.2 Mark the relationship of the hinges to the hood as shown, then, with the help of an assistant to hold the hood, remove the retaining bolts (arrows) from each hinge plate and lift off the hood

9.10a To remove the hood latch cover, release the push-in retainers (arrows) (1996 model shown, other model years similar)

9 Hood - removal, installation and adjustment

Removal and installation

Refer to illustration 9.2

Note: *The hood is somewhat awkward to remove and install; at least two people should perform this procedure.*

1   Open the hood, then place blankets or pads over the fenders and cowl area of the body. This will protect the body and paint as the hood is lifted off.

2   Make marks or scribe a line around the hood hinge to ensure proper alignment during installation **(see illustration)**.

3   Disconnect any cables or wires that will interfere with removal.

4   With an assistant supporting the weight of the hood, remove the hinge-to-hood bolts and lift off the hood.

5   Installation is the reverse of removal. Align the hinge bolts with the marks made in step 2.

Adjustment

Refer to illustrations 9.10a, 9.10b, 9.10c, 9.10d and 9.11

7   Fore-and-aft and side-to-side adjustment of the hood is done by moving the hinge plate slot after loosening the bolts or nuts.

8   Scribe a line around the entire hinge plate so you can determine the amount of movement.

9   Loosen the bolts or nuts and move the hood into correct alignment. Move it only a little at a time. Tighten the hinge bolts and carefully lower the hood to check the position.

10   If necessary after installation, the entire hood latch assembly can be adjusted up-and-down as well as from side-to-side on the radiator support so the hood closes securely and flush with the fenders. First, remove the hood latch cover **(see illustrations)**. To make the adjustment, scribe a line or mark around the hood latch to provide a reference point **(see illustration)**, then loosen the latch retaining bolts **(see illustration)** and reposition the latch assembly, as necessary. Following adjustment, retighten the mounting bolts.

11   Finally, adjust the hood bumpers **(see illustration)** on the radiator support so the hood, when closed, is flush with the fenders.

12   The hood latch assembly, as well as the hinges, should be periodically lubricated with white, lithium-base grease to prevent binding and wear.

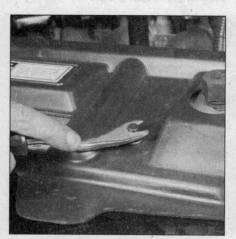

9.10b To release a push-in retainer, simply pry up the center part with a tool like this one or a flat-blade screwdriver

9.10c Mark the relationship of the hood latch to the crossmember to provide a visual indicator of the adjustment

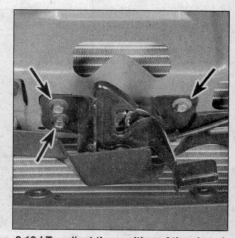

9.10d To adjust the position of the closed hood, loosen the hood latch bolts (arrows) and move the hood latch a little at a time, alternately closing the hood and noting its position in relation to the gaps between the hood and the fenders

9.11 Screw the hood bumpers in or out to adjust the hood flush with the fenders (left bumper shown, right bumper identical)

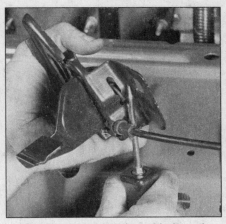

10.2a To disconnect the cable from the hood latch mechanism, pry the cable ferrule out of the latch assembly . . .

10.2b . . . and disengage the cable end plug from its slot in the latch

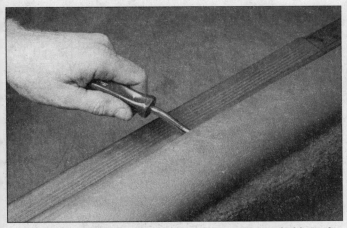

10.6a Gently pry the carpet retainer loose with a suitable tool

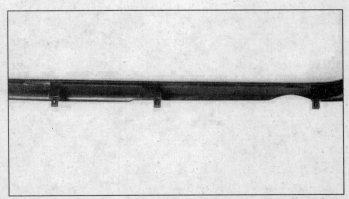

10.6b There are three locating pins under the front door portion of the carpet retainer on sedan models (shown) and two more pins under the rear door portion. On coupes there are four pins under the front door part

10 Hood latch and release cable - removal and installation

Warning: *The models covered by this manual are equipped with airbags. Always disable the airbag system (see Chapter 12) before working in the vicinity of the impact sensors, steering column or instrument panel. Failure to follow these procedures may cause accidental deployment of the airbag, which could cause personal injury.*

Hood latch

Refer to illustrations 10.2a and 10.2b

1   Scribe a line around the latch to aid alignment when installing, then remove the retaining bolts to the radiator support **(see illustration 9.10d)**. Remove the latch.
2   Disconnect the hood release cable by disengaging the cable from the latch assembly **(see illustrations)**.
3   Installation is the reverse of removal. Adjust the latch so the hood engages securely when closed and the hood bumpers are slightly compressed (see Section 9).

Release cable

Refer to illustrations 10.6a, 10.6b and 10.7

4   Disconnect the release cable from the hood latch assembly as described in Step 2.
5   Unclip the release cable from the engine wiring harness. Attach a piece of wire to the cable.
6   Working in the passenger compartment, remove the kick panel/carpet retainer (see illustrations), then peel back the carpet to expose the hood latch release cable and handle.
7   Remove the hood latch release handle retaining screw **(see illustration)**.
8   Trace the cable forward to the grommet where the cable goes through the firewall and pry the grommet out of the firewall. Pull the handle and cable rearward into the passenger compartment.

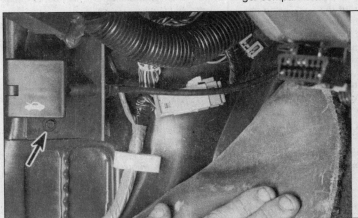

10.7 To detach the hood latch release cable handle, remove this retaining screw (arrow)

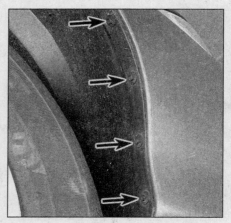

11.2a To detach the front bumper fascia from the splash shield, remove these four sheet metal screws (arrows) in each wheel well . . .

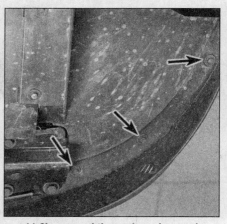

11.2b . . . and these three (arrows) underneath (right wheel well shown, left wheel well identical)

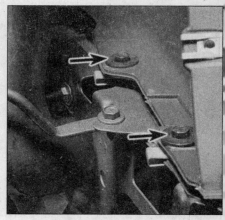

11.3 To detach the front bumper fascia from the fenders, remove these two bolts (arrows) from each fender

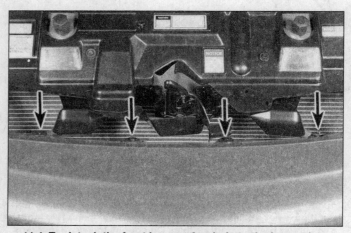

11.4 To detach the front bumper fascia from the impact bar, remove these four push-in retainers; to release each retainer, simply pry it up with a screwdriver (Chevrolet model shown, Pontiac models similar)

11.7 To detach the front energy absorber from the impact bar, drill out the nine pop rivets (five shown here, other four - located near ends of absorber - not visible in this photo); to locate the pop rivets, look for the semi-circular cutouts in the leading edge of the square above and below each rivet hole (non-Z24 model shown; Z24 models use six push-in retainers instead)

9   Disconnect the guide wire from the old cable and fasten it to the new cable.
10   With the new cable attached to the wire, pull the wire back through the firewall until the new cable reaches the latch assembly. Make sure that the grommet is properly seated on both sides of the hole in the firewall. Push on the grommet with your fingers from the passenger compartment side to seat the grommet in the firewall correctly.
11   Install the carpet and kick panel/carpet retainer.
12   Install the hood latch release handle retaining screw and tighten it securely.
13   The remainder of installation is the reverse of removal.

---

11   Bumpers - removal and installation

Warning: *The models covered by this manual*

are equipped with airbags. Always disable the airbag system (see Chapter 12) before working in the vicinity of the impact sensors, steering column or instrument panel. Failure to follow these procedures may cause accidental deployment of the airbag, which could cause personal injury.
Caution: *If the vehicle is equipped with a Delco Loc II or Theftlock audio system, make sure you have the correct activation code before disconnecting the battery.*

Front bumper
Refer to illustrations 11.2a, 11.2b, 11.3, 11.4 and 11.7
1   Raise the front of the vehicle and support it securely on jackstands.
2   Disconnect the bumper fascia from the left and right wheel well splash shields **(see illustrations)**.
3   Detach the bumper fascia from the fenders **(see illustration)**. **Note:** *Chevrolet*

models use two bolts to fasten the front bumper fascia to each front fender, while Pontiac models use two nuts and one screw to fasten the front bumper fascia to the fender.
4   Disconnect the bumper fascia from the front impact bar **(see illustration)**.
5   Before removing the bumper fascia, unplug the electrical connectors for the turn signal and parking lights (see Chapter 12).
6   Remove the bumper fascia.
7   To remove the front bumper energy absorber **(see illustration)** on most vehicles, drill out all nine pop rivets (Z24 models use six push-in retainers instead). To unlock a push-in retainer, pull the head out; to lock it into place, push the head down.
8   To remove the front bumper impact bar, simply remove the four impact bar retaining nuts (two at each end).
9   Installation is the reverse of removal. On all vehicles except Z24 models, you'll have to use new pop rivets.

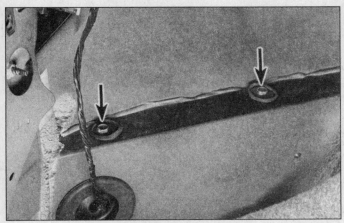

11.11 Inside the rear compartment, there are four rear bumper fascia retaining screws (arrows), two per side (left side screws shown)

11.12 There are four more rear bumper fascia retaining screws (arrows) - two per side - inside the rear wheel wells

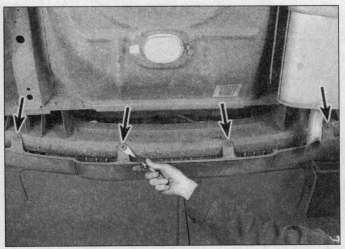

11.13 Remove these four push-in retainers (arrows) from the underside of the rear bumper fascia, then remove the fascia

11.15 To detach the rear bumper energy absorber, drill out the rivets (Pontiac Coupe and all Chevrolet models except the Z24) or remove the push-in retainers (Pontiac sedans and Chevrolet Z24 models); the number of rivets may vary - look for semicircular cutouts in the upper and lower edges of certain boxes, indicating a rivet in that box

Rear bumper

Refer to illustrations 11.11, 11.12, 11.13, 11.15 and 11.16

10   Raise the rear of the vehicle and place it securely on jackstands.

11   Working inside the rear compartment, remove the upper storage net retainers for access to the four rear fascia retaining screws - two per side **(see illustration)** - located inside the compartment. Remove these four screws.

12   Working inside the rear wheel wells, remove the four rear fascia retaining screws - two per wheel well **(see illustration)**.

13   Working underneath the rear fascia, remove the four push-in retainers **(see illustration)**.

14   Remove the rear bumper fascia.

15   To remove the rear bumper energy absorber **(see illustration)**, drill out the rivets (Pontiac Coupe and all Chevrolet models except the Z24) or remove the push-in retainers (Pontiac sedans and Chevrolet Z24 models).

16   To remove the rear bumper impact bar, remove the six retaining nuts (three at each end of the bar) from the stud plates **(see illustration)**.

17   Installation is the reverse of removal.

12   Fender (front) - removal and installation

Refer to illustrations 12.4a, 12.4b, 12.4c, 12.5, 12.8, 12.9a, 12.9b and 12.10

1   Remove the hood (see Section 9).

2   Loosen the front wheel lug nuts. Raise the vehicle, support it securely on jackstands and remove the front wheels.

3   Remove the splash shield **(see illustrations 11.2a and 11.2b)**.

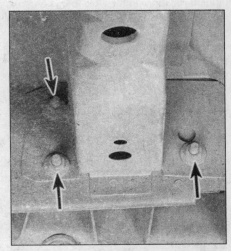

11.16 To detach the rear impact bar from the stud plates, remove six nuts (arrows) - three per side

12.4a To remove the wheel housing, release these three push-in retainers (arrows) in the upper part of the housing . . .

4   Remove the wheel housing and the fender flare **(see illustrations)**.
5   Remove the lower fender bracket bolts and the lower fender bracket **(see illustration)**.
6   Remove the front side marker light (see Chapter 12).
7   Detach the front bumper fascia from

the fender **(see illustration 11.3)**.
8   Remove the three fender insulator push-in retainers **(see illustration)** and remove the insulator.
9   Remove the two center fender bracket bolts and the upper fender bolt **(see illustrations)** and the center fender bracket.
10   Remove the two lower hood hinge bolts

(see illustration) and the lower hood hinge. Remove the two upper fender mounting bolts.
11   Remove the lower fender mounting bolts **(see illustration 12.4c)**.
12   Detach the fender. It's a good idea to have an assistant support the fender while it's being moved away from the vehicle to prevent damage to the surrounding body panels.
13   Installation is the reverse of removal.

13   Trunk lid - removal, installation and adjustment

Note: *The trunk lid is heavy and somewhat awkward to remove and install - at least two people should perform this procedure.*

Removal and installation

Refer to illustration 13.3
1   Open the trunk lid and cover the edges of the trunk compartment with pads or cloths to protect the painted surfaces when the lid is removed.

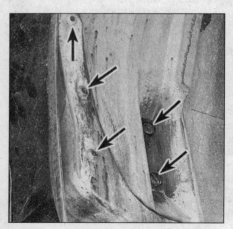

12.4b . . . and these two (right arrows), plus three more (not visible in this photo); to remove the fender flare, remove these three screws (left arrows) . . .

12.4c . . . and these two (right arrows); the two bolts (arrows) to the left of the fender flare are the lower rear fender mounting bolts

12.5 To detach the lower front part of the fender, remove these two bolts (arrows) and remove the lower fender bracket

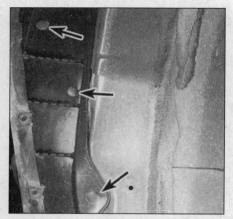

12.8 To remove the fender insulator, remove these three push-in retainers (arrows)

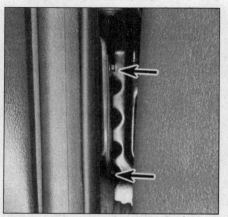

12.9a To detach the rear part of the fender, remove the center fender bracket bolts (arrows) . . .

12.9b . . . and the upper bolt (arrow)

12.10 Remove the lower hood hinge bolts (left arrows) and remove the lower hood hinge; to detach the upper part of the fender, remove the two bolts on the right (arrows)

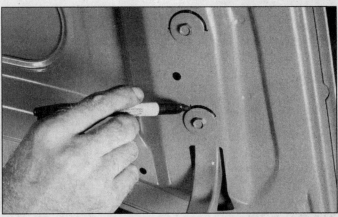

13.3 Before removing the four (two per side) trunk lid hinge bolts, be sure to mark the relationship of the hinge to the trunk lid to ensure correct alignment when the lid is installed

2   Disconnect any cables or wire harness connectors attached to the trunk lid that would interfere with removal.

3   Use a felt-tip marker or scribe to make alignment marks around the trunk lid hinge (see illustration).

4   While an assistant supports the lid, remove the hinge bolts from both sides and lift the trunk lid off the vehicle.

5   Installation is the reverse of removal. Note: *When reinstalling the trunk lid, align the hinge with the marks made during removal.*

Adjustment

Refer to illustration 13.12

6   Fore-and-aft and side-to-side adjustment of the trunk lid is done by moving the hood in relation to the hinge plate after loosening the bolts or nuts.

7   Scribe a line around the entire hinge plate as described earlier in this section so you can judge the amount of movement.

8   Loosen the bolts or nuts and move the trunk lid into correct alignment. Move it only a little at a time. Tighten the hinge bolts or nuts and carefully lower the trunk lid to check

the alignment.

9   If necessary after installation, the entire trunk lid latch assembly can be adjusted up and down as well as from side to side on the trunk lid so the lid closes securely and is flush with the rear quarter panels. To do this, scribe a line around the trunk lid latch mounting bolts to provide a reference point. Then loosen the bolts and reposition the latch assembly as necessary. Following adjustment, retighten the mounting bolts.

10   Adjust the bumpers on the trunk lid, so that the trunk lid is flush with the rear quarter panels when closed.

11   The trunk lid latch assembly, as well as the hinges, should be periodically lubricated with white lithium-base grease to prevent sticking and wear.

12   The effort required to raise or lower the trunk lid can also be adjusted, by moving the position of the ends of a pair of torque rods installed between the two trunk lid hinges (see illustration). Each rod can be adjusted up or down in one of three positions. To increase the effort required to raise the trunk lid, or to decrease the effort required to lower the lid,

relocate the rods down a notch. To decrease the effort needed to raise the lid, or to increase the effort needed to lower the lid, raise the rods a notch. To move a rod up or down, use a short section of pipe of a suitable diameter over the end of the rod; don't try to move a rod with your hand - it's too stiff.

14 Trunk lid latch, striker and lock cylinder - removal and installation

Caution: *If the vehicle is equipped with a Delco Loc II or Theftlock audio system, make sure you have the correct activation code before disconnecting the battery.*

Latch

Refer to illustration 14.2 and 14.3

1   On models with a remote release system, remove the locking clip, flip up the door on the latch assembly and disengage the release cable from the latch assembly.

2   Mark the relationship of the latch to the trunk lid (see illustration).

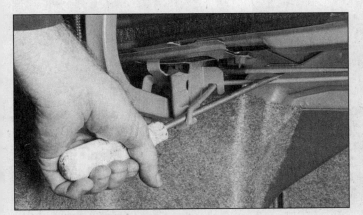

13.12 To readjust the tension on the trunk lid hinges, lever the ends of the torque rods up or down, one notch at a time, with a screwdriver as shown (raising the torque rods a notch makes it easier to raise the lid, and harder to lower it; moving the rods down a notch makes it harder to raise the lid, and easier to lower it)

14.2 Mark the relationship of the trunk lid latch to the trunk lid and remove the bolts (arrows)

14.3 To detach the lock release box from the latch assembly, release this push-in retainer (arrow)

14.6a The striker retaining nuts and reinforcement plate can be accessed through the gap between the rear bumper fascia and the body

14.6b You'll have to remove this sill plate to remove the striker

3   If you're replacing the latch or the lock cylinder, not just unbolting it from the trunk lid to swap it over to a new trunk lid, release the push-in retainer **(see illustration)** that secures the lock release box to the latch and detach the lock release box from the latch assembly. If you're repairing or replacing the trunk lid, rather than the latch and lock cylinder, it's not necessary to detach the lock release box from the latch assembly; simply remove both of them as a single assembly.

4   Remove the latch retaining bolts and remove the latch.

5   Installation is the reverse of removal. Be sure to align the latch carefully with the marks you made prior to removal.

Striker

Refer to illustrations 14.6a and 14.6b

6   Using a wrench inserted down into the space between the bumper fascia and the body, remove the two striker retaining nuts **(see illustration)**, remove the striker reinforcement plate, detach the sill plate **(see illustration)** and remove the striker.

7   Installation is the reverse of removal, but don't tighten the striker retaining nuts until you have closed the trunk lid and verified that the trunk latch and the striker are properly aligned.

Lock cylinder

Refer to illustration 14.10

8   Remove the trunk lid latch (see Steps 1 through 4).

9   Detach the lock release box from the latch assembly **(see illustration 14.3)**.

10   To detach the lock cylinder from the trunk lid on a Chevrolet model, pry off the retainer **(see illustration)**. To detach the lock cylinder on a Pontiac model, drill out the two rivets.

11   Installation is the reverse of removal. Don't forget the gasket between the lock cylinder and the trunk lid. On Pontiac models, install the new lock cylinder with new rivets, if available, or use nuts and bolts.

15   Door trim panel - removal and installation

Refer to illustrations 15.5a, 15.5b, 15.6a, 15.6b, 15.6c, 15.7, 15.8a and 15.8b

1   On models with power door locks and/or power windows, disconnect the cable from the negative terminal of the battery. **Caution:** *If the vehicle is equipped with a Delco Loc II or Theftlock audio system, make sure you have the correct activation code before disconnecting the battery.*

2   On Pontiac models, pull the inside door handle to the open position and carefully pry the upper edge of the handle bezel out of the door trim panel with a flat-blade screwdriver. Lift the bezel upward and remove it from the trim panel. On front doors, flip it over and unplug the electrical connector from the power door lock switch. Remove the bezel from the trim panel.

3   On Chevrolet models with power door

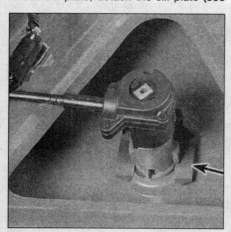

14.10 To detach the lock cylinder from the trunk lid on a Chevrolet (shown), pry off this retainer with a screwdriver; to detach the lock cylinder on a Pontiac model, drill out the two rivets

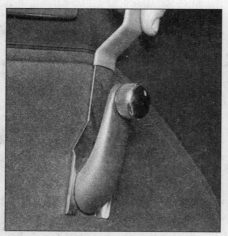

15.5a Use a window regulator handle removal tool to pop the handle retaining clip loose, then remove the handle

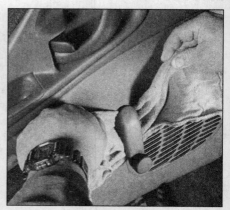

15.5b If you don't have a window regulator handle removal tool, work a clean shop rag up between the handle and the door trim panel from underneath as shown and pull up on the rag to pop the handle retaining clip loose, then remove the handle

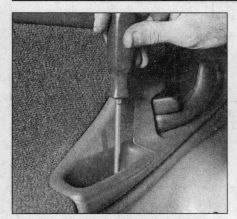

15.6a Remove the trim panel retaining screws inside this recess in the arm rest

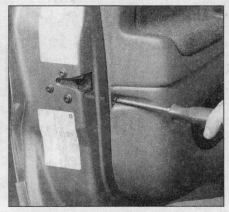

15.6b Remove all trim panel retaining screws from the rear (shown) and the front edges of the trim panel

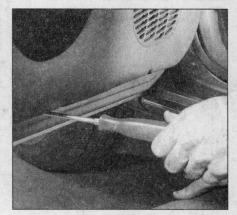

15.6c Remove all trim panel retaining screws from the lower edge of the trim panel (Chevrolet model shown, Pontiac models similar)

locks, pry the power door lock switch out of the door trim panel with a flat-blade screwdriver, unplug the electrical connector from the switch and remove the switch.

4   On models with power windows, pry the power window switch out of the trim panel with a flat-blade screwdriver, unplug the electrical connector from the switch and remove the switch.

5   On models with manually-operated windows, remove the window regulator handle **(see illustrations)**.

6   Remove the trim panel screws **(see illustrations)**.

7   Once all of the screws are removed, detach the trim panel from the door, disconnect any electrical connectors and remove the trim panel from the vehicle by lifting it up and away from the door **(see illustration)**.

8   If you're planning to repair or replace anything inside the door itself, you'll have to remove the water deflector between the trim panel and the door **(see illustration)**. To remove part of the deflector, simply peel it

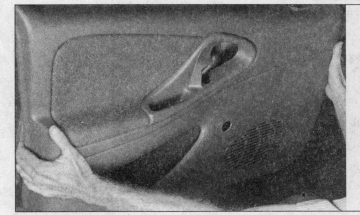

15.7 To detach the trim panel from the door, carefully lift it up, then away, from the door (Chevrolet model shown, Pontiac models similar)

loose from the door **(see illustration)**. If you need to remove the entire deflector, drill out the two rivets which secure the armrest hanger to the door and remove the hanger.

9   After you're done servicing the door component(s), reattach the deflector to the door. Use extra sealant if necessary. Make

sure that the deflector is securely attached to the door all the way around its perimeter. If you removed the armrest hanger, reattach it with a pair of suitable sheet metal screws or small bolts and nuts.

10   Installation is otherwise the reverse of removal.

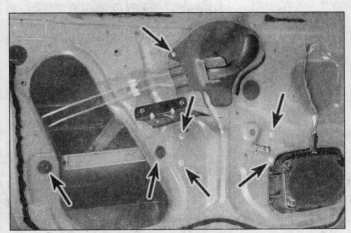

15.8a The water deflector is the plastic liner between the trim panel and the door. Locations of rivets and screws for the window regulator and door handle are indicated by arrows

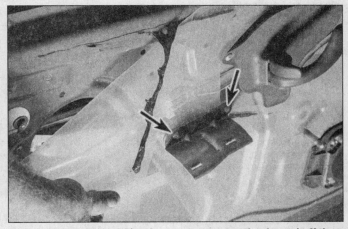

15.8b To get at the inner door components, simply peel off the deflector in the area in which you need to work; if you need to remove the entire deflector, drill out the two rivets (arrows) for the armrest hanger and remove the hanger

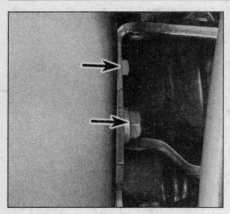

16.7a To detach the door from the vehicle, remove the upper hinge bolts (arrows) . . .

16.7b . . . and the lower hinge bolts (arrow). There are two bolts, but only one is visible

16.11 To adjust the door lock striker, loosen these Torx bolts (arrows) and move the striker up, down or sideways as necessary

16   Door - removal, installation and adjustment

Removal and installation

Refer to illustrations 16.7a and 16.7b

Note: *The door is heavy and somewhat awkward to remove and install - at least two people should perform this procedure. This procedure applies to both front and rear doors.*

1   Raise the window completely and disconnect the negative cable from the battery if equipped with power windows. **Caution:** *If the vehicle is equipped with a Delco Loc II or Theftlock audio system, make sure you have the correct activation code before disconnecting the battery.*

2   Open the door all the way and support it on jacks or blocks covered with rags to prevent damaging the paint.

3   Remove the door trim panel and enough of the water deflector to access all electrical wiring harnesses (see Section 15).

4   Unplug all electrical connectors, and detach all ground wires and harness retaining clips from the door. It's a good idea to label all connectors to aid the reassembly process.

5   Working on the door side, detach the rubber conduit between the body and the door. Pull the wiring harness through the conduit hole and remove the wiring from the door.

6   Mark around the door hinges with a pen or a scribe to facilitate realignment during reassembly.

7   Have an assistant hold the door, remove the hinge-to-door bolts **(see illustrations)** and lift the door off.

8   Installation is the reverse of removal.

Adjustment

Refer to illustration 16.11

9   Having proper door to body alignment is a critical part of a well functioning door assembly. First check the door hinge pins and bushings for excessive play. If the door can be lifted (1/16-inch or more) without the car body lifting with it the hinge pins and

bushings should be replaced.

10   Door-to-body alignment adjustments are made by loosening the hinge-to-body bolts or hinge-to-door bolts and moving the door. Proper body alignment is achieved when the top of the doors are parallel with the roof section, the front door is flush with the fender, the rear door is flush with the rear quarter panel and the bottom of the doors are aligned with the lower rocker panel. If these goals can't be reached by adjusting the hinge-to-body or hinge-to-door bolts, body alignment shims may have to be purchased and inserted behind the hinges to achieve correct alignment.

11   To adjust the door closed position, verify that the door latch is contacting the center of the striker. If it isn't, loosen the striker bolts **(see illustration)** and adjust the striker as necessary (up, down or sideways) to provide optimal engagement with the latch mechanism. Tighten the striker bolts securely once the striker is adjusted.

17   Door handles, lock cylinder and latch - removal and installation

1   Remove the door trim panel (see Section 15) and peel away the water deflector in the vicinity of the component you're planning to remove.

Inside handle

2   Drill out the rivet securing the inside handle **(see illustration 15.8a)**. Slide the handle to the rear to disengage its locating tabs from the door frame.

3   Pull out the handle, disengage the actuating rods from the backside of the handle and remove the handle. Note which rod is connected to which lever on the handle. The rods must be reattached exactly the same way when the handle is installed.

4   Installation is the reverse of removal. If you don't have a pop rivet installer, reattach the handle assembly to the door with a suitable sheet metal screw or a nut and bolt.

Outside handle

5   Lift up the outside handle and drill out the two handle assembly rivets.

6   Pull out the handle assembly, disengage the actuator rod from the lever on the backside of the handle assembly and remove the handle. Note how the rod is connected to the handle lever; it must be reattached exactly the same way when the handle is installed.

7   Installation is the reverse of removal. If you don't have a pop rivet installer, reattach the handle assembly to the door with nuts and bolts.

Lock cylinder

Refer to illustration 17.8

8   Pry off the lock cylinder retainer clip **(see illustration)** that secures the lock cylinder to the door.

9   Disengage the actuator rod from the lock cylinder lever and remove the lock cylinder.

10   Installation is the reverse of removal.

17.8 To detach the lock cylinder from the door, insert a large screwdriver through the small hole above the lock cylinder and pry off this retainer

17.11 To detach the latch assembly from the door, remove these three bolts (arrows)

18.3a To detach the window from the regulator assembly, remove this nut (arrow) . . .

Latch

Refer to illustration 17.11

11   Remove the screws securing the latch to the door **(see illustration)**.

12   Working through the large access hole, position the latch as necessary to disengage the actuator rods from the outside door handle and lock cylinder and the inside handle. Note how these rods are connected to the latch assembly. They must be installed exactly the same way during reassembly. Remove the latch assembly.

13   Installation is the reverse of removal.

18   Door window glass - removal and installation

Refer to illustrations 18.3a and 18.3b

1   Remove the door trim panel and the plastic water deflector (see Section 15).

2   Lower the window glass all the way down into the door.

3   Remove the regulator-to-window retaining nuts **(see illustrations)**.

4   Drill out the rivets which secure the sashes to the window **(see illustration 18.3b)**. Pull off the sashes and sash spacers and remove the window from the door by pulling it up and out.

5   Installation is the reverse of removal.

19   Window regulator - removal and installation

1   On models with power windows, detach the negative battery cable. **Caution:** *If the vehicle is equipped with a Delco Loc II or Theftlock audio system, make sure you have the correct activation code before disconnecting the battery.*

2   Remove the door trim panel and the plastic water deflector (see Section 15).

3   Remove the window glass assembly (see Section 18).

4   On models with power windows, unplug

the electrical connector from the window regulator motor.

5   On front doors, remove the window regulator bolts **(see illustration 15.8a)**.

6   Drill out the rivets that secure the window regulator to the door frame **(see illustration 15.8a)**.

7   Remove the regulator assembly.

8   Installation is the reverse of removal.

20   Outside mirrors - removal and installation

Refer to illustrations 20.2a, 20.2b and 20.3
Caution: *If the vehicle is equipped with a Delco Loc II or Theftlock audio system, make sure you have the correct activation code before disconnecting the battery.*

1   On models with power mirrors, disconnect the negative cable from the battery.

2   Remove the mirror trim panel **(see illustrations)**. On models with power mirrors, unplug the electrical connector from the

18.3b . . . and this one (arrow); the rivets holding together the sashes, sash spacers and window must be drilled out before the window can be removed from the door (upper arrow points to the rivet for the rear sash; rivet for front sash not visible in previous photo)

20.2a To get to the outside mirror retaining nuts, remove this Phillips screw . . .

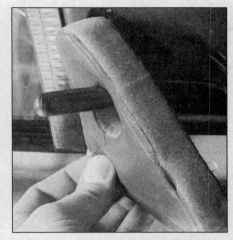

20.2b . . . and remove the triangular trim panel

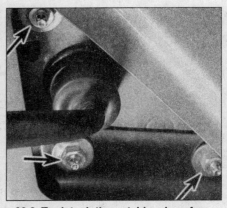

20.3 To detach the outside mirror from the door, remove these retaining nuts (arrows)

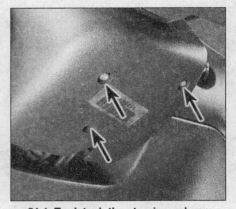

21.1 To detach the steering column covers from the steering column, remove these three screws (arrows) from the lower cover

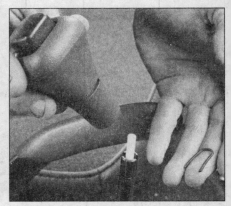

22.3 To detach the knob from the shift lever, pry out this retainer and pull the knob straight up

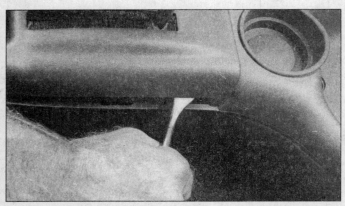

22.4a Pry the gear position indicator trim panel straight up to disengage the retaining clips . . .

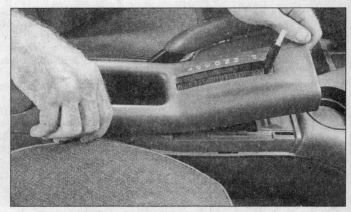

22.4b . . . then remove the trim panel

power mirror switch.
3   Remove the three mirror retaining nuts **(see illustration)** and detach the mirror from the vehicle.
4   Installation is the reverse of removal.

21 Steering column covers - removal and installation

Refer to illustration 21.1
1   Remove the three screws from the lower steering column cover half **(see illustration)** and remove the steering column covers.
2   Installation is the reverse of removal.

22 Center console - removal and installation

Refer to illustrations 22.3, 22.4a, 22.4b, 22.5a, 22.5b, 22.5c and 22.5d
Warning: *The models covered by this manual are equipped with airbags. Always disable the airbag system before working in the vicinity of the impact sensors, steering column or instrument panel to avoid the possibility of accidental deployment of the airbag(s), which could cause personal injury (see Chapter 12).*

1   Disconnect the negative cable from the battery. **Caution:** *If the vehicle is equipped with a Delco Loc II or Theftlock audio system, make sure you have the correct activation code before disconnecting the battery.*
2   Apply the parking brake lever and place the shift lever in the Neutral position.
3   On vehicles equipped with an automatic transaxle pry out the shift lever knob retaining clip and remove the knob **(see illustration)**. On vehicles equipped with a manual transaxle unscrew the shift lever knob and pry out the shift lever boot.
4   On vehicles equipped with an automatic transaxle pry out and remove the gear position indicator trim bezel **(see illustrations)**.
5   Remove the console retaining screws, raise up the console **(see illustrations)**, unplug any electrical connectors and remove the console from the vehicle.
6   Installation is the reverse of removal.

23 Dashboard trim panels - removal and installation

Warning: *The models covered by this manual are equipped with airbags. Always disable the air bag system before working in the vicinity of the impact sensors, steering column or*

instrument panel to avoid the possibility of accidental deployment of the airbag(s), which could cause personal injury (see Chapter 12).
1   Disconnect the negative battery cable.
Caution: *If the vehicle is equipped with a Delco Loc II or Theftlock audio system, make sure you have the correct activation code before disconnecting the battery.*
2   Disable the airbag system (see Chapter 12).

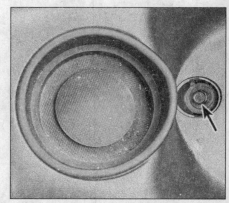

22.5a To detach the center console from the floor, remove this screw (arrow) from the front storage well . . .

22.5b . . . remove these two screws (arrows) from the mid-console . . .

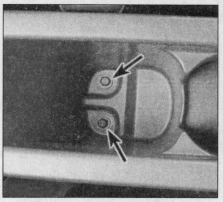

22.5c . . . remove these two screws from the rear storage well of the console . . .

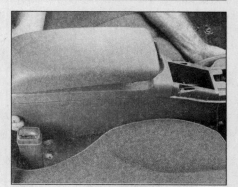

22.5d . . . then lift the console straight up and remove it (this Chevrolet console is typical; the number and location of retaining screws may vary slightly on different models)

23.6a To detach the center defroster grille, remove this retaining screw . . .

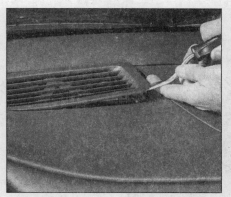

23.6b . . . then carefully pry the grille out of the instrument panel trim pad

23.9 To remove either end cap, simply pry it off as shown

Sound insulators

3   The sound insulators are the flat plastic trim panels underneath the left and right ends of the dash that must be removed to access everything located between the dash and the firewall (clutch pedal position switch, brake lights switch, cruise control switch, wire harnesses, etc.).

4   To remove either sound insulator, remove the screws along the trailing edge of the insulator (three screws for the left insulator, two for the right) then tilt the trailing edge of the insulator down, unplug any electrical connectors, then pull it to the rear to remove it.

5   Installation is the reverse of removal.

Defroster grilles and vent grilles

Refer to illustrations 23.6a and 23.6b

6   To remove the center defroster grille on Chevrolet models, remove the retaining screw, then gently pry up the upper grille **(see illustrations)**. To remove the center defroster grille on Pontiac models, simply pry the grille out of the dash using a small flat bladed screwdriver. Try not to scratch the plastic trim around the grille or the dash surface. To remove the smaller defroster grilles at the left and right ends of the instrument panel trim pad on Chevrolet models, simply

23.12 Remove the instrument panel trim pad retaining screw (arrow) in the recess for the center defroster grille (Pontiacs have two screws in this area)

pry them out.

7   To remove a left or right vent grille, remove the retaining screw and pry off the grille.

8   Installation is the reverse of removal.

Instrument panel end caps

Refer to illustration 23.9

9   To remove either end cap on a Chevrolet model, simply pry it off **(see illustration)**. To remove either end cap on a Pontiac model, remove the retaining screw.

10   Installation is the reverse of removal. Make sure the grommets for the locating pins are in good shape, then align the locating pins

on the back of the end cap with their respective grommets. If any of the grommets are cracked or torn, replace them (or the end cap may not stay on).

Instrument panel trim pad

Refer to illustrations 23.12, 23.14a, 23.14b, 23.16a, 23.16b and 23.17

11   Remove the center defroster grille (see Step 6).

12   Remove the retaining screw(s) in the center defroster grille opening **(see illustration)**. Chevrolet models have one screw; Pontiacs have two.

13   On Pontiac models, remove the valance

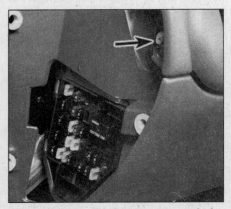

23.14a Remove this instrument panel trim pad retaining screw (arrow) from the left end . . .

23.14b . . . and this screw (arrow) from the right end

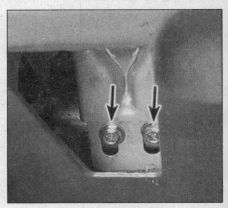

23.16a Inside the glovebox area, remove these two bolts (arrows) from the passenger airbag module bracket . . .

23.16b . . . and remove these three instrument panel trim pad retaining screws (arrows)

23.17 Lift the instrument panel trim pad straight up to pop the three locating pins above the instrument cluster loose from their respective holes in the instrument cluster trim plate

23.20a To detach the instrument cluster trim plate from the instrument panel, remove this screw (arrow) . . .

23.20b . . .this screw (arrow) . . .

23.20c . . . and this one (arrow)

retaining screws and the valance (the valance is the trim piece between the instrument panel trim pad and the windshield).

14   Remove the instrument panel end caps (see Step 9), then remove the screws located under the end caps (see illustrations).

16   Open the glovebox and remove the retaining bolts from the passenger side airbag module bracket (see illustration),

then remove the instrument panel trim pad retaining screws (see illustration).

17   Carefully inspect the perimeter of the trim pad and remove any remaining retaining screws (Pontiacs have more screws along the upper front edge of the trim pad), then grasp the panel securely and detach it from the instrument panel (see illustration).

18   Installation is the reverse of removal.

Instrument panel cluster trim plate (Chevrolet models)

Refer to illustrations 23.20a, 23.20b, 23.20c, 23.21 and 23.22

19   Remove the instrument panel trim pad (see steps 11 through 17).

20   Remove the instrument cluster trim plate retaining screws (see illustrations).

23.21 Work a prying tool around the perimeter of the instrument cluster trim plate in the area surrounding the heater/air conditioning controls and the radio, gently prying the trim plate loose

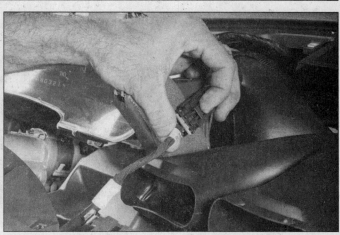

23.22 Pull the instrument cluster trim plate toward you and unplug the electrical connector for the trim plate wire harness (it's not necessary to unplug the individual connectors for the dimmer switch or for the cigarette lighter unless you're replacing those components)

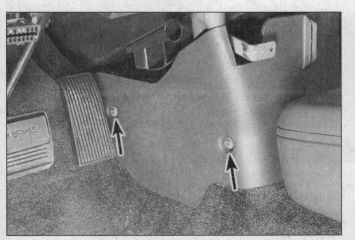

23.28 To remove the heater core/air conditioning evaporator trim panels, remove these two screws (arrows) from the left panel and the other two screws from the right panel . . .

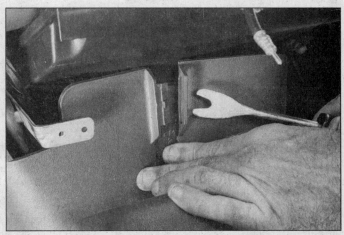

23.29 . . . then disengage the locking tab and slot in the middle and pull the two trim panels apart

21 Carefully pry the trim plate loose in the area around the heater/air conditioning controls and the radio **(see illustration)**.

22 Lift up the trim plate and pull it toward you, then unplug the electrical connector for the trim plate wiring harness **(see illustration)**. Remove the trim plate.

23 Installation is the reverse of removal.

Accessory trim plate (Pontiac models)

24 Remove the accessory trim plate-to-instrument panel retaining screws.

25 Open the glove box door and remove the rest of the accessory trim plate retaining screws.

26 Carefully pry the accessory trim plate to the rear to detach it from the instrument panel.

27 Installation is the reverse of removal.

Heater core/air conditioning evaporator trim panels

Refer to illustrations 23.28 and 23.29

28 Remove the four trim panel retaining screws **(see illustration)**.

29 Disengage the locking tab and slot in the middle and pull the trim panels apart **(see illustration)**.

30 Installation is the reverse of removal.

24 Instrument panel - removal and installation

Refer to illustrations 24.7, 24.8a, 24.8b, 24.8c, 24.8d and 24.8e

Warning: *The models covered by this manual are equipped with airbags. Always disable the air bag system before working in the vicinity of the impact sensors, steering column or instrument panel to avoid the possibility of*

accidental deployment of the airbag(s), which could cause personal injury (see Chapter 12).

1 Disconnect the negative battery cable.

Caution: *If the vehicle is equipped with a Delco Loc II or Theftlock audio system, make sure you have the correct activation code before disconnecting the battery.*

2 Disable the airbag system (see Chapter 12).

3 Remove the sound insulators, defroster grilles, end caps and instrument panel trim pad, and instrument cluster trim plate (Chevrolet models) or accessory trim plate (Pontiac models) (see Section 23).

4 Remove the heater and air conditioning control assembly (see Chapter 3).

5 Remove the radio (see Chapter 12). Remove the steering wheel (see Chapter 10), the combination switch and the windshield wiper switch (see Chapter 12) from the steering column.

6 Remove any air distribution duct retain-

24.7 To detach the glovebox light, remove these two screws

24.8a To detach the left end of the instrument panel, remove this screw (upper arrow) and nut (lower arrow)

24.8b To detach the center part of the instrument panel, remove these three screws (arrows)

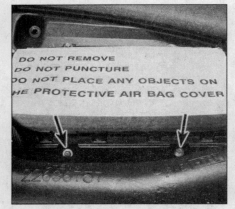

24.8c To detach the upper right part of the instrument panel, remove these two screws (arrows)

24.8d To detach the glovebox part of the instrument panel, remove these two screws (arrows)

24.8e To detach the right end of the instrument panel remove this nut (arrow)

ing screws. (The air distribution duct must be detached from the instrument panel but it's not really necessary to remove it to remove the instrument panel.)

7　Detach the glovebox light **(see illustration)**.

8　Remove the instrument panel retaining screws **(see illustrations)**.

9　Disengage the instrument panel assembly from the body by lifting it up and back slightly.

10　Reach behind the instrument panel and unplug any electrical connectors that may still be connected.

11　Installation is the reverse of removal.

25 Seats - removal and installation

Front seat

1　If you just want to repair or replace the seat itself, or you want to remove the seat to create more room to work under the dash, unbolt the seat from the adjuster assembly.

Locate the four bolts - one at each corner - securing the seat to the adjuster assembly (the bolt heads face down). Remove all four bolts.

2　Tilt the seat up, unplug any electrical connectors underneath and remove the seat.

3　If you want to replace the seat adjuster assembly, or you need to remove the adjuster to remove or replace the carpet, unbolt the adjuster from the floor. The seat adjuster assembly is bolted to the floor with four bolts.

4　Installation is the reverse of removal. Be sure to tighten all bolts securely.

Rear seat

5　Unlatch the rear seat back and tilt it forward.

6　Unhook the outer side belt retractor from the rear seat back.

7　Remove the spacer from right key pin.

8　Slide the seat back to the right and disengage the left key pin from the left key slot.

9　Slide the seat back to the left and disen-

gage the right key slot from the right key slot.

10　Remove the seat back.

11　Press the seat cushion retainer to the rear with a screwdriver.

12　Lift the seat cushion up and remove it.

13　Installation is the reverse of removal.

26 Seat belts - check

1　Check the seat belts, buckles, latch plates and guide loops for any obvious damage or signs of wear.

2　Make sure the seat belt reminder light comes on when the key is turned on.

3　The seat belts are designed to lock up during a sudden stop or impact, yet allow free movement during normal driving. The retractors should hold the belt against your chest while driving and rewind the belt when the buckle is unlatched.

4　If any of the above checks reveal problems with the seat-belt system, replace parts as necessary.

Chapter 12   Chassis electrical system

Contents

	Section		Section
Airbag - general information	25	Headlight housing - removal and installation	15
Antenna - removal and installation	12	Headlights - adjustment	16
Bulb replacement	17	Horn - check and replacement	21
Circuit breakers - general information	5	Ignition switch and key lock cylinder - removal and installation	10
Combination switch - removal and installation	8	Instrument cluster - removal and installation	19
Cruise control system - description and check	23	Power window system - description and check	24
Daytime Running Lights (DRL) - general information	18	Radio and speakers - removal and installation	11
Electric side-view mirrors - description and check	22	Rear window defogger - check and repair	13
Electrical troubleshooting - general information	2	Relays - general information	6
Fuses - general information	3	Turn signal/hazard flasher - check and replacement	7
Fusible links - general information	4	Windshield wiper/washer switch - removal and installation	9
General information	1	Wiper motor - check and replacement	20
Headlight bulb - replacement	14	Wiring diagrams - general information	26

1   General information

The electrical system is a 12-volt, negative ground type. Power for the lights and all electrical accessories is supplied by a lead/acid-type battery which is charged by the alternator.

This Chapter covers repair and service procedures for the various electrical components not associated with the engine. Information on the battery, alternator, ignition system and starter motor can be found in Chapter 5. It should be noted that when portions of the electrical system are serviced, the negative battery cable should be disconnected from the battery to prevent electrical shorts and/or fires.

Caution: *If the vehicle is equipped with a Delco Loc II or Theftlock audio system, make sure you have the correct activation code before disconnecting the battery.*

2   Electrical troubleshooting - general information

A typical electrical circuit consists of an electrical component, any switches, relays, motors, fuses, fusible links or circuit breakers related to that component and the wiring and electrical connectors that link the component to both the battery and the chassis. To help you pinpoint an electrical circuit problem, wiring diagrams are included at the end of this Chapter.

Before tackling any troublesome electrical circuit, first study the appropriate wiring diagrams to get a complete understanding of what makes up that individual circuit. Trouble spots, for instance, can often be narrowed down by noting if other components related to the circuit are operating properly. If several components or circuits fail at one time, chances are the problem is in a fuse or ground connection, because several circuits are often routed through the same fuse and ground connections.

Electrical problems usually stem from simple causes, such as loose or corroded connections, a blown fuse, a melted fusible link or a bad relay. Visually inspect the condition of all fuses, wires and connections in a problem circuit before troubleshooting it.

If testing instruments are going to be utilized, use the diagrams to plan ahead of time where you will make the necessary connections in order to accurately pinpoint the trouble spot.

The basic tools needed for electrical troubleshooting include a circuit tester or voltmeter (a 12-volt bulb with a set of test leads can also be used), a continuity tester, which includes a bulb, battery and set of test leads, and a jumper wire, preferably with a circuit breaker incorporated, which can be used to bypass electrical components. Before attempting to locate a problem with test instruments, use the wiring diagram(s) to decide where to make the connections.

Voltage checks

Voltage checks should be performed if a circuit is not functioning properly. Connect one lead of a circuit tester to either the negative battery terminal or a known good ground. Connect the other lead to an electrical connector in the circuit being tested, preferably nearest to the battery or fuse. If the bulb of the tester lights, voltage is present, which means that the part of the circuit between the electrical connector and the battery is problem free. Continue checking the rest of the circuit in the same fashion. When you reach a point at which no voltage is present, the problem lies between that point and the last test point with voltage. Most of the time the problem can be traced to a loose connection. **Note:** *Keep in mind that some circuits receive voltage only when the ignition key is in the Accessory or Run position.*

Finding a short

One method of finding shorts in a circuit is to remove the fuse and connect a test light or voltmeter in its place to the fuse terminals. There should be no voltage present in the circuit. Move the wiring harness from side-to-side while watching the test light. If the bulb goes on, there is a short to ground somewhere in that area, probably where the insulation has rubbed through. The same test can be performed on each component in the circuit, even a switch.

Ground check

Caution: *If the vehicle is equipped with a Delco Loc II or Theftlock audio system, make sure you have the correct activation code before disconnecting the battery.*

Perform a ground test to check whether a component is properly grounded. Disconnect the battery and connect one lead of a self-powered test light, known as a continuity tester, to a known good ground. Connect the other lead to the wire or ground connection being tested. If the bulb goes on, the ground is good. If the bulb does not go on, the ground is not good.

Continuity check

A continuity check is done to determine if there are any breaks in a circuit - if it is passing electricity properly. With the circuit off (no power in the circuit), a self-powered continuity tester can be used to check the circuit. Connect the test leads to both ends of the circuit (or to the "power" end and a good ground), and if the test light comes on the circuit is passing current properly. If the light doesn't come on, there is a break somewhere in the circuit. The same procedure can be used to test a switch, by connecting the continuity tester to the switch terminals. With the switch turned On, the test light should come on.

Finding an open circuit

When diagnosing for possible open circuits, it is often difficult to locate them by sight because oxidation or terminal misalignment are hidden by the electrical connectors. Merely wiggling an electrical connector on a sensor or in the wiring harness may correct the open circuit condition. Remember this when an open circuit is indicated when troubleshooting a circuit. Intermittent problems may also be caused by oxidized or loose connections.

Electrical troubleshooting is simple if you keep in mind that all electrical circuits are basically electricity running from the battery, through the wires, switches, relays, fuses and fusible links to each electrical component (light bulb, motor, etc.) and to ground, from which it is passed back to the battery. Any electrical problem is an interruption in the flow of electricity to and from the battery.

3.1a The passenger compartment fuse block, on the left end of the instrument panel, is accessible after removing the cover; besides fuses, this block also houses at least one circuit breaker (arrow), such as the one shown here, which is an accessory circuit breaker (some passenger compartment fuse blocks also house circuit breakers for the power windows and other power accessories)

3.1b To access the fuses in the engine compartment fuse block, remove this cover; notice that the function and amperage rating of each fuse location is clearly indicated on the cover

3   Fuses - general information

Refer to illustrations 3.1a, 3.1b, 3.1c and 3.3

1   The electrical circuits of the vehicle are protected by a combination of fuses, circuit breakers and fusible links. The two fuse blocks are located on the left end of the instrument panel and in the engine compartment **(see illustrations)**.

2   Each of the fuses is designed to protect a specific circuit, and the various circuits are identified on the fuse panel itself.

3   Miniaturized fuses are employed in the fuse block. These compact fuses, with blade terminal design, allow fingertip removal and replacement. If an electrical component fails, always check the fuse first. The easiest way to check fuses is with a test light. Check for power at the exposed terminal tips of each fuse. If power is present on one side of the fuse but not the other, the fuse is blown. A blown fuse can also be confirmed by visually inspecting it **(see illustration)**.

4   Be sure to replace blown fuses with the correct type. Fuses of different ratings are physically interchangeable, but only fuses of the proper rating should be used. Replacing a fuse with one of a higher or lower value than specified is not recommended. Each electrical circuit needs a specific amount of protection. The amperage value of each fuse is molded into the fuse body.

If the replacement fuse immediately fails, don't replace it again until the cause of the problem is isolated and corrected. In most cases, the cause will be a short circuit in the wiring caused by a broken or deteriorated wire.

4   Fusible links - general information

Some circuits are protected by fusible links. Fusible links are circuit protection devices that are part of the wiring harness itself, that are designed to melt and open the

3.1c The engine compartment fuse block also contains several important relays; again, their functions are indicated on the cover

circuit when a short causes excessive current flow. Fusible links on these models are on the right (passenger's side) of the engine compartment, on the inner wheelwell. Fusible links are used in circuits which are not ordinarily fused, such as the ignition circuit.

Although the fusible links appear to be a heavier gauge than the wire they are protecting, the appearance is due to the thick insulation. All fusible links are several wire gauges smaller than the wire they are designed to protect.

Fusible links cannot be repaired, but a new link of the same size wire can be put in its place. The procedure is as follows:

a) *Disconnect the negative cable from the battery.* **Caution:** *If the vehicle is equipped with a Delco Loc II or Theft-lock audio system, make sure you have the correct activation code before disconnecting the battery.*

b) *Disconnect the fusible link from the wiring harness.*

c) *Cut the damaged fusible link out of the wiring just behind the electrical connector.*

d) *Strip the insulation back approximately 1/2-inch.*

e) *Position the electrical connector on the new fusible link and crimp it into place.*

f) *Use rosin core solder at each end of the new link to obtain a good solder joint.*

g) *Use plenty of electrical tape around the soldered joint. No wires should be exposed.*

h) *Connect the battery ground cable. Test the circuit for proper operation.*

5   Circuit breakers - general information

Circuit breakers protect components such as power windows, power door locks and headlights. On some models the circuit breaker resets itself automatically, so an electrical overload in a circuit breaker protected system will cause the circuit to fail

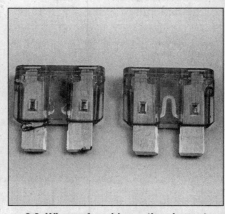

3.3 When a fuse blows, the element between the terminals melts - the fuse on the left is blown, the fuse on the right is good

momentarily, then come back on. If the circuit doesn't come back on, check it immediately. Once the condition is corrected, the circuit breaker will resume its normal function. Some circuit breakers must be reset manually.

6 Relays - general information

General information

1   Several electrical accessories in the vehicle, such as the fuel injection system, horns, starter, and fog lamps use relays to transmit the electrical signal to the component. Relays use a low-current circuit (the control circuit) to open and close a high-current circuit (the power circuit). If the relay is defective, that component will not operate properly. The various relays are mounted in engine compartment **(see illustration 3.1c)** and several locations throughout the vehicle. If a faulty relay is suspected, it can be removed and tested using the procedure below or by a dealer service department or a repair shop. Defective relays must be replaced as a unit.

Testing

2   It's best to refer to the wiring diagram for the circuit to determine the proper hook-ups for the relay you're testing. However, if you're not able to determine the correct hook-up from the wiring diagrams, you may be able to determine the test hook-ups from the information that follows.

3   On most relays, two of the terminals are the relay's control circuit (they connect to the relay coil which, when energized, closes the large contacts to complete the circuit). The other terminals are the power circuit (they are connected together within the relay when the control-circuit coil is energized).

4   Most relays are marked as an aid to help you determine which terminals are the control circuit and which are the power circuit.

5   Connect a fused jumper wire between one of the two control circuit terminals and the positive battery terminal. Connect another jumper wire between the other control circuit terminal and ground. When the connections are made, the relay should click. On some relays, polarity may be critical, so, if the relay doesn't click, try swapping the jumper wires on the control circuit terminals.

6   With the jumper wires connected, check for continuity between the power circuit terminals as indicated by the markings on the relay.

7   If the relay fails any of the above tests, replace it.

7 Turn signal/hazard flasher - check and replacement

Warning: *The models covered by this manual are equipped with airbags. Always disable the*

airbag system before working in the vicinity of the impact sensors, steering column or instrument panel to avoid the possibility of accidental deployment of the airbag(s), which could cause personal injury (see Section 25).
Caution: *If the vehicle is equipped with a Delco Loc II or Theftlock audio system, make sure you have the correct activation code before disconnecting the battery.*

1   1995 models are equipped with separate turn signal and hazard flasher units while 1996 and later models are equipped with a combination turn signal/hazard flasher. The turn signal flasher on 1995 models is located at the left side of the dash, to the right of the steering column. The hazard flasher on 1995 models is plugged into the "convenience center," which is mounted at the top of the left kick panel. The convenience center also houses the alarm module, if equipped, and the horn relay. On 1996 and 1997 models the combination turn signal/hazard flasher is plugged into the convenience center which is mounted at the top of the left kick panel. On 1998 and later models the combination turn signal/hazard flasher is mounted to the brake pedal bracket above the steering column.

2   You can determine whether a flasher unit is operating correctly by verifying that it makes an audible clicking sound when it's energized.

3   If a turn signal light fails to blink on one side or the other, and the flasher unit does not make its characteristic clicking sound, or if the turn signal indicator flashes much more rapidly than normal, a turn signal bulb is out.

4   If both turn signals fail to blink, the problem may be a blown fuse, a faulty flasher unit, a broken switch or a loose or open connection.

5   If the turn signal fuse has blown, look for a short in the wiring before installing a new fuse.

6   If the fuse is okay, verify that there's voltage to the flasher.

7   If there's voltage to the flasher, verify that there's voltage out of the flasher when it's energized. If there's no voltage to the flasher, check the combination switch (see

Section 8)

8   If there's voltage out of the flasher, check the wiring between the switch and the turn signals (turn signal flasher) or between the switch and all the running lights (hazard flasher).

9   To access the flasher units on all models it will be necessary to remove the left sound insulator panel.

10   To replace the hazard flasher on 1995 models or the combination turn signal/hazard flasher on 1996 and 1997 models, simply unplug it from the convenience center at the top of the left kick panel.

11   To replace the turn signal flasher on 1995 models or the combination turn signal/hazard flasher on 1998 and later models, unplug the electrical connector and disengage the flasher from its holder on the brake pedal mounting bracket.

12   Make sure that the replacement unit is identical to the original. Compare the old one to the new one before installing it.

13   Installation is the reverse of removal.

8 Combination switch - removal and installation

Refer to illustrations 8.3 and 8.5
Warning: *The models covered by this manual are equipped with airbags. Always disable the airbag system before working in the vicinity of the impact sensors, steering column or instrument panel to avoid the possibility of accidental deployment of the airbag(s), which could cause personal injury (see Section 25).*
Caution: *If the vehicle is equipped with a Delco Loc II or Theftlock audio system, make sure you have the correct activation code before disconnecting the battery.*

1   Detach the cable from the negative battery terminal and disable the airbag system (see Section 25).

2   Remove the steering column covers (see Chapter 11).

3   Remove the combination switch mounting screws **(see illustration)**.

8.3 To remove the combination switch, remove the indicated screws (upper arrows and lower left arrow); to remove the windshield wiper/washer switch, remove the combination switch and remove the windshield wiper/washer switch mounting screw (lower right arrow)

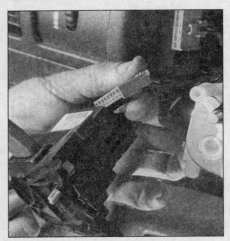

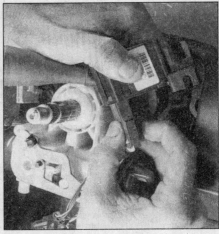

8.4 Detach the combination switch from the steering column housing assembly and unplug the electrical connector

9.5 Detach the windshield wiper/washer switch from the steering column housing assembly and unplug the electrical connector

10.4 To remove the ignition switch from the steering column housing assembly, remove these two screws (arrows)

4   Detach the combination switch from the steering column housing assembly and unplug the electrical connector **(see illustration)**.
5   Installation is the reverse of removal.

9   Windshield wiper/washer switch - removal and installation

Refer to illustration 9.5
Warning: *The models covered by this manual are equipped with airbags. Always disable the airbag system before working in the vicinity of the impact sensors, steering column or instrument panel to avoid the possibility of accidental deployment of the airbag(s), which could cause personal injury (see Section 25).*
Caution: *If the vehicle is equipped with a Delco Loc II or Theftlock audio system, make sure you have the correct activation code before disconnecting the battery.*
1   Detach the cable from the negative bat-

tery terminal and disable the airbag system (see Section 25).
2   Remove the upper and lower steering column covers (see Chapter 11).
3   Remove the combination switch (see Section 8).
4   Remove the windshield wiper/washer switch mounting screws **(see illustration 8.3)**.
5   Detach the windshield wiper/washer switch from the steering column housing assembly and unplug the electrical connector **(see illustration)**.
6   Installation is the reverse of removal.

10   Ignition switch and key lock cylinder - removal and installation

Warning: *The models covered by this manual are equipped with airbags. Always disable the airbag system before working in the vicinity of*

the impact sensors, steering column or instrument panel to avoid the possibility of accidental deployment of the airbag(s), which could cause personal injury (see Section 25).
Caution: *If the vehicle is equipped with a Delco Loc II or Theftlock audio system, make sure you have the correct activation code before disconnecting the battery.*
1   Disable the airbag system (see Section 25).
2   Remove the tilt lever, if equipped.
3   Remove the upper and lower steering column covers (see Chapter 11).

Ignition switch
Refer to illustrations 10.4, 10.5a and 10.5b
4   Remove the ignition switch retaining screws **(see illustration)**.
5   Detach the ignition switch from the steering column housing assembly and unplug the electrical connectors **(see illustrations)**.
6   Installation is the reverse of removal.

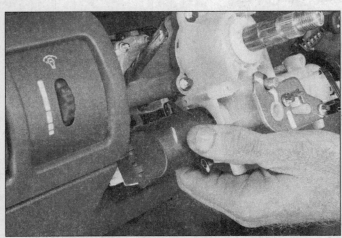

10.5a Move the ignition switch to the left to detach it from the steering column housing assembly . . .

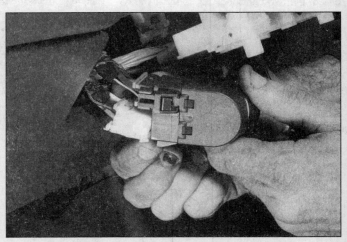

10.5b . . . then pull it back and down and unplug the electrical connectors

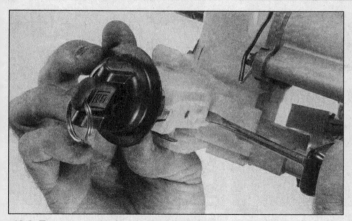

10.8 To remove the key lock cylinder, turn the ignition key to the Run position, depress the lock button with a screwdriver or other suitable tool, then pull out the lock cylinder

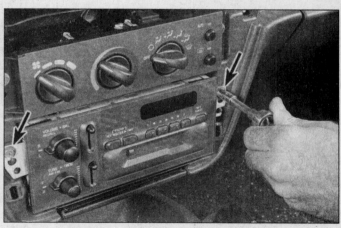

11.3 To detach the radio from the dash, remove these two screws (arrows)

Key lock cylinder

Refer to illustration 10.8

7   Turn the key to the Run position.

8   Depress the lock button **(see illustration)** and remove the key lock cylinder.

9   To install the key lock cylinder, turn the key to the Run position, depress the lock button and, rotating the key counterclockwise about five degrees, gently push the lock cylinder into place.

10   Installation is otherwise the reverse of removal.

11   Radio and speakers - removal and installation

Warning: *The models covered by this manual are equipped with airbags. Always disable the airbag system before working in the vicinity of the impact sensors, steering column or instrument panel to avoid the possibility of accidental deployment of the airbag(s), which could cause personal injury (see Section 25).*
Caution: *If the vehicle is equipped with a Delco Loc II or Theftlock audio system, make sure you have the correct activation code before disconnecting the battery.*

Radio

Refer to illustrations 11.3, 11.4a, 11.4b and 11.4c

1   Disable the airbag system (see Section 25).

2   Remove the instrument panel trim plate (Chevrolet models) or accessory trim plate (Pontiac models) (see Chapter 11).

3   Remove the radio retaining screws **(see illustration)**.

4   Pull out the radio and disconnect the electrical connections and antenna lead **(see illustrations)**.

11.4a Unplug the electrical connector(s) from the radio

5   Remove the radio from the instrument panel.

6   Installation is the reverse of removal.

Front speakers

Refer to illustration 11.8

7   Remove the front door trim panel (see Chapter 11).

8   Unplug the speaker electrical connector **(see illustration)** and remove the speaker retaining screws. Remove the speaker from the door.

9   Installation is the reverse of removal.

11.4b To detach the antenna lead from the radio, remove the hold-down screw . . .

11.4c . . . then pull out the antenna lead

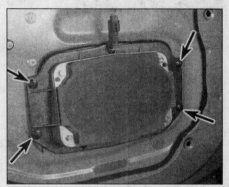

11.8 To remove the front speaker from the door, unplug the electrical connector and remove these four screws (arrows)

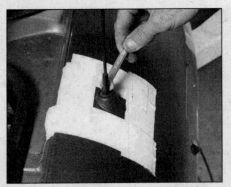

12.1 To detach the antenna mast from the bezel, loosen the nut at the bottom of the mast with a small wrench, back it off, and unscrew the mast

12.2a Peel back the carpet in the trunk area . . .

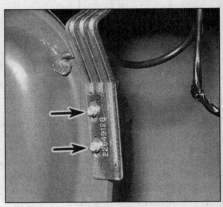

12.2b . . . then remove these two antenna bracket screws (arrows)

Rear speakers

10   Remove the rear seatback (see Chapter 11).
11   Remove one of the rear quarter trim panels.
12   Release the four plastic push-in retainers that secure the rear parcel shelf, disengage the rear seat belts from the slots in the parcel shelf and remove the parcel shelf.
13   To disengage either rear speaker, push down on the tab on front of the speaker spacer, lift the spacer and pull the speaker forward. Unplug the electrical connector and remove the speaker from the vehicle.
14   Installation is the reverse of removal.

12   Antenna - removal and installation

Refer to illustrations 12.1, 12.2a, 12.2b and 12.3
Caution: *If the vehicle is equipped with a Delco Loc II or Theftlock audio system, make sure you have the correct activation code before disconnecting the battery.*
1   Use a small wrench to remove the

antenna mast **(see illustration)**.
2   Open the trunk, peel back the trunk liner **(see illustration)** and remove the antenna base/bracket retaining screws **(see illustration)**.
3   Remove the antenna base/bracket from the outer bezel and the quarter panel then remove the antenna lead from the antenna base **(see illustration)**.
4   If the antenna lead is to be replaced detach the radio and disconnect the antenna lead from the backside of the radio (see Section 11). Then remove any retaining clips under the instrument panel securing the antenna lead.
5   To facilitate the removal of the antenna lead it will be necessary to remove the following interior trim panels: the right side kick panel, the right door sill plate and the right rear quarter trim panel. **Note:** *On 4-door models it will be necessary to remove the center pillar trim panel and the rear door sill plate.*
6   Attach a piece of stiff wire to the end of the antenna lead in the trunk compartment.
7   Working in the interior of the vehicle pull the antenna lead from the trunk compartment

into the passenger compartment.
8   Detach the wire from the end of the antenna lead and remove the antenna lead from the vehicle.
9   Fasten the end of the new antenna lead to the wire leading to the trunk compartment and pull the antenna lead into the trunk compartment.
10   The remainder of the installation is the reverse of removal.

13   Rear window defogger - check and repair

1   The rear window defogger consists of a number of horizontal elements baked onto the glass surface.
2   Small breaks in the element can be repaired without removing the rear window.

Check

Refer to illustrations 13.4, 13.5 and 13.7
3   Turn the ignition switch and defogger system switches to the ON position. Using a voltmeter, place the positive probe against the defogger grid positive terminal and the

12.3   Remove the antenna base/bracket from the outer bezel and the quarter panel, then detach the antenna lead (arrow)

13.4 When measuring the voltage at the rear window defogger grid, wrap a piece of aluminum foil around the positive probe of the voltmeter and press the foil against the wire with your finger

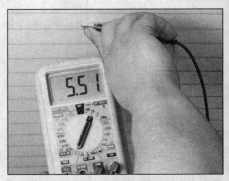

13.5 To determine if a heating element has broken, check the voltage at the center of each element - if the voltage is 6-volts, the element is unbroken - if the voltage is 12-volts, the element is broken between the center and the ground side - if there is no voltage, the element is broken between the center and the positive side

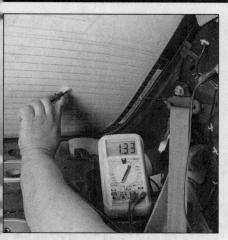

13.7 To find the break, place the voltmeter negative lead against the defogger ground terminal, place the voltmeter positive lead with the foil strip against the heating element at the positive terminal end and slide it toward the negative terminal end - the point at which the voltmeter reading changes abruptly is the point at which the element is broken

negative lead against the ground terminal. If the battery voltage is not indicated, check the fuse, defogger switch and related wiring.

4   When measuring voltage during the next two tests, wrap a piece of aluminum foil around the tip of the voltmeter positive probe and press the foil against the heating element with your finger **(see illustration)**.

5   Check the voltage at the center of each heating element **(see illustration)**. If the voltage is 6-volts, the element is okay (there is no break). If the voltage is 12-volts, the element is broken between the center of the element and the ground side. If the voltage is 0-volts the element is broken between the center of the element and positive side.

6   If none of the elements are broken, connect the negative lead to a good body

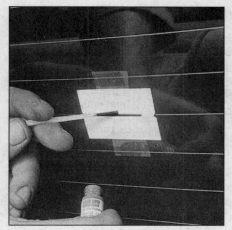

13.13 To use a defogger repair kit, apply masking tape to the inside of the window at the damaged area, then brush on the special conductive coating
•

ground. The reading should stay the same, if it doesn't the ground connection is bad.

7   To find the break, place the voltmeter negative lead against the defogger ground terminal. Place the voltmeter positive lead with the foil strip against the heating element at the positive terminal end and slide it toward the negative terminal end. The point at which the voltmeter deflects from several volts to zero is the point at which the heating element is broken **(see illustration)**.

Repair
Refer to illustration 13.13
8   Repair the break in the element using a repair kit specifically recommended for this purpose, such as Dupont paste No. 4817 (or equivalent). Included in this kit is plastic conductive epoxy.

9   Prior to repairing a break, turn off the system and allow it to cool off for a few minutes.

10   Lightly buff the element area with fine

steel wool, then clean it thoroughly with rubbing alcohol.

11   Use masking tape to mask off the area being repaired.

12   Thoroughly mix the epoxy, following the instructions provided with the repair kit.

13   Apply the epoxy material to the slit in the masking tape, overlapping the undamaged area about 3/4-inch on either end **(see illustration)**.

14   Allow the repair to cure for 24 hours before removing the tape and using the system.

14   Headlight bulb - replacement

Refer to illustrations 14.2, 14.3 and 14.4
Warning: *Halogen gas filled bulbs are under pressure and may shatter if the surface is scratched or the bulb is dropped. Wear eye protection and handle the bulbs carefully, grasping only the base whenever possible. Do not touch the surface of the bulb with your fingers because the oil from your skin could cause it to overheat and fail prematurely. If you do touch the bulb surface, clean it with rubbing alcohol.*

1   Remove the upper air intake splash shield.

2   Remove the headlight housing retaining bolts **(see illustration)** and pull the housing assembly out to access the bulb.

3   Working at the rear of the headlight housing, rotate the bulb holder counterclockwise to separate it from the housing while setting the housing aside **(see illustration)**.

4   Unplug the electrical connector from the bulb holder **(see illustration)**.

5   Without touching the glass with your bare fingers, plug the electrical connector into the bulb holder and install the bulb holder into the headlight housing.

6   The remainder of installation is the reverse of removal.

7   Make sure the headlights are correctly adjusted (see Section 16).

14.2 To detach the headlight assembly from the radiator support, remove these two bolts (arrows)

14.3 To disengage the electrical connector and headlight bulb holder from the headlight assembly, turn the holder counterclockwise and pull it out of the housing

14.4 Unplug the electrical connector from the headlight bulb holder

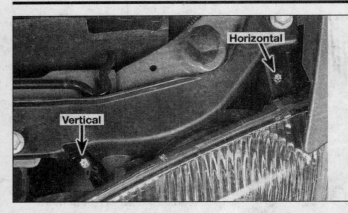

16.1a The headlight vertical and horizontal adjustment screws (arrows) are right behind the upper end of the headlight housing; you'll need a Torx-head tool for these screws (headlight trim piece removed for clarity)

16.1b The headlight vertical and horizontal adjustment screws can be accessed through the trim piece

15 Headlight housing - removal and installation

Warning: *The models covered by this manual are equipped with airbags. Always disable the airbag system before working in the vicinity of the impact sensors, steering column or instrument panel to avoid the possibility of accidental deployment of the airbag(s), which could cause personal injury (see Section 25).*

1   Remove the upper air intake splash shield (see Section 14).
2   Remove the headlight housing retaining bolts (see Section 14).
3   Remove the headlight bulb holders from the headlight housing (see Section 14).
4   Detach the headlight housing from the bracket and install the bracket on the new headlight housing.
5   Installation is the reverse of removal.
6   Adjust the headlights (see Section 16).

16 Headlights - adjustment

Refer to illustrations 16.1a, 16.1b and 16.3

Caution: *The headlights must be aimed correctly. If adjusted incorrectly they could blind the driver of an oncoming vehicle and cause a serious accident or seriously reduce your ability to see the road. The headlights should be checked for proper aim every 12 months and any time a new headlight is installed or front end body work is performed. It should be emphasized that the following procedure is only an interim step which will provide temporary adjustment until the headlights can be adjusted by a properly equipped shop.*

1   Headlights have two spring loaded adjusting screws, one on the top controlling up-and-down movement and one on the side controlling left-and-right movement **(see illustrations)**.
2   There are several methods of adjusting

the headlights. The simplest method requires masking tape, a blank wall and a level floor.
3   Position masking tape vertically on the wall in reference to the vehicle centerline and the centerlines of both headlights **(see illustration)**.
4   Position a horizontal tape line in reference to the centerline of all the headlights. **Note:** *It may be easier to position the tape on the wall with the vehicle parked only a few inches away.*
5   Adjustment should be made with the vehicle parked 25 feet away from the wall, sitting level, the gas tank half-full and no unusually heavy load in the vehicle.
6   Starting with the low beam adjustment, position the high intensity zone so it is two inches below the horizontal line and two inches to the right of the headlight vertical line. Adjustment is made by turning the top adjusting screw clockwise to raise the beam and counterclockwise to lower the beam. The adjusting screw on the side should be used in the same manner to move the beam left or right.
7   With the high beams on, the high intensity zone should be vertically centered with the exact center just below the horizontal line. **Note:** *It may not be possible to position the headlight aim exactly for both high and low beams. If a compromise must be made, keep in mind that the low beams are the most used and have the greatest effect on safety.*
8   Have the headlights adjusted by a dealer service department or service station at the earliest opportunity.

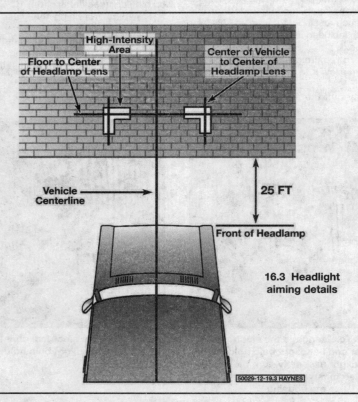

16.3 Headlight aiming details

17 Bulb replacement

Front turn signal and side marker lights

1   On all models except Pontiac GT models, remove the headlight assembly (see Section 15). On Pontiac GT models, unscrew the side marker lens from the bumper fascia.

17.9 To replace a back-up light bulb on a Chevrolet model (located in the trunk lid), turn the bulb socket counterclockwise and detach it from the lens housing, pull it down and remove the bulb from the socket (on Pontiac models, the back-up lights are located in the rear bumper fascia and can be replaced by unscrewing the lens from the fascia)

2   Twist the bulb socket a quarter turn counterclockwise, then remove the bulb assembly from the housing. **Note:** *On Chevrolet and some Pontiac models, the turn signal and side marker light sockets are screwed into separate housings. On other Pontiac models, they're in the same housing.*
3   Remove the bulb from the socket.
4   Installation is the reverse of removal.

Rear side marker lights and back-up lights (Pontiac models)

5   Remove the side marker or back-up light lens retaining screw(s) and pull the lens assembly out of the bumper fascia.
6   Detach the bulb socket from the lens assembly by turning it counterclockwise.
7   Remove the bulb from the socket.
8   Installation is the reverse of removal.

17.10a To gain access to the rear brake, taillight, turn signal and side marker light bulbs, release this push-in retainer and peel back the trunk liner . . .

Rear brake, taillight and turn signal bulbs; Chevrolet back-up and side marker lights

Refer to illustrations 17.9, 17.10a, 17.10b and 17.10c
9   To replace a back-up light bulb (in the trunk lid), simply turn the bulb socket counterclockwise, remove the socket **(see illustration)** and remove the bulb from the socket.
10   To replace a brake, taillight, turn signal or side marker bulb (in the body), detach the trunk carpet liner **(see illustration)**, peel it back, turn the bulb socket counterclockwise, remove the socket **(see illustrations)** and remove the bulb from the socket.

Trunk light

Refer to illustrations 17.11a and 17.11b
11   Pinch the ends of the socket retainer together as shown **(see illustration)** and pull down the retainer, socket and bulb **(see illustration)**.
12   Remove the bulb from the socket.
13   Installation is the reverse of removal.

17.10b . . . then remove the brake, taillight, or turn signal bulb . . .

License plate light

Refer to illustrations 17.14 and 17.15
14   Detach the two screws which attach the lens to the trunk lid **(see illustration)**.

17.10c . . . or the side marker bulb, by turning the bulb socket counterclockwise and pulling it out of the lens assembly

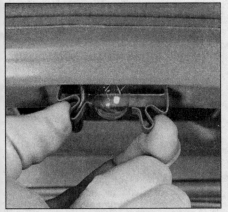

17.11a To replace the trunk lid light bulb, squeeze the ends of the retainer together as shown . . .

17.11b . . . then pull down the retainer and remove the bulb from the socket

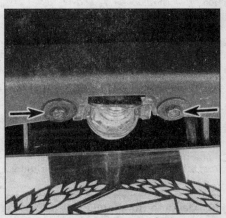

17.14 To detach the license plate light bulb from the fascia, remove these two retaining screws (arrows)

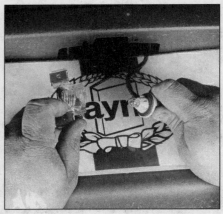

17.15 Pull the license plate light assembly down, then detach the bulb and socket from the lens assembly

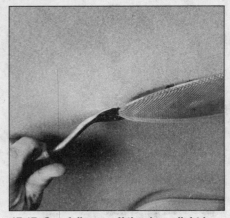

17.17 Carefully pry off the dome light lens

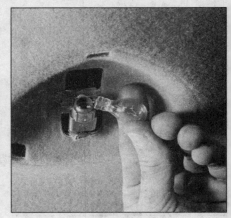

17.18 Remove the bulb from the dome light socket

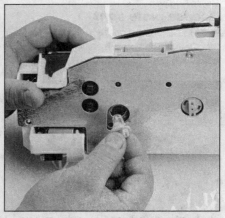

17.20 To replace an instrument cluster light bulb, turn it counterclockwise and pull it out

19.3a Unplug this electrical connector . . .

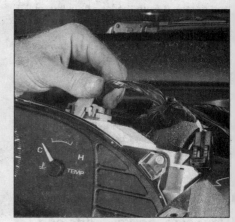

19.3b . . . and this one from the instrument cluster

15   Pull down the lens and socket, detach the socket from the lens **(see illustration)** and remove the bulb from the socket.

16   Installation is the reverse of removal.

Dome light

Refer to illustrations 17.17 and 17.18

17   Carefully pry off the lens **(see illustration)**.

18   Remove the bulb from the socket **(see illustration)**.

19   Installation is the reverse of removal.

Instrument cluster illumination

Refer to illustration 17.20

20   To gain access to the instrument cluster illumination lights, the instrument cluster will have to be removed (see Section 19). The bulbs can then be removed and replaced from the rear of the cluster **(see illustration)**.

18   Daytime Running Lights (DRL) - general information

The Daytime Running Lights (DRL) sys-

tem used on all Canadian and later US models illuminates the headlights whenever the engine is running. The only exception is with the engine running and the parking brake engaged. Once the parking brake is released, the lights will remain on as long as the ignition switch is on, even if the parking brake is later applied.

The DRL system supplies reduced power to the headlights so they will be bright enough for daytime visibility while prolonging headlight life.

A malfunction with the daytime running lights can be caused by failure of the DRL relay, which is located in back of the front impact bar, or by a failure of the microprocessor unit in the instrument cluster assembly.

19   Instrument cluster - removal and installation

Refer to illustrations 19.3a, 19.3b, 19.4a and 19.4b

Warning: *The models covered by this manual are equipped with airbags. Always disable the*

airbag system before working in the vicinity of the impact sensors, steering column or instrument panel to avoid the possibility of accidental deployment of the airbag(s), which could cause personal injury (see Section 25). The yellow wires and connectors routed through the instrument panel are for this system. Do not use electrical test equipment on these yellow wires or tamper with them in any way while working under the instrument panel.

Caution: *If the vehicle is equipped with a Delco Loc II or Theftlock audio system, make sure you have the correct activation code before disconnecting the battery.*

1   Detach the cable from the negative battery terminal and disable the airbag system (see Section 25).

2   Remove the instrument panel trim plate (Chevrolet models) or the instrument panel trim pad (Pontiac models) (see Chapter 11).

3   Unplug the electrical connectors from the instrument cluster **(see illustrations)**.

4   Remove the instrument cluster retaining screws **(see illustration)** and lift it from the dash **(see illustration)**.

5   Installation is the reverse of removal.

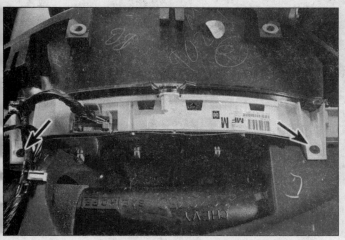

19.4a To detach the instrument cluster from the instrument panel, remove these two screws (arrows)

19.4b Make sure that everything is disconnected, then carefully lift the instrument cluster straight up and remove it from the instrument panel

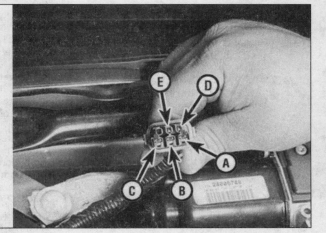

20.2 Use a voltmeter or test light to check for battery power at the wiper motor

A   Ground
B   Fuse output
C   Windshield wiper motor feed (High)
D   Windshield wiper switch signal (On)
E   Windshield wiper switch signal (Low/Pulse)

20.7 Use a small screwdriver to pry off the wiper arm nut cover, then remove the nut and pull the arm straight off its splined shaft

20 Wiper motor - check and replacement

Check

Refer to illustration 20.2
Note: *Refer to the wiring diagrams for wire colors and locations in the following checks. Keep in mind that power wires are generally larger in diameter and brighter colors, where ground wires are usually smaller in diameter and darker colors. When checking for voltage, probe a grounded 12-volt test light to each terminal at a connector until it lights; this verifies voltage (power) at the terminal.*

1   If the wipers work slowly, make sure the battery is in good condition and has a strong charge (see Chapter 1). If the battery is in good condition, remove the wiper motor (see below) and operate the wiper arms by hand. Check for binding linkage and pivots. Lubricate or repair the linkage or pivots as necessary. Reinstall the wiper motor. If the wipers still operate slowly, check for loose or corroded connections, especially the ground connection. If all connections look OK, replace the motor.

2   If the wipers fail to operate when acti-
vated, check the fuse. If the fuse is OK, connect a jumper wire between the wiper motor and ground, then retest. If the motor works now, repair the ground connection. If the motor still doesn't work, turn the wiper switch to the HI position and check for voltage at the motor **(see illustration)**. If there's voltage at the motor, remove the motor and check it off the vehicle with fused jumper wires from the battery. If the motor now works, check for binding linkage (see Step 1 above). If the motor still doesn't work, replace it. If there's no voltage at the motor, check for voltage at the wiper control module. If there's voltage at the wiper control module and no voltage at the at the wiper motor, check the switch for continuity (see Section 9). If the switch is OK, the wiper control module is probably bad.

3   If the interval (delay) function is inoperative, check the continuity of all the wiring between the switch and wiper control module. If the wiring is OK, check the resistance of the delay control knob of the multi-function switch (see Section 9). If the delay control knob is within the specified resistance, replace the wiper control module.

4   If the wipers stop at the position they're in when the switch is turned off (fail to park),
check for voltage at the park feed wire of the wiper motor connector when the wiper switch is OFF but the ignition is ON. If no voltage is present, check for an open circuit between the wiper motor and the fuse panel.

5   If the wipers won't shut off unless the ignition is OFF, disconnect the wiring from the wiper control switch. If the wipers stop, replace the switch. If the wipers keep running, there's a defective limit switch in the motor; replace the motor.

6   If the wipers won't retract below the hood line, check for mechanical obstructions in the wiper linkage or on the vehicle's body which would prevent the wipers from parking. If there are no obstructions, check the wiring between the switch and motor for continuity. If the wiring is OK, replace the wiper motor.

Replacement

Refer to illustrations 20.7, 20.8a, 20.8b, 20.8c and 20.9

7   Pry off the cover for the wiper arm nuts, unscrew the nuts and remove both wiper arms **(see illustration)**.

20.8a To detach the cowl screen, disconnect the windshield washer lines . . .

20.8b . . . release the push-in retainers (left arrow points to one, others not visible in this photo), remove the single retaining screw (right arrow) . . .

20.8c . . . and remove the cowl screen

20.9 To detach the wiper motor assembly, unplug the electrical connector (arrow) and remove the three retaining screws (arrows)

8   Disconnect the windshield washer line, remove the single retaining screw, release the five push-in retainers, and remove the cowl cover **(see illustrations)**.

9   Unplug the electrical connector from the windshield wiper motor **(see illustration)**.

10   Remove the three wiper motor assembly retaining bolts and remove the wiper motor assembly.

11   Detach the wiper transmission assembly from the wiper motor crank arm.

12   Detach the wiper motor crank arm from the wiper motor assembly.

13   Remove the three wiper motor retaining screws and detach the wiper motor from the bracket.

14   Installation is the reverse of removal.

21   Horn - check and replacement

Check

Refer to illustration 21.2

Note: *Check the CIG (cigarette lighter/horn) fuse before beginning electrical diagnosis.*

1   Remove the front bumper fascia (see Chapter 11).

2   Unplug the horn electrical connector **(see illustration)**.

3   To test the horn(s), connect battery volt-age to the horn terminal with a pair of jumper wires. If the horn doesn't sound, replace it.

4   If the horn does sound, check for volt-age at the terminal when the horn button is depressed. If there's voltage at the terminal, check for a bad ground at the horn.

5   If there's no voltage at the horn, check the relay (see Section 6). Note that most horn

relays are either the four-terminal or exter-nally grounded three-terminal type.

6   If the relay is OK, check for voltage to the relay power and control circuits. If either of the circuits is not receiving voltage, inspect the wiring between the relay and the fuse panel.

7   If both relay circuits are receiving volt-age, depress the horn button and check the circuit from the relay to the horn button for continuity to ground. If there's no continuity, check the circuit for an open. If there's no open circuit, replace the horn button.

8   If there's continuity to ground through the horn button, check for an open or short in the circuit from the relay to the horn.

Replacement

Refer to illustration 21.10

9   Remove the front bumper fascia (see Chapter 11).

10   Unplug the electrical connector **(see illustration 21.2)** and remove the bracket bolt **(see illustration)**.

11   Installation is the reverse of removal.

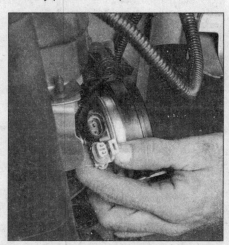

21.2 To test the horn, connect the horn to the battery with fused jumper wires; if the horn doesn't operate, replace it

21.10 To detach the horn from the bracket, remove this nut (arrow)

22 Electric side view mirrors - description and check

Note: *Check the INT LAMP fuse before beginning electrical diagnosis.*

1   Electric rear view mirrors use two motors to move the glass; one for up-and-down adjustments and one for left-to-right adjustments.

2   The mirror control switch, which is located in the left (driver's side) front door, can be rotated counterclockwise or clockwise to send voltage to the left or right mirror, respectively. With the ignition key turned to On (engine off), roll down the windows and operate the mirror control switch through all functions (left-right and up-down) for both the left and right side mirrors.

3   Listen carefully for the sound of the electric motors running in the mirrors.

4   If the motors can be heard but the mirror glass doesn't move, the drive mechanism inside the mirror is malfunctioning. Remove and disassemble the mirror to locate the problem (see Chapter 11).

5   If the mirrors don't operate and no sound comes from the mirrors, check the fuse (see Section 3).

6   If the fuse is OK, remove the door trim panel (see Chapter 11) and remove the mirror control switch assembly without disconnecting the wires attached to it. Turn the ignition key to On and check for voltage at the switch. There should be voltage at one terminal. If there's no voltage at the switch, check for an opening or short in the wiring between the fuse panel and the switch.

7   If there's voltage at the switch, unplug the electrical connector and check the switch for continuity in all its operating positions (refer to the wiring diagrams). If the switch does not operate properly, replace it.

8   Plug in the switch connector. Locate the wire going from the switch to ground. Leaving the switch connected, connect a jumper wire between this wire and ground. If the mirror works normally with this wire in place, repair the faulty ground connection.

9   If the mirror still doesn't work, remove the cover and check the wires at the mirror for voltage with a test light. Check with the ignition key turned to On and the mirror selector switch on the appropriate side. Operate the mirror switch in all its positions. There should be voltage at one of the switch-to-mirror wires in each switch position (except the neutral position).

10   If there isn't voltage at each switch position, check the wiring between the mirror and control switch for opens and shorts.

11   If there's voltage, remove the mirror and test it off the vehicle with jumper wires. Replace the mirror if it fails this test (see Chapter 11).

23 Cruise control system - description and check

1   The cruise control system maintains vehicle speed with an electronic servo motor located in the engine compartment, which is connected to the throttle linkage by a cable. The system consists of the electronic control module, brake switch, control switches, a relay, the vehicle speed sensor and associated wiring. Listed below are some general procedures that may be used to locate common cruise control problems.

2   Locate and check the CRUISE fuse (see Section 3).

3   Have an assistant operate the brake lights while you check their operation (voltage from the brake light switch deactivates the cruise control).

4   If the brake lights don't come on or don't shut off, correct the problem and retest the cruise control.

5   Inspect the cable linkage between the cruise control module and the throttle linkage. The cruise control module is located in the right rear corner of the engine compartment.

6   Visually inspect the wire harness and connector. Look for corrosion and damaged and broken wires.

7   The vehicle speed sensor is located on the transmission (see Chapter 7B). Raise the front of the vehicle and support it on jack stands. Unplug the electrical connector and touch one probe of a digital voltmeter to the orange wire of the connector and the other to a good ground. With the vehicle in Neutral and key On, measure the voltage while rotating one wheel with the other one blocked. If the voltage doesn't vary as the wheel rotates, the sensor is defective.

8   Test drive the vehicle to determine if the cruise control is now working. If it isn't, take it to a dealer service department or an automotive electrical specialist for further diagnosis and repair.

24 Power window system - description and check

1   The power window system operates electric motors, mounted in the doors, which lower and raise the windows. The system consists of the control switches, the motors, the regulators and the wiring harnesses.

2   The power windows can be lowered and raised from the master control switch by the driver or by remote switches located at the individual windows. Each window has a separate motor which is reversible. The position of the control switch determines the polarity and therefore the direction of operation.

3   The circuit is protected by a fuse and a circuit breaker. Each motor is also equipped with an internal circuit breaker, this prevents one stuck window from disabling the whole system.

4   The power window system will only operate when the ignition key is turned to On. Some models have a window lockout switch at the master control switch which, when activated, disables the switches at the rear windows and, sometimes, the switch at the passenger's window also. Always check these items before troubleshooting a window problem.

5   These procedures are general in nature, so if you can't find the problem using them, take the vehicle to a dealer service department or other properly equipped repair facility.

6   If the power windows won't operate, always check the fuse and circuit breaker first.

7   If only the rear windows are inoperative, or if the windows only operate from the master control switch, check the rear window lockout switch for continuity in the unlocked position. Replace it if it doesn't have continuity.

8   Check the wiring between the switches and fuse panel for continuity. Repair the wiring, if necessary.

9   If only one window is inoperative from the master control switch, try the other control switch at the window. **Note:** *This doesn't apply to the drivers door window.*

10   If the same window works from one switch, but not the other, check the switch for continuity.

11   If the switch tests OK, check for a short or open in the circuit between the affected switch and the window motor.

12   If one window is inoperative from both switches, remove the trim panel from the affected door and check for voltage at the switch and at the motor while the switch is operated.

13   If voltage is reaching the motor, disconnect the glass from the regulator (see Chapter 11). Move the window up and down by hand while checking for binding and damage. Also check for binding and damage to the regulator. If the regulator is not damaged and the window moves up and down smoothly, replace the motor. If there's binding or damage, lubricate, repair or replace parts, as necessary.

14   If voltage isn't reaching the motor, check the wiring in the circuit for continuity between the switches and motors. You'll need to consult the wiring diagram for the vehicle. If the circuit is equipped with a relay, check that the relay is grounded properly and receiving voltage.

15   Test the windows after you are done to confirm proper repairs.

25 Airbag - general information

Warning: *The models covered by this manual are equipped with airbags. Airbag system components are located in the steering wheel, steering column, instrument panel and center console. The airbag(s) could acciden-*

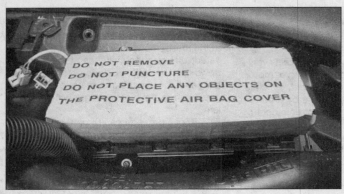

25.2 The passenger's side airbag is located on top of the dash, right above the glovebox (instrument panel trim pad removed); notice that the big yellow connector, known as the Connector Position Assurance (CPA) connector, has been unplugged to ensure that the passenger's airbag isn't accidentally deployed while you're working in that area

25.3 The forward discriminating sensor is located to the right of the hood latch, right in front of the radiator (the other one is located on the dash, just ahead of the passenger's side airbag)

tally deploy if any of the system components or wiring harnesses are disturbed, so be extremely careful when working in these areas and don't disturb any airbag system components or wiring. You could be injured if an airbag accidentally deploys, or the airbag might not deploy correctly in a collision if any components or wiring in the system have been disturbed. The yellow wires and connectors routed through the instrument panel and center console are for this system. Do not use electrical test equipment on these yellow wires or tamper with them in any way while working in their vicinity. **Caution:** If the vehicle is equipped with a Delco Loc II or Theftlock audio system, make sure you have the correct activation code before disconnecting the battery.

Description

Refer to illustration 25.2

1   The models covered by this manual are equipped with a Supplemental Inflatable Restraint (SIR) system, more commonly known as an airbag system. The SIR system is designed to protect the driver and passenger from serious injury in the event of a head-on or frontal collision.

2   The SIR system consists of two airbags - one in the steering wheel, one on top of the dashboard above the glovebox **(see illustration)** - and an impact sensor located below the hood latch. The arming sensor and the diagnostic/energy reserve module have been incorporated into one unit which is located under the instrument panel.

Sensors

Refer to illustration 25.3

3   There are two types of sensors. The two normally-open discriminating sensors, located next to the hood latch **(see illustration)** and in front of the passenger side airbag, are designed to close the airbag circuit when the change in velocity (i.e. the kind of sudden deceleration that can only occur as a result of an impact) exceeds a certain

threshold. A third sensor, the dual-pole arming sensor, located inside the center portion of the dash, is designed to close at low-level changes in velocity (lower than the discriminating sensors). The airbag cannot deploy until one of the discriminating sensors, and the dual-pole sensor, have closed the inflator module circuit. Once the electrical circuit between the crash sensors and the diagnostic module is closed, it inflates the airbags.

Diagnostic/energy reserve module (DERM)

4   The diagnostic/energy reserve module, which is located in the center part of the dash, contains an on-board microprocessor which monitors the operation of the system. It performs a diagnostic check of the system every time the vehicle is started. If the system is operating properly, the AIRBAG warning light will blink on and off seven times. If there is a fault in the system, the light will remain on and the airbag control module will store fault codes indicating the nature of the fault. If the AIRBAG warning light remains on after staring, or comes on while driving, the vehicle should be taken to your dealer immediately for service. The diagnostic/energy reserve module also contains a back-up power supply to deploy the airbags in the event battery power is lost during a collision. **Caution:** *Do NOT open the DERM case for any reason. Touching the connector pins or soldered components could cause damage from electrostatic discharge. A malfunctioning DERM must be replaced by authorized service personnel at a dealership.*

Operation

5   For the airbag(s) to deploy, an impact of sufficient force must occur within 30-degrees of the vehicle centerline. When this condition occurs, the circuit to the airbag inflator is closed and the airbag inflates. If the battery is destroyed by the impact, or is too low to power the inflators, a back-up power supply inside the diagnostic/energy reserve module supplies current to the airbags.

Self-diagnosis system

6   A self-diagnosis circuit in the module displays a light when the ignition switch is turned to the On position. If the system is operating normally, the light should go out after seven flashes. If the light doesn't come on, or doesn't go out after seven flashes, or if it comes on while you're driving the vehicle, there's a malfunction in the SIR system. Have it inspected and repaired as soon as possible. Do not attempt to troubleshoot or service the SIR system yourself. Even a small mistake could cause the SIR system to malfunction when you need it.

Servicing components near the SIR system

7   Nevertheless, there are times when you need to remove the steering wheel, radio or service other components on or near the instrument panel. At these times, you'll be working around components and wiring harnesses for the SIR system. SIR system wiring is easy to identify; they're all covered by a bright yellow conduit. Do not unplug the connectors for the SIR system wiring, except to disable the system. And do not use electrical test equipment on the SIR system wiring. **Always disable the SIR system before working near the SIR system components or related wiring.**

Disabling the SIR system

Refer to illustrations 25.10 and 25.11

8   Disconnect the cable from the negative battery terminal. **Caution:** *If the vehicle is equipped with a Delco Loc II or Theftlock audio system, make sure you have the correct activation code before disconnecting the battery.* Turn the steering wheel to the straight ahead position, place the ignition switch key in the Lock position and remove the key. Remove the airbag fuse from the fuse block (see Section 3).

9   Remove the steering column covers and the left sound insulator panel below the instrument panel (see Chapter 11).

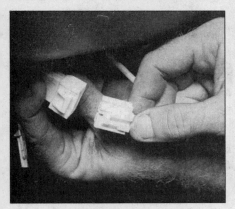

25.10 The driver's side airbag Connector Position Assurance (CPA) connector is located at the base of the steering column; always unplug it before removing the steering wheel or working in the area of the steering wheel

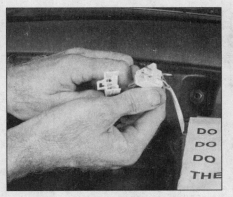

25.11 The passenger's side airbag Connector Position Assurance (CPA) connector is located to the left of the passenger's side airbag; always unplug it before removing the steering wheel or working in the area of the passenger's side airbag

25.15a To release the SIR coil from the steering shaft, remove this snap ring . . .

10 Unplug the yellow Connector Position Assurance (CPA) steering column harness connector (see illustration).
11 Before working in or around the passenger's side of the instrument panel, unplug the yellow Connector Position Assurance (CPA) passenger airbag harness connector (see illustration).

Enabling the SIR system

11 After you've disabled the airbag and performed the necessary service, plug in the steering column (driver's side) and passenger side CPA connectors. Reinstall the steering column lower trim panel, and the sound insulator panel.
12 Install the airbag fuse. Connect the negative battery terminal.

Centering the SIR coil

Refer to illustrations 25.15a, 25.15b, 25.16 and 25.18
13 Anytime some part of the steering system is disassembled for service or replacement, the steering column should be immobilized to ensure that the SIR coil doesn't become uncentered (moved). This can occur, for example, if the steering column is separated from the steering gear, or if the centering spring is pushed down, allowing the hub to rotate while the coil is removed from the steering column. If the coil becomes accidentally uncentered, re-center it as follows before reassembling the steering system:
14 Make sure that the wheels are pointed straight ahead.
15 Remove the coil assembly snap ring (see illustration) and remove the coil assembly (see illustration).
16 Holding the coil assembly with its bottom side facing up, depress the spring lock (see illustration) and rotate the hub in the direction of the arrow until it stops (the arrow is on the back of the coil assembly). The coil ribbon should be wound up snug against the center hub.

17 Rotate the coil hub in the opposite direction two and three-quarters turns, then release the spring lock. The coil is now centered.
18 Install the SIR coil and secure it with the snap ring. The tab will be at the top and the marks aligned when the coil is properly installed (see illustration).

26 Wiring diagrams - general information

Since it isn't possible to include all wiring diagrams for every year covered by this manual, the following diagrams are those that are typical and most commonly needed.
Prior to troubleshooting any circuit, check the fuse and circuit breakers (if equipped) to make sure they're in good condition. Make sure the battery is properly charged and check the cable connections (see Chapter 1).

25.15b . . . then remove the coil

When checking a circuit, make sure that all electrical connectors are clean, with no broken or loose terminals. When unplugging an electrical connector, do not pull on the wires. Pull only on the connector housings themselves.

25.16 To center the SIR coil, hold it with its underside facing up, depress the spring lock and rotate the hub in the direction of the arrow on the coil assembly until it stops

25.18 When properly installed, the airbag coil will be centered with the marks aligned (circle) and the tab fitted between the projections on the top of steering column (arrow)

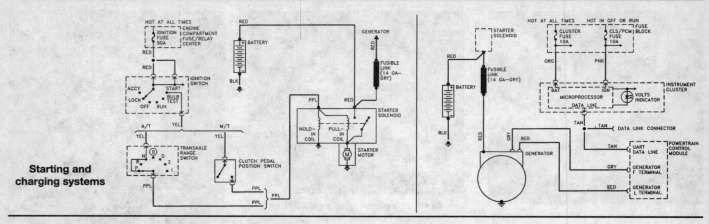

Starting and charging systems

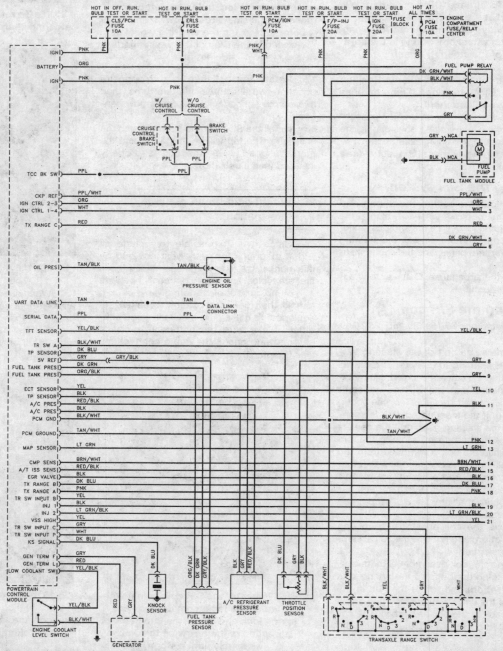

Engine control system (1 of 3)

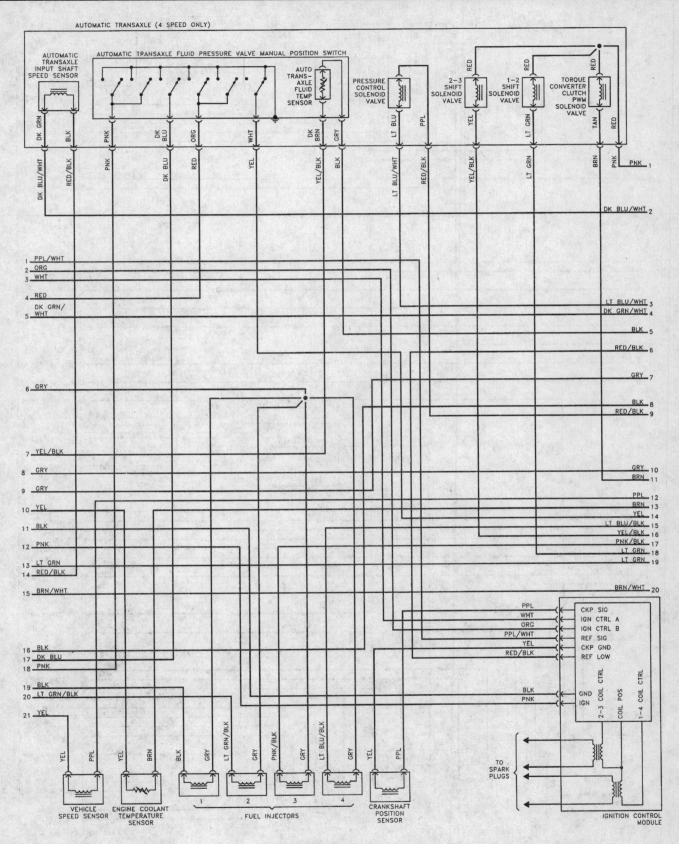

Engine control system (2 of 3)

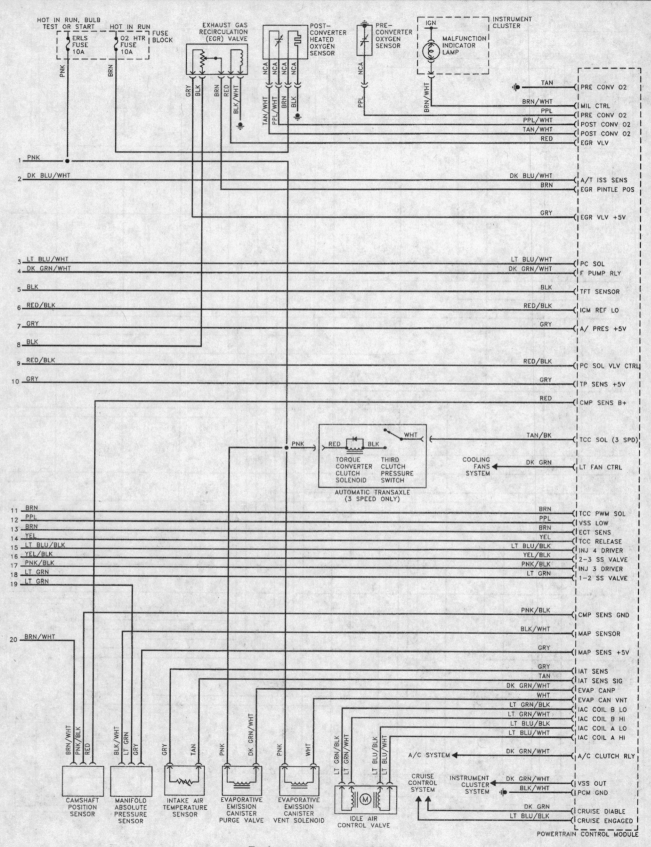

Engine control system (3 of 3)

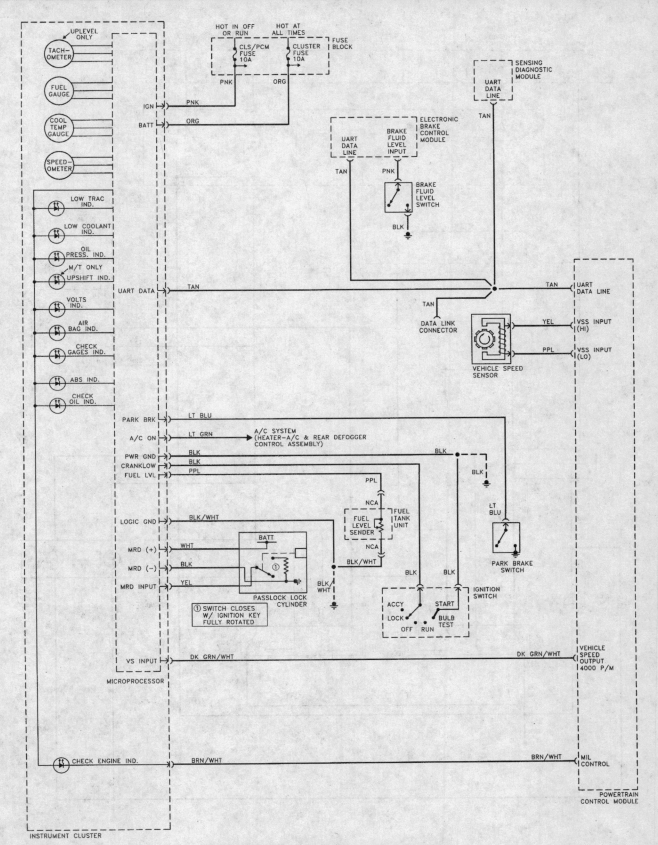

Instruments and engine warning system

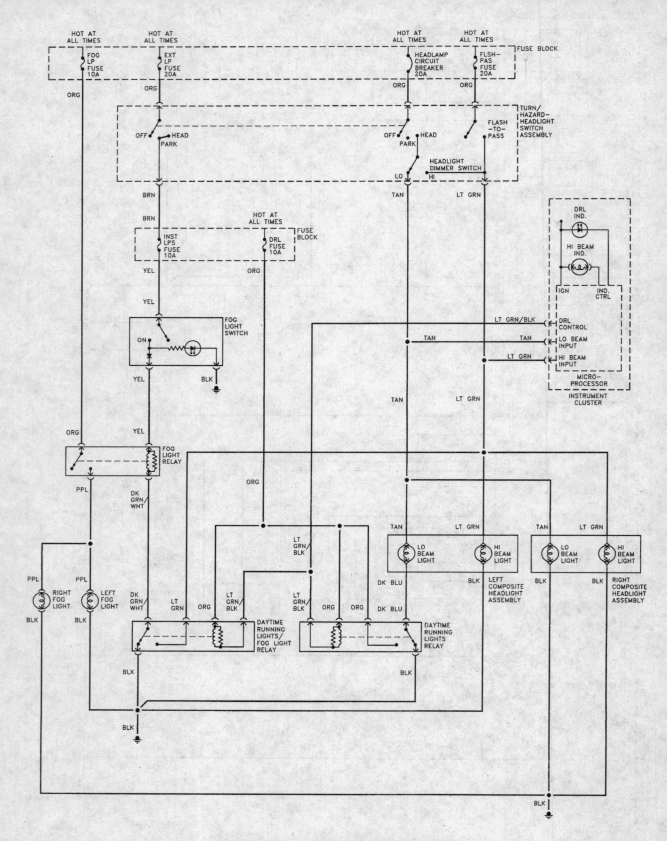

Headlight and foglight systems (1995 models)

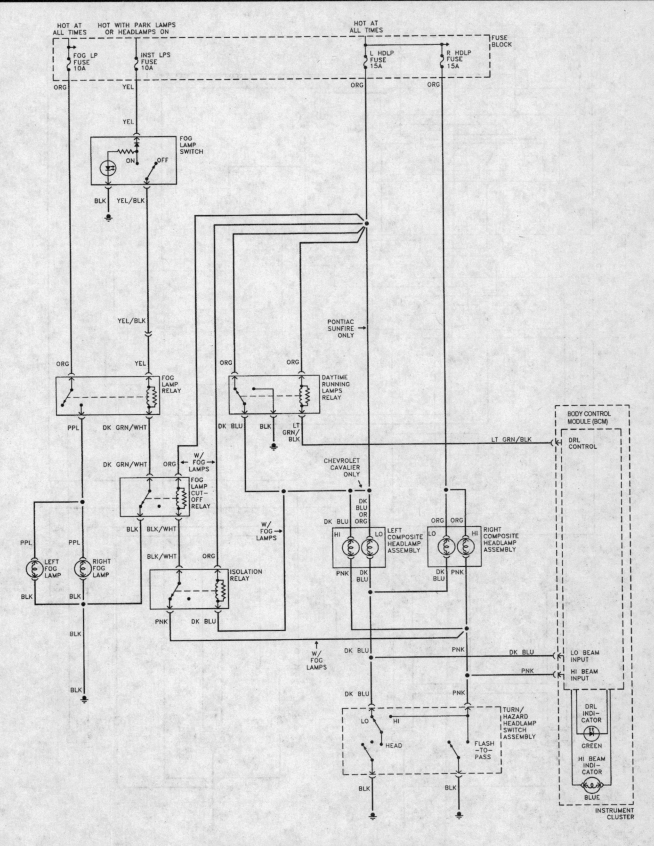

Headlight and foglight systems (1996 and later models)

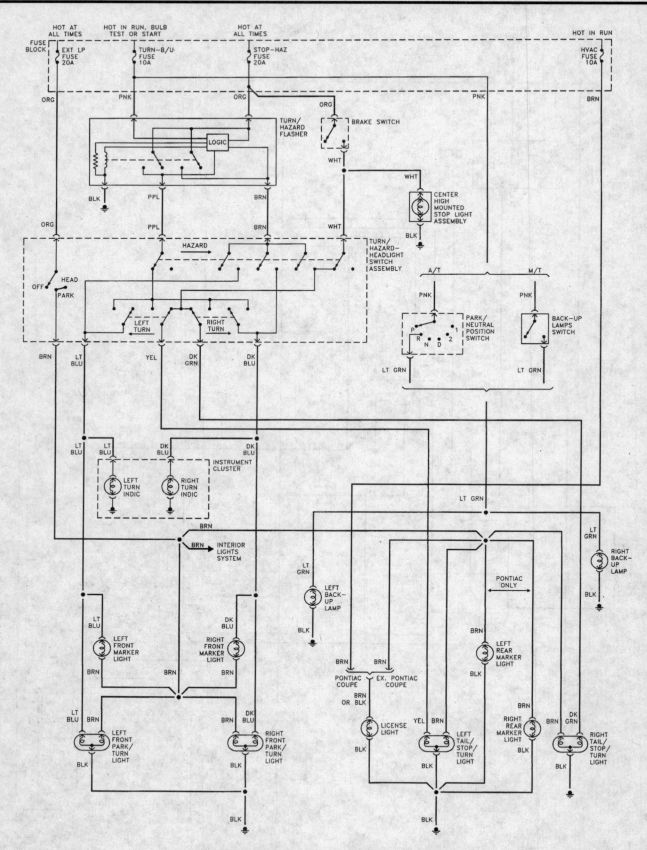

Exterior lighting systems, except headlights and foglights

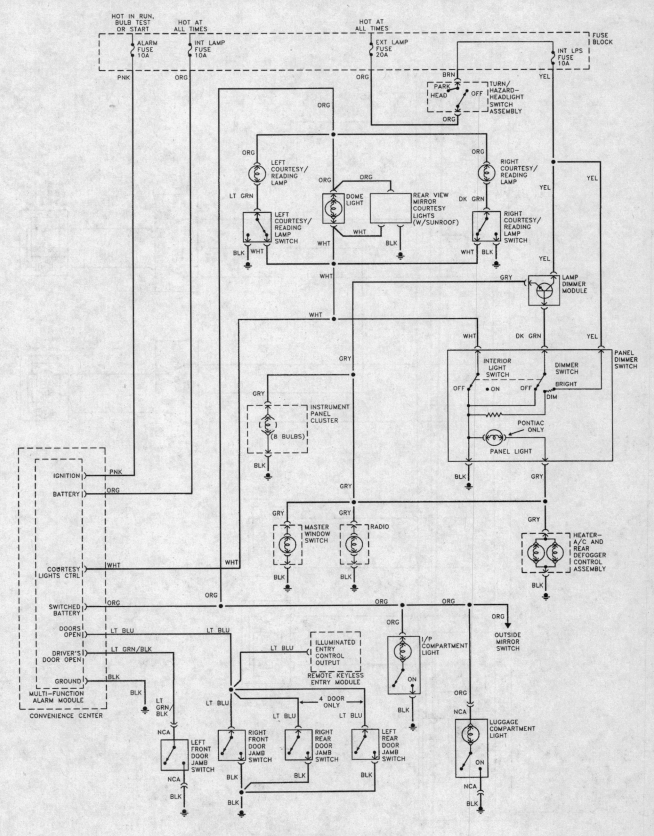

Interior lighting systems

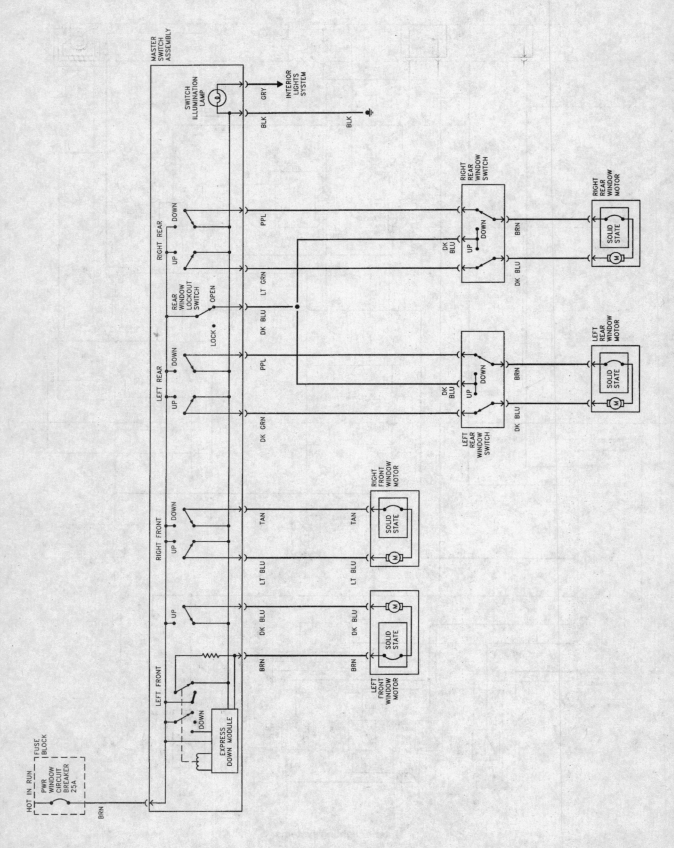

Power window system

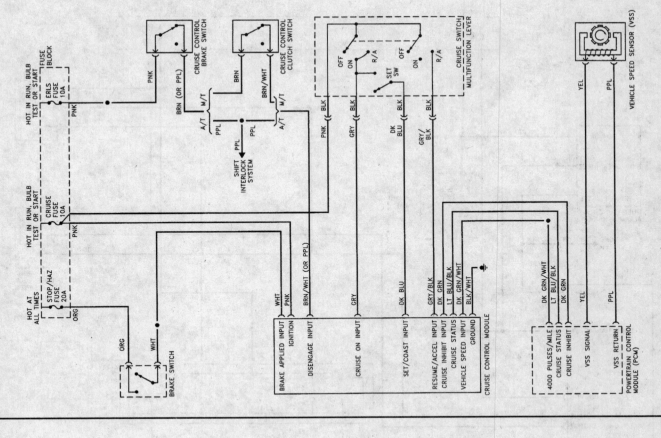

Cruise control system

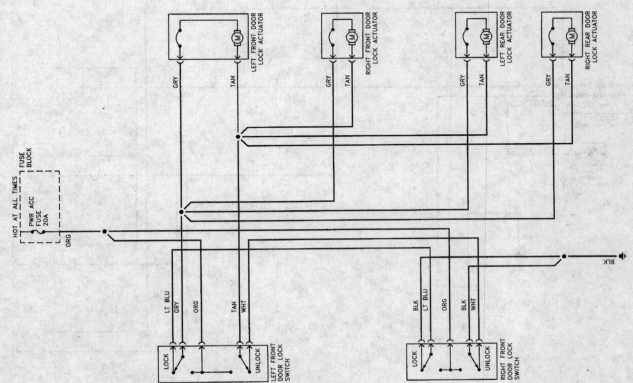

Power door lock system (without keyless entry)

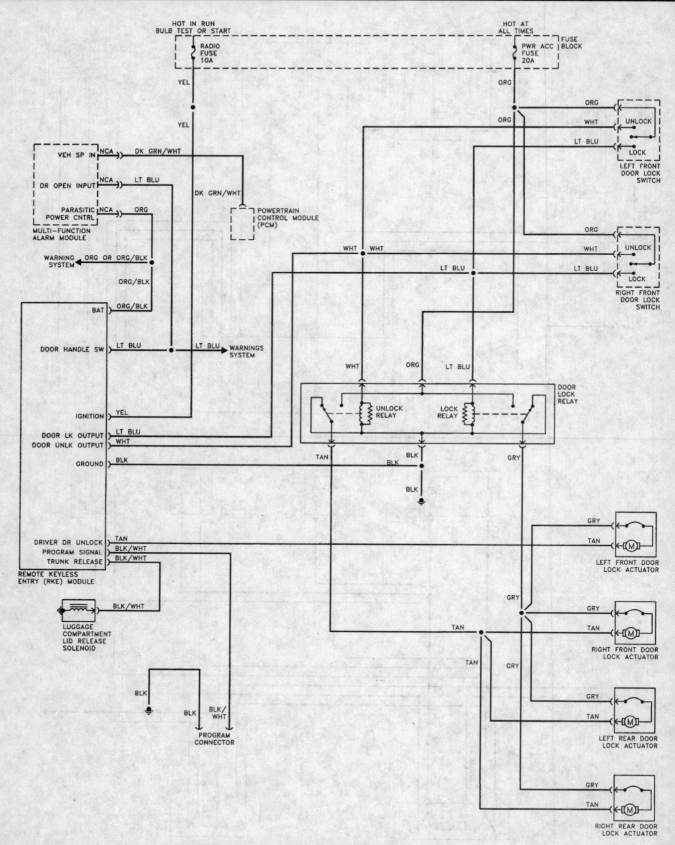

Power door lock system (with keyless entry)

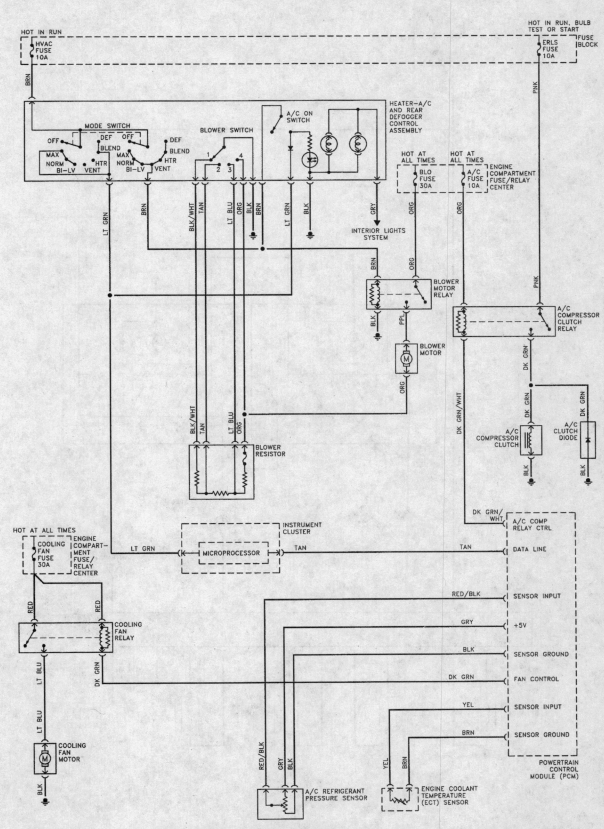

Heating, air conditioning and engine cooling systems

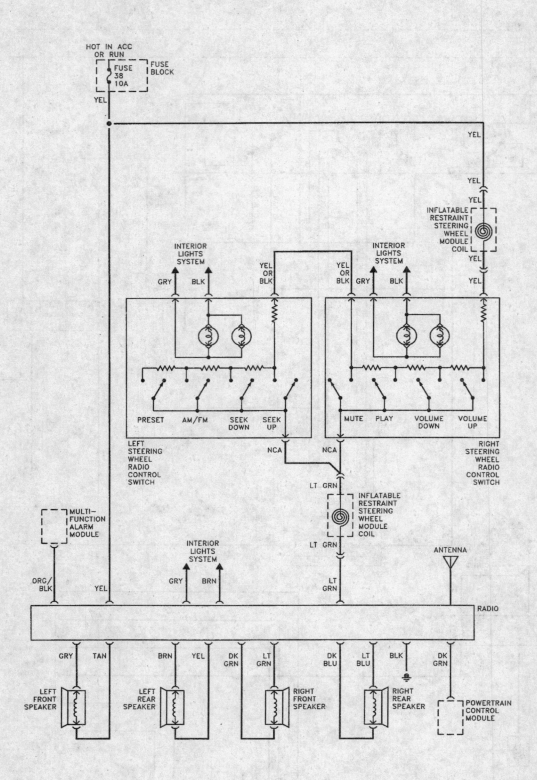

Radio, antenna and speakers

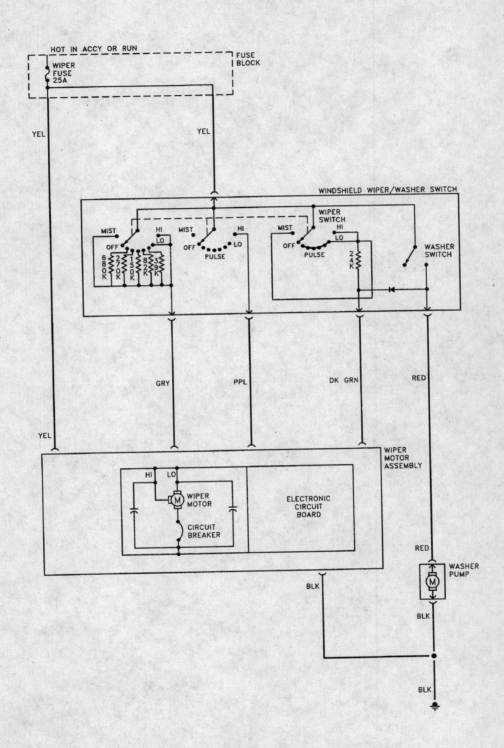

Wiper/washer system

Notes

Index

Notes

Haynes Automotive Manuals

NOTE: If you do not see a listing for your vehicle, consult your local Haynes dealer for the latest product information.

HAYNES XTREME CUSTOMIZING
11101 Sport Compact Customizing
11102 Sport Compact Performance
11110 In-car Entertainment
11150 Sport Utility Vehicle Customizing
11213 Acura
11255 GM Full-size Pick-ups
11314 Ford Focus
11315 Full-size Ford Pick-ups
11373 Honda Civic

ACURA
12020 Integra '86 thru '89 & Legend '86 thru '90
12021 Integra '90 thru '93 & Legend '91 thru '95

AMC
Jeep CJ - see *JEEP (50020)*
14020 Mid-size models '70 thru '83
14025 (Renault) Alliance & Encore '83 thru '87

AUDI
15020 4000 all models '80 thru '87
15025 5000 all models '77 thru '83
15026 5000 all models '84 thru '88

AUSTIN-HEALEY
Sprite - see *MG Midget (66015)*

BMW
18020 3/5 Series not including diesel or all-wheel drive models '82 thru '92
18021 3-Series incl. Z3 models '92 thru '98
18022 3-Series, E46 chassis '99 thru '05, Z4 models '03 thru '05
18025 320i all 4 cyl models '75 thru '83
18050 1500 thru 2002 except Turbo '59 thru '77

BUICK
19010 Buick Century '97 thru '05
Century (front-wheel drive) - see *GM (38005)*
19020 Buick, Oldsmobile & Pontiac Full-size (Front-wheel drive) '85 thru '05
Buick Electra, LeSabre and Park Avenue; Oldsmobile Delta 88 Royale, Ninety Eight and Regency; Pontiac Bonneville
19025 Buick Oldsmobile & Pontiac Full-size (Rear wheel drive)
Buick Estate '70 thru '90, Electra '70 thru '84, LeSabre '70 thru '85, Limited '74 thru '79 Oldsmobile Custom Cruiser '70 thru '90, Delta 88 '70 thru '85, Ninety-eight '70 thru '84 Pontiac Bonneville '70 thru '81, Catalina '70 thru '81, Grandville '70 thru '75, Parisienne '83 thru '86
19030 Mid-size Regal & Century all rear-drive models with V6, V8 and Turbo '74 thru '87
Regal - see *GENERAL MOTORS (38010)*
Riviera - see *GENERAL MOTORS (38030)*
Roadmaster - see *CHEVROLET (24046)*
Skyhawk - see *GENERAL MOTORS (38015)*
Skylark - see *GM (38020, 38025)*
Somerset - see *GENERAL MOTORS (38025)*

CADILLAC
21030 Cadillac Rear Wheel Drive all gasoline models '70 thru '93
Cimarron - see *GENERAL MOTORS (38015)*
DeVille - see *GM (38031 & 38032)*
Eldorado - see *GM (38030 & 38031)*
Fleetwood - see *GM (38031)*
Seville - see *GM (38030, 38031 & 38032)*

CHEVROLET
24010 Astro & GMC Safari Mini-vans '85 thru '03
24015 Camaro V8 all models '70 thru '81
24016 Camaro all models '82 thru '92
24017 Camaro & Firebird '93 thru '02
Cavalier - see *GENERAL MOTORS (38016)*
Celebrity - see *GENERAL MOTORS (38005)*
24020 Chevelle, Malibu & El Camino '69 thru '87
24024 Chevette & Pontiac T1000 '76 thru '87
Citation - see *GENERAL MOTORS (38020)*
24027 Colorado & GMC Canyon '04 thru '06
24032 Corsica/Beretta all models '87 thru '96
24040 Corvette all V8 models '68 thru '82
24041 Corvette all models '84 thru '96
10305 Chevrolet Engine Overhaul Manual
24045 Full-size Sedans Caprice, Impala, Biscayne, Bel Air & Wagons '69 thru '90
24046 Impala SS & Caprice and Buick Roadmaster '91 thru '96
Impala - see *LUMINA (24048)*
Lumina '90 thru '94 - see *GM (38010)*
24048 Lumina & Monte Carlo '95 thru '05
Lumina APV - see *GM (38035)*
24050 Luv Pick-up all 2WD & 4WD '72 thru '82
Malibu '97 thru '00 - see *GM (38026)*
24055 Monte Carlo all models '70 thru '88
Monte Carlo '95 thru '01 - see *LUMINA (24048)*
24059 Nova all V8 models '69 thru '79
24060 Nova and Geo Prizm '85 thru '92
24064 Pick-ups '67 thru '87 - Chevrolet & GMC, all V8 & in-line 6 cyl, 2WD & 4WD '67 thru '87; Suburbans, Blazers & Jimmys '67 thru '91
24065 Pick-ups '88 thru '98 - Chevrolet & GMC, full-size pick-ups '88 thru '98, C/K Classic '99 & '00, Blazer & Jimmy '92 thru '94; Suburban '92 thru '99; Tahoe & Yukon '95 thru '99
24066 Pick-ups '99 thru '03 - Chevrolet Silverado & GMC Sierra full-size pick-ups '99 thru '05, Suburban/Tahoe/Yukon/Yukon XL '00 thru '05
24070 S-10 & S-15 Pick-ups '82 thru '93, Blazer & Jimmy '83 thru '94,
24071 S-10 & Sonoma Pick-ups '94 thru '04, Blazer & Jimmy '95 thru '04, Hombre '96 thru '01
24072 Chevrolet TrailBlazer & TrailBlazer EXT, GMC Envoy & Envoy XL, Oldsmobile Bravada '02 and '03
24075 Sprint '85 thru '88 & Geo Metro '89 thru '01
24080 Vans - Chevrolet & GMC '68 thru '96
24081 Chevrolet Express & GMC Savana Full-size Vans '96 thru '05

CHRYSLER
25015 Chrysler Cirrus, Dodge Stratus, Plymouth Breeze '95 thru '00
10310 Chrysler Engine Overhaul Manual
25020 Full-size Front-Wheel Drive '88 thru '93
K-Cars - see *DODGE Aries (30008)*
Laser - see *DODGE Daytona (30030)*
25025 Chrysler LHS, Concorde, New Yorker, Dodge Intrepid, Eagle Vision, '93 thru '97
25026 Chrysler LHS, Concorde, 300M, Dodge Intrepid, '98 thru '03
25027 Chrysler 300 '05 thru '07
25030 Chrysler & Plymouth Mid-size front wheel drive '82 thru '95
Rear-wheel Drive - see *Dodge (30050)*
25035 PT Cruiser all models '01 thru '03
25040 Chrysler Sebring, Dodge Avenger '95 thru '05

DATSUN
28005 200SX all models '80 thru '83
28007 B-210 all models '73 thru '78
28009 210 all models '79 thru '82
28012 240Z, 260Z & 280Z Coupe '70 thru '78
28014 280ZX Coupe & 2+2 '79 thru '83
300ZX - see *NISSAN (72010)*
28018 510 & PL521 Pick-up '68 thru '73
28020 510 all models '78 thru '81
28022 620 Series Pick-up all models '73 thru '79
720 Series Pick-up - see *NISSAN (72030)*
28025 810/Maxima all gasoline models, '77 thru '84

DODGE
400 & 600 - see *CHRYSLER (25030)*
30008 Aries & Plymouth Reliant '81 thru '89
30010 Caravan & Plymouth Voyager '84 thru '95
30011 Caravan & Plymouth Voyager '96 thru '02
30012 Challenger/Plymouth Saporro '78 thru '83
30013 Caravan, Chrysler Voyager, Town & Country '03 thru '06
30016 Colt & Plymouth Champ '78 thru '87
30020 Dakota Pick-ups all models '87 thru '96
30021 Durango '98 & '99, Dakota '97 thru '99
30022 Dodge Durango models '00 thru '03
Dodge Dakota models '00 thru '03
30023 Dodge Durango & Dakota '04 thru '06
30025 Dart, Demon, Plymouth Barracuda, Duster & Valiant 6 cyl models '67 thru '76
30030 Daytona & Chrysler Laser '84 thru '89
Intrepid - see *CHRYSLER (25025, 25026)*
30034 Neon all models '95 thru '99
30035 Omni & Plymouth Horizon '78 thru '90
30036 Dodge and Plymouth Neon '00 thru '05
30040 Pick-ups all full-size models '74 thru '93
30041 Pick-ups all full-size models '94 thru '01
30042 Dodge Full-size Pick-ups '02 thru '05
30045 Ram 50/D50 Pick-ups & Raider and Plymouth Arrow Pick-ups '79 thru '93
30050 Dodge/Plymouth/Chrysler RWD '71 thru '89
30055 Shadow & Plymouth Sundance '87 thru '94
30060 Spirit & Plymouth Acclaim '89 thru '95
30065 Vans - Dodge & Plymouth '71 thru '03

EAGLE
Talon - see *MITSUBISHI (68030, 68031)*
Vision - see *CHRYSLER (25025)*

FIAT
34010 124 Sport Coupe & Spider '68 thru '78
34025 X1/9 all models '74 thru '80

FORD
10355 Ford Automatic Transmission Overhaul
36004 Aerostar Mini-vans all models '86 thru '97
36006 Contour & Mercury Mystique '95 thru '00
36008 Courier Pick-up all models '72 thru '82
36012 Crown Victoria & Mercury Grand Marquis '88 thru '00
10320 Ford Engine Overhaul Manual
36016 Escort/Mercury Lynx all models '81 thru '90
36020 Escort/Mercury Tracer '91 thru '00
36022 Ford Escape & Mazda Tribute '01 thru '03
36024 Explorer & Mazda Navajo '91 thru '01
36025 Ford Explorer & Mercury Mountaineer '02 thru '06
36028 Fairmont & Mercury Zephyr '78 thru '83
36030 Festiva & Aspire '88 thru '97
36032 Fiesta all models '77 thru '80
36034 Focus all models '00 thru '05
36036 Ford & Mercury Full-size '75 thru '87
36044 Ford & Mercury Mid-size '75 thru '86
36048 Mustang V8 all models '64-1/2 thru '73
36049 Mustang II 4 cyl, V6 & V8 models '74 thru '78
36050 Mustang & Mercury Capri all models Mustang, '79 thru '93; Capri, '79 thru '86
36051 Mustang all models '94 thru '03
36052 Mustang '05 thru '07
36054 Pick-ups & Bronco '73 thru '79
36058 Pick-ups & Bronco '80 thru '96
36059 F-150 & Expedition '97 thru '03, F-250 '97 thru '99 & Lincoln Navigator '98 thru '02
36060 Super Duty Pick-ups, Excursion '99 thru '06
36061 F-150 full-size '04 thru '06
36062 Pinto & Mercury Bobcat '75 thru '80
36066 Probe all models '89 thru '92
36070 Ranger/Bronco II gasoline models '83 thru '92
36071 Ranger '93 thru '05 & Mazda Pick-ups '94 thru '05
36074 Taurus & Mercury Sable '86 thru '95
36075 Taurus & Mercury Sable '96 thru '05
36078 Tempo & Mercury Topaz '84 thru '94
36082 Thunderbird/Mercury Cougar '83 thru '88
36086 Thunderbird/Mercury Cougar '89 and '97
36090 Vans all V8 Econoline models '69 thru '91
36094 Vans full size '92 thru '05
36097 Windstar Mini-van '95 thru '03

GENERAL MOTORS
10360 GM Automatic Transmission Overhaul
38005 Buick Century, Chevrolet Celebrity, Oldsmobile Cutlass Ciera & Pontiac 6000 all models '82 thru '96
38010 Buick Regal, Chevrolet Lumina, Oldsmobile Cutlass Supreme & Pontiac Grand Prix (FWD) '88 thru '05
38015 Buick Skyhawk, Cadillac Cimarron, Chevrolet Cavalier, Oldsmobile Firenza & Pontiac J-2000 & Sunbird '82 thru '94
38016 Chevrolet Cavalier & Pontiac Sunfire '95 thru '04
38020 Buick Skylark, Chevrolet Citation, Olds Omega, Pontiac Phoenix '80 thru '85
38025 Buick Skylark & Somerset, Oldsmobile Achieva & Calais and Pontiac Grand Am all models '85 thru '98
38026 Chevrolet Malibu, Olds Alero & Cutlass, Pontiac Grand Am '97 thru '03
38027 Chevrolet Malibu '04 thru '07
38030 Cadillac Eldorado '71 thru '85, Seville '80 thru '85, Oldsmobile Toronado '71 thru '85, Buick Riviera '79 thru '85
38031 Cadillac Eldorado & Seville '86 thru '91, DeVille '86 thru '93, Fleetwood & Olds Toronado '86 thru '92, Buick Riviera '86 thru '93
38032 Cadillac DeVille '94 thru '05 & Seville '92 thru '04
38035 Chevrolet Lumina APV, Olds Silhouette & Pontiac Trans Sport all models '90 thru '96
38036 Chevrolet Venture, Olds Silhouette, Pontiac Trans Sport & Montana '97 thru '05
General Motors Full-size Rear-wheel Drive - see *BUICK (19025)*

GEO
Metro - see *CHEVROLET Sprint (24075)*
Prizm - '85 thru '92 see *CHEVY (24060)*, '93 thru '02 see *TOYOTA Corolla (92036)*

(Continued on other side)

Haynes North America, Inc., 861 Lawrence Drive, Newbury Park, CA 91320-1514 • (805) 498-6703

Haynes Automotive Manuals (continued)

NOTE: If you do not see a listing for your vehicle, consult your local Haynes dealer for the latest product information.

40030 **Storm** all models '90 thru '93
Tracker - see SUZUKI Samurai (90010)

GMC
Vans & Pick-ups - see CHEVROLET

HONDA
42010 **Accord CVCC** all models '76 thru '83
42011 **Accord** all models '84 thru '89
42012 **Accord** all models '90 thru '93
42013 **Accord** all models '94 thru '97
42014 **Accord** all models '98 thru '02
42015 **Honda Accord** models '03 thru '05
42020 **Civic 1200** all models '73 thru '79
42021 **Civic 1300 & 1500 CVCC** '80 thru '83
42022 **Civic 1500 CVCC** all models '75 thru '79
42023 **Civic** all models '84 thru '91
42024 **Civic & del Sol** '92 thru '95
42025 **Civic** '96 thru '00, **CR-V** '97 thru '01, **Acura Integra** '94 thru '00
42026 **Civic** '01 thru '04, **CR-V** '02 thru '04
42035 **Honda Odyssey** all models '99 thru '04
42040 **Prelude CVCC** all models '79 thru '89

HYUNDAI
43010 **Elantra** all models '96 thru '01
43015 **Excel & Accent** all models '86 thru '98

ISUZU
Hombre - see CHEVROLET S-10 (24071)
47017 **Rodeo** '91 thru '02; **Amigo** '89 thru '94 and '98 thru '02; **Honda Passport** '95 thru '02
47020 **Trooper & Pick-up** '81 thru '93

JAGUAR
49010 **XJ6** all 6 cyl models '68 thru '86
49011 **XJ6** all models '88 thru '94
49015 **XJ12 & XJS** all 12 cyl models '72 thru '85

JEEP
50010 **Cherokee, Comanche & Wagoneer Limited** all models '84 thru '01
50020 **CJ** all models '49 thru '86
50025 **Grand Cherokee** all models '93 thru '04
50029 **Grand Wagoneer & Pick-up** '72 thru '91 Grand Wagoneer '84 thru '91, Cherokee & Wagoneer '72 thru '83, Pick-up '72 thru '88
50030 **Wrangler** all models '87 thru '03
50035 **Liberty** '02 thru '04

KIA
54070 **Sephia** '94 thru '01, **Spectra** '00 thru '04

LEXUS
ES 300 - see TOYOTA Camry (92007)

LINCOLN
Navigator - see FORD Pick-up (36059)
59010 **Rear-Wheel Drive** all models '70 thru '05

MAZDA
61010 **GLC Hatchback (rear-wheel drive)** '77 thru '83
61011 **GLC (front-wheel drive)** '81 thru '85
61015 **323 & Protegé** '90 thru '00
61016 **MX-5 Miata** '90 thru '97
61020 **MPV** all models '89 thru '94
Navajo - see Ford Explorer (36024)
61030 **Pick-ups** '72 thru '93
Pick-up '94 thru '00 - see Ford Ranger (36071)
61035 **RX-7** all models '79 thru '85
61036 **RX-7** all models '86 thru '91
61040 **626 (rear-wheel drive)** all models '79 thru '82
61041 **626/MX-6 (front-wheel drive)** '83 thru '92
61042 **626** '93 thru '01, **MX-6/Ford Probe** '93 thru '01

MERCEDES-BENZ
63012 **123 Series Diesel** '76 thru '85
63015 **190 Series** four-cyl gas models, '84 thru '88
63020 **230/250/280** 6 cyl sohc models '68 thru '72
63025 **280 123 Series** gasoline models '77 thru '81
63030 **350 & 450** all models '71 thru '80

MERCURY
64200 **Villager & Nissan Quest** '93 thru '01
All other titles, see FORD Listing.

MG
66010 **MGB** Roadster & GT Coupe '62 thru '80
66015 **MG Midget, Austin Healey Sprite** '58 thru '80

MITSUBISHI
68020 **Cordia, Tredia, Galant, Precis & Mirage** '83 thru '93

68030 **Eclipse, Eagle Talon & Ply. Laser** '90 thru '94
68031 **Eclipse** '95 thru '01, **Eagle Talon** '95 thru '98
68035 **Mitsubishi Galant** '94 thru '03
68040 **Pick-up** '83 thru '96 & **Montero** '83 thru '93

NISSAN
72010 **300ZX** all models including Turbo '84 thru '89
72015 **Altima** all models '93 thru '04
72020 **Maxima** all models '85 thru '92
72021 **Maxima** all models '93 thru '04
72030 **Pick-ups** '80 thru '97 **Pathfinder** '87 thru '95
72031 **Frontier Pick-up** '98 thru '04, **Xterra** '00 thru '04, **Pathfinder** '96 thru '04
72040 **Pulsar** all models '83 thru '86
Quest - see MERCURY Villager (64200)
72050 **Sentra** all models '82 thru '94
72051 **Sentra & 200SX** all models '95 thru '04
72060 **Stanza** all models '82 thru '90

OLDSMOBILE
73015 **Cutlass V6 & V8** gas models '74 thru '88
For other OLDSMOBILE titles, see BUICK, CHEVROLET or GENERAL MOTORS listing.

PLYMOUTH
For PLYMOUTH titles, see DODGE listing.

PONTIAC
79008 **Fiero** all models '84 thru '88
79018 **Firebird V8** models except Turbo '70 thru '81
79019 **Firebird** all models '82 thru '92
79040 **Mid-size Rear-wheel Drive** '70 thru '87
For other PONTIAC titles, see BUICK, CHEVROLET or GENERAL MOTORS listing.

PORSCHE
80020 **911** except Turbo & Carrera 4 '65 thru '89
80025 **914** all 4 cyl models '69 thru '76
80030 **924** all models including Turbo '76 thru '82
80035 **944** all models including Turbo '83 thru '89

RENAULT
Alliance & Encore - see AMC (14020)

SAAB
84010 **900** all models including Turbo '79 thru '88

SATURN
87010 **Saturn** all models '91 thru '02
87011 **Saturn Ion** '03 thru '07
87020 **Saturn** all L-series models '00 thru '04

SUBARU
89002 **1100, 1300, 1400 & 1600** '71 thru '79
89003 **1600 & 1800** 2WD & 4WD '80 thru '94
89100 **Legacy** all models '90 thru '98
89101 **Legacy & Forester** '00 thru '06

SUZUKI
90010 **Samurai/Sidekick & Geo Tracker** '86 thru '01

TOYOTA
92005 **Camry** all models '83 thru '91
92006 **Camry** all models '92 thru '96
92007 **Camry, Avalon, Solara, Lexus ES 300** '97 thru '01
92008 **Toyota Camry, Avalon and Solara and Lexus ES 300/330** all models '02 thru '05
92015 **Celica Rear Wheel Drive** '71 thru '85
92020 **Celica Front Wheel Drive** '86 thru '99
92025 **Celica Supra** all models '79 thru '92
92030 **Corolla** all models '75 thru '79
92032 **Corolla** all rear wheel drive models '80 thru '87
92035 **Corolla** all front wheel drive models '84 thru '92
92036 **Corolla & Geo Prizm** '93 thru '02
92037 **Corolla** models '03 thru '05
92040 **Corolla Tercel** all models '80 thru '82
92045 **Corona** all models '74 thru '82
92050 **Cressida** all models '78 thru '82
92055 **Land Cruiser** FJ40, 43, 45, 55 '68 thru '82
92056 **Land Cruiser** FJ60, 62, 80, FZJ80 '80 thru '96
92065 **MR2** all models '85 thru '87
92070 **Pick-up** all models '69 thru '78
92075 **Pick-up** all models '79 thru '95
92076 **Tacoma** '95 thru '04, **4Runner** '96 thru '02, **T100** '93 thru '98
92078 **Tundra** '00 thru '02 & **Sequoia** '01 thru '02
92080 **Previa** all models '91 thru '95
92082 **RAV4** all models '96 thru '02
92085 **Tercel** all models '87 thru '94
92090 **Toyota Sienna** all models '98 thru '02
92095 **Highlander & Lexus RX-330** '99 thru '06

TRIUMPH
94007 **Spitfire** all models '62 thru '81
94010 **TR7** all models '75 thru '81

VW
96008 **Beetle & Karmann Ghia** '54 thru '79
96009 **New Beetle** '98 thru '00
96016 **Rabbit, Jetta, Scirocco & Pick-up** gas models '75 thru '92 & Convertible '80 thru '92
96017 **Golf, GTI & Jetta** '93 thru '98 & **Cabrio** '95 thru '98
96018 **Golf, GTI, Jetta & Cabrio** '99 thru '02
96020 **Rabbit, Jetta & Pick-up** diesel '77 thru '84
96023 **Passat** '98 thru '01, **Audi A4** '96 thru '01
96030 **Transporter 1600** all models '68 thru '79
96035 **Transporter 1700, 1800 & 2000** '72 thru '79
96040 **Type 3 1500 & 1600** all models '63 thru '73
96045 **Vanagon** all air-cooled models '80 thru '83

VOLVO
97010 **120, 130 Series & 1800 Sports** '61 thru '73
97015 **140 Series** all models '66 thru '74
97020 **240 Series** all models '76 thru '93
97040 **740 & 760 Series** all models '82 thru '88
97050 **850 Series** all models '93 thru '97

TECHBOOK MANUALS
10205 **Automotive Computer Codes**
10206 **OBD-II & Electronic Engine Management Systems**
10210 **Automotive Emissions Control Manual**
10215 **Fuel Injection Manual, 1978 thru 1985**
10220 **Fuel Injection Manual, 1986 thru 1999**
10225 **Holley Carburetor Manual**
10230 **Rochester Carburetor Manual**
10240 **Weber/Zenith/Stromberg/SU Carburetors**
10305 **Chevrolet Engine Overhaul Manual**
10310 **Chrysler Engine Overhaul Manual**
10320 **Ford Engine Overhaul Manual**
10330 **GM and Ford Diesel Engine Repair Manual**
10340 **Small Engine Repair Manual, 5 HP & Less**
10341 **Small Engine Repair Manual, 5.5 - 20 HP**
10345 **Suspension, Steering & Driveline Manual**
10355 **Ford Automatic Transmission Overhaul**
10360 **GM Automatic Transmission Overhaul**
10405 **Automotive Body Repair & Painting**
10410 **Automotive Brake Manual**
10411 **Automotive Anti-lock Brake (ABS) Systems**
10415 **Automotive Detailing Manual**
10420 **Automotive Electrical Manual**
10425 **Automotive Heating & Air Conditioning**
10430 **Automotive Reference Manual & Dictionary**
10435 **Automotive Tools Manual**
10440 **Used Car Buying Guide**
10445 **Welding Manual**
10450 **ATV Basics**
10452 **Scooters, Automatic Transmission 50cc to 250cc**

SPANISH MANUALS
98903 **Reparación de Carrocería & Pintura**
98904 **Carburadores para los modelos Holley & Rochester**
98905 **Códigos Automotrices de la Computadora**
98910 **Frenos Automotriz**
98913 **Electricidad Automotriz**
98915 **Inyección de Combustible 1986 al 1999**
99040 **Chevrolet & GMC Camionetas** '67 al '87 Incluye Suburban, Blazer & Jimmy '67 al '91
99041 **Chevrolet & GMC Camionetas** '88 al '98 Incluye Suburban '92 al '98, Blazer & Jimmy '92 al '94, Tahoe y Yukon '95 al '98
99042 **Chevrolet & GMC Camionetas Cerradas** '68 al '95
99055 **Dodge Caravan & Plymouth Voyager** '84 al '95
99075 **Ford Camionetas y Bronco** '80 al '94
99077 **Ford Camionetas Cerradas** '69 al '91
99088 **Ford Modelos de Tamaño Mediano** '75 al '86
99091 **Ford Taurus & Mercury Sable** '86 al '95
99095 **GM Modelos de Tamaño Grande** '70 al '90
99100 **GM Modelos de Tamaño Mediano** '70 al '88
99106 **Jeep Cherokee, Wagoneer & Comanche** '84 al '00
99110 **Nissan Camioneta** '80 al '96, **Pathfinder** '87 al '95
99118 **Nissan Sentra** '82 al '94
99125 **Toyota Camionetas y 4Runner** '79 al '95

Over 100 Haynes motorcycle manuals also available

10-06

Haynes North America, Inc., 861 Lawrence Drive, Newbury Park, CA 91320-1514 • (805) 498-6703